RECLAIMING PARKLAND

RECLAIMING PARKLAND

Tom Hanks, Vincent Bugliosi, and the JFK Assassination in the New Hollywood

JAMES DIEUGENIO

WITH A PREFACE BY LISA PEASE
AND A FOREWORD BY WILLIAM DAVY

Skyhorse Publishing

Skyhorse Publishing books may be purchased in bulk at special discounts for sales promotion, corporate gifts, fund-raising, or educational purposes. Special editions can also be created to specifications. For details, contact the Special Sales Department, Skyhorse Publishing, 307 West 36th Street, 11th Floor, New York, NY 10018 or info@skyhorsepublishing.com.

Skyhorse® and Skyhorse Publishing® are registered trademarks of Skyhorse Publishing, Inc.®, a Delaware corporation.

Visit our website at www.skyhorsepublishing.com.

10 9 8 7 6 5 4 3 2 1

Library of Congress Cataloging-in-Publication Data is available on file.
ISBN: 978-1-62636-533-9

Printed in the United States of America

To my aunt and uncle, Louis
and Ernesta Spong, who raised me

Contents

Preface

With *Reclaiming Parkland*, Jim DiEugenio has performed a valuable service. Fifty years after the assassination of President Kennedy, with so many of the facts now available, it's truly hard to understand how so many figures in the media continue to get the basic facts of the assassination so wrong.

Jim approaches this subject from a new angle: by examining the built-in biases of these authors and filmmakers based on past projects and decisions. His revelations go a long way toward explaining how people as bright as Vincent Bugliosi or as lovable as Tom Hanks nonetheless fail to understand and correctly present this history.

In this book, Jim exams the recent books and scripts that Hollywood has made (and is making) into films and challenges their core theses. I, too, received a copy of the script of *Parkland* while it was still in development and was stunned at how overtly dishonest, in terms of the actual facts, it was. I've written screenplays. I understand the necessity of reshaping history in small ways to fit a dramatic narrative. I'm one of the first to say, and did say about *Charlie Wilson's War*, hey, it's just a film.

But I'm also a student of propaganda methods and techniques, and I know well how fictional presentations of history can inform or mislead an entire generation. I enjoyed *Charlie Wilson's War* because I'm an Aaron Sorkin dialog addict, and I wasn't expecting that any of the so-called history presented would be true. But I support the argument of others. Many people think they critically consume a film, only to refer to events from them later as if they were fact. Most people assume that if a film is purportedly based on a true event, it will be largely true in the important details. This is not always the case.

Ironically, that *was* the case with Oliver Stone's overly maligned film *JFK*. Sure, he combined several characters into new ones, compressed timelines, and changed what people had said. You have to do that to tell a more-than-three-hour story in three hours. But as someone who has studied the Kennedy assassinations—plural—for twenty years, I was amazed at how much director Stone and screenwriter Zach Sklar got right. I recognized dialog that came word for word from transcripts of Warren Commission testimony. I knew who the characters were meant to represent, even when the names had been changed or two or more people combined into a fictional character. But the essence of every scene was based on the facts as they were known at the time. So beyond being a fantastic moviegoing experience, which is all anyone should ever expect from a fictional story, it was also, remarkably, quite true to its subject.

The same cannot be said for *Parkland*, *Charlie Wilson's War*, and an upcoming film based on books by Lamar Waldron and Thom Hartmann. These presentations don't just distort history. They misrepresent it in ways so serious one can only call them propaganda.

That this is also true of Vincent Bugliosi's book *Reclaiming History*, however, is vastly more disturbing. It's not a film; it's a book. It is supposed to be a nonfiction presentation. Yet it is so rife, as Jim aptly demonstrates, with errors and distortion that it, too, can only properly be labeled propaganda.

In this presentation, Jim ranges far afield, giving us details of the Manson murders as reported in Bugliosi's most famous book, *Helter Skelter*, and examining in some detail a mock trial of Lee Harvey Oswald in which Bugliosi participated. Knowing how much Bugliosi had gotten wrong in *Reclaiming History*, Jim looked into those earlier cases to understand Bugliosi's biases.

Similarly, one can't really understand why Tom Hanks would produce a movie like *Parkland* without understanding who Tom Hanks is, what motivates him, and why he gravitates to certain types of projects.

Jim also considers the powerful and sometimes sinister relationship between the Pentagon, the CIA, and Hollywood. It may be harder than ever to get honest films made in the future if we don't confront this growing alliance.

A filmmaker in Hollywood shared a story with me that is relevant here. He had made a documentary about the JFK assassination. Before he went to the meeting where the studio executives were to vet his project, Oliver Stone had handed him a copy of the now-famous CIA memo that dictated instructions to its media assets as to how to refute notions that Kennedy was killed by a conspiracy. The filmmaker entered the room, and the atmosphere was jovial. He distributed the memo, ran to the restroom, and returned. Suddenly, the atmosphere in the room had turned stone cold. He soon found out why. The author of that CIA memo was one of the people at the vetting table, and the memo had just outed him to the other participants. It's a bit chilling to consider that the CIA is so deeply embedded in Hollywood that it has the ability to put the kibosh on projects it might feel threatened by. Perhaps that, more than anything, explains the trouble, as Jim discusses, that Salon founder and author David Talbot had when he tried to get a documentary made based on his book *Brothers*.

This book should initiate a discussion of the role that Hollywood increasingly plays in shaping, and often distorting, our history. Because once history is polluted, like the oil spilled by the Exxon Valdez in Prince William Sound, Alaska, it can take decades to clean up.

That's why this book is important. This is a book that seeks to dredge that sludge up and return a clearer history to us. I'm grateful to Jim for dedicating a significant portion of his life to this monumental task.

Jim did not embark on this journey alone. The book is laden with acknowledged contributions from many lesser-known researchers who have toiled for decades for the same reason Jim has: history actually matters. Our understanding of history determines our future course. If we figure out what happened, then we know what we need to do next. Perhaps the biggest reason some people prefer to read the false history is that it requires nothing of us. If Oswald alone killed Kennedy, there's no reason to change anything about one's life. But if the government lied to us, if the media is still lying to us, that tells us just how much was and is still at stake and that we need to take action if we wish to change course. Not everyone wants to confront that reality. Heck, my life would have been simpler had I never picked up Jim Garrison's fine book on the Kennedy assassination, *On the Trail of the Assassins*. The truth really is like the red pill in the film *The Matrix*: once you consume it, you can never go back to your previous mental state again.

If you, like most people, long to "fit in," you need what's in this book. This book will arm you with the means to defend whatever notion you had that caused you to read this far in the first place. If you tell people you don't believe Oswald acted alone, you will soon be labeled a "conspiracy theorist." (I correct those who mislabel me by noting I am actually a "conspiracy realist.") Be assured you are on the right path. Jim will give you the facts to refute the arguments your well-meaning but ill-informed friends may make. You are in good hands. And if you have a sense of humor at all, you will laugh. If you don't, schedule an appointment to get your funny bone checked.

—**Lisa Pease**, coeditor of *The Assassinations*,
August 2013

Foreword

When Vincent Bugliosi's bloated paean to the Warren Commission and its findings, *Reclaiming History*, was released in 2007, I wrote in a review at the time that the mainstream media's response could be summarized in one word: predictable.

Indeed, the *Washington Post, New York Times, Los Angeles Times,* and numerous television and radio outlets heaped praise on a book that nobody ever read. How could they? Bugliosi's book totals 1,612 oversized pages and weighs in at a whopping five-plus pounds. In addition, it includes a CD-ROM that contains another 1,128 pages of material. In his preface, Bugliosi admits that had they followed standard publishing conventions his work would have totaled thirteen volumes. Knowing a little something about deadlines and how newspaper reviews work, there is no way these reviewers could have (or would have) waded through thirteen volumes of material. This harkens back to when the Warren Commission released its twenty-six volumes of supporting testimony and exhibits and the *New York Times* printed a glowing review the very next day! That kind of feat would do Evelyn Wood proud.

The media lovefest played itself out early though and the book would have died the ignominious death it so richly deserved had not Forrest Gump come to the rescue. (Indeed, within a few short weeks, scores of copies of *Reclaiming History* started showing up in bookstore remaindered bins—its original $50.00 price tag now marked down to a measly $5.00.)

Shortly after publication, Tom Hanks and his partner at Playtone, Gary Goetzman, announced they had struck a deal with HBO to produce a ten-part miniseries based on Bugliosi's book. Like the mainstream media's Warren Commission worshippers before them, it is doubtful that Goetzman or Hanks ever fully read Bugliosi's book or its critiques prior to making the announcement.

However, years would pass and there would be virtual silence about the project from either Playtone or HBO. Finally, news started trickling out that HBO had dropped out of the project. It was then revealed that *Reclaiming History* had morphed into a feature film script titled *Parkland* that would focus on that venue and the prominent players from the tragic weekend of November 22–24, 1963.

In the interim though, several dogged researchers actually took the time to read Bugliosi's magnum opus and would write carefully thought out and impeccably researched critiques of that book. Foremost among these writers was Jim DiEugenio. Jim took on the unpleasant task of poring over Bugliosi's entire book, every chapter. He actually had the book out on his desk as he read the additional material on the CD. Does anyone think the reviewer for the *LA Times* did that? And being based in LA, Jim could further explore the Hollywood angle to this story that brought Hanks and Goetzman (and actor Bill Paxton) into the picture as well.

Jim then wrote a masterful ten-part demolition of Bugliosi for his CTKA website. Rather than heaping invectives upon the author (something Bugliosi delighted in), Jim's analysis was not only a tour de force in criticism but an invaluable reference work as well. There were things in that critique that many people had never known before. In other words, Jim was not just showing how wrong Bugliosi was, he was telling readers that there were still things about the JFK case that they did not know about.

Now, with *Reclaiming Parkland* DiEugenio has greatly expanded this masterwork. In addition to intensifying his masterful takedown of Bugliosi's central thesis (backed up with provable, incontrovertible research, by the way), Jim casts his net and shines disturbing new light on the Hollywood connection, revealing troubling new information on this bizarre nexus and how the *Reclaiming History* project evolved and morphed into its present form. This is arguably some of the most compelling material in this volume. This is a tough call to make because DiEugenio also conducts a reexamination into the Manson case and the whole Helter Skelter "fiction" that made Bugliosi a household name (and a very rich man). In fact—as with the JFK case—for many people, Jim will be alerting them to aspects of that sensational case they did not know about. How many books can one say that about? None except this one.

By tracing the Bugliosi timeline from Manson to JFK, DiEugenio goes behind the curtain and reveals the seamy underbelly of Hollywood, politics, and murder. Along the way we see how Hollywood has been compromised by the US intelligence agencies, emerging as a virtual Military/Industrial/Entertainment Complex—perhaps the most disturbing revelation in a book filled with many. And a message that has probably come to many readers far too late. They did not understand that what they were seeing on both TV and in the theaters was compromised.

Additionally, DiEugenio takes on the role of activist as he recounts the steps he took to try to prevent another Hollywood perversion of history. In 2011 Leonardo DiCaprio's production company took an option on the fatuous volumes put out by Lamar Waldron, *Ultimate Sacrifice* and *Legacy of Secrecy*. Readers familiar with these volumes will recall Waldron's twisted logic and mangled interpretation of Kennedy-era DOD documents that laid out *contingency* plans (one of many) for a possible invasion of Cuba. Waldron conflated these documents into actual battle plans for a full-scale military invasion of the island planned for early December 1963. Waldron further fantasized that the Mafia assassinated JFK rather than let the invasion take place (how's that for pretzel logic?). This idea, in many ways, is as far out as the Bugliosi/Hanks revival of the Warren Commission.

Few historians and even fewer Kennedy researchers fell for this nonsense, yet once again Hollywood jumped into the fray and preproduction, headed by DiCaprio's father, began on the Waldron "thesis."

Knowing this production was headed for disaster, not to mention easy discreditation at the hands of the mainstream media, Jim and Paul Schrade arranged for a meeting with Waldron, documentarian Earl Katz, and the senior DiCaprio himself. The tragic-comic results of that meeting that Jim recounts here would make a movie in and of itself, albeit a black comedy. David Mamet would be a good screenwriter for it. Needless to say, despite the warnings, Hollywood is going full speed ahead with the DiCaprio/Waldron sideshow.

Can one imagine if Oliver Stone tried to get *JFK* made in today's Hollywood? The good work generated from that film (i.e., the Assassination Records Review Board) could get set back years after the double-dose of Hanks and DiCaprio. One of the questions this book poses is this: Did what happened to Stone influence the film producers in the field after him? Did they now understand they could only go so far in the field afterwards? This is one of the triumphs of this book. It relates the epochal cultural struggle our nation has had in confronting the assassination of President Kennedy. A struggle that appears to have been lost in both television and films—much to the detriment of our citizenry and our country. Again, how many books pose and explore these types of questions?

But whatever the case in compromised tinsel town, tireless patriots like Jim DiEugenio will plug away, attempting to raise the public's consciousness with his organization, Citizens for Truth About the Kennedy Assassination (CTKA), and with good works like *Reclaiming Parkland*. As with the revised edition of *Destiny Betrayed* DiEugenio has written another book that is both indispensable and timeless—reclaiming our history in the process. And holding out hope for the recovery of our country.

—**William Davy,** author of *Let Justice Be Done*

Introduction

"Oh, you mean that four inch thing."

—Vincent Bugliosi to the author

Back in the nineties, Lisa Pease and I copublished a bimonthly journal called *Probe Magazine* that essentially chronicled new developments in the three assassinations of the sixties: John F. Kennedy, Martin Luther King, and Robert F. Kennedy. Several famous people subscribed or purchased it at the newsstand, including famed prosecutor Vincent Bugliosi. That illustrious magazine also contained a catalogue of items for sale. These were usually compendiums of documents that had been declassified by the Assassination Records Review Board (ARRB), a presidentially appointed panel set up after the release of Oliver Stone's film *JFK* to declassify records still being held by the government about President Kennedy's assassination. Every so often Bugliosi would call me about the availability of these documents. After a few of these calls, I began to understand Bugliosi was writing a rather voluminous book about the murder of President Kennedy. During one conversation he told me that his original plan was to publish the work as a three-volume set but the publisher had vetoed that idea on the grounds that it would be too expensive and no one would buy it. So, the final plan was to release the work as an oversized book with a CD attached. Although many reviewers have referred to *Reclaiming History* as being over 1,600 pages long, this is not really accurate.[1] When one adds in the two large files on the CD, the grand total is 2,646 pages.

It is important to understand this point because the two files on the CD are entitled Source Notes and End Notes. The former are footnotes, but the latter is really additional text. Presumably Bugliosi had envisioned the end notes as the other volumes of the three-book set. With that CD, what the prosecutor had originally foreseen was a three-volume set of 900 pages each.

When I asked Bugliosi why the book was so long, he quipped, "Well, I've got to knock down all that stuff you and Lisa wrote in *Probe*." He was joking, of course, but his book does, in fact, spend many, many pages arguing with the authors of other books. As I shall note later, much of this is done in what some might say is a very vituperative, mean-spirited way. In fact, Bugliosi's propensity in demeaning the critics of the Warren Commission is one of the most disheartening parts of the colossal volume.

In one conversation, I asked Bugliosi this important question: "How are you going to explain the differing entrance wounds in the back of Kennedy's skull?" The Warren Commission had decreed that the entrance wound of the fatal shot that killed the president entered at the base of his skull, but the 1969 medical review panel appointed by Attorney General Ramsey Clark moved this wound up to the top of the skull, near the cowlick area. The House Select Committee on Assassinations kept it there for their investigation in the seventies. I was surprised at the way Bugliosi replied to my question about this crucial matter. The illustrious prosecutor nonchalantly said, "Oh, you mean that four inch thing? Well, that's one of those things that falls into place once we know Oswald did it."

I was mystified by this reply. Was Bugliosi really justifying the bizarre fact that this is a murder case where one bullet left two different entry points by saying, well, that doesn't really matter since we know Oswald fired them both? As we shall see in the chapter on the autopsy, the strange maneuvering of this wound raises some of the most profound questions about the JFK case. Those questions do not even begin to be answered by saying, "Well, we know because Oswald did it." In fact, they indicate the opposite. And to frame the question around the phrase "Well, we know because Oswald did it" is precisely the faulty methodology the Warren Commission used. In other words, they had come to a conclusion before they evaluated the evidence. And this is what brought them into eternal disrepute.

This exchange with Bugliosi began to raise my antennae about what to expect from his book. After all, the former prosecutor was a distinguished and well-reviewed author. *The Betrayal of America* (2001), about the incomprehensible Supreme Court decision in the *Bush v. Gore* case in the 2000 election was a well-argued polemic. *No Island of Sanity*, his 1998 book on the Paula Jones case, was an insightful examination of the faulty reasoning of the Supreme Court in not delaying the Jones civil suit which, of course, allowed President Clinton to be deposed while in office and led to Clinton's impeachment debacle.

In addition to Bugliosi's interesting books on the political scene, there is the impressive list of his true crime books; not just the giant bestseller *Helter Skelter* (1974), but also *And the Sea Will Tell* (1991) and *Till Death Us Do Part* (1978). Bugliosi has become a wealthy man not only because so many of his books became bestsellers (*Helter Skelter* alone has sold seven million copies) but also because of the film rights that were sold for some of his books. For instance, the one under discussion here.

So, there is no doubt that in addition to being an accomplished attorney, Bugliosi is also a respected author. Which is why so many expected so much more from his book.

The Nonreview Reviews

Reclaiming History was well reviewed, but that was to be expected. Any book that supports the original Warren Commission verdict of Lee Harvey Oswald as the lone assassin of JFK is not going to be roundly criticized in the mainstream media (hereafter referred to as the MSM). So, when I read the positive reviews in, say, the *New York Times,* I took this with a large grain of salt. The *New York Times* had irresponsibly accepted the Warren Commission verdict in September 1964 without even reading the twenty-six volumes of evidence, which were not released until the following month. Once the newspaper had done that, they then had to taper and censor all of their subsequent coverage in order to not admit they had made a huge error which had resulted in misleading their reading public about who had killed their president.[2] In fact, this censorship extended as far as editing book reviews that were too favorable to critics in their original form and consciously bypassing the regular book review editor by assigning reviews of Kennedy assassination books to certain writers in advance.[3]

This is just one example of how controlled the press is in regard to President Kennedy's assassination and books like *Reclaiming History.* The review of *Reclaiming History* in the *Wall Street Journal* which appeared on May 20, 2007, is another example. This review was written by Max Holland. For twenty years, perhaps no other single person has more vociferously attempted to revive the moribund Warren Commission through a variety of media—books, newspaper editorials, TV specials, academic journals, and magazine articles—than Max Holland. In 2001, he became the first author working outside the government to be given a Studies in Intelligence Award from the Central Intelligence Agency. This might have been because in the fall of 2001, an article of his on the JFK case appeared on the CIA's own website. Today, he supports the Commission and demeans its critics through his own website, www.washingtondecoded. com. As with the *New York Times* practice of prescreening writers, giving Holland the assignment to review Bugliosi's book was guaranteeing the result in advance.

Another example of this would be the review of *Reclaiming History* in the *Atlantic,* which echoed the *New York Times* practice. That review was written by novelist Thomas Mallon, who in 2002, five years before the publication of *Reclaiming History,* had written a nonfiction book entitled *Mrs. Paine's Garage.* Previously, the work of Carol Hewitt, Steve Jones, and Barbara LaMonica had brought serious suspicion about the enigmatic figures of Ruth and Michael Paine; Mallon's book was an apologia for them. It ignored or discounted all the evidence those three writers, and many others, had recently brought to bear on the pair.[4] The *Atlantic,* which is one of the worst periodicals on this subject, allowed Mallon to begin his review with the following: "Several years ago I spent a portion of one November afternoon in Irving, Texas, inside the home garage where Lee Harvey Oswald had hidden his rifle in the months before he killed John F. Kennedy."[5] Mallon then described Ruth Paine as "an admirable Quaker who, as a young housewife, became innocently enmeshed in the assassination. . . ." He added that Ruth was a person of "idealistic nature and fine character." As we will see, it is highly doubtful that Oswald ever had a rifle in the Paine garage and even more doubtful that it was the rifle the Warren Commission accused him of having. We will also see that the character of Ruth Paine is, to say the least, not as saintly as Mallon implies. Therefore, this "review" of *Reclaiming History* was typical MSM: "hear no evil, see no evil, say no evil" on the JFK case. The editors made sure of that in advance.

The reaction from the *Los Angeles Times* was also rather predictable.[6] As Warren Commission critic Pat Speer has noted, it looks like this particular review of *Reclaiming History* was written with the help of Bugliosi's publicist. In a taped interview conducted before the release of the book, Bugliosi said he wanted his work to be considered "a book for the ages." Well, on cue, Jim Newton's review ended with the following two sentences: "With this work, Bugliosi has definitively explained the murder that recalibrated modern America. *It is a book for the ages.*"[7] (Emphasis added.) Nice press if you can get it, and if the subject is the JFK murder and your name is Vincent Bugliosi and the paper is in your hometown, you *can* get it.

Knowing how the MSM deck was stacked, I was not impressed with the "reviews," simply because, in the best sense, they were not really reviews. These writers had been made to genuflect before the MSM's massive sell-out to the Warren Commission. The dog and pony show surrounding *Reclaiming History* recalled the orchestrated reaction that greeted Gerald Posner's now discredited 1993 tome *Case Closed.* That blatant panegyric for the Warren Commission was published by Random House. It was commissioned by editor Bob Loomis, a man who has always defended the Commission. Harold Evans, who was chief of Random House at the time of the book's publication, came up with the idea of running a four-part ad in the *New York Times* in August 1993 depicting photos of six prominent critics and accusing them of being guilty of misleading the American public. That ad campaign culminated in the boldfaced and false blurb, "One Man. One Gun. One Inescapable Conclusion."[8]

Evans was half of a high-powered couple. He was married to the famous magazine editor Tina Brown. After Brown began editing the online magazine *Daily Beast,* she hired her husband's former client as, of all things, an investigative reporter. Posner was rather quickly exposed as being a serial plagiarist. It was so bad, Brown had to fire him in 2010. None of this caused the MSM to retract its endorsement of *Case Closed.*

If Harold Evans had done an editorial job instead of being an unrestrained PR man, he could have prevented the whole unraveling of both his client and his book. After the book was published, some interested parties did what Evans should have done in advance—they did a textual review and noticed that certain witnesses were saying for Posner what they had never said before, even under oath. This was quite unusual and some authors decided to cross-check Posner's work which neither Loomis nor Evans had done. Posner testified before Congress on November 17, 1993, that two of Kennedy's pathologists had changed their stories for him on the aforementioned subject of the placement of Kennedy's skull wound. The Random House author said under oath that both Drs. James Humes and Thornton Boswell had told him Kennedy's head wound was at the top of the skull. Dr. Gary Aguilar, a prolific writer on the JFK case, called both men. They both denied saying this to Posner. In fact, Boswell twice said to Aguilar that he never spoke to Posner at all.[9] This leaves open the distinct possibility that Posner, among his other suspected crimes, perjured himself before Congress. Posner also stated that when he interviewed bystander James Tague, the third man shot in addition to President Kennedy and Governor John Connally, Tague said he could not tell which shot hit him. Previously Tague had said it was not the first shot. When both Aguilar and Harold Weisberg called Tague, he also said he never talked to Posner, and further insisted to both men that he was not hit by the first shot.[10] There were other witnesses, like Carlos Bringuier and Harold Norman, who disputed the quotes Posner had attributed to them.[11]

Yet, none of these serious faults halted the MSM's chorus of acclaim for Posner's book. As one can see by just looking at the trade paperback version, the book was acclaimed by the usual suspects: the *New York Times, Newsweek, Time Magazine,* and by historians and fellow lawyers like Robert Dallek and Jeffrey Toobin. Evidently, none of them noticed the discrepancies in what certain witnesses told Posner versus what they had previously said under oath. Or, perhaps, the "reviewers" were not informed enough to notice the discrepancies. Was this the reason they got the assignments in the first place?

To be sure, there were some negative reviews of *Reclaiming History.* Most of these were collected and published on the Mary Ferrell Foundation website.

Some of these were written by authors I respect, like Gerald McKnight and David Wrone and Gary Aguilar. The problem I had with these reviews is that they were relatively narrow in their focus and also rather brief. In other words, it appeared that virtually no one had read all of the 2,646 pages of Bugliosi's book. In fact, when I asked Gary Aguilar if he had read the entire book, he unforgettably replied, "Are you crazy!"

So I decided to read the entire almost 2,700 pages of *Reclaiming History*. In the process, I assembled an entire binder full of notes. After doing so, I can understand what Aguilar meant. One of the most startling things about *Reclaiming History* is that Bugliosi did very little original research in the twenty-one years he says he spent writing it. (As we will see, that figure is likely inflated.) For instance, although Bugliosi spends over one hundred oversized pages going after both Jim Garrison and Oliver Stone's film *JFK*, it seems apparent from reading both the pages and the footnotes that he never went to any of the places he discussed. This includes New Orleans, the Cuban exile training sites around the Crescent City, and the Clinton-Jackson area in Feliciana Parish where Oswald was seen with Clay Shaw and David Ferrie. This is a serious failing of *Reclaiming History*. To work on this book as long as Bugliosi did, to have the reported million-dollar contract he had, to have a secretary—Rosemary Newton—and two cowriters, and to apparently never have left one's office to do a field investigation of a crime as complex as the JFK case is really inexplicable. Other writers who did not have anything like these advantages, *did* go to that area, and they *did* interview witnesses, and they *did* find new evidence and testimony which shed valuable light on the case.[12]

One of the most disturbing characteristics of *Reclaiming History* is the startling amount of bile, disdain, and invective that the prosecutor heaps on the critics who actually do perform such field investigation. It's almost as if he is predisposed against doing such elementary detective work. This is really paradoxical coming from a criminal lawyer.

A Simple Case?

Maybe that attitude stems from another puzzling comment the prosecutor made to me in another conversation. In discussing Bugliosi's work on the Robert F. Kennedy assassination, I compared the two cases and said that the JFK case was just as complex as the RFK case, if not more so. (For example, Sirhan never went to Mexico City and, to my knowledge, there was not a prior attempt to kill RFK in another town, as there was with JFK in Chicago.) Bugliosi shot back with, "It's not complex. It's a simple case. The writers make it complex."

What can one say about such a comment from a man who, in most other aspects of his literary career, has displayed the traits of intelligence, gravitas, insight, and honesty? A case is not simple when it has been inquired into seven times by various government agencies: (1) the initial FBI investigation (1963); (2) the Warren Commission inquiry (1963–64); (3) the Jim Garrison investigation (1966–70); (4) the Rockefeller Commission (1974–75); (5) the Senate's Church Committee (1975–76); (6) the House Select Committee on Assassinations (1976–79); and (7) the Assassination Records Review Board (1994–98).

What is astonishing about these seven inquiries, spread over thirty-five years, is that they varied so much in their findings. For example, the initial FBI investigation did not buy the infamous Single Bullet Theory: the idea that one bullet went through both John Kennedy and Governor John Connally as they sat in the back of the presidential limousine in Dealey Plaza in Dallas. As many have noted, to say there is no Single Bullet Theory is tantamount to saying there were two assassins. After reading the entire report and the accompanying twenty-six volumes of evidence, Jim Garrison, the district attorney of New Orleans, came to the conclusion that the Warren Commission was a haphazard investigation at best and was wrong in every single aspect of their conclusions, including that Oswald killed President Kennedy.[13]

In the 1970s, the Church Committee concluded that, contrary to what the Warren Commission had stated and also contrary to what Bugliosi implies in his book, the FBI and the CIA did not serve the Warren Commission well.[14] In fact, important information was not channeled to the Commission. If anything, this concept—that the FBI and CIA kept crucial information from the Commission—has grown even more ominous and looms larger today than it did in 1975. The House Select Committee on Assassinations (HSCA) concluded there was a 95 percent possibility of a second gunman in Dealey Plaza, and it criticized the methodology of the Commission in no uncertain terms. Even in 1994, thirty years after Kennedy's assassination, it turned out that the government was hiding as much information about Kennedy's murder as it had revealed in the previous three decades. Once it closed shop, the ARRB declassified about 2 million pages of records, which is the same number of pages of documents on this case that the National Archives housed prior to the creation of the Board. In fact, a new location, called National Archives II, at College Park, Maryland, had to be created to store all these new documents. (Bugliosi perhaps does not know this since it appears all of his searches for documents were done on the phone or by mail.)

After surveying the above concise summary of seven inquiries in thirty-five years, how can anyone call the differing results "simple"? Especially when, even today, there are still scores of records that were not declassified or located by the ARRB. Take, for example, the taping of Air Force One messages on the day of the assassination. Years after the ARRB closed down, a more inclusive version of the tapes stored in the Archives surfaced that exposed new information about General Curtis LeMay. Lemay's assistant was trying to locate his inbound plane as Kennedy's body was being flown back to Washington. This revelation even provoked the MSM to discuss the LeMay vs. Kennedy issue.[15] In the over 2,600 pages of *Reclaiming History,* you will see all of two references to LeMay even though Bugliosi discusses the Cuban Missile Crisis and Vietnam and LeMay was vociferously opposed to Kennedy's policies in both instances.

As noted above, what many people found disturbing about Bugliosi's approach to the JFK case were the radically different conclusions he had come to about the RFK case. As we shall see, throughout *Reclaiming History* Bugliosi heaps all kinds of harsh insults on the critics of the Warren Commission. In fact, he even outdoes the MSM in trying to render the term "conspiracy theorist" as a reflexive, automatic pejorative. Yet, listen to Vincent Bugliosi during a civil trial involving the Robert Kennedy case:

> "But recent revelations . . . have indicated that there is a little more credibility to the word 'conspiracy'. If there is a conspiracy here, it could possibly involve people in the highest levels of our government."[16]

Bugliosi went beyond that a few moments later:

> "We are talking about a conspiracy to commit murder . . . a conspiracy the prodigious dimensions of which would make Watergate look like a one-roach marijuana case."[17]

A bit after that he described how conspiracies were constructed:

> "Conspiracies are proven bit by bit . . . until . . . you have a mosaic. They are proven by circumstantial evidence. Conspiracies are conceived in shadowy recesses. They are not hatched on television in front of 5,000,000 witnesses." [18]

Vincent Bugliosi is anything but dumb, so he must have been aware that in publishing *Reclaiming History*—where one of his methods was to demean and ridicule the critics of the Warren Commission in extreme terms—someone would probably go back and look up his contrary language on the same subject in the Robert Kennedy case. Therefore, he supplies a reason for why he had such differing views on the two cases. In his end notes section, he says that the evidence of the number of shots fired at RFK in the kitchen pantry at the Ambassador Hotel outstrips the number of bullets that the alleged assassin, Sirhan Sirhan, could have fired."[19] Having studied that case, I agree with that statement, but having studied the JFK case even longer, it is hard for me to believe that Bugliosi could not see that the same problem applied to the earlier case. There is just too much evidence that more than three shots were fired in Dealey Plaza. We shall look at that evidence in a future chapter.

This observation indicates the overall plan of Bugliosi's book. From an in-depth analysis, it seems that Bugliosi has done the following: the material the prosecutor thinks he can deal with adequately is included in the main text; the material he thinks he may have some difficulty with, he places in his end notes; and the material he does not wish to deal with, he leaves out.

Bugliosi's (Nonbinding) Pledge

This relates to one of the most curious statements in the entire book. In the introduction, the prosecutor writes, "My only master and my only mistress are the facts and objectivity. I have no others." Then follows one of the most questionable sentences in the entire book:

> "The theorists may not agree with my conclusions, but . . . I intend to set forth
> all of their main arguments, and the way they, not I, want them to be set forth,
> before I seek to demonstrate their invalidity."

He closes out this pledge by writing the following:

> "I will not *knowingly* omit or distort anything."[20] (Emphasis in the original.)

To anyone who really knows the JFK case, this was perhaps the most ill-advised statement in a book that—as we shall see—literally bubbles over with them. And, for the life of me, I cannot understand why his editor let Bugliosi keep it in the book. Clearly, Bugliosi made his name as an assistant district attorney. *Reclaiming History*, as we shall see, was instigated by a TV trial in which he participated as a prosecutor. Prosecutors do not normally help the defense make their case, and whatever Bugliosi may say, his book is designed as a giant prosecutor's brief. This is one reason, as we shall also see, it is so vitriolic in tone. No objective person can read *Reclaiming History* without coming to that conclusion. But, besides that, the JFK case is so huge and complicated that no author can simply go through the entire case and present both sides of each issue. With the four million pages that have been declassified to date,

that would take a series of books at least as long as the twenty-six volumes of
the Warren Commission. That kind of assignment would also take a writer
with a much more scholarly and detached attitude toward the evidence than a
prosecutor has. Bugliosi's claim about presenting the critics' arguments as they
wanted them presented was simply a silly one to make. It is confounding as to
why he made it. Let us preview how faulty it is by taking just four examples,
which we will revisit later in this discussion.

First, there is the polygraph examination the Warren Commission gave
to Jack Ruby. Predictably, the Commission went to the FBI for this assignment.[21] Bell Herndon was a fourteen-year veteran of the FBI and had a long
background with the polygraph machine. He explained to the Commission
that there were three physical indications the machine was designed to capture: respiratory patterns, heart rate and blood pressure, and something termed
GSR, or galvanic skin response. GSR measures the response of skin and muscle tissue to internal stimuli and can be very revealing of emotions in certain
subjects.

Years later, the House Select Committee on Assassinations (HSCA) hired a
three-man panel to review the results of Herndon's work. This panel concluded
that Herndon violated a host of polygraph rules and regulations in this test. At
least ten of them to be exact.[22] Taken as a whole, these would have been enough
to invalidate the test, which, quite naturally, Herndon said Ruby had passed.
But the panel went even further in criticizing Herndon's test. They discovered
that Herndon set the GSR device at only 25 percent of its maximum power at
the start. He then actually lowered it from there.[23] The panel noted this was
the opposite of normal practice. Because of this, the panel considered the GSR
reading to be a complete waste. So, the HSCA is undermining one of the findings of the Warren Commission. So much for this being a simple case.

The HSCA report on this subject is twenty-one pages long. In his behe-
moth book, Bugliosi devotes all of two pages to the subject. In his end notes, he
reveals that he did read the panel's report,[24] but he does not mention Herndon's
subterfuge with the GSR setting. And of Herndon's multitude of violations of
protocol, the prosecutor mentions only two. To put it mildly, this is not how
a responsible and knowledgeable critic would address the subject—or present
the evidence about it—because this exam goes to the heart of whether or not
Ruby was lying during his examination and whether or not the FBI deliberately
covered up that perjury.

Let us now go to a second important piece of evidence. Some would call
it the most important and exculpatory piece of evidence in this entire case:
Commission Exhibit 399. This is, of course, the infamous Magic Bullet—the

projectile that the Warren Commission says went through two people, President Kennedy and Governor John Connally, making seven wounds and smashing two bones, yet emerging from this travail in almost pristine condition. From almost the beginning, most informed people have questioned whether or not this was possible, or whether someone substituted CE 399 into the record to make a ballistics link to Oswald's alleged rifle. If the latter is the case, it means someone probably planted the ersatz bullet.

In late 1966, explosive evidence surfaced which gave credence to the substitution concept. Author Josiah Thompson interviewed Parkland Hospital Security Chief O. P. Wright. President Kennedy was rushed to Parkland Hospital for emergency treatment after he was shot, and that is where CE 399 was discovered. When Thompson showed up for the interview with a picture of CE 399 depicting a copper coated, round nosed, military jacketed bullet, Wright immediately told him that was not the bullet he turned over to the Secret Service. He said he had turned over a lead colored, sharp pointed, hunting round.[25] Wright had a very familiar background in firearms since he used to work for the sheriff's department. Thompson wrote that if this was true, it indicated that either the FBI or the Secret Service had switched the bullet and therefore the assassination was, at least in part, an "inside job."

It is clear from his footnotes that Bugliosi knows about the Wright/Thompson interview because he read Thompson's 1967 book *Six Seconds in Dallas,* but he left this particular interview out of his book. Again, no serious critic would do that in presenting the case for Oswald's innocence.

Let us conclude this discussion of Bugliosi's pledge to present the evidence the way the critics would by mentioning the investigation by the ARRB of the medical evidence. When the Board was set up it was allowed to do special investigations if there was any kind of ambiguity about particular evidence in the record. There is much "ambiguity" about the medical evidence in the JFK case, and therefore board counsel Jeremy Gunn and military records analyst Doug Horne conducted many interviews with witnesses from both Parkland Hospital in Dallas and Bethesda Naval Hospital in Maryland. The latter was where the actual autopsy of Kennedy was performed. Some of this Gunn/Horne material was quite interesting. Two of their interviews were more than interesting: those with pathologist James Humes and with medical photographer James Stringer. These interviews brought into question the authenticity of both the autopsy X-rays and the photographs.

In the first instance, Gunn asked chief pathologist Humes to look at an X-ray of Kennedy's skull. In his autopsy report, Humes had described a trail of metal particles that began at the lower rear of the skull (the occipital area) and extended to the top of the skull in the supraorbital area. This would have roughly corresponded with what the Commission said happened with the fatal headshot which killed Kennedy: it came in at the bottom of the skull and exited at a *higher* point, above the right ear on the right side of the head. The pro em is this: no such trail of fragments exists on the X-rays today. Gunn han ered this point home in an interview he did with Humes.[26]

> Gunn: "Do you recall having seen an X-ray previously that had fragments corresponding to a small occipital wound?"
> Humes: "Well I reported that I did, so I must have. But I don't see it now."

What happened to those fragments is a mystery we will return to in our chapter on the autopsy evidence. The point is that Bugliosi does not furnish this quote in his book, but almost any critic, especially a medical expert, would do so in presenting the problems with the autopsy evidence.

And almost any medical expert would present another exchange from the ARRB depositions. Bugliosi spends many pages in his book discussing the mystery of Kennedy's lost brain[27] because this important exhibit is nowhere to be found today. Bugliosi lays into Horne with no reservations for saying that the pictures of Kennedy's brain in the National Archives are not actually his and are most likely pictures of a different brain. Bugliosi then leaves out perhaps the most explosive interview in the entire ARRB canon. Autopsy photographer John Stringer was asked if he took basilar photos—ones shot from underneath—of the brain. He said he had not, even though there are such photos in the National Archives.[28] Stringer also said there were identification tags used in his shots of the brain, yet these are absent from the brain photos in the archives.[29] When shown actual photos of the brain from the National Archives, Stringer was genuinely puzzled since the edge numbers on the film revealing both the film used and the technique employed were not used by him. Gunn then asked him, in light of all this, would he be able to identify the photographs before him as pictures of the brain of President Kennedy. Stringer replied simply and powerfully: "No, I couldn't say that they were President Kennedy's. . . . All I know is, I gave everything to Jim Humes, and he gave them to Admiral Burkley."[30] Needless to say, in keeping with the topic, this startling piece of sworn testimony does not appear in *Reclaiming History*.

As the reader can see, each of these four instances involves very important issues in the Kennedy case. And in each of them, Bugliosi's text would seem to contradict his introductory statement about presenting the defense case as the critics would want their case presented. The number of instances contradicting Bugliosi's statement could easily be multiplied by a factor of five, and in fact, I did just that on an online forum.[31] In trying to understand why the prosecutor would say such a thing at the start of his book, my only explanation would be that perhaps he wanted his readership to think that he had actually neutralized every single important argument the critics had ever made, and that while doing so, he posed their questions in their own manner. Such is not the case.

To say the least, the rhetorical combination of this dubious pledge plus the vitriolic tone was very off-putting. Perhaps because of Bugliosi's confrontational tone and because of the faults in the book, there were at least three threats of litigation over *Reclaiming History*: by Mark Lane and Joan Mellen against Bugliosi, and by Bugliosi against Gary Aguilar.[32]

Another rather disturbing aspect of the celebrated author and his self-proclaimed "magnum opus" was his reluctance to appear at Dr. Cyril Wecht's 2008 conference and defend his medicolegal findings among those who were at least as knowledgeable about the case as he was.[33]

As many foresaw, even with the good reviews, even with a few high profile media appearances, the "cinder block" of a book did not sell well. The publisher, W. W. Norton, then tried to revive the book and recoup its losses by releasing an abridged version of the work called *Four Days In November*. This did not work well either. The combination of a major publishing house, a high profile author, and a big ad campaign had somehow crashed and burned.

Tom Hanks Rescues *Reclaiming History*

But then, like a deus ex machina from a medieval play, Hollywood entered the picture. And this is why *Reclaiming Parkland* is not just about the Kennedy assassination and Vincent Bugliosi's (very long) take on it, this is also a book about the connections between Washington on the East Coast and the film colony on the West Coast. It's a subject that very few writers have discussed at any length or depth. The purchase of the film rights to *Reclaiming History* by Playtone—the production company owned by Tom Hanks and Gary Goetzman—gave me the opportunity to explore the connection between these two power centers. I came away rather surprised; surprised by how politically close the two cities are, and how, largely speaking, they mutually support each other in order to maintain the status quo. This happens both overtly and covertly. For instance, it was not discovered until months after its release that the CIA demanded and got changes in the film *Zero Dark Thirty*, changes that the CIA thought would make them look good.[34] In this book, I try to briefly tell the story of how people like Hanks and Goetzman got into a position of wielding such power that they could control the picture of how America sees a key historical event, and I try to explain something that may seem puzzling:

how men who grew up in the tumultuous sixties could then, once in a position of power, bear a movie message for us that is very little different than the flag waving and empty patriotism of the MSM. For Hanks and Goetzman, it appears the assassinations of the sixties have all been solved. They would have us believe that the CIA is a benign institution; that the Agency had no role in Watergate or the Iran/Contra scandal, that the October Surprise did not happen—neither Richard Nixon's 1968 version, nor Ronald Reagan's 1980 version, that there was no Agency complicity in the importation of heroin into the USA during the Vietnam War, or of cocaine during the illegal war against Nicaragua's Sandinista government in the eighties, and, finally, that George W. Bush was not elected president twice in two stolen elections. That would seem to be the America Playtone presents.

The problem for Hanks, Goetzman, and Playtone is that most thinking Americans understand that all of the above *did* happen, and that these events have had a crushing effect on our democracy, or what is left of it. Hanks can produce as many movies about going to the moon, about the British rock invasion of the sixties, or from the works of MSM historians like Stephen Ambrose and David McCullough as he can stomach (and he apparently has a large appetite for this stuff), and he can also produce films that cover up or ignore the true circumstances of President Kennedy's death. Hanks actually seems to think he is saying something truthful and that he is deepening and expanding the consciousness of the public. It is this aspect of the phenomenon that helps show that Hollywood really has not changed that much since the days of the studio moguls.

How did such an arrangement come to pass? How does it maintain itself? How is it exhibited in the purchase and transformation of *Reclaiming History*? Although most of this book is about Vincent Bugliosi's misguided attempt to revive the preposterous Warren Commission, a smaller but significant part is about the crushing disappointment that the New Hollywood has proven itself to be.

Part 1:
How a Calamity Befell Us

CHAPTER ONE

The Prosecutor

"People say I'm an extremely opinionated person. If opinionated means that when I think I'm right I try to shove it down everyone's throat, they are correct. . . . As for arrogant, I am arrogant and I'm kind of caustic. . . . The great majority of people I deal with are hopelessly incompetent, so there's an air of superiority about me."

—Vincent Bugliosi, *Playboy Magazine*, April 1997

Vincent Bugliosi was born in 1934 in the northern Minnesota town of Hibbing. He attended a Catholic school, played sports in high school, and became quite proficient at tennis. He eventually became Minnesota's State High School Champion and Northwest Junior Champion. He was good enough at tennis to win a scholarship to the University of Miami, Florida. After graduating from Miami, Bugliosi entered the service. He rose to the rank of captain in the army.[1] After leaving the service, he then attended UCLA Law School. He graduated in 1964 as president of his class.[2]

Shortly after passing the bar exam, Bugliosi joined the Los Angeles District Attorney's office. In a relatively short amount of time, Bugliosi became one of its busiest and most efficient prosecutors. In the little less than nine years he was there, Bugliosi lost only one felony case, while winning more than one hundred.[3]

One case in particular would rocket Bugliosi into the stratosphere of lawyer-celebrities: the one known as the Tate/LaBianca Murders. On the morning of Saturday, August 9, 1969, the housekeeper for film director Roman Polanski and his wife, actress Sharon Tate, discovered the first of five corpses in the Polanski home in the Bel Air section of Los Angeles. The police eventually discovered four more bodies at the site. In addition to Sharon Tate, there was mens' hairstylist Jay Sebring, coffee heiress Abigail Folger, her boyfriend Victor Frykowski, and recent high school graduate Steve Parent, who had been visiting his acquaintance, caretaker William Garretson.

The very next evening, the bodies of Leno LaBianca and his wife Rosemary were found in their home in the Hollywood district of Los Feliz. These two gruesome discoveries formed the beginning of the infamous Tate/LaBianca murder cases. Since both homes were in the city of Los Angeles, the local DA's office handled the cases. Aaron Stovitz, the head of the Trials Division, picked the thirty-five-year-old Bugliosi to aid him. Forgetting about both the Charles Lindbergh child kidnapping case and the assassination of President Kennedy, assistant Bugliosi was quick to ordain the multiple homicides as "the case of the century."[4]

Due to the huge amount of publicity the murders generated, the first judge, David Keene, placed a gag order on the attorneys. During the trial, the DA felt that Stovitz violated that order. Stovitz was therefore removed from the proceedings.[5] Bugliosi now became the lead prosecutor in the case.

Susan Atkins was already in jail due to suspicion in another homicide. While at Sybil Brand Institute, Atkins told inmates about being present inside the Tate home and being driven to the LaBianca home on the nights the killings occurred. She allegedly admitted this not once, but twice, to two different detainees: Ronnie Howard and Virginia Graham. In November, through Howard, news of her confession eventually got back to the authorities.[6] A few days later, Graham got in contact with the Los Angeles Police Department. The police then taped Graham's testimony about her conversation with Atkins.[7] A couple of hours later, LAPD began to question other people who had been involved with Charles Manson, a name Atkins had revealed to Howard and Graham.

Atkins's lawyer arranged to have his client tape her confession for him. On December 3rd, he then presented this to Stovitz, Bugliosi, and the police.[8] Caballero allowed this evidence to be entered to the grand jury. In return, Atkins's testimony could not be used against her in court. Based on this grand jury testimony, Manson and others who had been named by Atkins were charged with the murders. Manson was not that difficult to find since he had just been charged with arson and auto theft in Inyo County, a desolate place about 175 miles northeast of Los Angeles. But, as Stovitz later said, if Manson had not set fire to a bulldozer, they might never have found him up in the deserted Death Valley.[9]

After many weeks of pretrial motions, attorney juggling, and jury selection, the trial began on July 24, 1970. Including its penalty phase, the joint trial went on for nearly nine months. Judge Charles Older sentenced the convicted defendants to death on murder and conspiracy charges on April 19, 1971. In 1972, in the case of *People v. Anderson*, the California Supreme Court voted to eliminate the death penalty. Therefore, the death sentences were commuted to life in prison.

Already in the limelight because of the deluge of publicity about the trials, Bugliosi decided to write a book about his experiences on the case. A major publisher, W. W. Norton—the same publisher that released *Reclaiming History*—teamed the first-time author with an experienced writer, Curt Gentry. The book was published in 1974. Entitled *Helter Skelter,* it quickly became a bestseller, and it stayed on the bestseller list a long time because a much watched two-night television film, broadcast in April 1976, kept it there when the book was released as a mass-market paperback. *Helter Skelter* eventually sold over seven million copies, becoming the number one bestselling true crime book ever.

Looking Back at *Helter Skelter*

I had never read *Helter Skelter* prior to preparing this book, but after reading it, I decided to do some supplementary research on that case. I was rather surprised by what I found. The spectacular success of the book and TV film seems to have blinded many people to some central issues about both that book and the case itself. In this discussion of Bugliosi as author/prosecutor, it seems appropriate to, however belatedly, review those issues in this setting.

In light of the attitude taken in *Reclaiming History,* it seems important to note that Bugliosi and the DA's office achieved the convictions of Manson and the others on the vicarious liability clause of the criminal conspiracy statute. In a conspiracy trial, this means any member of the conspiracy can be held liable for the crimes committed by his coconspirators in furtherance of the plot, even if the final act did not actually include certain members of the plot.[10] It was on this legal ground that Manson was convicted of the murders in Tate/LaBianca. This was necessary since Manson was not present at the scene during either set of murders. (On the second night, he had been on the scene but left before the murders took place.) Therefore, as shown at this trial, Bugliosi thoroughly understands this concept in law, for he himself used it quite pointedly in this case. For instance, during his summation to the jury, the prosecutor said, "Manson thought he would get off by not killing anyone. Well, it's not that easy . . . The law of conspiracy has trapped these murderers even as the killers trapped their victims."[11] Therefore, demeaning the generic idea of conspiracy as a "theory"—as Bugliosi does throughout *Reclaiming History*—reveals a rather short memory on his part.

Another interesting aspect of *Helter Skelter* to note in comparison to *Reclaiming History* is this: Bugliosi spends page after page criticizing the police work in the Tate/LaBianca cases. At times, he actually names the people he thinks are responsible for the errors or delays in the investigation. Yet, in *Reclaiming History*, he does not even note, let alone complain about, the delay that the Warren Commission had in deposing Sylvia Odio after her first contact with the FBI.[12] And Odio is an important witness to a pre-assassination plot to kill President Kennedy. One who Bugliosi himself tends to believe.

In *Helter Skelter*, Bugliosi complains throughout the first hundred or so pages about the failure of the police to link the two cases—Tate and LaBianca—even though there were signs they were related. In *Reclaiming History*, he refuses to see any relationship between the failed attempt to kill President Kennedy in Chicago in early November with the successful attempt three weeks later to kill him in Dallas.

In *Helter Skelter*, the prosecutor looks with skepticism on what he considers a questionable judgment of accidental death in the case of Manson follower John Philip Haught. Yet, in *Reclaiming History*, he displays no such skepticism over the questionable death scenes of any number of important witnesses such as Gary Underhill, George de Mohrenschildt, and FBI domestic intelligence chief William Sullivan.

In *Helter Skelter*, the prosecutor notes that although the firearms weapon used by one of the murderers was actually discovered by a bystander and sent to a San Fernando Valley police station, it took a while for the weapon to get downtown.[13] Yet, in *Reclaiming History*, he makes no complaint about how long it took the Dallas police to send three bullets recovered from patrolman J. D. Tippit's shooting scene to the FBI to be tested. Or that, on the original police report, there was no mention at all of recovered cartridges. Yet six days later, four were entered.[14]

Although we could go on much longer in this vein, let us note one last comparison example. In *Helter Skelter*, Bugliosi is at pains to show how difficult it was for Ronnie Howard to relay information about the Atkins confession to the authorities even though she was in jail at the time.[15] Yet, in *Reclaiming*

History, he is nonplussed by the failure of the Dallas Police to accept an offer to speak to Rose Cherami, a witness who had potentially explosive evidence about two Cubans planning to assassinate President Kennedy in Dallas.[16]

To anyone familiar with the two cases, it would appear that the prosecutor had a healthy sense of disdain for professional incompetence and negligence back in 1969. To be charitable, it appears that the quality left him as he aged.

Former New York homicide prosecutor Robert Tanenbaum termed the Tate/LaBianca trial a "motion picture case." That is, one in which you have an eyewitness (in this case, two of them) plus you have the forensic exhibits to corroborate what that eyewitness says. It is hard for the defense to surmount this kind of case. And, in fact, as author George Bishop notes in his book on the trial, the defense attorneys felt the case was a "lost cause" from the start.[17] As Bishop stated it, "under the present circumstances, the scales of justice seemed heavily tipped in favor of the people."[18] So it would seem that in this regard, Bugliosi and Gentry were indulging themselves in a bit of literary license for the purpose of building drama in *Helter Skelter*. Once Atkins started talking to Ronnie Howard, the case, as Bugliosi himself said, was broken.[19] From there, it was not uphill, but downhill.

Even though Bugliosi tried to make the case sound difficult, that downhill "slalom run" was greatly aided by the negative publicity surrounding the events. To give just one example, well in advance of the trial, on December 14, 1969, with the help of journalist Lawrence Schiller, the *Los Angeles Times* published the Atkins confession. Then, just five days later, *Life Magazine* featured Manson on its cover with a maniacal glare in his eyes, the caption reading: The Love and Terror Cult. This was months before jury selection took place, therefore it was well-nigh impossible to find anyone who had not been exposed to the deluge of advance publicity, yet the judge would not allow a change of venue. The grounds being that the publicity was so omnipresent it was unlikely any city in the USA was unaffected by it.

Bugliosi's Motive for Murder: The Beatles

Today, one of the most controversial aspects of the Tate/LaBianca trial is the motive put forth for the crimes. Let us detail that motive here so the reader can examine it in the full and vivid scope of its grandiosity.

As author Ed Sanders notes, in prison Manson learned to play the guitar and proved to be an adept student with a pleasant voice. When he was released in March 1967, Manson was interested in developing a musical career. In fact, he had developed some leads in prison to help him in this pursuit. In 1968, the Beatles recorded Paul McCartney's song "Helter Skelter." The title came from a

London amusement park ride.[20] That song, which would be a strong influence on the heavy metal movement, was released on the *White Album*. Let us try and follow Bugliosi's attempt to fit that song into a motive for the murders.

Revelation 9:15 refers to four angels being let loose for an indeterminate amount of time to "slay the third part of men." According to Bugliosi, Manson follower Paul Watkins and Gregg Jakobson (who along with his friend Terry Melcher was trying to promote Manson's musical career) said Manson interpreted this to mean that one third of mankind, the white race, would die during this apocalypse. Bugliosi said Manson somehow related this slaughter of the white race to the amusement park song "Helter Skelter" and thought it was also signaled on the *White Album* through songs like "Blackbird" and "Revolution Number 9." After an apocalyptic race war, the Black Muslims would be the only faction standing. However, they would not be able to make order out of chaos and would turn to Manson and his followers, who would now come out of a bottomless pit mentioned in the first verse of Revelation 9. By this time, they will have multiplied into the tens of thousands and now Manson and his followers would retire the Black Muslims and rule the world.[21] Bugliosi was apparently convinced of this theory by the fact that one of the attackers had written the words "Healter Skelter" in blood on the refrigerator at the scene of the LaBianca murder. Even though it was spelled wrong, and even though what happened there was not Paul McCartney's amusement ride and therefore could not have connoted these wild images of a race war, let alone the Book of Revelation—Bugliosi now had his overall paradigm.

As the reader contemplates this mind-numbing Bible/Beatles concoction he or she should recall this fact: Bugliosi is the man who cannot find one credible conspiracy theory in the JFK case.

The motive was pure Bugliosi. To his credit, Aaron Stovitz, who was technically the lead lawyer, *never* bought the idea of "Helter-Skelter." In fact, he stayed skeptical about it until his death.[22] But Stovitz looked at the case differently than Bugliosi. To Stovitz, it was another murder case and it was to be treated as such; Bugliosi did not see it that way. In fact, when he heard Stovitz interviewed on the radio saying just that, he came into work the next day in a state of bewilderment. He explained to his colleague that Tate/LaBianca was not just any other case; that it was unlike any other crime ever committed in "the whole history of mankind." When Stovitz resisted this, Bugliosi would not let up: "This has got to be the biggest murder case that ever happened."[23] His brow furrowed in a state of agitation, he then walked out.

After this confrontation, Stovitz's superior, J. Miller Leavy, walked into the room. Having overheard some of the conversation, he had a revealing colloquy with Stovitz. "Vince getting excited?" he asked. Stovitz pointed up to a discolored acoustic tile in the ceiling, "He was just up there," he said. "Sticking to the ceiling," said Leavy. "Like a pizza," Stovitz replied.[24] This is an important anecdote for the reader to remember. Although both men appreciated Bugliosi's skills as a prosecutor, they understood his innate excitability and flair for hyperbole.

Which would later come in handy. For as trial chronicler George Bishop wrote, Bugliosi appeared to believe in the Helter Skelter theory more than Manson did.[25] To Bishop, Manson was essentially a con man who sold bits and pieces of his half-baked ideas to different people he thought could help him or he needed to frighten so he could control them. As Bishop noted, the idea that the wily ex-con actually could or meant to put it all together into a cohesive philosophy, this was something beyond Manson.[26] For instance, why on earth would the Muslims ever turn to Manson, and why were there never any further home invasions? Shouldn't Manson have ordered attacks on at least one African American home? But, as Bishop also points out, selling this wild phantasmagoria was not beyond Bugliosi. The prosecutor had a fine sense of theater and was very much at home, stage center in a courtroom.[27] Therefore, the seasoned lawyer could make this fantastic scenario saleable to a jury. And as the prosecutor pointed out to that jury, motive may be considered evidence of guilt.[28] What worse motive could there be than the creed he was reciting?

Was "Helter Skelter" an Urban Legend?

As noted above, it's an open question whether the prosecutor himself ever really bought the warlock's alchemy because when confronted with Stovitz's skepticism over it, Bugliosi said that he would abandon it instantly if someone could come up with something better.[29] But he told Stovitz that there was so little money stolen that robbery was an unrealistic motive. As if that were the only alternative.

In *Helter Skelter*, there is an interesting, almost throwaway line to the effect that drugs had nothing to do with the crimes.[30] At that point in the book, it is couched in terms of the perpetrators using drugs that night. As we shall see, it appears that the prosecutor does not want the reader to contemplate that angle in any manner, but when one examines the evidence chronicled outside of *Helter Skelter,* one has to question why the statement exists as it does. As it turns out, at least two of the perpetrators *were* on speed the night of the Tate murders, which vitiates the point the prosecutor is trying to make about Manson's control over the killers and his design of the murder scene.

But even more curious, in author George Bishop's description of the trial, there is very interesting testimony from an LAPD narcotics officer[31] who stated that marijuana, hashish, cocaine, and Methylenedioxyamphetamine were found at the scene of the Tate murders.

Bugliosi and Gentry mention this, but only in passing. It's almost as if they mention it only in order to dispose of it.

Maintaining the Helter Skelter mythos allows Bugliosi and Gentry to make their recurrent and ridiculous comparisons of Manson with Adolf Hitler. The problem being that, taken in their proper context, these comparisons are as goofy as the Beatles/Bible concept. The idea that a band of social misfits who had to freeload off an elderly, near-blind owner of an obsolete movie ranch—George Spahn—who now made his money renting horseback rides, can be compared to what Hitler, Goebbels, Roehm, Goering and Himmler did in Germany is so nutty as to be risible.

But further, Manson could never do what Hitler did since, due to his appearance and poor speaking skills, he could never go public as the face of a mass movement. Therefore, he could never attract the type of people with the formidable abilities of say a Joseph Goebbels, Heinrich Himmler or Reinhard Heydrich. Within five years of taking control of the Nazi Party, Hitler was ready to stage a coup in Bavaria, the largest state in Germany. At the end, Manson could not even stay in control of a deserted ranch in Inyo County, a place so remote and empty that, as a policeman said, "You could hide the Empire State Building out there and no one could find it."[32] From there, where was Manson going to strike? At the local Gila monsters and cactus plants? The comparison is simply preposterous. At the same time that it aggrandizes a pimp, drug dealer, and con artist, it softens the true horror of the German national tragedy of Nazism, let alone the millions who perished through its industrialized engines of destruction. And it points out a problem with *Reclaiming History* that will be discussed later: Bugliosi's shortcomings as a historian.

I have taken this long to discuss this book and this case because Bugliosi made his name on it. It belongs to him and is supposed to show the prosecutor at his absolute best. Much of the public considers it his finest literary effort, and they know him through this book. It is also a case in which the forensics evidence was not questionable—there was really no arguing about the gun used that night or the fingerprints discovered at the scene. As we will see, this is not at all the case with the Kennedy assassination. In fact, it's the opposite. Both the genuineness of the evidence in the JFK case and chain of possession of that evidence is extremely questionable. Although few can fault Bugliosi's performance in Tate/LaBianca purely as a prosecutor, as shown above, one *can* fault his performance as an investigator. The two roles do not serve the same function or purpose. As we shall see, the FBI investigation upon which the Warren Commission, and Bugliosi, rely, was compromised from the start in the Kennedy case. Yet, Bugliosi the investigator accepted it.

To give Bugliosi his due, he has written at least two well-argued political polemics: *No Island of Sanity* and *The Betrayal of America*. He deserves kudos for those books, and I personally congratulated him about the latter for his work in the *Bush v. Gore* case. Bugliosi then forwarded his earlier book on the Paula Jones case to me. I thought that was also a good book. The evidence would seem to indicate that when Bugliosi works with relatively simple and tangible cases—cases in which the investigation has already been concluded or there is little investigation to do—he does good enough work and is well worth reading in that regard. But it would seem that as both author and lawyer, he does not handle scope and complexity well.

Which is why he should have never taken on the JFK case.

CHAPTER TWO

The Producers

"I totally believed there was a conspiracy, but after you read the book, you are almost embarrassed that you ever believed it. To think that guys who grew up in the sixties would make a miniseries supporting the idea that Oswald acted alone is something I certainly wouldn't have predicted. But time and evidence can change the way we view things."

—Gary Goetzman, *Daily Variety*, June 7, 2007

If by saying he "read the book" in the above quote means producer Gary Goetzman actually read the entire 2,646 pages of Vincent Bugliosi's *Reclaiming History* I would be very surprised. I would also be very surprised if Goetzman and his producing partner, Tom Hanks, were familiar with the 2 million pages of declassified documents related to the Kennedy murder that the Assassination Records Review Board (ARRB) had declassified by 1998 when they closed their doors after four years. To even seriously contemplate that someone like Goetzman or Hanks did such a thing is simply a nonstarter.

So how did Hollywood power players more comfortable on the Beverly Hills cocktail circuit or practicing their tennis game enter into such a confusing maze as the murder of President Kennedy? In the *Daily Variety* story quoted above, reporter Michael Fleming writes that the idea was hatched after Hanks,

Goetzman, and their colleague actor Bill Paxton had a conversation about the JFK case. They then decided to look at Bugliosi's book, which had just been published by W. W. Norton.

So *Variety's* scenario has three Movieland mavens sitting at Spago's and deciding to debate the JFK case—figuring out how an entrance wound could make a larger hole than an exit wound (which it did in this case) and how and why Oswald left the Marines early to go to Russia—out of the blue. If that sounds a bit strained to the reader, he should not feel alone. It sounded strained to me too. Because prior to this, Goetzman had produced—or coproduced—such film fare as *Modern Girls, Amos and Andrew, Miami Blues, The Ant Bully, The Polar Express, My Big Fat Greek Wedding,* and *Mamma Mia!*. His partner on the last four titles was Tom Hanks, who had also produced the films *Cast Away* and *Evan Almighty* with Goetzman.

What could provoke a spontaneous conversation about a forty-five-year-old murder mystery that shook the foundations of the republic between such La La Land insiders?

In the Beginning

It turned out that Mr. Fleming's trade magazine report was incomplete. In a later appearance on Tavis Smiley's talk show, Bill Paxton was more accurate in what had actually transpired. Paxton had a personal interest in Kennedy's assassination. Back in November 1963, Paxton's father had taken him to see President Kennedy, Vice President Lyndon Johnson, and Governor John Connally as they emerged from the Texas Hotel in Paxton's hometown of Fort Worth the morning of the assassination, Kennedy's last stop before Dallas. Paxton, who was almost nine years old, went back to school that day and heard the news that Kennedy had been killed. As he told Smiley, "And I couldn't really kind of grapple, I couldn't really comprehend what had happened . . . I just saw him, I thought, that can't be."[1]

Decades later, in 2007, Paxton was at a Dallas film festival near Dealey Plaza and decided to walk over to the Sixth Floor Museum. One of the employees there dug out the extant film of Kennedy that morning in Fort Worth. In one of the shots, there was young Paxton on his father's shoulders.[2]

Paxton's memory was rekindled the same year *Reclaiming History* came out. When he returned to Los Angeles, Paxton learned about the upcoming publication, most likely through the *Los Angeles Times.* As we have seen, that *Times* article was probably done with the help of Bugliosi's PR man. Paxton, unaware he was being manipulated, then had his "eureka!" moment. As he told

Smiley, "Has anyone ever just told this story without bias, without an agenda, without a conspiracy? Just tell it as a human interest story." Apparently—and as we will see, mistakenly—Paxton thought that *Reclaiming History* was the answer to his question. He then took this book to Tom Hanks and Goetzman. Hanks told Paxton it was going to be their next project.[3]

The cooperation between the *Los Angeles Times* and Bugliosi's publicity machine was well oiled.[4] The author of the *Times* review, Jim Newton, had just penned a 600 page laudatory book on the life and career of Chief Justice Earl Warren. The idea that a biographer like Newton would then find fault with a book that discounts and disguises the greatest failure of Warren's career is, to say the least, naïve. But the point is, the publicity machine for *Reclaiming History* had succeeded. The radio and TV appearances, the laudatory reviews, had done the trick. Just one month after the book was published, Fleming's story appeared in *Daily Variety*. The Hanks/Goetzman producing entity, Playtone, had purchased the rights to *Reclaiming History*.

About three months later, HBO had jumped on board. Colin Callender, president of HBO films, announced that his cable channel would carry a ten-part miniseries based upon the book. At that time, Paxton was starring in the HBO series *Big Love*, which was also produced by Playtone. With typical Hollywood hyperbole, Callender bellowed the following about the producers of *The Ant Bully*: "We are delighted that Tom, Gary, and Bill brought this amazing project to HBO. The successful creative partnership we have enjoyed with them over the years imbues us with a confidence, an excitement, and the knowledge that Bugliosi's riveting book will make a very powerful transition to screen."[5] Bugliosi now joined in the media acclamation of the new partnership which would bring the truth about November 22, 1963, to a wide audience. After saying that he was "really excited to be working with people of the immense stature of Tom Hanks, Gary Goetzman, and Bill Paxton," he then said that the vast majority of the public believed the *falsehood* that there was a conspiracy to murder President Kennedy. (Emphasis added.) Working with this new triumvirate, the prosecutor must have felt confident he could make people see the light.[6] Paxton added, "This is the greatest story that's never been told. Based on the facts and evidence that Vincent Bugliosi so masterfully presents, it's a story that has haunted me and my generation our whole lives . . ." Paxton concluded that with the fiftieth anniversary of Kennedy's assassination looming ahead, "We felt it was the right time to pursue this subject."[7]

As this book will show, none of what was prognosticated in these 2007 stories ever happened. *Reclaiming History* was not Playtone's next project. No multipart miniseries was ever produced, and the evidence suggests that it was never seriously contemplated. The film that will emerge from all this hullabaloo does not even bear the title of Bugliosi's book. Finally, HBO will not produce this mutated offspring for its channel. But, considering the way the film world works, that was really beside the point. As Fleming revealed, Peter Miller of PMA Literary Agency, Bugliosi's book-to-film agent and one of the best in the business, had done what he was expected to do: make the book into a media event to the extent that his manufactured crescendo would prove irresistible to someone in the film world. Whether these purchasers read the book, or understood what it said, was irrelevant. Sales is marketing, and Bugliosi's sales agents knew that in the superheated world where literary agents meet Hollywood Honchos, flash and frill is more important than content and substance. After all the bluster in the *LA Times* over Jim Newton's "book of the ages," Goetzman was throwing overboard all that Age of Aquarius stuff. After all, Paxton was in Fort Worth at the age of eight. He had to know, right?

Wrong. It's very clear from his statement on the Tavis Smiley show that Paxton was uniquely unqualified to inform any prospective buyer about the merits of *Reclaiming History*. It's true that Bugliosi's book features no conspiracy in it, which, as we shall see, was the point of the book from its inception. But for any informed person to say *Reclaiming History* is without bias, without an agenda, and is told chiefly as a human interest story is simply nonsense. As we shall see in enormous detail, *Reclaiming History* is an extremely biased book because the author had his mind made up before he wrote the first word. In fact, two million pages of previously declassified documents could not change Bugliosi's attitude toward the subject even though some of these documents were truly startling. But since Bugliosi had contracted out to write a book that hewed to the Warren Commission line while he personally demeaned the report's critics, this new evidence was irrelevant to his contractual arrangement.

Paxton was likely unaware of all this subterranean stuff that had been going on for decades, or he would not have said that *Reclaiming History* featured a tale that had never been told. The story told by Bugliosi's book was one of the stalest and hoariest in contemporary history; the same discredited story as told by the Warren Commission back in 1964. One of the most surprising things about *Reclaiming History* is that there is so little that is new in it. That Paxton could say that the book tells a tale that has not been told reveals that he did not bother to consult anyone to do an academic peer review of the book. (As we will see in a later chapter, Giorgio DiCaprio and Earl Katz did allow for this. They just didn't care for the results.)

The evidence would indicate that Paxton was starstruck by the fact that a lawyer of Bugliosi's stature had become interested enough in the JFK case to write a long book about it. Paxton probably thought that if Bugliosi agreed with the Warren Commission, then other lawyers who had contact with the case must be of the same persuasion. If that is what he thought, Paxton was simply wrong because once we get beyond the Warren Commission, Vincent Bugliosi is more the exception than the rule.

How did these men get into such a position to make such momentous public decisions about highly controversial and very important historical issues, and further, to be able to work the levers of power to actually act upon them? To understand that, one must understand Tom Hanks.

Tom Hanks Becomes an Actor

Tom Hanks's image is that of the All-American northern California boy who was born in the Eisenhower era and grew up under presidents Kennedy and Johnson.

Young Tom began to watch a lot of television, a habit that would stay with him through late in his teenage years and well into college. He was especially keen on watching the NASA Gemini and Apollo projects to the point that he says he did not miss any of those launchings.[8] He has also said he enjoyed the twenty-six-installment British TV series "The World at War." Other favorites were the American series anthology program "Biography" and *Star Trek*. (It is important to remember these viewing habits, for they had an indelible effect on Hanks.)

It was at Skyline High School that Hanks began to find his way and his vocation. Near the school was the First Covenant Church where Hanks actively participated in all the activities offered there: choir, Sunday services, and Bible readings.

It was at Skyline High that Tom met Rawley Farnsworth, the drama teacher there. Hanks took every class Rawley offered[9] and also acted in many of Farnsworth's productions like *Twelfth Night*, *The Night of the Iguana*, and *South Pacific*. According to observers, he was especially good in the last.

After he graduated, Hanks went to Chabot Community College in Hayward, California. A friend and former Farnsworth student, John Gilkerson, encountered him one day and asked what he was doing. When he learned that Hanks wasn't acting, Gilkerson advised him to get into some plays. Hanks later said that this was when he first began to pursue an acting career.[10]

Hanks then began to act in college productions, take drama classes, and see productions of plays in community theater. He then went to Sacramento State to study theater. Vincent Dowling, artistic director of the Great Lakes Shakespeare Festival, was a guest director at Sacramento State and was impressed by Hanks's enthusiasm. He invited Hanks to go to Cleveland with him.[11] Immersed in theater, Hanks left college before graduation.

Dowling was not just a director, but also a distinguished actor who had been with Ireland's storied Abbey Theater for two decades. Under his supervision, Hanks appeared in Shakespearean plays like *The Taming of the Shrew* and *The Two Gentlemen of Verona*.

Hanks decided to move to New York with his live-in girlfriend, Susan Dillingham, who took the stage name Samantha Lewes. In 1979 he performed in an off-Broadway play, Machiavelli's *The Mandrake*. That play provided him with an important connection. A girl in the production knew a talent manager who was looking for clients. The manager arranged for Hanks to sign with J. Michael Bloom Agency, which had offices in both New York and in Los Angeles. Bloom was good at handling young actors and launching their careers, knowing once they hit it big they would bolt for one of the A-list agencies.[12]

In 1980, Hanks was sent on an audition for an ABC situation comedy called *Bosom Buddies*. He was cast as a colead with Peter Scolari, moved to LA, and began making $9,000 per episode.

Tom Hanks Becomes a Star

Bosom Buddies ran for just two years. Like most TV sitcoms, it had a basically unbelievable premise: two up-and-coming ad agency employees disguise themselves as women in order to live in an apartment they can afford. Hanks showed the energy and fine timing of a natural comic performer, and when the show was cancelled, he did several TV guest spots. One was on *Happy Days*. That show's star, Ron Howard, was trying to branch out into film directing and when he was preparing his romantic fantasy film *Splash*, he remembered Hanks and offered him the role. *Splash* became the surprise hit of 1984. Hanks was now a star and in demand as a comic movie actor.

One can argue that over the next ten years Hanks appeared in some of the worst American films of the last three decades: *The Man with One Red Shoe*, *The Money Pit*, *Dragnet*, *The 'Burbs*, *Joe Versus the Volcano*, and *The Bonfire of the Vanities*. The last was so atrocious that Julie Salamon wrote a bestselling book on how Hollywood managed to make a sow's ear out of Tom Wolfe's silk purse.

In 1993 and 1994, Hanks began to turn his film career around. He was offered two very good roles in the films *Philadelphia* and *Forrest Gump*. Both films did well at the box office; the latter picture actually smashed records. And Hanks did something very rare: he won an Oscar two years in a row.[13]

It was on the set of *Philadelphia* that Hanks met Gary Goetzman. Goetzman, who started his career as a child actor, appeared in Jonathan

Demme's women's prison picture *Caged Heat* at the age of twenty-two. He then appeared in Demme's *Handle with Care, Last Embrace*, and *Melvin and Howard*. In 1984, Demme asked Goetzman to coproduce his Talking Heads concert film *Stop Making Sense*, which started a successful music supervising career for Goetzman with his partner Sharon Boyle. In 1991, Demme had Goetzman executive produce the smash hit, multi-Oscar-winning thriller *The Silence of the Lambs*. Two years later, Goetzman did the same for Demme's 1993 film, *Philadelphia*, where the producer/actor/music supervisor met the actor/star whose career was about to both mushroom and branch out into other areas of the film industry.

The Star Becomes a Producer

In 1996, Goetzman and Demme helped Hanks produce *That Thing You Do!*, a film Hanks wrote and directed. It was an amusing piece of ephemera about an American rock group amidst the British rock invasion. Shortly thereafter, Hanks began to make films inspired by his youthful TV watching habits, starting with the 1998 HBO miniseries *From the Earth to the Moon*, a twelve-part series adapted from Andrew Chaikin's book *A Man on the Moon*. Hanks, who had appeared in Ron Howard's film *Apollo 13*, coproduced the series with Howard, Howard's partner Brian Grazer, and Michael Bostick. Hanks directed the first episode and wrote or cowrote four others.

Hanks's biographer, David Gardner, has interesting and revealing comments as to why the actor picked this project for his miniseries producing debut. Most people who lived through the sixties recall it as an exciting time; one of hope, change, dynamism, and ultimate disappointment due in large part to the extinguishing of that hope through the assassinations of four leaders: JFK, Malcolm X, Martin Luther King, and Robert Kennedy. It seems that Hanks does not remember the sixties that way at all because he grew up in a broken home with parental neglect. In speaking of the decade, he said, "I remember those as some of the worst years of my life. It was hell." He continued in that vein: "Our world was very, very polarized. If you had long hair, you were a good guy; if you had short hair you were a bad guy. We mistrusted just about anything that had to do with the government.[14]" Gardner then builds on this point of view as expressed by Hanks himself to the *New York Times*.

> "To Tom . . . the space missions were among the few lasting, happy memories he had of the era. But for many, they were mistrusted along with everything else the government of the time was involved in. It was a historical viewpoint Tom had a

vested interest in changing. In essence, he wanted to reclaim the '60s for his own
generation by giving the space program a context he felt it had been denied."[15]

To say that this is a shallow view of what went on in that turbulent decade
does not even begin to describe the inanity of these comments. To reduce that
cataclysmic, and ultimately tragic decade to a long-haired versus short-haired
dialectic—one which recalls Westerns setting white-hatted heroes against
black-hatted villains—seems to reveal a mind and mentality that, like Bugliosi, cannot handle complexity. To put it mildly, what happened in the sixties
did not reduce to a simple schema revolving around long-haired versus short-
haired young men. And the American government *was involved* in some very
bad—some would say evil—activities and endeavors. Today, no intelligent,
scholarly, and objective observer can deny that. From the quote above, it seems
that Hanks wants to try.

In the quote that began this chapter, Gary Goetzman says the scales have
finally fallen from his eyes. Is it hard to believe that someone born in the sixties
now believes the Warren Commission, and even wonders how he could ever
have believed the JFK case was a conspiracy? In light of the above, no, it's not
hard to believe. If Hanks and Goetzman's comprehension of the sixties is at
this level—that of a not-so-curious high school junior—then it's quite easy to
understand that a complex event like the Kennedy assassination seemed not
within the producers' cognitive abilities to begin with.

This insight into Hanks's consciousness is bolstered by the new foreword
he wrote for Chaikin's book upon its reissue in 1998 to accompany the broadcast of the miniseries:

> "The thing that still fuels me in my day-to-day life and what I want to convey to
> my children, and to the audience, is that if mankind can figure out a way to put
> twelve men on the moon, then, honestly, we can solve anything."

He went on to add that the stories of the astronauts who landed on the
moon are among the very finest stories ever told. In fact, at the end of Part 4 of
the series, the script literally says that the success of Apollo 8 in 1968 redeemed
the assassinations of King and RFK that year because a woman named Valerie
Pringle said so. She wrote to the astronauts, "You saved 1968."

Such a viewpoint is rather juvenile and ahistorical. For many people, the
Apollo mission did not prove that America can solve any problem. If it did,
the country would not be in the declining position it is today. At best, like the
Manhattan Project, it proved that a nation that spends enough money and
provides enough resources to a large group of scientists can achieve a highly

technical goal. (The comparison with the Manhattan Project is made in the very first minutes of Part I of the series. A segment Hanks directed.)

But, like the Manhattan Project, the questions to ask are: What was the effect? Did the creation and dropping of the atomic bomb have a beneficial effect on America and the world? For those involved in that sector and in that industry, perhaps it did. But what about the rest of us? The same comparison can be applied to the Apollo mission. Yes, the missions were splendid scientific and technical achievements. Yes, like the power of the atomic bomb, they were spectacular to watch. But what effect did they have on the rest of us afterwards? Today, the idea of manned space travel has been all but abandoned. The idea of *mass* manned space travel is nothing but a far in MW off fantasy, especially for a fiscally bankrupt nation like ours. The Apollo mission greatly benefited NASA, and the astronauts, scientists, and technicians involved, and their related suppliers—the defense industries. It was an expensive inspiration for the country—when this country could afford it. But to proclaim it the declaration of a national will just seems silly today.

It's relevant to compare *From the Earth to the Moon* with Phil Kaufman's film about the Mercury mission, *The Right Stuff*. Based on Tom Wolfe's bestselling book, Kaufman took the materials of that book and made something original from it. Differing with Wolfe's viewpoint, he applied his own theme to the materials without really altering them. Unlike Hanks, Kaufman took a historical perspective on Mercury. He did so by adroitly and effectively juxtaposing that mission with the story of daredevil jet test-pilot Chuck Yeager. By doing so he made the mission into a historical marker. No one who has seen that film can forget the last three sequences: Lyndon Johnson feting the astronauts with a giant barbecue in the Astrodome; Yeager trying to break the altitude record for a jet plane and crashing while doing so; and Gordon Cooper setting a record for orbits of the earth. By artfully juxtaposing and intercutting them, Kaufman said something about the ending of one aeronautical age and the beginning of another. Beyond that, he posed the question of whether or not this was actually a good thing for America. He further asked: Compared to Yeager, were men like Cooper even pilots at all? These are the things that a real filmmaker does with history. This is what he or she is supposed to do. *From the Earth to the Moon* has none of this. It is little more than a pageant which chronicles a historical event. As Aristotle wrote, it is nothing but mimesis: art duplicating life; art at its most simplistic.

Hanks and Spielberg Meet Stephen Ambrose

In 1998, the same year that HBO broadcast Hanks's first miniseries, the actor starred in Steven Spielberg's *Saving Private Ryan,* a film that coupled his desire to "save the sixties" with another goal: To commemorate World War II as the Good War and to depict the American role in it as crucial. It is important to note Hanks's reaction to seeing the film at a private screening:

> "When I saw the movie for the first time, I had the luxury of being in a room by myself, so I wept openly for a long time. I have never cried harder at a movie, or almost in real life, than at the end of this one—it was just so painful. I think an absolutely unbelievable thing has occurred here, and I am part of it, and I sort of can't believe it."[16]

Maybe he can't believe it because the real events didn't happen anywhere close to those depicted in the film. In doing some World War II research, the late Stephen Ambrose discovered the story of Fritz Niland who was in the 101st Airborne that had parachuted into France as part of D-Day. While in France, Niland told his friends one day that he was leaving because his brother Bob had been killed during the Normandy invasion. He later learned that two of his other brothers had also been killed that week—one in Europe and one in the Pacific. Under the Army's sole survivor policy, he was removed from combat. It turned out that one brother did not actually die but survived a Japanese prison camp,[17] so, in reality, the sole survivor rule did not even apply. There was no search mission as the film depicts, and therefore there was no rounding up of a patrol to find Ryan/Niland. There was no sniper incident either, and there was no mistaken identity faux pas as depicted in the film. No one took out a machine gun nest at an abandoned radar station. There was no putting down a near mutiny with the survivors of the patrol. And there was no culminating tank battle over a bridge with Captain John Miller dying and telling Ryan, "James . . . earn this. Earn it." That scene did not exist since there was no Captain Miller. And since there was no Miller, there was no ending scene with Ryan in a Normandy cemetery standing over Miller's grave asking his wife if he was worthy of Miller's (nonexistent) sacrifice.

In reality, a military chaplain, Rev. Sampson, found Niland in France with very little difficulty. He told him he was going home. He was shipped back to England and then to the USA. That was it. As far as the coda goes, Peter Niland, Edward's son, laid flowers at the Normandy graves of his two uncles in 1974.

So, at the age of forty-two, what exactly was Hanks breaking down and tearing up about? Especially since he knew all this because he had met Niland's son. Therefore, Hanks knew the film was 90 percent fiction.

The Niland story was first reported in Ambrose's book *Band of Brothers*, and the now deceased Ambrose was a consultant on *Saving Private Ryan*. This is where Ambrose met Spielberg and Hanks. Ambrose talked them into contributing hundreds of thousands of dollars to preserve a pet project of his in New Orleans—the National World War II Museum.

Hanks's meetings with Ambrose and Goetzman, plus his work with Spielberg on the World War II film, combined to launch Playtone, the film production company set up by Hanks and Goetzman. It was named after the fictional recording company in Hanks's film *That Thing You Do!* Its first major TV production was the HBO miniseries adapted from Ambrose's *Band of Brothers*.

Ambrose made his reputation with his two-volume biography of Dwight Eisenhower. This quickly became the standard reference work in the field. The historian said on television that the idea for the biography came from Eisenhower, who had read one of his Civil War books, and that he would give up two days a week from his teaching job at Johns Hopkins to interview the former president.[18]

It turned out that these were both misrepresentations. Tim Rives, the deputy director at the Eisenhower Library, discovered that it was Ambrose who proposed to Eisenhower that he be his official biographer. This was done in a letter written in September 1964. The next month, Ambrose sent Eisenhower another letter along with two of his books. In the letter, he wrote that, "I would like to begin a full scale, scholarly account of your military career." In other words, Ambrose proposed himself to Eisenhower. It was not Eisenhower's idea at all.[19]

It now gets worse. It appears that, as with Gerald Posner, Ambrose created interviews. Eisenhower's retirement years were tightly controlled and documented by his appointments secretary Robert Schultz. Far from the hundreds of hours and two days a week scheduling, Eisenhower only met with Ambrose three times—a total of five hours—and they were never alone together. Ambrose's first major book on Eisenhower, *The Supreme Commander*, came out in 1970. In the notes to that book, Ambrose cited nine interview dates. Schulz's records make clear that seven of those dates are impossible since Eisenhower either was not at his home in Gettysburg or was meeting with someone else.[20]

Later on, when the actual biography was published, Ambrose covered his tracks. His notes were not specific as to a date. They just said, "Interview with DDE." The range of subjects covered by these interviews was rather extensive:

Brown vs. Board of Education case, Douglas MacArthur, quitting smoking, President Kennedy, the Rosenbergs, Dien Bien Phu. As library director Tim Rives said, the discussion of such a wide array of topics, in addition to the main subjects of the book—Ike's presidency and military career—seems staggering for such a relatively brief amount of time. This is why Rives doubts the authenticity of some of the interviews. In addition, the dates Ambrose gave for interviews with Eisenhower's brother Milton also do not check out.[21]

Ambrose Switches sides for Political Gain

But to me that is not even the worst of it. In 1988, James Bacque was preparing *Other Losses*, his startling book about American war crimes and abuses against German POWs. He sent a copy of the manuscript to Ambrose. Ambrose wrote him back with high praise for the work. He wrote, ". . . you have the goods on these guys, you have the quotes from those who were present and saw with their own eyes." He then concluded with, "You really have made a major historical discovery, the full impact of which neither you nor I nor anyone can fully imagine." In a postscript, he even said he had written a letter to Alice Mayhew, his editor at Simon and Schuster, about the book.[22]

Bacque then visited Ambrose at his home in the summer of 1988. Ambrose now went through the final draft of the book and made some final corrections and suggestions. In other words, Ambrose was editing a book he had already read and had high praise for.[23] The book was then published in four foreign countries where, as Ambrose predicted, it created a storm of controversy. But it was all documented, much of it with records from the US Army archives.

When the book was later published in America, Ambrose at first did the right thing by giving a few interviews supporting the work. But during a guest lecturing spot at the US Army War College, Ambrose suddenly did a backflip somersault. He first set up a seminar panel attacking the book. And as with the Oliver Stone film, he then criticized the book on the front page of the *New York Times Book Review*.[24]

As Bacque notes, the book was the same book Ambrose had read in advance and then praised. And Ambrose himself did not do any research to counter any of the claims in the book. It seems his visit with the Army War College was enough to remind him of what was within the boundaries of the "canons of history." Implicating a Republican military hero and president in an unspeakable crime was not within those canons.

As Bacque concluded, this decision to switch sides was not really all Ambrose's fault. The American establishment does not really value accuracy in the historical record. What it really wants is a "pleasing chronicle which justi-fies and supports our society."

"We should not wonder when a very popular writer like Ambrose is revealed to be a liar and plagiarizer, because he has in fact given us what we demand from him above all, a pleasing myth."[25]

Which helps explains why Ambrose was Hanks's favorite historian.

CHAPTER THREE

You Call This a Trial?

"One of the prerequisites for a trial is a live defendant."

—Mark Lane in *"Vinnie, it is Round"*

If Tom Hanks was really interested in historical truth rather than popular acceptance, he would have examined the origins of *Reclaiming History*. If something begins under false circumstances, the odds of it ending up as a trustworthy and sturdy product are not good. Imagine a trial in which a man would be tried for murder and during the proceedings:

1. The doctor who performed the autopsy on the victim and the two doctors who assisted him would not be testifying;
2. No eyewitness testified that the accused was in the position he needed to be in order to execute the crime;
3. The prosecution would call twice as many witnesses as the defense;
4. The defense would not present the best exculpatory evidence for the accused;
5. Scientifically false evidence was used by the prosecution, without objection by the defense;
6. The defense could not use 2 million pages of evidence that the prosecution was hiding;
7. The accused could not testify in his behalf as to where he was at the time of the crime or what his occupation really was.

Would anyone consider such an exercise to be in any way genuine? Vincent Bugliosi did. And this was the genesis for his book *Reclaiming History*. In the Introduction on page xxiv, the author writes, "Obviously, were it not for my participation in this docu-trial . . . the book would never have been written." Originating with this false foundation makes the book the literary equivalent of the Leaning Tower of Pisa.

Vince and Gerry go to London

It all began with a mock trial, *United States v Oswald*, Bugliosi did for London Weekend Television in 1986. Bugliosi was the prosecutor and another high-profile trial lawyer, Gerry Spence, was Oswald's defense attorney. Some twenty-one hours of video were cut down to four-and-a-half hours for the version broadcast on Showtime Channel. The Dallas jury ended up convicting Oswald.

As noted above, Mark Lane has pointed out that one necessity of a real trial is a live defendant. In the 1993 mock trial done for HBO of James Earl Ray in the Martin Luther King case, Ray testified. In this case, there is no doubt that Lee Harvey Oswald would have been the most important witness. By far. Oswald could give information that no one else could and he could also corroborate important testimony about such crucial issues as where he was at the time of the shooting and his associations with people like David Ferrie, Clay Shaw, and Guy Banister. There was simply no way one could compensate for Oswald's absence. How prosecutorial is Bugliosi? It's not enough that he tries to deny this crucial fact, he actually tries to say the opposite is true. Incredibly, in *Reclaiming History*, the author argues that *it's better* for the cause of truth that Oswald died.[1]

That was by no means the only flaw in the production. Dr. Cyril Wecht presented the medical evidence for the defense and Dr. Charles Petty for the prosecution. Neither one was in any way associated with the actual autopsy, a crucial failing because of all the controversy surrounding that aspect.

Related to the idea of the best exculpatory evidence, Sylvia Odio was not there. She is probably the most important witness alive providing evidence before the fact of a conspiracy concerning the anti-Castro Cubans and the Central Intelligence Agency.

Defense attorney Gerry Spence was unprepared as evidenced by his ultimate selection of witnesses and his cross-examination of some of the prosecution's witnesses. Spence could have mounted a much stronger attack against witnesses like Petty, film and photograph expert Cecil Kirk, and chemist Vincent Guinn.

The trial never moved out of London, whereas the actual evidence is at the National Archives in Washington. The attorneys were never allowed to present this actual material, and the jury was never allowed to see it. This is quite important in a case where there is much indication of evidence tampering. As a point of comparison, the King mock trial was held in Memphis, the scene of the crime, the location of many witnesses, and much of the evidence. Just one witness, the defendant, Ray, was examined for five hours.[2] The entire legal proceeding in London took all of three days![3] The King mock trial in its raw footage form, lasted over twice as long: fifty-four hours over ten days of filming.[4] The budget of the King mock trial was over three million dollars,[5] which allowed extensive new research to be performed. There was almost nothing new that was presented in the London trial. (One exception will be revealed later.) In fact, contrary to what Bugliosi tries to convey, the show looks like a low-budgeted quickie production. For example, there was not even a projection screen used for showing exhibits. They were shown on what appeared to be 27-inch TV sets.

That the jurors were not allowed to visit the National Archives in Washington to see the actual exhibits is very important. In the Kennedy case, there is a difference between seeing a visual representation of an exhibit, and actually handling that exhibit in front of you. For instance, marksmen who tested the particular rifle in question said it had a defective sight, the bolt was too difficult to work with, the firing pin was rusty, and the trigger pull was a "two-stage operation" that threw off their aim. The experts deemed that this rifle in evidence was so unreliable that they did not practice with it for fear that pulling the trigger would break the firing pin.[6] This cannot be conveyed by using a picture or looking at a substitute rifle. As we shall later see, this particular problem is not limited to the rifle.

Gerry Was Not Ready

But there was also one other problem that Bugliosi and the producers should have taken into account. The fact that they did not betrays a certain unmistakable bias in the proceedings. The defense attorney in the King mock trial was William Pepper. Pepper had been Ray's attorney for a number of years, therefore he was very familiar with all the ins and outs of that unusual case. I have studied both the King and JFK cases and being familiar with both of them, my opinion is that the Kennedy case is more complex. Yet, this production used Spence—a man who had absolutely no previous experience in the JFK field—as Oswald's attorney. In order to properly defend Oswald, one must be familiar with both the original and the revised official story. Because, buried deep in the record of that long and invented official story are many, many time bombs, plus alleged "experts" who were actually fulfilling agendas. (In fact, Bugliosi used one of them, Vincent Guinn, at this ersatz trial.) But if one is not thoroughly familiar with those reams of material, one does not know what questions to ask to expose those problems in the evidentiary record.

In regards to this key point, in a talk Bugliosi did at the Sixth Floor Museum in Dallas on May 24, 2007, he proudly proclaimed that Spence had two attorneys in his law firm study the Kennedy case for three months.[7] Anyone familiar with the JFK case understands the absurdity of the statement. To say that two lawyers can even *begin* to assimilate the mountains of evidence and testimony in the JFK case in three months is preposterous. In just the Warren Commission, Church Committee, and HSCA inquiries, there are *forty-nine volumes* of testimony and exhibits to digest. Bugliosi had the advantage since he was presenting the official story at the time, upheld by alleged authorities and alleged scientific reasoning. And he had the further advantage of using the HSCA version of that official story that was more assiduous in making the case against Oswald and did not publish much of its raw data. Therefore, the underpinnings of the HSCA inquiry were not exposed at the time.

Bugliosi Inflates a Show Trial

With all the constraints placed upon it, the trial's outcome could not come close to a real legal proceeding, plus it was biased in favor of the prosecution. But Bugliosi actually took it seriously. He used it to submit the first draft of his JFK book, originally entitled *Final Verdict* and extensively revised to become the quite different *Reclaiming History*.

In his book, Bugliosi states that he was first contacted in March 1986 by the producer for London Weekend Television (LWT), Mark Redhead. Redhead wanted him to serve as the prosecutor in a mock trial of Oswald.[8] Although Bugliosi says he always had turned down previous attempts to become involved with such "artificial courtroom settings," LWT had put together the "closest thing to a real trial of Oswald that there would likely ever be, the trial in London being the only 'prosecution' of Oswald ever conducted with the real witnesses in the Kennedy assassination."[9]

The problem is that the majority of witnesses at the trial were not eyewitnesses to the assassination. Dr. Petty and Dr. Wecht had no role in the original autopsy, nor were expert witnesses called by Bugliosi or Spence. Bugliosi writes that through hard and difficult work, LWT "had managed to locate and persuade most of these original witnesses . . . to testify in the television trial of Oswald." From what I could see, there were four eyewitnesses to the events in

Dealey Plaza at this mock trial, whereas in 1993 in Dealey Plaza as part of a JFK symposium, the late Larry Harris assembled four times as many eyewitnesses and he placed them in their positions in Dealey Plaza at the time of the assassination. In other words, without the finances of a television station and staff, Larry Harris managed to do a better job than LWT did.

But the prosecutor now goes further. He calls these people who he and Spence questioned for a few minutes, "the *key* witnesses to the assassination."[10] (Emphasis added.) When the original autopsy doctors are not in attendance, when Marina Oswald is not there, when no eyewitness at the trial puts the accused in the right place at the time of the murder, and when the accused himself is not there, how can anyone call these witnesses "the key witnesses to the assassination"? One has to surmise, as with *Helter Skelter*, the prosecutor is exercising a bit of literary license.

But in his attempt to transform this TV production into a real trial, Bugliosi actually writes that there was not one critical witness missing in London who he would have needed in a real trial of Oswald.[11] How about Oswald? Or his wife Marina? How about an actual doctor who did Kennedy's autopsy? With a statement like that, one has to wonder if anyone edited *Reclaiming History* for Bugliosi.

With all this important background material now established, let us now review what Bugliosi felt was as close to a real trial as the late Lee Harvey Oswald will ever get.

Bugliosi began his witness list with Wesley Frazier,[12] who was an acquaintance of Oswald's from his job at the Texas School Book Depository. Most of the time in a murder trial, the prosecution's first witness is someone who puts the accused in a position to commit the crime. Bugliosi could not do so because the witness used by the Commission for that purpose had passed away in 1983. His name was Howard Brennan. From a purely forensic view, this was probably fortunate for Bugliosi as problems with Brennan as an eyewitness to Oswald being in the sixth floor window are myriad. Since there really is no one else to put Oswald there, there was no one else to call in this regard.

Therefore, Bugliosi called Frazier. Frazier usually gave Oswald a ride back to Irving on weekends so he could visit his wife. But this time, on November 21, Oswald had asked for a ride on Thursday. After spending the night in Irving, Oswald walked to Frazier's place on Friday morning. Oswald approached Frazier's automobile that morning and placed a bag in his back seat. Oswald said the bag contained curtain rods, the reason Oswald had given him for wanting to go to Irving on Thursday in the first place.

Frazier's story is susceptible to vigorous cross-examination in every aspect, but this can only come from long and excruciating study which one cannot do in three months. What Bugliosi did here is what the Warren Commission did with Frazier. They wanted to try to show that somehow Oswald had a broken down rifle in that bag, a bag that only Frazier and his sister saw Oswald carry, and a bag that somehow disappeared once they got inside the Book Depository. To the point that the Dallas Police somehow forgot to photograph it, even though it was supposedly laying on the sixth floor of the depository, to incriminate Oswald. Once it disappeared, the police then substituted a different bag which they carried outside the building.

Now, this is just the beginning of the problems with Frazier's story. But knowing where the prosecutor was headed with Frazier, it was the defense counsel's obligation to raise doubts about Frazier's credibility right off the bat.

Instead Spence got Frazier to say that Oswald was a good guy and he kind of liked him. He also got him to admit that he felt the shots came from the grassy knoll area. And that was about it. Therefore, Bugliosi was allowed to enter the "Oswald and the paper bag" story into the record without obstruction.

Charles Brehm, a Dealey Plaza witness, testified next. He had brought his young son into the Plaza to watch the motorcade that day. Brehm testified that he felt the shots came from behind the car, that there were three shots, and the third one missed. Brehm could have been neutralized by confronting him with his own testimony in 1966, contained in Mark Lane's *Rush to Judgment,* where he said that bits of Kennedy's head came flying toward him. "It seemed to have come left, and back . . ." and ". . . over in the area of the curb where I was standing."[13] Brehm was on the quad opposite the grassy knoll behind and to Kennedy's left when the president's head exploded. Brehm was quoted by a reporter only minutes after the assassination as saying that he "seemed to think the shots came from in front of, or beside, the President."[14] It was only when he talked to the FBI on November 24th that Brehm said he felt the shots came from behind the motorcade.[15]

If Spence had read the first newspaper report to the witness, the FBI report, and the Lane interview, he could have introduced the possibility of Bureau intimidation in the investigation. Instead, Spence used the Zapruder film to try and contradict Brehm's notion of direction.

Norman Changes His Story for Elmer Moore

The prosecution's next witness was Harold Norman, one of the witnesses on the fifth floor who said he heard something above him, like someone working a gun bolt and shell casings dropping three times. Toward the end of Bugliosi's direct examination, he asked the witness a rather leading question: "Is the sound of those . . . ejections of the cartridge cases and the falling to the floor something you will recall the rest of your life?" To which Norman said yes.

If Spence had been up to speed, he should have walked over to the witness and said in a loud, clear voice, "Mr. Norman, forget about the rest of your life. You couldn't even remember that noise for four days!" Spence then should have read to the witness Norman's FBI report from November 26th. In this first statement to the authorities, there is no mention *at all* of those three noises he just said he would never forget for the rest of his life.[16] But further, there is nothing in the record that says Norman said anything like this to anyone *prior* to that time. In that FBI report, Norman said that after the first shot, he stuck his head out the window, looked up, and was hit with some dirt particles. That action was corroborated by five witnesses; James Jarman, who was on the same floor as Norman, plus four witnesses on the street who said they saw him look out the window.[17]

Norman's new and improved story did not surface until his Secret Service interview on December 2, 1963, twelve days after the assassination and eight days after the FBI interview. This version contains no mention of him leaning out the window and looking up toward the sixth floor to get dirt particles in his eyes. And it's hard to hear cartridge cases falling above you if your head is outside the room.

One of the Secret Service agents who helped Norman alter his story was Elmer Moore, who emerged as one of the chief architects of the alleged cover-up. In addition to massaging the Norman story, he was instrumental in getting Malcolm Perry to change his first day pronouncement about the direction of the shot which caused Kennedy's throat wound.

Bugliosi, Boone, and Baker

The next two witnesses called by Bugliosi were local Dallas law enforcement officers, Eugene Boone from the sheriff's office and Marrion Baker from the police department. Boone, who had been in the vicinity of the scene and heard shots, had run over to Dealey Plaza and onto the grassy knoll. Bugliosi asked him if he found any evidence of an assassin having being there. Boone said no and that he then went over to the sixth floor of the depository. Bugliosi then asked a real Arlen Specter type leading question as he showed him a picture of some boxes arranged near the window: "You could almost say there was a sniper's nest around that window," he said, to which Boone replied, "Yes." Spence finally objected to that query as a leading question, which the judge sustained, but since Bugliosi had already signaled what he wanted to hear, when the prosecutor rephrased the question more properly as to what he saw, Boone replied that the row of boxes looked like an attempt to hide something on the other side. Bugliosi then questioned the witness about his discovery of the rifle. He asked him why he at first thought this was a German Mauser instead of an Italian-made 6.5 Mannlicher Carcano rifle. Boone, apparently recalling all the problems this question had caused back in 1964, replied that the term "Mauser" only referred to a bolt action rifle and that, even though he was a sheriff's deputy, he was not an expert in identifying weapons. This was the excuse given by the Warren Commission for the German Mauser identification.[18]

Spence should have reserved the right to impeach Boone with a rebuttal witness. That rebuttal witness should have been photographer Tom Alyea. Since Spence himself asked Boone about the arrangement of the shells, Alyea could have been used to rebut both that testimony and Bugliosi's contention about the arrangement of the "sniper's nest" of boxes.

Bugliosi Reels in Tippit

Bugliosi then called Ted Callaway to the stand. This was odd, and it was surprising that Spence did not object because Callaway was not even in Dealey Plaza at the time of the shootings. Callaway is a witness to the shooting of police officer J. D. Tippit later that same day. Despite the fact Callaway did not actually see the Kennedy shooting, Bugliosi apparently wanted to drag him in to make the jury think that if Oswald killed a police officer, it must have been because he killed President Kennedy.

That Bugliosi was allowed to bring in a witness to a separate murder case was extremely disturbing. That neither the judge nor the opposing counsel objected, would seem to indicate that, contrary to what the prosecutor writes in his book, there *was* some kind of scripting to the whole affair.[19]

What makes this all even worse is this: When Spence put on his case, he never argued the Tippit murder at all. He did not bring in one witness or one exhibit to counter what Bugliosi had done, and which had been so prejudicial to his client. Therefore, Bugliosi's "signature murder" of Tippit by Oswald was allowed to linger in the minds of the jury. For comparison purposes, there was another mock trial of Oswald held in June 2013 by WFAA TV in Dallas. The judge ruled the Tippit case could not be brought into court, and Oswald was acquitted.[20]

Lovelady v. Oswald, Oswald in the Theater

Spence used the famous Ike Altgens photograph of the Man in the Doorway twice. Once with eyewitness Brehm and once with law enforcement officer Baker. The idea was to suggest that Oswald was really watching the motorcade from the front steps of the Book Depository and therefore he could not be on the sixth floor shooting Kennedy. Bugliosi now decided to recall Wesley Frazier, Oswald's colleague, to the stand. He asked him if he knew who the man in the picture was. Frazier said it was Billy Lovelady. When asked how he knew that, Frazier replied that he was standing right behind Lovelady in the picture, although you could not see him because of the shadows from the overhang.

The prosecution's next witness was Johnny Brewer. Brewer worked at Hardy's Shoe Store right down the street from the Texas Theater, the place where Oswald would be apprehended. Brewer testified that he had been listening to the radio and heard some bulletins about a policeman being shot nearby. He then saw a man in the foyer of his shop. He said the man looked like he was trying to act furtive so as not to be noticed. When the man walked out of the foyer and towards the theater, Brewer followed him outside and said that he did not see him pay to get into the theater. He then walked up to the attendant, Julia Postal, and she said she had been distracted by the sirens and did not recall selling anyone a ticket. (In reading Postal's testimony, it's an open question if she ever saw Oswald go by her into the theater.[21])

Brewer then went inside but could not find Oswald. He asked for the house lights to be turned on. Brewer pointed out Oswald to the police, who had been called. Oswald was arrested, and as Brewer stated to Spence, a policeman now said, "Kill the president, will you!"

After Tippit was killed, witness Warren Reynolds followed a suspect to a nearby Texaco station near an old house where Reynolds thought the killer was hiding. Reynolds and the police, who had followed him, now discovered an abandoned jacket under a car.[22] When this jacket was found, Officer J. T. Griffin phoned it in on the police radio saying he thought the jacket belonged to the suspect they had now focused on in or near the house. When Sgt. Gerald Hill radioed back, he said he had a man in his car who could *identify* the suspect.[23]

Now, why is this relevant to what Bugliosi was selling the jury on in the Tippit case: that there was no other suspect in that case? Because although Reynolds had followed the suspect for a block, he refused to state the suspect was Oswald. Two days after he was interviewed by the FBI, he was shot in the head at his place of work.[24] Apparently, Reynolds felt there was a connection between his being shot and the Tippit murder, because in July 1964, when he testified before the Warren Commission, he now changed his story and said the man he followed *was* Oswald.[25]

And then there is the jacket. When it was originally discovered, the message that went out over the police radio that it was white.[26] This jacket somehow later turned into a gray-colored jacket.[27] Since the Warren Commission heavily relied upon Marina Oswald as a witness, and since she said her husband only had two jackets, one gray and one blue, this probably had some influence on how this color transformation occurred.[28]

So, at best, what Bugliosi told the jury was simply wrong. By any reasonable evaluation, the man Reynolds had followed from the Tippit scene was not Oswald, even if Spence could not get this information into the record by cross-examining Johnny Brewer, he could at least have stated it to the jury during his summation.

At around 1:30 PM, the police now moved into the parking lot at Jefferson Branch Library, which was two blocks from the scene of Tippit's murder at 10th and Patton. Adrian Hamby drove his car to work that day and was walking through the parking lot. As he did so, two plainclothes policemen stopped him and asked him what he was doing. The nineteen-year-old boy said he worked at the library. They told him to tell his supervisor to lock all the doors. Two officers had seen an unidentified white male running across the lawn of the library. In fact, a message now went out on the radio: "He's in the library, Jefferson, East 500 block." Every car in the area now moved toward the library.

Therefore, the police did have other suspects in the Tippit slaying. And once Bugliosi tried to claim the opposite, and once the judge erroneously allows him to do so, Spence is obligated to counter this. But further, after presenting all the intriguing facts, Spence could have then posed a very pointed question: Where was Lee Harvey Oswald when all these leads were being radioed in and all these searches were taking place? This is one of the biggest mysteries in Bugliosi's "simple case." Why did it take Oswald almost a half hour to walk eight blocks? It is multiplied by the fact that no one saw him cover the distance, even though he was proceeding at the rate of about three minutes per block.

Bugliosi Channels Robert Blakey

Since this mock trial took place in 1986, Bugliosi was able to use the findings of the HSCA. And since the final chief counsel of that committee made much of the use of "scientific evidence" Bugliosi decided to utilize their authorities instead of the Warren Commission's. A key advantage for the prosecutor in doing so was that the working files of the HSCA were sealed at this time, not to be declassified until the creation of the Assassination Records Review Board in 1994. What made this even more advantageous for Bugliosi was that the Warren Commission published twenty-six volumes of evidence after working for less than one year. The HSCA published only twelve volumes after being in session for almost three years. Therefore, there was no paper trail of raw data available to counter their so-called scientific findings.

Cecil Kirk was only twenty-five years old in 1963. Even at that young age, he was enlisted to work for the Warren Commission.[29] In his early career he had worked for the FBI before going over to the Washington City Police Department.[30] Spence should have used this point in his questioning because once the HSCA was formed, the first chief counsel, Richard Sprague, said he would not use any experts from the Warren Commission inquiry since its work was so compromised it was now discredited. But further, these men would have an interest in upholding its basic findings. But Sprague's replacement counsel, Robert Blakey, ignored this dictum more than once.

Kirk was called to do two things: comment on the Zapruder film, and discuss the famous backyard photographs of Oswald with the alleged weapons used to kill Kennedy and Tippit while holding an extreme left publication. Kirk said that the film showed Kennedy being hit three times. Based on the film, he said the first shot missed. With two shots left, the film revealed that Kennedy was hit twice and Governor Connally, riding in front of him, was hit once. Kirk also said that the first shot came as early as Zapruder frame 162. He based this on the fact that Connally shifted his head from left to right. Kirk said that this meant Connally was looking toward the Book Depository, even though the motorcade had passed that building. Kirk said that the second shot occurred right before Kennedy disappeared behind the Stemmons Freeway sign. He then said the evidence for this shot hitting both men is that as Kennedy's hands go up to his throat, Connally's left shoulder is higher than his right shoulder. Kirk then froze Zapruder frame 313 that showed the moment the fatal shot hit Kennedy. He said that since the brain matter is going forward, the shot came from the rear.

One of the largest problems that the Commission had was the timing problem of the shooting sequence. Since they placed the first shot at some time after Kennedy disappeared behind the freeway sign, this allowed only six seconds between the first and last shots. That time frame now left a very difficult problem: getting off three shots in six seconds with a manual bolt action rifle at a moving target drifting away from the sniper. From the mid-sixties to the mid-seventies, the critics of the Warren Commission hammered away at this point. This new analysis by Kirk and colleagues helped alleviate this problem by saying the first shot was fired much earlier and missed the car. Thus, Blakey and Kirk now stretched out the firing sequence another two seconds.

The problem with this hypothesis is the same problem the Warren Commission had with it; there simply is nothing on the film that substantiates this. To grab at Connally shifting his sight from one side to the other shows how single-minded you are in the pursuit of your aim. After all, the man was in a motorcade with spectators on both side of him. Further, nobody in the car except Connally exhibited that motion at that time. Realizing how valueless this was as evidence, Kirk now brought out Rosemary Willis, the little girl in red in Dealey Plaza that day who was jogging along at Kennedy's right and then stopped running. Kirk tries to tie this in to shore up his forlorn Connally motion.

However, Kirk's attempt to tie Willis into the hypothesis is also problematic. Although Spence did not point it out, when viewing the girl's movements on a clear copy of the Zapruder film, it is clear that they do not back up this circa frame 160 shot because the girl does not begin turning to her right at that frame. She is running and looking in that direction from the start, beginning in the Z frame 140s. She starts to slow down just before frame 190,[31] which would be too late for Kirk's purpose. At his website, Don Roberdeau has gone even further in exposing Kirk's use of Willis. When the girl gazes back, she is looking at the west end of the Depository, at the opposite end of the so-called Oswald window. She then jerks her head around further to the west and stares at the stockade fence atop the grassy knoll. On November 2, 1978, she told the HSCA that she saw a man behind the wall there who disappeared instantly. In other words, if Spence had been prepared, Rosemary was actually a good witness for the defense. Therefore, in this regard, the Commission was more honest than the HSCA. But since Kirk worked for both, what does that make him?

There is something possibly even worse about the use of Rosemary Willis that Spence could have used to really have a go at Kirk. Her father, Phil Willis, was a photographer who took some important photos in Dealey Plaza that day. He brought both his daughters with him: Rosemary and Linda Kaye. Rosemary did not testify to the Commission but Linda Kaye did. She told the Commission that when the first shot sounded, Kennedy stopped waving and grabbed his throat and leaned forward. She could not tell where the second shot went. She then saw Kennedy struck in the head.[32] As she told the Commission, she was standing right in line with the Stemmons Freeway sign, about twenty feet from the limousine, at the time of the shooting.[33]

If Spence had been well prepared, he would have noted that Linda Kaye had testified under oath in 1964 but Rosemary didn't say anything until over a decade later, and was not under oath at the time she said it. Spence's obvious question to Mr. Kirk would have been: Why did you use her instead of her sister? It would have been nice to hear the answer to that question. Researcher Pat Speer, who has made an extensive survey of the witnesses in Dealey Plaza, has concluded that Linda Kaye was correct. The first shot that sounded hit Kennedy and there was no "early" shot at frame 160.[34]

Incredibly, Bugliosi had Kirk testify on a medical matter. Kirk used the (slightly) forward spray of material from Kennedy's skull as evidence the bullet struck him from behind. As Milicent Cranor explained to me in 2008, according to medical-ballistics experts, whether a perforating bullet goes back-to-front—or front-to-back—it is the *top* of the head that opens widest. This is due to exploding brain, or cavitation. The rapid displacement of brain along the bullet path thrusts open the skull wherever it meets the least resistance, often along suture lines. In such cases, brain and blood go in many directions. So this is an issue a photo analyst should not have been speaking about. And Spence could have exposed Kirk on this point as a blatant propagandist who was talking about things he knew nothing about as long as it supported the Warren Commission.

If Spence wanted to further wreck Kirk, he would have called HSCA photo analyst Robert Groden as a rebuttal witness. Groden would have analyzed the film with much more logic and evidence as to more than three shots. But more directly, he would have pointed out two serious errors in the record Bugliosi was making. First, according to the published HSCA report, there were four shots, and one came from the front.[35] Further, since the HSCA and Kirk said that Kennedy was hit right before he disappeared behind the freeway sign in the film, that shot could not have been fired by Oswald because the Commission determined that the line of sight from the sixth floor window would be obstructed by the branches of an oak tree at that time.[36] The Commission wrote that these branches would have obstructed an assassin's view from frames 166 to 210. Therefore, through skillful cross-examination, or through defense witness Groden, Spence would have shown that Kirk's HSCA determined that Oswald did not fire two of its four shots. Therefore, at the least, Oswald had accomplices. And further, that both Bugliosi and Kirk—who had to have been aware of this—had kept it from the jury.

Spence's Lost Opportunity with Petty

Bugliosi's next witness was the late Dr. Charles Petty. Petty was one of the most vocal members of the HSCA. As we shall see in our chapter on the autopsy, there was a definite reason he was chosen to be on that panel. Petty replaced Dr. Earl Rose as the medical examiner in Dallas in 1969.[37] In 2003, he told CNN that the Kennedy autopsy was done well.[38] This is an autopsy about which even Michael Baden, who helmed the HSCA medical panel, said, "Where bungled autopsies are concerned, President Kennedy's is the exemplar."[39] For any pathologist to try and conceal that fact reflects extremely poorly on his objectivity in this case. Which is probably why Bugliosi chose him.

Petty recited the now familiar Bugliosi creed. He stated that Kennedy was struck by only two bullets, and none from the front. The bullet which struck him in the skull broke up into smaller fragments and these were most prominent in the right front area of the head. He added that the extremely fast rearward motion of Kennedy toward the back of the car was not caused by a bullet, but a neuromuscular reaction. Petty said bullets do not cause these kinds of strong, visible movements in real life, only in movies. Governor Connally reacted a bit late to being struck by the same bullet due to a delayed reaction because different people react to trauma differently. But he was hit by the same bullet that went through Kennedy's back and exited his throat. It was no surprise that this bullet emerged in nearly pristine condition since it was a full metal jacketed bullet. When asked if this was possible, he said, "Yes, of course."

Spence started his cross-examination of Petty with questions about the nonavailability of Kennedy's brain. These questions, although not well posed, elicited some fascinating medical replies from Petty. If nothing else, they revealed Petty's bunker mentality on the case. When Spence asked him if it was important to inspect the brain if a bullet traveled through it, Petty gave a memorable answer: "It would be nice if the brain were available." When Spence asked Petty if it was not essential to see the brain, Petty replied with something even stranger: "It's not essential to see the brain." He then added that he had the photos and X-rays instead. When asked if the HSCA looked for the brain, Petty gave an even more puzzling answer: "Not really." This is simply false because, as Spence pointed out to Petty, the HSCA interviewed over twenty people trying to find out the location of the brain. To this Petty replied, "We asked but we did not look for it." However, it is clear from the record that contrary to Petty's testimony, the HSCA made an extensive and unsuccessful effort to find Kennedy's brain. Petty then reiterated that it was not really essential to examine Kennedy's brain since he had the photographs and X-rays.

If Spence really knew the Kennedy case, he could have begun to take Petty apart piece by piece. However, Spence was not that well versed in the medical evidence, and also the HSCA records had not yet been declassified. There are undoubtedly missing photographs in this case and the available photographs are terribly posed and shot. As shall be seen, there is also strong evidence from the man who was said to have photographed Kennedy's brains that the photos Spence is concentrating on are fakes. In other words, due to their own lack of due diligence in this regard, the HSCA fell for a hoax.

Spence could have brought into the record the fact that it was not just Kennedy's brain that was missing, but also exhibits like tissue slides taken from wounds of the brain and the back, tissue slides from the brain, and internal photos of Kennedy's chest.[40] With these missing exhibits entered into the record, plus the fact that there is no evidence the brain was properly sectioned, the following question could have been posed: "Dr. Petty, how do you know, with certainty, from which direction the bullet entered President Kennedy's head?" And if he had replied that there is no pictorial evidence of an exit wound at the rear of the head, Spence could have replied that there were over twenty witnesses at Parkland Hospital in Dallas who saw a gaping hole in the rear of Kennedy's skull.[41] Is that not proof the fatal shot came from the front, and therefore was not fired by Oswald? What happened to that gaping hole? And does the fact that it disappeared make confidence in those photos look rather naive?

The most obvious question Spence could have asked is "How do wounds move in corpses?" For that is what happened in this case. The HSCA, which Petty served on, moved the head wound up four inches, from the base of the head to the cowlick area, and the wound in the back two inches down. In normal cases this does not occur, but it did in this case. Why? Who or what was wrong? Was it the autopsy doctors or the photographs that are mistaken? Spence could have also asked: "Why was the back wound not dissected at autopsy?" and "What kind of murder by gunshot wound case had there ever been where the two wounds in the deceased were not properly tracked for directionality?" In the Kennedy case, neither the back wound nor the head wound was tracked properly. Spence could have also asked Petty: "Since that back wound was not dissected, how do you know that the back wound actually went through and exited the throat?"

The autopsy in this case was simply a horror, so bad, that to this day, it is not possible to know precisely what happened to President Kennedy because the proper procedures were not followed. And in Chapter 7, we will try and understand why they were not.

Spence's cross-examination showed that unlike a real trial, exhibits and documents were not properly prepared in advance. To present a document, one should have a copy ready for the opposing attorney to inspect before it is read in court. Spence had not done this with a report from the HSCA medical panel, so he tried to lighten up the proceedings by sitting next to Bugliosi at the prosecutor's table and reading it from there. If you can believe it, Bugliosi then stood up, skipped seventeen lines and started reading a different section of the volume during Spence's cross-examination. Since the show was not meant to be serious, the judge started laughing.

Bugliosi, Lutz, and Guinn

Monty Lutz, a ballistics expert, was Bugliosi's next witness. Lutz also served with Blakey's HSCA, and with almost his first answer he showed just how biased he was. Bugliosi flashed a photo of CE 399, the "magic bullet" image, on a TV screen. Not once, but twice, Lutz said that this bullet was found on Governor Connally's stretcher. After Lutz said it twice, Bugliosi then repeated it as if it were an established fact, although, as shall see in Chapter 5, it is anything but an established fact. Bugliosi needed to get this into the record, for if CE 399 is found anywhere else, the indications are that it was planted and Oswald was framed.

It was stunning to watch Judge Lucius Bunton not say one word as Lutz and Bugliosi repeatedly uttered these untruths. There is a doctrine in law that decrees that when important information is conveyed to the jury, about which the witness has no direct knowledge, a foundation must be laid and the attorney must specify that he will then follow up on this matter. There were no facts in evidence before Lutz testified to demonstrate that the magic bullet was found where he said it was. But yet, through all this, Bunton just sat there.

More incredible was that Spence did not object. He had two grounds on which to do so. The one stated above, but also because Lutz was not deemed an expert on this aspect of the Kennedy case. That is, the provenance of CE 399. Right then and there, Spence should have asked the judge to strike the testimony about where the bullet was found and to instruct the jury to disregard it. Spence then should have asked for a 402 hearing with the jury out of the room. This hearing decides if certain evidence or testimony is admissible. After this, I have very little doubt that Lutz would not have been able to mislead the jury with this testimony that was very prejudicial to the defense. But it does show that Lutz was arguing from a position not founded in the factual record.

If Lutz had not been able to mislead the jury, Bugliosi then asking Lutz if CE 399 was connected to the rifle in evidence would be meaningless as it was not established to have been found on Connally's or Kennedy's stretcher.

Lutz was then asked about the two bullet fragments found in the front seat of the car. He said the same; that these were ballistically linked to the rifle in evidence that he called the "Oswald rifle." And then thereafter, as with the "Connally stretcher bullet," Bugliosi called it "Oswald's rifle," which should have been objected to.

Bugliosi asked if it was possible to fire the rifle in evidence three times with accuracy in eight seconds, the time span allowed for by Kirk's fraudulent testimony about an "early shot" at frame 160. Lutz said that this was certainly possible not just for him, but for a layman! Bugliosi then went even further by asking if it would have been easy for a layman to accomplish this. Lutz topped the prosecutor by saying it would be "quite easy" and said he himself did this with the rifle in evidence. Again, Spence should have objected because the experts who first tested this weapon said it was so unsafe and in such poor condition that they dare not use it. Lutz using this actual weapon indicates someone had worked on it in order to refurbish it for use. If that was the case, it had lost its value as evidence. Again, either Bunton or Spence should have struck this testimony from the record, admonished the jury to disregard it, and demanded a 402 hearing on the issue.

Lutz then got even wilder. He said that with a Mannlicher Carcano rifle, he set up three targets on a rifle range to simulate the three Warren Commission shots. He then performed five tests. He claimed he fired the weapon three times and hit all three targets in 3.6 seconds. This was amazing, since it took 2.25 seconds for the FBI to just work the bolt on the Mannlicher Carcano. [42] Bugliosi offered no evidence how this occurred. There was no unedited film, no synchronous timing mechanism offered, and no neutral witness. And Judge Bunton said nothing.

Spence asked Lutz if his test was conducted from an elevated site six floors off the ground. He said it was conducted on a rifle range. Spence then asked if the targets he fired at were moving or stationary. Lutz admitted they were stationary. But to show just how determined Lutz was to cloud that fact, the witness tried to say that the president was also stationary in Dealey Plaza. Spence rightly cut him off before he finished this ridiculous statement. Lutz then said something contradictory. He said that he missed the target even under those ideal conditions, yet he had previously said that on one of the five attempts he did hit all three targets. Bunton never asked for clarification on this issue.

Dr. Vincent Guinn, the prosecutor's next witness, was presented as an expert in bullet lead analysis. Through analysis of certain trace elements, he was supposed to relate certain fragments in Connally to CE 399 and other fragments from Kennedy's skull to the large bullet fragments in the front seat of the car. After so doing, he said there was "solid evidence" there were only two bullets that struck both Kennedy and Connally. Bugliosi tried to hammer this point home by again saying that CE 399 was found on Connally's stretcher. Again, neither the judge nor Spence objected. Bugliosi ended his direct examination with what today we can show as ludicrous. He posed a hypothetical question to Guinn: "If fifty people had fired at Kennedy that day, your science indicates that they all missed except Oswald." To which Guinn agreed.

Spence countered that Guinn only examined a very small sample of the fragments in Kennedy's brain. He also showed that Guinn did not examine copper fragments in the car and questioned the authenticity of the evidence. Guinn made a highly questionable statement at this point. He told Spence he had no reason to doubt the authenticity. Spence let that statement stand. If Spence had been one of the lawyers who knew the case quite well, he would have pounced on that. By Guinn's own admission, the wrist fragments that were originally tested in 1964 had vanished by the time Guinn began his work for the HSCA. Guinn added that the missing fragments are presumably still around somewhere, "but where they are, I have no idea."[43] After his HSCA testimony, Guinn told reporters it was only after he got the evidence from the National Archives "that he discovered that he was testing fragments different from those originally tested." When he weighed the particles, he found that none of the individual weights corresponded with those noted when the FBI attempted the tests in 1964.[44] In a tape-recorded interview, he actually theorized how a substitute piece of lead from CE 399 could be given to him disguised as a fragment from Connally's wrist.[45] That taped interview should have been played back to the witness after he said he had no doubts about the authenticity of the evidence. He would have been impeached by his own words.

Shaneyfelt, Delgado, and Ruth Paine

Former FBI agent Lyndal Shaneyfelt, the prosecution's next witness, had been J. Edgar Hoover's prime agent on a wide variety of technical issues dealing with the JFK case.

Shaneyfelt was called to certify two major points as a handwriting expert. First, that it was Oswald's writing on the envelope to Klein's Sporting Goods ordering the rifle in question, and second, that Oswald had written his so called Historic Diary, which Bugliosi used to show Oswald was a communist. Spence's cross-examination brought out the interesting fact that in his examination of the envelope, he only had a copy to work from. The original had been destroyed.

Nelson Delgado was a curious choice by the prosecutor. Bugliosi may have called him so Spence could not use him as his witness. Delgado said that Oswald read Russian papers, read Karl Marx, and was a follower of Fidel Castro. Delgado was in Oswald's Marine unit in Santa Ana, California, and saw Oswald practice with a rifle, so Bugliosi tried to make the argument that although Oswald scored at the lowest rung in his test before being released, he had scored higher prior to that. The implication was that Oswald was preoccupied with going home. On his cross-examination, Spence elicited from Delgado an interesting piece of information of which I was not aware. In fact, it was the one new piece of information in the whole production. Delgado had left the country after the Warren Commission hearings because he felt the FBI was trying to harm him because of his testimony. Bugliosi made a mistake here. He tried to ridicule Delgado by suggesting, in essence, that if the FBI wanted to get him, he would not be here today.

Ruth Paine was Bugliosi's final witness. Ruth befriended Marina Oswald after meeting her within the White Russian community in Dallas. She told Bugliosi that she helped get Oswald his job at the Book Depository.

Bugliosi then tried to make a very large deal about Oswald's visits with his wife while she was at Ruth's home. He said that invariably up until the week of the assassination, Oswald would visit on weekends, but he broke that routine on November 21. Spence should have pointed out that since Oswald started work on October 16, this routine was only one month old. But further, he had not come out the previous weekend before the assassination.[46] Bugliosi's so-called ironclad incriminating routine was broken twice in six opportunities.

Bugliosi also drew from Ruth that the Thursday night before the assassination, Ruth went down to the garage about 9 PM. The overhead light was on, and it was her impression that Lee Oswald left it on. The question called for a conclusion and since this was Bugliosi's witness and it was clear where he was headed, it was bound to be biased against Oswald. But neither Judge Bunton nor Spence objected.

Bugliosi then honed in on the reason given by the Warren Commission for Oswald wanting to visit his wife on Thursday—to pick up some curtain rods. Bugliosi elicited that Oswald did not ask Ruth for curtain rods and she did not see Oswald with any that night. She actually did have curtain rods in her garage, but they were still there the next day.

Bugliosi then asked a series of questions that, in my view, should all have been objected to since they called for conclusions. Ruth Paine was his witness and since he was well versed from her Warren Commission testimony and various articles and interviews in what she would say about Oswald, he knew how prejudicial these statements would be. For instance, he asked her how Oswald viewed the world around him. How she could know, seeing Oswald as little as she did, is puzzling. But Ruth had been playing her role for a very long time so she replied on cue, "I think he saw the world as hostile, and he had very little good to say about other people." Bugliosi then topped himself. "Were you able to discern how Oswald viewed himself?" Again, Judge Bunton said nothing. Ruth actually began to answer this question with, "I think he had kind of an inflated . . .," but finally, Spence objected. The point is this: If Oswald was some kind of low level intelligence agent and informant, then it would be quite natural to keep that role from most of the people around him.[47] Bugliosi had to have understood this point before he asked the question.

In spite of Spence's objections, Ruth was still able to get into the record that Oswald thought he was something special and others did not see him that way but that others might in some time. The implication being that this is the kind of guy who would kill the president so the world would know who he really was.[48]

It is in reference to Ruth Paine that Bugliosi writes in his book that Oswald was not really a necessary witness at this mock trial because he had the woman at whose residence he spent the night before the assassination and she "testified to Oswald's storing the murder weapon on the garage floor of her home."[49] The problem with this is that Ruth Paine never testified to this at this show trial and not before the Warren Commission either. In fact, she said that not only did she never see a rifle in her home, but that when she packed the Oswalds' things to take to Dallas from New Orleans, she did not see a rifle among them.[50] In other words, not even Ruth Paine was enough for the prosecutor. Spence's cross-examination tried to show that he could make some guilt by association claims about Ruth as she had just done with Oswald. For instance, was it just a coincidence that she was living with Marina at the time of the assassination, and that she helped Lee get a job at the Book Depository? He also got her to admit that she was somewhat taken aback by Oswald's call to her from jail and his presumption of his innocence. When Spence pressed her on this, she refined it to say that she was surprised that he felt so unattached to the event. Spence should have replied with: "Maybe that was because he *was* unattached to the event?"

Spence's Anemic Defense

Spence called seven witnesses, half as many as the prosecution, and in my opinion, they were not well chosen. Bill Newman was a Dealey Plaza witness who testified to hearing shots coming from behind him, behind the picket fence up on the grassy knoll. Another witness, Tom Tilson, said he saw a man resembling Jack Ruby at the scene taking off in a car after the murder, but Bugliosi duly noted times that Ruby was accounted for just before and just after the time Tilson said he saw him. Spence called FBI agent Jim Hosty as a hostile witness to get into the record that after the assassination, the FBI had destroyed a note that Oswald had left for Hosty in the Dallas office. Paul O'Connor, who removed Kennedy's brain at Bethesda Medical Center, stated that there was hardly any brain left when the body arrived. Bugliosi tried to impeach him by saying that this differs from the autopsy report which says there was a sizeable brain entered into evidence. Bugliosi accused O'Connor of not saying anything about this matter to the HSCA, although once the HSCA records were declassified, it turned out that he *had* said this to that body.

The core of Bugliosi's case were his four "expert" witnesses from the HSCA: Kirk, Petty, Lutz, and Guinn. In response, Spence only called one expert witness: Dr. Cyril Wecht. He had other options. Spence could have called Dr. Charles Wilber who wrote a book to demonstrate step by step just how bad the Kennedy autopsy was.[51] He could have called Dr. Robert Shaw who operated on John Connally at Parkland. Shaw always insisted that the bullet that went through Connally was not the same one that went through Kennedy. Spence could have tried to locate Carlos Hathcock, the greatest Vietnam-era sniper of his day, who said he tried several times to duplicate what the Commission said Oswald did, but could never do it. Spence could have called Josiah Thompson or Ray Marcus to discuss the provenance of the all-important CE 399 to demonstrate all the questions about the chain of possession of that crucial exhibit. Spence could have called Dr. Forrest Chapman to indicate the forensic problems with CE 543, one of the shells found at the so-called sniper's lair. The combination of Chapman's work with Marcus and Thompson would have indicated that both CE 399 and the shells were planted.

The problem with not calling any authorities allows the sophistry and evasion of the Warren Commission advocates to appear forensically sound. Also, it leads to the implication that you have no authorities on your side. We will encounter many other witnesses who Spence could have called later in this book. To me, the only really effective witness Spence used was Dr. Cyril Wecht. Watching Bugliosi cross-examine him was painful. Wecht was developing hard evidence about the serious problems in the Single Bullet Theory, how bullets tested by the Commission did not look anything like CE 399, and criticizing the amateurishness of the autopsy. Bugliosi implied these were not pieces of evidence, but opinion better off in a summation. They were not opinion. They were facts the prosecutor did not like.

HSCA investigator Eddie Lopez was called as a witness, but since his excellent report about a CIA plot related to Mexico City was not declassified at the time, he could not really discuss it. Bugliosi tried to neuter his implications about Mexico City by saying that since the motorcade route was not firmed up until November 14th and Oswald had been in Mexico City six weeks before, such a notion was nonsense. The problem with this is that the decision to go to Dallas was made several months before that. Once Dallas/Fort Worth was firmed up for a one-day visit, a motorcade through the downtown area was also included. In fact, Kennedy insisted on this himself.[52]

Seth Kantor, Spence's final witness, had already written a book on Jack Ruby. Kantor did well enough, showing a chart of Ruby's phone calls and how they skyrocketed in the latter part of 1963, and how Ruby was in contact with

Mafia enforcers at that time. Kantor had also seen Ruby at Parkland Hospital the day of the assassination, and also saw the lack of security for the abandoned presidential limousine outside. Where Spence could have used Kantor more effectively was in Ruby's actual entry into the Dallas Police basement to kill Oswald. Incredibly, there was no mention of the HSCA determination that Ruby did not come down the Main Street ramp, as the Commission said he did. He came in from an alley to a back door in the building that someone had left unprotected. This should have been made clear with maps and narration because it indicated that the police security that day was compromised.

I have tried to outline the myriad shortcomings of this alleged trial. I could go on for many more pages. It seems clear to me that, either by design or by accident, the proceedings favored the prosecutor. But one really can't blame Spence so much for the verdict. For the simple matter is that no ingénue can master the JFK case in a matter of three months. We can blame producer Mark Redhead for thinking anyone could do so.

To show how Bugliosi tried to cloud the imbalance in the production, he names Paul Hoch in the notes to his book as an outside consultant to the trial. He then adds that Hoch "leans toward the conspiracy theory" side of the argument.[53] This is simply wrong. Hoch does not lean toward the conspiracy side. After engaging in several discussions with Hoch, it seems to me and to many others that he leans toward the Warren Commission side. Which does not mean he impacted the result; it means that Bugliosi is trying in as many ways possible to tilt the reader's perceptions in his direction.

Before purchasing *Reclaiming History,* Tom Hanks should have had someone do a review of this grotesquely imbalanced mock trial. That would have told him something about the auspices of *Reclaiming History.* There is no evidence he did anything of the kind.

Part 2:
Exposing *Reclaiming History*

CHAPTER FOUR

On First Encountering
Reclaiming History

*"The conspiracy theorists are guilty of the very thing they accuse
the Warren Commission of doing. . . . There is no substance at
all for any of these theories, they're all pure moonshine . . . . I'm
basically telling them that they've wasted the last ten to fifteen
years of their lives."*

—Vincent Bugliosi, *U.S. News and World Report*, June 3, 2007

Vincent Bugliosi is a likeable person. He has the personal attributes of humor,
self-effacement, and intelligence. He has written three valuable books about
the Clinton/Bush years: *No Island of Sanity*, *The Betrayal of America*, and *The
Prosecution of George W. Bush for Murder*. I would recommend any of these three
books. They all have two common traits that give them virtue. First, they are all
brief and can be read in a day or two. Second, in all three cases, the author had
the facts, the law, and morality on his side. This, of course, makes it easy going:
a kind of downhill roller coaster ride.

    Reclaiming History has none of these advantages. First of all, the three
books mentioned above are Chihuahuas in size. The Kennedy assassination
book is the size of an Irish wolfhound. Not only is the book over 1,600 pages

long (2,600 pages, if you include the text on the CDs), it is oversized and the font size is small.

As the publisher W. W. Norton foresaw when the volume was first published in 2007, the inordinate length doomed the book to, what was for Bugliosi, poor sales. Even though the author got a few national media appearances, and even though the mainstream reviewers were kind, the book was remaindered in a year. Norton then tried to redeem its investment by reissuing one section of the book in trade paperback. This section, the first of *Reclaiming History,* is entitled "Four Days in November," and is the version repackaged for publication with the Playtone film *Parkland.*

But to understand the author's original intent and what Hanks and Goetzman bought into, let us examine the structure of *Reclaiming History.* The book has a rather long introduction and is then divided into two "books." Book One, subtitled rather pretentiously "Matters of Fact: What Happened" contains fifteen chapters. The first chapter, "Four Days in November," is a kind of hour-by-hour reconstruction in narrative form of November 22 to November 25 in a series of descriptive scenes; a kind of combination of novel with play that allows facts to be presented in their real-time continuum rather than out of context. If you can allow for the biased presentation—which means you have to be very familiar with the facts—this is the best part of the book. The other chapters in Book One cover things like the subsequent investigations of the murders committed that weekend, the Kennedy autopsy, the Zapruder Film, a long biography of Lee Harvey Oswald, evidence of Oswald's purchase of the rifle, his presence in the so-called sniper's nest, what happened on the grassy knoll area, Oswald's possible motive, and a summation of his evidentiary guilt as presented by the author. This comes to well over half of the book's text.

Book Two contains nineteen chapters and is titled, again rather pretentiously and also rather sneeringly, "Delusions of Conspiracy: What Did Not Happen." The first word of the title tells you almost all you need to know about this long section. The first two chapters introduce the concept of conspiracy and then outline the history of the critical community in the JFK case (Bugliosi disdains that rubric, opting instead for the more pejorative "conspiracy community"). He then goes through various aspects that the critics of the Warren Commission have investigated such as the idea of the Second Oswald and suspicious deaths. He profiles authors Mark Lane and David Lifton and offers chapters on various suspects in the case like the Mob, the CIA, LBJ, and the KGB. He concludes this part with an examination of the Sylvia Odio story and her possible relation to the Cuban exiles in a plot with Oswald, a long, strident all-out attack on Oliver Stone's film of *JFK,* and a summary chapter matching the end of the first book on why he concludes there was not a conspiracy.

How did the book get so long? In discussions with me, Bugliosi disclosed that the first draft of the book was entitled *Final Verdict* and focused largely on the London trial. But two events followed upon the completion of that first draft. First, Oliver Stone's film *JFK* created a media uproar which lasted for about a year. Second, as a result of that incredible controversy, the federal government created the Assassination Records Review Board tasked with declassifying the remaining classified files on the JFK case. They ended up taking four years to do so and declassifying, in whole, or in part, 2 million pages of documents. Therefore, at each stage, Bugliosi revised and expanded his draft.

Bugliosi Pummels the Critics

To describe the book's length and overall design does not really tell you what the volume is about. It leaves out the book's tone and attitude which is, for this work, integral to understanding it. To begin to comprehend why this is important, one must understand that there are two sides to Bugliosi: the charming, bright, witty raconteur and the pugnacious courtroom prosecutor we meet in this book. The experience is like knowing a nice gentleman who happens to be a boxer. You have a pleasant conversation with him in his dressing room, and five minutes later in the ring he is hell-bent on separating his opponent's head from his neck. To give the reader a taste of Bugliosi transformed, consider the following quotes:

"Waiting for conspiracy theorists to tell the truth is a little like leaving the front-porch light on for Jimmy Hoffa."[1]

". . . in the conspiracy community of the Kennedy assassination, where one's peers have turned their mother's pictures against the wall and are telling even bigger lies themselves, and where the American public is unaware of these lies, not only is this type of deception routinely accepted by most members of the community, but the perpetrators are treated as celebrities who lecture for handsome fees and sign autographs at conventions of Warren Commission critics and conspiracy theorists."[2]

"Although I had commenced my work on the case with a completely open mind, I found there was absolutely no substance to their charges and that they have performed a flagrant disservice to the American public. Dissent is what makes this country the great nation that it is, but this was not responsible dissent. This was wanton and reckless disregard for the facts of the case."[3]

"But the very best testament to the validity of the Warren Commission's findings is that after an unrelenting, close to forty-five-year effort, the Commission's fiercest critics have not been able to produce any new credible evidence that would in any way justify a different conclusion."[4]

I can assure the reader that this small sampling is just the beginning. Later on, the ideas of medical critics like David Lifton and Doug Horne are referred to in the strongest terms as being "unhinged," "delirious," and "obscenely irresponsible."[5] In talking about Dr. David Mantik, who Bugliosi acknowledges has an MD and PhD, he explains Mantik entertaining some of their ideas like this: ". . . within the world of insanity there is an internal logic. By that I mean one can frequently have a perfectly intelligent conversation with an insane person if one is willing to enter that person's world of insane suppositions."[6]

Inevitably, with this kind of attitude, there are several instances throughout the nearly 2,700 pages where the author equates the critics of the Warren Commission with those who believe that Elvis is still alive or in alien abductions or someone who claims he took a picture of heaven.[7] It is nothing if not an argumentative book. One can classify it in two ways: an argument by intimidation and an argument by sheer verbosity. By combining both techniques, we get a queer form of polemic, one that consists of ad hominem attacks, argument by *ad nauseam,* and a peculiar authorial positioning which implies that if something is longer or bigger, it must be better. The reader should just give in to the impression that if a book is that long, it must be that good. In many instances, as in this one, it just means the book is longer.

The Prosecutor Slips Early

In his long, pugnacious introduction, Bugliosi begins to lose ground right at the start. Like filmmaker Robert Stone, who made *Oswald's Ghost,* in his attempt to attack the critics he tries to portray them as doing what they do for "handsome fees," and claims fans pay them for autographs.[8] Here's the big problem with this attempt at a pecuniary motive: Bugliosi has never been to the functions he is describing, so how can he know what happens there? He has been *invited* to attend, but he has not shown up. I can assure Mr. Bugliosi that I have been to many of these seminars and conferences since 1992 and onward, and no researcher I know has ever been paid to appear. No writer has ever been paid for an autograph. On the contrary, writers almost always pay for their own transportation, accommodations, and meals. In other words, authors who go to these affairs are *losing money.* They go for the opportunity to share new ideas or discoveries with others. That Bugliosi presented it that way, without doing any homework, shows his paramount desire to demonize the critics in the eyes of the reader.

In his introduction, Bugliosi makes a statement and uses an example that provides a recurring motif: an attempt to show that much of the work of the critical community is unfounded. He states that the critics have always written that no rifleman has ever duplicated Oswald's feat at the Texas School Book Depository of firing three shots and scoring two hits in the head and shoulder areas in less than six seconds. He says that this charge is not accurate. He then points to an example in the Warren Commission Report of a mysterious soldier named Miller (no first name given) who, according to a commanding officer, actually bettered Oswald's feat. Bugliosi's implication is that this information has been out for years but the critical community has ignored it since it would undermine their arguments. Therefore you cannot trust them with even the evidence in the Warren Commission volumes.[9] However, this implication is unfounded. You can read about this episode on Warren Commission critic Michael Griffith's website and in Sylvia Meagher's classic critique of the Warren Commission, *Accessories After the Fact.*[10] In fact, Meagher goes into this specific subject and testimony at greater length than Bugliosi does. But why would she if, as the prosecutor says, it undermines her case for Oswald's innocence?

Examining the testimony completely does not undermine the critics' case at all. Three "master marksmen" took two tries at duplicating what Oswald was supposed to have done. As Meagher explains it, these "master marksmen" were rated at the very top of the scale, not by the Marines, but by the National Rifle Association. In other words, they were even better than the top shooters in the armed services by a level of two or more classes; so proficient they qualified for open competition and even the Olympic Games! Now compare this to Oswald, who barely made the lowest class possible when he left the Marines in 1959. How can one equate the two? Further, while these men practiced all the time, there is no known credible witness who saw Oswald target practice with the rifle in question. One wonders why the Commission allowed the military to select these marksmen and not a shooter more comparable to Oswald. The results show why. Of the three men, only one of them bettered Oswald's time. But here's the catch, Oswald was firing from sixty feet up at a moving target, while the three experts were firing from thirty feet up at still targets. As Meagher notes, wouldn't it have been quite simple to just rope off Dealey Plaza, put these guys in the sixth floor window, place a convertible in the street below, and try a true experiment? If this was not done, why not? Neither in the text at this point, nor in the corresponding end note section does Bugliosi tell you about the different settings or pose the question as to why they were not the same. But several sentences later, after giving the reader this incomplete information, he pillories the critics as being "so outrageously brazen that they tell lies . . . about verifiable, documentary evidence. . . ."[11] A few pages later, in discussing how the critics have sliced and diced Gerald Posner's book, he comments that they are "going to have a much, much, much more difficult time with me."[12] As we shall see, that did not turn out to be the case.

Bugliosi then makes an even more dubious statement. He writes that he is only after facts and objectivity and will therefore set forth the critic's arguments the way *they want them set forth* before invalidating them. (Emphasis added.) Then he adds, "I will not *knowingly* omit or distort anything,"[13] (emphasis in original) which he tries to qualify by saying there may be references in the millions of pages on the subject that he simply never encountered. But how could he have missed those pages about the expert marksmen in Meagher's book when he sources her book often and uses her name frequently, usually in a negative way.

Although I will try not to excessively repeat that sentence about omitting or distorting anything, it is violated quite often in Bugliosi's book. My question is: Why did he write such a thing? And why did his editor, Starling Lawrence, let him keep it in the introduction? Clearly, whatever Bugliosi says, his book is a prosecutor's case. This case is so big, and so many pages have been written and documents declassified, that to give both sides of each issue would necessitate a work the size of the Warren Commission report. To write such a work would require someone with pure objectivity, which no one has. One must concentrate on certain areas, present evidence for your thesis, try to note the other side's objections, at least minimally, and then give sources for the reader to consult from that side if he wants to review their argument more completely. If one can do that, then you have acquitted yourself well. But to write what Bugliosi does on the matter of presenting both sides of each issue is just not possible or even desirable. It's even a bit silly to try.

Who Wrote What?

Before proceeding further, we should describe the book's attributes. There can be little doubt that Bugliosi has done a ton of reading in the field. And not just on the assassination itself. There are discussions here about the life and presidency of John Kennedy. For instance, Bugliosi does an adequate job in conveying what happened at the Bay of Pigs and discussing the two major reports: The Taylor Report done for President Kennedy and Lyman Kirkpatrick's Inspector General Report for the CIA. In addition, the amount of secondary sources consumed for the work is impressive. In reading the text and looking at the footnotes, it is clear that Bugliosi has really read much of the material and entered it into the book. The author could hold his own with almost any scholar on JFK's career and life.

However, in any serious and lengthy discussion of *Reclaiming History* it is hard to dodge the issue of Bugliosi collaborating with other writers, and to wonder who was responsible for which parts of the book. More than once, and in public, author David Lifton has stated that *Reclaiming History* was a cooperative venture and that the other two writers were the late Fred Haines and Dale Myers. A look back at Bugliosi's writing career certainly advances precedents for this claim. About half the books Bugliosi has written have been co-ventures. Since *Reclaiming History* turned out to be such a large undertaking, and Bugliosi wrote at least four books in the meantime, it would seem natural that this recurring practice would reappear. By reading what Lifton has to say on this issue and by talking to him about it, it seems to me that Lifton has sound sources. According to him, Fred Haines, the first person brought into the project, spent a lot of time, at a fee of $50,000 per year, complementing Bugliosi's work. It was Haines's idea to structure the opening section as a narrative, and Haines did a lot of work on the Oswald biography section, which I feel is one of the worst parts of the volume. According to Lifton, when Haines became ill and had to drop out of the project, Myers was then brought on board. Myers did a lot of work on the technical aspects of the case, like the acoustics evidence and photography, until he and Bugliosi had a falling out. Therefore Myers's name does not appear on the front cover of the book. And since a settlement was arranged, he is not allowed to talk about the issue. Although Bugliosi specifically names both Haines and Myers in his acknowledgments, none of this rather messy backstory is described. According to Lifton, both Haines and Myers were, at different intervals, scheduled to get a "with" credit on the front cover of the book: that is, the authorship would read Vincent Bugliosi with Dale Myers. Lifton believes that as much as a third of *Reclaiming History* may actually be the work of these two other men. Interestingly, in his acknowledgments section, Bugliosi credits Myers as having more of a writing role than Haines.[14] This cooperative venture makes it hard to specifically criticize parts of the book because it is difficult to figure out who wrote what. But since Bugliosi finally assumed sole cover credit, and since he probably had final say over what went into the book and how it was composed, I will continue to refer to him as the author.

There is another reason this point should be discussed. Bugliosi makes little or no effort to be gentle in his disagreements with the critical community. In addition to the comments made above, he writes: ". . . simple common sense, that rarest of attributes among conspiracy theorists . . ."[15]; "But conspiracy theorists are not rational and sensible when it comes to the Kennedy assassination."[16]; ". . . silliness is what all of the conspiracy allegations are about. . . ."[17]

In this regard though, the falling out with Myers probably helped. Why? Because the ctka.net website contains an interview John Kelin did with Myers in 1982. Titled "I Don't Think Lee Harvey Oswald Pulled the Trigger," it reveals that Myers used to be one of those nutty conspiracy theorists Bugliosi spends so much time belittling. In this interview, he talks about the assassination of JFK being a covert intelligence operation, how Kennedy's death opened up America to the dark side of its government, how he can prove beyond a reasonable doubt Oswald did not pull the trigger on either the president or the police officer, how he believes there was a shooter on the grassy knoll, and finally how, at the time of the murder, Oswald was actually on one of the lower floors of the building. If anything, the releases of the Assassination Records Review Board seem to favor the concept of conspiracy. Yet, either Bugliosi does not know about what, to him, must be considered Myers's sordid past, or he doesn't care. Not telling the reader about it certainly spares both of them a lot of uncomfortable explaining and some possible puzzling looks from the reading audience.

Finally, there is one other point that needs to be addressed in this aspect. Like most authors who undergo a St. Paul type conversion on the road to Damascus, Myers today does not talk a lot about his previous position or how complete his makeover was. Like most who undergo a total conversion, they wake up in their new incarnations despising who and what they were. In other words, the zealotry in their new direction is even more rabid than in the original. There is no better example of this than Myers getting on national television in 2003 and proclaiming via his Gerald Posnerian computer simulation that the Single Bullet Theory is not just a theory anymore. Because of the Myers produced magic, it was now the single bullet fact. Yet, this simulation has been thoroughly skewered at least four times since then.[18] The amazing thing about these critiques is that there is very little overlap in the deconstructions. Which means that on every possible angle, the Myers simulation was open to very effective attack. Some of these appeared way before Bugliosi's book was published, yet in the end notes to his book Bugliosi lavishly praises the Myers simulation[19] without reference to any of the effective critiques of what Robert Harris has called a "propaganda cartoon." Again, what happened to presenting the critics' arguments as they themselves wanted them presented?

Bugliosi's Love Affair with CE 139

Bugliosi spends over 2,600 pages trying to say that the facts come neatly together in the Kennedy assassination. The centerpiece of the prosecutor's case is Oswald's alleged ownership of the rifle in evidence—Commission Exhibit

139. Bugliosi actually uses the dead man's denials of this ownership as evidence against him.[20] He discards the denials and devotes two chapters in Book One convicting Oswald based on the rifle evidence: "If there is one thing that is now unquestionably certain, it is that Lee Harvey Oswald ordered and paid for one Mannlicher Carcano Rifle that was found on the sixth floor of the Texas School Book Depository. . . ."[21]

However, as we shall see, the rifle allegedly ordered by Oswald is not the same model or length as that which was found on the sixth floor. But before getting into that chain of possession issue, one problem with claiming that this rifle was the one found at the so-called sniper's nest is that it was not the first weapon reported by the authorities. The first reports of the rifle were of a 7.65 German Mauser, not the 6.5 Mannlicher Carcano. The press, DA Henry Wade, and the police made these reports all in the space of the first twenty-four hours.[22] On November 23, Deputy Constable Seymour Weitzman executed an affidavit in which he said that he and Deputy Sheriff Eugene Boone discovered the Mauser on their search of the sixth floor of the book depository. The description in the affidavit is quite specific. Boone later testified to the Warren Commission that Captain Fritz and Lt. Day also identified it as a Mauser.[23] In fact, Boone filed two reports on the day of the assassination saying the rifle he found was a Mauser.[24] What makes this testimony so startling is that one does not have to be familiar with rifles to see that there is a serious problem here because on the rifle in evidence it is clearly stamped "Made in Italy" and "Cal, 6.5." How could anyone say the rifle was a Mauser if it read that it was made in Italy? The Warren Commission assigned this troublesome episode to the Speculations and Rumors section of the Warren Report and said it was all a mistake.[25] Predictably, Bugliosi agrees.[26]

This glib explanation is only *the beginning* of the problems with the rifle. A very interesting photo essay on the subject by Jerry McLeer on his website makes points about the differing style numbering in the different pictures of the serial number. McLeer also noted that when the HSCA test-fired the rifle in evidence, there were differences in the land and groove impressions as originally fired by the FBI,[27] a perfect example of having photos and models but not having the original evidence submitted at the mock trial.

But yet, not even this tells the whole puzzling story about the rifle. There is a serious question as to who ordered the rifle and when. The Warren Commission states that Oswald ordered the rifle on March 12, 1963, in Dallas and sent a money order for $21.45 to Klein's Sporting Goods in Chicago. He allegedly ordered the rifle through an ad in *American Rifleman* and had the weapon sent via his alias of A. Hidell to his post office box.[28]

Bugliosi discounts an important and sensible question: If you were planning on shooting the president, why would you do it with a rifle that you ordered through a mailed money order when you could very likely buy a rifle over the counter with cash and leave no paper trail?

The FBI and Warren Commission state that, although the envelope was mailed on March 12th, it arrived and was deposited by Klein's at the First National Bank of Chicago the following day.[29] The late David Belin who did the questioning on this point,[30] never blinked an eye at how an order could be shipped 700 miles, be received at the Chicago post office, delivered to Klein's, and then deposited at the bank all in one day. Before the advent of computers no less. During the mock trial, Bugliosi had FBI agent Lyndal Shaneyfelt certify that Oswald had sent the envelope to Chicago. Evidently, the FBI never noticed the date markings or the dates on the alleged bank deposit slip. Or if they did, the Bureau saw nothing wrong with any of it.

Once the envelope arrived at Klein's, the company microfilmed the mailing envelope and the order coupon but not the money order for $21.45.[31] It then gets even more interesting. As the late Raymond Gallagher wrote in the pages of *Probe Magazine*, ". . . the bank deposit slip, the extra copy provided by the bank at time of transfer, reads February 15, 1963, not March 13—one month *before* Oswald sent the coupon. . . . Of course, if the February date is correct, then C2766 could not be the correct serial number on the rifle in the so-called backyard photographs."[32] (Emphasis added.)

The alleged money order deposited by Klein's at First National Bank of Chicago has none of the endorsements that the bank's vice president, Robert Wilmouth, says it should have: stamps for the First National Bank of Chicago, the Federal Reserve Bank of Chicago, or the Federal Postal Money Order Center in Kansas City. This is evident by looking at the order itself.[33] Wilmouth never testified before the Warren Commission. Further, the FBI did not find Oswald's latent fingerprints on the money order.[34]

The alleged coupon used to order the rifle is just as dubious. In his 1998 *Probe* article, Gallagher noted a discrepancy that Sylvia Meagher first pointed out back in 1967. The rifle found on the sixth floor was not the model that the Commission said Oswald ordered in March 1963. The Commission states that Oswald used a coupon from the February issue of the *American Rifleman* to order his Carcano.[35] A copy of this ad does not appear in the Warren Commission Report. Instead, a copy of the November 1963 Klein's ad appears (at Vol. 20 p. 174). But *that* ad did not appear in the *American Rifleman*. It appeared in *Field and Stream*. If this ad appeared in November, what could it possibly have to do with the case against Oswald? Unless he ordered two rifles, which no one says he did. Further, the first ad is for a 36-inch Carcano rifle weighing 5.5 pounds, the one the Commission says Oswald ordered. The November ad is for a longer rifle of 40-inches weighing 7 pounds. The rifle in evidence by the Warren Commission is allegedly 40.2 inches long, and with sling and sight weighs in at 8 pounds. In other words, by all accounts, the rifle the Warren Commission says is Oswald's is not the rifle that the Commission says he ordered.

Falling Out of Love with CE 139

For decades, the Italian government had several factories making modified versions of the Mannlicher Carcano rifle. There were at least two 40-inch versions of the rifle and several versions of the 36-inch model. There were well over a million of the former made and over two million of the latter.[36] And here is the rub: Although FBI agent Robert Frazier tried to state that there was only one of *this type* of Carcano with the serial number C 2766—and that a letter prefix with a four digit number was the serial number standard—there is evidence in the Warren Commission volumes to contradict him. As Meagher pointed out, the report does not specify whether Frazier's "type" refers to the model, the year of manufacture, or the category of Mannlicher Carcano rifle.[37] In fact, the owner of Empire Wholesale Sporting Goods Limited told the Bureau that in the thirties, Mussolini ordered all arms factories in Italy to manufacture the Mannlicher Carcano. And since many companies manufactured the same rifle, ". . . the same serial number appears on weapons manufactured by more than one concern. Some bear a letter prefix and some do not."[38]

Researcher Thomas Purvis owns a 36-inch Mannlicher Carcano carbine made at the Gardone factory in 1940. The serial number on this rifle is C 5522. Obviously, to get to that progressive number, the Gardone factory had to have stamped a previous rifle as C 2766. In an article at the JFK Lancer, Martha Moyer writes in "Ordering the Rifle" that John Lattimer had a 40-inch Carcano with the serial number C 2766.[39] So if you do the math as to the millions of Carcano rifles and the multiple factories where they were made, you can imagine how many of the models had the C 2766 serial number on them.

How do we know the rifle in evidence is the same one that Oswald allegedly ordered, if indeed he did? As Purvis has noted, a real clue as to this riddle is that if you follow the FBI investigation of the rifle, the agents appear to have gone to Crescent Firearms, the wholesaler, before going to Klein's, the retailer. That may be, as Gallagher noted in his seminal *Probe* article, because of yet another dichotomy. Louis Feldsott of Crescent Firearms informed the Commission that he had sold this particular rifle, serial number C 2766, to Klein's on June 18, 1962. He also said that he informed the FBI of this on the evening of November 22, 1963.[40] Yet, William Waldman of Klein's said that the shipment of 100 rifles, which included the serial number of C 2766, was ordered from Crescent on January 24, 1963, and received in Chicago on February 22, 1963.[41] As Gallagher noted in his article, there appears to be a six-month discrepancy between the records of the two men. Feldsott was never sworn and deposed in order to resolve this important discrepancy.[42]

It appears that Waldman lied to the Commission on this point. The actual invoice record of C 2766 disappeared after it was shipped from Genoa, Italy, to a warehouse in New Jersey in 1960.[43] When Fred Rupp of Crescent Firearms picked up their order of the rifles from this warehouse, the paper trail does not include any records for the specific carton containing C 2766. That carton number was 3376. That information *was* included in the original form with which the rifles came into the country. After October 24, 1962, there are no specific records of Crescent moving that carton from the New Jersey warehouse,[44] even though Rupp moved 434 of the Mannlicher Carcanos in question. But the Warren Commission needed to make that specific connection from Crescent to Klein's, so when Commission counsel David Belin asked Waldman if a specific invoice showed that carton 3376 was shipped to Klein's, he said it did.[45] But when one looks at the form, that carton is not checked off as being in receipt.[46] All the other forms displayed by the Warren Commission to show this transaction took place are either undated or unsigned. And it appears that the Klein's microfilm records disappeared while in FBI custody.[47]

The Other Side of the Transaction

Bugliosi, quoting Frazier, first discounts the serial number issue. Then later on in the end notes section he says it doesn't really matter since we know that the rifle in evidence is Oswald's. With discrepancies in the work schedule cards and postal markings and bank deposit slip, this is hardly a clean-cut case.

To show how much is missing from *Reclaiming History,* there is also a question on the *other* side of the transaction: Did Oswald pick up this particular rifle at his post office box? In order to ship firearms, the seller had to ship with a form 2162. When the Commission examined local postal inspector and FBI informant Harry Holmes, surprisingly, the issue of form 2162 did not come up.[48] Because if a form 2162 signed by Oswald or Klein's had turned up, it would have helped in demonstrating that the transaction took place.

Why would it not have gone all the way? Because there was another regulation violated in the mail transaction. Postal regulation No. 355.111 dictates that "Mail addressed to a person at a P. O. Box who is not authorized to receive mail shall be endorsed 'addressee unknown' and returned to sender where possible." Klein's sent the rifle to A. Hidell, and not Oswald. Because the postal application form was made out in Oswald's name, when the package arrived and the postal worker saw that there was no box there in that name, it should have been stamped "addressee unknown" and sent back to Klein's. This was a serious problem for the Commission—and they knew it. How did the rifle get through in defiance of two postal regulations?

Harry Holmes helped the Warren Commission out on this one. He said that packages are treated differently than letters in this aspect. When a package arrives, a notice is placed in that person's box and anyone who had a key to Oswald's box could pick up the package—without showing his or her ID.[49] What Holmes left out was they would still have to sign form 2162. But in his testimony to Wesley Liebeler on this point, Holmes brought no regulations with him to show this overriding kind of action was routine. To prove that Holmes was quite conscious of this problem, he said that in part 3 of the post office box application, Oswald could have written down a name other than his own, and this person could have been allowed to pick up any mail. Meaning that if he had a "Hidell" identification, he could have picked up the parcel post package, since he had written it down in part 3. But Holmes also said that on the post office box in Dallas, number 2915, this part 3 of the form was discarded. Even though the one for Oswald's box in New Orleans was still intact. And on that application, Oswald had written down "Hidell."[50] So in his dialogue with Liebeler, Holmes now tried to say that it was the New Orleans office that was in violation of regulations.[51] They should not have kept the application.

As researcher Gil Jesus has shown, it appears to be the other way around. It was Dallas that was in violation of regulations. The post office was required to keep the application forms for two years after the box was closed. Therefore, it would appear that Holmes was being less than honest in his testimony. But further, it appears he was being less than candid for a reason. For as Jesus also points out, the FBI filed a report on this issue. They concluded that "Oswald did not indicate on his application that others, including an 'A. Hidell,' would receive mail through this box in question, which was Post Office Box 2915 in Dallas."[52] The evidence would indicate that the FBI and the Warren Commission knew they had a serious problem in explaining how Oswald could have picked up the rifle in violation of the two regulations.

FBI informant Harry Holmes was used to dodge the problem. Holmes's subservience to the Bureau was so extreme that his family contacted JFK Lancer group and asked them to understand his behavior in the context of the times, when the FBI was perceived as an honorable institution and he was just doing his duty in the JFK investigation.

It is clear Holmes was alerting the FBI to subversive mails being sent to Oswald. In fact, he alerted agent James Hosty that Oswald was in contact with the Fair Play for Cuba Committee in New York. (Bugliosi leaves out this part of Holmes's role in the case.) But we are to believe that Holmes never told the FBI about this three-foot-long package the "commie" Oswald got from Klein's Sporting Goods in Chicago, one of the largest sellers of firearms in America at the time. Holmes also testified that the post office made exhaustive inquiries into the handling and delivering of that large package to Oswald's box, but, incredibly, no one remembered doing it.[53] Even though Oswald would have had to have shown he was Hidell.

Since Marina Oswald was a favorite witness of the majority of the Warren Commission (Allen Dulles, John McCloy, Gerald Ford, and Warren himself), it follows that she would be a favorite of Bugliosi's. But somehow Bugliosi wants us to forget what she said about this issue in one of her first secret service interviews. Marina said that she never saw Oswald with a scoped rifle. In fact, until she saw the rifle in evidence on television she did not know that rifles with scopes existed![54] Although Klein's did put scopes on the 36-inch model rifle, they did not put scopes on the 40-inch model. The HSCA interviewed Klein's in-house gunsmith on this point, something the Commission did not do.[55] The question then becomes how did the 40-inch model on the sixth floor attain a scope?

On Sunday, November 24, a Dallas TV reporter got an anonymous phone call saying that Oswald had his rifle sighted in on November 21st at a gun shop in Irving. The reporter called in the information to Detective Turner at Dallas Police HQ. This was the second tip Turner had about this information (the first included the information that the rifle came from Klein's). On November 25th, the FBI turned up at Dial Ryder's house in Irving. Ryder worked at a local gun shop and had a repair ticket with Oswald's name on it.[56] When shown a photo of Oswald, Ryder said he associated the man with someone who had brought in an Argentinian rifle about two weeks before and had a scope mounted on it.[57] There is no record of the FBI trying to find out who this man was.

What makes the Ryder story fascinating is a related piece of testimony. Gertrude Hunter and Edith Whitworth testified to the Commission that Oswald, his wife, and two daughters, came into Whitworth's furniture shop in Irving looking for a gunsmith who had formerly occupied the locale, and whose sign "Guns" had not yet been removed. Oswald had an object wrapped in paper with him about 15-inches long. He said he wanted to have the plunger (i.e., the firing pin) on his rifle fixed.[58] (The rifle found in the Book Depository did have a defective firing pin.) Mrs. Whitworth recalled that she may have directed him to the Irving Sports Shop where Ryder worked. Hunter corroborated Whitworth.[59] As Sylvia Meagher noted, the Commission did all it could to discredit the two women. The last thing in the world they wanted was corroboration that someone was impersonating Oswald on the eve of the assassination.[60]

There is one more interesting point to be made about the Ryder/Whitworth incident. Prior to the Ryder story, the FBI had given the price of the rifle purchase as $12.78. After the Ryder story created headlines in Dallas, the FBI now changed the purchase price to $19.95. Probably because the latter price was the price of the rifle with scope added.

The rifle is the centerpiece of Bugliosi's questionable case against Oswald. Every single step of the transaction, on both the mailing side and the delivery side, is vulnerable to doubt. It is all documented with exhibits and testimony and printed regulations. And you will find very little about any of these serious problems in *Reclaiming History*. Which, again, belies the author's claim to present the critics' arguments as they wish to have them presented. And to show just how coerced Bugliosi's witness Marina Oswald was, we must not forget that at first she said she had never seen a rifle with a scope. But before the Warren Commission, Marina uttered her exquisitely rehearsed line when shown the rifle in evidence: "This is the fateful rifle of Lee Oswald."[61] However, on the Oprah Winfrey show of November, 22, 1996, Marina said, "I was a stupid girl and right now if you show me my husband's hunting rifle I am not sure because up to this date I know nothing about this rifle. . . .. It was a stick with metal. That's all a rifle is to me to this day."

Although we have touched on some of the major problems with the rifle, it is possible to bring up several more that are just as troubling. For example, the FBI could never prove which precise deposit of Klein's included Oswald's alleged money order.[62] Which brings into further question whether or not Oswald ever mailed payment for it. If Bugliosi missed all of the above, it demonstrates the difference between being a good investigator and being a good lawyer. Unfortunately for Bugliosi, the value of a lawyer's case relies upon the quality of the investigation behind it. And in the JFK field, there exist much better investigations than those done by London Weekend Television.

CHAPTER FIVE

Oswald's Defense

"There was not one speck of credible evidence that
Oswald was framed."

—Vincent Bugliosi, *Reclaiming History*, Introduction

In 2003, at Dr. Cyril Wecht's forensic symposium on JFK at Duquesne University, attorney Jim Lesar turned to Arlen Specter and asked, "Mr. Specter, how would you get CE 399 into evidence?"

Bugliosi, who was invited to that conference, chose not to attend. It would have been interesting to hear his answer. If Oswald had lived, the prosecution would have had to establish the validity of CE 399, the bullet the Warren Commission says went through both President Kennedy and Governor Connally. That trajectory contains the single-bullet theory. Without it, there are more bullets than provided for by the three shells found on the sixth floor thereby necessitating another assassin, *ergo* a conspiracy. But at a real trial, not the farcical one in London, in order to introduce CE 399, the witnesses who discovered it would have had to ID it before it was admitted as evidence. Which would have meant calling another 402 hearing. For, as Lesar noted, any defense lawyer worth his salt would have been all over this piece of evidence, realizing that it was the key to acquitting his client and exposing a frame-up. Needless to say, none of this was done at the London sideshow.

But in Pittsburgh, there were lawyers who really knew the case. So before letting Specter answer the question, Lesar turned to Bob Tanenbaum, the first deputy counsel of the HSCA. Tanenbaum said admitting it would be a problem since you had both a chain of custody question *and* an identification question. Specter then blustered through actually naming Darrell Tomlinson as a witness; Tomlinson would not be a good witness. In fact, Tomlinson would blow up Bugliosi's carefully scripted testimony of Monty Lutz as to where the bullet was found.

The Sorry Trail of CE 399

Josiah Thompson's *Six Seconds in Dallas* has become a controversial book. Despite having its detractors early on, at least one section of that work is still valuable: Thompson's discussion of which stretcher CE 399 was discovered on at Parkland Hospital. In a long, detailed, and illustrated analysis he concludes that the bullet was not discovered on either Kennedy's or Governor Connally's stretcher. From the description given by senior engineer Darrell Tomlinson, the man who first discovered it, Thompson concludes that the bullet was found on Ronald Fuller's stretcher, a little boy brought into the emergency ward at about 1:00 PM.[1] Specter did not want to hear this so, if you read his interview of Tomlinson in Commission Volume 6, you will see that he is intent on shaping his story.[2] Specter understood how deadly it was to the chain of possession of CE 399 if that bullet was found on any other stretcher but Connally's. In fact, even before Tomlinson testified before the Commission, Specter had told Allen Dulles that the bullet was found on Connally's stretcher and not Kennedy's.[3]

Like Specter, Bugliosi does not like Thompson's work here either. He knows just how dangerous it is to his case. For if CE 399 was found on any other stretcher but Connally's, then what is the proof that it went through both men? So the prosecutor handles it on the CD in his end note file. (For in his prosecutorial zeal, Bugliosi makes the whole chain of custody issue of CE 399 disappear! He calls it a "giant non-issue. Since we know that the bullet was fired from Oswald's Carcano rifle, and wasn't found on Kennedy's stretcher, it had to be found on Connally's stretcher."[4]

Almost unbelievably, Bugliosi then writes that the discovery of CE 399 on Connally's stretcher is one of the few points that virtually everyone agrees upon! This is so wrong it is hard to comprehend how he wrote it. On this very same page, Bugliosi writes two other puzzlers. He writes that ". . . we know it wasn't found on Kennedy's stretcher." Yet, this is what Commissioner Allen Dulles thought before Specter had to correct him.[5] Second, to save the chain of possession issue, he writes that FBI agent Elmer Lee Todd's initials are on CE 399. This is false and it betrays the prosecutor's serious failings as an investigator.

As Tanenbaum said to Lesar, it was not just the chain of possession issue which a 402 hearing would have examined. There was also an identification issue. After Tomlinson picked up the bullet, he gave it to Parkland security officer O. P. Wright. In an FBI Airtel of June, 20, 1964, it is said that neither man could identify the bullet. As Thompson stated in the footnotes to his book, when he interviewed both men in 1966, neither could positively identify CE 399 as the bullet they found that day.[6] But in a subsequent FBI memo forwarded to the Warren Commission, the Bureau said that both men stated that CE 399 "resembled" the bullet they picked up and it "appears to be the same."[7] But in fact, in 1966, when Thompson interviewed Wright, Wright was adamant about this. He actually told Thompson the bullet he found was a sharp-nosed, lead-colored projectile, not a round nosed, copper colored cartridge like CE 399.[8] Wright knew what he was talking about since he used to work in the Sheriff's office. This, of course, brings into question whether or not the FBI and Warren Commission reports on these identification interviews were accurate. Or did they misrepresent something?

The FBI Cover-Up

Many years later, Thompson, joined by Dr. Gary Aguilar, found out what really happened. Bardwell Odum was the FBI agent said to have shown Tomlinson and Wright CE 399 after which they now said it resembled the bullet they saw that day. Years later, when the two investigators finally tracked Odum down, he said he didn't recall doing any such thing.[9] Bugliosi confronts this rather startling discovery, which clearly implies that the FBI lied in two ways. First, he says that perhaps Odum forgot the original episode. This seems doubtful. Was there ever a bigger case Odum worked on than this? In addition, Odum told Aguilar and Thompson that he knew Wright, "and would certainly not have forgotten such an episode if it had ever happened."[10]

The second technique employed by Bugliosi is really beneath him and any dignified discussion of the JFK case at this time. He says that implying the original reports are false is to say the FBI was in on the conspiracy to kill Kennedy. Therefore, he actually wants Aguilar and Thompson to say that.[11] (This is not an exaggeration, and the reader can check this footnote out himself.) But if one reads what Aguilar wrote about this in *The Assassinations*, he says no such thing. So why should he be asked to admit something he is not even implying? These are both meant to detract from the legal issue at hand for the prosecution: In a real court of law, not London Weekend Television's, the onus would be on Bugliosi to get CE 399 into evidence.

But here's the rub. Why would you want to? In challenging the claims by journalist and author Jim Marrs that much of the Kennedy evidence could not be admitted into court, Bugliosi replies that he could get 95 percent of it into evidence.[12] But why? Why would you want people like Tomlinson and Wright testifying that the bullet was found on the wrong gurney and is not the original bullet? And further, why would you ever want Odum saying he never showed the projectile to them? How could this possibly benefit the prosecution? It would, in fact, be a tremendous setback to the prosecution's case, both in practical terms, and also in the sense that the jury would now question the efficacy of the other evidence. Certainly you would want to keep those witnesses off the stand and try and convict Oswald with some other type of evidence while hoping the defense would not try and introduce the exhibit or the testimony. In other words, you would keep your fingers crossed.

There is even more evidence to certify that the Magic Bullet concept was always phony. At a press conference after operating on Governor Connally, Dr. Robert Shaw said that he had not yet taken the bullet out of Connally's leg. Shaw said it was in his left thigh and would be taken out before he went to the recovery room. How could Tomlinson have found the bullet outside of Connally's leg before surgery if it was still in Connally's leg after surgery?[13] Perhaps because, as Robert Harris has shown in a recent essay, it is now possible to demonstrate Connally was hit by a separate bullet.

As Connally stated in his autobiography, a bullet fell out of his body and was picked up by a nurse, Audrey Bell. This was acknowledged by DA Henry Wade who said he saw the nurse with a bullet in her hand, which was taken from Connally's gurney.[14] This bullet was given to Dallas Highway Patrolman Bobby Nolan. Nolan took it to the Dallas police that evening. He was interviewed by the FBI the next day. In that report they confirm the bullet came from Connally's left thigh. As Harris proves, the FBI knew this would create a problem, especially if the bullet could not be linked to Oswald's alleged rifle. So they smudged the evidence by saying the nurse had really retrieved a *group* of fragments from Connally and had given those to a highway patrolman. This was untrue; she gave her fragments to hospital administrator Jack Price. Again, it appears the FBI was intent on covering up the true facts of the case.[15] In Bugliosi's discussion of this issue, he ignores the facts of the story up until Nolan was interviewed the day after. He then tries to say Audrey Bell had the fragment the whole time and then muses as to what could have happened to the bullet if it was *not* planted.[16]

But actually it's even worse than that. When Thompson went looking a few years ago for security officer Wright, he learned that he had passed away. But he did manage to locate his widow who had also worked at Parkland Hospital at the time of the assassination as one of the nursing supervisors. She reported to Thompson that on the day of the assassination, more than one nurse approached her and said they had also picked up bullets that day.

One of the more interesting discoveries of the ARRB was an FBI evidence envelope from Dallas. As Michael Griffith points out, although the envelope was empty, the cover indicated it had contained a 7.65 mm rifle shell found in Dealey Plaza after the shooting. The envelope was dated December, 2, 1963, so the shell was found sometime between November 22 and December 2, 1963. This important piece of evidence had been hidden for three decades, perhaps because it matched the caliber of the Mauser rifle reportedly first found.

In addition to this shell is Mark Oakes's work on the famous photo of what appears to be FBI agent Robert Barrett picking up a bullet slug in Dealey Plaza that day.

I bring these points up because a common practice these days among "Krazy Kid Oswald" advocates like Robert Stone and Bugliosi is to ask: If there were more than three bullets fired, where did they go? The above begins to answer that question, but it also exposes the emptiness of the charge. Because in any real crime scene investigation, Dealey Plaza would have been immediately cordoned off and then details of Dallas Police, supplemented by FBI technology, would have been channeled into the entire area. There would have been a foot-by-foot systematic check for shells, bullets, weapons, and anything else lying around from the shooting. That did not happen. Further, as Seth Kantor testified and the photos show, when Kennedy's limousine got to Parkland Hospital, it was not secured. In other words, like the stretcher inside the hospital, it was possible to go ahead and plant evidence. So this "Where did it go?" question is really a slick rhetorical device that makes Warren Commission critics defend and rely upon the sorry crime scene practices that took place afterwards.

Before leaving this issue of evidence tampering with bullet projectiles, let me state that there is even more to be said about the issue, of which Bugliosi does not seem cognizant. And it further undermines his untenable assertion that there is not a speck of evidence to indicate Oswald was framed.

The Telltale Shells

Let us now address the matter of ammunition and cartridge cases. The FBI did an extensive search of all the gun shops in the Dallas area and they could find only two places which handled this type of ammunition. Neither of them recalled selling anything to Oswald.[17] There were three cartridge cases found on the floor at the scene, and there was one live round in the weapon. The evidence says that Oswald had four bullets. No ammo company sells bullets by the round. They sell them by the box, usually twenty per box. This presents a real quandary. Because no extra ammunition, or boxes, were found in Oswald's personal effects.[18] Did someone give him four bullets and say, "See if you can kill Kennedy with those?" Did he ask someone for the ammo? Did he buy them in New Orleans or Mexico? What happened to the other sixteen rounds and the container box or boxes? This is one of those enduring mysteries about this case for which no one, including Bugliosi, has ever offered a satisfactory conclusion.

The Warren Commission labeled one of the shells reportedly found on the sixth floor, CE 543. The problem is that it is a dented shell. As ballistics authority and expert marksman Howard Donahue has said, this dented shell could not have been used to fire a bullet that day. The weapon would not have fired properly.[19] As Josiah Thompson notes, it also had three identifying marks revealing it had been loaded and extracted from a weapon at least three times before. These were not found on the other shells. As Thompson further notes, "Of all the various marks discovered on this case, only one set links it to Oswald's rifle, and this set was identified as having come from the magazine follower. Yet the magazine follower marks only the last cartridge in the clip. . . ."[20] The last cartridge in the clip was the live round, not this one. Further, the clip contained no fingerprints,[21] and neither did any of the cases.[22]

One of the things Thompson did was to test whether CE 543 could have been dented when it was discharged. It could not.[23] Bugliosi solves this problem the same way Gerald Posner did.[24] He says it was dented during firing.[25] He uses Monty Lutz from the HSCA as his authority. But when Mike Griffith asked Howard Donahue about this particular issue, Donahue replied that, "there were *no shells dented in that manner by the HSCA* . . . I have never seen a case dented like this."[26]

Griffith also communicated with British researcher Chris Mills on this evidentiary point. Mills, who experimented with a Mannlicher Carcano rifle on this issue, said that the only way he achieved this denting effect was by using *empty* shells, and he had to repeat the experiment sixty times to get the same effect. Mills concluded this could only occur with an empty case that had been previously fired, and then only occasionally.[27]

Author Michael Kurtz noted that the shell "lacks the characteristic indentation on the side made by the firing chamber of Oswald's rifle."[28] He then adds that forensic pathologist Forrest Chapman concludes that CE 543 was probably "dry loaded." Because the dent was too big to support a bullet, it was not fired from the Carcano. Chapman also noted that "CE 543 had a deeper and more concave indentation on its base . . . where the firing pin strikes the case. Only empty cases exhibit such characteristics."[29] And Kurtz adds that when the FBI fired an empty shell for comparison purposes, it also contained the dent in the lip and the deep firing pin impression. Kurtz also concluded that CE 543 could not have been fired from the Carcano that day.[30]

The FBI analysis of the other two hulls is also at odds with the official story. Only one of the shells, CE 544, had markings revealing it had been ejected from the bolt of the rifle in evidence. The other two had markings made by the magazine follower, which would have only marked the last round in the clip.[31] Yet, neither was the last round. Neither CE 544 nor CE 545 bear the markings of a firing pin from the rifle in question. This suggests that both had been loaded into the firing chamber and that CE 544 was ejected through the bolt action, but CE 543 was not.[32] Therefore only one of the shells was actually ejected through the bolt of the weapon.

We should think back to what photographer Tom Alyea said about the shells, that they were all within the distance of a hand towel. That is not how they are arranged in the Warren Commission photos. As Alyea and Allan Eaglesham indicate, the shells were picked up and then dropped again by either Captain Fritz or police photographer R. L. Studebaker. For, as the subsequent FBI experiments showed, the dispersal pattern after ejection would not have been anywhere that neat.[33]

As Gil Jesus and Barry Krusch have noted, the Dallas police markings on the shells raise further questions. The first officers who handled the shells should have marked them. But the man who placed them in the evidence envelope, Lt. J. C. Day, told the Commission on April 22, 1964, that they were not so marked at the time; in other words those initials were not carved at the crime scene. And further, he said that the envelope had not been sealed when it was returned to him that night at 10 PM. In a letter to the Commission dated April 23, 1964, Day wrote that one of the hulls, CE 543, has only the initials GD on it. Yet when George Doughty was interviewed by Day, Doughty did not recall handling the shell. Later—as Krusch has pointed out in his book *Impossible*—in an affidavit of June 23, 1964, Day reversed himself. He said that he *had* initialed CE 543 *with* Doughty. In Day's original story that particular shell was not sent to Washington with the other two. It was kept by Fritz in his desk drawer. But as Krusch shows, with this new affidavit, the story changes and it is CE 544 that stays in Dallas, not CE 543. How could Day have confused the two shells if CE 543 had a significant dent in it?

In light of all this puzzling evidence about the shells which raises so much doubt and so many questions, Bugliosi's reliance on Monty Lutz was rather ill-advised.

Bugliosi and Guinn vs. Aguilar

Bugliosi's reliance on Larry Sturdivan is even worse. Dr. Gary Aguilar did a long review of *Reclaiming History* for the legal publication *Federal Lawyer*.[34] In that review he focused on Bugliosi's use of the Neutron Activation Analysis (NAA) for bullet lead analysis done by Vincent Guinn for the House Select Committee on Assassinations. Enamored by Robert Blakey's HSCA experts, the prosecutor actually used Guinn at the London show trial. But by the time *Reclaiming History* was published in 2007, the use of NAA for the purpose of bullet identification and linkage was collapsing around the prosecutor's ears. Yet Bugliosi actually spent four pages on this issue to tie the bullet fragment evidence to Oswald's rifle.[35] In those four pages in the text, there is not a hint that the whole procedure had been exposed as forensically false, but, as Aguilar discussed at length in his review, such was the case: NAA for bullet lead analysis has been thoroughly and completely discredited. To the point where the FBI has announced it will not use it in court anymore. Before *Reclaiming History* was published, Texas A&M statistics professor Cliff Spiegelman had already denounced this technique as questionable. And he directly challenged its use in the JFK case. There have now been two published studies by two teams of experts that have completely invalidated the underpinnings of this test. In addition to the Spiegelman-Tobin study, there was another by statistician Pat Grant and metallurgist Rick Randich. The latter study had already been released before *Reclaiming History* was published.

But there had been so much material published even by 2004, that the man who inspired Bugliosi to use the test at his mock trial had already denounced it two years before *Reclaiming History* was published. In 2005, at a conference in Washington, HSCA Chief Counsel Robert Blakey let it be known that he was jettisoning bullet lead analysis. He actually called the test "junk science."[36] The previous year, in July 2004, Tobin had written a long analysis for a legal journal exposing the faults in Guinn's assumptions.[37] Tobin had been a metallurgist for twenty-four years at the FBI laboratory. Perhaps no one knew more about the process than he did. In that article—published three years before Bugliosi's book came out—he predicted that bullet lead analysis would not withstand a strong Daubert standard hearing.[38] And Daubert was the legal standard to apply for a judge admitting so-called expert testimony. Tobin pointed out that "recent testing yields results at odds with the premises, and there is no meaningful peer reviewed and referenced literature supporting" the theory.[39]

In fact, Tobin actually came up with a citation which showed that *Guinn himself* had objected to the FBI overselling the accuracy of what came to be known as CBLA, or Comparative Bullet Lead Analysis.[40] As Tobin put it, the most obvious manner in which CBLA could be challenged was to ask the question: Did the available research data validate the specific theory on which the expert was testifying? The answer to that question by these two teams was: No, it did not. For instance, as far back as 2002, Pat Grant found error rates in the process as high as 33 percent.[41] Which is simply unconscionable for a legal venue. So, from a sheer statistical viewpoint, the process was questionable. As one judge asked, if the jury did not know how many bullets were out there, and how big the original melt was, how could they accord the analysis probative value?[42] Because of this research, the National Academy of Sciences (NAS) warned the FBI to review the whole CBLA process before continuing with it. As Tobin notes, this was in 2004. Again, three years before *Reclaiming History* was published.

But this research went on beyond 2004. I had an opportunity to sit in on a small conference conducted by Randich and Grant arranged in San Francisco by Gary Aguilar. Here, the basic flaw in Vincent Guinn's work was pointed out. Since he was a chemist and not a metallurgist, he had no knowledge of the way that metals melt in the smelting process and how this would impact the trace elements one gets from drawing samples. In other words, because of the way the elements coagulate in the smelting process, the position of sample drawn from the bullet will have a strong effect in determining the trace element particles you end up comparing.[43] Which makes the process arbitrary.

Bugliosi was aware of the Randich/Grant study and even though his book was published before the Spiegelman/Tobin study was peer reviewed, this was still three years after the NAS announcement. The FBI was going to stop using the practice at trial because the witness would have been in danger of being indicted for perjury. And, in fact, Guinn himself had contradicted the basis of his methodology at different points in his career.[44] He had said that elemental traces varied widely within even one bullet. In other words, one could get a low concentration of antimony in one area but a higher one somewhere else in the bullet. In other words, there was no uniformity inside the bullet. The trace elements were arranged almost at random, but he never explained why. The fact that he seems to have been unaware of this shows Guinn did not know about the crystallization formations in the smelting process noted above.

Guinn was also wrong about the uniqueness of the lead used by Western Cartridge Company for Mannlicher Carcano bullets. Guinn falsely said that this lead "was found to differ sharply from typical bullet leads." Western Cartridge Company Mannlicher Carcano bullets do not differ sharply from most bullet leads. It seemed different to Guinn because he compared the lead alloy to unjacketed handgun rounds. At the private conference in San Francisco in 2006, Randich stated that the lead used in these WCC MC bullets is much like other metal-jacketed rounds. Randich said that outside of .38 and .22 handguns, most bullet manufacturers use the same lead alloy most of the time. (He placed the figure at 75 percent.) This, in and of itself, sticks a harpoon in Guinn's work since it says that the lead alloy for an MC bullet, far from being unique, is, more often than not, the same alloy that say, rival company Remington would use. With this, Guinn's concept of the singular identifiability of Mannlicher Carcano ammunition is negated.

In San Francisco, Randich and Grant projected a chart that measured the trace elements of five pieces of evidence Guinn analyzed: the bullet left in the rifle at the so-called sniper's nest, the bullet that Oswald allegedly fired at General Walker, and the three samples from the Kennedy assassination. The values varied widely especially for the "sniper's nest" bullet and the Walker bullet. Peter Dale Scott surmised that it appeared that those two bullets came from a different type of gun or type of ammunition. Right before this chart was placed on the overhead, Randich spoke about how trace metal values can vary widely in a particular run if one of the ingots used for the metals has been replaced on the production line. I then asked him if, theoretically, all of these bullets could have come from the same box even though they displayed such a wide variety of trace elements. He said yes, theoretically they could. The next question was, "Then what's the basis for this science?" Randich replied, "You're talking to the choir."

Rahn's Budapest Caper

In light of the above, it is amazing that Bugliosi does what he can to blunt the impact of these discoveries on the viability of Vincent Guinn's work. In fact, his five-page discussion of the matter in his end notes spends about 75 percent of that space defending Guinn, rather than in elucidating the technical discoveries of this new work, which invalidates Guinn.[45] Incredibly, the prosecutor never mentions the two major errors: that Guinn came to his faulty conclusion because he compared the WCC/MC metal alloy with *handgun* bullets, and that the alloy used for the former bullets was unique when it was not. Nor does he explain that Guinn was not a metallurgist, therefore he knew nothing about the segregation process during smelting which meant that if you took one sample from one area and another sample from a close distance away, the trace elements results would be different. Since Guinn tested so few particles, the process was invalidated statistically.

In his end notes, the prosecutor praises a two-part article by Ken Rahn and Larry Sturdivan, but he does not state where it was published or in what journal. Rodger Remington tracked this article down. It was published in *Journal of Radioanalytical and Nuclear Chemistry* in Budapest, Hungary.[46] Why publish there? With the rising tide against CBLA brought about by Spiegelman, Tobin, Grant, and Randich, these two Warren Commission stalwarts could not get an article published in America. Also, the journal they published in had no visible background or experience in articles on CBLA.[47] Third, the issue in which the two-part article was published contained a tribute to Vincent Guinn, who had passed away in 2002. The publication solicited articles from friends and colleagues, and then published the tribute in 2004. Clearly, as Remington points out, Sturdivan and Rahn were trying to get something into the record to blunt the impact of the CBLA being undermined by the scientific community. Since Rahn's field is atmospheric chemistry and Sturdivan's is physics, it is unclear why they should be allowed to publish in a peer-reviewed journal about CBLA in the first place. But revealingly, like Cecil Kirk, Sturdivan had done work for the Warren Commission and also served as a witness for Robert Blakey's HSCA.

When the movement to form the HSCA was heating up in the mid-seventies, many people desired that the people hired by the committee be completely separated from the Warren Commission. This was in order to avoid the danger that the results of technical tests would be the same for the HSCA since the original people involved would have a bias against having their work overturned. Yet, both Guinn and Sturdivan *did* work for the Warren Commission.[48] Despite this, HSCA chief counsel Blakey had no problem having Sturdivan testify about the ballistics of the Carcano. In addition, Sturdivan's fields of specialty are statistics and physics but he testifies as an authority on things like ballistics, wound configuration, trajectory analysis, and for Bugliosi, NAA. Besides his lack of credentials, he, along with Kirk and Guinn, would have a hard time admitting that the verdict he helped create back in 1964 may have been wrong. For Bugliosi to use Sturdivan is almost like trotting out the likes of Gerald Ford to testify to the thoroughness and efficacy of the Warren Commission investigation (which he does).[49]

This issue of the prosecutor's use of CBLA—along with his use of Sturdivan and Guinn—is an important one. Bugliosi writes about Guinn's work for about eight pages and then places the information that impeaches Guinn in the CD notes, not the main text. Therefore, reading the text, the reader would still think Guinn's work has some validity. Bugliosi minimizes how effective the new discoveries in the field are, and he praises the Budapest work of Rahn and Sturdivan without saying it was published there. In the main text, he actually quotes from Guinn's testimony at the ersatz London trial for about a page. Including Guinn's most extreme, and now embarrassing, statements. Bugliosi then concludes, ". . . from the *NAA evidence alone*, it was now possible to state, with a high degree of probability, that the so-called pristine bullet, the "magic bullet" (CE 399), had indeed been the bullet that smashed into Governor Connally's wrist."[50] (Emphasis added.)

It is only *after* saying that and using Guinn in the text that the author finally begins to explain why this work is now discredited. And he does this on the attached CD. And listen to how he does this: he says that the forensic value of CBLT ". . . may not be true, at least not anymore."[51] But yet, if CBLT has now been discredited, then the process must have been faulty back in 1963 when it was first used on the Kennedy case. There are no "mays" about it.

Bugliosi also says that ". . . no one has successfully challenged the findings of Dr. Guinn in the Kennedy assassination. . . ." At the conference described in San Francisco, Rick Randich did just that. Spiegelman said that his findings indicate the fragments could have come from three or more bullets, and if that is so, ". . . then a second assassin is likely, as the additional bullet would not be attributable to the main suspect, Mr.Oswald."[52] Bugliosi then writes that the "conspiracy community has been quick to seize on the new findings about NAA as a weakness in the case against Oswald."[53] My question to the prosecutor: How are Spiegelman and Randich members of the "conspiracy community"? They and their illustrious colleagues have shown Guinn's work to be untenable. Their work invalidates Guinn's concepts for *everyone*. Bugliosi then tries to say that Guinn stated that WCC MC ammunition had different elemental compositions within the same box of bullets. Yet, as noted above, Randich proved this was wrong. The overwhelming majority of rifle bullets are made from the same lead alloy. To top off this discussion, like at the London sideshow, the prosecutor refers to CE 399 as the "Connally stretcher bullet." And he says that it was fired from "Oswald's rifle."[54] As if these are accomplished facts. They are anything but.

I have concentrated so far on what prosecutors call "core evidence." That is: the alleged weapon, the ammunition, CE 399, the shells found at the scene, and the NAA tests used to link the fragments to Oswald's rifle. Consider the legal state of this evidence. Today, the NAA could not be used. Any prosecutor would have to think twice before he even tried to get CE 399 and cartridge case CE 543 into evidence. How could you even talk about the ammunition if you cannot even prove Oswald purchased it? And as I have taken time to show, there is a string of unanswered questions about whether or not the rifle in evidence was ordered by Oswald under the circumstances described in the Warren Report. Bugliosi's mantra is that the JFK case is a simple case, it's the Warren Commission critics who make it complicated. However, the critics created none of the testimony, exhibits, or evidence noted above. It was all placed into the record by others: the FBI, the Dallas Police, and the Warren Commission. Bugliosi can argue against this record or try to explain it away until the cows come home, but these facts existed before he arrived on the scene, they exist right now, and they will exist when he leaves.

The Walker Shooting

At times in *Reclaiming History*, Bugliosi uses a narrative form, that is, he tells the story in straight chronological order. That form has its advantages. It also has drawbacks. You end up using pieces of evidence which later have a dubious provenance.

Like the Commission, Bugliosi concludes that Oswald took a shot at Gen. Edwin Walker in April 1963. The Dallas Police never even considered Oswald a suspect in the Walker shooting for the eight months they investigated that case. And the evidence used by the Warren Commission to link him to the crime did not surface until after the assassination. In fact, one of the pieces, the bullet fired that night, was transformed in caliber and color by the Warren Commission to tie it to Oswald's alleged rifle.

As Gerald McKnight notes in his fine section on the Walker shooting in *Breach of Trust*, the Dallas Police always referred to the bullet fired into Walker's home as being a steel-jacketed 30.06 bullet.[55] And in the report filed by Officers Van Cleave and McElroy, they note the projectile as being steel jacketed.[56] Both local Dallas newspapers and an Associated Press story referred to the bullet as a 30.06 in caliber.[57] In less than three weeks after the assassination, the FBI changed the bullet to a 6.5 caliber, *copper*-jacketed bullet. Which meant they could link this projectile to Oswald. And, in fact, the bullet today in the National Archives, allegedly tied to the Walker case, is copper coated.[58] Yet, none of the Dallas police officers who handled the slug were called to testify before the Warren Commission.

Through the work of Randich and Grant, the elemental trace values of the so-called Walker Bullet are different from those found at the Kennedy crime scene. In a March 27, 1964, memorandum, the FBI concluded that "the lead alloy of the bullet recovered from the attempted shooting of General Walker was different from the lead alloy of a large bullet fragment from the car in which President Kennedy was shot."[59] Two FBI agents, Henry Heiberger and John Gallagher, performed tests on the bullet for the FBI. The former was never called by the Commission and the latter was never asked about the matter.[60]

Ruth Paine Produces the Walker Note

There were two other pieces of physical evidence used to link Oswald to the Walker shooting. One consisted of five photographs of Walker's house found in the garage of Ruth and Michael Paine, where many of Oswald's belongings were stored after his return from New Orleans. The second, a handwritten note in Russian allegedly left for Marina by Lee, ominously concludes he may be in jail and how to find him there.[61] This note has no date on it and does not refer to Walker at all, on either page. Nor did it have Oswald's latent fingerprints on it.[62] How can one possibly write a note that fills up almost both sides of a sheet of paper and not get fingerprints on it? The fingerprints of Marina, who was supposed to have found the note, were absent also. The FBI report on this issue, dated December 12, 1963, was not included in the Commission's twenty-six volumes of evidence. And when the FBI's fingerprint expert, Sebastian Latona, appeared before the Commission, he was not asked about this issue.

Gil Jesus points out internal problems with what the note says. For example, it says that Oswald's checks were mailed to him and Marina should cash them. But as Jesus points out, the evidence is that they were not mailed to Oswald. And how could Marina cash them if they were not made out to her? Marina is supposed to take clippings about Oswald to the Embassy, presumably the Russian embassy. Yet, the Commission story is that Marina could not read English newspapers at the time. And why would the Russian Embassy want clippings of one American citizen shooting at another American citizen? There is also advice to go to the Red Cross. For what reason should Marina go to the Red Cross afterwards? How would that occur if Oswald was arrested for a shooting?

The problem with the pictures *and* the note is that they both surfaced via Ruth Paine after the assassination. The photos were found in her garage and the note was found in a book she turned over to the Irving Police on November 30.[63] Several Dallas Police officers who searched the Paine residence for two days for evidence immediately after the assassination somehow had failed to find the note.

The books Ruth turned over were titled *Our Child* and *Book of Helpful Instructions*. Ruth said it was urgent Marina have the books as she could not get along without them since she used both every day.[64] This reportedly happened on November 30th, but something preceded it by one day that may have been the impetus to link the dead Oswald to the Walker shooting. On November 24th, a reporter named Hasso Thorsen for the West German newspaper *Deutsche National Zeitung* called Walker. He tried to elicit a statement to the effect that Oswald had fired at him. When questioned on his response by the Warren Commission, Walker said he told Thorsen that no, he did not think it was Oswald, but on November 29, an article appeared in that West German newspaper that said Walker had reported that it was Oswald who *had* fired on him.[65] No one knows where this information came from. And the next day, Oswald's incriminating note appears for the first time.

Marina's testimony about the note is contradictory in the extreme. On December 2, 1963, she said she never saw the note.[66] The next day, she said the note was written by Oswald before the Walker shooting.[67] She also contradicted herself about where the note was located. First she said it was on a dresser in their bedroom,[68] but in 1964, before the Warren Commission, she said the note was located in Oswald's "private room."[69] But as Jesus points out, the most puzzling part of Marina's testimony was that the note was not left for her in case a catastrophe struck. Marina says that on the night of the Walker shooting, she just happened to be drawn into Oswald's private room, which was about the size of a closet. And that is where the note was *found*, not left.[70] In fact, the Secret Service agents around Marina were also skeptical. For on December 4, five days after Ruth delivered the note in Marina's book, Ruth Paine was visited by two Secret Service agents who returned the "Walker Note" because they thought it was from her.[71]

The Walker Witnesses

The Dallas Police who investigated the crime suspected there was more than one person involved. When the FBI got involved later, they interviewed the two principal witnesses, Kirk Coleman and Robert Surrey. Coleman said that after he heard the shot he ran outside and he saw two men driving away in separate cars. When the FBI interviewed Coleman, he described the two men and neither one fit Oswald's description. He also said that one car had its motor running with the headlights on.[72] Before escaping, one of them men looked back at him. Because of this, Coleman was fearful for his life. He told the Dallas Police he would like to keep his name out of the papers.[73] Coleman did not appear before the Commission.[74]

Coleman's account of the shooting was backed up by Robert Surrey, a Dallas businessman who supported Walker's rightwing political causes. Surrey told two FBI agents that just forty-eight hours before the shooting, he had driven up to Walker's house and had seen two "well-dressed men in suits and ties" peering into Walker's windows. The pair did not see him, so he continued watching them from a nearby yard. After about thirty minutes, they drove away in a car without a rear license plate. Like Coleman, Surrey said he'd never seen either man before and that neither one looked like Oswald.[75]

Bugliosi deals with all this in the main text of *Reclaiming History* by presenting it largely in his biography section of Oswald which was cowritten with Fred Haines, a screenwriter who suggested that this section be written in narrative form. Bugliosi presents the note as being discovered by Marina on the night of the Walker shooting[76] without noting Marina's differing accounts of this episode. Further, he has Oswald admitting to the shooting, which he never did. He then says that the FBI first began to look at Oswald as a suspect in the Walker case on November 30, without mentioning in the main text, the convenient timing of the West German article and the Ruth Paine book transfer.[77] In discussing the Walker bullet, Bugliosi does not mention, at least in this section, how both color and caliber changed when it was transferred from the DPD to the FBI. As for the DPD and FBI investigations, which concluded two men were involved, he consigns it to an on-page footnote without any comment.[78] He mentions the fact that one of the photos taken outside Walker's home and found in the Paines' garage had the license plate cut out.

In light of this, what does Bugliosi use to bolster his Walker case? He says, "We know that Oswald attempted to murder General Walker because he confessed to his own wife that he did; nothing further is required to make the point."[79] However, in a secret report about Marina, the HSCA did not agree.[80] They had serious problems with Marina's testimony.

One of the things Bugliosi maintains from Marina Oswald is the idea that Lee allegedly kept a notebook with maps, notes, and pictures about the Walker shooting. This notebook was supposed to have been burned by Oswald.[81] When the HSCA asked Marina if the notebook contained photos, she replied "I think so." When asked if the photos were attached to pages in the notebook, she said, "I don't remember right now." When asked the fate of the notebook, Marina said, "I don't know."[82] This HSCA testimony came about a year after publication of the long book *Marina and Lee,* on which Marina cooperated for a number of years.

The obvious question was posed by Commission lawyer Wesley Liebeler: if Oswald was guilty in the Walker shooting, why would Oswald keep the photos and the note around for almost eight months?[83]

Bugliosi deals with the slug and how it changed in color and caliber over eight months by saying that because of the malformations in the bullet, the police could not identify the weapon of origin. But on November 30, since they thought there was a connection between the Walker and Kennedy shootings, the FBI reexamined the bullet. Robert Frazier said that the *general characteristics* of the slug were consistent with the alleged Oswald rifle.[84] (Emphasis added.) Bugliosi writes that by "general characteristics," the FBI meant four lands and grooves and a right-hand twist to its rifling. Carol Hewett was more candid. Hewett, who, in addition to being an authority on the Paines, is also very good with firearms, showed how worthless and deceptive Frazier's statement was. "Since practically all rifles have a 4-groove right-hand twist, this means that the Walker slug resembled just about all other fired rifle bullets in the world."[85]

As for the mutating color and caliber, the prosecutor buries this at the end of a small-type, on-page footnote. For Frazier now said something perhaps even sillier: "some individuals commonly refer to rifle bullets as steel-jacketed bullets when they actually in fact have a copper alloy jacket."[86] For anyone who has ever seen the WCC/MC copper jacketed bullets, this statement is so far-fetched it begs belief. Wisely, Bugliosi leaves it without comment.

The Paines, the Baron, and Walker

Hewett makes an interesting observation before the Warren Commission about Michael Paine's testimony concerning the Walker shooting. After first meeting Marina through George DeMohrenschildt, Ruth arranged to have dinner with both the Oswalds and her estranged husband Michael at her home. When discussing this with the Commission, Michael "without hesitation" stated that the dinner occurred on April 10.[87] This would have exonerated Oswald because it would have given him an alibi. Later on, Michael's testimony was amended to incorporate Ruth Paine's date for the dinner of April 2, supported by her calendar which, as we shall see, contained some bizarre markings. As Hewett noted, Ruth was never asked if the April 2 marking was made before or after the event. And she also notes that April 2 is a Tuesday. Which meant Oswald was skipping his typing class.[88] But further, in another odd calendar notation that Ruth was never able to explain, the word "Marina" appears in the Russian Cyrillic alphabet on April 10—the date of the Walker shooting—with an arrow pointing to April 11. Two weeks after the Walker shooting, the date of April 24 is also marked on Ruth's calendar. This time with both Marina and Lee's name on it. According to Ruth, she just happened to go on that date to their home when Oswald was packed to leave for New Orleans. (If that statement is true, then the date had to have been written afterwards. Which now makes the date for dinner questionable.)

Commission counsel Albert Jenner was not completely convinced this was the coincidence Ruth made it out to be. But this coincidence now allowed Ruth to bring Marina and her daughter June to her place in Irving. And since Michael and Ruth were estranged, it allowed Ruth to accommodate Marina and June in her two bedroom home. After living with Ruth for a few weeks, Marina was driven by Ruth to New Orleans in early May 1963. This allowed for a precedent to pick her up from New Orleans in September, thereby storing the Oswald belongings in her garage from which the photos of Walker's house would surface.

In light of this record, the Walker shooting now became Marina's excuse before the Warren Commission as to why she wanted Lee to move to New Orleans.[89] Oswald moving to New Orleans became the occasion for Marina to first move in with Ruth. (Unforgettably, she also said that she did not return the "Walker note" to Oswald because "He forgot about it.")

As I wrote in the 2012 edition of *Destiny Betrayed*, the Paines always tried to minimize their associations with George and Jeanne DeMohrenschildt.[90] In May of 1963, Marina had returned records and a record player she had borrowed from George to Everett Glover via Michael Paine. Glover had been the host for a gathering that DeMohrenschildt designed to introduce the Oswalds into Dallas's White Russian community which included the Paines.[91] The Baron (George's nickname) had already left for Haiti by the time of this return. So these items were now placed in his storage unit. On November 25, Ruth told the FBI that Glover was now staying at the Baron's residence. So the Paines were well aware of the status of DeMohrenschildt, and Glover as his caretaker, even when the Baron was absent from Dallas.

When George and his wife returned to Dallas in February of 1967, something odd happened. Three years after the assassination and three years after the controversial backyard photographs had been taken from the Paines' garage, still another backyard photograph now surfaced. This one turned up amongst the *record albums* in DeMohrenschildt's storage unit.[92] It should be noted that DeMohrenschildt had made a joke about the Walker shooting to Oswald in April of 1963, asking him how he could have missed his target. The Commission said this visit took place on April 13,[93] three days after the Walker shooting. During that same visit, Jeanne reportedly said she saw the rifle used in the shooting at Oswald's Neely Street apartment. Yet, according to Marina, the rifle was supposed to be buried at that time and was not recovered until April 14, Easter Sunday night.[94] That visit was the last time George saw Lee and Marina.[95] Was their mission now complete in their introducing the Oswalds to the Paines and the attempt to incriminate Oswald in the Walker shooting?

If so, with the buried rifle, it appears that someone could not keep their story straight.

But even with that, DeMohrenschildt showed that he was only half-joking about Oswald. Not long after the Walker shooting, George stopped by the home of fellow White Russian Natasha Voshinin. He told her that although he had had a benign view of the communist in their midst, he had now changed his mind. He now told her, "That scoundrel took a potshot at General Walker. Of course Walker is a stinker, but stinkers have a right to live." She then added that he told her something about the rifle. Which, of course, was supposed to be buried. Natasha now called the FBI, which may be how the FBI decided to link the two cases several months later.[96]

What makes this later discovery of another backyard photograph so intriguing is that it was made amidst the spiraling controversy about the JFK case that had caused New Orleans DA Jim Garrison to secretly reopen the Kennedy case. This particular version of the photograph was unusual in two ways. Photographically, it had a wider field of view, a higher resolution, and a thicker border. It was so unusual that today it is called the "DeMohrenschildt version" of the photograph. Secondly, it was signed, so it seemed timed in order to quell any doubt about the photos being faked. The back of the photo was inscribed "To my friend George from Lee" and dated "5/IV/63" the Cyrillic version of April 5, 1963. In different handwriting is a satiric comment, "Hunter of Fascists, Ha! Ha! Ha!" Although the latter inscription was attributed to Marina, she denied writing it, and it appears to be written over a pre-existing script.

After this photo was found, the Paines had dinner with the DeMohrenschildts. The discussion was about the Kennedy assassination and this new photo in particular.[97] It has never been explained as to how it got into the storage unit, but Jeanne said the Paines had access to the unit.[98] But at that dinner, apparently one matter was left dangling. And as with Jeanne seeing a rifle that, according to Marina, was buried underground, the reader might suspect that someone was undoing the thread on the quilt. In the Baron's manuscript, "I'm a Patsy, I'm a Patsy," he describes the excited Jeanne finding the photo in storage. He then writes that they could not understand how the inscription could be to George since he was in Haiti on April 5, 1963. This is not true. The couple left for Haiti a bit more than two weeks later.[99] But more to the point, in trying to figure out how the photo got in their belongings, DeMohrenschildt writes that, after the assassination, Glover was so spooked because he knew the Oswalds that he left town with no forwarding address. The reader should recall that Ruth Paine told the FBI that Glover was staying at *DeMohrenschildt's address* after the assassination. So who is lying? George or

Ruth? And why? Unfortunately, the HSCA never figured this one out because they never called Ruth or Michael to be deposed. And DeMohrenschildt died under mysterious circumstances the day his subpoena arrived.

It is often said that the Paines' garage was the haven for, as Oswald termed it, "the so-called evidence" against him. But it wasn't just the items in the garage; it was also the Paines themselves. And, in one case, the Paines were still discovering things thirty years later. In November 1993, on a *CBS Reports* entitled "Who Killed JFK: The Final Chapter," Michael Paine told Dan Rather that when he went to pick up Oswald for an April 2, 1963, dinner engagement, Oswald proudly showed him a photo of himself holding up a rifle with a newspaper.[100] Although he had several opportunities, Michael never told this story about the photos to the FBI or the Warren Commission in 1963 or '64. And as with the late arriving "DeMohrenschildt version" of the photos, this new story tends to prop up their authenticity by saying they were not manufactured late in the day. But as Hewett points out, if this new tale is true, and Michael knew about the rifle, then why did he say he thought Oswald had camping equipment under a blanket in the garage instead of a rifle? And why, knowing Oswald had a rifle in his house, would he not check under the blanket himself to be sure? By coming out with the story so late, he avoided answering these questions under oath. Most researchers and authors tend to think that the first association of Oswald with the Walker incident was the November 29 conservative German newspaper article mentioned above. That was followed the next day by Ruth producing the "Walker note." And that article was the beginning of the "blame the Kennedys for their own deaths" meme. It said that Attorney General Robert Kennedy had intervened back in April 1963, and that intervention prevented Oswald from being arrested for the crime. Since the Dallas Police had a 30.06 steel-jacketed bullet in hand, and Oswald was never a suspect for them, it is hard to understand why RFK would intervene. But as Hewett notes, there was a previously published comment associating Oswald with the Walker shooting that appeared on the *day after the assassination*, in the November 23 issue of the *Houston Post*. There, Michael Paine suggested "that Oswald may have been involved in the Walker affair"[101] Which is stunning, considering how fast Michael made this deduction and the fact there was no evidence to make it with. Recall, the two best witnesses, Surrey and Coleman, gave descriptions not matching Oswald, and the bullet had yet to be transformed. In looking through Bugliosi's index, I could not find this quote attributed to Michael Paine. But it tends to undermine his pronouncement that there is not a speck of evidence to indicate Oswald was framed.

Bugliosi had Ruth Paine deliver her decades-old story about going down to the garage on the evening of the twenty-first and discovering the light was still on. Her assumption was that Lee had been down there. In other words, he picked up something—like the rifle—and was dumb enough to leave the light on. But he would also have had to put together the brown sack, with the tape appending it all, and break down the rifle to fit inside. As Carol Hewett noted in the January 1996 issue of *Probe,* Marina Oswald stated that Lee watched TV that night and he then retired at about 9 PM. She stayed up until 11:30 PM and never saw Lee go down to the garage. If there was a light left on, it was likely by Michael Paine, who testified that he would often stop by to use his tools which were stored there. So much for Ruth's eager attempt to incriminate Oswald.

Bugliosi's Chief Witness: Marina

Marina Oswald said things that incriminate Oswald in the Walker shooting. In an FBI interview of December 11, Marina said Oswald had been at the Walker home prior to April 10, but he had not shot at Walker that previous time. Why? Because he knew there was a gathering scheduled at the church near Walker's house a few days later and, ". . . he wanted more people around when he attempted the assassination." In other words, he wanted more witnesses on the scene. (I could not find this part of Marina's testimony in *Reclaiming History.*) In this interview she also said that when Oswald returned on the night of April 10, he did not have a rifle with him. He told Marina "he had buried the rifle in the ground far from the actual spot of the shooting. He then mentioned a field and the fact that the field was near a railroad track."[102] He then retrieved it on Sunday, the fourteenth.

As more than one critic has pointed out, this creates another problem for Bugliosi and the official story. Did Oswald bury the rifle in the ground using his bare hands? How would the rifle then be protected from damage with no protective cover around it? Why did the FBI examination on November 23 reveal no traces of dirt? And if no particles were found, what did Oswald use to clean the weapon since there was no rifle cleaning solution found among his belongings afterwards?

In his end notes, Bugliosi quotes a Secret Service report of December 10 stating that Marina said Oswald buried the rifle. But not where. What makes this odd is that Marina was explicit a day later with the FBI that Oswald buried the rifle in the ground. By leaving this explicit direction out, Bugliosi now says that Oswald did not say where he buried the weapon.[103] Realizing his silly argument, Bugliosi then writes that even if Oswald did bury it in the ground, "it's a non sequitur to conclude that he would have been incapable of disassembling the weapon thereafter and cleaning it completely."[104] By leaving out those specific parts of the evidence, Bugliosi again does not live up to his pledge to make the critics' arguments as they themselves would want them made. And the reader may now see why.

After a long analysis of the evidence given by Marina and the DeMohrenschildts in the Walker case, and showing how their testimony collided in mid-air and was not even consistent in its own terms, critic Sylvia Meagher came to the conclusion that "Marina Oswald fabricated the whole story of the attack on General Walker."[105] I agree that is a highly plausible thesis. But with the work of Carol Hewett, it seems Marina had some help from the Paines. And that help ended up leaving the Baron out in the cold.

Bugliosi Marches On with Marina

The official story maintains that both the backyard photos and the Walker photos were taken with an Imperial Reflex camera. As I pointed out in the second edition of *Destiny Betrayed*, the evidence trail of this camera leaves it an open question as to whether or not Marina had it when she took the backyard photos on March 31, 1963.[106]

Further, Marina has claimed that at the time these were the only pictures she ever took. If the only photos Marina ever took turned out to be as momentous as these, wouldn't she recall how she worked the camera? Marina didn't. When testifying before the HSCA, she was asked four different times how she took the backyard photos. Clearly, they were trying to test her on this because the HSCA staff had clear doubts about her credibility as a witness. Each time she replied that you used the camera by raising it to your eye and lining up the shot through the viewfinder. For example, consider this question: "This camera, do you recall whether to take pictures with this camera you would look down into the viewfinder or whether you would hold the camera up to your eye and look straight ahead?" She replied that you look straight ahead. Wrong answer. With this type of camera you held it at your waist and looked down into the large rectangular viewfinder.[107]

When originally asked by the Warren Commission if she recalled the day she took the backyard photos, Marina replied that it was toward the end of February or the beginning of March. There were two problems with this. First, the alleged rifle was not shipped until the third week of March. Second, the newspapers being held by the Oswald figure in the photos were not sent until late March. The date ultimately decided on was March 31.[108]

One of Bugliosi's key scenes in the "Four Days in November" section is Marina and Oswald's mother, Marguerite Oswald, setting fire to a version of the backyard photograph so that the police cannot incriminate Oswald in the Kennedy murder.[109] This is supposed to prove that Marina took the photos and was therefore trying to protect her husband. But when the HSCA asked her if she ever destroyed any of the photos she took of Lee, she replies: "Apparently I did. I forgot completely about it until somebody spoke about it. I think I did." They then ask her how many photos she destroyed. She said she did not recall. When asked *how* she destroyed the photo, she said: "Well, I have been told I burned it. . . ." She is then asked if anyone was with her when she did so. She again replies that she does not remember.[110]

Marina first said she thought she only took one photograph and there were two identical pictures. She then said it turned out to be two different poses.[111] But two more pictures surfaced: the DeMohrenschildt version, and one which Dallas policeman Roscoe White had. As noted, the DeMohrenschildt version looks like it was made with a different camera. And the White version has Oswald in a different pose. So one could argue that there are actually four pictures, not one, as Marina originally thought.

If we follow Marguerite's testimony, there was a *fifth* photograph, that was inscribed "To my daughter June." Oswald was holding the rifle up above his head with both hands, which is a completely different pose.[112] And it was this one which Marina and Marguerite had in the wake of the assassination. Question for the prosecutor: Why would Oswald sign a picture over to his two-year-old daughter? Apparently, the Commission could not figure that one out either. They dropped the line of questioning.

In light of all this, one has to wonder, was someone manufacturing all these photos if Marina originally said she took just one?

Marina's Credibility

In view of Marina's testimony in both the Walker case and concerning the photos, it's surprising that she is Bugliosi's chief witness. Late in the book, Bugliosi goes to visit Marina. He had commented early on that her credibility was good, but later when she started talking to the critical community, it plunged.[113] This appraisal is not accurate. Marina's credibility has always been in question. She was always afraid of being deported and therefore was a very cooperative witness, but the fact that she *was* so cooperative and yet still made many contradictory statements should be key in appraising her value as a witness. She has made contradictory statements on Oswald's rifle practice, on Oswald's activities the night of the Walker shooting, and on the ammunition he allegedly had. When asked by J. Lee Rankin if she had ever seen him clean his rifle, she replied, "Yes, I said before I have never seen it before. But I think you understand I want to help you . . ."[114] Yes, we understand. The woman was in a dilemma.

It is not accurate, as Bugliosi writes, to say the early official bodies trusted Marina. In late June 1964, Fredda Scobey, a member of Warren Commissioner Richard Russell's staff, wrote him a three-page memo on this point. In referring to other members of the staff, she wrote that several of them would be at a meeting to discuss the question of whether or not Marina should be further cross-examined. Scobey writes that: "Marina directly lied on at least two occasions . . . her answers could be a skillful parry of the questions. . . . It does seem to me that if her testimony lacks credibility there is no reason for sheltering her. The above spots where her veracity was not tested are perfectly obvious to any person reading the report . . . and it might become a policy matter whether this decision to brush her feathers tenderly is well advised."[115]

Not just Russell and Scobey had doubts about Marina. As James Hosty revealed in his book *Assignment Oswald*, the Warren Commission had Marina wiretapped because apparently there was some suspicion she was a KGB agent. But beyond that, there were several Commission staff lawyers who argued against using Marina. The original authors of Chapter 4 of the Warren Report entitled "The Assassin" were Joseph Ball and David Belin. In their draft they did not want to rely very much on Marina Oswald. Ball found her to be "at *best*, an unreliable witness."[116] (Emphasis added.) This chapter was rewritten by Norman Redlich, who included the Walker shooting, even though Marina's testimony was the main piece of evidence used in the Walker case, and the Commission was saying—in this same chapter—that Marina fabricated a similar episode of Oswald trying to kill Vice President Richard Nixon.[117] In fact, Redlich himself had called Marina a liar to the Secret Service, the FBI, and the Commission,[118] but he still rewrote the chapter relying on her testimony. The rewrite of the chapter took three months. When it was over, Wesley Liebeler read it and was so discouraged that he wrote his famous twenty-six-page Liebeler Memorandum.[119] He said that what Redlich had done "read like a brief for the prosecution." He then added that "this sort of selection from the record could seriously affect the integrity and credibility of the entire report."[120]

But to go further with Marina, in the last few weeks of the Commission's life, Richard Russell, Senator John Sherman Cooper, and Representative Hale Boggs flew to Texas to question Marina on their own. (Notably absent were Commissioners Earl Warren, Allen Dulles, Gerald Ford, and John McCloy.) Like Scobey, they thought she had been less than forthright on certain key points.[121] Therefore, unlike what Bugliosi tries to portray, Marina's testimony had been under fire almost from the beginning. Almost half of the Warren

Commissioners and a substantial number of staffers did not want to rely on her to any large degree.

In 1978, the HSCA also grew wary of Marina's highly questionable testimony. They collected all of her statements to the FBI, Secret Service, Warren Commission, and HSCA and drew up a secret report on the matter entitled "Marina Oswald Porter's Statements of a Contradictory Nature." The list of contradictory statements ran on for twenty-nine pages. Several of the pages were on the Walker incident. The report concluded they could not agree with the Warren Commission on Oswald's involvement in the Walker incident simply because of her credibility issue.[122]

However, Bugliosi defends Marina's role as chief witness by attacking Sylvia Meagher's attempt to show the conflicts in her testimony.[123] This does not present a full and accurate picture. For it is not just the critics who had a problem with Marina. It is also the Warren Commission and the HSCA staffers. In light of that, plus what I have pointed out here, any defense of Marina's testimony today is simply ill-founded.

Bugliosi on the Paraffin Tests

Like every Warren Commission revivalist since James Phelan, Bugliosi understands how large a problem the paraffin test poses for those who wish to convict Oswald. This test, done on Oswald by the Dallas police, showed he had no gunshot residue on his face from discharging a rifle. Bugliosi recycles the old canard that since the Mannlicher Carcano rounds were so tightly sealed in the chamber, the nitrate powder and gas could not escape onto Oswald's cheek, even with the rifle up to his face.[124] The truth is the opposite, and it appears that the FBI knew about it and then lied about it.

Former FBI agent Bill Turner did not buy FBI agent Cortland Cunningham's testimony about no residue escaping onto the gunman's face. Writing for the magazine *American Jurisprudence*, Turner conducted his own tests with Vincent Guinn (who, as we have seen, Bugliosi trusts in other matters). Turner and Guinn found that the weapon discharged nitrates in abundance.[125]

The original paraffin test done by the police came back positive for Oswald's hands and negative for his cheek. But the Commission decided to throw it out since the test was susceptible to false positives (i.e., the nitrates could react to elements besides the nitrate chemical reagents). The Dallas police said that the cast of Oswald's right hand revealed a "typical" pattern revealing he had fired a handgun.[126] This is not really accurate. In the declassified Dallas records, the actual outlines of these casts were now made available. It is clear that the greater amount of nitrates appear on the palm of each hand, not on the back side.[127] That would not be the case if Oswald had been firing a handgun, since the palm of his right hand would have been holding the weapon. In reality, the results on his hands seemed to indicate that the nitrates came from something Oswald touched that day.

The paraffin test was an obstacle that J. Edgar Hoover tried to surmount. He had the rifle particles even more finely tested than with paraffin casts. These tests were done in secret and no one was ever supposed to know about them. The FBI used the Neutron Activation Analysis process at Oak Ridge, Tennessee, to test the paraffin casts themselves.[128] The NAA test revealed that the deposits on the paraffin casts could not be associated with the rifle cartridges.[129] However, Hoover said that the test was flawed because it could not differentiate between gun powders. The truth was that someone had contaminated the samples in advance, probably by excessive handling of the casts.

In February 1964 Guinn performed official tests to show that any firing of the Mannlicher Carcano would produce detectable traces of gunpowder on the shooter. His tests, which proved that one could detect gunpowder on casts whether one used a chemical agent or not, were even worse for Hoover: they showed that these traces would be apparent not just on the cheek, but also the hands of the shooter.

When the Commission got back these results, Redlich wrote a memorandum to Dulles saying that, "At best, the analysis shows that Oswald may have fired a pistol, although this is by no means certain." Even Redlich had to admit, "There is no basis for concluding that he also fired a rifle."[130] When a prosecutor as zealous as Redlich writes something like that, then one has to understand just how bad the testing was for the Commission. Both Hoover and Redlich made sure that the actual test results were hidden from view. It took Harold Weisberg years to pry them out of the National Archives. So what Redlich and Hoover did was dual edged. They neutralized the paraffin test and they buried the further NAA testing from the public. So when Cunningham told the Commission, "I would not expect to find residue on the right check of a shooter," he did so as part of an FBI cover-up.[131]

Incredibly, Bugliosi cites the paraffin test to say that Oswald had gunpowder residue on his hands.[132] Without either (1) describing the pattern of the nitrates, or (2) describing the evidence that Oswald had been reading a newspaper that day, which would leave those traces.[133] He does not refer to the further atomic testing over which Hoover demanded complete secrecy, even though the call from Guinn to the FBI discussing the issue are in Gerald McKnight's book, which it is clear Bugliosi has read. By exposing Cunningham's deception, Guinn revealed that the rifling of the Mannlicher Carcano is so poor that when

Guinn tested it, the shooter got gunshot residue on *both* cheeks.[134] How and why Bugliosi could not see through this obvious Hoover-orchestrated cover-up is one of the many mysteries in *Reclaiming History.*

Bugliosi on the Rifle Tests

The prosecutor also tries to revise the judgment about Oswald being a poor shot.[135] He says the critics have been wrong on this point for years. According to him, Oswald actually was capable of attaining the amazing feat of precision shooting that the Warren Commission says he did: firing three shots in six seconds with a manual bolt action rifle, and getting two direct hits at a target moving away from him at a maximum range of almost three hundred feet. The record doesn't support this remarkable thesis. After weeks of practice and intensive training, Oswald managed to attain a sharpshooter classification by two points, one classification above the lowest possible, using a semi-automatic rifle firing at still targets. The next time he took to the range he was even worse. He fell into the lowest category possible, that of marksman. And, at a score of 191, he missed falling out of that category completely by just two points.

As Nelson Delgado said, Oswald on the firing line was "a pretty big joke" because he got a lot of complete misses, something that Delgado stated a good shot never did.[136] Further, in the film *Rush to Judgment*, Delgado told Mark Lane that Oswald just was not that interested in weaponry. He was always being criticized for not taking proper care of his rifle or cleaning it regularly.

Another Oswald service cohort, Sherman Cooley, was interviewed by author Henry Hurt for his book, *Reasonable Doubt*. Cooley, a veteran hunter, was just as derisive as Delgado: "If I had to pick one man in the whole United States to shoot me, I'd pick Oswald. I saw the man shoot. There's no way he could have ever learned to shoot well enough to do what they accused him of doing in Dallas."[137] James Persons told Hurt about Oswald's below average coordination, which he thought was the major factor in his very poor marksmanship.[138] Hurt, who interviewed dozens of Oswald's fellow Marines, said that this eyewitness testimony was universal. "On the subject of Oswald's shooting ability, there was virtually no exception to Delgado's opinion that it was laughable. Many of the Marines mentioned that Oswald had a certain lack of coordination that they felt was responsible for the fact that he had difficulty learning to shoot."[139]

As with the paraffin test, there is evidence that the FBI and Warren Commission knew just how bad a shot Oswald was. Realizing how much it hurt their case, they then tried to cover it up. In the interview Mark Lane did with Delgado, Oswald's former Marine colleague said that the FBI did not like what he had to say about Oswald's poor shooting skills. He told Lane that they tried to "break down" and get him to change his story. As he specifically said, "They tried to disprove it. They did not like the . . . statement that Oswald, as far as I knew, was a poor shot." And as we know from the London mock trial, Delgado was shot at and fled the country, which is testimony I could not find in *Reclaiming History*. (Even more odd is the fact that Bugliosi writes that Delgado was called by the defense, but, in the DVD, Delgado was a prosecution witness.[140])

The Warren Commission also realized something was lacking in this aspect of their case. When Marine Corps officer Eugene Anderson testified about Oswald's poor final shooting performance, he tried to attribute it to the inhospitable atmospheric conditions: "It might well have been a bad day for firing the rifle—windy, rainy, dark."[141] Apparently, the Commission did not consult the US Weather Bureau, but Mark Lane looked this up. The records reveal that there actually were ideal conditions: ". . . it was sunny and bright and no rain fell."[142] Even the late Wesley Liebeler, assistant counsel for the Commission, understood that what they were doing with Oswald's rifle abilities was exaggerated and unjustified: "The fact is that most of the experts were much more proficient with a rifle than Oswald could ever be expected to be, and the record indicates that fact. . . . To put it bluntly, that sort of selection from the record could seriously affect the integrity and credibility of the entire report. . . ."[143]

That kind of biased "selection from the record" bothered even Liebeler. It didn't bother Bugliosi.

Bugliosi, Vickie Adams, and Oswald's Alibi

Like Gerald Posner, Bugliosi wants to put Oswald somewhere on the upper floors of the Texas School Book Depository (TSBD) near the time of the shooting. Like Posner, he cites differences between what a witness told one agency versus what he or she told another, despite the common knowledge that many witnesses in this case have complained that what the FBI, the Warren Commission, or the Dallas Police have recorded is not what they actually told them. Among these was Victoria Adams.

Adams is one of the central witnesses whose testimony places Oswald on the lower floors of the TSBD at the time of the shooting. She and her acquaintance Sandra Styles were on the fourth floor looking out the window at the motorcade. After hearing the shots fired, they ran down the stairs, during which time Adams said they neither saw nor heard anyone behind them.[144] This is crucial because police officer Marrion Baker told the Commission he saw Oswald about 75–90 seconds after the murder drinking a Coke on the second floor. So, if Oswald was on the sixth floor, he had to have been tearing down those stairs to get to where Baker saw him at that point in time.

The Commission realized Adams presented a problem, and acted on it in a number of ways. First, as revealed in Barry Ernest's book *The Girl on the Stairs*, they did not perform any time tests with her, as they did with Marrion Baker coming up the front stairs of the building. Incredibly, it does not appear that the Commission interviewed Sandra Styles. The FBI did talk to her but the actual interview is not filed with interviews of the other TSBD employees.[145] According to author Gerald McKnight, this Styles record was deliberately made rather hard to find.[146] But further, the records of two other corroborating witnesses on the fourth floor office of publisher Scott Foresman, where Adams worked, are not in the volumes.

It appears that the Commission went even further to weaken Adams's testimony. And Bugliosi buys it. The Commission says that after Adams got down the stairs, she noticed employees Bill Shelley and Billy Lovelady and told them what she had seen from the window. But the Warren Report said that the two men had been to the railroad yards at the time of the shooting and then returned to the TSBD. So, in order for them to have done that, Adams had to have come down later than what she said. Yet in the affidavits that Shelley and Lovelady gave on the day of the assassination, there is no mention of them running to the railroad yards after the shots. Bugliosi buys this also.[147] He even attacks Sylvia Meagher for bringing the discrepancy up. Meagher noted that there was no mention of the railroad yards in the first day affidavits of either man.[148] Bugliosi notes this is true, but he then says that it is "terribly deceptive" for Meagher to state so. Why? The author says the first day statements are relatively brief. I have a question for the prosecutor: How many words does it take to say, "I went over to the railroad yards." It's a brief and simple sentence, but we are to believe that although both men did so, neither man wrote it down. When in fact, if they did run over there, there must have been a reason, such as perhaps seeing everyone else run over or hearing shots from the area. The railroad yards are across the street from the Depository and up behind the grassy knoll and picket fence.

Bugliosi says that Meagher does not tell the reader the affidavits are one paragraph. She didn't have to. She essentially printed Shelley's on the page.[149] And it appears that Shelley signed two affidavits that day. There is nothing about the rail yards in either one. Even though he had not one, but two paragraphs in which to do this.[150]

David Belin, who examined Adams, offered her a map of the first floor to draw where she arrived once she and Styles completed their run down the stairs, Commission Exhibit 496. However, CE 496 does not include the map. Instead there is Oswald's application form for work at the Depository. And if one looks at the surrounding exhibits, that application form is completely out of place. This switch had to be deliberate. For Bugliosi, pointing out contradictions in testimony is a "terribly deceptive" act by Meagher; but Belin's act of disappearing evidence is not even worth noting? It would certainly seem that Belin and the Commission were aware of how important a witness Adams was. And they set out to undermine her.

The Warren Commission Report fudged the time in which Adams said she left the fourth floor to head down the stairs.[151] They said she left "within about one minute" after the shots rang out. They then use the later testimony of Shelley and Lovelady to neutralize her story and say she was mistaken, but the Report does not say that this new Lovelady and Shelley testimony does not correspond to their first day affidavits.

The Commission fudged her testimony, refused to interview the woman who was right next to her, and then appears to have altered the testimony of two other people in order to negate the weight of her actions. Bugliosi sneers at Meagher's implication that there was collusion between the Commission and Lovelady and Shelley over Adams. But just look at the testimony of Lovelady on this issue. He mentions "Vickie" before Commission counsel Joseph Ball does. Ball then asks, "Who is Vickie?" as if he does not know who Lovelady is talking about. Lovelady replies that she works for Scott Foresman but he *doesn't know her last name*. But then Ball, who did not know who "Vickie" was, now fills in her last name! Lovelady tops it all by saying he "believes" that is her last name,[152] even though he brought her name up first. Meagher was correct in suspecting this was a dog and pony show originating behind the scenes.

In Ernest's book, we find out why the dog and pony show was necessary. In the 1990s he discovered a document in which J. Lee Rankin was advised that Adams wanted to correct her Commission testimony. But at the end of her Commission testimony it says she *does not* wish to do so. She will leave it up to Belin and the Commission.[153] But at the end of this letter, the very last sentence reads, "Miss Garner, Miss Adams's supervisor, stated this morning that after Miss Adams went downstairs she (Miss Garner) saw Mr. Truly and the policeman come up."[154] Obviously, if the two men had come up after, then Adams left within seconds of the shots, not a minute. The date of this letter was June 2, 1964. Even with this letter in Rankin's hands, the Warren Report then wrote that Adams "actually came down the stairs several minutes after Oswald and after Truly and Baker as well,"[155] when, in fact, they had corroborating evidence the opposite had occurred.

Barry Ernest also tracked down Adams and Styles, who corroborated each other on the key points. First, they both left the rear of the office within seconds, before the limousine disappeared beneath the underpass.[156] Second, neither Styles nor Adams saw Lovelady or Shelley when they got to the first floor.[157] When told Adams's testimony made reference to Shelley and Lovelady being on the first floor when the two women arrived, Styles said, "I can't imagine why Vicki would have said that—if she did."[158] The reader should note those last three words.

When Adams was shown her ultimate testimony in the Commission volumes, she was puzzled. She did get to correct her deposition, and she told Ernest that she did not remember the part about Shelley and Lovelady being in there: "If it had been in there, and since I didn't see them, I would have edited it out."[159] She suspected her testimony had been doctored but she could not prove it since she never had the original.

When Ernest asked her to re-create those crucial seconds, Adams said that the distance from the window to the door was about 50–70 feet. And the two "had to run around a group of three tables, like banquet tables, and then out the door to the stairway."[160] This would be a distance of about ten yards. Adding in the slight delay in negotiating the tables, this would take about fifteen seconds at a brisk walk.[161] If one adds in the few seconds past the last shot, with the car drifting toward the underpass, then Adams and Styles were on the stairwell about twenty seconds after the last shot. It is hard to imagine that they would not have seen or heard Oswald on those rickety old wooden steps. The Commission could have done a dual experiment, one with an FBI agent running down from the sixth floor window, and one with an agent quickly walking from the Styles/Adams window. There is no evidence they did so, and I could not find anywhere in *Reclaiming History* where Bugliosi scores them for this lack. Yet, in a February 25, 1964, internal memorandum, both Belin and Ball noted how important this would be in light of Adams's testimony. They also said that Oswald would have had to descend to the second floor in a short amount of time "if he were the assassin." The memo said that neither Styles nor Adams saw anyone on the stairs. It concluded with, "We should pin down this time sequence of her running down the stairs."[162] The reader should recall that Bugliosi criticized what he thought were delays and missteps in the police investigation of the Tate/LaBianca case. However, in his discussion of this issue, he makes no criticism of the failure to perform this simple reconstruction. And it should be noted that it was Ball and Belin who suggested it. Was it just a coincidence that these were the two attorneys who examined, respectively, Lovelady and Adams?

In his book, Barry Ernest reconstructed the Adams investigation and found a crucial moment where the Lovelady and Shelley construct appears to have been inserted. In Adams's November 25, 1963, FBI interview, there was no mention of Lovelady or Shelley. But in February, she was visited by Dallas Police Detective Jim Leavelle, who said there had been a fire at the police headquarters and her file had been burned. That was the pretext for the visit. But further, Adams had moved since the assassination, had left no forwarding address, and had no phone in her name.[163] Those circumstances and the mythical fire indicate how badly the authorities needed to get in contact with Adams. It was at this point that the Lovelady-Shelley business gets inserted into the record.[164] Whether Bugliosi was aware of this, I do not know, but it is an important point that the prosecutor does not bring up.

Barry Ernest did something that Bugliosi did not do: he found both Adams and Styles. Both witnesses were alive in 2007 when *Reclaiming History* was published (although Adams passed away later in the year). He also found Dorothy Garner, the witness who certified the Adams/Styles story for Rankin but whose testimony never made it into the record. Barry contacted Garner after his book came out. In an email communication with me in July 2013, he said Garner stated that both Sandra and Vickie left the window within seconds. She followed them out to the fourth floor landing. While she was there, she did not see Oswald come down, but she did recall Baker coming up the stairs. Dorothy recalled being interviewed very briefly by someone from the Warren Commission, but as of today, no one can find the record of this interview. Finally, thanks to Barry Ernest, the evidence about this is out in the open.

In the twenty-one years he was working on the book, the prosecutor had ample opportunity to locate Garner, Styles, and Adams. If he had, he would have found out what Belin and Ball did on this point. Belin did an off the record interview with Adams first. He then challenged her memory: "Now, Miss Adams, don't you think you could be wrong?"[165] He also advised her that when the stenographer came in and he asked her if she wanted to add anything, she was to decline the offer. As noted in the volumes, she waives her right to correct the transcript. But, oddly, the transcript was delivered to her at work and she did request corrections but not one was made.[166] This seems odd because Ernest found the actual stenographic copy of the Adams testimony that jibes with the Commission volumes. It says that Adams declined to make any correction at the end of the deposition. But, it is unsigned.

When Ernest asked the archives how this could be, they replied that there were actually *two* versions of Adams's testimony. The second one is signed, with the corrections, and declassified two months after the Ernest book first appeared, twelve years after the ARRB closed shop. Ernest now asked to listen to the actual tape made during the interview. He wanted to hear if Belin actually gave Adams a diagram of the first floor on which to mark where she saw Lovelady and Shelley when she came down—that alleged exhibit which now showed as Oswald's employment application in the volumes. According to the JFK Act, passed for the ARRB, these tapes do exist. What Ernest found out in reply is utterly fascinating. The Adams tape is missing and cannot be found. And so are Lovelady's and Shelley's. Remember, Bugliosi calls this a simple case and it is the writers who make it complicated. Question for the prosecutor: unless he believes in a conspiracy even wilder than his Beatles/Bible/Helter Skelter one, it was not the writers who deep-sixed those tapes.

Whether or not Bugliosi knew the sordid aspects of what happened to Adams, they are not in his book and he ends up supporting the Warren Commission subterfuge about Lovelady and Shelley.[167] This means that Bugliosi could go after Carolyn Arnold, a secretary in the Book Depository who told the FBI that she had seen Oswald on the first floor at about 12:25 PM.[168] As with Adams, the authorities did a dance with Arnold's statement to read that she saw Oswald "a few minutes before 12:15 PM."[169] This would allow Oswald the necessary time to go back up to the sixth floor after she saw him. Like Styles, Arnold was never called before the Commission as a witness.

Fifteen years later, reporter Earl Golz sought out Arnold, who was still working at the Book Depository. She was shocked at what the FBI had done to her testimony.[170] Considering what we just saw with Adams, it's not surprising that Bugliosi actually uses the original FBI report to discredit Arnold.[171] He says that her 12:25 time was first told fifteen years later.

Bugliosi also uses what Oswald was supposed to have said during interrogations to get him out of where Arnold said she saw him. He even uses the statement signed by TSBD employee Virgie Rackley that says she accompanied Arnold outside. He says Rackley stated she did not see Oswald at any time that day.[172] But this statement pertains to her accompanying Arnold outside, not being with her inside. And it's inside where Arnold said she saw Oswald.

Further, Bugliosi does not reveal what the FBI is doing in the statements he has chosen to quote from with Rackley. These statements, from Commission Exhibit 1381, are similar to form letters. The Bureau used them ostensibly to account for where the TSBD employees were at the time of the shooting. But there are two other key sentences in the statements. First, that each employee saw no stranger on that day inside the building, and second, that they did not see Oswald at the time JFK was killed. So clearly, the FBI is trying to close down any avenue to conspiracy, and also to cut off Oswald's alibi by saying that at the exact time of the shooting, these witnesses did not see Oswald. Arnold did not see Oswald at the exact time of the shooting, she saw him a few minutes before. (Bugliosi does not reveal that Arnold also said in her CE 1381 statement that after the shooting she never returned to the Depository that day. This will figure into another myth that he tries to promulgate, that there was a Depository roll call, with Oswald the only missing employee.)

According to the FBI, Bonnie Ray Williams told them that he had been on the sixth floor eating his lunch until about 12:05. But before the Warren Commission, Williams denied saying this.[173] When the Commission asked him for his best recollection in this regard, he said that he left the sixth floor at around 12:20. Consequently, the Commission ended up believing him. Bugliosi does not. In the main text, he has him leaving the sixth floor at somewhere between 12:06 and 12:12.[174] On what new forensically sound and decisive evidence does he base moving the time back? He says it should not have taken Williams that long to eat his lunch.[175]

These are not random mistakes in the recording of important testimony. In each dispute, the original testimony has been altered in one direction: it allows the Commission the leeway to put Oswald on the sixth floor. Without the alterations, you can't. Between Williams on the sixth floor at 12:20, Arnold on the first floor at around 12:25, and Adams on the stairs right after the shooting, Oswald's placement on the lower floors at the time of the murder is all but puncture proof. Another witness, Jack Dougherty, was on the fifth floor at the time of the shooting.[176] Once he heard a shot, he took an elevator to the sixth floor. As revealed in the Adams testimony, that elevator is within a few feet of the stairs. He did not see Oswald either.

Bugliosi, who apparently wants to isolate Arnold, says she was the only person to see Oswald on the lower floors anywhere near that late. This is not really accurate. Oswald said he ate lunch on the first floor with two African Americans in the room while he was there. Oswald recalled one of them being called "Junior" and although he did not recall the other's name, he said he was kind of short. James Jarman's nickname was indeed Junior and his friend Harold Norman was a bit short. Norman, who ate lunch on the first floor, did recall someone else being there. At about 12:15, Jarman walked over to pick him up and watch the motorcade.[177] It would seem that Oswald put himself on the first floor after the noon hour. And this is where his cohorts at work said he usually ate lunch.[178] This is important because the first sighting of a rifleman on the sixth floor at the west end, farthest away from the "sniper's lair," was by Arnold Rowland at 12:15.[179] If Oswald was in the lunchroom on the first floor, this could not have been him.

All students of the JFK assassination are familiar with the peculiar case of Charles Givens. Givens was interviewed by the Dallas police and the FBI on November 22. He talked about his whereabouts on that day: about taking his lunch period and visiting a friend in the parking lot before the murder. He said he worked on the sixth floor until 11:30. To the FBI, he added two pieces of information. At around 11:30, as he was going down, Oswald told him to send an elevator back up to him on the sixth floor. He then said that at 11:50, he had seen Oswald reading a paper in the so-called domino room on the first floor, a place where some employees ate lunch.[180] Bolstering this, employee Eddie Piper also said he saw Oswald on the first floor at noon,[181] and Bill Shelley said he saw Oswald on the first floor at around 11:50.[182]

As many writers have shown, Givens changed his story for the Commission. On April 8, 1964, before Mr. Belin, he now said that he forgot his cigarettes on the sixth floor and went back up around noon where he saw Oswald there near the southeast corner window. This made no sense in light of his previous testimony. Why would Oswald ask for an elevator to go downstairs, just to go back upstairs? But yet this nonsense was printed in the Warren Report.[183] Belin then asked him if he had ever seen anyone reading a paper in the domino room—the first floor lunchroom—at 11:50. Givens reversed his story and said no.[184] What had happened in the meantime?

As Sylvia Meagher pointed out, Lt. Revill of the Dallas Police approached Robert Gemberling of the FBI and said that since he had dealt with Givens on a drug charge, he thought he could get Givens to change his story for money.[185] That conversation was in February 1964. What makes the implication quite convincing is that on May, 13, 1964, Revill told the Commission that he encountered Givens that day, and Givens told him that he had seen Oswald on the sixth floor.[186] In his testimony Revill named two corroborating witnesses, a Detective Brian and Captain Fritz. However, when the Commission called these men, they did not ask them about Revill's story.[187] If Revill was aware of this on that day, why didn't he make a report about it himself? And why did Givens not say anything about it that day either? After all, Oswald was arrested by the police at about 1:50 PM. The rifle and shells had been discovered on the sixth floor even earlier. There were hours to explore this connection. Therefore, Givens should have been a prime witness right then and there. But he was not.

Bugliosi is so desperate to put Oswald on the upper floors that he says we should believe Givens's April testimony before the Commission and not what he said in November. He justifies it by using Revill's May testimony as corroboration![188] He can do this with the unwitting reader since he does not present Givens's evolving testimony in order, or Revill's cooperation with the FBI, or the lacunae in Revill's story as to why he never made a report on the day of the assassination after Oswald was arrested.

Bugliosi is so obsessed with putting Oswald on the upper floors that he ignores the fact that Revill's later testimony is inconsistent with his earlier statements in this regard. In his book, Bugliosi says Revill talked to Givens about Oswald during the search inside the Book Depository.[189] Yet Givens was locked out of the building after the assassination. Revill then escorted him to police HQ for questioning.[190] So how could Givens be questioned by Revill inside the TSBD if he was locked out and then escorted to Dallas HQ? And the obvious question is this: If Givens told Revill about Oswald on the sixth floor at that time, why didn't Revill alert the DPD questioners, since he sent him over to the DPD in the first place?

Let us give the last word on this issue to the murdered defendant. Oswald maintained during his brief period of detention that he had been on the first floor at the time of the assassination. When police homicide chief Will Fritz questioned him, "Oswald said he was leaving the building shortly after the shooting when two men, one with a crew cut, approached him, identified themselves as Secret Service agents, and asked for the location of the nearest telephone."[191] Fritz's description of what Oswald said was quite similar to what shows up in Secret Service agent Thomas Kelley's notes of his own interview with Oswald. Down to the description of the man with a crew cut.[192]

The Secret Service finally interviewed two men who they thought fit Oswald's descriptions, Pierce Allman and Terrance Ford, both employed by TV station WFAA. They were both in Dealey Plaza that day and after hearing the shots they ran into the TSBD to look for a phone. They reported to the Secret Service that a man in front of the building who matched Oswald's description directed them to a phone. Later, when the men were again interviewed, neither was able to positively identify a photo of Oswald as the man who directed them. However, the report noted that Allman had a crew cut and "carried his press pass in a leather case similar to cases carried by federal agents and police officers."[193] If the two reporters heard the shots and ran up to the building and saw Oswald, then it seems Oswald must have been on or near the first floor at that time as he said he was. In his entire chapter on this issue, Bugliosi never mentions Allman or Ford.

The Roll Call and the Lineups

Bugliosi likes to repeat previous Warren Commission shibboleths about Oswald, whether they are accurate or not. For instance, he repeats the myth about Oswald being the only absentee from a so-called Book Depository roll call. Two of his sources are an article by Kent Biffle written eighteen years after the fact, and Commission Exhibit 3131 which does not contain any information pertinent to his point (it pertains to fingerprints on the boxes).

Many years ago, Jerry Rose wrote an article which began to expose this canard.[194] First of all, more than one business was located at the Depository. Such a roll call, if there had been one, could not account for everyone in that building. As Mark Bridger pointed out in 2007, there is no evidence that any such roll call, in the normal usage of that phrase, ever took place.[195] At the most, there was an informal head count by Roy Truly of his own book warehouse employees, and the time for it is not definite. And even there, Oswald was not the only one missing. As Bridger points out, so was Givens.[196] As Bridger shows, Bugliosi appears to have borrowed this roll call device from the Warren Commission, Dallas DA Henry Wade, and Gerald Posner, among others. As Bridger notes, it has little substance.

Second, as Rose pointed out, in March 1964 it was discovered that there were *several* people missing from the TSBD from their lunch hour until 1:30. In fact the statements made in Commission Exhibit 1381—which Bugliosi sources more than once—reveal that several of them, like Gloria Holt and Carolyn Arnold were locked out or failed to return to the TSBD after the shooting. Holt stated that she was told by others the building would be shut down and so she went home. If other people said this to her, then they must have done the same thing.

Bugliosi even tries to salvage the outrageous lineups that the Dallas Police put Oswald in on the twenty-second and the twenty-third. He acknowledges that there are honest objections to their composition, but he says they were probably inconsequential in the final analysis. He uses the example of a good identification as William Whaley, the cab driver who picked up Oswald and delivered him to his rooming house.[197] He ignores the fact that Whaley's identification had little if anything to do with whether or not Oswald committed the crimes he was accused of. But he also leaves out the fact that Whaley saw two pictures of Oswald before he went to the lineup.[198] Bugliosi also uses another cab driver, William Scoggins, who was at the Tippit murder scene. According to Bugliosi, he is a good lineup witness who identified Oswald. On this occasion, Oswald was shouting out how it was unfair to place him in a lineup in which he was wearing only a T-shirt while others wore sport coats. How could Scoggins not pick him out? But yet, Bugliosi missed reporting the fact that outside the lineup, when a series of photos were shown to him by the FBI, he was not sure about which was Oswald.[199]

The Tippit Murder

With regard to the murder of Patrolman J. D. Tippit, Bugliosi thinks there is no question about Oswald's guilt in this incident also. He deals with the mismatching of cartridges and bullets in an on-page footnote in his End Notes section.[200] Two Winchester and two Remington shells hit the officer, but the bullets were three Winchesters and one Remington. How does the prosecutor solve this problem? He says that one shot missed. And he does not in any way note the paradox of what he says in this instance with what he said previously about the murder of JFK. With JFK, Bugliosi promulgates the myth of Oswald the excellent shooter, but in this case he wants us to believe this crack shot somehow missed at very close range. Also, as noted previously, with the JFK shooting Bugliosi demands to know where the extra bullets or shells went if there were more than three shots. There is an answer to that question, but in this instance there is none that I know of. No one has ever found this missing bullet, but the prosecutor does not even pose the question.

FBI agent Cortland Cunningham could not match the bullets recovered from Tippit's body to Oswald's alleged handgun,[201] although the shells became key. Bugliosi does not deal at all with the late-arriving and discovered cartridge cases. Once the FBI found they could not match the bullets to the weapon, the cases were sent to the Bureau six days later. Even though these pieces of evidence were not entered onto the original evidence summary.[202]

Were these matching cases the ones found at the scene? Witness Domingo Benavides gave Officer James Poe two shells. Sergeant Gerald Hill told Poe to mark them with his initials. When Poe examined the shells for the Commission, he could not find his initials on any of them.[203] Benavides was the closest eyewitness to the crime. He was not invited to lineup and he refused to name Oswald as the killer. He was then threatened and his brother shot. He changed his mind and did identify Oswald. Acquilla Clemmons and Mrs. Donald Higgins also said they would not identify Oswald as the killer. There were some witnesses who said they did see Oswald running from the scene, but as Sylvia Meagher pointed out, the lineups for these witnesses were highly questionable.

Bugliosi dismisses the now unmarked shells as an issue that cannot be resolved. He then adds, "but such unresolvable points are common in the investigation of a complex, multifaceted murder investigation."[204] From here, he goes on to relate what he calls another such mystery started by FBI agent James Hosty in his book *Assignment: Oswald*. Hosty wrote that after Tippit's body was taken away by ambulance, Captain Westbrook found a man's wallet near the pool of blood where Tippit's body had been.[205] The wallet was Oswald's. This seriously conflicts with the official story, which has the DPD taking Oswald's wallet from him on the ride from his arrest at the Texas Theater to City Hall. There is even film of this incident made by TV station WFAA. Westbrook told FBI agent Bob Barrett that the identification was for a Lee Harvey Oswald and Alek Hidell. In the film, there are three men handling the wallet. Bugliosi tries to save the day by concluding that in spite of the witness testimony to the contrary, it was Tippit's wallet, not Oswald's.[206]

Here's the problem with this desperate hypothesis. At 2:00 PM that afternoon, three police officers went to Methodist Hospital to recover Tippit's effects. They were placed in an envelope and taken to DPD headquarters where they were checked in at the Identification Bureau at 3:25 PM. One of the effects was Tippit's wallet.[207] Incredibly, Bugliosi dismisses this fact. Even though the only item carried to the hospital was Tippit's handgun, he says that someone may have brought his wallet from the scene to the hospital, even though the only wallet picked up was the one with Oswald's ID.

But as desperate as Bugliosi is to escape this "too many wallets" dilemma, he cannot because the Warren Report says that Oswald supposedly left his wallet in a dresser drawer at the Paine's the morning of the assassination.[208] That makes three wallets. Since Bugliosi does not mention this fact, he does not have to address the troubling evidentiary point that even if he is totally unjustified in transforming the Oswald/Hidell wallet into Tippit's, that still leaves an extra wallet to explain.

A witness said that the killer of Tippit leaned onto the police car and therefore the police had the car dusted for prints. But, according to Bugliosi, only smudged prints were found.[209] The police later told the Commission that the prints were not legible.[210] Bugliosi goes on for a full paragraph about how this is not uncommon. He says, "Contrary to popular belief, this is typical." He goes on to say that actually it's quite rare to find clear fingerprints of the suspect at the scene.[211]

However, the House Select Committee on Assassinations said that there *were* clear prints taken off the car. Detective Paul Bentley told that body in 1978 that Officer Doughty "lifted good prints from the exterior section of that door immediately below the rolled-down window."[212] Both the good and bad prints are located at the Dallas Municipal Archives. The Warren Commission examined neither. Dale Myers took the prints to a fingerprint technician in Wayne County, Michigan, named Herbert Lutz, who compared the good car prints with Oswald's. They did not match.[213] It is very hard to believe that Bugliosi did not know this. Myers, one of his unnamed ghostwriters, quotes from pages all around this section of *With Malice* in his End Notes.

One can understand from a prosecutorial point of view why Bugliosi would resist the second wallet at the scene and the non-Oswald fingerprints on the car. If he accepts them, then it is clear that someone tried to frame Oswald for the Tippit shooting. Since the prints were not Oswald's, then either the assailant was not him or there were two of them and the killer dropped a mock-up of Oswald's wallet at the scene to frame him. If the killer *was* Oswald, why would he do that? But making Bugliosi's stance even more unsustainable, he says in his introduction that he could find no "speck of credible evidence that Oswald was framed."[214] If the above exculpatory evidence of the prints and the wallet is not credible, then what on earth is?

Then there is the question of how Oswald got to 10th and Patton in time to shoot Tippit. The distance from his rooming house to that scene is 9/10 of a mile. Earlene Roberts, the rooming house manager, said she last saw Oswald outside her window at about 1:04.[215] The most credible witnesses as to the time of the shooting, with watches, like T. F. Bowley, place the shooting at 1:10 or before.[216] It seems highly unlikely that Oswald could have covered that distance in six minutes or less. In fact, two researchers who walked the distance at a power-walk stride both said it took about fourteen minutes to do so.[217] Helen Markham, who timed the shooting when she was waiting for her bus to go to work, said the shots rang out at about 1:07.[218] When I interviewed the late Larry Harris, who was the foremost authority on the Tippit case, he placed the shooting at either 1:08, or 1:09.[219]

About this issue, whether or not Oswald was at the scene of the crime at all, Bugliosi makes one of the most astounding statements in the entire volume. He understands what a hole this puts in his case if Oswald is not there, so he writes, "Of course, even if Bowley is correct and Tippit was killed at 1:10 or earlier, it would be irrelevant, since we know Oswald killed him."[220] Is Bugliosi saying that even if Oswald could not have been at the scene of the crime, he still committed the offense? He adds here that, how Oswald got to the scene is only academic. No, it's not. If someone drove him, then he had accomplices. Therefore, the case becomes a conspiracy.

But what was Tippit doing that day? The Dallas Police had a hard time explaining what Tippit was doing in Oak Cliff when all the other police cars were headed for Dealey Plaza. The Warren Commission was eventually given three transcripts of the Dallas Police radio logs from the twenty-second. It was on the second log that an order appeared for two officers, Tippit and Nelson, to move into Oak Cliff at 12:45.[221] But the way it showed up in a delayed fashion caused some suspicion, especially since five witnesses saw Tippit arrive at the GLOCO service station on the Oak Cliff side of the Houston Street viaduct at

12:45.[222] According to these witnesses, he sat in his car and watched traffic cross the bridge for about ten minutes.

As with the rifle, Bugliosi says there is no question that Oswald ordered and picked up the .38 Smith and Wesson revolver that he says was used to kill Tippit. He deals with this in his biographical section on Oswald.[223] And he adds that Oswald posed with the handgun in the famous backyard photographs. This transaction was handled at the delivery end by a private mail delivery company called Railway Express Agency (REA). REA had to abide by state laws to ship firearms, including a "certificate of good character" needed to be shown to the employee. There also must have been a proof of ID submitted on a 5024 form filled out for small firearms like revolvers and pistols. And this all had to have been done at REA headquarters as the post office would not handle a private mail company's cargo. REA should have sent a postcard to Oswald's box. He then should have walked over to REA and given his identification and certificate of good character and this should have all been recorded in the REA office books.

As John Armstrong notes, there is no evidence at all that REA ever sent a postcard to Oswald's post office box to pick up the handgun.[224] There was no 5024 form either or a signature of receipt by Oswald or Hidell for the package. In sum, there was no proof as to either the identity of the individual who picked up the package or the date he picked it up on.[225] There was no proof that the transaction was ever completed and payment forwarded to the originating company Seaport Traders. Further, there was no proof that REA remitted payment to Seaport for the handgun. The Warren Report shows no bank transactions to certify this exchange.[226] But even beyond that, there is no proof at all that the FBI ever visited REA in Dallas to talk to anyone who gave the revolver to Oswald or Hidell. If one looks askance at the credibility of Marina Oswald, and if one thinks the backyard photographs are specious, then the chain of possession of the .38 Smith and Wesson begins on November 22, 1963.

The above constitutes a summary of what a real defense of Oswald would have touched upon in the Kennedy, Walker, and Tippit crimes. At the end of Book 1 in *Reclaiming History*, Bugliosi has a chapter entitled "Summary of Oswald's Guilt." Here he lists what he calls fifty-three pieces of evidence which point to Oswald as the assassin of Kennedy, the killer of Tippit, and the man who shot at Walker. In his book *Biting the Elephant*, Rodger Remington takes over 100 pages to analyze this bill of particulars. He concludes that sixteen of them did not include citations, five of them concerned expert testimony which would be challenged at trial, three of them consisted of "someone said" type of evidence, three were rhetorical questions, two were Bugliosi labeling Oswald with "consciousness of guilt," three more consisted of Bugliosi saying Oswald "made no sense" or Oswald was "telling posterity" or Frazier saying he saw Oswald "carry the bag." Finally, five others were Bugliosi saying a certain fact was such because "we know it is."[227]

That makes for a pretty sorry record for a prosecutor, especially one who has used almost 2,700 pages in selling the reader on the belief that the defendant has no defense at all.

CHAPTER SIX

Bugliosi on the Zapruder Film and the Autopsy

*"... within the world of insanity there is an internal logic.
By that I mean one can frequently have a perfectly intelligent
conversation with an insane person if one is willing to enter
that person's world of insane suppositions."*

—Vincent Bugliosi on Doug Horne in *Reclaiming History*

In this section, we will examine how Vincent Bugliosi addresses two areas of pertinent physical evidence: the twenty-six-second color film made by Abraham Zapruder in Dealey Plaza and the autopsy performed at Bethesda, Maryland, the evening of the assassination. Combined, these two chapters make up one of the largest sections of *Reclaiming History,* nearly 270 pages. And in both cases the material in the End Notes is longer than that in the main text.

Is the Zapruder Film Superfluous?

Bugliosi's initial approach to the Zapruder film is as if the film is unnecessary, almost superfluous, to understanding the crime. He writes that the other physical evidence is "absolutely conclusive" as to the number of shots fired, which he says is three.[1] As stated in Chapters 4 and 5, he bases this largely on the cartridge evidence found on the sixth floor.[2] He also writes that it is "absolutely conclusive" that the shot that hit President Kennedy went on and struck Governor Connally.[3] This, of course, refers to CE 399, the virtually pristine bullet that went through two men, made seven wounds, smashed two of the hardest bones in the human body, and then reversed and popped out of Connally's thigh and onto John Connally's stretcher at Parkland Hospital. This is what the prosecutor terms "absolutely conclusive" evidence in President Kennedy's murder.

Here is what Bugliosi considers dubious evidence. In discussing the images on the Zapruder film he will now describe two crucial pieces of evidence. First, in referring to the stunning backward movement of Kennedy's body that bounces him off the back seat, he writes of "the *apparent* backward snap of the president's head at the moment of the head shot."[4] (Emphasis in original). Second, in referring to the time lag between Kennedy reacting to being hit and Connally's discernibly later reaction, he writes "the *alleged* delayed reaction between Kennedy and Connally around the time the Warren Commission claimed they were hit by a single bullet."[5] (Emphasis in original.) He then concludes that neither of these "allegations"—the rapid rearward movement and the "delayed reaction"—is actually true.[6]

Explaining why the Warren Commission decided upon the "delayed reaction" hypothesis, Bugliosi says that the FBI and Secret Service reenactments in Dealey Plaza did much to decide the issue. When the Commission found that the sixth floor window, Kennedy's back, and Connally's back existed along a straight line, this "substantiated" the Single Bullet Theory.[7] However, given the configuration of Dealey Plaza, how could they not line up in a straight line? And how could this, in and of itself, prove that (1) Oswald did it, and (2) the Single Bullet Theory (SBT) was viable? The prosecutor's logic here is lacking. (And so is his consistency. Later on, relying on unnamed ghostwriter Dale Myers, he will insist that Kennedy and Connally are *not* lined up straight.)

Further, in these reenactments, the bullet firing sequences were different than what the Warren Commission maintains. As Chuck Marler notes in *Assassination Science*, the Secret Service reenactment of December, 5, 1963, ended up showing "three 'X' markings on Elm Street—ones that correspond to President Kennedy's location at Zapruder frames 208, 276, and 358." The three "X"s represented rifle shots from the Texas School Book Depository Building "and is contrary to the Warren Report."[8] For instance, the Warren Commission said only two shots hit the limousine, not three, and the last shot was at frame 313, not 358. How does this "substantiate" the Commission's conclusions?

Richard Russell Gets Duped

Bugliosi then describes the infamous September, 18, 1964 Warren Commission executive session hearing which contained the debate on finalizing the Single Bullet Theory (SBT). Senators Richard Russell, John Sherman Cooper, and Representative Hale Boggs were the skeptics, against John McCloy, Allen Dulles, Representative Gerald Ford, and Chief Justice Earl Warren as those who espoused at that time the SBT. Bugliosi describes the debate and how Russell wanted his dissent against the SBT described in a footnote. This was parried by Warren and McCloy. The settlement was that the SBT would be described in the *Warren Report* as "persuasive" but not "compelling."

What Bugliosi leaves out of his description in the main text is that Chief Counsel J. Lee Rankin deliberately made no stenographic record of this meeting. A woman was present to assure Russell there would be a stenographic record of both the meeting and his objections. But there was none. As Gerald McKnight notes in *Breach of Trust,* all that is left of this meeting is a six-page memorandum "of some housekeeping items and innocuous motions."[9] Russell never found out about Rankin's trick until years later.[10] Bugliosi deals with this important issue in his End Notes. There he writes that "it is not known if the stenographic notes of this meeting were ever typed up."[11]

But if they had been, would they not have showed up in fifty years? Especially after the Assassination Records Review Board declassified all the other executive session transcripts? Even after J. Lee Rankin's son turned over all the rest of the Warren Commission remnants he had to the Board? Strangely, Bugliosi also writes that "No one has ever suggested that important matters were discussed at the session. . . ." Everyone knows that this debate about the SBT language was the main subject of the meeting because there is a transcript of a call between Russell and President Johnson in which Russell describes what really happened at the meeting.[12] And the six-page summary does not include either this debate or any reference to Russell's footnote motion. At the very end of his discussion of this key issue, Bugliosi brings up McKnight's treatment of the matter. He says that McKnight *might* be right in his conclusion.[13] (Emphasis added.) He does not advance a benign explanation as to how McKnight could be wrong. Or why there is no verbatim transcript of this meeting today. This is how far the prosecutor will go in his advocacy for a group as underhanded and dishonest as the Warren Commission. In this instance they actually deceived their own members in order to make it appear that they were united on their most unbelievable, but necessary, premise.

From here, Bugliosi goes on to examine the SBT in light of the Zapruder film. He prefaces his analysis with this absolute: ". . . since we *know* Kennedy and Connally were not hit by separate bullets, we know, before we even look at the film, that it *cannot* show otherwise."[14] (Emphasis added.) With that preface, the reader has an idea of what to expect. The objective is to talk you out of what you see and into what the Warren Commission insisted upon.

Myers Trips Up Bugliosi

The author begins his demonstration with a factual error. Bugliosi states that Governor Connally was not lined up in front of President Kennedy but was actually a half a foot inboard of him.[15] His faulty source for this is Dale Myers. As researcher Pat Speer notes in his critique of Myers, the House Select Committee on Assassinations diagrammed the car in Exhibit 11-19. The seat is actually 2.5 inches in from the door. Myers later realized Speer was right and, while admitting it on his website, he tried to blame the mistake on the late Peter Jennings's careless narration during the horrendous 2003 ABC special on the JFK case. Myers pleaded innocence even though he himself had slid the seat over six inches in his ersatz "simulation" for ABC. Further, it does not seem that the former ghostwriter for Bugliosi has told his former writing partner about this error. On his book tour, Bugliosi was still spouting this "half foot" phony argument. What makes it even worse is that, as we will see, Kennedy is hit before he goes behind the freeway sign, so at the time the Warren Commission says the SBT occurs, he is grabbing his throat and pulled *inward* from the side of the car. Therefore lining himself up with Connally.

If you go to Dealey Plaza and look out the sixth floor of the Texas School Book Depository you will see that there is a clear right-to-left horizontal angle from that vantage point to the car below. So if any assassin tried to fire at Kennedy from this perch, the trajectory does not align for an exit through his throat and then an entrance into the *right side* of Connally's back. So Myers did his bit of trickery to fix that problem for the MSM. And Bugliosi, for whatever reason, followed this folly. But it's worth noting, Bugliosi actually went even further than this. In his End Notes to his chapter on the Zapruder film, he actually fully endorses Myers Motion, that is, Myers's phony 3-D computer re-creation of the Zapruder film. He calls it "a remarkably compelling view of the assassination of President Kennedy."[16] He goes on to add that Myers's magic bullet contraption is consistent with both the Warren Commission's version of the SBT and the HSCA's version. Yet he does not note here that the HSCA's photographic panel stated that JFK was hit *before* he went behind the freeway sign. Myers says he was hit when he was behind it. Further, the Warren Report never pinpointed the frame in the film where the SBT happened. They just said it probably occurred during frames Z 210-225.[17] It then acknowledged there was no reaction visible in Connally at this time. Consequently it came up with its infamous "delayed reaction": Connally had been struck by a bullet that tore through three limbs of his body and shattered two hard bones, but he didn't know it since this was a "glancing blow,"[18]

This infamous "delayed reaction" is another problem Myers covered up for ABC and newscaster Peter Jennings, who had hired him. Myers names frame 223 as the time the SBT struck. This, even though, as Milicent Cranor has graphically proven, Connally does not seem to be reacting at this time. As Josiah Thompson clearly demonstrated in *Six Seconds in Dallas,* the clearest visible reaction time for Connally is right around frame 237. Myers and his cohort, Todd Vaughn, like to say that the shoulder drop visible directly after this is an "optical illusion." The problem is that Thompson actually measured this drop against a constant: the top of the car door. He then put the results of the measurement on a graph. So it is no "optical illusion."[19] It is this clear separation in reaction time that Myers's 3D contraption tries to conjure away. As Cranor proved, part of how he does this is by changing the positioning of Kennedy's hands and the expression on his face.

Dr. Robert Shaw Doesn't Buy the Magic Bullet

Bugliosi's second reason for accepting the SBT in spite of the Zapruder film is just as specious. He says there is a lack of physical evidence of any second gunman. This, of course, discounts the backward movement of Kennedy's body. Bugliosi also then states there were no remnants of a second gunman, and he specifically states a lack of other bullets or shell casings. As I showed in Chapter 5, this is simply wrong. There were such artifacts found. He then goes on to say that the bullet hole in Connally's back was ovoid, not circular, and this proves the bullet had hit something to make it lose its stability in flight. Yet, the angle of Connally's body at the time of impact could also affect this shape. And what Bugliosi leaves out is that the shape of Kennedy's wound in his jacket is even more ovoid than Connally's jacket (JFK=1 x 1.5 cm, JBC=1.5 x 1.7 cm). Another important point left out of this is the opinion of two Dallas doctors who worked on Connally: Robert Shaw and Charles Gregory. Thompson asked them if they felt Connally was hit with the same bullet that hit JFK. They said no. Why? Because no fibers from the victim's clothes were carried into the wound. This contrasted with the wound in Connally's wrist which had a number of cloth fibers. As Thompson concluded: "The absence of any cloth fibers in the back wound, together with its clean-cut edges, suggested to both physicians it had been caused by a pristine bullet . . . both were convinced that the President and the Governor had been hit by different bullets."[20]

Next, Bugliosi writes that there was not enough time to get off a second shot from the Mannlicher Carcano to hit Connally right after JFK had been hit. Which, of course, is an argument that works both ways. His fifth and last reason is that since only three bullets were fired, this leaves no more bullets in the scenario, since one missed and hit bystander James Tague. This is a perfect example of what is called circular reasoning. Or reasoning from a predetermined conclusion.[21]

After seventeen pages of all this prefatory material, Bugliosi finally gets to what he sees on the film.[22] He borrows the first leg of his scenario from Gerald Posner. He says the first shot, which missed, was fired at frame 160. Posner used Cecil Kirk's "fact" to place the shot this early: namely Rosemary Willis turning backward toward the TSBD at this time. We have already exposed this as false in Chapter 3, but it points out just how hard it is to find any evidence for a shot on the film at this point. And what Bugliosi dredges up is so weak and imprecise, it is not worth criticizing.[23] For example, as Pat Speer notes, one can't believe in this early shot because Kennedy is in front of the Book Depository and is smiling at the crowd and waving to a group of spectators on his right.[24]

Bugliosi Creates a Spinning Magic Bullet

Now, on the other hand, there is a serious problem with this right off the bat. How could Oswald miss at this point, yet score two direct hits while the car is further away? What Bugliosi says here is worth noting. He writes that "since the oak tree started to obscure his vision of Kennedy at the time of frame 166 . . . he necessarily would have felt very hurried and hence rushed the shot."[25] Well, one logical response to this is: Why didn't he fire a few frames earlier then? But further, how could a man who is about to get two direct hits, miss the closest shot by about 200 feet! Which is how far bystander James Tague was from the kill zone. (In this section, the author never specifically mentions the distance problem.) Bugliosi tries to counter this by saying that the Tague hit was not really a bullet but a fragment. But get this: Bugliosi says it was from a bullet aimed at the car that bounced off the pavement.[26] So here you have a ricochet that went almost 200 feet. And then ricocheted again off a curb and wounded James Tague in the face. But it left no copper as it hit the curb near Tague even though these Mannlicher Carcano bullets are copper coated. (The FBI did an analysis and said they found no copper there.[27]) Apparently, Bugliosi wants us to believe that by bouncing off the pavement, this impact precisely sheared the jacket from the lead core—*as the bullet was spinning!* Sort of like it was getting a cheap haircut. Can anyone imagine such precision? Sort of like the Sundance Kid shooting a man's holster off his waist without wounding him. Second problem: Why did no one find this sheared off jacket? According to Bugliosi, it was laying on the pavement right in the middle of Dealey Plaza. Yet no one saw it.

Bugliosi has a problem here that he does not want to own up to. See, J. Edgar Hoover never bought this single bullet fantasy. In the FBI's version, all three bullets hit the targets. Two for Kennedy, and a separate one for Connally. He is not getting any cooperation from Hoover, because although Hoover does not buy the fantasy, the FBI is stuck with explaining how Tague got hit without a copper trace on the curb. They never did. And the Commission avoided giving the public two different scenarios by not printing the FBI report in the volumes when they were published.

In the restored Zapruder film—that is with the frames that were lost due to a printing error put back in—it is quite clear to any objective observer that Kennedy was hit *before* he went behind the freeway sign. In fact, when first projected by Robert Groden at the 1993 Harvard Conference, it was actually kind of shocking since it was so obvious. This is also what the photographic panel of the House Select Committee on Assassinations had concluded. But Bugliosi cannot allow this. The reason being that this hit could not have been fired by Oswald since, except for a fraction of a second, his view was blocked by the branches of an oak tree. So Bugliosi now goes into prosecutorial overdrive. He says that Kennedy was still waving at the crowd as he disappeared behind the sign.[28] This is simply not true on the restored version. But in spite of that, Bugliosi concludes that Kennedy was hit between frames 207-222.

Before commenting on why this is hard to swallow, let us first make one easy observation: You cannot see Kennedy at Bugliosi's chosen frames. He is hidden by the sign. But you can see Connally. There is not anything discernible to indicate he is hit at Z 222.[29] So if Kennedy is hit before he goes behind the sign, and Connally is not hit even after he emerges from behind it, the likelihood is they were not hit by the same bullet. There goes the SBT due to the timing problem with the rifle. It would have been quite difficult for Oswald to have fired the manual bolt action rifle that fast. And this is why I think Bugliosi and Posner place the first shot as early as they do despite the paucity of evidence. They have to stretch out the firing sequence in order to make it more believable to the public.

From here, Bugliosi goes on to the fatal headshot on the Zapruder film. Quite naturally, Bugliosi uses Larry Sturdivan's film of the shooting of a goat to endorse the so-called neuromuscular reaction explanation for the backward movement of Kennedy's body in the film[30] As Randy Robertson pointed out at the Duquesne Conference of 2003, if this was the case then Kennedy's arms as well as his legs would have been extended. Because in the film Sturdivan showed to the HSCA, the goat's front and back legs extended outward before the goat died after being shot. Yet Kennedy's arms stay at his sides, precisely as they were before the bullet struck. And since Kennedy did not die immediately afterwards, this can be no last dying spasm. Sturdivan is a statistician and a physicist. Why is Bugliosi using him for a medical opinion? If one recalls, Bugliosi also used him for Comparative Bullet Lead Analysis. Sturdivan turned out to be wrong on that also.

Bugliosi Repeats Cecil Kirk's Error

Another visual Bugliosi uses to endorse his shot from the rear at Z 313 is a still film of Kennedy's head tilting slightly forward at the time the bullet explodes. Bugliosi plays this up quite strongly: for him it proves this shot came from the rear. He makes his discovery of it quite dramatic.[31] If the reader recalls, this was the Cecil Kirk fallacy we exposed through medical researcher Milicent Cranor in Chapter 3. Namely that, according to medical-ballistics experts, with a through and through bullet, whichever direction it enters from is irrelevant. It will be the top of the head that opens widest. This is due to the phenomenon of cavitation. (Please see the discussion of Kirk in Chapter 3 for a fuller explanation.)

Two other things about this photo also escaped Bugliosi. It appears that the *front* of JFK's head is being impacted at this frame. And it appears to be a lot of damage. And as Doug Horne points out in his book *Inside the ARRB*, Tom Robinson of Gawler's Funeral Home, who helped pick up Kennedy's body from the autopsy room, says he saw a hole in Kennedy's right temple. It was in the hairline, and is actually partly visible in some photos. It was a neat wound and "did not have to be hidden by make-up, and was simply plugged by him with some wax during the reconstruction." Robinson recalled it being about a quarter inch in diameter.[32]

The third argument Bugliosi uses to counter the backward movement of JFK is this: a 6.5 mm Western Cartridge bullet could not have the kind of impacting force to drive JFK backwards as shown in the film. Bugliosi also then asks himself: How does a human body react when being hit by a bullet?[33] I found this self-query slightly humorous. Bugliosi is in his seventies. So he was alive during the Vietnam War. He apparently forgot one of the most famous images from the Tet offensive. This is the film taken in Saigon during the uprising when an Army of South Vietnam officer summarily executes a suspected Viet Cong guerilla. He fires his pistol into his head at close range. The impacting force drives the victim backward and drops him to the ground.

Hard to believe Bugliosi could have forgotten that famous image when he asked himself that question.

Another point Bugliosi does not bring up here is one that HSCA investigator L. J. Delsa brought up with me in New Orleans. He said the first time he watched the film, he said to himself that the shot from the front must have been from a weapon of a larger caliber than the one from behind. This, of course, also indicates a second assassin. Which is probably why Bugliosi does not mention it.

Bugliosi Defends the Worst Autopsy Ever

Bugliosi begins his chapter on the autopsy with two quite dubious statements. In the very first paragraph, he states that he does not agree with the assertion that many authorities have pronounced about the episode, namely that JFK's autopsy was botched.[34] What makes this entering statement so startling is that, as he acknowledges on the same page, Bugliosi's own chief expert has stated such! Dr. Michael Baden has written for the record that, "Where bungled autopsies are concerned, President Kennedy's is the exemplar."[35] So what Bugliosi does here would be like a DA disagreeing with his own expert witness in court. The second questionable statement he makes at the start is that only two shots hit Kennedy, they were both from the rear, and this "remains unassailable." As we shall see, it is not.

The prosecutor now says that the House Select Committee on Assassinations was too harsh in their treatment of the original autopsy doctors (i.e., James Humes, J. Thornton Boswell, and Pierre Finck). In fact, he calls their critique of their work "considerably overstated."[36] Perhaps nothing in the book is more revealing of just how committed the author is to defending the Warren Commission. And yet at the same time having it both ways. For later on, he actually agrees with the changes that the HSCA made in the original autopsy—the raised entry point on the head, and the lower point on the back. (Although, as we shall see, at times he even quibbles with this.)

Why Bugliosi does this seems strange. What he seems to be trying to do is to soften the critique of the autopsy and actually vouch for the competence and skill of the pathologists.[37] But this leaves him with a huge problem: If he is right about their competence, then how does one explain why the autopsy was so poor? He mentions the idea—as Pierre Finck testified to at the trial of Clay Shaw—that the military controlled the autopsy. He then tries to counteract this powerful testimony by saying that Finck said that there were no generals in charge of the autopsy. But Finck added that he didn't have to take orders from generals ". . . because there were others, there were admirals . . . and when you are a Lt. Colonel in the army you just follow orders. . . ."[38]

To further remove the doctors from responsibility for their work product, Bugliosi says that the Kennedy family must have limited the autopsy. This idea has been so completely and repeatedly discredited by writers like the late Harold Weisberg and Gary Aguilar that it's puzzling that the author even surfaced it. Both Humes and Boswell said this was not the case before the Assassination Records Review Board.[39] Humes once told a friend that he was ordered not to do a complete autopsy, but the orders were *not* from RFK.[40] The HSCA concluded that the Kennedys did not interfere with the autopsy. A very good proof of this being the fact that Robert Kennedy left blank the space marked "restrictions" on the form he signed authorizing the autopsy.[41] The commanding officer of the Naval Medical Center, Admiral Galloway, said the same. And he was quite specific: ". . . no orders were being sent in from outside the autopsy room either by phone or by person."[42] Now, in light of Galloway's words, since the Kennedys were out of the room, the interference had to have come from inside. For, as Bugliosi argues, if there was no interference, then these eminently qualified doctors would have given the president an excellent and complete autopsy. Rather than, as Harold Weisberg has written, one more suiting to a bowery bum.

Jim Humes Fabricates a Cover Story

To illustrate the lengths Warren Commission stalwarts must go to in order to deny that the military limited the postmortem, consider the following: When Pierre Finck testified at the Clay Shaw trial he recalled Humes being flustered by this interference and asking the question, "Who's in charge here?" Finck further testified that an army general, who was neither a pathologist nor doctor, replied, "I am." [43] This is about as clear as it gets in figuring who was running things that night. When this episode was depicted in Oliver Stone's film *JFK,* it became necessary to construct a cover story to conceal the truth. So Humes now told his friend George Lundberg, the editor of the *Journal of the American Medical Association,* the following fairytale in order to make it go away. Before the autopsy commenced, he saw a man with a camera in the building. He did not want to chase him so he went to the loading dock and saw some generals milling around. He asked, "Who's in charge here?" When he found out, he told the officer to remove the guy with the camera.[44] Bugliosi, predictably and dutifully, repeats this tall tale.[45] But as Gary Aguilar notes, and Bugliosi does not, Finck *could not* have been referring to this "loading dock" episode at the trial. Why? Because Humes places this loading dock incident before the autopsy started. Finck did not arrive until after the autopsy began. Therefore, it could not take place at a loading dock. Second, Finck testified that this incident happened not before, but while the autopsy was in progress.[46] This is how desperate the late Jim Humes was to get himself off the hook. It's a painful human predicament that Bugliosi does not seem to understand.

But yet, in the face of all the above, Bugliosi insists that the military did not control the autopsy. Now anyone can read Finck's Shaw trial testimony.[47] There, one can see the true answer to this question. Not only were the doctors constrained by the military, but Finck was uncomfortable in admitting to this fact. For instance, when prosecutor Alvin Oser asked him if he saw the autopsy photos in advance of signing either the first autopsy report or the supplementary report of a few days later, it is clearly hard for Finck to admit that he did not. In fact, he actually tried to dance around the fact that he had previously said he *did* see the photos. When Oser had this answer read back to him, Finck actually tried to blame his previous misleading answer on a stenographic error. He finally admitted he did not see the photos until—get this—1967. And then when Oser asks Finck the simple question as to why he did not dissect the track of the back wound, which allegedly exited the neck, well, the colloquy gets almost painful to read. Oser had to ask him this question seven times! Oser even has to ask the judge to order Finck to answer the question. Finally Finck answers with: "As I recall I was told not to but I don't remember by whom."[48]

Question for the prosecutor: If RFK had told him not to—or Kennedy's physician George Burkley had done so—wouldn't Finck have recalled it? And wouldn't he have readily answered the question since it would have gotten him off the hook for his negligence? The answer is obvious. And it renders silly the idea that it was the Kennedys and not the military that limited the autopsy. An autopsy so bad that fifty years later we still can't figure out what precisely happened to President Kennedy.

The Probes Don't Connect

What makes the above question to Finck so vital today is that, after the work of the ARRB, we can now see that the failure to dissect this wound seems to have a rationale behind it. Because in reading both the interviews conducted by Chief Counsel Jeremy Gunn, along with the declassified interviews of the HSCA, the evidence indicates that this wound did not transit the body. Compelling evidence for this is the new information about the probing of the back wound with a malleable instrument done that night at Bethesda Naval Center. Both pathologist Robert Karnei and photographer Robert Knudsen say that the probing revealed that the back wound was clearly below the throat

wound.[49] Further, and even worse for the Warren Commission and SBT advocates, photographer George Knudsen and assistants Paul O'Connor and James
Jenkins said the angle of the probe was steeply downward.[50] Jenkins actually
told William Law that from his observation, the trajectory to connect the two
was impossible.[51] And there were photos taken of this which—no surprise—do
not exist today.[52] Finally, at least six witnesses, including radiologist John Ebersole, pathologist Robert Karnei, and FBI agents Jim Sibert and Francis O'Neill
said the instrument used could not find an exit point.[53] All of this seems strong
evidence that the back wound (1) did not connect to the neck wound, and (2)
was not a through and through wound.

And this is just the beginning of the problems with the alleged track of this
back wound. Another problem is this: If this bullet entered and exited as the
Warren Commission said it did, then why are the cervical vertebrae intact? As
Dr. John Nichols pointed out at the trial of Clay Shaw, if the bullet followed
the path as specified in the autopsy report, then certainly the vertebrae would
have been broken. David Mantik has taken this point even further with skull
and neck X-rays of patients. He has projected these at certain conferences, like
the ASK seminar in Dallas in 1993. These geometrically dramatize this point.
Further, as Pat Speer has pointed out, why, on the original measurements, is
this anterior neck wound (1) too small for the Mannlicher Carcano 6.5 mm
bullet and (2) smaller than the entry on the back.[54] Also, as Henry Hurt has
written, why were no metal traces found on either Kennedy's shirt or tie, "traces that should have been there if a bullet had caused the damage"[55] Finally,
as Milicent Cranor discusses in her fine essay, "Trajectory of a Lie," wound
experts Vincent DiMaio and J. C. Aguilar have written that in a "shored exit
wound," such as JFK's anterior neck wound with the shirt tight around the
neck, there (1) should have been an abrasion collar, and (2) should have been
skin on Kennedy's shirt. There was neither. Further, in a shored exit wound,
the abrasion collar looks "scalloped or punched-out." According to Malcolm
Perry, who saw it close up, this was not the case. (More on Perry later. Cranor's
important essay can be read at the historymatters.com website.)

In fifty years, no credible evidence has yet surfaced that connects this
back wound to this anterior neck wound. In retrospect, this may be why the
pathologists were ordered not to dissect the wound. Because if they had, there
would be no continuous track to be found and that would have created some
serious problems. It would have strongly suggested shots from two directions
and therefore two assassins. This is one reason why assistant James Jenkins felt
like he did after the autopsy. He told author William Law: "I felt what we saw
that night was nothing related to the pathology report. There was no relation

to it. I came out of the autopsy totally expecting them to say there were two shooters. One from the right and one from behind."[56]

In fact, Bugliosi seems confused by this issue himself. On page 421 he writes that Dr. Charles Petty explained to him that the back wound was lower than the throat wound anatomically, but since Kennedy was leaned forward, it could have exited at his throat, which was actually higher. But then, just three pages later, on page 424, he writes that it is clear from autopsy photos that the back wound was clearly above the neck wound. Is this a photo that Petty did not see? Since Petty was on the HSCA forensic panel, how could that possibly be true? Whatever his problem, Bugliosi has a devil of a time convincing the reader that these two wounds connect. And part of that problem is the diagrams he prints on page 422. In them, he tries to account for this dubious path by leaning President Kennedy forward by an amount that simply is not seen in the Zapruder film until after JFK is clearly struggling in pain. Which is after he emerges from behind the sign. But yet, the HSCA photographic panel concluded he was hit in the back *before* he went behind the freeway sign. If you look at those several frames before he disappears behind the sign, the lean simply does not exist for Bugliosi's depicted trajectory to work. I believe this is one reason why many who advocate for this forward lean place this back hit behind the sign. Simply so they can say that this lean exists in a place where no one can see it.

But as Josiah Thompson pointed out, it's even worse than that. The HSCA finally decided that the angles through JFK and Governor Connally were 11 degrees *upward* through Kennedy, and 27 degrees downward through Connally. So the official story has this Magic Bullet not hitting any bone as it traverses Kennedy's neck since, as Nichols and Mantik have shown, no cervical vertebrae reveal this. Yet, this military jacketed bullet—which was good at holding trajectory—deflects a total of 38 degrees, while striking nothing but soft tissue! This is very hard to believe. And this is one of the major problems Cyril Wecht had with Michael Baden's leadership of the HSCA's forensic panel. Bugliosi writes that Wecht did not understand this forward lean issue.[57] This is not accurate. Wecht did understand it, but he said the lean is not present in the Zapruder film at the points necessary. Wecht was very clear about why he disagreed with Baden on this point. And he talks about it at length in Chip Selby's fine film *Reasonable Doubt*. He said Kennedy does not exhibit this lean as he disappears behind the sign; and he does not exhibit it just as he emerges from it. So what are we to believe? That he was in this position for only the fraction of a second when he was behind it? Wecht didn't buy it. Bugliosi does.

Arlen Specter Reports for Work

What is so interesting about this trajectory problem in *Reclaiming History* is that Bugliosi likes the way the HSCA handled it. At least some of the time. But he says the Warren Commission mishandled it. Yet something he does not make clear is this: the HSCA *had* to handle it this way because they detected something on the autopsy photos that either the autopsy doctors missed, or was not there in 1966–67. The HSCA said there was an abrasion collar on the back wound which indicated directionality. And the direction was from below. Now here is a question for the ages: How could a bullet fired from sixty feet above, following an unobstructed path, enter its target at an upward angle? There is no credible answer to that question in Bugliosi's book.

When you combine this with the fact of the actual placement of the back wound, which is below the neck wound, then its panic time for the official story. And the Warren Commission knew it. This is why they lied about it. As James Sibert said, "Well, the way they got that was by moving that bullet hole in the back, keeping moving it until they got it to the base of the neck so it would come out . . . the anterior part of the neck, you know, as an exit wound."[58] Both Sibert and Francis O'Neill, who observed the autopsy for the FBI, have said there was nothing stated the night of the autopsy about a path connecting the two wounds.[59] They both said this was all created after the fact, without the body in front of the doctors. And, in fact, it is now possible to create the trail that led to such folly.

It appears to begin with a visit Arlen Specter made to James Humes. At this meeting there was preliminary discussion of the wounds. Specter actually described this meeting at the Duquesne Conference in 2003. And how Humes would not talk to him unless the top Navy brass OK'd it first.[60] But after this initial hesitancy, the two became friends. After all, they needed each other. Humes and Boswell later admitted to meeting with Specter 8–10 times before their Warren Commission testimony.[61] Specter, working with the commander of the Medical School at Bethesda, John Stover, and also Admiral Galloway, then sent Humes and Boswell to Bethesda Naval Hospital to see a young man of twenty-two named Harold Rydberg.[62] To this day, Rydberg does not understand why he was chosen to draw the wound illustrations for the Warren Commission.[63] He had only studied medical art for a year. Rydberg told William Law that Humes and Specter could have easily gotten a much more experienced illustrator from Walter Reed or the University of Maryland for the job. Rydberg later figured out that one reason he was chosen is that a veteran medical illustrator would not have gone along with the forlorn exercise. Why was it forlorn? The two doctors appeared before him with nothing: no pictures, no X-rays, no official measurements. They were equipped only with their memories.

But they did have one thing: Humes and Specter had already decided on the Single Bullet Theory.[64] They had to because Humes was going to testify in just three days, that is, on March 16, 1964. Rydberg later deduced that the reason they showed up with nothing in hand was that they wanted no paper trail. As we will see, if they had come properly prepared, the illustrations were so wrong that this would have proved they were lying to Rydberg to attain a desired end result. But since they came with nothing, they could just say they remembered things incorrectly. Once the illustrations were done, they were placed in a safe and then given to Admiral Galloway. Galloway then gave them to the Commission to use for Humes's testimony.[65]

But, as noted, the actual drawings give the game away. Which may be why they are not in the Warren Report but stuffed away in the volumes.[66] As James Jenkins told William Law, the doctors instructed Rydberg to draw renditions that fit the conclusions the Commission needed; not depictions of what they saw during the autopsy. Even though he had 2,700 pages, these drawings are not in Bugliosi's book. Yet you can find them in much smaller books like Charles Crenshaw's and Josiah Thompson's. These drawings were made in the first two weeks of March, that is, only three months and three weeks after the pathologists performed the most important autopsy in American history. Yet if one looks at the drawings Humes and Boswell instructed Rydberg to sketch, they made two unbelievable errors. In the profile view of the throat wound, with JFK depicted as erect, they placed the posterior wound up into Kennedy's neck. That is, they moved the back wound upwards to make it align with a theoretical exit in his throat. Then, completing their mission, they told Rydberg to draw a flight path connecting the false points.

The Rydberg Drawings

The diagram they instructed the young illustrator to draw for the head wound is just as wrong. They had Rydberg place Kennedy's head in a much more anteflexed position—looking down into his lap—than he is at Zapruder frame 313. This false positioning allows for a shot from behind and low in the skull to exit the right side of the head. To sew it all up, they had Rydberg draw another flight path through this false position. It is hard to believe that these errors are accidental or can be chalked up to a lapse of memory. Since, as with almost all of these "errors," they point in one direction: They use false evidence to make the case against Oswald as the lone assassin.

What makes this supposition all the more tangible is what Specter did with Humes when he testified on March, 16, 1964. At this point in time, the Commission had blowups of individual frames of the Zapruder film. Which they could have given Rydberg. But Specter did a funny thing when Humes testified. He waited until Humes was in mid-testimony, *after* Rydberg's diagram of the head shot had already been entered into the record. Then, and only then, did he show Humes the prints of frames Z 312 and 313. The clever prosecutor now posed an artfully framed query. He asked Humes if the prints depicted Kennedy's head in "approximately the same position" as it was in Rydberg's CE 388. On cue, Humes replied, "Yes sir." Allen Dulles later rammed the point home by asking Humes if Kennedy's head posture was "roughly the inclination that you think the President's head had at the time." Humes again said yes. No one on the Commission asked to actually compare the Rydberg drawing with the Zapruder film prints.[67]

Bugliosi spends exactly one paragraph on this entire episode. And that paragraph is not in the text.[68] He admits that Rydberg's drawings are not accurate. But he does not explain how they *could* have been made accurate if the Commission—and Specter—wanted them to be. He notes that CE 385 depicts Kennedy in an upright position for the back wound. He then writes that JFK was never in this position. Maybe not exactly, but he is close to this in the frames leading up to his disappearance behind the freeway sign. And if he was shot there, as the HSCA photographic panel says, then in addition to his being concealed by the branches of an oak tree, it is very hard to make the trajectory from a lower back wound to a higher neck wound work. He also admits that Rydberg's CE 388 is not accurate with the positioning of Kennedy's head. Incredibly, he adds that the drawings "therefore could only have *confused the Warren Commission staff.*" (Emphasis added.) He can write this because he does not describe how Specter and Dulles influenced Humes. Which reveals that the two knew precisely what was wrong with the Rydberg depictions, and they wanted it that way.

Bugliosi also does not pinpoint these very interesting facts: the Commission never interviewed FBI agents Francis O'Neill and James Sibert, or Kennedy's personal physician George Burkley. The agents were shocked by this.[69] Specter had read their eyewitness report on the autopsy, which did not buy into the SBT. He then tried to discredit their report by saying that Sibert made no contemporaneous notes and O'Neill destroyed his.[70] Neither accusation is true. But Specter conveyed this lie about their report to Warren Commission Chief Counsel J. Lee Rankin.[71] The Sibert-O'Neill report placed the back wound too low to exit through the throat. And Burkley's death certificate did the

same. Consequently, these three important witnesses were not interviewed by
the Commission. And neither the FBI report on the autopsy nor the Burkley
death certificate appears either in the Warren Report or the twenty-six volumes.[72] This all reveals that, far from being "confused," the clever and ambitious
Specter understood quite early what he was doing. And he manipulated the
evidence to arrive at his desired goal: the fantastic SBT.

What Was the Autopsy Report Based Upon?

The reader will note I have taken some time to describe Finck's testimony at the
Shaw trial and the Specter/Rydberg/Humes episode in detail. That is because
it is important to show just how compromised the autopsy doctors had become
by early 1964. And this is not all there is to indicate they were compromised.
For example, before the ARRB, Humes admitted that he destroyed not just
the first draft of the autopsy report, but also the notes it was based upon.[73] And
the ARRB further discovered that some mysterious figure also confiscated the
contemporaneous notes that the meticulous Finck had prepared.[74] What this
does of course is open up the possibility that, as with the Rydberg drawings,
the autopsy report in evidence today is not based upon facts discerned on the
evening of November 22, 1963, but upon later necessary revisions to make it
align with an evolving story.

Gerald McKnight makes a strong case that this actually happened. As he
deduces, Commission Exhibit 397 contains the surviving notes, which are just
a few pages. Yet the autopsy report is a six-page, single-spaced document. In a
two-page analysis, McKnight shows that of approximately ninety facts in the
autopsy report, about sixty-four cannot be found in the official notes. And he
further writes, "Some fifteen of these pieces of information involve measurements and numbers that are not found in the published record."[75] And this is
one of the most maddening things about the autopsy report in evidence today:
its lack of specific measurements and locations about the head wound and the
back wound. Which should have been in the notes.

As McKnight further reveals, the story that Humes has told about
the destruction of his notes and report does not jibe with the record. In a
meticulous reconstruction, the historian establishes a paper trail that ends on
November, 26, 1963, with White House physician George Burkley handing
"the autopsy notes and the holograph draft of the final report" to the Secret
Service. [76] Before the HSCA, Humes admitted to the time of his wholesale
destruction by burning. It was when Oswald was shot by Ruby. Which was
Sunday, November 24. This is doubly interesting. First, with Oswald dead,
there would be little need for the notes to be preserved for a criminal trial. If

Oswald had lived, they would be absolutely necessary because without them, a sharp defense attorney could question the factual foundation of the report. After November 24, the legal pressure for preserving these were gone. Second, many of the alterations to the first draft appear to have been done in the office of Admiral Galloway that very Sunday.[77] This is also the day that Nicholas Katzenbach issued his infamous memorandum to White House assistant Bill Moyers which laid out the official story about Oswald as the lone assassin.

As most people know, the actual destruction of the autopsy draft and notes was originally said to have been done by Humes, at his home and in his fireplace. His excuse? He did not want those notes "stained with the blood of our beloved president" to come into the possession of some crass souvenir hunter. This is another deception that collapsed before the ARRB. It was revealed that the draft in question had been written in the privacy of his home. So, how did JFK's blood get on it?[78] This was one of the points at which Humes, caught up in a web of deception and contradiction, became flustered. When asked for a more realistic reason, he first replied that it may have been errors in spelling which caused him to do what he did. Then he said he could not remember, and he apologized for not recalling. But he also offered this: that he might not have "even ever did that."[79] That is, burned the documents.

If it is the last, then the revisions made in Galloway's office were made with the originals intact. Which makes their subsequent disappearance even more provocative. As McKnight notes, they may have survived to November 26 with Burkley.

Again, Bugliosi deals with this issue not in the text, but in his End Notes.[80] He manages to mention the date of November 24 without tying it to Oswald's murder. He mentions the revisions made in the report without placing them in Galloway's office. He does not describe the lack of factual basis in the report when it is compared to the extant notes. Therefore he doesn't have to raise the question: Where did these facts come from? And he doesn't detail how the ARRB pierced Humes's cover story about the burning of the first draft. (He actually says Humes had become confused on this point.) This latter exclusion allows him to write that if Humes did do such a heinous thing, why would he admit to it? As outlined above, it may be because he didn't do such a thing. And he knew that his superiors in the navy, who were cognizant of that fact, and their cohort on the Warren Commission, Specter, would cover that lie for him.

The Pathologists Rehearse for the Media

The doctors were first co-opted by the army and navy brass on the evening of the autopsy. Arlen Specter then further compromised them before the Warren

Commission. From here on in, there was no turning back. But the problem was this: The Commission had published twenty-six volumes of evidence. And one of the exhibits was autopsist Thornton Boswell's autopsy face sheet. This placed the back wound low, about 5–6 inches below the neckline. Second, the volumes also published frames from the Zapruder film. The frames were small, black and white, and of poor quality. But they revealed enough to entice some people to go to the National Archives and view the real thing. One of those interested was Josiah Thompson. As we shall see, with these exhibits, the critical community now began to doubt the credibility of the autopsy.

In 1966, Edward Epstein published *Inquest*. In this book he showed clear and large photos of Kennedy's jacket and shirt. To those who had purchased the Warren Commission volumes, this created a serious problem. The bullet holes in those two pieces of clothing depicted a wound well down in the back, as Boswell's drawing showed. It was not in the neck as Humes and Boswell had instructed Rydberg to draw. It also now made sense why, as Finck later said, "I was denied the opportunity to examine the clothing of Kennedy. One officer who outranked me told me that my request was only of academic interest."[81] If he *had* seen the clothes, how could he have thought the back wound could have exited at the level of the throat?

How does Bugliosi deal with this important point, namely the autopsy doctors not being able to inspect the clothing? He leaves out the quote by Finck saying a superior officer overruled him. He then says the Secret Service had picked up Kennedy's clothing at Parkland Hospital. But, since the Secret Service was in attendance that night at Bethesda, why didn't Finck's superior officer just ask them to produce the clothes for the doctors? Specter seemed cognizant of this problem also. When he was running the Warren Commission's reenactment of the assassination, he used Connally's actual jacket. But he didn't use Kennedy's.[82] So it is hard to escape the assumption that Specter and the autopsy doctors knew where the entry hole in the back was. Or that Epstein was correct, since Boswell's autopsy face sheet coincided with the photos.

But caught in the tangled web, Boswell now had to backtrack on his own diagram. Part of the reason for the Justice Department review of the medical evidence in 1966 seems to be to counteract the effect of Epstein's book. For after this review, on November 25, 1966, Dr. Boswell gave an interview to the *Baltimore Sun*. He told the newspaper that "If I had known at the time that this sketch would become public record, I would have been more careful." He now moved up the wound from down in the back to just below the collar of JFK's shirt. The *New York Times* picked up this story also. Boswell now asserted that he and Humes just recently inspected the photos on November 1 and there was "absolutely no doubt in our minds now" about the single-bullet theory.[83] The idea that Epstein's book was part of the reason for this review was made clear by an Associated Press article of the previous day by Jack Miller. Miller wrote, "In an interview, Boswell said that when he examined the autopsy photographs for the first time Nov. 1, the pictures showed clearly that the wound was in the neck. The photographs are in the National Archives and are not available to the public. One of the critics of the Warren Report, Edward Epstein, used the diagram (the autopsy face sheet) and the FBI reports to suggest the possibility that there may have been a second assassin. But Epstein . . . conceded in the current issue of *Esquire* magazine that if the autopsy photos showed the wound in the neck, there would be no further doubt about the autopsy report and that second assassin would be ruled out."[84]

Since the public would not be able to see the photos for five more years, Boswell knew his lie was safe from exposure. For the autopsy photos, which have since been published, show the wound clearly in the back. Not the neck. If Boswell saw the photos just three weeks earlier, how can we believe this was just a mistake? It is more likely that the government was using a willing tool to ridicule and demean the critical community. Bugliosi does not mention this strange and mendacious upward migration in 1966 by Boswell.

Humes Lies for Rather

But Boswell's stooping was not enough. The critical community was gaining steam in late 1966 and early 1967. There was another review of the autopsy materials in late January 1967. For this one, Pierre Finck was brought back from Vietnam to take part. We complain today about a press complicit with the government, for example, the false circumstances bandied about by the media for the Iraq War. Well, this phenomenon is not new for those who follow the Kennedy assassination. As the 1966 review was done for the partial benefit of the print media, the 1967 review seems planned with the cooperation of broadcast media. In fact, Warren Commissioner John McCloy was an adviser for a CBS special on the JFK case, which had been planned as early as December 1966.

In May 1967, the Justice Department wrote a letter to Humes and said CBS had requested to interview him for its upcoming special. They were therefore giving him permission to talk to CBS. The Justice Department then prepared a script for Humes to follow when he was questioned by CBS reporter Dan Rather. This script was clearly meant to reinforce what Boswell had previously done, that is, neutralize Epstein by revivifying the SBT. The Justice Department wanted Humes to say that 1) a bullet "entered the back of the neck and exited through the throat," 2) that the autopsy face sheet portrayed this wound too low, and 3) Humes's review of the autopsy photos and X-rays supported the conclusions of the Warren Commission (i.e., the Single-Bullet-Theory). Humes dutifully told Rather that the photos clearly showed that the wound was exactly where the doctors stated it to be in their Warren Commission testimony and as was shown in the Rydberg drawings.[85] Which was false. Bugliosi mentions Humes's story for CBS, but he does not tell the reader it was scripted by the Justice Department.[86]

But the critics were not just confining themselves to the questions about the Rydberg depiction of the SBT. On January 14, 1967, the *Saturday Evening Post* ran a cover story previewing Josiah Thompson's upcoming book, *Six Seconds in Dallas*. As Russell Fisher, director of the Clark Panel later stated, Attorney General Ramsey Clark got hold of the proofs of Thompson's book after this article appeared.[87] What he saw must have startled him, because, as Fisher continued, one reason the Clark Panel was convened and its findings released was to "partly refute some of the junk" in the book.

Thompson did to the Rydberg drawing of the Kennedy headshot what Epstein did to his drawing of the SBT. He brought it under the most serious questioning. And he did it by visually dramatic means. He simply placed Zapruder frame 312, the frame right before Kennedy's head explodes, on the same page with what the doctors told Rydberg was the path of this bullet through Kennedy's skull.[88] In other words, Thompson corrected the lie that Dulles and Specter created with Humes. For at Zapruder frame 312, Kennedy's head is not in approximately the same position as Rydberg depicted it in his drawing.

As Thompson showed, if Oswald is the assassin, Kennedy's head is not in the proper position to make this flight path work. The trajectory does not align for an entrance at the bottom of the skull with an exit at the top above the right ear. For that to work, the bullet would have had to have been fired from the level of the trunk of the limousine. Tasked by Clark, forensic pathologist Russell Fisher now went to work. Before describing the result, it is important to note that Fisher was later brought in to review the mysterious death of CIA Officer John Paisley. Paisley's body was found floating in Chesapeake Bay in 1978. Understandably, the original coroner who saw the body said he was murdered because he was shot through the head, had indications of rope burns on his neck, and was weighted down with two diving belts when the body was recovered. As one commentator said, "Strapping on two sets of diving belts, jumping off the boat with a gun in hand, and then shooting yourself in the water is, to be charitable, a weird way to commit suicide." Further, the fatal head wound was through the left side of his brain. Yet, Paisley was right-handed. Finally, no blood, brain tissue, weapon, or expended cartridge was found on board Paisley's boat. Did he take it all with him when he jumped overboard? None of this was a problem for Fisher. He ruled the case a suicide.[89]

Fisher Rescues Clark from Thompson

Well, Fisher worked this same magic for Clark. He took care of the trajectory problem posed by Thompson in a rather easy manner: He simply moved the wound on the back of the skull up by four inches! This was a milestone in the medical evidence for this case. The autopsy doctors had placed the entrance wound in the head at the level of the external occipital protuberance (EOP). This is near the bottom of the rear of the skull. Fisher was raising it to the level of the cowlick. It is hard to believe that the autopsy doctors, who had the body in front of them for hours and manipulated the scalp, could have made such a serious error, but this is what the Clark Panel insisted had happened. And to show even further that this third review in two years was politically motivated, Clark did not release the results of this inquiry until January 16, 1969—almost eleven months after the panel was convened. It just happened to be the day Jim Garrison's prosecution of Clay Shaw finally began after being delayed for almost two years. Can there be any doubt that the government was out to neuter the work of the critics? And if they had to force the doctors to falsify the facts, or if Russell Fisher had to miraculously elevate wounds, so be it.

Now, it is necessary here to chart a path directly from Maryland, where Fisher operated, to London Weekend Television where Bugliosi and Spence starred in their farcical trial. If one recalls Bugliosi's medical witness, the man who said, "It would be nice if the brain were available," was Charles Petty. Was there a reason Petty was so nonchalant about the loss of valuable exhibits in the JFK case? As we saw in the Paisley case, Russell Fisher could be made to compromise medical facts for reasons of national security. Pat Speer had surfaced some interesting facts about Petty's career. From 1960 through 1967, Petty worked as Fisher's assistant in the Maryland state medical examiner's office. Then, two years later, he was hired by the city of Dallas to replace Earl Rose as coroner. In 1977, he coedited a book with Fisher, which was funded by the Justice Department. In 1978, he testified before the HSCA. He followed Dr. Cyril Wecht and was tasked with refuting Wecht's rejection of the SBT.[90] Therefore, it is no coincidence that Petty then followed in Fisher's footsteps as chief advocate for Fisher's new and modified version of Kennedy's autopsy. The one that was supposed to "refute some of the junk" in Thompson's book.

We have spent some time on the historical aspect of the interaction of the pathologists with both the media and the government. It is necessary in order to understand the confusion about the medical facts of the case in the early years. That confusion was brought on by the attempts in Washington to counteract the holes poked in the Commission's autopsy case. To counteract these points, the autopsy doctors were trotted out and given permission to speak—but only after being briefed and scripted. And they willingly read their lines, even if the script differed from the facts. They apparently felt safe since a shroud of secrecy existed and they knew their side would protect them. Which is what happened. It is important to remember this rather sordid part of the story in regard to *Reclaiming History*. For Bugliosi attempts to portray the pathologists as competent, uncompromised, and if they committed errors, they were honest errors. In light of the above, this is untenable. And it is now about to get worse.

Humes's Particle Trail Disappears

As mentioned in the introduction, on February, 13, 1996, the following exchange occurred between staff attorney Jeremy Gunn and Jim Humes as part of the ARRB inquiry into the medical evidence:

Q: Do you recall having seen an X-ray previously that had fragments corresponding to a small occipital wound?
A: Well I reported that I did, so I must have. But I don't see it now.

I could not find this exchange in *Reclaiming History*, yet it is surely one of the most gripping and important revelations of the Assassination Records Review Board. Some would say it holds the key to the medical evidence in the JFK case. Humes here is denying both his own autopsy report, and what he himself said he saw during the autopsy of President Kennedy. When Gunn, the chief counsel of the ARRB, pressed him ever so slightly on this point, ARRB researcher Doug Horne said Humes became visibly frustrated. To the point that, if Gunn would have asked him one more question, Humes would probably have stalked out.[91]

To understand why this point was so sensitive with the late pathologist, we must return to what Charles Petty's role model and benefactor, Russell Fisher, did with the rear skull wound. We must also be reminded that Thompson's visual exposure of the falsity of the Rydberg head shot partly provoked that review. The problem was simple. The Commission's story was that Oswald was firing from sixty feet up. This downward head shot hit Kennedy low on the rear skull, but it exited at a *higher* point, above the right ear on the right side of the head. So now you had a second bullet that, although it entered going downward, exited going upward. What makes this even more fascinating is that in the autopsy report, Humes wrote that there was a trail of metal fragments that connected the entry in the occipital region to the top of the skull in the supraorbital area, that is, above the eye socket. Which, at least, would be evidence that this indeed did occur. The insurmountable problem is this: No such trail exits in the X-rays we have today. And this is what Gunn was questioning Humes about. How could he have made such a grievous error? Humes couldn't explain it. Hence his agitation.

To really understand the depth of this problem we must return to Russell Fisher and the main reason why he raised this rear skull wound. It is on the basis of something that reversed the pattern of Humes's errors as described above. In the above ARRB questioning, Humes saw something—the trail of metal particles—that later bodies did not. Well, with the Fisher Panel, Fisher saw something that Humes allegedly did not. And it's a doozy. Fisher observed that there was a 6.5 mm fragment near the top of the rear skull table. Of course, the size and shape of this fragment fits the exact description of the ammunition fired by Oswald. So the question then became: How the heck did all the autopsy doctors and radiologists and FBI agents miss it if Fisher saw it?

Fisher Saw It, Why Didn't Humes?

Again, Jeremy Gunn questioned Humes on this particular point. After drawing his attention to it, Humes commented on this 6.5 mm fragment like this: "The ones we retrieved I didn't think were the same size as this. . . ." Gunn then asked him if they were smaller or larger. Humes replied, "Smaller, considerably smaller. . . . I don't remember retrieving anything of this size. . . . Truthfully, I don't remember anything that size when I looked at these films."[92] When Gunn interviewed J. Thornton Boswell about this fragment, he said the same, "No. We did not find one that large. I'm sure of that."[93] When William Law asked FBI agent James Sibert if he saw this fragment the night of the autopsy, he also responded in the negative, ". . . there was nothing like that."[94] Further, he said that he recalled no one in the room mentioning it either.[95] His FBI partner, Francis O'Neill, said the same: "If there was such [a fragment] as that, it certainly wasn't pointed out to me."[96] John Ebersole was the Navy MD who was in charge of radiology during the Kennedy autopsy. When David Mantik called him in 1992, the two radiologists were having a nice conversation about a number of things. Yet when Mantik asked him why the Clark Panel found the 6.5 mm fragment but Ebersole did not, Ebersole promptly terminated the conversation and hung up on him.[97] Jerrol Custer, the X-ray technician, told

William Law all the bullet fragments he saw were small.[98] (In an interview with Dr. Gary Aguilar for this book, he told me the 6.5 mm fragment would have been at least 50 percent larger than the second largest fragment retrieved that night.)

Concerning this key point, these last four witnesses are crucial. First, Custer and Ebersole were involved in actually taking the X-rays, and were therefore experienced in looking at them. The two FBI agents were formally tasked with retrieving bullets and fragments for the FBI lab. Recall, this is the evening of the assassination. Oswald is still alive. These fragments would be prime evidence at his trial. Yet they recall nothing like this fragment either being on the X-rays or being mentioned by anyone else. Taken together, this testimony strikes one as being probative. It is very hard to say this fragment existed on the X-rays seen during the autopsy at Bethesda. If it did, it would be incompetence of a preposterous degree. Actually, almost frightening.

Bugliosi does not mention this incredible "error" in the text of *Reclaiming History*. In fact, he never mentions at all how it would be possible for all six witnesses mentioned—and more—to miss such a crucial exhibit in what would have been a murder case. He calls this key exhibit ". . . the presence of what appears to be a bullet fragment . . . embedded in the back of the skull."[99] He then adds that Dr. Mantik believes this 6.5 mm fragment did not exist on November, 22, 1963, and was later imprinted onto the X-rays. As he usually does, Bugliosi then questions the logic of anyone doing such a thing: "How could this . . . implicate Oswald?" he asks.[100] The reader should note two things here. Bugliosi is not denying its existence. Further, he does not relate its curious provenance. Those are matters of evidence. He shifts from that to supplying motive. Then he implies, well geez fellas, how does that help the official story?

Let's help the prosecutor. Well, Mr. Bugliosi, how about its size for one? It matches the alleged ammunition used by Oswald. Secondly, maybe because it helps with the trajectory problem outlined earlier? If the entry point is on the bottom of the skull, how could the bullet exit higher on the right side? That trajectory is made easier with Fisher's new and improved higher entry point. (Recall, Fisher was supposed to refute the junk in Thompson's book. This is how he did it.) Third, it helps cure the problem of JFK's head not being nearly as anteflexed as needed at Z frame 312. With this new and higher entry point, it need not be. As noted, Specter and Dulles had weakly disguised this point. Fourth, it also helps with the metal particle fragment trail being too high in the suborbital area for the low entry point. That makes four ways the Fisher Panel and its discovery helped in the case against Oswald. And, somehow, the prosecutor could not see any of this?

Fisher's Solution Creates New Problems

But yet, as novelist Walter Scott wrote, when we "practice to deceive," we sometimes build a tangled web that is difficult to navigate. The new 6.5 mm "discovery" ameliorated some problems, but it created some of its own.

The first one was this: The autopsy doctors would not sign off on it. The Clark Panel did not consult with them when they first switched the location in 1968. But the next Kennedy investigation, the HSCA, was much more public and much more reported upon. So the HSCA had to consult with the original autopsy team. Michael Baden, the head of the HSCA's Forensic Pathology Panel, was all on board with the new cowlick location. He and the overwhelming majority of the panel wanted Humes, Boswell, and Finck to switch from the EOP location to the new higher one. And in the newly declassified HSCA interviews, it is clear that the autopsists were quite reluctant to do so. For one thing, having had the body in front of them, Finck said they had the opportunity to manipulate the scalp.[101] And before the HSCA, he actually described the separation of the scalp from the skull in detail.[102] Second, all three were utterly unconvinced by the photographic evidence the HSCA used (i.e., the appearance of a red spot at the cowlick area). To many this looked like nothing more than a spot of dried blood. When HSCA medical investigator Andy Purdy asked Pierre Finck what inference "would you draw if you saw just that?" Finck replied "On the basis of the photograph alone, nothing."[103] The HSCA was so intent on flipping the autopsists that one of their doctors even asked Finck to look at this red spot with a magnifying glass! To which Finck replied, that it would be embarrassing.[104] Finck was so baffled by the HSCA's insistence on making the red spot at the cowlick the new entry wound that he posed a remarkable question about both the spot and its provenance: "I don't know what it is. How are these photographs identified as coming from the autopsy of President Kennedy?"[105] This from a man who said he actually directed photos to be made of the entry wound in the skull![106] (As we will see, there is a question about at least one set of photos from the autopsy not being Kennedy's.) Dr. Boswell candidly said about the Fisher Panel revising elevation of the head wound, "I never believed this."[107]

Petty Berates Humes: Get on Board Fisher's Train!

According to HSCA investigator Andy Purdy, when he first talked to Dr. Humes, he seemed unaware of any great discrepancy between the Clark Panel and his own work. When Purdy described this split in opinion on where the rear entry wound on the skull was, Humes strongly disagreed. Purdy wrote,

"Dr. Humes stated categorically that his physical measurements are correct and emphasized that he had access to the body itself. . . ."[108] Then before Baden's panel, Dr. Humes even pointed out a paradox in the photographic evidence: Although the red spot was visible in the color photograph, he added "I almost defy you to find it in that magnification in the black and white."[109] Further, as David Mantik has observed, in years of research on the JFK case, he has yet to find one witness at either Parkland Hospital or Bethesda who has ever testified as to noticing this red spot at the cowlick area, let alone identifying it as an entry hole.[110] In fact, Purdy told the ARRB that when Humes refused to budge on this issue, Dr. Charles Petty—Bugliosi's medical witness—took him outside and yelled at him.[111]

Now, it is true that Humes eventually relented to the HSCA's pressure and, on camera, pointed to the cowlick location as the entry wound.[112] But it is clear that this was for show trial purposes only. Because two years later, in a phone interview with Harrison Livingstone, he insisted that his autopsy was correct in 1963: the entry was at the EOP. As Livingstone wrote, he got the impression Humes would never retreat from this position, "he was very strong on this issue."[113] And when Humes was interviewed by both the *Journal of the American Medical Association* in 1992 and by the ARRB in 1996, he stood by his original location.[114]

The way Bugliosi deals with this issue is rich. This is what he says on page 395: "How have the three autopsy pathologists reacted to this apparent gaffe in their report? Not very well I'm afraid. By and large most people don't want to admit they made a mistake. The three autopsy surgeons were no exception." The reader should note the prosecutor's choice of the word "gaffe" for a mistake all three made that turned out to be the biggest one of their careers. Those kinds of instances are not normally referred to as "gaffes." But Bugliosi is caught between a rock and a hard place. He doesn't want to admit the pathologists were not up to the job and should never have been chosen to perform it in the first place, but he also does not want to admit that, hey, if they *were* up to the job, how the heck did they miss the 6.5 mm fragment, which is as plain as day on the X-ray? And finally, the last thing in the world he wants to admit is what is obvious to most objective persons: All three of them missed it because it was not there in 1963. Therefore, he has to defuse the scope and depth of the issue—which is enormous—by calling it an "apparent gaffe."

It is imperative to add two more key points about the "discovery" of the cowlick location for this wound. First, Dr. Petty seems to have had a change of heart about this point later on. In 1993, in *JAMA*, Petty seemed to agree with Humes on this elevated placement. He wrote that, "There were no bullet defects other than those described by Humes in his report." [115] Again, Bugliosi used Petty as his London trial medical expert. Yet in *Reclaiming History*, I could find no note of Petty's subsequent mild relenting on his admonishment of Humes.

Finally, let me add what I consider an absolutely crucial revelation in this "wandering head wound" saga. At the Duquesne Conference of 2003, Dr. Randy Robertson projected on screen a document that tells us a lot about how obsessed the HSCA really was in its mad pursuit of this "wound in the cowlick" goal. Robertson had unearthed the document from the newly released HSCA files as declassified by the ARRB. Dr. Michael Baden clearly felt no one would ever see it, let alone show it in a public forum with him in attendance. What was it? It was a personal note from Baden to Ida Dox, the artist the HSCA employed to render lifelike renditions of the Kennedy autopsy photos. The note instructed her: "You can do better than this." Attached to Baden's note was a photo of a skin laceration from a medical textbook. Baden was clearly telling his employee that he wanted this cowlick spot to be embellished to look like a *real* gunshot wound. And right after Robertson flashed this on the screen Gary Aguilar, who had seen the actual photos in the National Archives, chimed in. He exclaimed, "The actual autopsy pictures do not have those raised edges like that!" This clearly indicates that the "red spot" was altered by Dox for public consumption—read "deception"—to give it depth and a "crater look." Something it does not actually have. Since Bugliosi turned down his invitation to attend this conference, he was unaware that his own chief medical witness was falsifying evidence. Unaware of this declassified exposure, he prints the embellished Dox drawing of the rear skull wound as representing the "entrance wound."

Fisher's Second Magic Bullet

But the above is only the beginning of the problems with this new and improved cowlick location. What Fisher apparently did not realize is that he had now created a second magic bullet. Because when one analyzes this new autopsy, it is very hard to explain the 6.5 mm fragment in any other terms. And although the American public is generally aware of the mythological properties of the pristine version of CE 399 (i.e., the back-neck magic bullet), the critical community has not done a good job in presenting the almost equal absurdity of this new one. But since Bugliosi has to accept Fisher's placement of this newfound fragment—or admit the evidence is falsified—the author should explain why it is so unbelievable.

Consider what Bugliosi is maintaining: Oswald is firing from the sixth floor at a target that is now about 250 plus feet away. The military jacketed

Western cartridges manufactured for the Mannlicher Carcano rifle are said to be quite stable in their flight path. So this bullet is flying through nothing but air at a downward trajectory and strikes Kennedy's skull in the cowlick area. Would it not strike nose first? Yet the nose and tail of this projectile (CEs 567 and 569) were reportedly found in the front of the limousine. As David Mantik has written in *Assassination Science:* "How is it possible for a nearly complete cross section from somewhere *inside* the bullet to embed itself on the *outside* of the skull?"[116] Because this is what the Fisher panel, and later the HSCA forensic panel, would have us believe. Namely that a bullet traveling at almost 2,000 feet per second striking the top of the head would immediately break into thirds. In the space of a nanosecond, it would then presumably flatten sideways and leave the middle third of the bullet up against the *outside* of the skull. Even though that part of the bullet should not have struck the skull first. So it appears the nose of this bullet did not even penetrate the back of the skull before it shattered. Then the other two fragments hurtled through the head and into the front of the car. Why did I say "flatten sideways"? Because if it did not, then the rear portion of the bullet just hopped over the middle portion stuck outside the skull. It then proceeded to follow the front portion through the skull. Yet, the exit for this bullet path is out the top of the right ear. Wouldn't they then have gone outside the side of the car since JFK was next to the door?

I have referred to the London trial being a Little League World Series game. Perhaps that overvalued it. Can one imagine if Spence had charted this new and unheard of ballistics phenomenon on a graph, and then asked Petty to explain how it all happened in the space of an instant? And then asked him, "What are the odds of one case having two Magic Bullets of equal absurdity within six seconds of each other?" That dialogue may have equaled the famous Ealing Studio British comedies for its quality of droll humor.

Now, Bugliosi wants us to believe that the first Magic Bullet, CE 399, went through two people, caused seven wounds, and smashed two bones. Then miraculously, it emerged almost completely intact. This other bullet, upon entering one layer of bone, broke into thirds immediately upon contact. Also, this military jacketed bullet started off going from right to left, then on its trajectory through the skull, went left to right. Because, in width, the new bullet entrance was about in the center of the skull. Yet, its exit is on the right side. And let us add one more anomaly: The stray 6.5 mm fragment is not actually at the new entry site. It is located 1 cm. below it.[117] Go figure.

Understandably, Bugliosi does not describe this bizarre phenomenon in anything like the detail I have. That's because—as with CE 399—no ballistics expert can explain or remember such a thing happening. Howard Donahue could not even recall a nose from a bullet doing such a thing.[118] Larry Sturdivan, a man who Bugliosi actually believes at times, has said the same. He actually wrote, ". . . to have a cross section sheared out is physically impossible."[119] Has Bugliosi now become a conspiracy theorist?

Mantik notes another problem with the new fragment. It is the only piece of evidence to indicate this new trajectory. By that he means that there is no corresponding entry hole in the skull on the anterior-posterior X-ray (i.e., front to back). On the lateral, the fragment is 1 cm below a fracture line. Therefore, the fracture lines do not actually emanate from it. As Mantik writes, "Unless they unequivocally extend to this 6.5 mm object they cannot represent fracture lines caused by a posterior skull bullet." And finally, the mysterious trail of dust-like particles at the front of the skull lies above this new cowlick entrance.[120]

So let's add up the prosecutor's case. No witness at Parkland or Bethesda ever saw the red spot at the cowlick in 1963. No witness who saw the X-rays at Bethesda recalls the 6.5 mm fragment. The autopsists manipulated the scalp from the skull and say the entry bullet hole was well below it. No other corroborating physical evidence on the X-rays jibes with this new location. Now, in evaluating this forlorn fragment and five years late entry hole, it is important to quote a standard guide to court procedure, *McCormick on Evidence*. It reads in part:

> "The principle upon which photographs are most commonly admitted into evidence is the same as that underlying the admission of illustrative drawings, maps, and diagrams. . . . a photograph is viewed merely as graphic portrayal of oral testimony, and becomes admissible only when a witness has testified that it is a correct and accurate representation of the relevant facts personally observed by the witness."[121]

Can one imagine presenting the 6.5 mm fragment in court when the X-ray technicians and autopsists deny its existence? Or the "red spot" cowlick entry that the photographers and pathologists did not see? Again, one could not get this evidence into court under this standard. But, even if you could, why would you want to? As with CE 399, it would be an evidentiary debacle with the court and the jury.

How Did It Happen?

So are there any clues as to how this bizarre upward migration and this impossible object materialized? Consider the following. According to X-ray assistant Jerrol Custer, his boss, Dr. John Ebersole, made a weird request to him right after the assassination. After being called to the White House by the Secret Service, Ebersole returned to Bethesda and asked Custer to do a strange thing. Ebersole asked him:

> "I need you to do a special duty. I have skull fragments here and I've got bullet fragments. I want you to tape the bullet fragments to the skull fragments—and take X-rays of the different densities. This is for a bust of Kennedy."[122]

Consider this for a moment. Kennedy has just been killed by having his head blown apart. Now a bust is being prepared to depict the bullet fragments as they ripped his head open? Was it for J. Edgar Hoover's private enjoyment? Custer said he just looked at Ebersole in disbelief. But, he told Law, "When you're in the service, you don't question what an officer tells you to do. You do it."[123] During this videotaped interview, Law asked Custer what he was really thinking at the time. Custer said, "Well . . . I won't say it on camera."[124] Custer felt that this may have been an initial, exploratory attempt to manipulate the X-rays.[125] A few weeks later, Ebersole gained access to the National Archives and, still working on measurements for the Kennedy "bust," reviewed the skull X-rays. He actually drew lines on them. When the HSCA asked him about this, he said one of the lines was to "get a line from the highpoint of the forehead back to the occipital."[126] This, of course, would align with the original particle trail that Humes wrote about in his autopsy report. The trajectory that does not exist on the X-rays today. Recall, when David Mantik asked Ebersole about the provenance of this 6.5 mm object and why he did not see it in 1963, Ebersole promptly hung up on him. Does the above help explain why?

Understandably, I could not find this fascinating tale in Bugliosi's mammoth book.

Is there a sound reason to believe this elevated location as advocated by Fisher and Michael Baden of the HSCA? If so, it escapes me. And if Bugliosi argues, as he does, that the pathologists were competent, his defense of them is seriously compromised. Simply stated: Competent pathologists do not make mistakes about fatal bullet holes.

What Happened to Kennedy's Brain?

At the beginning of this chapter, I quoted Bugliosi going after Doug Horne on his thesis that there were actually two examinations of the Kennedy brain. And that the evidence is that there was a subterfuge and substitution for the exhibit. Bugliosi termed this whole idea as part of the realm of insanity and condemned David Mantik for even considering it.

This may be one of the worst parts of *Reclaiming History*. As we showed, Bugliosi pledged he would not leave anything out of his book concerning the critics' arguments before he neutralized them. In reading this part of his book, it looks like he did it again. For one does not have to believe every part of Horne's argument to understand that there is a very real question about the viability of the photos that contend to show Kennedy's brain.

There is a lot of evidence to show that, at both Parkland and Bethesda, many witnesses said they saw a brain that was severely damaged. FBI agent Frank O'Neill said half the brain was gone and that a significant portion was missing from the rear.[127] Mortician Tom Robinson said that a large portion of the brain was gone "in the back" and "that the portion of the brain that was missing was about the size of a closed fist."[128] Dr. Boswell, during his ARRB interview, said that about a third of the brain was missing.[129] In an interview he gave to the *Journal of the American Medical Association*, Jim Humes said that 2/3 of the right cerebrum was gone.[130] Floyd Riebe recalled for the ARRB that he saw the brain removed but there was only about half of it left.[131] FBI agent James Sibert commented that "you look at a picture, an anatomical picture of a brain and it's all there—there was nothing like that."[132] James Jenkins said that the brain was so damaged on the underside that it was hard to introduce needles for perfusion with formalin.[133]

At Dallas's Parkland Hospital Dr. Robert McClelland said that "probably a third or so, at least, of the brain tissue and some of the cerebellar tissue had been blasted out."[134] Dr. Ronald Jones said that "as the president lay on the cart with what appears to be some brain hanging out this wound with multiple pieces of skull noted next with the brain and with a tremendous amount of clot and blood."[135] Dr. Perry described a gaping wound at the rear of the skull "exposing lacerated brain." Further in his testimony before the Commission, he states "there was severe laceration of underlying brain tissue."[136] Dr. Charles Carrico described an avulsive rear skull wound in which the brain had both cerebral and cerebellar shredded and macerated tissue. And this was exhibited both in the wounds and on the hanging skull fragments.[137] Before the body left, Nurse Diana Bowron packed the head wound with gauze squares at Parkland. She later recalled that much of the brain, about a half from both sides, was gone.[138]

All the above is consistent with what we see on the Zapruder film: a terrific head explosion with matter ejecting high into the air. It is also consistent with the very first witnesses in and around the car. As we know, Jackie Kennedy turned over pieces of her husband's skull and brain to a doctor at Parkland Hospital. Motorcycle policemen Martin and Hargis recall being splattered with blood and brain.[139] As revealed by Doug Horne in Volume 4 of *Inside the ARRB*, a Secret Service agent recovered a piece of brain from the car.[140]

Here is the problem. In light of all the above testimony from a wide variety of witnesses, plus the Zapruder film, when one looks at the HSCA's artist rendition of the existing brain, it surprises, because it is pretty much an intact brain.[141] Even Earl Rose of the HSCA noted that the underside of this brain does not match the description of the head wound described by the pathologists.[142] Which becomes the first problem in the photos. For in the depositions taken for the ARRB, photographer John Stringer said he shot no basilar views of the brain, that is, from underneath.[143] So where did those views come from if Stringer did not take them? And why don't they reflect the witness testimony?

Then there is the weight of the brain. That weight is 1500 grams. This is surprising. Since the average weight of a brain for a forty to forty-nine year old male is 1350 grams. If one even allows for a period of formalin fixing afterwards, Kennedy's brain actually has *more volume than a normal brain!* Which is shocking considering that, as we have seen, it had been blasted away, went flying through the air, was left in the car, and even landed on other people in Dealey Plaza. What makes this fact even more intriguing is that according to records, the brain was not weighed the night of the autopsy at Bethesda Medical Center.[144] This is inexplicable. However, in Thornton Boswell's testimony to the ARRB, he recalled that it actually was weighed.[145] It is hard to figure which is worse: if it was weighed and the results eliminated, or if it was not weighed at all. One has to wonder, since this is so inexcusable, if this was part of the annotated record that was later destroyed.

In 1965, in a report for his military superiors, Pierre Finck wrote that the brain was weighed in at 1500 grams on November 29.[146] Finck was noted for being meticulous and taking good notes. This creates another problem because Jim Humes told the *Journal of the American Medical Association* that he turned over the autopsy exhibits to Admiral George Burkley, Kennedy's personal physician, to be stored in the National Archives. But Burkley said the brain would be interred with the body on the twenty-fifth. So what could Finck have been writing about on the 29th if the brain had already been buried at Kennedy's funeral?[147] It should be noted that if Humes is correct, the brain had to have been unsectioned. Because the time frame would not allow near enough time for the proper formalin soaking to make sure the brain could be easily sectioned for examination of bullet paths.

When one turns to the supplementary autopsy report, one sees something quite odd. This report included a separate brain examination with notations on other vital organs like the spleen and kidneys. The actual autopsy protocol is signed by all three autopsy doctors, but it is not dated.[148] The supplemental autopsy report is signed only by Humes. There is a date at the top of the first page, December 6, but it is handwritten,[149] which indicates, since the rest of the report is typed, that this date was added later. The description given in this report appears to describe much more disruption and laceration to the brain than the pictures or drawings show. The report says that when viewed from below, the disruption and lacerations are obvious. Which returns us to Dr. Earl Rose and the basilar (underneath) views that Stringer does not recall taking. Rose said the inferior side of the brain was relatively intact. Rose did not understand that, since a bullet came in low on the skull in the original report.[150] Therefore there should have been much more trauma, which Humes does describe in his supplemental report. There he talks about "disruption of the right cortex"; "longitudinal laceration of the mid-brain through the floor of the third ventricle"; a "1.5 cm tear through the left cerebral peduncle"; and "irregular superficial lacerations over the basilar aspects of the left temporal and frontal lobes."[151] This report could fit a shot coming in from low in the hairline. Does it fit a shot high in the cowlick area? And if Humes's description is accurate about all these disruptions and lacerations, why does Rose say they aren't there? Is it because the basilar photos Rose saw would fit a shot passing through high in the skull? The photos that Stringer says he did not take?

As the reader can see, once all the evidence is entered into the record, Doug Horne does not seem to inhabit a world of insanity anymore. In fact, in his discussion of the issue in the text, Bugliosi does not bring up any of this testimony about how much of the brain was missing. He does bring it up in his End Notes. He then, like magic, completely dismisses it. How? Through HSCA Chief Pathologist Michael Baden. This is now what happens. Baden says that people who say a lot of the brain is missing are wrong. How can he be so certain? Baden says that he saw the photos in the archives and instructed Ida Dox to draw the diagrams based on them. Baden assures the prosecutor, the "whole brain was still there . . . less than an *ounce or two* of his brain was actually missing from the cranial cavity."[152] (Emphasis added.) This is the guy who instructed Ida Dox to alter the blood drop on Kennedy's skull to make it look like a bullet wound, who says the FBI took pictures at the autopsy that night, and who cannot even orient the autopsy photos correctly in public.[153] And now, in defiance of fifteen witnesses and the Zapruder film, Baden says only an ounce of two of the brain was missing. And Bugliosi buys it.

Now, what happened to the brain after Humes gave it to Burkley is a mystery. But no matter when this transfer to Burkley happened, the precise date cannot be proven. And with the handwritten date on the supplementary report, no one can determine when that examination took place either, or who, besides Humes, was there. But the question avoided by Bugliosi rigorously throughout this long discussion is this: Why is there no record of any brain sectioning being scheduled or done? Or if it was done, where are the photos of it? Again, this is inexplicable. But further, why did Humes's story about when he turned over these artifacts change so much? Was he trying to make excuses for each investigation for not sectioning the brain?

In Bugliosi's over twenty pages denigrating Horne, there was one piece of Stringer's testimony that was absent. Under examination by the ARRB he wrecked Petty's excuse for not having the brain and much of Bugliosi's and Baden's argument for there being no volume from the brain missing. We have seen where Stringer said he took no basilar views of the brain, but he also said he used identification tags in his photography. There are none in the photographs.[154] Jeremy Gunn then asked him if based on those facts he would he be able to identify the photographs before him as the brain of John F. Kennedy. Stringer said, "No, I couldn't say that they were President Kennedy's. . . . All I know is, I gave everything to Jim Humes, and he gave them to Admiral Burkley."[155]

It then got worse. Stringer had identified to Gunn the types of film he used for both black and white and color pictures. The type of film used in the archived brain photos is Ansco. Stringer was genuinely puzzled when he discovered this because not only was it the wrong film, but it was used in a photographic technique called a press pack, which he did not use. This was betrayed by a series number in the pictures, something which Stringer was almost stunned to see.[156] Stringer also did not recognize the film used in the color shots of the brain.[157] And, of course, there were no photos of the brain sections.

In addition to not informing the reader about any of the above during his vicious attack on Horne, Bugliosi also does not mention Stringer's specific memory of the sectioning. Or how he took the photos. He said it was with a light box shooting down on the sections as they were cut. When asked if they were small pieces or cross sections he said, "If I remember, it was cross sections." When asked the purpose, Stringer said, "To show the damage."[158] One last thing left out by Bugliosi—when Jeremy Gunn asked Stringer if he recalled the brain looking like the photos in front of him when he shot it, he said no because in the photos in front of him, the cerebellum was intact. In the brain he saw and the photos he took of it, it was damaged and cut.[159]

Recall what Bugliosi's witness Charles Petty said to Gerry Spence about the brain not really being necessary or essential. When Spence asked why, Petty replied he had the photos and X-rays. Can one imagine if Spence had known about Stringer at that time? Petty would have been made to look silly.

One last thing about all the sound and fury about Horne and the sectioning. By not trying to get to the bottom of why or if it was ever done, the prosecutor avoids a really precarious admission. The official story has President Kennedy being hit twice by gunshot wounds. Once through the back and once through the head. This must be the only modern autopsy in the annals of medicine where, even though that happened, neither wound was dissected.

Summing up

So far, we have traced some very strange things in the JFK medical evidence. We have shown that:

1. The military limited the autopsy.
2. Arlen Specter co-opted Humes and Boswell's recollections of the bullet wounds.
3. No credible evidence exists to connect the back and neck wounds.
4. Humes destroyed the notes and the first draft of his autopsy report.
5. Specter did not interview Kennedy's personal physician who signed his death certificate.
6. The pathologists did not look at the photos or examine Kennedy's clothes before writing their report.
7. In 1966, the media, Justice Department, and Boswell conspired to lie about the location of the back wound to the public.
8. In 1967, Humes did the same.
9. In 1968, a secret panel raised the fatal head wound four inches up JFK's skull.
10. In 1977, the pathologists strongly disagreed with this new entry point.
11. Michael Baden ordered his artist to embellish the photos to make this new location more credible.
12. According to two ballistics experts, the part of the bullet located in the X-rays at this new location cannot be there.
13. John Stringer testified that he did not take the pictures of Kennedy's brain that are in the National Archives.

Let us close this chapter with another very troubling issue in the JFK autopsy. One which shows that a government agent deliberately changed a witness's testimony to make the SBT plausible. It's the kind of behavior—witness tampering in a homicide—that should be an affront to any criminal lawyer. But especially a prosecutor.

Before the creation of the ARRB very few people in the critical community had ever heard the name of Elmer Moore. And that was the way it was supposed to be. Today, scores of people know the name. And a few, including Gary Aguilar and Pat Speer, see him as one of the crucial components of the medical evidence cover-up. In fact, things were still being revealed about him as late as 2003, after the ARRB had been shut down for five years. At the Duquesne Conference of 2003, Arlen Specter revealed two things about Mr. Moore that no one had ever known before. First, this Secret Service agent who, at the time of the assassination, was stationed in San Francisco, eventually became the bodyguard to Earl Warren while he was on the Warren Commission. Why any of the Warren Commissioners would need a bodyguard is puzzling. Their work was done almost entirely in secret. So if no one knew what they were doing, how could anyone object to it? And further, object to it so strongly that they would either want to hurt or kill them? Also, no other Commissioner was detailed a personal bodyguard. The second thing Specter revealed about Moore was equally extraordinary. Earl Warren did see the autopsy photos. Specter knew this because Moore had them and wanted to show them to him also. These dual Specter revelations about Moore were stunning. But to appreciate them in full, one has to have known a little bit about Moore in advance.

It had always been a mystery as to why Dr. Malcolm Perry essentially reversed his story about President Kennedy's neck wound. On the day of the assassination, Perry was the doctor at Parkland who had performed the tracheostomy on the dying president. Therefore he would have had the closest and longest look at this neck wound. During a press conference in Dallas right after Kennedy died, Perry appeared with Dr. Kemp Clark, the professor of neurosurgery who pronounced JFK dead. On three occasions during the press conference, Perry declared that the wound in the neck was an entrance wound.[160] The day after the assassination, he said the same thing to reporters from the *Boston Globe*.[161]

These public pronouncements were made well before the creation of the Warren Commission. But when Arlen Specter studied the record, he understood how deadly they were to the creation of his two main goals: 1) the Single Bullet Theory trajectory, and 2) Oswald as the lone assassin. When Perry testified before the Commission, something had clearly happened to him. First, after testifying that the wound had edges which were not ragged but clean, he then qualified this by saying that they were neither clean cut nor were they very ragged. When asked by Specter if by the appearance of the neck wound, it could have been either an entrance or an exit, he replied, "It could have been either." Specter even got Perry to say the SBT was possible if the throat wound was an exit. Gerald Ford asked Perry if the reporting of his news conference was accurate or inaccurate. Perry replied with the latter. And Allen Dulles chimed in by saying that Perry should now issue a public correction about his November 22, 1963, remarks. Which, of course, with Perry's appearance there, now had been neutralized.[162]

It had always been a mystery as to why Perry and other Dallas doctors could have changed their original remarks and gone along with the SBT for the Warren Commission. So, like Humes with the HSCA and the upper level entry wound, Perry threw out his professional ethics for a show trial presentation. The ARRB made it possible to find out how this happened. It was not a pretty picture. And Moore was in the middle of it.

As Gary Aguilar wrote in *Probe*, after November 22, 1963, Moore began to hang around Parkland a lot. He had clearly done much work on the medical and ballistics aspects of the assassination. And by December 11, he had turned Perry around on the trajectory issue. Up until this time, the Dallas doctors had been talking freely with the press, including the *Saturday Evening Post*. They still thought the neck wound an entrance. Armed with the official autopsy report, Moore now began to turn the tide, and their minds. Perry was now saying that the neck wound was an exit, and it was exiting at a downward angle.[163] Moore evidently had good contacts in the press also. The first known media report of a transiting bullet (one that exited the throat) appeared in the *Dallas Times-Herald* on December 12, 1963, just one day after Moore got Perry to sign on to the official story.[164] So Allen Dulles got Perry to issue his Orwellian public "correction."

The revelation about Moore's massaging the doctors' testimony was first revealed to the Church Committee back in 1975. A man named Jim Gochenaur said he had met Moore while living in Seattle in 1970. Moore had told him he was the liaison between the Warren Commission and the Secret Service. He said that as a member of the Secret Service, he had to do what he was told.[165] And one of his tasks in this new Warren Commission function was getting Dr. Perry to change his story. So he admitted to pressuring Perry to alter what he had said. Moore added something quite revealing. He said he had to do this since there was no conclusive evidence at this point as to where the shots had come from. Here, Moore is essentially saying the Commission had to badger Perry to make the case against Oswald.

Moore also revealed that on the *day of the assassination* he flew from California to Washington. He then was detailed to Dallas on November 29. Once there, he immediately got into contact with the Dallas doctors.[166] What makes this timing interesting is that Nurse Audrey Bell told Harrison Livingstone that when she saw Perry the next day, on November 23, he looked tired and worn. He then told her that he had been getting calls that night from Washington.[167] This may have been Moore, but if not, Moore was surely continuing the assignment. (This also brings into serious doubt the story that Humes knew nothing about a wound in the neck until the next day.) There is also evidence that Moore and the Secret Service got their own agents to change things that they had said to FBI agents Jim Sibert and Francis O'Neill on the night of the autopsy.[168] This was a way of further discrediting the Sibert-O'Neill report and therefore neuter how it differed from the Commission's conclusions.

Gochenaur provided some private insight into Moore. Moore said he later felt badly about pressuring Perry into altering his story, but Gochenaur also added that the longer Moore talked, the scarier he got. He seemed to have to rationalize what he had done for the Commission. He did this by going on a long and violent rant about Kennedy. He said JFK was a pinko who was selling out the Free World to the communists. By the time the conversation was over, Gochenaur was actually frightened.[169]

This is the man who was now entrusted to be a bodyguard to Earl Warren. In his January 1, 1976, appearance before the Church Committee, Moore showed up with an attorney. During his interview it became clear why he had hired one. He said he understood that talking a witness out of his testimony in a criminal case constituted a felony. Then things got really interesting. Moore informed the Church Committee that after his Dallas assignment, he then met with Earl Warren and convinced him he needed Secret Service protection while on the Warren Commission. And as Specter mentioned in his Duquesne talk, Moore was in the room when Jack Ruby was questioned in Dallas. But, as this above fact shows, Moore was there for much more than "protection." He admitted to having daily talks with Warren. And as we have seen with Perry, we can imagine what those talks were like.

Pat Speer has unearthed documents that reveal the whole "protection" side of Moore's function to be a cover story. Warren wanted Moore to help "the Commission for an indefinite period to assist in its work."[170] Secret Service Chief Rowley in a similar December 8 memo wrote that Moore was assigned to "furnish any service, assistance, and cooperation the Commission considers necessary." As Gerald McKnight notes in *Breach of Trust*, after the January 22, 1964, Warren Commission meeting concerning Oswald being a possible FBI informant, J. Lee Rankin instructed his secretary to give all the excess material—tapes, notes, carbons—to Elmer Moore to be incinerated.[171] Moore was much more than a bodyguard. He was someone's mole at the highest level of the Commission. Whose mole he was is an intriguing question.

But let us return to Specter. With Moore actually showing him the autopsy photos, we know for a fact that he himself knew the Warren Commission's SBT was a lie. Just as we know that his ballet with Humes about the positioning of Kennedy's head at the time of the fatal shot was a charade. For, as even Bugliosi has to note in this aspect, Gerald Ford altered the Warren Report before it was printed. At the last minute, Ford changed the wording of the location of the back wound in the text. He raised it from the back to the neck. This, of course, makes the SBT trajectory more possible. Bugliosi notes this incident. He actually makes it into a debate about the intentions of the Commission. He says either this was a mistake, or the Commission "deliberately changed the facts to solve the high-exit-wound problem."[172] He then comes down for the innocence of the Commission. That is, this was nothing but a benign error. But Specter's belated confession about Moore creates a huge problem for this "benignity" because the autopsy photos reveal this wound to be unquestionably in the back. Moore, Warren, and Specter all saw the photo. So, unless they were blind, they had to know that what Ford did was not borne of benignity. But from malignancy.

Bugliosi says he spent twenty-one years writing and researching the 2,700 pages of *Reclaiming History*. Elmer Moore's name is not in the book.

CHAPTER SEVEN

Bugliosi vs. Garrison and Stone

"NSAM 273 does not, as Stone's audience was told, reverse NSAM 263. In fact, it specifically reaffirms Kennedy's decision to withdraw 1,000 troops by the end of 1963. . . ."

—Vincent Bugliosi, *Reclaiming History*

It is with a sadness approaching trepidation that I address the part of *Reclaiming History* that deals with the investigation of New Orleans DA Jim Garrison and Oliver Stone's film treatment of it in his 1991 movie *JFK*. But as disappointing and unrewarding as *Reclaiming History* is, this particular chapter—90 pages in the text and 128 in the End Notes—is perhaps the low point in the volume.

Garrison's Lost Files

In any serious and scholarly presentation of the Garrison inquiry today, one would have to include the fact that there have been reams of documents discovered that alter the calculus of a factual database from which to draw. This, of course, is why books like James Kirkwood's *American Grotesque* are obsolete today. The Assassination Records Review Board did a fair enough job in trying to secure the files of, and related to, the Garrison investigation. One source of new material were the files left behind by Garrison in the DA's office. These were held by the man who succeeded him, Harry Connick.

To secure and keep two sets of files—certain Grand Jury records and the file cabinets from Garrison's office—there followed a long legal struggle between Connick and the Justice Department. Connick fought the Justice Department for over a year before a federal court ordered him to turn the file cabinets over to the ARRB.[1] It turned out that once Connick had gotten into office, he went about systematically incinerating the court records and investigative files of his predecessor on the Clay Shaw case.[2] The ARRB was lucky to manage to eventually secure these five file cabinets after a bruising court battle with Connick. For there was material in those particular file cabinets on interesting suspects and witnesses like Kerry Thornley, Clyde Johnson, Emilio Santana, and Bernardo De Torres.[3] As we will see, Vincent Bugliosi ignores virtually all of it.

Bugliosi and Connick

This background material is important because Bugliosi actually uses Connick as a witness against Garrison. But the prosecutor does not tell the reader about Connick's role in the attempted destruction of the Clay Shaw files. What makes it worse is that it's the same old tired boilerplate that has been proven to be completely and utterly false. Connick tells Bugliosi that even before Garrison charged Clay Shaw, Garrison was viewed by the legal community as someone who could not make charges stick in cases he brought.[4] Which is ridiculous. The truth is just about the opposite. Garrison tried many cases as an assistant DA, and rose to be First Assistant under Malcolm O'Hara. Once he became DA, Garrison significantly reversed the losing record of his predecessor, Richard Dowling.[5] In 1995, I spoke to John Volz, the late U.S. Attorney in New Orleans who had served as first assistant to Garrison, and had stayed for a few months in Connick's office after he defeated Garrison in 1973. I asked Volz how he would compare the two DAs. He smiled at me and said, "There is no comparison at all. Connick couldn't convict someone if the guy's name was on the bullet."

But it wasn't just that Connick was a poor prosecutor. Leon Cannizzaro, the man who succeeded Connick, called Connick's failure to turn over blood evidence in a robbery case which resulted in a death penalty, "the unethical actions of a rogue prosecutor."[6] In fact, Connick's office was so bad, and his office so corrupt that even the Supreme Court criticized it. Justice Ruth Bader Ginsburg wrote that Connick deliberately let inexperienced prosecutors with virtually no training try high-stakes cases. The aim would be to defy the 1963 *Brady v Maryland* decision which required the state to turn over exculpatory evidence to the defense. In her searing opinion on a Connick case that went to the Supreme Court, she cited the DA's own words, namely that he had stopped reading law books when he took office in 1974.[7] In the famous John Thompson case, the defendant was weeks away from being executed in 1999, when an investigator found a blood report from the crime scene which did not match Thompson's blood. A former prosecutor then revealed that the man who tried the case, Gerry Deegan, confessed to him while dying that he intentionally hid the report in 1985 to secure a conviction.[8] Even when this was revealed, Connick retried Thompson. The jury found him not guilty in thirty-five minutes.

And it's not just one successor to Connick who criticizes his unethical practices. Eddie Jordan, who succeeded Connick in office, called the DA's office conduct in another case "inexcusable."[9] Take another overturned capital case, the 1995 Juan Smith case. Cannizzaro tried to bring the case to court again. The Supreme Court could not understand why he even bothered to defend Connick's practice of not giving the defense the early statements of a key eyewitness.[10]

In addition to not revealing any of this about his witness, Bugliosi writes that Connick told him that Oliver Stone *never asked* about these Garrison files left in his office when the famous director met with him before he started filming his 1991 movie *JFK*.[11] Question: How could Stone know about them without the HSCA document, which had not yet been declassified? But what Bugliosi does not say is that Connick has changed his story on this point. Back in 1995, Connick told propagandist Gerald Posner that he told Stone *he had the files*, and the director expressed no interest in seeing them.[12] When Stone saw this, he accused Connick of lying. He replied to Posner that "I never had anything like the conversation with Harry Connick Sr. that is described in your article. And he never said anything remotely like the words he is quoted as using."[13] It's pretty easy to measure who is lying here. Because as I note in my previous book, in an interview with Connick about these files at least three years after he talked to Stone, Connick was not aware he had them.[14] It was my interview that alerted him to the fact he did. So how could he have told Stone about them if he didn't know they were there? The famous prosecutor couldn't figure that out?

In spite of Connick, the ARRB has now made it possible to take a whole new look at Garrison. As I did in the second edition of *Destiny Betrayed*. But even though the ARRB has contributed mightily, no one will ever be able to truly evaluate the case Garrison could have mounted. And this is an issue that any responsible writer must address. Because as has been shown, Garrison's office was studded with double agents quite early, for example, Bill Gurvich and Gordon Novel.[15] Therefore, his records were being ransacked from the beginning. What makes this problem easy to explain is that one of the men in charge of those files was a likely infiltrator, namely Tom Bethell. Garrison mentions this problem in the documentary film about him called *The Jim Garrison Tapes* (1992). He describes an investigator who came into his office with a briefcase that got larger all the time. Garrison understood after the fact—as he usually did—that he needed the bigger case to accommodate the files he was pilfering. So while the investigation was ongoing, Garrison was losing valuable information.

But after Shaw's trial, more information was lost. Connick admitted that he did destroy some files. We also know that Garrison himself lost some of these materials. He mentioned it in a letter he wrote to Zachary Sklar, who was editing his book *On the Trail of the Assassins* at the time. He wrote he had stored some files in a friend's garage, but that somehow the cabinets were stolen from the place. I also know from the late photography expert Richard Sprague that certain files that Garrison had given to Bud Fensterwald at the Assassination Archives Research Center in Washington also disappeared. Sprague specifically mentioned files on the mysterious Fred Lee Crisman. Obviously, any person interested in doing a genuine evaluation of Garrison would have to conclude that such a thing is not really possible today because of these lost materials. I would estimate that what we have today is probably less than half of the records of the actual Garrison inquiry.

Bugliosi's Sources

As I said above, any serious and scholarly treatment of Garrison today would have to incorporate all, or most, of the above facts. That is, the new documents, plus an acknowledgement of what was lost. If you include almost none of it, then you can easily be accused of having an agenda. So let us do an accounting. Bugliosi lists 297 footnotes to this 90-page text chapter. But this is not entirely accurate since a lot of the references have multiple citations. So the real number is probably closer to 360–370. Now, excluding things like transcripts of the Shaw trial and the preliminary hearing—which could have been attained by Bugliosi on his own—and footnotes that were multisourced, I counted less than twenty references to the new ARRB documents. Which comes to less than 10 percent of the information in the chapter. In fact, Bugliosi's citations to the works of people like Patricia Lambert, James Kirkwood, Edward Epstein, and Milton Brener come to double the new document count. This tells us a great deal of course. In fact, it's actually embarrassing to compare this ratio of new material with Bill Davy's fine book on the Garrison inquiry, *Let Justice Be Done*. Davy has more references to the new documents in his first section—focused only on David Ferrie—than Bugliosi has in this whole banal and tedious chapter. But that's not the clincher. The clincher is this: Bugliosi's chapter is ninety pages long; Davy's is eight. But you will learn more about Ferrie, Oswald, and New Orleans in those eight pages than you will in all of *Reclaiming History*.

One of the things that Bugliosi tries to do is actually defend the late James Phelan. Which is hard to do since the declassified files of the ARRB show that Phelan was a government agent whom they could rely upon to write scripted stories.[16] I also showed that during the Clay Shaw trial, Phelan had a house rental to which he invited all the journalists in town to cover the trial. They would assemble each night and he would pass out refreshments as he outlined their next day stories. On the day the Zapruder film was shown, he knew he had a problem. But, miraculously, he took out a piece of chalk, walked over to his portable blackboard, and outlined the vagaries of the so-called jet effect. This was supposed to explain why Kennedy's body rocketed backward *toward* the shooter.[17]

Now, if Bugliosi thinks that Phelan rented the house on his own, provided the refreshments out of his own pocket, and thought up the "jet effect" himself, then perhaps he believes in the Easter Bunny also. Phelan was not just in New Orleans to cover up Kennedy's assassination as an individual reporter. He was there to cover it up for the national media. And through them, the entire American public. This is why many of the more interesting aspects of the Shaw trial never had any impact. For example, the startling testimony of pathologist Pierre Finck. And from what we know—and what Bugliosi ignores—Phelan did this for the FBI or with the help of his longtime editor and benefactor Bob Loomis.[18] For Bugliosi to tap dance around this issue of journalists as undisclosed agents is inexplicable. Did he think what Judy Miller did at the *New York Times* to scare the public into the Iraq War was OK?

Shaw was a Liberal, Oswald didn't Know Ferrie

If Bugliosi is willing to use witnesses like Connick and if he is going to whitewash Phelan, then we already know what this chapter is going to be like. As with the discredited and obsolete James Kirkwood (who Bugliosi actually calls Kirkland at one point), we know he is out to perform a hatchet job on Garrison. It doesn't take long to discern this. As we have seen, Bugliosi trots out—via Connick—the same old tired and false arguments about Garrison being an irresponsible and incompetent lawyer and DA. But that is only half of it. Whenever someone does something like that, the other shoe has to drop. Which is the elevation into sainthood of Clay Shaw. Unbelievably, *Reclaiming History* actually calls Shaw a political liberal.[19] This deception was started by Shaw himself in order to camouflage any motive he could have for participating in a conspiracy to kill President Kennedy.[20] It has been exposed as a deception for decades. Incredibly, Bugliosi recycles it as if it's new.[21]

Since Bugliosi makes a silly attempt at whitewashing Shaw's true politics and deep ties into the CIA, it's natural that he also attempts to follow in Lambert's fatuous steps with David Ferrie and Oswald. He actually tries to say that they didn't know each other.[22] I'm not kidding. He actually tries to wish away the photo that surfaced in the nineties of Oswald with Ferrie at a Civil Air Patrol (CAP) picnic.[23] He then writes something that is really kind of shocking. He tries to imply—through some tricky wording—that prior to the discovery of this photo, there had only been one witness who placed Oswald together with Ferrie in the Civil Air Patrol, namely Ed Voebel.[24]

To write something like that in 2007 takes chutzpah galore. Anthony Summers wrote a good book called *Conspiracy* on the JFK case in 1980. That is way before the photo surfaced and before the ARRB started declassifying the secret files. Summers wrote that six witnesses testified that Oswald and Ferrie were in the CAP together.[25] And all Bugliosi had to do was interview the HSCA investigators in New Orleans—L. J. Delsa or Bob Buras—and he would have found out that the total was even more than that. This inexplicable failure may explain his reluctance to use the files of Jim Garrison. Because back in 1967 Garrison had seven witnesses who attested to this fact.[26]

Bugliosi also tries to use the Gerald Posner canard about Ferrie being expelled from the CAP squadron. Therefore there might be some question about whether or not Oswald was actually in Ferrie's squadron, or if Ferrie was just hanging around his old squad while the photo was taken.[27] This particular technique reminds one of Posner's cheap trick in *Case Closed* in not telling the reader that Oswald's voting registration attempt in Clinton, Louisiana, actually took place in two cities—Clinton and Jackson—and not just one. For, as Peter Vea discovered many years ago, Ferrie was expelled from the CAP squadron at Lakefront Airport, and then started his own nonchartered squadron at Moisant Airport. This fact is established in an FAA report on Ferrie from 1963.[28] The documentary record indicates that Oswald first met Ferrie at Lakefront for some classes and then actually joined the CAP at Ferrie's breakaway Moisant squadron in 1955.

The best accumulation of testimony establishing this fact is by John Armstrong in his interesting Oswald biography called *Harvey and Lee*. He spends four pages quoting the testimony of the witnesses who state that Oswald was in Ferrie's CAP squad.[29] This includes the student who first got Oswald interested in joining the CAP, Fred O'Sullivan. O'Sullivan says that Ferrie left the Lakefront squad and started his own squad at Moisant. Another witness Armstrong quotes is the man who took the picnic photo of Ferrie with Oswald, Chuck Francis. (Armstrong quotes Francis as saying he actually testified about this to the FBI, along with the fact that he had photographed the two together.) Another CAP witness is Jerry Paradis who was interviewed back in 1978 by the HSCA. Paradis stated, "I specifically remember Oswald. I can remember him clearly, and Ferrie was heading the unit then. I'm not saying that they may have been there together. I'm saying it was a certainty."[30]

Need more? In 1964, Ferrie himself told Thomas Clark, a friend who worked at his filling station, that he was Oswald's instructor in the CAP.[31] But the capper in all this is the following. Almost everyone knows that Ferrie was hectically looking for his library card in the wake of the assassination. He visited Oswald's landlady, Jessie Garner, to see if Oswald had left it behind.[32] He even visited a neighbor of Oswald's, Doris Eames, to inquire whose card Oswald was using at the library that summer.[33] Clearly, Ferrie was frantic about preventing any linkage between himself and Oswald after the assassination. (Which, in a case that was not so politically charged, Bugliosi would use his favorite prosecutor's term: Ferrie was exhibiting "consciousness of guilt.")

But Ferrie was not just trying to prevent a linkage between the two through his library card—which he had apparently let Oswald borrow that summer. He was also trying to stop anything from happening then that happened in the nineties, that is, the exposure of a CAP photo of him and Oswald. How do we know this? Because Ferrie called a former CAP student of his named Roy McCoy right after the murder of Kennedy. McCoy wasn't home at the time, so Ferrie talked to his wife. He asked her about any photos that Roy might have from his Civil Air Patrol days when Ferrie was in charge of their squadron. This FBI report, dated November 11, 1963, then includes the following statement: "Ferrie also asked Mrs. McCoy whether the name of Oswald was familiar to her." Later, Roy McCoy naturally concluded that Ferrie was trying to find any photos of Oswald's CAP days to prevent any association between him and the instructor.[34]

What Bugliosi tries to do here inevitably sounds like Posner in his book *Case Closed* writing the following: "There is no credible evidence that Oswald knew . . . David Ferrie" (page 148 of the hardcover edition). This is utterly and completely false and Ferrie himself knew it. Or else he would not have been trying to conceal it.

Why does Bugliosi do this? Because he understands that the CAP episode opens up a real Pandora's Box with Oswald. Because Ferrie had a genuine liking for and influence over his cadets. As the HSCA investigators discovered, one of Ferrie's functions as a CAP instructor was to encourage and recruit young men into the Marines. And as Bill Davy interestingly points out, during Oswald's time in the CAP, his mother Marguerite "recalled being visited by a man in uniform who she presumed was a Marine Corps recruiter. Her visitor encouraged her to allow her son Lee to quit school and join the Marines."[35] Since Oswald was underage at the time, this may have been a friend of Ferrie's impersonating as a recruiter. But yet, Oswald did try and join the Marines later, even though he was underage. He failed. But it is right after this that he does two rather contrary things. He starts to assiduously study his brother's Marine Corps manual, and he also starts talking to his pals Palmer McBride and William Wulf about Marxism. Hmm. Yet Ferrie was a clear and militant right-winger. Yet we must recall, as another CAP cadet said, Ferrie talked about getting orders from military intelligence.[36]

Clearly, if one presents the totality of the evidence, it would indicate that Oswald's friendship with Ferrie had a powerful, perhaps crucial, effect on his life. It very likely inspired his joining the Marines and later becoming an intelligence operative. Which is one reason why Posner, and now Bugliosi, try to make it disappear. They need to maintain the Warren Commission mythology of Oswald as the disaffected Commie. Sorry Mr. Prosecutor. The sum total of the evidence indicates the opposite.

Keeping Oswald Out of 544 Camp Street

Again, like Gerald Posner, Bugliosi is intent on keeping Oswald out of Guy Banister's office at 544 Camp Street.[37] He uses information from the bizarre 1993 PBS *Frontline* Special on Oswald. Namely, that contrary to what everyone has ever written or said, the addresses 544 Camp Street and 531 Lafayette Street did not lead to the same offices (i.e. Guy Banister's office). Bugliosi writes that the Camp Street entrance only went to the second floor. You had to go into the other address to get to Banister's office.[38]

This was an issue begun by a very circumspect witness, Sam Newman, during the HSCA hearings. Newman, the owner of the building, had always been very evasive about who he rented to and when, and if he knew Oswald was there.[39] The HSCA staffers did not believe him when he said he did not know Oswald was there, and there is testimony that does impeach him.[40] He drew a diagram of the building which said the two entryways did not actually lead to the same place. Gus Russo then got a guest on his 1993 PBS *Frontline* program, "Who was Lee Harvey Oswald?" to say the same.

But then how did Bill Turner do just that back in 1967 while on assignment for *Ramparts* magazine? Years ago, Turner told me firsthand about his experience of entering both addresses and walking up the stairs to the same small coven of offices. (Bugliosi knows Turner well. He could have called him and asked him about this since it figures in his book *Deadly Secrets*.) Jim Garrison made the very same discovery, which he describes in his book *On the Trail of the Assassins*.[41] He writes the following: "So both entrances—544 Camp and 531 Lafayette—led to the same place." Further, Turner told me that he and Garrison discussed this exact point when they met. Did both investigators have the wrong address? When the news of Garrison's investigation broke worldwide, scores of reporters flew into town to talk to the DA and other witnesses and suspects. Many of them were hostile to Garrison from the start. And I have mentioned two of them: James Phelan and Hugh Aynsworth. If what Gus Russo and Bugliosi are saying were true, wouldn't one of these anti-Garrison reporters have easily found out about it and written about it back in 1967? Recall this too: both Phelan and Aynseworth were tied into the FBI. Hoover despised what Garrison was doing. Wouldn't the Director have gotten the word to them if this were so?

No one in the other office at 544 Camp Street recalled the presence of Oswald or had him on their roster of members. (For example, there was a union office at the building.) Yet there are a number of witnesses who can attest to a relationship between Oswald and Banister. And many of them saw Oswald at 544 Camp Street. In the second edition of *Destiny Betrayed* I list these witnesses and also people who corroborate talking to them about seeing Oswald there. It comes to a total of thirteen. And it is topped off by two INS agents named Wendell Roache and Ron Smith. They testified to the Church Committee that they tracked illegal Cuban exiles into the Unites States. They noticed Ferrie since he was with them so often. They tracked Ferrie to 544 Camp Street. But they also saw Oswald there in the summer of 1963. Corroborating Banister's secretary Delphine Roberts, they said he had his own office there,[42] which further undermines Newman. In fact, Banister also admitted this. When Oswald was arrested in August 1963, he had some flyers with the 544 Camp Street address on it. Since his old employer, the FBI, interviewed him while he was in jail, Banister heard about this and snarled, "How is it going to look for him to have the same address as me!"[43] The other question of course is: Why would Oswald stamp the address on it if he was *not* there?

This whole issue about the layout of the building cannot be settled since the structure was razed in 1973. But as the reader can see, the point is used by the prosecutor as a diversion. For there is no doubt today that Oswald was there. And this then becomes a serious question for the prosecutor to explain. For if Oswald was really a communist, why would he be associated with both Ferrie and Banister? But what makes it all worse for Bugliosi is something I could not find in his book. The CIA had started an anti-Fair Play for Cuba Committee campaign back in 1961. Among other things, they were infiltrating the FPCC with double agents in order to try and discredit the group. The two men running that program were David Phillips and Jim McCord.[44] Therefore, Oswald was a prop in a playlet designed by those two men and stage managed by Banister. Which undermines to great effect Bugliosi's obsolete effort to maintain the façade of Oswald the communist.

Denying Shaw was Bertrand

In his book, Garrison discusses four witnesses who admitted to the fact that Shaw used the alias of Bertand.[45] And he would have found more if he had not shut down so many places in the French Quarter during his crackdown on the B girl drinking vice. Joan Mellen found two more people—Rickey Planche and Barbara Bennett—who would have attested to this but resented what Garrison had done in his campaign against the clip joints.[46] Of course, Bugliosi takes the Posnerian route and says throughout that Shaw did not use this alias,[47] but this is more nonsense. Today, with all the declassified files we have, it is clear that what Bugliosi is saying is, in his favorite pejorative, simply moonshine. Because today, it's not just sources dug up by Garrison, but also the FBI. The FBI also knew Shaw used this name in the homosexual underworld of the time. Lawrence Schiller, longtime FBI informant, had done his own investigation and told the LA FBI office he found five sources in that milieu who told him that Shaw was known by other names including Bertrand.[48] But even before that, the FBI had developed two sources independently who said Shaw used the alias of Bertrand.[49] Today, when one combines all these sources, the number is well into the double digits.[50] This is why Dick Billings wrote in some of his early notes for *Life*, "Evidence that Shaw is actually Bertrand is popping up everywhere."[51] And now we even have Dean Andrews, the man who started the whole Clay Bertrand chase, on the record as admitting to Harold Weisberg that Shaw was Bertrand.[52]

As the declassified files reveal, even outside of Banister's office, Shaw/Bertrand and Ferrie were acquainted. One of the most interesting group of ARRB released files were those on Freeport Sulphur (now named Freeport McMoRan). Based on these files, Lisa Pease did an absolutely scintillating two-part essay in *Probe*.[53] It revealed the fact that Banister knew about a business venture which involved shipping nickel ore from Cuba to a Canadian front company. Ferrie flew an official of Freeport along with Shaw on an exploratory trip to organize the venture.[54] Garrison had not just a file on this but at least two witnesses.[55] Gaeton Fonzi was also interested in this interesting angle, and he actually connected the enterprise to David Phillips.[56] One can tell how potent this essay is by observing the fact that the name Freeport Sulphur is not in Bugliosi's index. In addition to this, there are at least three other witnesses in Garrison's files who connected Shaw with Ferrie: L. P. Davies Jr., Charles Krop, and Betty Rubio.[57] And guess what? None of them are in Bugliosi's book.

As the reader can see, in spite of Bugliosi's persistent denials, we have clearly connected Ferrie, Oswald, Banister, and Shaw. And beyond that, several authors have shown how they all connect to the CIA. For instance, Ferrie himself admitted he was involved in Operation Mongoose. And he trained Bay of Pigs participants at a camp supervised by David Phillips.[58] There is no doubt that Banister was involved with the Bay of Pigs operation and Mongoose.[59] Finally, on the outside of their activities, lurk CIA mid-level managers like Howard Hunt—who helped establish Sergio Arcacha-Smith's Cuban Revolutionary Council—and David Phillips. Arcacha-Smith was also seen at 544 Camp Street. To establish all of these relationships and to place them in a network is anathema for *Reclaiming History*, of course, because now one can actually begin to define how a conspiracy could actually work. To top it off, CIA Counter-Intelligence Chief James Angleton prepared a memorandum attempting to supply Howard Hunt with a cover story for him being in Dallas on the day of the assassination.[60] Further, before he died, a weeping Phillips admitted to his brother that he was also in Dallas that day.[61]

In light of all the above, it's clear why Bugliosi is in full denial overdrive. Because by persons, actions, and locations, that is, from New Orleans to Mexico City to Dallas, you can now piece together the outline of a conspiracy to kill President Kennedy.

Oswald in Clinton and Jackson

As time has gone on, the Clinton-Jackson incident has gained both more credibility and more importance in studies of the Kennedy assassination. That refers to the famous sighting of Clay Shaw, David Ferrie, and Oswald in late summer of 1963 in two small towns in sparsely populated East Feliciana Parish, approximately ninety minutes north of New Orleans. As was the case with many JFK assassination occurrences, Jim Garrison was the first official to seriously investigate this intriguing affair. Since it shows Oswald in close proximity with two people he is not supposed to know—and who would blow his Marxist cover—the Warren Commission never mentioned it. The FBI knew about it through witness Reeves Morgan.[62] As we shall see, the Bureau acted on it, but concealed what they did. Which is more poison for Bugliosi since, as we will soon see, he is actually going to vouch for J. Edgar Hoover's investigation of JFK's murder.

Today, there are at least four good renditions of this important incident. One by Jim Garrison in his book *On the Trail of the Assassins*; one by William Davy in his fine book, *Let Justice be Done*; one by Joan Mellen in *A Farewell to Justice*; and one by me in the second edition of *Destiny Betrayed*.

I will briefly summarize the facts as they can be adduced today with the help of the declassified files of the ARRB. Oswald appeared first in the town of Jackson, which is about ten miles west of Clinton. He walked into the barbershop of Edwin McGehee and started talking to him about finding a job. McGehee thought the best place for him would be the local state hospital, which Oswald apparently did not know was a psychiatric hospital. He also referred him to two people who could help him: state representative Reeves Morgan and local voter registrar Henry Palmer. Oswald, probably that evening, visited the home of Morgan who lived in Clinton. Oswald asked him about getting a job at the hospital as an electrician. Morgan said he could not put him ahead of his own constituents. He advised him that it would help if he took the Civil Service exam or was registered to vote. Oswald was observed at the Morgan home by both his daughter Mary, who was inside the house, and his son Van, who was playing outside on the front lawn. Van recalled that the driver of the black Cadillac waiting for Oswald had a shock of white hair.

The next day, a voter registration drive was taking place in Clinton. Since this was 1963, it was an emotionally charged situation as there were strong elements in the parish of the White Citizens Council, and even worse, the Klan. But the voter registration group, the Congress of Racial Equality (CORE), had set up a drive to register African American voters. A black Cadillac drove into the midst of this campaign. Since the black registrants were accustomed to the FBI monitoring their efforts, they paid special attention to the auto. Corrie Collins, the chapter leader, identified the three people as Clay Shaw, David Ferrie, and Lee Harvey Oswald. William Dunn, another CORE volunteer, corroborated Collins. Registrar Palmer walked outside his office and saw Oswald immediately, since he was the only white man in line. Several witnesses—including Charlotte Greenup, James Bell, Robert Thomas, Eddie Spears, and Gloria Wilson—vividly recalled the car. Henry Clark stated in an affidavit that he saw a well-dressed man in a suit outside the car who was well over six feet tall and resembled an actor (Garrison thought this to be Jeff Chandler). He also saw a man with unusual hair using a pay phone. He swore that the first was Shaw—who did resemble Chandler—and the second was Ferrie.

With all the teeming interest about the car, Palmer asked local Sheriff John Manchester to approach the auto and try and get an identification. Manchester did so. He approached the tall man in the suit. The man said he was with the International Trade Mart in New Orleans. Manchester requested his driver's license and asked him if he had anything to do with the voter drive. The man said no. Manchester asked for his name and the man said it was Clay Shaw. Manchester looked at his license and the name matched. Manchester reported back to Palmer that the man was with the ITM. When Oswald was in line to register, Palmer asked him for an ID. Oswald gave him some separation papers from the Marines. When asked for local references, Oswald named two doctors—Pierson and Silva. When the HSCA subpoenaed the records of the hospital, incredibly, both names were on the list of doctors employed at the time. (How Oswald knew this is an interesting mystery, which has never been solved.) Palmer would also later identify the trio as Oswald, Shaw, and Ferrie.

Probably the next day, Oswald appeared at the hospital. The receptionist, Bobbie Dedon, directed him to the personnel office. He filled out an application for secretary Maxine Kemp, which another person, Aline Woodside, recalled seeing. [63]

Jim Garrison first investigated this incident in 1967. It was re-investigated by the HSCA, which did not do as good a job as it should have done. There has been a documentary film made on the subject called *Rough Side of the Mountain*. Bill Davy, Peter Vea, and I have been to the scene twice to talk to the surviving witnesses. Joan Mellen did her own investigation for her book. And today, the ARRB has declassified and collected the surviving statements and records of witnesses from the two official investigations. There was even a picture taken of the car parked in Clinton with the occupants inside.[64] It is quite an impressive amount of material. Today, no objective observer can deny the event occurred.

Bugliosi is not an objective observer. He is a Holy Warrior fighting the infidels besieging the Temple of the Warren Commission. So he spends twelve pages going after everyone, and I mean everyone, involved.[65] To read those twelve pages is to see a lawyer using every trick in the book—and then some—to get rid of what attorneys call "bad facts." That is, things that hurt his case. And although Bugliosi wants to separate *Reclaiming History* from *Case Closed,* there are very few places in the book where he resembles Gerald Posner more than he does here.

For instance, he actually tries to use Marina Oswald as a witness against Oswald being on the scene.[66] This is because in one of his early statements, McGehee described a car different than the Cadillac in front of his shop. Based on this, if the reader can believe it, Bugliosi asked Marina if she had been in Clinton or Jackson. And he actually uses her denial as evidence against the event happening! First of all, McGehee's shop was located in Jackson not Clinton, and this is the only time this other car is mentioned. Further, McGehee testified that he never actually saw Oswald exit or enter the car he drove up in. This other car had a bassinet in it. Garrison later determined that there was a laundromat next door and that was what this car was there for. Bugliosi must be cognizant of this if he read Bill Davy's book, which he says he did. Because it's all there in black and white, on page 299.

Then follows a puzzling passage, which was hard to decipher, except to say that Bugliosi may be capitalizing on the simmering racial politics of the area for an argumentative point. For example, he uses a local rightwing lawyer, Richard Kilbourne, to cast doubt on the witnesses and the event ever happening.[67] But most informed commentators know that Banister had contacts with the white legal establishment in the area and also the segregationist element there. Who, of course, had no love for JFK. Bugliosi leaves this fact out.[68] Bugliosi even quotes a letter from Garrison's office acknowledging the fact that the black witnesses are afraid to testify because of those elements, so they will have to win their trust. This is why some of the African American witnesses were hesitant at first to identify any of the trio. Bugliosi then uses this against Garrison and those witnesses by casting aspersions on the phrase "win their trust."[69]

And now Bugliosi goes absolutely Posnerian. He says that Garrison used a faked composite photograph to "revive" the testimony of the Clinton witnesses.[70] We are now in Posnerland for sure because this is what Posner did to try and discredit the famous CAP picnic photo of Oswald and Ferrie. He said this would be just like Garrison since he had forged two photos previously. Big problem for Posner: He had no evidence for this. Now what is Bugliosi's evidence for this photo being forged? Does he present technical analysis? No. Does a credible witness back this story up? No. Does the author even show us the picture to point out faults and proof of forgery? No. Here is the sum total of his case: the proof the photo was fake was that Garrison didn't use it at Shaw's trial! As if there could be no other reason for Garrison not doing that.

Why Bugliosi was stooping to Posnerian depths was truly befuddling for me because I knew the story behind this picture years ago and it was hard to believe the prosecutor did not, since his colleague Patricia Lambert wrote about the photo. After thinking it over, I believe I've hit upon the reason why Bugliosi now became Posner. It's because he wants to discredit the fact that there actually *was such a photo taken at the time*. Since that goes a long way in proving the event happened—and lawyer Bugliosi does not want to admit that "bad fact." So what does he do to negate that evidentiary impact? He first describes the photo incorrectly and then misrepresents the reason it was not used. He says that the photo depicted Shaw and Oswald in the front seat, but Garrison's investigator—who actually had the photo—did not describe it that way. Anne Dischler described the picture as actually looking like *Ferrie* and Oswald were in front. I believe Bugliosi is incorrect because the clear majority of witnesses described *Shaw* in front. Bugliosi switches Shaw with Ferrie so he can say Garrison used the picture to "revive" their testimony. Which he could not do with Ferrie in front.

What he doesn't say is this: The car was parked for hours in Clinton and Shaw got up and walked around for a while. Ferrie used a pay phone. And that's when Ferrie probably slipped in front and that's when the picture was snapped. The actual reason the photo was not used at trial is because it was taken at a distance and at a bad angle. Therefore the identifications were not probative. Garrison tried to have the photo enlarged but it lost too much resolution.[71]

Bugliosi also says that Garrison removed two state investigators from the Clinton investigation: Anne Dischler and Francis Fruge.[72] Wrong again. By all accounts, Garrison wanted to keep them both. They were turning up a lot of good evidence, which the DA wanted to expand upon. The state police removed them from his staff. This was when *Life* magazine was pressuring Gov. John McKeithen to turn on Garrison.[73] Bugliosi then uses Lambert's long interview with Dischler to try and discredit both her and witness Corrie Collins. Dischler was later shocked at what Lambert did with her notebooks and their interview and issued a statement saying that Lambert had twisted around important facts in order to design her own scenario which was not the truth about what happened in Clinton.[74] What was the Lambertian scenario? The idea was to get Oswald out of Clinton and to substitute a worker at the hospital named Winslow Foster for him. There is no support for this in the record.

Bugliosi also tries to say that if the event would have happened, then why didn't the witnesses talk about it themselves, or report it, or offer it to the media? When I read this, I dropped my eyelids and shook my head. This proved that in twenty-one years Bugliosi never went to the scene. Because the witnesses did talk to each other about what they saw. All he had to do was interview them. Which he did not. Or their kids. Which he did not. Because they told their children about it. And then their children talked to each other about it. I realized this the first time I visited Jackson. I tried to talk to Ed McGehee, but he was too sick to come out of the house. His daughter was visiting him and she knew all the details of Oswald's appearance at his barbershop and his traversing the area. We drove a few blocks around town—a few blocks is all there is—and stopped to get a bite to eat. Because I was there, she struck up a conversation with the son of another witness to the incident who just happened to be there. And he knew all about it also. Almost everyone in both towns is aware of the so-called Oswald visit. But if you don't go there, you can say otherwise.

As to his question about offering it to the media, well, I have a question in reply: What media? Jackson has about four thousand people in it. Clinton about two thousand. The entire area of Clinton is 2.8 square miles. At the time, the entire parish contained less than 20,000 people. That doesn't make for a real big media hub, Mr. Prosecutor. Not a real big echo chamber—maybe a few hundred yards or so. And you won't make a lot of big advertising dollars with a population base like that either. Again, only someone who has never been there could write these things.

Bugliosi states that Reeves Morgan testified that he had alerted the FBI to Oswald's presence in Clinton after the assassination. He then writes that the FBI says they have no record of this. Bugliosi finds this denial credible. It turns out that the FBI did get this call, and Elmer Litchfield of the Baton Rouge office later admitted this.[75] Further, Morgan's call very likely caused a visit by an FBI agent to the psychiatric hospital. For employee Merryl Hudson recalls that a few days after the assassination an FBI agent appeared and visited the personnel office there. The agent flashed a photo of Oswald and said, "He is supposed to have turned in an application."[76] Again, if you never leave your home in Pasadena, how do you find out these things? It can only be done in a field investigation, where one link leads to another.

Finally, as he often does, Bugliosi asks for the reasoning behind it all. Why would Oswald be trying to get a job in the area? That wasn't the point. Recall, Banister had some contacts in East Feliciana. Shaw and Ferrie probably sold Oswald on the idea of going up there as an extension of what he had just done with the FPCC. As Philip Melanson postulated many years ago in *Spy Saga*, the idea was to smear CORE with a communist. But unknown to Oswald, the real and underlying agenda was to get Oswald's application into the hospital. Which, as revealed in his conversation with McGehee, Oswald did not know was a mental hospital. As Garrison came to believe, it would have been easy for a contact in the hospital to change the file over from an employee to a patient file. And come the assassination, this would clinch the image of Oswald as not just a Commie, but also a demented Commie. Two things altered the plan. First, it was unnecessary because the media bought the Commie angle so readily all by its lonesome. Second, Shaw and Ferrie did not expect the huge turnout for the CORE drive. Since it was so big Oswald waited in line for hours. Consequently, too many people got too long a look at the pair of accessories.

To say, as Bugliosi does, that it did not happen is just not supportable today. There is the picture, and then there is the application form that three, perhaps four people saw. I say "perhaps four" because something Bugliosi does not tell you is that in addition to witnesses Dedon, Kemp, and Woodside, Bob Buras of the HSCA heard of another person who saw the application. His name was Dale Booty. But when Buras tracked him down, Booty wouldn't talk. He said, "I prefer not to get involved."[77] Probably because the application ended up disappearing. And that was probably as a result of Morgan's call.

But Booty's reluctance could also have been because of what happened to some other witnesses in the area. Joseph Cooper was a local policeman who Garrison was going to call before the Grand Jury. Right before he was to be called, he was in a serious accident. While he was injured, the State Police tried to steal his files.[78] As Jim Olivier discussed at a talk at JFK Lancer in 2003, Gloria Wilson was also a witness. She also identified Oswald, but she told her boyfriend that she had seen him there before. (If she did it may have been through the operation of nearby Marydale farms, apparently a Cuban exile training ground owned by Shaw's partner at the ITM, Lloyd Cobb.) Gloria Wilson died in 1964. It happened so fast, and she was so young—only nineteen—that friends thought she had been poisoned. When Garrison's investigators found out about this, they also found out she had kept a diary at her place of work. The diary was stolen.[79] In July 1968, witness Andrew Dunn, while being held in a Clinton jail on charges of public intoxication, was found hanged.[80]

Others, like lawyer Billy Kline, were intimidated by the aforementioned rightwing forces in town like fellow attorney Richard Van Buskirk, who had been associated with Banister.[81] There was also Gladys Palmer, a potentially very important witness, who was talked to by local rightwing heavies Jack Rogers and Ned Touchstone.[82] She then forgot all about seeing Oswald. There were even others who, as late as the HSCA, were not located. In 1977, Robert Blakey got a lead from local investigator Ronald Johnston. He said he knew two witnesses who saw Shaw and Oswald together in the Clinton courthouse. The witnesses maintained that the pair then proceeded on to the hospital. Blakey didn't act on this for almost a year. The next HSCA call to Johnston was a brief contact report that said Johnston would get in touch with the witnesses. Looking through the files, Bill Davy never found any follow-up report on that matter.[83]

In summary, there were literally dozens of witnesses to the Clinton-Jackson incident. And Bugliosi looks silly trying to deny it. And if the Warren Commission had investigated the episode properly in 1964, it had the potential to unlock the case. Which is probably why they and the FBI did not investigate it at all. The opposite happened. The FBI likely confiscated Oswald's application and then erased the record of Morgan's call. The same FBI that Bugliosi thinks did a crackerjack job investigating the JFK case. Whew.

In retrospect, if Gerry Spence really understood the case, he would have called Lou Ivon as a witness in London. Ivon was Garrison's chief investigator. With his testimony about these events in New Orleans, Bugliosi's whole picture of Oswald as the communist malcontent would have been exploded. As would Ruth Paine's support for it.

Bugliosi vs. Stone on Vietnam

Bugliosi spends many, many pages going after the film *JFK,* and its screenwriters Oliver Stone and Zachary Sklar. He even goes after a main thesis of the film: That Kennedy was disengaging from Vietnam at the time of his death. That thesis has been supported by several historians since the film was released, since the ARRB declassified many documents on this issue. In fact, since 1991, some distinguished books have been published which support the thesis with strong new evidence, for example, David Kaiser's *American Tragedy,* Gordon Goldstein's *Lessons in Disaster,* and Jim Blight's *Virtual JFK.*

In his book, Bugliosi makes two stunning statements about the issue. He says that the evidence that Kennedy was withdrawing from Vietnam is conflicting and ambiguous at best.[84] He also says that what LBJ was going to do there was not really certain.[85]

In looking over Bugliosi's lengthy bibliography, there was an amazing missing entry. It was a book by historian Fredrik Logevall published in 1999, several years before the release of *Reclaiming History.* When I saw it was not listed, I again shook my head in disbelief. For no responsible scholar can even begin to approach the issue of Kennedy versus Johnson unless they have this book in hand. It proves beyond any doubt that from the moment Johnson took office, until the moment he was inaugurated in 1965, there was never any doubt that America was going to war in Vietnam. And further, that Johnson deliberately lied about this issue throughout his election campaign in 1964. Logevall was at a conference on this issue held by historian Jim Blight, which was the basis for the book *Virtual JFK.* There he said that the difference between the two men was that Johnson was clearly an undiluted Cold Warrior and a firm believer in the Domino Theory. No one who studies Kennedy's career, especially his early visit to Saigon in 1951, can say that about JFK.

Which leads to another missing book in the prosecutor's bibliography. Again, this was published many years before *Reclaiming History*. That is Richard Mahoney's *JFK: Ordeal in Africa*. That book shows that Kennedy was very much opposed to the imperial designs in Africa and Asia of President Eisenhower, Secretary of State John Foster Dulles, Vice President Richard Nixon, and CIA Director Allen Dulles. Once one reads that book, one begins to see why Kennedy was determined not to allow combat troops into Vietnam. And once one reads Logevall, one understands why Johnson bucked Kennedy's firm policy about this *in 1961* on his visit to Saigon.[86] He recommended to South Vietnamese President Ngo Dinh Diem that he request Kennedy send troops to help him. This, after Kennedy had already made it clear he was not going to commit troops. So as early as 1961, the differences in approach to Vietnam are already in the record.

As John Newman notes in his milestone book *JFK and Vietnam*, Kennedy had based his withdrawal plan on taking advantage of the differences between what the real battlefield conditions were and what the Pentagon said they were. Knowing that the American-backed South Vietnam effort there was failing, the Pentagon was disguising this with a whitewash of how bad things really were. Therefore, Kennedy was going to hoist the generals on their own petard: If things were going so well, then we were not needed anymore.

One of the most important pieces of information in Newman's book is that Johnson had access to *the true intelligence reports* which made it clear that the American effort was not working. He got these through his military aide Howard Burris.[87] The record shows LBJ was aware of the real conditions in the spring of 1962. Since he had already tried to coax Diem to ask Kennedy for troops in 1961, these reports must only have fortified his belief that American troops were needed to stem the tide. Or else the Domino Theory would sweep all of Southeast Asia under a Red Horde. Therefore, the idea that the Pentagon was not really sure about Johnson's attitude in Vietnam, that is simply not supported by both who the man was, and what he was doing in the White House on this issue in 1961 and '62.

Concerning the differences between NSAM 263 and NSAM 273, first let us dispose of the obvious. Johnson never removed the first thousand troops as Kennedy's NSAM 263 had forecast. Because, as is made clear in the book *Virtual JFK*, Johnson was playing to the media: He wanted to create the illusion that there was no breakage in policy, when in fact he was planning for that split within days of taking office. The important difference was that the latter order reversed Kennedy's previous one by allowing for direct American naval involvement in the Tonkin Gulf.[88] This in turn led to the Tonkin Gulf Incident in late summer of 1964. LBJ had already been preparing for that, since he had already had the war resolution to attack Vietnam in hand.[89] The reason he had it in hand was because he understood that the Pentagon was, in part, lying about the true conditions of the war. At his first meeting on this issue, held just forty-eight hours after Kennedy was killed, he had made it clear to all that his approach in Vietnam was much more militant, much more confrontational than JFK's. He then sent Secretary of Defense Robert McNamara to Vietnam for a fact-finding trip. From that first meeting, McNamara understood what Johnson wanted. Therefore, when he returned, he presented the real conditions on the ground. This was the basis for NSAM 288,[90] which was the designing of full scale battle plans against North Vietnam. In other words, something Kennedy never asked for in his three years as president, Johnson had now achieved in three months. This was the basis for the Tonkin Gulf Resolution which Johnson now used as a declaration of war against Vietnam.

If one looks in the index to *Reclaiming History*, one will not find any reference to NSAM 288.

A Tapestry of Lies?

In his all-out war against screenwriters Stone and Zachary Sklar, Bugliosi is intent on telling his reader that there is not one episode in the film that can be trusted. In fact, he actually calls the picture a "tapestry of lies." [91] Now, let's step back from Bugliosi's superheated diatribe and try to be fair and objective about the issue. When one is making a film based upon true events, one is allowed dramatic license. One has to make allowances for the compression of episodes over time into a feature film. Also, one has to allow for the ebb and flow of interest and emotion in order to capture and sustain audience interest. Many films made in America do not even obey those basic rules. As we have seen *Saving Private Ryan* is largely a fairy tale. It is about 95 percent fiction. Did Bugliosi scream about that one? Take Brian De Palma's *The Untouchables*. The high point of the film, the roof top chase between Frank Nitti and Eliot Ness, never happened. Neither was there any near gunfight between Capone and Ness in a hotel lobby. Neither did one of Ness's men get strangled with an electrical wire in an elevator by Nitti in police headquarters. Did Bugliosi write the *LA Times* and protest this? The list could go on and on. The fact is that much of this attack on the film is not artistic nor does it deal with the issue of dramatic license. It is mostly political. And much of it was spearheaded by compromised reporters like Hugh Aynesworth who have campaigned for Oswald's guilt, literally, from the day of the assassination.

Therefore, let us have a discussion from a rational point of view. Let us do a detailed discussion of the opening narrative of the film and then a general discussion of the rest to see how the film stacks up in use of dramatic license. This discussion is based upon the Director's Cut of the film. Since it is longer, it should benefit Bugliosi's argument because it should contain even more deceptions. I will discuss some of the flashbacks, but as there are so many, to discuss them all would slow down the discussion and make this section as interminable as Mr. Bugliosi's book. These scenes take up about the first hour of the film.

1.   The first scene is Jim Garrison getting the news of the assassination through an assistant. This scene is just about as it happened and it is described in Garrison's book. They then go to a bar and watch the TV coverage. *This is accurate and the only difference is that in the film it is investigator Lou Ivon who brings him the news. In real life, it was lawyer Frank Klein. Since Klein's character is not in the film, this is a legitimate use of dramatic license.*

2.   The second scene is Guy Banister and Jack Martin in a bar drinking and watching the same coverage. Banister is making insulting remarks about Kennedy, as if he is glad to see him gone. *This is accurate and if anything understated as to Banister's feelings about Kennedy being gone.*

3.   Martin and Banister walk back to Banister's office. Once inside, Banister notices something missing from his files. He accuses Martin of stealing from him. Martin makes an unwise comment about what he has seen there that summer and Banister pistol whips him to the floor. *This is, if anything, understated. There are some reports that Martin was actually trying to take Oswald's files from Banister. And the comments that Martin made were actually even more provocative in tone about what had happened there that summer and with Kennedy. The beating was so bad that if Banister's secretary Delphine Roberts had not intervened, Martin felt Banister may have killed him.*

4.   While watching TV at home, Garrison sees Jack Ruby correct the Dallas DA as to what group Oswald worked for that summer. It was not the Free Cuba Committee, but the Fair Play for Cuba Committee. *This is accurate, and Ruby did look like he was impersonating a reporter.*

5.   After watching TV coverage of the case, Garrison calls a special meeting about gathering information on Oswald's stay in New Orleans that summer. *This is accurate, and Garrison describes it in his book as taking place on a Sunday, as it does in the film.*

6.   At the meeting, they get news about David Ferrie's association with Oswald and his strange trip to Texas on November 22, 1963. *This is*

accurate down to the lawyer who gave them the information, Herm Kohlman.

7. Garrison calls in Ferrie for an interview. Ferrie denies he knew Oswald and says he decided to go ice skating and goose hunting in Texas the day Kennedy was killed there. Garrison does not buy the story and turns him over to the FBI. *This is accurate, but it's actually worse. Garrison found out that not only did Ferrie not take any guns to shoot geese, but at the skating rink he stood by a pay phone like he was awaiting a phone call. He never skated. Further, when he was turned over to the FBI, he lied to them also. In addition to denying any association with Oswald, he even said he never owned a telescopic rifle or even used one, or would even know how to use one.*

8. The FBI dismisses Ferrie and they say it was not their idea to question him anyway. *This is accurate, but it's even worse than depicted. The fact that Ferrie lied continually through his interview and the FBI did not call him on anything suggests that J. Edgar Hoover did not give one iota about who killed President Kennedy.*

9. Upon hearing that the FBI did not detain Ferrie, Garrison drops his investigation. *This is both true and false. In a formal sense, Garrison did drop the investigation, but he stayed interested and started reading literature on the case. He also appears to have done two or three reports on certain elements in the case.*

10. On a plane trip with Senator Russell Long in the fall of 1966, Garrison discusses the Kennedy case and hears Long's doubts. *This is accurate, except in the film the plane appears to take off from Washington not New York. But in September of 1966, Garrison flew to New York for a trip with New Orleans oil man Joseph Rault. On the way back, Long joined them and this conversation took place.*

11. Inspired by the Long conversation, Garrison ordered the twenty-six volumes of the Warren Commission and began to pick apart the evidence, including the testimony of Lee Bowers, Oswald's study of Russian in the Marines, and also about the three tramps arrested in Dealey Plaza. *This is generally accurate. Garrison ordered three sets of the volumes: one for his home, one for his car, and one for his office. He knew the volumes and their problems very well, including Bowers's testimony about the cars driving in behind the picket fence on the grassy knoll. Garrison did not get interested in the tramps or hoboes until he was given that information by photo expert Dick Sprague in late 1967.*

12. Garrison now goes down to 544 Camp Street and discovers Banister's office at the address Oswald placed on his pro-Castro flyers. *This is accurate and Garrison describes it in his book. The information about Oswald getting in a street fight with a Cuban exile and getting arrested and asking for an FBI agent to interview him while in jail and Banister learning about Oswald putting his address on his flyer is all in the record. The only thing we do not know for sure is if Banister confronted Oswald about his mistake in putting his address on the flyer. But, through Delphine Roberts, we know Banister was upset about it, and it seems a natural assumption that he told him about it.*

13. Garrison interviews Jack Martin and discovers what Banister was really up to at 544 Camp Street. It was a meeting place for Cuban exiles and Banister did things like supply and ship weapons for training camps during Operation Mongoose. The authorities eventually busted the camps on Kennedy's orders in 1963. Oswald was at 544 Camp Street and had an office there. Delphine Roberts came in one day to complain about Oswald's leafleting, and Banister said it was OK since he was with them. Clay Bertrand came into 544 Camp Street once and Banister showed him around. *This is accurate, including Oswald being at the training camps. The only questionable part of this is Bertrand/Shaw being at 544 Camp Street. But there is no doubt Banister and Shaw knew each other and Shaw called him at his office. Therefore this seems a legitimate use of dramatic license.*

14. Garrison meets with Dean Andrews who tells him about Oswald being in his office, the mysterious Clay Bertrand who paid him to do some work for him, and Bertrand calling him to defend Oswald in Dallas the day of the assassination. He asks him who Bertrand really was and Andrews will not tell him for fear of his life. *This is generally accurate except for the implication that Bertrand sent Oswald to Andrews's office. This is ambiguous. Andrews was asked once if Bertrand was with Oswald when he visited his office and Andrews did not really deny it. Later, as noted in this chapter, it was discovered that Andrews told Harold Weisberg that Shaw actually was Bertrand.*

15. Garrison goes into a state prison to meet with a convict named Willie O'Keefe. O'Keefe tells him about meeting with Bertrand, various sexual encounters Bertrand paid him for, meeting Oswald at Ferrie's, and a gathering with Ferrie, Bertrand, and a man named Leon Oswald where they talked about assassinating Kennedy. *If one allows that O'Keefe is a composite character, a narrative device that is usually*

accepted, this is generally accurate. O'Keefe is made out of four Garrison witnesses: Ray Broshears, William Morris, David Logan, and Perry Russo. Logan was in prison when Garrison's staff interviewed him, which is why this scene takes place where it does. Morris and Logan had met with Shaw and had homosexual trysts with him. Broshears had met with Ferrie and Bertrand. Russo was at Ferrie's and met Oswald there and was at the gathering where the assassination of Kennedy was talked about. But according to him, at this gathering Bertrand did not say as much as the film says he did.

16. Garrison meets with four members of his staff at a restaurant to discuss what they have discovered about some witnesses and about Oswald. The witnesses are Bowers, Rose Cherami, and the tramps. Garrison learns that Cherami and Bowers are dead. The discussion about Oswald is a fast montage sequence which tries to lay in all the contradictory information about Oswald's life that makes him such a complex character—his defection to Russia, his association with the White Russians in Dallas, his offering of radar secrets to them, the Russians sending him to Minsk and giving him a nice apartment and stipend. It ends with a discussion of the late arriving palm print on the alleged rifle in evidence, one that the FBI did not notice when they got it from Dallas. *This is all accurate, and today seems understated. Oswald's life has come more into focus with the work of writers like Lisa Pease, John Newman, and John Armstrong. The characters of George DeMohrenschildt and Ruth and Michael Paine today are even more well-defined. These three could have been portrayed in an even more sinister light.*

The Rest of the "Tapestry of Lies"

As the reader can see, if one allows for the use of a modicum of dramatic license, there really is nothing in the first hour that can be strongly objected to. Reports about how wildly unfounded the film is have been so exaggerated as to be grotesque. Rather than go through the entire film like this, one can say that, with several exceptions, the film is generally acceptable in its use of dramatic license. It certainly compares quite favorably with the largely fictitious *Saving Private Ryan* or the violent fabrications of *The Untouchables*, or a whole slew of other rapaciously licentious films. If the film were made today, with all the declassified information we have, it could have been even more accurate and even more detailed.

There are some things that one can certainly object to. Stone would have been well-advised not to have used the Three Tramps, as today they appear to have been just that: tramps. The identification of the Babushka Lady—a mysterious woman with a camera in Dealey Plaza—as Beverly Oliver is not strong enough to be used in a film that the entire media was gunning for in advance. And it is through this identification that Stone places Ferrie at Ruby's bar in Dallas. Garrison's interview with Clay Shaw goes a bit overboard toward the end with Garrison accusing Shaw to his face of plotting to kill Kennedy. The appearance of Garrison on *The Tonight Show* was hard to script since the tape is very difficult to locate. Garrison's meeting with the man called Mr. X (Fletcher Prouty) in Washington did not take place until years afterwards. Stone could have built this scene around former CIA agent Richard Case Nagell, a man Garrison did meet with during his investigation and who did give him much valuable information. At the trial of Clay Shaw, Stone throws in several people who did not actually testify, like some Parkland doctors, and presents some evidence that Garrison did not actually present, like battered bullets from Warren Commission tests. Garrison did present one of the prosecution's final arguments but it was not as elaborate or involved with the assassination plot in Dealey Plaza as this one. But this can be justified as dramatic license since it is the climax of the film.

Many critics have gone after the film for things said that are clearly labeled as speculation or theorizing. For instance, Garrison conceptualizing that Oswald may have infiltrated a Cuban exile plot against Kennedy in Dallas. This should clearly be allowed on the grounds of dramatic license. And Garrison does say in the film during his summation that he is going to theorize as to what really did happen.

As the reader can see, Stone's film is not even close to being a "tapestry of lies." Today, with all the evidence of the ARRB, parts of it seem to be actually understated. And if the film could be reshot today, it would be even more convincing since we have so much more documented evidence about almost every angle of the case.

The media went after the film for three reasons: They had bought into the Warren Commission cover-up almost immediately, they joined in the trashing of Jim Garrison in 1967, and they never made the connection between JFK's assassination and the escalation of the Vietnam War. They were derelict in their duties and the American public suffered for it. This film shoved that failure in their faces. And, understandably, they did not like that.

I don't understand Bugliosi's excuse.

CHAPTER EIGHT

Bugliosi on the First Forty-Eight Hours

"I can't believe that!" said Alice. "Can't you?" the queen said. . . .
"Try again, draw a long breath and shut your eyes!"

—Lewis Carroll, *Through the Looking Glass*

What I am going to do here is chronicle some of the unbelievable things done by the first official investigators of the John F. Kennedy assassination. Which, of course, were the Dallas Police (DPD). One of the most startling things about *Reclaiming History* is this: Bugliosi finds almost nothing wrong with how the DPD handled either the JFK case or their detention of Oswald. In fact, he has little but fulsome praise for them, saying that in forty-eight hours they accumulated enough evidence to "prove his guilt beyond all doubt."[1] Amazingly, he even tries to excuse their responsibility for the murder of Oswald by shifting the blame to city manager Elgin Crull.[2] A man whose name is hard to find anywhere in the literature.

Bugliosi decided to take an absolutist stance on this case. Everything is seen in terms of black and white. Therefore when he trots out his representatives of Dallas law enforcement, he presents what they say as unequivocally true. Some examples of the people he uses are police officer Jim Bowles who later became Dallas Sheriff, the late District Attorney Henry Wade, and, most frequently, Wade's assistant in the DA's office, Bill Alexander. He then pulls out all the stops in his paean to Captain Will Fritz, the longtime chief of the robbery and homicide division. This was a chief of homicide who admitted he had no formal training in forensics.[3] Bugliosi has to do this since Fritz was the man who, along with Wade, was essentially running the investigation of Lee Oswald.[4] So if you pose questions about Fritz, you pose questions about the overall efficacy of the DPD's Kennedy investigation. Bugliosi doesn't want to do that, so he systematically eliminates them. He then tries to portray the Dallas Police as the crime-detecting equivalent of Scotland Yard. With Fritz as something like Sherlock Holmes.

Virtually all the book's praise of the DPD is self-serving and self-sustaining. That is, it comes from inside the DPD or DA's office and is just reverberated by Bugliosi. Bugliosi ran a risk here. Since there was no independent outside standard involved in his appraisal, there was no control factor in what he wrote. Therefore, the uninitiated reader was relying on the author's judgment.

Bugliosi's Perfect Bad Timing

Unfortunately for the author, as with his claim about there being no instances of LAPD officers framing African Americans, the pretty portrait he drew of the DPD also blew up in his face. Because right after the book was published an outside standard did emerge. In 2006, Dallas elected Craig Watkins, its first black DA. He was the first DA in over a half century who was not from—to put it kindly—the good ole boys network. To put it unkindly, well, let's use Watkins own words to describe what preceded him: "There was a cowboy kind of mentality and the reality is that kind of approach is archaic, racist, elitist, and arrogant."[5] Watkins never worked for Wade or met him. Therefore, once in office, he was free to go ahead and review many of his cases with an independent eye. What was the result? No other county in America—and almost no state, for that matter—has freed more innocent people from prison in recent years than Dallas County where Wade was DA from 1951 through 1986.[6]

In the review Watkins instituted, nearly thirty convictions, three for murder, have been overturned so far. And there are over 200 more to go. This review has caused both the DA's office and the DPD to be exposed for what they really were.

Watkins has said that many of the cases won under Wade "were riddled with shoddy investigations, evidence was ignored, and defense lawyers were kept in the dark."[7] Take for instance, the case of James Lee Woodard. Woodard spent twenty-seven years in prison for a murder that DNA testing later showed he did not commit. But what makes it worse is that "Wade's office withheld from defense attorneys photographs of tire tracks at the crime scene that didn't match Woodard's car."[8] A lawyer overseeing the review said that many corners were cut to get the case finished. And it was hard for her to be precise about who was more involved in that: the DA's office or the detectives running the case. Another person involved in the review, a professor of criminology at UT, has commented that it was a "win at all costs" mentality. "When someone was arrested, it was assumed they were guilty. I think prosecutors and investigators basically ignored all evidence to the contrary and decided they were going to convict these guys."[9]

There was another case reversal in which the man accused of rape had a solid alibi. As the *Dallas Morning News* reported, Johnnie Earl Lindsey was at work when the crime was committed, and his supervisor vouched for his alibi. Plus, he had time cards to prove it. The case made against him was based upon eyewitness testimony and faulty police lineups. Sounds familiar.[10]

Another reason that Wade was successful in the face of good evidence could be his penchant for stacking the jury against minorities. At Wade's request, assistant DA Jon Sparling actually wrote a manual on how to pick a jury. Some of guidelines make for interesting reading. Take this for starters: "You are not looking for any member of a minority group which may subject him to oppression—they always empathize with the accused." Here's another: "Look for physical afflictions. These people usually sympathize with the accused." These kinds of rules manipulated the racial makeup of juries. In any year, up to 90 percent of qualified black candidates were kept off felony juries. Even when confronted with these statistics, Wade was not convinced his office systematically excluded minorities from juries.[11] How could he? Here's a guy who, in 1963, issued a memo telling his prosecutors, "Do not take Jews, Negroes, Dagos, Mexicans or members of any minority race on a jury, no matter how rich or well educated."[12] If you read *Reclaiming History*, there is no evidence that Alexander ever told the author about any of these memos.

One could possibly make an excuse for Bugliosi since most of these explosive revelations emerged after his book came out. But note, I said "most." For instance, as the reader can see, this last memo surfaced in 2004. Which is three years before *Reclaiming History* was published. Even before that, in 2001, a month before Wade passed away, DNA evidence was used to reverse a rape conviction.[13] Before that, in 1988, Errol Morris released his documentary film *The Thin Blue Line* which showed how the Dallas DA's office had framed Randall Adams for the murder of a police officer. In that case, possibly as many as five witnesses felt free to commit perjury. Adams was later freed, but the actual killer, David Harris, who all but confessed during the film, was not then charged. Harris later went on to kill again and was executed by lethal injection. In that film, it is revealed that the hidden motto of Wade's office was, "Any prosecutor can convict a guilty man. It takes a great prosecutor to convict an innocent man."

But *way* before even the Adams case emerged, back in 1983, there was the Lenell Geter case. Geter was a black engineer who was convicted of armed robbery and sentenced to life in prison. It's almost superfluous to write the following: Even though he had an alibi, he was picked out of a police lineup. After a year in jail, the case attracted so much adverse publicity to his office that Wade agreed to a new trial. Yet, because of the questionable evidence and the strong belief that Geter was singled out because he was an available African American, Wade dropped the case. It's hard to believe that Bugliosi completely missed this one. Why? Because it became a *cause célèbre.* It was so high profile that in 1984 *Sixty Minutes* ran a famous segment on it that helped get Geter out of jail. After he was released, there was a 1987 TV film made on the subject entitled *Guilty of Innocence: The Lenell Geter Story.* I guess Bugliosi missed them both. And apparently, his buddy Alexander didn't tell him about it.

To makes this all a bit worse, Bugliosi chose Bill Alexander to be his main witness from that office. In his discussion of the man, it is difficult to locate the fact that he was dismissed by Wade in 1967. At that time, when he was asked by a reporter if Earl Warren should be impeached, Alexander famously replied that no, Warren should be executed, preferably by hanging. As Joseph McBride notes in his book *Into the Nightmare,* Alexander told an author, "And as far as anybody giving a particular rat's ass about John Kennedy getting his ass wiped in Dallas, who cares?"

The DA's Office Hid JFK Files Too

There is something else that Watkins has managed to reverse in Dallas. As most people know, the ARRB was supposed to have collected all the outstanding documents from each level of government involved in the Kennedy case. They visited Dallas back in 1994. And in fact, the Dallas Police turned over several thousand pages of documents to the City Manager's office before the visit. But the DA's office was not as forthcoming. And apparently, Bugliosi's main source, Mr. Alexander, wasn't either. In early 2008, fourteen years after the ARRB visit, Watkins unearthed twelve boxes of materials that the DA's office failed to surrender to the ARRB. In fact, there were even more pages in this cache than what the police originally turned over. This is double trouble for Bugliosi because 1) Throughout the book, he states that the ARRB got everything and therefore only nutty conspiracy theorists could say otherwise, and 2) When the news media called his trusted source about why this was not turned over years ago, Mr. Alexander refused to be interviewed.[14]

All of the above is meant to do two things. First, it shows how willingly and thoroughly Bugliosi has sided with, not just the official story, but with the bodies involved in creating that story. To make one telling point of comparison: as we saw in the last chapter, Bugliosi recycled all the tired and provably false tales about Jim Garrison being a poor and corrupt DA. And he used untrustworthy sources like Harry Connick to do so. And he then ignored the huge scandals that took place under Connick, which were much worse than anything under Garrison.

But here, where the charges of corruption and malfeasance are utterly true and backed by solid evidence, he decided not to investigate. Instead he maintained an open ear to Hugh Aynesworth's buddy Bill Alexander, a man who clearly has a stake in not telling him the real story when, in fact, he had to have known what was really going on and was therefore part of the cover-up. Again, this is the danger of advocacy journalism. If you get too close, it may backfire. And Bugliosi somehow didn't anticipate that.

With the author's make-believe version of the Dallas Police cast aside, let us examine some of the controversial practices of that now exposed department while they had their most important suspect ever in their hands.

Wesley Frazier's Gun Sack

George O'Toole's concise but interesting book, *The Assassination Tapes,* was one of the first to show an interest in Wesley Frazier. O'Toole was one of the very first people to actually investigate the man. Linnie Mae Randle was Frazier's sister and when O'Toole called to interview him, she told him that he was away in the service, which was a misleading half-truth. It's true that at the time of the conversation, Wesley Frazier was in the army, but he came home each weekend and stayed in the same town where she lived, Irving. So it would have been easy for O'Toole to interview him. But neither Linnie nor her brother wanted to be interviewed by O'Toole. And this was pretty much a firm policy of theirs for decades. Wesley and Linnie Mae appeared on very few TV programs since 1964. And in fact, even to this day, Wesley is handled very gingerly by the likes of FBI/CIA associated journalist Hugh Aynesworth and his partner in the Dallas cover-up Dave Perry. At some appearances in public, Aynesworth sits right next to Frazier. Let us try and understand why.

The Warren Commission tells us that Ruth Paine called the Texas School Book Depository at the suggestion of a neighbor who told her that her brother had just been hired there. [15] The neighbor was Linnie Mae Randle. Oswald was hired and started work there in mid-October. He was living in town while his wife Marina was staying with the Paines in the Dallas suburb of Irving. On weekends, Oswald would hitch a ride with Wesley to Irving to see his family, and he would drive Oswald back to work on Monday. On Thursday, the 21st, Oswald asked Frazier if he could drive him to the Paines to see his family. This is probably because he had not gone out on the previous Friday and had a quarrel with Marina that week.[16] But the Commission tries to explain this visit otherwise. So there follows in the Warren Report a sentence that has become enshrined in assassination literature since 1964, by both critics and Commission defenders alike—neither side questioning it. It goes like this: "Oswald told Frazier that he would like to drive to Irving to pick up some curtain rods for an apartment in Dallas."[17]

As written, this statement is not accurate. Oswald did not admit to saying this. It originates with Frazier. And the other detail that goes with it, namely that he said he carried those curtain rods in a long paper bag to work on Friday, is also not accurate. Oswald did not say that either. Will Fritz wrote a report after Oswald was killed in which he said that when he confronted Oswald with Frazier's story about the curtain rods, the suspect denied it.[18] Oswald maintained that he carried a lunch bag to work on Friday.[19] Yet this long paper bag story was injected into the press so quickly and forcefully that even as able a critic as Sylvia Meagher accepted it. She and Mark Lane did not argue about who was telling the truth, Frazier or Oswald. Instead they argued over how long the bag was. This story about the long paper bag had to wait for decades to be seriously challenged. But challenged it is.

The first problem with the story is this: Jack Dougherty saw Oswald as he entered the building that morning after he left Frazier's car. He was specifically asked about the long bag, he didn't recall it.[20] No one else saw it either.[21] This is a package that the Commission says was three feet long.[22] One way to have tested Oswald's story about carrying a lunch bag to work would have been to have interviewed the driver of the catering truck that visited the work site each morning. There is no evidence that this was done.[23] This is an important point because Frazier said that Oswald always carried his lunch except for *that* day.[24] So if Oswald did not buy his lunch that day, then what was he eating on the first floor? Also, there is no affirmative evidence from the Paine household that Oswald picked up any curtain rods. Ruth Paine, who helped incriminate Oswald every way she could, said he took no rods from their household.[25] Marina Oswald said the same.[26] No witness saw Oswald transport the paper bag to the Paine household, or is on record as seeing the long paper bag at the Paines.[27]

Depository witness Troy West is interesting in this regard. As Harold Weisberg notes, the Commission states that this long paper bag was made from paper and tape secured from the Depository.[28] West had worked at the place for sixteen years. He said he never left his station, even for lunch. He was the man in charge of dispensing the paper and tape for packaging. When asked if Oswald ever approached his desk for paper or tape he said he did not.[29] Further, West established that the tape would automatically be dispensed from the machine while wet. To take it out dry, you would literally have to take the tape out of the machine first.[30] Which neither West, nor anybody else, saw Oswald do.

FBI agent James Cadigan did not mention that he found any oil or grease marks on the inside of the sack.[31] Yet, the rifle in evidence was soaked in a lubricant called Cosmoline before being transported across the ocean in order to prevent corrosion.[32] Further, the Commission story says the gun was disassembled by Oswald when it was in the sack. Therefore, both the interior and exterior of the weapon would have been touching the paper. Yet, none of this left any oil or grease markings on it.

The Invisible, Noiseless Package

British detective Ian Griggs has done experiments in disassembling the Mannlicher Carcano. It turns out that the Commission and the FBI were deceptive in this. When actually disassembled, the rifle has to be broken down into twelve parts to isolate the wooden stock. Unless the smaller parts are placed in an envelope, they will bounce around in the package and make noise. Which Wesley Frazier did not report hearing. Finally, when this is done, and Griggs did it, the stock is inevitably scratched by the metal parts. Yet this scratching is not seen on the rifle in evidence today.[33]

Now, the Commission says the rifle was disassembled in a gun sack. It was on the back seat as the two men were driving to work, at approximately 7:30 AM in start and stop traffic. Therefore, one would have to think that the twelve parts the rifle was broken into had to have been moving ever so slightly against the paper. At least one or two of them? The Commission sure hoped so. Because they asked FBI agent Cadigan that specific question. Did the paper have any bulges or creases in it? Cadigan said he could not find anything like that that he could associate with the rifle.[34]

According to the Commission, specifically Marina Oswald, the weapon was stored in a blanket at the Paines' garage. One would think that if the rifle had been stored in that blanket for almost two months, there would be plentiful fibers transferred from the blanket to the paper but there were only two types found. FBI agent Paul Stombaugh could not find enough of the fibers to make a positive identification since there were too many types of fibers in the blanket that were not found on the paper. What is interesting is how the FBI agent said he found them. He said he found them just by tapping the top of the sack.[35] Yet in the photos of the gun sack as it is being taken from the Depository, the police are holding it in a straight up position by one hand on the bottom. Therefore, the fibers should have dropped out as it was carried down the stairs. Is there a way that so few fibers could have been found on the paper *after* the paper was taken into evidence? Yes. Because when the Dallas Police stored the evidence, there is a photo of the blanket sitting right next to the gun sack.[36]

Let's add this up. According to Troy West, who never left his station, Oswald never approached him to secure the paper or tape the Commission says he used to prepare the package. If he had, in order to make sure the tape was wet and sticky, he would have needed to tape the package in front of West, which West would have surely remembered. Yet, in spite of that fact, no one saw Oswald carry the package with him to the Paines. Not even Frazier. (Think about all that for a few seconds.) Further, no one at the Paines' residence recalls the package or Oswald asking for curtain rods. [37] There are no scratches, creases, or malformations in the paper that were traced to the rifle. There are no lubricants from the gun on the paper. And the cloth fibers found on the paper cannot be identified to the blanket it was allegedly wrapped in even though the Commission says it was lying inside it for almost two months. (It would have been an interesting experiment to have actually wrapped the rifle in the blanket for seven weeks to see how many fibers were transferred to it.) Finally, once Oswald left Frazier's car, no one saw him carrying a long bulky package inside the building. So, besides Frazier—I will get to Linnie Mae Randle's testimony later—how did the Commission link Oswald to the bag?

Through a right palm print and the left fingerprint of his index finger.[38] Think how silly this is. In all the necessary handiwork of securing the paper, preparing this three foot package, taping it together, putting the rifle inside, carrying it into the building, and finally taking it out of the package—Oswald got one single fingerprint on it. Further, there were no other prints on the bag. How could that be if, as we shall see, the police told the Commission that two of them—possibly three of them—picked it up and delivered it to HQ? Now, the part of the palm that left the print was from the right hand, the "heel" or "ulnar" side, the side of the hand near the little finger.[39] The fingerprint came from the left index finger at the first joint.[40] In other words, Oswald carried the 40-inch, eight pound rifle, across his body with the left index finger at the top and the base of the palm of his right hand at the bottom. And no one else saw him in this unforgettable position with a three foot package inside the Depository. Now, if during Oswald's questioning for twelve hours by the police, he was shown the paper he was supposed to have secured and cut to make the package, then perhaps he touched it with those parts of his hands.

The Differing Documents, and Bugliosi's Excuse for Them

What makes this print evidence even more questionable is that there are two differing documents on the FBI analysis of the paper. Way back in 1977 Gary Shaw discovered two FBI documents. They said two contradictory things about the same exhibit. One document said that paper samples from the Depository were "not identical" with the bag in evidence. The other said the samples had the same "observable characteristics" as the bag in evidence. This indicated that the Bureau realized that the bag created a problem for them and that the Dallas Police were wrong about where the paper came from. They therefore changed the first document with precise language to the second one with the vague language to give themselves legal leeway. Because if they admitted the paper did not come from the Depository, then where did it come from? Shaw, and researchers Jack White and Ed Tatro, believed the Bureau altered a document in order to frame Oswald.

As Pat Speer notes, Bugliosi deals with this issue in his End Notes. Bugliosi says that since the reports were from different days, it is obvious that further investigation by Hoover of later paper samples straightened it all out. Speer comments that there is a big problem with Bugliosi's solution: Both reports were created on the same day, November 30, 1963. And since the further paper samples Hoover tested did not arrive until December 1, how could they have been tested for these November 30 documents? Further, Bugliosi leaves out the fact that the FBI later offered two differing explanations for the differing documents: one by Public Affairs Officer William Baker, the other by the actual author of the documents, Vincent Drain. They both offered differing but benign explanations. It turns out they were both wrong. It now appears that the bag in evidence did not match the Depository paper samples and that the document was later altered to say it did.[41]

This would indicate that the bag in evidence today was manufactured after the fact. Speer makes a cogent argument on his website that this happened. He shows that the paper bag allegedly found in the Depository, carried outside, and photographed by the press that day does not appear to be the same paper bag returned by the FBI to the Dallas Police four days later. And it is surely not the paper bag that Wesley Frazier said he saw Oswald cupping in the palm of his hand beneath his shoulder. The fascinating thing about his study is that it appears that not only did the Dallas Police not photograph the bag where they say they found it, but they do not appear to have photographed it at all until November 26![42]

Was there a reason why the FBI did not want to state that the paper and tape used in creating the gun sack were identical to those found in the Depository that day? There does seem to be a reason for that, and that reason seems to be to avoid the issue of who actually made the sack and when. Although the FBI did not ultimately say the paper and tape on the bag were identical to those that went into the making of the gun sack, the Warren Report could not resist stating that they did say that.[43] In the original November 30, 1963, FBI report on the assassination (sometimes called the Gemberling Report, after FBI agent Robert Gemberling) it did say that the paper was originally found to be identical to the samples found in the Depository on the day of the assassination. But that statement was included among a list of corrections that J. Edgar Hoover wanted made in the report.[44] He did not want to use the word "identical,"[45] he wanted to use the phrase "same observable characteristics." But in examining Cadigan's testimony, he conducted a series of tests in which the two samples did not differ. And when asked if they were identical, the answer was that they were.[46]

So why did Hoover want to backtrack from that identical comparison? As former police investigator Gil Jesus points out, the FBI was covering up the perfidy of the Dallas Police. As we have seen earlier, under Wade and Fritz the police were quite efficient in the art of the frame-up. A point Bugliosi ignores. Once a rifle was found, there had to be a way for Oswald to transport it inside. And since, as we shall see, the police could never prove one was found on the sixth floor, it appears they decided to help their case along against Oswald. For as Jesus shows, although the Book Depository got shipments of tape and paper in large batches, every roll of paper and roll of tape within the batch was *not the same*. For example, the source from which the Depository got its tape was not a manufacturer but a supplier.[47] And in fact, the tape used varied in color and thickness, as can be seen by photos.[48] The FBI computed that the Depository used 8.6 rolls of tape every three days or almost three per day. Which means that a roll of tape was consumed in a bit under three hours. Therefore, the tape could not be identical. This was why when the FBI made a replica sack a few days after the assassination, they discovered that both the tape and paper were noticeably different than in the exhibit attributed to Oswald.[49] What this evidence clearly suggests is that the Dallas Police manufactured this alleged gun sack on the day of the assassination. The FBI understood that, and they tried to steer the Commission away from this "identical" term for fear it would expose what had really happened.

But further, Cadigan also testified that the markings on the tape in evidence were identical to those samples taken from the Depository on the twenty-second. That is, the spinning wheel markings of the dispenser.[50] This indicated that the tape was not taken out of the dispenser and used to paste the paper sack together elsewhere. Which would have had to have been the case if the Commission was correct about Oswald preparing the gun sack. Again, this would strongly suggest that the paper sack was constructed at the wrapping table inside the Depository. The two policemen present when that tape sample was taken were Lt. Day and Det. Studebaker.[51] As we shall see, both were involved with the "discovery" of the gun sack on the sixth floor.

Who Discovered the Gun Sack?

As Speer notes, the Dallas Police could not tell a consistent story on what was discovered first, the bag or the rifle. They could not tell a consistent story on who dusted the bag. Lt. Day says he did this on the scene, but no one on the scene backs him on this. Others say it was Det. Studebaker who dusted the bag.

But it's even worse than that. The DPD can't even tell a coherent story as to who found the bag. Day said the bag was found near the shells. Yet when Luke Mooney described the discovery of the shells, he mentioned no bag. But, as Griggs points out, if Day was telling the truth, Mooney had to have been standing on the bag as he stood over the shells![52] When David Belin asked Deputy Sheriff Roger Craig if he saw any long sack laying in the floor, Craig replied that he did not.[53] Sgt. Gerald Hill said he didn't see the long sack even though he wasn't really asked the question.[54] In his obtuse answer, Hill referred to Det. Hicks. Yet when Hicks was asked if he saw a long paper sack, he replied "No sir; I don't believe I did."[55] Lt. Day said he found it and building foreman Roy Truly could back him on this because no one else viewed it. But Truly said he didn't even know things were found in the southeast "sniper's lair" part of the sixth floor.[56] And Truly was never asked one question about this paper sack.

The police now relied on Detectives Johnson, Montgomery, and Studebaker to save the day. Listen to Montgomery: "Let's see—the paper sack—I don't recall for sure if it was on the floor or on the box, but I know it was just there—one of the pictures might show exactly where it was."[57] Of course, there was no picture. And we are to believe Montgomery didn't know that.

A further problem with Montgomery and Johnson was that although they allegedly saw such a bag, they couldn't decide who picked it up and unfolded it. Johnson said Montgomery picked it up and unfolded it, but Montgomery said nothing about unfolding it and firmly denied picking it up.[58] Montgomery passed that buck onto Studebaker. Studebaker is the man who photographed much of the evidence. But somehow, he did not photograph the bag *in situ*, or even on the floor where it was found. For he admitted the bag did not even show up incidentally in any related photos he took on the sixth floor. He also said he put a piece of tape on the bag where he thought he saw a possible print. There was no such visible print or tape on the bag when received by the FBI.[59] But here is the capper with Studebaker, when asked how long the bag was, he said it was between three and four feet long.[60] This is almost twice as long as the bag Frazier testified to. In other words, the man who should have seen the bag first did not, even though he was standing on it. And the man who did see it, and should have photographed it, did not take the picture. What makes it even worse is that it appears that it is *this* bag that was photographed outside the Depository by the press. Speer has some fun showing the difficulty in matching this package to the bag in evidence today. And further that the Dallas Police did not photograph any bag until November 26. After Oswald was dead.

In light of all the above, even Police Chief Jesse Curry had doubts about the paper bag. As Speer notes, in describing the bag in a picture, Curry wrote: "A paper bag *probably* constructed from wrapping paper and tape at the Texas School Book Depository. . . . This is *probably* the same bag which was found on the sixth floor by investigators." (Emphasis added.) Here, the Police Chief— the man ultimately responsible for the case against Oswald—actually used the qualifier "probably" not once, but twice. Finally, Speer shows that the second bag, the one in evidence today, was very likely cut down in size from the Commission's larger bag, the one described by Studebaker. It had to be in order to fit the allegations of Wesley Frazier about a different bag. Which indicates just how important Frazier was to the official story in this regard.[61]

The Midnight Polygraph

"I'm not familiar with it."

—Det. R. D. Lewis to George O'Toole

The above statement shows just how deep the deception inside the DPD about Wesley Frazier went. Det. Lewis is denying a police report saying he gave Frazier a polygraph exam the evening of the assassination.[62] It is hard to believe he did not recall the test he administered since the conditions surrounding the exam were bizarre. For starters, it took place at midnight on November 22, 1963. Second, it took place on the direct order of Capt. Fritz.[63] Third, Lewis had gone home for the day and was likely preparing for bed when he was called back to conduct the polygraph. Lewis was so much in denial about the test that when O'Toole asked him about it he replied, "What day was Kennedy shot on?" O'Toole said it was a Friday. Lewis then asked, "What, what was the date?" After a few more moments of this jousting, Lewis finally admitted he recalled it: "I do remember running some guy regarding a package and knowing Oswald and curtain rods and so forth."[64] But he still said he couldn't remember the exact day, or the results, or the guy's name. In fact, in trying to recall Frazier's name he made a curious choice of words: "If my life depended on it I couldn't remember."[65] If we believe him, Lewis couldn't recall the events of the biggest day in the history of the Dallas Police Department. Or the most important polygraph he ever ran on midnight of that day. As O'Toole notes, Lewis wasn't alone in this regard. Det. Stovall also tried to feign amnesia about being present for this polygraph. Even though he was.[66]

What makes the amnesia even harder to swallow is the description of the polygraph as rendered in Jim Bishop's 1967 book, *The Day Kennedy Was Shot*. Bishop was an Establishment journalist who sold the official story. So his book was written with the cooperation of the Dallas authorities and even Judge Brown, who had presided over the Ruby trial. In fact, Bishop writes that police employees who had previously been told not to talk were allowed to speak to him. Bishop describes a tense midnight scene in which Frazier could not emotionally compose himself. Therefore, it was difficult for Lewis to attain any valid contrasting readings on the machine. Bishop actually used the phrase "controlled hysteria" to describe the readings Lewis was getting to even innocent questions.[67] According to Bishop, there were five people in the room "and there wasn't one who expected to learn anything from Wesley Frazier. All they had managed to do was scare the wits out of him."[68]

As O'Toole notes, this test broke established guidelines in more ways than one. There is no evidence of a pre-interview, and it was done at the end of the day. Whereas examiners like to give the tests at the beginning of the day when the subject is fresh. So from the description above, any polygraph examiner would predict that the results of the test would be inconclusive. But they would be wrong. According to the police report, Frazier passed the test.[69] What makes that unexpected result even more surprising is the following: In addition to "forgetting" about the test, Lewis did not sign the police report, and he did not testify to the Warren Commission. Why not? Because, as Australian researcher Greg Parker discovered, the actual test and readings are nowhere to be found today. Of course, this raises all sorts of questions about what the test was really about and its validity. Yet this is the police force with which Bugliosi cannot find serious fault.

Why Did the Police Polygraph Frazier?

How Frazier was placed in the hot seat on November 22 is not an easy story to put together. It appears to begin with the visit by the Dallas Police to the Paine household on the afternoon of the twenty-second. During this visit Linnie Mae Randle walked over to the Paine house and told them about her brother giving Oswald a ride to work. She apparently told them about a bag in the back seat. She then told Det. Adamcik where her brother Wesley was. The DPD then had the Irving police arrest Wesley Frazier and take him into custody. Frazier was picked up by the DPD at around 7:15 PM. The police then did a search of both his car and his home. The most interesting thing they found was a .303 Enfield rifle with clip and ammo.[70] Why is that interesting? Because as Walt Brown has confirmed in his Master Chronology of the Kennedy Assassination, this was the very first rifle reported as found by the police that day, even before the 7.65 Mauser. With that in mind, it doesn't take a great leap to understand why Frazier's reactions were "controlled hysteria" during his midnight polygraph. After this search, Frazier and his sister were taken to the station where they filled out affidavits. They left and were then called back for the polygraph. (There are two versions of Frazier's affidavit, one with no date and one with the twenty-second on it. There is no date on the police report that makes up CE 2003.)

The reader may have noticed: I have minimized the testimony of Linnie Mae. I do so because in my view it is highly questionable. Her testimony about seeing Oswald put something in the back of Frazier's car has been vitiated by a few authors, including John Armstrong. As he notes in his book *Harvey and Lee,* if one looks at the photos of the Randle home in the Commission volumes, it is hard to believe Randle's story about seeing Oswald opening the door to Frazier's car from where she was looking because her view would have been blocked by the carport wall.[71] And both Linnie and Wesley said his car was parked on the far side of the car port, beyond the wall.[72] If you read Linnie's testimony, she saw Oswald first that morning.[73] Yet she said nothing to Wesley about it. Their mother, Essie Williams, was also at home that morning. She is the one who told Wesley about Oswald being outside.[74] Yet, she did not mention the bag to the FBI.[75]

Linnie Mae said that when she saw Oswald cross over to Frazier's car that day, he was clutching the bag from the top and it almost touched the ground as he carried it. But then, on the next page of her testimony, she forgets what she just said. When Joseph Ball asks her how Oswald was dressed, she can only describe his shirt since she says she only saw him from the waist up! But then how could she tell how close the sack was to the ground? Further, Wesley

Frazier does not corroborate Linnie's story. He says that while he was preparing to go to work, Linnie was fixing his lunch and that she never told him Oswald was there. Now, if you saw your brother drop off Oswald the night before, if you saw Oswald walk across the street and up your driveway, and then open the back door of the car and place a package on the seat, wouldn't you turn and tell Wesley that the man he was driving with was coming to the door? She did not.[76] Wesley's mother did.

One other point about Linnie and Wesley's story, Frazier told HSCA investigator Jack Moriarty that he said he always locked his car since it was situated outside, not inside a garage. The problem then became, how did Oswald get the package into the back door if it was locked? Wesley now said that that particular door was broken.[77] Moriarty was so puzzled by this that he said to Frazier: "You figure that one out OK?"

At the Book Depository

Wesley Frazier has always said that he and Oswald drove into the parking lot at work together that morning. Oswald then got out and picked up his package. Then, for some unknown reason, Oswald sprinted up ahead of him. When asked if he usually did that, Frazier replied no. They usually walked up together. This was the first time it happened. So therefore Frazier got this long look at Lee carrying the much storied package.[78] Commissioner Gerald Ford was greatly interested in this part of Frazier's story, since it somehow implied that Oswald was hiding something from Frazier. (How Oswald could keep it from everyone else was not important.) A funny thing happened to Frazier's story during the HSCA investigation. Edward Shields was a coworker of Frazier's who worked at the warehouse building north of the Depository. Shields had been questioned by the Warren Commission, but he was not asked about anything other than where he was at the time of the shooting.[79] The HSCA went further. They asked him if he saw Frazier in the parking lot that morning. He said he did, and that Frazier was alone. Someone he knew asked Frazier where his friend was. Frazier said, "I dropped him off at the building."[80]

But that's not the clincher. As noted, the early critics—Harold Weisberg, Sylvia Meagher, and Mark Lane—all bought into Oswald and the curtain rod story even though that story was delivered secondhand through Wesley Frazier. Yet when Oswald's apartment owner, Gladys Johnson, was asked if the room Oswald lived in had curtains on its curtain rods, she said it did. When asked if Oswald ever mentioned bringing in new curtains or rods, she said no. Her testimony was minimized by Weisberg's discovery of the famous Black Star Photo Agency picture taken by Gene Daniels. On the twenty-third Daniels took a photo of Mrs. Johnson adjusting the curtains standing atop Oswald's bed. This photo did much to persuade some that Frazier was repeating what Oswald had told him. Yet, as former detective Ian Griggs points out, Howard Roffman wrote Daniels a letter inquiring about the circumstances of the picture. Daniels wrote back that the lady asked him not to take any photos at the time since she had to adjust the curtains. *The reporters had disturbed the room* and she didn't want anyone to see it like that.[81] Daniels shot the picture anyway. Therefore, the photo does not support the story Frazier recited about Oswald and the curtain rods.

To show just how invested the Dallas Police are in Frazier's story, consider this: When this new information about the Daniels photo put a big question mark next to it—as in why would Oswald say that to Frazier if he didn't need any curtain rods—they came up with a fallback position. In Larry Sneed's book *No More Silence,* the revised version now became that Oswald was bringing the rods for someone else. This is how necessary it is for the DPD to protect Frazier.

Bugliosi's discussion of this complex, multilayered, and deliberately buried issue is grade school stuff. As mentioned above, he gets the FBI report on the paper samples wrong. He then argues about the length of the rifle and if there were curtain rods found by the police at the Depository.[82] He actually writes that Oswald's "fingerprints" were on the bag, leaving out the fact that it was one index finger and there were likely two bags. R. D. Lewis's name is mentioned once, but not in regard to Frazier's polygraph. I could find no mention of the Enfield at Frazier's house either. He even writes this: ". . . the general description of the bag given by Frazier and his sister matched the bag found in the sniper's nest." I really don't know what he is talking about here since the bag tested by the FBI was not just significantly smaller, but was actually discolored by the test they did.[83] But further, there was no photo of the bag made *inside* the Depository so how does he know what was found "in the sniper's nest." Third, if you look at the Commission testimony I just cited, you will note something quite disturbing. Pat Speer has noted that the bag photographed by the press outside the building does not look like the bag returned to the DPD by the Bureau on the twenty-sixth. But in the testimony by FBI agent James Cadigan quoted above, it is revealed that there was actually a third bag![84] This was a "replica" bag made by the Bureau at the Depository on December 1 and used to present to witnesses for "identification purposes"! According to the FBI, they had such a difficult time getting a print off the bag sent them by the police that it was discolored and not really recognizable. Witnesses were supposed to identify a bag that was not in existence on the day of the crime. Only the

Warren Commission could let the FBI get away with such a thing. Bugliosi not only makes no criticism of it, he doesn't even tell the reader that it happened.

The story of this (these) paper bag(s), Wesley Frazier, his sister, and the curtain rods can be challenged every single step of the way from Troy West to whether or not there were one, two, or three bags eventually submitted into evidence. To me, like Oswald ordering the rifle, the paper bag has been accepted for way too long. And so has Wesley Frazier. As Roger Feinman has written, one way to look at the episode is this: By the early evening of the twenty-second, the DPD had very little besides the notoriously bad eyewitness Howard Brennan, who couldn't be relied upon to put Oswald on the sixth floor. As Police Chief Jesse Curry later admitted, they had no one who put Oswald in the building with a gun in his hand.[85] Therefore, they needed Frazier and his "Oswald carrying a package" story. This is the man Bugliosi used to open his prosecution in his phony London trial. If this case were ever reopened, he would be one of the first witnesses called to the stand. And he would be there a very long time. The reason is easy to understand: If there is no gun sack, there is no gun.

Where Did the Bullets Go?

Let us continue with some more of the work done by the DPD that Bugliosi can find no serious fault with.

As noted in Chapter 5 titled "Oswald's Defense," Bugliosi raises no questions about the bullet audit or collection procedures of the Dallas police. What he does with the bullet apparently found by DPD detective Buddy Walthers is a case in point.[86] This incident was captured by photographers Jim Murray and William Allen shortly after the assassination. Walthers and another man both bend over to examine something in the grass. The other man inserts something in his pocket. According to Bugliosi, they were just testing sod. He concludes, as he always does, that this is all much ado about nothing. There are two problems with his analysis. Mark Oakes did an excellent job researching this subject many years ago and made a filmed report on his investigation of the incident. He makes a strong case that the man next to Walthers was FBI agent Robert Barrett. Barrett's friend, FBI agent Robert Gemberling, is the person who helped ID Barrett. What does Bugliosi do? Predictably, he calls Barrett. Barrett says it was not him, and that is that. I could have saved Bugliosi the trouble on that one. It's sort of like J. Edgar Hoover denying Oswald was an FBI informant to the Warren Commission and Bugliosi believing it (which, of course, he does). Secondly, he says that Walthers only talked about the bullet to some people, for example, Alvin Maddox of the sheriff's department. But in a 1996 interview with Oakes, Maddox said he actually saw the bullet.

Let's take another example in this regard. The *Dallas Times Herald* reported on November 24, 1963, that "Dallas Police Lt. J. C. Day of the crime lab estimated the distance from the sixth floor corner window the slayer used to the spot where one of the bullets was recovered at 100 yards." When George O'Toole called Day about this and the matter of the second rifle found in the Depository, Day broke off the conversation and referred him to the Warren Report.[87] Of course, that makes no sense because the Warren Report says there was only one bullet found at Parkland Hospital and there were two fragments of a bullet found in the limousine. If you add those two to the hit to James Tague, 200 feet away, and add in this one, then that makes four bullets. Bugliosi mentions this report by Day, sloughs it off, and does not mention O'Toole's call to Carl Day.[88] As he usually does, he says that for the report to be true then the DPD was in on the conspiracy, "an allegation for which there is no evidence."[89] Not true Mr. Prosecutor. They would have to have been in on the cover-up. Which is a different thing. Which they could have done for different motives, like CYA, since the president had been killed in their town. And it didn't have to be planned in advance or hit upon spontaneously within a few minutes of the shooting. As we have seen with Wesley Frazier, it could have happened many hours later.

Then there is the famous Aldredge bullet strike. Within a day or two after the assassination, Dallas resident Eugene Aldredge saw a four-inch-long bullet mark in the middle of the sidewalk along Elm Street. He did not tell the FBI about it since he assumed the mark had surely been noticed and would be discussed in the Warren Commission volumes. When he realized this was not the case, he contacted the FBI and told them about it. He also told them that Carl Freund, a reporter for the *Dallas Morning News,* had also looked at the mark and had decided it was a bullet strike. Less than a week after calling the FBI, he and a friend went to look at the mark. He now saw that it was still visible, but it had been filled in with a mixture of concrete and asbestos. And a crude attempt had been made to alter the mark to make it look like it was weather-worn. In its report on the mark, the FBI admitted to finding it and described it as being four inches long and a half inch wide. Why did they dismiss its significance? Because it could not have been made by a shot fired from the sniper's nest window in the Depository. The window they have Oswald firing from.[90] I could not find Aldredge's name in the index to *Reclaiming History.*

The German Mauser

It would have been interesting if O'Toole would have had the opportunity to talk to Day about the second subject he wanted him to address. That is, the second rifle found in the building. Because as previously noted, there were several reports that a German Mauser was located before the Mannlicher Carcano was discovered. In addition to the affidavit by Seymour Weitzman, the report by Deputy Sheriff Eugene Boone, and Boone's testimony about Fritz and Day identifying the weapon as a Mauser, there is also the testimony of Treasury Agent Frank Ellsworth who was on the scene that day. He said the Mannlicher Carcano was discovered on the fourth or fifth floor by a couple of local detectives. It was not discovered on the same floor as the cartridges. Ellsworth recalls talking about this with others. His idea at the time was that the assassin carried the rifle down a floor or two and then dropped it.[91]

One reason that O'Toole was interested in talking to Day about the second rifle was that he had done a PSE test on Deputy Constable Weitzman when he appeared on the 1967 CBS special about the *Warren Report*. By this time of course, Weitzman had been forced to take back his original affidavit saying he identified the weapon as a 7.65 Mauser. O'Toole found near-maximum stress throughout Weitzman's renunciation of his first identification.[92] When he tried to find Weitzman in Dallas in 1973, he discovered he was not with the sheriff's department anymore. He then tried to locate him but was unsuccessful. One more thing to add in this regard, as Sylvia Meagher points out in *Accessories After the Fact*, when Weitzman was deposed in Dallas by assistant counsel Joe Ball, they discussed an interview he did for the FBI in which it appears he described the rifle in detail. That FBI report is nowhere in the twenty-six Commission volumes.[93]

In 1997 author Noel Twyman first published evidence questioning whether or not there were two or three shells found at the so-called sniper's nest. Twyman presented photos and documents showing that the DPD sent not three but two shells to be examined by the FBI. This matches the documents turned up by John Hunt which show two shells arrived in Washington that night. Bugliosi admits this but he explains it by saying that Will Fritz kept one shell in Dallas for "comparison tests."[94] Question to the prosecutor: Weren't those tests being done in Washington that night by the Bureau? Bugliosi tries to dodge this question by saying that Fritz was trying to find out where the shells had been purchased. Really? And you needed a sample to compare the ones on the shelf with the ones in evidence? Let me add one more thing about this shell issue. When Twyman's book first appeared and this issue was raised, the ARRB did an inquiry about it. They discovered an odd thing. When they interviewed the policemen still alive involved with the search of the sixth floor, each of them passed the buck. That is, no one would take responsibility for discovering the shells. The police then said that this happened a lot. The name credited to a discovery was not always correct. Go figure.[95]

Sebastian Latona vs. Lt. Day

As I said, Bugliosi backs the DPD all the way, therefore he finds no problem at all with one of the most highly controversial areas of their investigation: the fingerprint tests. In fact, he actually calls it probative evidence in the case.[96] Again, this is quite puzzling. In his web essay on the subject, Michael Griffith noted that Lt. Day said that he had lifted a palm print from the rifle barrel before the rifle was sent to Washington late on the evening of the twenty-second. Yet when FBI expert Sebastian Latona got the rifle, not only did he find no prints of any value anywhere, he found no evidence of any fingerprint traces or of a lift.[97] Further, Day took no photograph of this palm print either before or after he says he lifted it. Former NYC Deputy DA Robert Tanenbaum told me this is standard procedure for any respectable police department. You do this to guard against losing the print in the lift. Latona said the same thing.[98] But Day didn't do it with this palm print. Further, Latona said there was no note on the rifle about where to look for the palm print.[99]

Now, Bugliosi says that Day did not do this since he was alerted the FBI was taking the rifle to Washington.[100] The implication being that everything was rushed and impromptu. Interestingly, in this paragraph the author supplies no time frame for when Day was alerted to this fact, and when the rifle then left Dallas. Day said this call came in at around 8:00–8:30 PM. Yet, by his own admission, Day took a photo of the rifle at 9:00–9:30.[101] Why did he not take a photo of the palm print then because the rifle did not actually leave until shortly before midnight?[102] By not supplying the time frame, Bugliosi avoids the question of what Day did with the rifle for those intervening hours. And if the print was there, why on earth did he not lift it at that time?

Now, the evidence was returned to Dallas from Washington on the twenty-fourth. One would think that Day would have certainly jumped on the rifle at this point and finished the job he was halted from doing. He didn't. He didn't get to work until the twenty-sixth. This was the day the evidence was sent back to Washington. Yet, Day's palm print did not arrive there until the twenty-ninth! Whereas the other prints from the Depository arrived on the twenty-seventh.[103]

As Michael Griffith pointed out, Day had two opportunities to forward the lift with the rifle yet the palm print did not arrive in Washington until one week after the assassination. Bugliosi does not even point this out to the reader. In fact, he does the opposite. After noting the date of the 29th, two lines later,

Bugliosi announces that his palm print now precluded Oswald from saying he was not in possession of the rifle.[104] The prosecutor ignores the fact that Oswald had now been dead for five days. So his verdict is postmortem.

It is interesting in this regard to note something the author does not. District Attorney Henry Wade was the chief spokesman for the DPD during Oswald's two days in detention. He held press conferences on Friday and Saturday night yet he did not mention any palm print either evening even though he was asked about them. But he did mention it on Sunday night, after Oswald's death.[105] This was after Oswald's autopsy and around the time of the delivery of the corpse to the local funeral parlor.

Now, as Griffith notes, even the Warren Commission had problems with the late arriving palm print. Chief Counsel J. Lee Rankin asked the FBI to question Day about it. Here is what makes this episode fascinating. The man they sent to question Day was FBI agent Vincent Drain. Drain was the man responsible for transferring the evidence on the evening of the twenty-second. Drain says he was never told by anyone in the DPD about any such palm print when he picked up the evidence.[106] Day said he *did* mention it. So when Drain went to interview Day for the FBI about his palm print, Day refused to sign any sworn statement—knowing Drain would contradict him.

But Bugliosi has an out for that. He brings us Rusty Livingstone. Livingstone says Drain was distracted when Day told him this, so he didn't hear it.[107] Evidently Bugliosi kept a straight face when he heard this. Drain is hearing about a print on the rifle that killed JFK and he was distracted. By what, pray tell? A heart attack?

Livingstone is the Dallas cop who waited thirty years to copublish a book called *First Day Evidence*. This book came out in 1993, right after the time of Oliver Stone's film *JFK*. Livingstone now pronounced that not only did they have a palm print, but also a fingerprint within an inch of the trigger guard. As many have asked—but not Bugliosi—why did Rusty wait almost three decades to tell us this? Consider all the pressure the DPD had been under during the first forty-eight hours, then during the ten months of the Warren Commission. Consider how they were being questioned by the FBI and the Commission and the press about the late arriving palm print. Why did they not make this fingerprint public during the first forty-eight hours or the ten-month life of the Commission? Why did they keep this evidence under wraps? Further, and equally inexplicable, why did they then not give it to the HSCA fifteen years later? Did Rusty know Oliver Stone was going to make a movie and he might be able to make some money with a book before he died? It is all too bizarre to contemplate. Yet, Bugliosi asks none of these questions. But as we saw in the last chapter, he poses all sorts of interrogatory flatulence about, for example, the photograph Jim Garrison had in Clinton. Yet Rusty Livingstone's three-decade-old prints leave him strangely silent. With the behavior of the DPD in this regard, I have little doubt they will have another surprise for us at the fiftieth anniversary. And Bugliosi will pose no question about its rather late arrival.

Bugliosi does what he can to cut off any speculation that anyone was taking fingerprints off Oswald's corpse at Miller Funeral home. Eventually, he admits it happened. And he admits that the FBI must have done it.[108] (He doesn't have much choice since the director was wiping black ink off Oswald's fingers.[109]) But he tries to limit what could actually have been done. First, he makes all kinds of excuses for agents being there in the first place. He says they had to have multiple fingerprint samples. Yet, everyone knows the DPD fingerprinted Oswald multiple times. Even sets of prints where they say he "Refused to Sign." (Which is an essay in and of itself. Why would Oswald refuse to sign his own fingerprint card?) Second, he uses Day—of all people—to say that he does not think it's possible to transfer a print from a print card to another object.[110] FBI agent Drain says not only can it be done, he thinks the DPD did it: ". . . because they were getting a lot of heat by Sunday night. . . . Something like that happened."[111]

Baker vs. Baker

Like Wesley Frazier and his dubious curtain rod story, the Warren Commission immortalized the famous scene in the Book Depository where Marrion Baker confronted Oswald drinking a soda. The critics accepted it. Oliver Stone then memorably depicted it in his 1991 film *JFK*. Since the incident has attained iconic status, we all understand what it conveys and what it is supposed to mean. Dallas Patrolman Marrion Baker was traveling in the motorcade. He heard the shots. He drove up to the Texas School Book Depository. He met Oswald's supervisor Roy Truly. They ascended to the second floor. Baker somehow saw a figure through a door window in the lunchroom there. He accosted him with his gun drawn and said to Truly, "Do you know this man, does he work here?" Truly replied that he did and they turned around and continued back up the stairs. As with Frazier's curtain rod tale, everyone on both sides accepted it. In the Frazier instance, the question became not was it true but how long the bag was. In this instance, the argument centered over whether or not Oswald could have come down from the sixth floor and walked into the lunchroom in time for Baker to see him in front of a soda machine (which, as we have seen, has now been decided with the work of Barry Ernest on Vickie Adams), or, as authors like Howard Roffman and Don Thomas argued, whether or not Baker could have even seen Oswald through the glass window in the door. If he did not, then he had likely come up to the lunchroom from the first floor. No one questioned whether or not it happened. And in one version Baker told, Oswald had a Coke in his hand. In another he did not.

That last discrepancy should have told us something. For how, on the day of the assassination, could Baker have not recalled such a revealing detail. Or how could he have let someone talk him out of it. Because in the version printed in the Warren Report, Truly added that Oswald's hands were empty. Yet as Sylvia Meagher points out, as late as September of 1964, Baker was still writing about the Coke in Oswald's hands.[112] Someone actually drew a line through that bit of information. What makes this interesting is that Baker wrote this six months after he gave his Commission testimony, in which he said there was nothing in Oswald's hands.[113] In other words, Baker never got his story straight.

Another indication as to how Baker's testimony was evolving is the version of it in Gary Savage's book, *First Day Evidence*. In that version, he says he encountered Oswald on the first floor. Truly identified him as an employee, and they left him there as they proceeded into the building. But then Baker adds something interesting, "The investigator from Washington contacted me for my recollection of what happened, but I guess they weren't interested in what I said."[114] As we will see, probably because the improvement wasn't quite good enough yet for the Commission. Because Oswald was still on the first floor. Yet, this version pretty much coincides with Oswald's own story.[115]

The first person I ever heard who actually questioned the provenance of this story was David Lifton. He asked whether, on the surface, it made any sense. Because as Truly tells it, Baker hailed Oswald, Oswald walked toward him, and Baker essentially had his gun within three feet of his stomach. As Lifton commented, "Was Baker going to shoot him for drinking a Coke?" I smiled at the cleverness, but I didn't actually question the incident.

Today I do. Why? Because the final Commission version does not even resemble the incident that Baker described on the day of the assassination. On that day Baker executed an affidavit in which he described this encounter himself. He describes going up the stairs with Truly. Then this startling passage follows: ". . . as we reached the third or fourth floor, I saw a man walking away from the stairway. I called to the man and he turned around and came back towards me. The manager said I know that man he works here. I then turned the man loose and went on up to the top floor. The man I saw was a white man approximately thirty years old, 5'9", 165 pounds, dark hair and wearing a light brown jacket."

This affidavit exists in two forms, a handwritten and typed version. Unlike the handwritten one, the typed version has no cross-outs and is phrased more grammatically. But they both say the same thing. Baker signed them both on the twenty-second. Note the stunning differences between the affidavit and the incident as described in the Warren Report. In the affidavit there is nothing about seeing Oswald through a window in the door. Nothing about the lunchroom. Nothing about a Coke. They weren't even in any room, but near a stairway. And the guy he saw does not appear to be Oswald. He was older, heavier, and he was wearing a brown jacket.

For me, what certifies that Baker is being honest here is that when he went down to the police station to write his affidavit, Oswald was *in the same room* with him. Which Baker described as a small room, so small that he had to almost fall over Oswald to get out.[116] In other words, he was in the same room with Oswald and he still did not name him in either version of his affidavit. According to the Commission, he had just stuck a gun in this guy's stomach.

Toward the end of the evening, the DPD began to realize that Baker's first day testimony could prevent the noose they were preparing from setting around Oswald's neck. So when Det. Marvin Johnson made out an undated report either that evening or the next day, he transmitted Baker's first day information accurately—except for one thing not in the affidavit. He wrote, "Officer Baker later identified Lee Harvey Oswald as the man he had seen on the 4th floor. . . ." At the very end of this report, and completely out of chronological order, Johnson adds that Baker identified Oswald at the station in the small room. Yet, Baker told the Commission that he was making out the affidavit at the time in the room. And Oswald's name is not in it![117]

Then, four months later, Baker's testimony was in its final dry-cleaned and altered version for the Warren Commission. Baker ID's Oswald, but now he is a guy in the second floor lunchroom.[118] In other words, the guy in the jacket on the fourth floor stairway was gone, not to be seen again. If you are counting, that is four different versions of this story.

But let me add this about Baker's Warren Commission testimony. He still denied that Oswald was dressed like the man he saw. Second, assistant counsel David Belin had to admonish him about his revealing body language—he told him to look at him when he answered questions.[119] Third, Allen Dulles understood the problem Baker's police station nonidentification of Oswald presented. So he tried to make the time they shared the same room as brief as possible. Finally, Dulles and Belin took this interview off the record no less than five times.[120]

In tracing the evolution of this story, it is necessary to follow how Oswald's words were also transmuted. As Anthony Summers writes in *Conspiracy,* Oswald maintained that he was on the first floor eating his cheese sandwich lunch at the time of the shooting.[121] (Which, by the way, is the lunch he maintained he brought from home.[122]) On November 23 James Hosty and Jim Bookhout wrote an FBI report. Based on Oswald's November 22 questioning, the authors' wrote that Oswald said he ate lunch on the first floor, but went up to the second floor to get a Coke. It is not specified in this report when he went to the second floor. But more importantly, there is no mention of Oswald getting a gun stuck in his stomach by Baker.[123] Which Oswald certainly would have recalled and reported. On the 24th, after Oswald is shot, Bookhout rewrites this report by himself. Now, Bookhout has Oswald remembering the Baker gun in his stomach.[124] Notably, before the Commission, Hosty had an opportunity to alter this memo also. He chose not to.[125] Another example of this evolution, when postal inspector Harry Holmes wrote a long memorandum recalling what Oswald said in his interviews, there was no mention of Oswald at the soda machine, the Coke in his hands, or of Baker pointing the gun at him.[126] When pressed by the Commission, he could not recall Oswald saying anything about the second floor encounter with Baker. But David Belin later prompted Holmes about the Coke: "Did he say anything about a Coca Cola or anything like that . . .?" This was clearly a leading question. And then Holmes recalled it, five months after he wrote the memo.[127] But he only recalled what Belin prompted him about: the Coke and the machine. There was nothing else about Baker and Truly.

In nearly every instance where one reads of his interrogations, Oswald is mentioned as having seen two black workers at lunch in the "domino room" on the first floor.[128] And as Summers notes, this was corroborated.[129] Now, Jack Dougherty told the Commission that he was on the fifth floor at the time of the assassination, near the west elevator.[130] This would have had to be very close to the stairway where the Commission has Oswald allegedly tearing down at the time. Dougherty never mentioned seeing him.

Let me note one more point about why I think the Baker-Oswald incident may have been created. In most accounts, Bonnie Ray Williams is said to have been on the sixth floor eating his lunch until about 12:15–12:20. (Bugliosi, as noted earlier, makes him a fast eater and has him out of there at about 12:09.) But there is evidence that Williams was there until even later. After Jarman picked up his lunch and Norman quickly ate in the domino room, they both went outside for the motorcade. Norman and Jarman did not walk up to the fifth floor for a bird's-eye view until the announcement was made that the motorcade was on Main Street. At the earliest, this came on the police radio at 12:22. And in fact, Jarman told the Commission that they went up between 12:20 and 12:25.[131] The two went inside and rode an elevator up. Williams said he joined them down there after lunch.[132] This must have been at 12:25. It is clear from reading Williams's testimony that the FBI and the Commission wanted him to change his story and have him leave the sixth floor as early as possible. To the point of the Bureau writing down things he did not say. And the reason for the witness tampering? To give Oswald more time to set up his so-called sniper's nest, that is, the shield of boxes and the gun rest. Bugliosi does not mention the clear tampering with Williams's testimony. (I won't even discuss Mrs. Robert Reid who says she saw Oswald walk through her office at about 12:33. I don't find her credible. One reason being that, as Don Thomas has shown, Oswald was out of the building by 12:33.[133])

Now, let us interconnect this material to explain why Bugliosi leaves it out. With Williams on the sixth floor until 12:25 and Dougherty where he was on the fifth floor at the time of the shooting, Oswald could not have been where the Commission says he was at the time Kennedy was killed. With the Baker incident now dubious, this most likely leaves him on the first floor. When he exactly bought the Coke, no one knows. But it was not when Baker said he did. And this is the reason I believe the incident was created after the fact. Getting Oswald from floor six to floor two was improbable enough. Getting him from floor six to floor one would have been impossible. And the weight of this new evidence suggests the DPD, FBI, and Warren Commission understood that. So they created this phony forty-year-old argument over Oswald speeding down the stairs by altering Baker's first day affidavit. Just like they created the ersatz forty-year-old argument about the length of the curtain rod bag.

Recall, Baker, like Wesley Frazier, was a prosecution witness at the London trial. Spence never confronted him with his first day affidavit to impeach him. But further, who was the man he confronted on the stairwell, and where did he go?

The Cops and the Backyard Photographs

Before finishing up with the climax of the DPD's excellent performance, that is the murder of Oswald by Jack Ruby while he was literally in their arms, let us note an episode that attracted attention to them in 1993. At this time, the DPD had let their files be catalogued by the City Manager's office under the guidance of Cindy Smolovik. Reporters Ray and Mary LaFontaine searched the new releases and discovered the so-called ghost photograph. This was a cut-out of the famous backyard photograph of Oswald with rifle and handgun. It is called a cut-out because the figure of Oswald is actually removed. In other words, it appears to be part of the process of matte insertion to create a composite—the process actually depicted in Oliver Stone's film *JFK*. Along with this photo, there was also picture of a Dallas police officer named Bobby Brown in a pose similar to Oswald in the backyard of the Neely Street house. This was the house where Marina supposedly shot the picture of Oswald.

Brown's story was that this was done at the request of the Secret Service a few days after the assassination. So what about the image being removed from the photo? Brown told author Gary Savage that he had his image removed from the photo because he did not want to be identified with it. When Savage asked him why he would want his image removed from a reenactment: "He was adamant . . . that he only wanted to take himself out of the photograph since it was the background that was the subject and not himself. He said he did this entirely on his own. . . . He said he cut his image out of a developed photograph and placed a white piece of paper behind it. . . ."[134]

As Savage later found out, Brown was not telling him the truth. For the image removed from the photo was not Brown's but Oswald's. As writer John Johnson discovered, this can be proven by comparing this altered photo with the 133-C version of it in the Warren Commission volumes.[135] Further, if Brown was only interested in the photo's background, he could have just studied the photographs the DPD attained from Ruth Paine's home over the weekend of the assassination.

In light of this, Brown then amended his answer. He then said it was done when they got the photos back from the FBI. The idea was not to insert anything into the removed area of the photo, but just to get Oswald's image onto a blank white background. Of course, it was all his idea, "I just did it to be doing something."[136] But if we believe Brown, that would produce Oswald in a seasonally adjusted photo from November, and the originals were allegedly taken in March. What would the evidentiary value be of such an exercise? Further, Brown had a weak explanation for the two thin vertical white lines on the ghost photograph. He said they were the cut lines where Oswald's image was removed. But it was not removed along neat vertical lines. As the LaFontaines suggested, the lines could also have betrayed the use of an overlay of acetate where the inserted figure could be fit into the picture before going to a copy camera.[137]

Another interesting thing to note. The pose struck by Brown did not recall the two photos originally removed from the Paine home. It was a different pose. His pose resembled a photo pilfered from the Dallas Police, which did not show up until the widow of Roscoe White returned it in 1975.[138] Further, as Johnson notes, there were actually two of the ghost photos in the archives. The silhouette was the same but the backgrounds were slightly different. One has the two vertical lines visible, in the other they are removed. As Johnson notes, someone went to some trouble with an airbrush to do so.

All quite interesting and with a difficult to believe story by Bobby Brown to explain it away. When you look up Brown's name in Bugliosi's index, you will not find anything relating to his role in this affair. In fact, I could not find any mention of the episode in the entire book.

Bugliosi and the Murder of Oswald

One of the worst parts of the Warren Report was its inquiry into Ruby's activities at Dallas Police HQ on November twenty-second and twenty-third. Even worse was its examination of how he entered the basement with such exquisite timing on the twenty-fourth and how the DPD made it rather simple for him to kill Oswald.

When Oswald was murdered on television, it was perhaps the most shocking live event in American history. After the shock died down, the obvious question became: Why did Ruby do it? Ruby's initial rationale, to spare Jackie Kennedy the ordeal of testifying at Oswald's trial, was so strained as to be humorous. Yet the author repeats that here without comment.[139] This is a story that Ruby's trial lawyer, Melvin Belli, said he was sure was false.[140] But Bugliosi also adds the "Sheba defense." Ruby would never leave his dog Sheba in the car if he had planned such a thing.[141] If that isn't good enough for you, he quotes someone using the old standby for prosecutors: "He liked to be in the middle of things no matter what it was."[142] But the author is really covering the waterfront on this one. He later quotes someone else: "He was a great patriot and he thought he was doing a great favor for the people of the United States."[143] He then pulls out the capper, he uses Dr. Renatus Hartogs, the psychiatrist who examined Oswald: "Ruby appears to have felt he had the right to avenge the murder."[144] This motley collection seems to me to fulfill the old cliché of throwing enough mud on the wall in hopes something will stick. It's because these excuses are so unconvincing that many came to the conclusion that Ruby was sent to silence Oswald.

Bugliosi tries to cut that off by using his own particular timing to prevent Ruby from coming into the basement at the moment that Oswald walked down the corridor. Here Bugliosi makes two questionable assumptions. The first is that we know when Ruby got into the basement. The second is that we know how he got there.[145] The fact is that neither is known for certain. For instance, there is some testimony that he was there for three minutes, which all but eliminates him getting there from the Main Street ramp.[146] Bugliosi also tries to shorten the time frame Ruby had from the Western Union office to walk over to the nearby City Hall. He says it took two minutes or so.[147] It is actually four minutes from the time stamp on the money order he sent—11:17—to when Oswald was shot, which was 11:21.

Bugliosi wants us to believe the old Warren Commission reconstruction: That Ruby walked over to the Main Street ramp and then strolled down into the basement about two minutes before the shooting. And Ruby, that well-known friend of many Dallas cops, did this in plain sight of a number of witnesses who did not see him. This would include reporter Terrance McGarry and taxi driver Harry Tasker.[148] There was also a police witness, Don Flusche, who was in position opposite the ramp to see Ruby walk down it at the proper time. He said he did not see him. (Flusche is an interesting witness who we will return to later.) Further, he was also missed by three police officers who drove out the ramp while Ruby was allegedly walking down.[149] Two of the policemen in the car, Sgt. Putnam and Lt. Pierce, were absolutely certain Ruby did not come down the ramp at the time they were leaving. And Pierce knew Ruby.

Why is this important? Because the basis of the Commission's case is that this car blocked the view of the man who was guarding the ramp against unauthorized entries. That man was Officer Roy Vaughn. The Commission said that when the Pierce car was driving out, Ruby walked down the ramp and into the basement. In all the intervening years, there is no credible witness who said he saw Ruby come down the ramp at the time the Commission said he did. There are problems with witnesses like Napoleon Daniels.[150] One of the Commission's problems with Daniels was that he said he saw the man he thought was Ruby walking down the ramp when no car was coming up. Which would imply that Vaughn was either irresponsible or he let Ruby in on purpose. Three other witnesses could be mentioned in this regard, Jim Turner, William J. Newman, and K. H. Kroy. But the first only saw Ruby two thirds of the way down the ramp, and as we shall see, there was another way Ruby could have secured that position. Newman could not identify the man he saw as Ruby. And K. H. Kroy's identification was equivocal.[151]

In addition to shaving the time off Ruby's walk, Bugliosi also says that if Ruby had planned ahead to kill Oswald, it is inconceivable he would not have been in the basement well in advance of the transfer. Why? Because "He knew it would most likely be the last chance he would ever have to silence him. There are no ifs, ands, or buts about this."[152] There aren't Mr. Prosecutor? Perhaps Bugliosi missed the WFAA TV broadcast that morning which stated that, after he arrived at the county jail, Oswald would be allowed to be questioned by members of the press.[153] And if you recall, Ruby disguised himself as a press representative on Friday night when he corrected a statement about Oswald. So the distinct possibility exists that if Ruby's timing was off at City Hall, he could have just followed the caravan over to the county jail. Bugliosi also asks: Well, why didn't Ruby try to polish off Oswald on Friday or Saturday? As we will see, Ruby did not have such a great opportunity as he did on Sunday. But further, Oswald did not make his attempted call to military intelligence officer John Hurt until Saturday night. For many people, that call was a pretty good indication that Oswald was at least thinking of revealing who he really was. Since the Dallas Police have always maintained that there was no stenographic record or taping of his interrogations, as far as we know, that was the first sign Oswald might talk. The morning after, he was dead.

Now, let's give the unexpurgated version of how Ruby's actions put him in the right place at the right time. Police dispatcher Billy Grammar got a phone call the evening before Oswald's murder. The caller said words to the effect, "You have to change the plan. If not, *we* are going to kill him." (Emphasis added.) Grammar knew Ruby, and he said Ruby called him by name. The next day, when Grammar heard that Ruby had killed Oswald, he retroactively put the voice together with the man. He concluded the murder was planned. (Grammar's interview is on YouTube. His name is not in Bugliosi's index.)

Both Jim Marrs and Anthony Summers write that there is uncertainty about Jack Ruby's movements on the morning of the twenty-fourth.[154] In fact, even the Warren Report admits this.[155] Ruby and his roommate George Senator said that Ruby stayed in his apartment until about 11:00 AM. Yet, when the cleaning lady called about two hours earlier in the morning, the voice on the other end sounded terribly strange to her. She wasn't sure it was Ruby's.[156] She continued by saying even though she had been his employee for a long time, Ruby did not seem to comprehend who she was or why she was calling. Further, three TV technicians—Warren Richey, Ira Walker, John Smith—said they saw Ruby near their broadcast van outside the police station before 10 AM. Ruby asked them, "Has Oswald been brought down yet?"[157] A church minister said he was on an elevator with Ruby at 9:30, and Ruby's destination was the floor where Oswald was.[158] Yet, Ruby *was* at his apartment about an hour later. He got a call from one of his employees, Karen Carlin, to wire her some funds. He got off the line and went to Western Union, which was about a minute's walk from City Hall. That morning, George Senator was at the Eatwell Café near the police station when he heard Oswald was shot. He called one of Ruby's lawyers to represent his roommate, *before* he knew Ruby was the killer.[159]

A day or two after the murder, Senator had a meeting in his apartment with Ruby attorney Tom Howard and two members of the press, Jim Koethe and Bill Hunter. What was discussed is unknown. But the three men who met with Senator were all dead by March of 1965.[160] For days after the shooting, Senator acted like a man "overwhelmed with fear." He refused to sleep at the apartment and soon left Dallas altogether.[161] Summers postulates that it may have been Senator who took the early call from the cleaning lady. Which could have left Ruby out and about.

Like fanatical Warren Commission assistant counsel David Belin, Bugliosi repeatedly states that it would have been all but impossible for Ruby to have timed his visit to the Western Union office. The reason being that Oswald's transfer time was indefinite. All that had been decided was that it would be after 10:00 AM.[162] He can insist on the miraculous timing since he leaves out most of the above. If Ruby did not answer the cleaning lady's call then he could have been at City Hall checking on the status of the transfer. Which is what the testimony of the TV technicians and the minister suggests. He then received the Carlin call at approximately 10:20. It only takes about 15–20 minutes to drive from Ruby's to City Hall.[163] Some of this time was allegedly taken up by Ruby taking a bath. But why would you take a bath to wire money? What makes this alternative scenario so interesting is this: Many years ago, a *Probe* subscriber named Ray Gallagher sent the author a photo. It depicted a picture of Western Union taken from one of the open doors behind City Hall. It was an eye-opener. The proximity was such that you could signal someone. In other words, Ruby's timing did not have to be exquisite. He could have just been waiting in his car at Western Union for the proper moment. It's hard to believe that no one in twenty-one years ever pointed this out to Bugliosi. But if they did not, then it tells us a lot about whom he was consorting with for two decades.

Which brings us to the reason for Ruby being at Western Union. As alluded to earlier, he received a call on Sunday morning from an employee named Karen Carlin. Originally, on Saturday night, she wanted a very small advance of $5.00 on her salary, which Ruby gave her through an acquaintance.[164] As Australian researcher Greg Parker first indicated to me, it would literally take pages to analyze the four interviews in the Commission volumes of Bruce and Karen Carlin. As Greg realized, they are that odd. But let us be brief. First, it seems there was official pressure being exerted on the Carlins to go along with the "rent and groceries" excuse for the wire transfer on Sunday morning. Yet when the FBI interviewed the Carlin landlord, a funny thing happened. There was no question to Weldon Thomas about late or delayed rent payments.[165] Realizing that this posed a problem, the Secret Service went back to interview him on March 31. It turns out that 1) The payment schedule was rather informal,

2) There was never any argument if it was late by a few days, and 3) Thomas never presented a demand for payment. So what was the urgency about the Sunday wire? Interestingly, the landlord told the Secret Service he never even talked to Karen about the payments at all. Bruce handled them. Yet, in the Commission hearings, Karen is supposed to be the one who broached the subject with Ruby—even though Bruce Carlin talked to Ruby on Saturday night. About the crucial point of whose idea it was to send the money by Western Union, Karen first says it was Ruby's.[166] When Counsel Leon Hubert tries to talk her out of this, Carlin suggests she has had this done to her before by saying, "I won't say for sure about anything. I'm not for sure about nothing anymore." So when Hubert later says, "It was his idea wasn't it?" on cue, she neutralizes her previous testimony by saying, "I don't remember." Karen understood from experience.

What makes this even more interesting is Bruce Carlin's earlier Commission testimony. There seems to be difficulty in Bruce keeping his "rent and food" story in line. He got so confused on this matter that he almost gave the game away. Listen to what he says:

> "As far as the money going for rent and groceries, because *I didn't know that I would have to remember*, and in fact I talked to Mr. Tom Thomas about it, because somebody from the . . . FBI or Secret Service had called to clear up a number of these things on the phone. In fact, they called almost *in the middle of the night* . . . ."[167] (Emphasis added.)

The clincher in that tantalizing mouthful is this: Tom Thomas was not an FBI agent. He was Carlin's colleague from work. And near the end of his second interview, Bruce complained about the harassment by the FBI and Secret Service and how he even lost a job over his testimony![168] Clearly, the pressure was being applied to cooperate with the story he didn't know he had to remember. And before Hubert deposed Bruce Carlin he admitted he pre-interviewed him in the hallway. Further, the Carlins did something fairly rare for Warren Commission witnesses. They brought a lawyer. And the lawyer actually asked questions.[169] How sure did the Commission need to be about what the Carlins were going to say? According to an undated DPD record which probably was transmitted in April 1964, Karen revealed that she had been interviewed by the FBI and Secret Service *seven times*.

During his testimony Ruby made an interesting statement about the pretext for the Western Union wire. Plain and simple, Ruby said he got a call from one of his girls on Sunday morning for money. By putting it out there like that, Ruby makes it sound like 1) she instigated the Sunday call, and 2) it was unexpected. Yet the Carlins' story is that this call had been pre-arranged *by Ruby*. He then says he told her, "Can't you wait until payday?" and she replied, "Jack, you are going to be closed."[170] Yet the thing about waiting for payday had already been discussed the night before. So there was no reason to bring it up on Sunday morning. Finally, Ruby announced he was going to be closed through Sunday, which was the day of this call.[171] In other words, according to Ruby, she could have come in for the money the next day. (In regard to Ruby's penchant for confabulating, one of the most interesting aspects of the HSCA inquiry was their finding that the FBI's polygraph of Ruby was probably faked. This will be discussed in the next chapter.)

There is another piece of Ruby's testimony that makes the Sunday morning wire transfer even more suspicious. Just four sentences before Ruby mentioned the call from Carlin, he went out of his way to describe his Sunday drive to Western Union. He specifically noted he drove by the County Building, the place where Oswald was to be transferred within the hour. He says he saw a crowd outside and therefore thought Oswald had already been moved. What a convenient sight, and at the perfect time. Right before he is about to murder Oswald. Ruby was indulging himself in a large dose of CYA in all these statements,[172] which none of the Commission members present challenged him on. And neither does Bugliosi.

The HSCA Finds Don Flusche

Unlike Bugliosi, the HSCA seriously questioned the Warren Commission version of Ruby strolling down the Main Street ramp. And it should be noted, Ruby himself gave out signals it was false. For in the version of his story given to the Commission he said no one was near him when he walked down the ramp.[173] Yet the Commission says there were at least four people near him: Vaughn and the three policemen in the car. If what Ruby had said was so, then either Vaughn was in on the conspiracy or he was unbelievably negligent. One reason the HSCA disagreed with the Commission on Ruby coming down the ramp is that Ruby was inconsistent in his testimony, and because of the delay within the police department of getting the story to Chief Curry.[174] Another reason was the testimony of the aforementioned Sgt. Flusche. He told HSCA investigator Jack Moriarty that he was in perfect position to watch the ramp at the time since "he was standing diagonally across from Main Street ramp on the opposite side of the street during the period in question."[175] He saw the Pierce car exit the ramp and he saw the commotion inside the basement when Oswald was shot. He told Moriarty that he knew Ruby, and "There was no doubt in his mind that Ruby did not walk down the ramp and, further, did not walk down Main Street anywhere near the ramp."[176] There are indications the DPD deliberately hid Flusche's testimony from both their internal inquiry and the Commission. And, in fact, when a member of the police inquiry heard of Flusche's testimony years later, he said, "It tends to dispute the findings of the investigative team I was assigned to."[177] So the HSCA decided that Ruby came in an unsecured door through an alley.[178] This would have placed him around the end of the ramp and in position to see the Pierce car go by Vaughn. In fact, according to the HSCA, Leon Hubert brought out this point with witness Jim Turner, but it was cut out of the Warren Report.[179] Now, in his Warren Commission testimony Ruby here told another whopper. He said that he did not hide behind anyone once he was in the basement, "unless the television cameras can make it seem that way." Well, perhaps the video feed was altered, because it sure looks like Ruby is hiding behind someone as he eagerly awaits Oswald.[180]

The Horns Get Edited Out

In 2007, Ray Marcus called me and asked an odd question. He said, "Jim, what version of Oswald's killing have you seen?" I said, "What do you mean, what version?" He said: "The one with one horn, two horns, or no horns?" I said I had seen the one with one horn. Marcus then explained that the original version has two horns but through the years, this version has been edited, and I had seen one of the edited versions. He said, "I'll send it to you. You'll understand why immediately." He was correct about the understanding. The first horn goes off at almost the exact second that Oswald emerges from the office and into the corridor. The second horn goes off about a nanosecond before Ruby plunges forward to shoot Oswald. Once you're aware of it, it is almost eerie to watch. Bugliosi describes the horns. He doesn't describe the timing.[181] Ruby made this all even stranger in 1965. Because he then wrote a note in which he alluded to the horns. In a letter secured by Bill Diehl of the *St. Louis Post Dispatch*, he talks about being gravely ill and going to a hospital. He closes with, "If you hear a lot of horn-blowing, it will be for me, they will want my blood." Now I guess someone like Bugliosi could say he was referring to St. Gabriel. But yet, Ruby was Jewish.

But besides that, there is something else Bugliosi doesn't describe about this haunting, harrowing episode. As Oswald walks out the corridor, Bugliosi's much praised Capt. Fritz walks so quickly out in front of him that he separates himself from the suspect by several feet. This breaks protection for Oswald. It leaves him exposed from the front, allowing Ruby to shoot him. But making it worse, as you watch this on film, please look at Fritz. After the first shot goes off, everyone is looking in the direction of Oswald. Everybody except one person: Fritz. He doesn't turn around until Ruby is trying to get off his second shot. In all the photos of Oswald being shot by Ruby, the pictures are cropped so you don't see Fritz looking the wrong way. To say the least, it is all very bizarre. Further, before bringing Oswald out, the police had discussed a four pocket formation to protect Oswald. Fritz sprinted out front and broke it. Bugliosi makes nothing of it. This may be a major reason why Fritz refused to give interviews about the assassination.[182]

The Cover-Up

Later on, there was a cover-up inside the criminally corrupt DPD. Roy Vaughn was set up to take the rap for the actual guilty parties. According to Ruby biographer Seth Kantor, one of the men Ruby shielded himself behind before he shot Oswald was policeman Blackie Harrison.[183] When this concealment was pointed out to him, Ruby exploded in rage.[184] The day Harrison was supposed to be polygraphed about Oswald's killing, he was on tranquilizers in order to disguise his reactions. Therefore his test turned out inconclusive.[185] Lt. Jack Revill, who was in on the inquest, said he was never satisfied with Harrison's statement on the issue.[186] Patrick Dean, the man in charge of security that day, failed his polygraph even though he wrote his own questions! And when the HSCA went looking for the record of the test in 1979, like the record of Frazier's polygraph, they couldn't find it.[187] The HSCA concluded that Patrick Dean was a key figure in Oswald's shooting.[188] In fact, while subduing Ruby, Dean reportedly blurted out "Man, you got me in one hell of a shape." Ruby actually apologized to Dean at the time.[189] Yet Dean would not arrange for a deposition with the HSCA and he refused to reply to written questions in the form of an affidavit.

But here's the clincher. Unlike Bugliosi, *even the Commission* understood something was wrong with the police in this whole episode about Ruby's entry and Oswald's murder. Assistant counsel Burt Griffin told Summers, "I always thought all along about the Dallas police that anything that would get them into trouble or embarrass them, they would lie to us. No question about that."[190] And, in fact, Griffin found Dean to be lying about whether or not Ruby could have gotten through a door in an alley that runs along City Hall. Dean said Ruby would have needed a key to enter the door into the basement. Three members of the building's maintenance staff said this was false.[191] Because of this type of deception, assistant counsel Burt Griffin blew up at Dean and composed a memo in which he wrote: 1) Dean was derelict in securing all the doors to the basement, 2) Griffin had reason to believe Ruby did not come down the ramp, and 3) He suspected Dean was now part of a cover-up and was advising Ruby to say he came down the Main Street ramp even though he knew he didn't.[192]

Under pressure from Texas authorities like Henry Wade, Commission Chief Counsel J. Lee Rankin backed away from Griffin's memo in which Griffin suggested Dean be made a target of further inquiry. What does Bugliosi say about this riveting incident? He buries it at the bottom of a page next to an asterisk in his footnote section. He inexplicably says Griffin was reprimanded for "using too much discretion." (Huh?) He then says only Dean complained to the Commission. Thereby leaving out the whole Texas pressure aspect. And he does not mention the detailed accusations of the six-page memo.[193]

Today of course, everyone knows that Ruby later described the outlines of a large conspiracy that manipulated him into shooting Oswald and then taking the fall. In the Diehl letter described earlier, Ruby says that the shot taken at Gen. Walker's home was to make believe Oswald was a crackpot, so there would then be no discernible motive in his killing of Kennedy: he was nutty and the public would leave it at that. In a 1996 interview, former sheriff's deputy Al Maddox said that Ruby slipped him a note before he died saying he was part of a conspiracy and his role was to silence Oswald. In an interview shortly before his death with psychiatrist Werner Teuter, Ruby said the assassination of Kennedy was "an act of overthrowing the government." He added he knew who had had Kennedy killed and that he was framed to kill Oswald.[194] In a famous interview he did in an almost empty courtroom, Ruby said that everything pertaining to his situation had not surfaced yet: "The world will never know the true facts of what occurred—my motive, in other words." When asked if the truth would ever come out, Ruby replied, "No." Because those who had placed him in such a position would never let the world know the true facts, he explained. When asked if these people concealing the truth were in high positions, he said, "Yes."[195]

End Game

From Friday night onward, Ruby had stalked Oswald through police headquarters for two days. He equipped himself with notebook and pen to pass himself off as a reporter for a Jewish newspaper to gain entry into the press room on Friday night.[196] According to reporter Wes Wise, he was even near the county jail on Saturday to check when the transfer would take place.[197] On Sunday, with the help of the police, he was moved into position to attain his goal. And he did. Unforgettably, Det. Don Archer described Ruby in custody after Oswald's shooting. He said Ruby was very hyper:

"He was sweating profusely. I could hear his heart beating. He asked for one of my cigarettes. I gave him a cigarette. Finally . . . the head of the Secret Service came up . . . and he told me that Oswald had died. This should have shocked Ruby because it would mean the death penalty. . . . Instead of being shocked, he became calm, he quit sweating, his heart slowed down. I asked him if he wanted a cigarette, and he advised me he didn't smoke. I was just astonished. . . . I would say his life had depended on him getting Oswald."[198]

Ruby was relieved because Oswald now would never talk. By silencing Oswald he could now get a lenient sentence on perhaps a mental derangement plea or maybe even voluntary manslaughter. Which would mean a maximum of five years in jail.[199] With Oswald dead, there would be no need to answer those troubling queries that were bothering him so much. Oswald's death closed out any questions about Ruby being involved with Cubans from New Orleans in gunrunning operations. Of Ruby being seen by two credible witnesses at Parkland Hospital Friday afternoon. About Julia Ann Mercer seeing him drop off a young man carrying a package to a point near the end of the stockade fence in Dealey Plaza an hour before the assassination. Ruby gambled on a five-year sentence rather than the possibility of facing all that if Oswald had talked. That reason makes a great deal more sense in explaining Ruby's act than Bugliosi saying Jack needed to be "in the middle of things no matter what it was."

I could go on with the perfidy of the Dallas Police. For instance, we could mention the work done by Ian Griggs on the lineup allegedly attended by Howard Brennan, the controversial witness putting Oswald on the sixth floor for the DPD and the Commission. Griggs interviewed the people who were supposed to be viewing the lineup with Brennan. No one else recalled him being there.[200] We could talk about how the police tried to say Oswald tried to shoot someone in the theater, when in fact the bullet in the chamber was never struck by a firing pin. Or the fact that even though Oswald was frisked in the theater, he suddenly ended up with five bullets in his pocket two hours later.

By any objective measurement the sorry tale told above represents an atrocious performance by the Dallas Police. What provoked it was the murder of J. D. Tippit. The combination of having to solve the biggest murder ever in Dallas, plus having Oswald also be suspect as a cop-killer proved too much to handle for an ill-equipped, already compromised police force. Whoever planned the two murders understood that. They knew the combination of killing Kennedy and Tippit would overload a corrupt bureaucracy and crack it. In fact, police officer Jim Leavelle later all but admitted this to author Joseph McBride. He said, that to him, the murder of Kennedy was "no different than a south Dallas nigger killing . . . it was just another murder inside the city lines of Dallas. I've handled hundreds of them." He told McBride about Tippit, "What some people don't realize is that when a police officer gets killed, that takes precedence over the shooting of the president, because that's close to him." The author should note that phrase "nigger killing," and not just for the racism it reveals. But because as many suspected, and as McBride confirmed, the Dallas Police had a large percentage of Klansmen in it. Which would mean that because of Kennedy's civil rights crusade, for those officers, the JFK case would be a "nigger killing" even though Kennedy was Irish.

Unlike Bugliosi, Jesse Curry, chief of Dallas Police, ended up criticizing his force's unsatisfactory result. Years later, he wrote that the Warren Commission had yielded to political pressure. After viewing the Zapruder film, he thought that President Kennedy and Governor Connally had been hit by separate bullets. He did not believe Oswald had acted alone, or perhaps even at all: "We didn't have any proof that Oswald fired the rifle, and never did. Nobody's yet been able to put him in that building with a gun in his hand."[201]

With all this sorry information now in front of him, the reader can decide whose estimation of the Dallas Police is more on the mark: Mr. Bugliosi's or Mr. Watkins's.

CHAPTER NINE

Bugliosi and the FBI

"Hoover lied his eyes out to the Commission."

—Commissioner Wade Boggs

To believe *Reclaiming History*, one has to ignore the character, life, and record of the man who once said, "Justice is only incidental to law and order." That man, J. Edgar Hoover, ran the FBI for over four decades. One also had to deal with the ramifications of what the statement means. But Vincent Bugliosi *has* to ignore it. He has to make the reader believe that once the FBI took over the investigation, J. Edgar Hoover led a flawless, relentless inquiry to find out who killed President John Kennedy.

Before reading *Reclaiming History*, I thought that Bugliosi would recognize the huge problem this presented for him. That is, he would understand that he had to level with the reader on the issues of who Hoover was, what he stood for, and his relationships with the Kennedys and how that almost guaranteed the FBI's problematic inquiry into the JFK case. With what we know about J. Edgar Hoover and the Bureau today, Bugliosi couldn't deny that the FBI caused the Warren Commission major credibility problems. For, as we shall see, even members of the Commission admitted this. Yet he does no such thing. If anything, he actually goes the other way. He actually tries to—there is no other word to use—*praise* the work the FBI did. In this day and age, that is almost shocking.

But since Hoover and the FBI were by far the main investigative arm for Bugliosi's Holy Grail (i.e., the Warren Commission), they are part of the faith he must protect and uphold. At any cost.

Since the book is so (unnecessarily) long, there are two parts to Bugliosi's defense of the FBI. The first part is where he lays in the background of the agency; let's call it the historical backdrop. The second part is where he attempts to analyze and evaluate their performance. As we will see, Bugliosi curtails both parts. But one can see his dilemma. For how could the FBI's conclusions be accurate if their practices were so flawed? In other words, it would make the reader think: How could they have done all that wrong yet got it right? So in his writing on the FBI, Bugliosi somewhat resembles a trapeze artist doing a high wire act. He has to walk a very narrow and delicate path. If he veers an inch from that straight and narrow trail, he's in the net below.

J. Edgar Hoover Exposed

Unfortunately for Bugliosi, many of us are not concerned with walking the straight and narrow with the likes of J. Edgar Hoover, Clyde Tolson, and Cartha DeLoach. Time and knowledge have taught us what they were really about. Therefore, we are not on a high wire walk with him. We can actually veer from that preordained path without fear of falling.

In the eighties and nineties, there were four lengthy biographies that transformed the image of Hoover and the FBI forever. They were, in order, *Secrecy and Power* by Richard G. Powers, *The Boss* by Athan Theoharis, *J. Edgar Hoover: The Man and the Secrets* by Curt Gentry, and *Official and Confidential* by Anthony Summers. While he was alive, there had been journalistic hints and traces of just what an ogre J. Edgar Hoover actually was. But since he was in such a powerful position, he and his toadies could keep a lid on most exposés of the Bureau. But after his death, and with the accumulation of declassified files on many despicable FBI campaigns, for example, COINTELPRO operations against Martin Luther King and the Black Panthers, the image of the Bureau took a terrible beating. From which it has yet to fully recover.

Consider this statement by Bugliosi: "J. Edgar Hoover, since his appointment as FBI director in 1924, at once formed and effectively ran perhaps the finest, most incorruptible law enforcement agency in the world. . . ."[1] This statement is hard to swallow whole but the use of the word "incorruptible" makes it indigestible. Now, right after this, Bugliosi spends about four pages on a relatively brief overview of some of the unsavory acts committed by Hoover's FBI. He does mention a few of the COINTELPRO operations Hoover authorized,[2] and he does call Hoover a megalomaniac who was "beset by obsessions, paranoia and insecurities. . . ." But he tries to give himself an out by saying that there is no credible evidence saying that Hoover ordered the death of President Kennedy.[3]

Bugliosi furthers this red herring by writing in his End Notes the following statement: "Since many conspiracy theorists suspect FBI Director J. Edgar Hoover of being behind the assassination . . ."[4] Here's the problem: I know of no credible Warren Commission critic of any stature, of any generation, who holds to this position. What almost every credible critic believes is that Hoover deliberately covered up the true circumstances of the assassination. (And, as we shall see, the evidence for this is simply insurmountable.) So the pertinent questions then come down to: 1) Why would Hoover do such a thing, and 2) were there precedents for this type of behavior?

Why Hoover Did What He Did

Concerning the former, one major motivation for Hoover is something that Bugliosi seriously underplays. That is, the conflicts between Hoover and the Kennedys, and the FBI Director's lifetime friendship with Lyndon Johnson. (The latter is something Bugliosi almost completely ignores.) In the four pages footnoted above, and to a slight extent in his End Notes, Bugliosi barely mentions just how serious these conflicts were.[5] But in reality the Kennedys thought Hoover was a weird and bizarre personality. In fact, Robert Kennedy actually called Hoover senile, frightening, and "rather a psycho."[6] Let's spell out what Bugliosi underplays:

1. In 1961, Attorney General Robert Kennedy was about to begin the largest campaign against the Cosa Nostra in American history. Yet, this was a group that Hoover actually denied even existed. RFK had to drag Hoover into this campaign, and it is questionable if Hoover ever would have done it on his own.

2. President Kennedy was the first president to actually take an interest in and move on civil rights. This was something that Hoover would have never taken action on in a hundred years. Because, as every recent commentator has demonstrated, he was a racist.

3. Hoover was still devoting a large amount of resources to anti-communist activities in 1961. RFK thought this was silly and started discouraging it. He famously commented that a large percentage of these so-called communists were FBI informants.

4. RFK was perhaps the first Attorney General who actually exercised some degree of authority over Hoover. For instance, he had a pri-

vate line into his office.[7] Another instance: he made Hoover withdraw from private circulation a negative dossier he had compiled on Martin Luther King. (Which, after JFK's death, Johnson OK'd the circulation of.[8]) To say the least, Hoover resented this imposition on his domain. He called RFK an "arrogant whippersnapper" and a "sneaky little sonofabitch."[9]

5.   Because of the above, RFK had planned on replacing Hoover after President Kennedy won reelection.[10] This was something that Hoover could feel confident that his friend Lyndon Johnson would not seriously consider. In fact, Johnson waived the mandatory retirement age when Hoover reached seventy years old.

The conservative Director did not like the liberal Kennedys, either personally or politically. And he hated RFK. One close acquaintance describes Hoover as being almost driven over the edge by his relationship with his boss, Bobby Kennedy.[11] Hoover would rant and rave about the Attorney General, "saying god-awful things" about him. "He despised him and didn't hide the fact."[12] Hoover was much closer to Johnson on the issues of anti-communism, and the pettiness of his personal politics—what we call the "politics of personal destruction" today—than he was to the Kennedys. For example, one thing that RFK grew to resent was Hoover's constant attempts to drive a wedge between himself and King.[13] Hoover did this by using his eternal standby: King was a pinko who had agents of Moscow in his camp. This old ploy was something that the unsophisticated Johnson would fall prey to. And as LBJ ratcheted up the Vietnam War, and as King grew more opposed to it, Hoover convinced Johnson that the anti-war movement was communist inspired.[14] As Johnson and King fell out over the war, the president welcomed the "sex tapes" Hoover gave him on King. Johnson actually played them for his friends.[15] Another way to phrase the antagonism between the two was as David Talbot did: RFK and Hoover represented to each other what was wrong with America.[16]

All of the above is crystallized in Hoover's phone calls to the Attorney General on the day of the assassination. Hoover never called RFK at home. But on this day he did. After RFK's wife gave him the phone, Hoover told him the following: "I have news for you. The president's been shot."[17] As Talbot describes it: "Hoover's voice was blunt and matter of fact. Kennedy would always remember not just the FBI chief's words, but his chilling tone." Twenty minutes later Hoover phoned again and said, "The president's dead" and promptly hung up. Hoover could be so cavalier and carefree since he knew that Johnson felt the same way about RFK as he did. He knew that, caught between himself and Johnson, Bobby Kennedy would now be reduced to being just another Attorney General—who Hoover could largely ignore. Which is what happened. After President Kennedy died, at first Hoover did not answer Robert Kennedy's direct line phone calls. He'd just let the phone ring. Then, after a decent interval, he had the phone removed from his office and put on his secretary's desk.[18] RFK got the message. Two weeks after the assassination, he said to a colleague, "Those people don't work for us anymore."[19] And in fact, to use just one example, although the war against organized crime did not disappear, it significantly declined after 1963.

As Oswald's identity became known, let us add one other factor as to why Hoover would be eager to brush the facts of the assassination under the rug quickly. If Oswald was an FBI informant, it would have been deadly to the Bureau's image as a crime-fighting organization to have him implicated in an assassination plot. That image was something Hoover had taken great time and effort to build in the public's consciousness.

With the above background sketched in, the question can be asked: What would be in it for Hoover to seek out a complex and multilayered conspiracy to kill President Kennedy? Wouldn't he just want to go ahead and ratify anything the Dallas Police did to get the thing over with, thereby covering up Oswald's informant status and also subjugating RFK? Which, as many have demonstrated, is what he did.

The Horrendous History of an Ogre

Now the necessary second question to pose in relation to Hoover's behavior in the JFK case was: Were there precedents for cutting corners, altering testimony, and faking evidence in Hoover's background and record? In light of the books I mentioned above, this is almost a humorous question to ask. And it refers back to Hoover's doctrine about law and order preceding justice. When Hoover was in on any kind of case that was high profile or politically charged, he had no compunctions about being Machiavellian in his approach to the law or the court system.

And we can start right at the beginning of his career. Hoover was in on the planning, the execution, and the eventual prosecution of one of the largest violations of civil rights, the constitution, and legal procedure in American history. Namely the infamous Palmer Raids of 1919–20. This is where thousands of Americans were abducted out of their homes, beaten, detained, tried, and deported simply because they were suspected of being leftists or union sympathizers. (Hoover detested both.) After they were illegally detained, Hoover wanted no bail or lawyers for those in jail,[20] even though he later admitted that the raids were illegal. After all, the man did have a law degree.[21] This was such a miscarriage of justice on a large scale that Hoover later tried to deny his involvement in it. When, in fact, he was one of the two main operators running it from headquarters.[22]

But that's not the worst of it. Hoover was furious that this operation turned out to be so controversial, so he started keeping files on the lawyers who opposed the raids and defended the innocent.[23] And it later was discovered that Hoover and the other perpetrators had planted agents provocateurs and informants inside of union cells to manufacture evidence for the subsequent trials.[24] It is hard to believe, but in this over 2,600 page book, the author does not even mention the Palmer Raids and Hoover's role in them.

A special target of Hoover's wrath at this time was the great leftist labor leader Emma Goldman. He was determined to have her deported. How did he achieve this? He altered the trial testimony of Leon Czolgosz, the assassin of President McKinley, to make it look like she had encouraged him to shoot the president.[25]

What is important to realize about both these heinous acts is this: Hoover was not even director of the FBI at the time. So between 1919 and 1963, he had forty-four years to hone his craft in the fields of violating legal rights, misrepresenting the facts of a case, altering and planting evidence, and perpetuating cover-ups. To go through the myriad times he did this would take a small book. So let's just mention a few instances.

In the famous Lindbergh kidnapping case, Hoover had his longtime assistant—some would say his flunky—Charles Appel say that Bruno Hauptmann's handwriting matched the samples on the ransom demands. Even though *Hoover knew* that Hauptmann's fingerprints did not match "the latent impressions developed on the ransom notes and the ransom money." Hoover later wrote that he harbored serious doubts about the state of the evidence against Hauptmann. And Charles Lindbergh indirectly commented on Hoover's role in that case by saying that, if not for the FBI's role, Hauptmann would have never been apprehended, brought to trial, and finally executed. Hoover always resented Lindbergh for making that revealing remark.[26]

In 1934, some of the most powerful corporate interests in America were worried about the populist aspects of FDR's New Deal. After visiting Europe and studying how fascism had grown there through the use of veterans groups, they decided to use that strategy in a military takeover of the White House. They approached General Smedley Butler to be their accomplice. They actually told him they wanted to stage a coup d'état by his leadership of a half million veterans. They would first remove the vice president and secretary of state, then force Roosevelt to resign. The campaign was already in operation, had millions in financing, and the DuPont family would use their company Remington Arms to create the weaponry needed. After nearly a year of meetings with the coup plotters, Butler took his testimony to Hoover. What did the Director say about this treasonous act? That there was no evidence a criminal statute had been violated so he didn't have the authority to start an investigation.[27]

Whatever one thinks of the Alger Hiss case, the FBI either planted or built the famous Woodstock typewriter to link Hiss to the documents in Whittaker Chambers's possession. Because the typewriter in evidence could not have belonged to the Hisses.[28] I should add here, Hoover later admitted that to alter a typewriter to match a known model could be done.[29]

Harvey Matusow was a former journalist and stage actor who later worked as a campaign aide to Joseph McCarthy. He provided information smearing folk singer Peter Seeger and hurting his career, and labor leader Clinton Jencks which sent him to prison. In 1955 Matusow wrote a book in which he confessed that he had been an FBI agent and was paid by the Bureau to perjure himself about members of the American Communist Party.[30]

In addition to being a prime mover behind the Palmer Raids, which caused the first Red Scare, Hoover was just as instrumental in causing what is referred to as the second Red Scare in the late forties and early fifties. He did this by aiding Richard Nixon and his cohorts at the House Un-American Activities Committee and his cohort Joseph McCarthy in the senate. As Gentry notes in this regard, Hoover understood that the testimony, information, and evidence he funneled to Congress was, in most cases, not reliable. He did it because he understood that in the congressional arena the standard of proof would be reversed; the accused *would have to prove his innocence*.[31] This resulted in the ruination of lives through things like blacklists, the destruction of reputations, and at least a dozen suicides. As Gentry concluded, McCarthyism was in large part the creation of Hoover.

When President Eisenhower wanted to set up a Civil Rights Commission, Hoover argued against it by manufacturing evidence that the Ku Klux Klan was pretty much defunct. Which was completely false.[32]

In 1956, Hoover launched the first of the illegal COINTELPRO operations. These escalated in time to include the famous attempt to blackmail Martin Luther King into committing suicide, and the—no other word will do—murderous campaign against the Black Panthers which resulted in the death of several members, including Fred Hampton and Mark Clark.[33] The tactics used included penning false and inflammatory letters and planting agents provocateurs within the ranks.

When anyone would rise up and try to expose Hoover's unethical and illegal practices, Hoover would manufacture evidence, pass it on to his allies in the media, and it would be used to destroy them. An example would be Hoover's campaign against Congressman Cornelius Gallagher. First, the FBI wiretapped his telephone, and then they broke into his home to steal documents. Hoover then used the fruits of these illegal acts to concoct a story that Gallagher was a tool of the Mob and that a gangster had died in his home while lying in bed with his wife. As Anthony Summers has written, there was no evidence for any of these accusations in any of the files of any government agency at the time. Hoover created it all—including phone transcripts—and destroyed Gallagher's political career in order to quell criticism of his illegal practices. And also to serve as a warning to others. [34]

Hoover's regime was so unethical and full of cronyism that its effects on the FBI lasted long beyond his 1972 death. For example, in the nineties, chemist Fred Whitehurst went public with how the fabled FBI crime lab had contaminated and misplaced evidence and even changed his reports in order to strengthen cases for the prosecution.

Before we begin to examine what Bugliosi calls the FBI's fine investigation of the JFK case, it is necessary to underline the point made above: Hoover was not at all uncomfortable with the manipulation—and the sometime creation—of testimony and evidence. And he did it in a variety of ways. This is a part of the man's record that is simply inescapable today. But Bugliosi does not address it in his book. Secondly, in most of the above cases, the accused at least had the benefit of an attorney. In the Kennedy case, Oswald never had a lawyer—either in life or in death. And the body that was meant to represent him, the Warren Commission, joined Hoover in his effort to frame Oswald and shove any evidence of conspiracy under the rug. In other words, for a man like Hoover, rigging the Kennedy case was a walk in the park.

Hoover Begins the Cover-Up

As former FBI agent William Turner wrote in his book, *Hoover's FBI,* many observers date the beginning of Hoover's decline from the work he did on the Kennedy assassination. How concerned was J. Edgar Hoover about who actually killed President Kennedy? On November 23, he was at the track with his longtime companion and colleague, Clyde Tolson. Between races, Hoover conducted the investigation from an office phone there, with Tolson running down the bets.[35] In order to quiet domestic fears of any kind of foreign conspiracy, both Lyndon Johnson and Hoover desired a report as quickly as possible.

But Hoover had another reason in mind. He wanted to get his report out before Bobby got over his period of mourning.[36]

This FBI report was the first official inquiry into the assassination. It was submitted on December ninth. If anyone thinks I have somewhat overplayed Hoover's animus for the Kennedys and his desire to have the JFK case eliminated from his docket as quickly as possible, then all they have to do is read this report. Today it is referred to as the FBI Summary Report.[37] The title placed on it by Hoover was "Investigation of Assassination of President John F. Kennedy: November 22, 1963." In light of what we know today it is a shoddy, pathetic and—there is no other way to term it—a deliberately deceptive piece of work. Although the document fills about 400 pages, the actual written report itself is about one hundred total. And, at that, it makes plentiful use of subheads. Plus the typing is double-spaced. As to the quality of the inquiry, this report mentions the alleged bag found near the Depository window as the bag that Wesley Frazier says Oswald carried to work that day. It later shows a picture of this alleged bag, yet it does not tell the reader that no picture of the bag was taken by the Dallas Police as it was lying on the sixth floor. In other words, Hoover was exonerating by honoring the horrendous practices of the Dallas Police.

And that's just the beginning. This report spends all of two pages on the murder of Patrolman J. D. Tippit. And because the Dallas Police held the autopsy report on his death so closely, the report has him being shot three times instead of four times. Yet of those two pages, less than half of them describe the actual circumstances of the shooting. Most of the material is a description of Oswald as an "avowed Marxist, a former defector to the Soviet Union and the self-appointed Secretary of the New Orleans Chapter of the Fair Play for Cuba Committee, a pro-Castro organization." Later on, the report identifies one witness to the shooting, Mr. Scoggins. They then identify another, who I suspect is the notorious Helen Markham—yet since they do not name this witness, I cannot be sure. And, if you can believe it, that's about it for the murder of Tippit. To list just one glaring omission: there is no mention of the timing problem. That is: How could Oswald have reached the scene of the crime as fast as he did if he was last seen by his landlady standing at a bus stop at 1:04?[38] This would mean that, according to a witness who checked his watch, Oswald traversed the nearly mile distance in about six minutes. There is also no mention of the first police reports, which described the shells found at the scene as being ejected from an automatic. Yet Oswald was supposed to have been carrying a revolver.[39]

This was the first time that any official body tried to pin the murder attempt of Gen. Walker on Oswald. Which actually reverses what the Dallas Police did about that case. Since, in eight months, they never even considered Oswald as a suspect in that case. The FBI report revises the DPD verdict in all of 1.5 pages. It uses two pieces of evidence in this regard. The testimony of Marina Oswald, and the mysterious note describing what Marina should do if her husband ever got into trouble. It leaves out the fact that the note surfaced *after* the assassination of JFK through the very suspicious Ruth Paine. And although Oswald wrote well over a page of this note, his fingerprints were not on the paper.[40]

How does the FBI deal with the incredibly important episode of Oswald in Mexico City? In less than three pages. But unbelievably, the report spends less than one page, actually two paragraphs, on what he did once he got to his Mexico City hotel. In other words, there is no enumeration of the number of trips to both the Soviet and Cuban consulates, no discussion of the phone calls made or the taping of those calls, not even any mention of any specific witness who saw Oswald there. And of course, there is no noting of what happened to the photos and audio tapes of both consulates by the CIA. No mention of all the problems the FBI had in obtaining records of Oswald's mode of entry and exit into the country, including the destruction of the bus manifests for both his way there and back.

The discussion of the murder of Oswald by Ruby is just as slipshod. Subtracting the biographical material, it's about twenty-six pages. It includes this gem of a sentence, "Ruby refused to advise the FBI how he got into the basement or what time he entered." And evidently, Hoover was not real interested in those actual circumstances. Because, if you can believe it, the name of Officer Roy Vaughn is not in the index to the report. This is the policeman who was stationed at the Main Street ramp to check on any unauthorized persons entering the police basement. Since Ruby said he entered that way, and Vaughn said he did not, Hoover prevents any dissonance in the report by not bringing up the differing accounts on this key issue. I should add here, to indicate how thorough the FBI inquest into this key issue is, the report includes exactly two exhibits in regards to this shooting. The first is the famous photo of Ruby killing Oswald. The second is a diagram of the City Hall basement. That's it.

In the entire report there is not one mention of either George DeMohrenschildt, Michael Paine, or David Ferrie. Even though, as we know today, the FBI was almost immediately aware of all these people and how important they were in Oswald's life. Finally, the report is not annotated. So in the vast majority of instances, the reader does not know where the information is coming from. A large part of the report consists of a biography of Oswald. This begins in Volume 1 on page twenty-two and ends about fifty pages later. In other words, it consumes about half of the actual written report. The rest of the report is a collection of exhibits the FBI got from the Dallas Police.

The Commission Rejects the FBI Report

Just how lacking in distinction was the summary report? Once it was presented to the Warren Commission they decided they could not make it the keystone of their inquiry. In fact, it was not included in the publication of the twenty-six volumes. That tells you how abysmal it was.

But there was more to it than that. In a Warren Commission executive session transcript of January 22, 1964, Chief Consul J. Lee Rankin expresses his reservations about how Hoover conducted the investigation. Because in Rankin's previous and lengthy experience with the FBI, "it is hard to get them to say when you think you have got a case tight enough to convict somebody . . . the FBI, they don't do that. They claim that they don't evaluate. . . ." But in this case they had. They concluded that Oswald shot Kennedy by himself and Ruby shot Oswald by himself. Further, the two men did not know each other and there was no conspiracy in either case.

Rankin also noted the fault in Hoover's investigative methodology: "Secondly, they have not run out all kinds of leads in Mexico or Russia and so forth. . . . But they are concluding that there can't be a conspiracy without those being run out. Now that is not my experience with the FBI."

Former FBI agent Bill Turner noted this same point to this author. The thing that struck Turner as being so bad about Hoover's JFK investigation was that individual leads were not followed to their ultimate conclusion. As he described it, there were three main steps in any FBI inquiry: 1) Collection of all pertinent leads, 2) the following out of all leads to their ultimate end, and 3) collating of all information garnered into a complete and accurate report.

Turner said that without the second phase, the third phase was not really possible. And that is what he found so appalling about the FBI report on JFK. To him, it was so apparent that step two had been systematically and rigorously circumvented *that there had to have been interference from above.* FBI agents just did not proceed like that unless they were advised to do so. Therefore, as noted by Rankin, for Hoover then to have broken with FBI policy a second time, and specifically named Oswald as the sole killer, that was even more extraordinary. For by the time the report was submitted, Hoover was aware that Johnson would be appointing the Commission. In other words, the FBI would not be the final arbiter of a verdict in the Kennedy case. They would be serving a client: the Warren Commission. Yet Hoover had come to a conclusion for the Commission before they had even begun their work or assembled their staff.

As Rankin put it, "They are concluding that Oswald was the assassin . . . that there can't be a conspiracy. Now that is not normal . . . Why are they so eager to make both of these conclusions?"[41] In fact, there are indications that this is what Johnson wanted. When Sen. Richard Russell tried to beg off serving because of the time involved, Johnson replied, "There's not going to be any time to begin with. All you got to do is evaluate a Hoover report he's already written."[42]

The underlying problem was that Hoover never wanted the Commission to exist.[43] But once Johnson constructed it, Hoover actually wanted to helm it. Failing that, he did the next best thing. He sent them a report that was not just descriptive, not just informational, but it was conclusive in every aspect. In this regard, upon reading the FBI report, Sen. Russell was as surprised as Rankin: "They have tried the case and reached a verdict on every aspect."[44] Returning to that January 22 transcript, Rankin came to the same conclusion: "They would like us to fold up and quit. . . . They found the man. There is nothing more to do. The commission supports their conclusions, and we can go home and that is the end of it." As Wade Boggs added, "This closes the case, you see."

Both Turner and Rankin were correct. Hoover had broken with traditional FBI investigatory structure. As Curt Gentry writes, the titular head of the FBI investigation, Alan Belmont, got the drift. The day of Oswald's murder, he wrote Clyde Tolson that he was sending two supervisors to Dallas to review the findings on the Oswald matter and prepare a memo for the Attorney General setting out the evidence showing Oswald is responsible for the shooting that killed the President.[45]

The agents in the field also got the drift: Oswald had acted alone. Therefore any evidence to the contrary would be most unwelcome. As FBI supervisor Laurence Keenan told Anthony Summers: "Within days we could say the investigation was over. Conspiracy was a word that was verboten. The idea that Oswald had a confederate or was part of a group or a conspiracy was definitely enough to place a man's career in jeopardy. . . . Looking back, I feel a certain amount of shame. This one investigation disgraced a great organization."[46]

FBI agent Harry Whidbee, who worked on the Kennedy investigation, said it was a "hurry up job. . . . We were effectively told: 'They're only going to prove Oswald was the guy who did it. There were no conspirators, and there was no international conspiracy.'. . . I had conducted a couple of interviews and those records were sent back again and were rewritten according to Washington's requirements."[47] While working for Jim Garrison, Mark Lane conducted a May 1968 interview with FBI employee William Walter. It reinforced Whidbee's testimony about Washington rewriting FBI reports. For Walter told Lane that initial reports were rewritten in Washington to support the official story.

Congressman Don Edwards was a former FBI agent who investigated the JFK case. He said, "There's not much question that both the FBI and the CIA are somewhere behind the cover up. I hate to think what it is they are covering up—or who they are covering for."[48] And there are the words of FBI counter intelligence Chief William Sullivan, who admitted: "There were huge gaps in the case—gaps we never did close.[49] Both the FBI and the CIA are somewhere behind the cover up. I hate to think what it is they are covering up—or who they are covering for."[50] One must also add the revelations by former FBI agent Don Adams in his recent book, *From an Office Building with A High Powered Rifle*. Among many, here are just two. First, when he reported to Dallas to support the FBI inquiry, he watched the Zapruder film with two other agents. Afterwards he said to his colleagues, well, it's obvious Kennedy was hit from two different directions. They replied that they knew that. But Hoover and Tolson didn't want them to go down that path, so they couldn't. He also wrote that, years later, when he sent away for his reports on rightwing extremist Joseph Milteer, he found they had been rewritten. From all this inside information, there is no doubt that the FBI had changed its operating procedure, and they also decided early that they would rewrite reports that did not conform to Hoover's goal.

Hoover's Reaction to the Assassination

It is interesting and illuminating to trace Hoover's reaction to Kennedy's murder in regards to his attitude about the case against Oswald. Within two hours after Oswald's arrest, Hoover was "quite convinced they had found the right party."[51] It is crucial to note here that this was before the FBI had received any of the evidence from the Dallas Police. The next day, once he began to get reports from his analysts about the evidence, he told Johnson "The case as it stands now isn't strong enough to be able to get a conviction."[52] On Sunday, after Ruby killed Oswald, Hoover told Johnson the following: "The thing I am most concerned about is having something issued so we can convince the public that Oswald is the real assassin."[53] This telling comment actually preceded the more famous one in the Justice Department memo by Nicolas Katzenbach, which states a very similar aim thusly: "The public must be satisfied that Oswald was the assassin." And it may be that Katzenbach took his cue from Hoover. In other words, the true facts of the case didn't matter. What mattered was the perception in the public mind that Oswald was the killer of Kennedy. Everything else could be swept under the rug in order to attain that goal. And in fact, the next day, Hoover was the source of a story to the Associated Press saying that all available information indicated Oswald was the lone assassin in the murder of President Kennedy.[54] (We will discuss Bugliosi's weird interpretation of the Katzenbach Memorandum in the next chapter.)

Hoover himself later confirmed, on two occasions, that his actions in the JFK case were not an attempt to seek justice but to maintain law and order. Just a few months after the assassination, but after the FBI report had been submitted, he told a friend in the privacy of his office that the case was a mess, that it was just a lot of loose ends.[55] Then, while on vacation in the late summer of 1964, a close acquaintance of the Director's talked to him about the Kennedy case. He asked him if Oswald was the actual killer. Hoover replied, "If I told you what I really know, it would be very dangerous to this country. Our whole political system could be disrupted."[56] Obviously, if Hoover believed his own report he would not have said anything like this. The Director understood his own report was pabulum for the public. In his mind, justice had nothing to do with it. He was maintaining law and order.

None of the above means a lick to Bugliosi. He terms the efforts of Hoover and the FBI in the Kennedy case an "excellent job of investigation."[57]

The FBI on the First Day

"There is not a scintilla of evidence to support that proposition [of an FBI cover-up in the JFK case]."

—Vincent Bugliosi, *Reclaiming History*

What can one say about the above statement? Except that the author is correct in only one way. It is true that there is not a scintilla of evidence to support an FBI cover-up in the JFK case. There is a mountain of evidence to support it. But since *Reclaiming History* presents the prosecution's case, Bugliosi has to write the above. Why? Because the FBI was the prime investigative arm of the Commission. And it wasn't even close. They did 25,000 interviews and submitted 25,400 pages of materials. The Secret Service was a distant second at 1,550 interviews and 4,600 pages.[58] So if you discredit the FBI, you discredit the Commission. Bugliosi does not want to do that.

There is compelling evidence that the FBI was complicit in the cover-up the very night of the assassination. And it comes from two sources. And it impacts on the viability of what is perhaps the most crucial piece of evidence in the JFK case. This, of course, is CE 399.

Connie Kritzberg was a reporter for the *Dallas Times Herald* at the time of the assassination. Kritzberg had just been promoted to Home Editor, but she was switched to the city desk for Kennedy's visit. After Kennedy's murder, she interviewed Kemp Clark and Malcolm Perry at Parkland Hospital. She submitted her story to her editors and left the office just before 9 PM. Her story appeared in the next day's edition entitled "Neck Wounds Bring Death to President." (She did not title the story.) In that article she described two wounds to Kennedy. An entrance wound in the front of the neck and the principal wound at the back of the head which "was either an exit or tangentially exit wound." The next sentence was this: "A doctor admitted that it was possible there was only one wound." Connie did not write that sentence. When she read it, she immediately called her editor, who she recalled as being Tom LaPere. She asked him, "Who added that sentence to my story?" He replied quickly, "The FBI."[59]

Does Bugliosi think that FBI agents enter newspaper offices on their own, at random, and ask to see the next day's stories for editing? They don't. They do it only with permission from above. And as we shall now see, this was coordinated for a purpose.

Perhaps the most important evidence in a murder case is the ammunition, especially when it is recovered from the body, or at the crime scene. Both the FBI and the Commission tell us that CE 399 is the one that ended up in Parkland Hospital and was found by hospital senior engineer Darrell Tomlinson and security chief O. P. Wright. Wright then turned it over to the Secret Service. The Secret Service transported it to Washington and gave it to the FBI, specifically to agent Elmer Lee Todd.

Now, from almost the beginning of the controversy about the Warren Commission, CE 399 has been under perpetual fire. And from a variety of different angles. We have touched on some of these already. From the very beginning, when Tomlinson found the bullet and turned it over to Wright, there was a serious question about whose stretcher it was recovered from. Tomlinson always believed that Commission counsel Arlen Specter had juggled his testimony in this regard. As we have seen, Josiah Thompson wrote that the evidence would indicate that Tomlinson found the nearly pristine bullet on the stretcher of a little boy named Ronald Fuller. Specter understood that this would be dangerous to admit for the Commission. It would denote the bullet was planted. So Specter first tried to rattle Tomlinson. When this would not suffice, the Commission just ended up printing the following statement: "Although Tomlinson was not certain whether the bullet came from the Connally stretcher or the adjacent one, the Commission has concluded that the bullet came from the Governor's stretcher."[60]

But, as noted, security officer O. P. Wright made things even worse. Since he used to work for the Sheriff's Department, he was quite familiar with weapons and ammunition. So when Thompson interviewed him in 1966 he showed him a photo of CE 399. Wright's response devastates the Commission. He said no, and then produced a lead colored, sharp pointed, hunting round. Which is completely different from the copper colored, round nosed, military round in evidence today. (In Bugliosi's rather brief discussion of this issue, he mentions Tomlinson and Thompson's analysis of the stretchers. He leaves out Thompson's interview of Wright, Wright's rejection of CE 399, and his production of a hunting round. See his End Notes, pp. 430–431)

Jim Marrs notes a rather interesting thing about Wright. Even though he was clearly an important witness, the Commission does not appear to have interviewed him. In fact, his name is not in the Warren Report. So when Thompson went looking for him in 1966, the information he garnered clearly shed backward light on the work of Arlen Specter and the Commission. And as we have seen in Chapter 5, the evidence indicates that Hoover fabricated interviews with Wright and Tomlinson in order to validate the chain of possession of the Magic Bullet. The question then became: Was Wright avoided because Specter and Hoover knew that his testimony would undermine their case against Oswald?

The work of John Hunt shows that such was the case.

Hunt is the kind of person to keep in mind when we hear Bugliosi ridiculing the critical community as a bunch of irresponsible goofballs who are in this endeavor for handsome speaking fees and autograph payees—neither of which exist. Hunt didn't have the huge advance Bugliosi did. But, on his own dime, he went to the National Archives and he stayed there. And he brought something with him that was important to his quest: a magnifying glass. Actually, two of them. And because of this, he managed to surface first day information you will not find in *Reclaiming History*. Information that the *LA Times,* and Thomas Mallon, and Tom Hanks do not want to broadcast. Once he gathered this important information, he didn't market it in a book or go on any media tour. He wrote two important essays and put them on the web for all to see.[61] They raise the most profound questions about what Hoover knew and what he was up to.

As Hunt states it, he wanted the answer to one question: Is bullet CE 399 sitting in the National Archives today, the same bullet that was recovered at Parkland Hospital. As noted above, the story goes that Wright handed the bullet to Secret Service agent Richard Johnsen.[62] Johnsen then took the bullet to Washington where he gave it to his boss James Rowley.[63] At the White House, Rowley then gave it to FBI agent Elmer Todd. And Todd delivered it to Robert Frazier at FBI HQ.[64] As Josiah Thompson notes in his book, when Johnsen gave the bullet to Rowley, Johnsen composed a receipt to mark the delivery. There are two quite interesting things in his short note. He admitted that it was not known who occupied the stretcher the bullet was recovered from.[65] He actually seemed to describe Ronald Fuller's stretcher. Second, he certified the time that he gave the missile to Rowley as 7:30 PM.

Here begins a monumental problem for the official story. FBI analyst Robert Frazier had been alerted to the fact that evidence was coming in from Dallas that evening. So he was waiting for its arrival. When Todd walked in with the bullet, Frazier did what he did a thousand times before. He noted the time of delivery and the name of the man who gave him the exhibit.

As Hunt states, there are some things missing from the FBI files in regards to Frazier's notes on this bullet. But there was enough left over to piece together a chain of custody. In fact, Frazier composed a document entitled "History of Evidence." On the top line he wrote that he received the bullet from Todd at 7:30 PM. And Frazier wrote another document, called "Laboratory Work Sheet." This also certifies that he got the bullet from Todd at 7:30. It describes it as "Bullet from Stretcher."

The obvious question presented by these documents is this: How could Frazier at FBI HQ have received the bullet from Todd at FBI headquarters in Washington before Rowley gave it to Todd at the White House? Both men were in two different places at the time. But it's even worse than that. Because Todd noted the time he got the bullet from Rowley on the envelope he received from him. Todd wrote down the time as 8:50 PM. Question for the Prosecutor: How could Todd have given CE 399 to Frazier before he got it from Rowley? As Hunt concludes his essay—aptly titled "The Mystery of the 7:30 Bullet"— either there were two bullets or the FBI switched the bullets. Either would be fatal to the Warren Commission. The latter would show, as Thompson wrote, that the assassination was, at least partly, an "inside job." That is, it was aided, (i.e., covered up) by agents of either the Secret Service or FBI.[66] If the former is the case then this means there were four bullets. And therefore the Commission conclusion about Oswald as the lone assassin is negated.

But really, it's even worse than that. In Thompson's book he writes about the transaction between Todd and Frazier like this: "They both marked the bullet with their initials."[67] Thompson sources this to a Justice Department report, which in turn contains two pages of an FBI report on the rifle bullet from the stretcher.[68] And as Thompson notes, the FBI document does say Todd identified his initials on CE 399. On June 24, Todd took CE 399 and showed it to Rowley and Johnsen at the White House. It was necessary for them to do this since their initials were not on the bullet. So now we have Tomlinson, Wright, Johnsen, and Rowley all failing to identify CE 399.

But surely, Todd's initials were on it? After all, it said so in the FBI report. And Bugliosi, who apparently never visited the National Archives to inspect the bullet, uses the aforementioned FBI report to tell the reader that such is the case.[69] Hunt, on a Motel 6 budget, went to Washington. He did what Bugliosi—who could have stayed at the Sheraton—did not. He photographed the bullet in sequential rotation. Therefore, the reader can see its entire circumference. Todd's initials are not on CE 399 today. So if Todd did mark a bullet on November 22, 1963, that bullet is not in the National Archives. Hunt is the kind of person that Bugliosi pulls out all the stops to ridicule in *Reclaiming History*. A researcher who puts himself out at personal sacrifice for no personal gain. Needless to say, Elmer Todd is mentioned exactly one time in the book.[70] And that one reference in support of Hoover's deception is wrong. John Hunt's name is nowhere to be found in the entire book. Even though his essay was published a year before *Reclaiming History* came out.

Earlier, in Chapter 5, we saw how, beyond a reasonable doubt, the FBI switched the bullets in the Gen. Walker case in order to incriminate Oswald in that shooting attempt. It is now shown—also beyond a reasonable doubt—that the Bureau pulled a similar trick with CE 399. Either the bullet was switched or a second bullet was made to disappear. If that does not constitute an FBI cover-up then Bugliosi will have to show us what does.

And we're just getting started.

Hoover Makes the Tague Hit Disappear

Commission Counsel Lee Rankin once said about Hoover that, before he served on the Commission, he did not think Hoover would deliberately lie. But let us see how Hoover now lied about more crime scene evidence. Since a prosecutor like Bugliosi would consider that core evidence, or, in some cases, "hard evidence." Which should remain untouched for evidentiary purposes.

Bugliosi understands that the James Tague bullet strike in Dealey Plaza is a serious problem for upholders of the Commission, in two senses. First, Tague was positioned under the triple underpass, out of the target zone by a distance of well over 200 feet. So how could Oswald have scored two direct hits, yet fired a shot that missed by that much? (Bugliosi does not mention this distance problem in his discussion of the Zapruder film.) The other serious problem with this strike is that there was no detection of copper at the scene where it bounced off the curb to hit Tague. This is hard to swallow, especially if you have seen a copper coated Mannlicher Carcano bullet. We saw how Bugliosi worked his spinning, shearing magic with the copper being stripped off as the bullet rotated off the street.[71] After that piece of magic, the bullet was then posed in such a way as to recoil off the street and propel itself well over 200 feet. And still had the kinetic energy to displace part of the curb. Yet, where did the sheared jacket go? Because it is not in evidence today.

This particular incident is one reason why the Warren Commission did not print the FBI report in its twenty-six volumes. Hoover had two men at the autopsy in Bethesda. They were Frank O'Neill and Jim Sibert. They wrote a report on the autopsy that differs in important ways from the report eventually submitted by pathologist James Humes. For instance, they wrote that the bullet in the back did not penetrate the body, and it entered at a much steeper angle of 45 degrees. But, most relevant to this discussion, they said that all the shots fired hit either Kennedy or Connally, and a separate bullet hit the governor. In other words, no Single Bullet Theory. As we will see, Hoover was intent on keeping this particular bullet accounting sequence intact. (Bugliosi tries to say that the reason Hoover rejected the SBT was that he did not have the autopsy report.[72] He ignores the fact that long after he did have the autopsy report, Hoover wrote: "We don't agree with the Commission, as it says one shot missed entirely. We contend all three shots hit."[73])

Tague was struck in the cheek, and both he and a policeman saw a bullet strike on the curb next to him.[74] Photographers heard about it, and a picture of the strike was in the newspapers that weekend. As Gerald McKnight notes, the FBI office in Dallas knew about Tague the weekend of the murder, well before the initial report was submitted.[75] In fact, Tague had reported the strike to the FBI in December.[76] So there had to be a reason why they avoided it. When Tague held a press conference about his experience, the local agents tried to smear him in their reports as a publicity seeker.[77] Even though Tague was a law-abiding citizen with no record who held a managerial position in which he supervised two hundred employees.[78] This attempted concealment extended to the Warren Commission. For when the Commission questioned photographers Tom Dillard and Jim Underwood, they asked no questions about Tague. Even though they had seen and photographed the bullet strike.[79] In April of 1964, David Belin interviewed a policeman who was on the scene. He tried to tell Belin about a bystander who appears to have been Tague. He actually mentioned it twice. Belin ignored the information.[80] In fact, in an early draft of the report, the Commission stated that "the Secret Service checked the area where the bullet reportedly struck near the Triple Underpass but could find no indication that a bullet had struck near the street in that area."[81] The Commission appears to have at least tried to follow Hoover's lead in this regard.

At the end of May, Tague returned to Dealey Plaza. He was about to visit relatives out of state and he wanted to film the mark of the bullet strike. A

funny thing happened when he went to aim the camera. He found out that the
mark had disappeared.[82] Yet, there had been photographs taken of it that survived. Now, with publicity rising in Dallas, Commission counsel Arlen Specter
suggested that Tague be deposed and that the FBI look into the matter. After
the mark was gone, of course.

The report submitted by the Bureau to the Commission is memorable in
its phrasing: "No nick or break in the concrete was observed . . . nor was there
any mark similar to the one in the photographs. . . ."[83] The report then went on
to offer reasons why the mark was now not visible. They authors said it might
have been the rain, or the brushes of a street cleaning machine. How either one
of those could *fill in* a bullet crease is something only Hoover could explain.
At this point, about eight months after the fact, Wesley Liebeler finally went to
Dallas to talk to Tague. The FBI alerted Dallas that they wanted the curb strike
located. Dallas agent Gordon Shanklin said the attempt had been "aborted."[84]
Hoover realized the stalling could not continue so he sent analyst Lyndal Shaneyfelt to examine the curb.

The results of all this may explain why Hoover was reluctant to investigate
originally. Tague was unwavering in his depiction of what happened. He felt
a sting on his cheek, looked down, and saw a piece missing from the curb.
Which is what he told the FBI on December fourteenth.[85] He was backed up
by Deputy Sheriff Buddy Walthers, a nine-year veteran who said there was no
doubt it was a fresh ricochet mark. But as Henry Hurt notes, a very peculiar
thing happened during the Tague deposition. Liebeler revealed that 1) he knew
about the other photos and 2) he knew that Tague had tried to shoot the mark
with a motion picture camera.[86] (Emphasis added.) Tague was stunned at this
revelation. It clearly suggested the FBI was tailing him.

Shaneyfelt had the spot where the mark had appeared sawed out and flown
back to Washington. After spectrographic analysis he concluded that the trace
elements were lead and antimony. No copper. Harold Weisberg sued to get the
exact strip of film used during spectrographic analysis. The FBI claimed that
it had been somehow destroyed or discarded during routine housecleaning.
(How evidence in the JFK case could be considered routine is puzzling.) The
FBI was so arrogant that it even questioned whether or not the mark had been
patched![87]

This episode reveals that the FBI originally tried to conceal the evidence
of the Tague strike, even though they knew it happened; that they at first tried
to smear and then surveilled James Tague to neutralize his attempts to get the
word out about this bullet; that they also knew that someone had filled in the
mark, therefore compromising its value as evidence; that they then tried to
cover that fact up with absolutely risible excuses, and then, when they could

conceal it no more, they gave a report on most of this to Liebeler; and finally, that they stonewalled Weisberg when he tried to get the raw data on which Shaneyfelt's test results were based upon.

How does Bugliosi deal with all this? He places it in the End Notes section.[88] Like the FBI, he tries to ridicule Tague because he became close to Weisberg and eventually wrote a book. He also agrees with the FBI and Hoover that the strike had to be a *fragment* ricochet. And because he is so tied into the Commission, since the strike was absent copper, this must mean the Mannlicher Carcano bullet jacket had been sheared. He cannot bring himself to admit that the projectile may have been a different type of bullet. Although he discounts Gerald Posner's idea of a tree branch doing the shaving of the copper coating, he actually says it is "possible." (To anyone who has ever actually seen the Western Cartridge Company ammunition, this is risible.) Surprisingly, he begins the FBI's role in the whole sorry affair on August 5, 1964. Thereby curtailing their prior and lengthy guilty knowledge, and disposing of the fact that what Shaneyfelt did in August, the FBI could and should have done the weekend of the assassination. And he makes no mention at all of Weisberg's lawsuit and struggle, and the FBI's lame excuses as to why they could not turn over the evidence he wanted.

There is one other important piece of information that Bugliosi leaves out of this discussion. In July, Chief Counsel Rankin wrote Hoover a letter. He asked, quite sensibly, at what point did this projectile pass over the limousine and where it originated from. Hoover replied on August 12 with a letter Rankin probably wishes he had never received. He said that after a microscopic study of the Zapruder film and the angle that projectile hit the curb, they decided that the missile was moving in a "general direction away" from the Texas School Book Depository.[89] Which, of course, means it could have been fired from almost anywhere in the building at anything outside it. The letter then got worse. It said that the bullet was fired at Zapruder frame 410 and at an elevation of eighteen feet above street level. So Oswald got two direct hits and then fired over the top of the car by about fifteen feet. He then stayed in the window for about five seconds after he killed Kennedy. Hoover then added that the angle of the strike was thirty-three degrees. As Gerald McKnight notes, if Hoover was right and this were a direct shot, it could not have been fired from the so-called sniper's lair. It was perhaps for this reason that the Commission stated "the mark on the south side of Main Street cannot be identified conclusively with any of the three shots fired."[90]

Recall what Bugliosi said in his introduction. That he would only set forth the critical arguments the way the critics want them set forth. He then added, that "I will not knowingly omit or distort anything."[91] I could not find this letter from Hoover in *Reclaiming History*. The problem is that it's clear he read Gerald McKnight's book, because he quotes it elsewhere.

Mercifully, I will leave it at that.

Hoover Fudges the Films and Re-creations

On top of the above, we have already seen how Hoover did everything he could to falsify the results of the paraffin tests. Harold Weisberg was also part of the effort to secure those records. But the indefatigable researcher was also critical of the so-called FBI reenactment of the assassination. Previously, the Bureau had a reputation—deserved or not—for doing precise work. As Bill Turner noted above, this collapsed with the JFK case. From his observations of the photos, Weisberg noted that some of the landmarks—like the signs—had either been altered or were removed.[92] Groundskeeper Emmett Hudson confirmed this to the Commission. He said hedges and shrubbery had been trimmed. All three road signs had been moved. And the Stemmons Freeway sign had been replaced.[93] Jim Marrs interviewed Chester Breneman, a surveyor who participated in both the FBI-Secret Service reenactment in May and in a much earlier one for *Life* magazine. He and his fellow surveyor, Bob West, were shocked that the car used for the simulation was not just a different model, but a different make. The Bureau accepted a Cadillac for the original Lincoln.[94] Yet the elevation of this car was thirteen inches higher than the Lincoln. How could this be an honest reconstruction if this car placed its passengers that much higher? For as everyone knows, the Single Bullet Theory is so finely balanced on the head of a pin that if you take out one variable, it collapses. Yet this was a major adjustment.

Breneman confirmed much of Hudson's testimony. He told Marrs that the original Stemmons Freeway sign had been removed. Further, the two men were told not to factor in any bullet strikes on the south side of Elm—apparently a reference to the Tague hit.[95]

This leads to the handling of the photographic evidence by the Bureau. In an early report unearthed by Harold Weisberg, and commented on by him in the DVD, *The Garrison Tapes*, the FBI actually reported that the Zapruder film had little evidentiary value. On November 25, 1963, the FBI issued a report on the Bronson film which depicts the Book Depository at the time of the first shot. The report says that ". . . the film failed to show the building from which the shots were fired." When asked by the Warren Commission the reason the assassin did not fire on the limousine as it progressed up Houston Street, Hoover replied, "The reason for that is . . . the fact that there are some trees between this window on the sixth floor and the cars as they turned and went through the park."[96] Which, as Robert Groden and others have pointed out, is false. And Hoover probably knew this since the FBI had done extensive study and reporting on the film. As more than one author has noted, when the Warren Commission printed frames from the Zapruder film in its volumes, some of them were transposed so "the certain perception of the front-to-rear shot is removed. The FBI took responsibility for the faulty sequence, and in 1965 Director J. Edgar Hoover called the transposition a printing error."[97] Since it was in receipt of a copy of the film from the Secret Service within two days of the assassination, the CIA did its own study of the Zapruder film quite early in the process.[98] They concluded that the first shot came before Zapruder film 210. They also concluded that there were two assassins, since they had the second shot at just 1.6 seconds after the first. Which is too fast a time to recycle the rifle. Since the CIA analysis clashed with the Commission's, Hoover cooperated on a cover story that said the Agency did not get a copy of the film until December 1964, when they requested it for "training purposes."[99]

But Hoover's deceptions about the films were not limited to just Abraham Zapruder's. Anyone who has read Josiah Thompson's early book on the JFK case, *Six Seconds in Dallas*, will remember the importance he attributes to the Hughes film. In fact, he uses it to build the memorable climax of that book. This takes place on pages 234–248, where Thompson—in his idiosyncratic way—uses witness testimony, photos, and film frames to build a powerful visual case that there were two men in the "sniper's lair" window both before and after the shots were fired. One of the capstones of this demonstration is his use of frames from the film made by Robert Hughes. Let us quote some of the relevant text: "Some eighty-eight frames of Bob Hughes's 8-millimeter film show what appear to be two figures on the sixth floor of the Depository within five seconds of the first shot." Then discussing one of the figures, he writes, "it may very well be the gunman in the sniper's nest getting into firing position. The other figure appears 10 or 12 feet to the left in the second pair of windows from the corner. . . . In some of the eighty-eight frames . . . that figure appears clearly." This is one of the most memorable passages in the literature from the first generation of critics.

What did Hoover do with this evidence? When accounts surfaced about what the Hughes film showed at the time of the assassination, Hoover set himself to work doing what Bugliosi says he did not do: He covered it up. He sent a report to the Warren Commission on the matter. The said report included one frame of the film. (Recall, Thompson talked about eighty-eight frames.) He assured the Commission—based upon that one frame—that the entire footage showed no such suspicious figures or actions.[100]

Hoover Fiddles with the Testimony

One of the worst things a law enforcement agency can do is to deliberately discount, distort, and rewrite testimony. Or intimidate a witness. Yet examples of this abound in the FBI's inquiry of the Kennedy case:

- The FBI tried to get Nelson Delgado to change his testimony about Oswald's terrible shooting skills in the Marine Corps. (Mark Lane's film *Rush to Judgment*)

- The Bureau tried to get Delgado to say that Oswald was proficient in Spanish. When Delgado knew he was not. (WC Vol. VIII, pp. 248–49)

- FBI agents reported that Delgado was not a top rifleman, when he was one of the highest scorers in his troop and wore an expert badge. (Ibid, p. 238)

- The FBI tried to discourage Arnold Rowland from telling his story about seeing an elderly black man around the time of the assassination on the sixth floor. (Harold Weisberg, *Whitewash II*, p. 80)

- Ken O'Donnell and Dave Powers were told by the Bureau not to tell the Commission what they believed: namely that shots came from the right front of the motorcade. (*Vanity Fair*, December, 1994, p. 88)

- The Bureau tried to get Depository witness Bonnie Ray Williams to alter his story about what time he left the sixth floor before the assassination. Which, concerning Oswald's alibi, is a crucial point. (WC Vol. III, pp. 172–173)

- FBI agent Regis Kennedy falsified a report about Dean Andrews receiving a phone call from Clay Bertrand (Clay Shaw) to defend Oswald. (William Davy, *Let Justice be Done*, pp. 51–52)

- Ken Dowe, a local radio announcer, provided information that Ruby called the police on Saturday asking when Oswald would be transferred. The FBI told him that it wasn't important. (Sylvia Meagher, *Accessories After the Fact*, p. 319)

- Alfred Hodge told FBI agents that he saw Ruby at the police station on the twenty-fourth. The agents left that out of their report. (WC Vol. XV p. 501)

- When the FBI first questioned Marina Oswald about Lee's rifle practice, she could not recall any such instances. Two months later she recalled three. One of which was impossible, since the rifle had not been shipped yet. (Meagher, p.132)

- When Marina Oswald was hesitant in answering their questions, the Bureau told her that she would have to if she wanted to stay in the USA. (WC Vol I, pp. 79–80)

But it's actually even worse than that. Because there is a multitude of evidence that the FBI decided quite early that they were going to cover up the fact that Oswald was not what the media pointed him out to be. Or what Hoover made him out to be in the summary report (i.e., a dedicated and loyal Marxist).

In addition to their roles in the Walker shooting, Ruth and Michael Paine helped the Bureau make Oswald's Minox camera disappear, and they further aided in substituting one allegedly owned by Michael Paine to take its place. This helped the FBI explain the discrepancy between the DPD inventory and the FBI inventory of evidence. Since the latter list had deep-sixed the Minox. The Minox, a miniature camera often used for espionage, would have indicated Oswald was an undercover intelligence agent. Especially since he already owned two other cameras for personal use. Why would the rather lower class Oswald spend money to buy a third camera, and especially an expensive Minox? To cover up his attempt to erase this revealing item, Hoover actually instructed the local Dallas FBI chief to contact the Dallas Police, Marina Oswald, and Ruth Paine.[101]

The FBI knew about Oswald's association with David Ferrie in New Orleans. For instance, when the Bureau interviewed Chuck Francis, the man who took the famous CAP photo of Oswald with Ferrie, he told them about the association between Dave and Lee.[102] The FBI also knew about Ferrie frantically searching for any evidence that could surface in the wake of the Kennedy assassination that would link Oswald to himself. They knew Ferrie had visited a neighbor of Oswald's, Doris Eames, to inquire whose card Oswald was using at the library that summer.[103] And they also knew Ferrie had called a former Civil Air Patrol member named Roy McCoy to seek out any photos he may have had of the two in the CAP.[104]

The FBI also knew, and covered up, its knowledge of Oswald being in the Clinton–Jackson area in the summer of 1963. We know this through the research of Joan Mellen, who talked to an FBI agent who worked that area.[105] She also found out that the Bureau then visited the hospital personnel office where Oswald was advised to go by Clay Shaw and David Ferrie. The FBI also had no interest in any of the startling information that State Trooper Francis Fruge had garnered from Rose Cherami. We know this because Fruge later told radio broadcaster Jim Olivier that he contacted the Lafayette office of the FBI. They had no interest in interviewing her.[106]

As noted above, the FBI altered a report about Dean Andrews to make it seem like he was under hospital medication when he received a call from Clay Bertrand. This was probably done because the Bureau knew that Clay Shaw used that alias and this clue would then lead them to Shaw.[107] How do we know this as a logical deduction? In a stunning disclosure by the Assassination Records Review Board, FBI officer Cartha DeLoach told the number two man at the FBI that "Shaw's name had come up in our investigation in December 1963 as a result of *several parties* furnishing information concerning Shaw."[108] (Emphasis added.) This point was furthered at the trial of Clay Shaw when FBI agent Regis Kennedy testified that 1) He had been involved in the Bureau's JFK inquiry prior to his visit to Andrews, and 2) He had been seeking Clay Bertrand in connection to that inquiry.[109] Regis Kennedy is the same FBI agent who knew Shaw had done work for the CIA in Italy for five years during his association with Permindex. He very likely found this out during his Bertrand/Shaw inquiry back in 1963.[110]

The FBI, DeBrueys, and Oswald

It is clear that Hoover had to have known about Oswald's association with Guy Banister and 544 Camp Street. For starters, John Newman revealed a quite compelling piece of subterfuge in his book *Oswald and the CIA*. He wrote that the New Orleans FBI office had deleted from the final draft of a memo to Washington the following interesting information: "Several Fair Play for Cuba pamphlets contained the address 544 Camp Street."[111] This FBI dodge about Banister and Oswald went even further. For when the Bureau forwarded its very few and skimpy reports on Banister to the Warren Commission—in which they did not question him about Oswald—they failed to use the 544 Camp street address. They used the alternative address of 531 Lafayette.[112] This may have some significance for the Commission did print one flyer Oswald had been distributing that summer. This was the famous Corliss Lamont pamphlet entitled "The Crime Against Cuba." But on that particular document, Oswald had stamped the address 544 Camp Street.[113] So even if they had tried to connect the two, which I doubt they would have, they could not.

As mentioned above, in spite of all this guilty knowledge, the FBI summary report portrayed Oswald as a Marxist loner. They could do that since none of these associations are mentioned. Same with the Warren Report.

It is interesting to note that it appears that the FBI point man on Hoover's Minox camera caper was Warren DeBrueys. As John Armstrong has noted it was DeBrueys who went to the Dallas Police property clerk H. W. Hill.[114] DeBrueys was one of the FBI agents who tried to convince Hill and Officer

Gus Rose that they actually did not find a Minox camera but a light meter. Armstrong also notes in his book that DeBrueys was one of the agents involved in creating the new and revised evidence inventory list.[115] He was also one of the agents on the scene in New Orleans, and later in Dallas, who spoke fluent Spanish and had informants inside the Cuban exile camp. Joe Newbrough, an employee of Banister, told Jim Garrison that he saw both DeBrueys and Regis Kennedy at frequent meetings of the Cuban exile group named the Christian Democratic Movement. They were in the company of David Ferrie.[116] According to a CIA report, a fellow denizen of Banister's office, namely Sergio Arcacha-Smith, was another close contact of DeBrueys.[117] Jim Garrison found out that DeBrueys was so involved with Banister, Ferrie, and the Cubans in New Orleans that "instead of operating out of local Bureau headquarters, he had a special office at the Customs House on Canal Street, close to the scene of anti-Castro activity."[118] When Garrison called DeBrueys before the Clay Shaw grand jury, he pleaded executive privilege. On orders sent down by the Justice Department.[119]

When I interviewed DeBrueys at his home in suburban New Orleans in the summer of 1995, he revealed to me that right after the assassination, he was detailed to the Dallas office of the FBI and he was one of the top FBI agents involved in the research and composition of the shabby FBI summary report. In fact, he seemed to take credit for being the first agent to realize that Oswald had actually taken a shot at Gen. Walker. His evidence for this: Since Oswald shot at Kennedy in the head, and whoever shot at Walker aimed at his head, then they must have been by the same shooter. (I can assure the reader, the man was serious.) DeBrueys also told me he read few, if any, books on the JFK case. That turned out to be another humorous statement. Because when upon wandering into his study later, there was a whole shelf of books on the Kennedy assassination. At least fifteen of them.

Perhaps the most tantalizing information about DeBrueys and Oswald in New Orleans comes in the aftermath of Oswald's arrest after his altercation with Carlos Bringuier on August 9, 1963. As most readers know, this incident took place four days after Oswald allegedly first approached Bringuier about helping his group in their struggle *against* Castro. John Newman points out something very interesting about the August 5 date. Up until that time, although the Bureau said they knew Oswald was in New Orleans, they did not know his address.[120] This address was not ascertained until August fifth. Newman says that this is a startling coincidence. Because this was the date on which Oswald broke out of his low-profile phase and into a highly visible action phase against the Fair Play for Cuba Committee. And it began with his approach to Bringuier. We are to believe that the Bureau could not find out this defector's address for three months. Both Newman and Anthony Summers postulate that a more logical answer to the FBI not knowing his address is the cooperation going on between the Bureau and the CIA over both groups' penetration of the Fair Play for Cuba Committee. Summers discovered documents in the CIA ARRB releases that acknowledged that fact.[121]

But on August 9, he was passing out pro-Castro leaflets. Bringuier and two friends heard about this and rushed over and accosted him about this. As John Newman notes, this confrontation is dealt with in the Warren Report in three sentences. But the man who booked Oswald, Lt. Frances Martello said something interesting about it. He said that Oswald "seemed to have set them up so to speak, to create an incident, but when the incident occurred he remained absolutely peaceful and gentle."[122] Once arrested, he asked to be interviewed by the FBI. And he specifically requested DeBrueys. He told Martello, "Tell them you have Lee Oswald in custody."[123] A young FBI clerk took Martello's call early on a Saturday morning. Oswald had told Martello to relay a number with his name to the local Bureau office. John Quigley was the only field agent on hand. Walter searched the files with the number relayed from Martello. He found two sets of related files on Oswald. One related to espionage and Cuba. But there was also a security file with the name of both Oswald and DeBrueys on it. This file was locked up with those of people doing ongoing surveillance and classified as paid informants. Walter later told Jim Garrison that the files looked to him as if the FBI was in regular communication with Oswald. Martello kept much of this information about Oswald secret since he had been a police informant for Guy Banister at an early stage in Banister's career. The FBI knew about Martello's limited hang out so they sent the House Select Committee on Assassinations the wrong file on him. An error which was not corrected.[124]

Perhaps the cinching argument about the FBI–CIA cooperation on undercover operations against the FPCC is this: On September 16, the CIA sent a message to the FBI saying that they were "giving some consideration to countering the activities of the FPCC in foreign countries" and to planting deceptive information which might embarrass the Committee. The next day, Oswald applied for a tourist card at the New Orleans Mexican consulate for his much storied trip to Mexico City.[125]

There is also anecdotal evidence to the effect that the FBI understood that Oswald was an informant to the Bureau at the time he was working as an agent provocateur into the FPCC for the CIA. Harry Dean has said that he recognized who Oswald was immediately after the assassination because he himself had done the same type of thing to the FPCC for the CIA and FBI.[126]

Joseph Burton was a former FBI informer who infiltrated Marxist and radical groups. He was sometimes accompanied by a woman from New Orleans on these missions. She told Burton that she and her husband knew Oswald was affiliated with the New Orleans FBI office. Later on Burton asked his contact at the Bureau about this. He confirmed the information.[127]

How does Bugliosi deal with all the above? This is what he says about the FBI's delay in finding Oswald's address in New Orleans: "It is not clear from the record how the FBI got Oswald's address on Magazine Street. . . ."[128] To which a good reply would be: "OK, but doesn't that kind of beg the question 'How does he react to the abundant evidence that Oswald was an informant within the Cuban exile community?'" He ignores almost all the evidence adduced above. He then tries to reduce the allegations about DeBrueys to the infamous dispute between the FBI agent and Orest Pena. This devolved into a prolonged and bitter battle between the two, with Pena saying DeBrueys physically threatened him and DeBrueys saying Pena ran a bordello out of his bar. Bugliosi does not elucidate or trace this dispute in any detail at all. That approach may have shed some light on how it all started. Instead, he blames most of it on Mark Lane.[129]

Bugliosi and the FBI Informant Story

The final way he deals with it is enlightening. As many commentators have written—including Joseph Green at ctka.net—very early in the Warren Commission inquiry, in January 1964, they were confronted with a report that Oswald was an FBI informant. Bugliosi attributes this story to reporter Lonnie Hudkins.[130] He then recites the familiar tale of Hugh Aynseworth and Bill Alexander misleading Hudkins with a disinformation story about Oswald being an FBI agent. Why? To test if their phone lines were tapped! That is, they made up the story and assigned Oswald an informant number to see if the story would get out. If it did, they knew the FBI was listening.[131] If that sounds a bit too credulous I should add here, Bugliosi also proffers that Hoover signed an affidavit saying that all agents who had any contact with Oswald had sworn he was not an informant.[132] He adds that Hoover was under penalty of perjury when he submitted this affidavit without adding that if the Commission had gone after Hoover their investigation would have closed down. Because the FBI by this time—February 6, 1964—was doing about 80 percent of the investigatory work for them.

There are two integral things that Bugliosi leaves out of this sordid tale. First, not everyone signed the affidavits Hoover requested from them. (Which is incredible in and of itself. Since Hoover ran the Bureau with almost dictatorial powers.) As Tony Summers pointed out, two agents refused to submit affidavits to Hoover in this regard. Summers tried to interview one of them. This was New Orleans agent Milton Kaack. As Summers related it, Kaack became apoplectic when the author asked him about the matter. He cried, "No, no! . . . You won't get anything out of me" and then he hung up.[133] Which is an interesting reaction for someone who supposedly had nothing to hide.

But the second aspect Bugliosi leaves out is even more fascinating. What Hoover did not tell the Commission is this: He commissioned a forceful and thorough inquiry into the origins of this "Oswald is an FBI informant" story in order to find out how it actually surfaced. Unlike Bugliosi, he apparently did not buy into Alexander and Aynseworth. In fact, the results of this secret inquiry were not declassified until 1977. The trail went from Washington DC, to the radical right to Sen. Ralph Yarborough and ended with the secretary of the Communist Party in Texas. Hoover assigned Cartha DeLoach to head the investigation. In true FBI fashion, DeLoach collected all the leads, then followed them out, and filed an accurate report. That report did not come to fruition until February 10. In other words, four days *after* Hoover submitted his "sworn deposition under penalty of perjury" to the Commission.[134] Which tells you, if you did not know already, how little he thought of the Commission.

DeLoach started with Julian Sourwine. He was the general counsel of Kennedy-hater Thomas Dodd's senate subcommittee on internal security. Sourwine said he was familiar with the allegations and knew from where they came. But, he said, his source was reluctant to talk. DeLoach told him he would have to do so. Three days later, Sourwine gave up his name. It was Philip Corso, on the staff of Sen. Strom Thurmond. Corso told the FBI that his source was located in the CIA. Corso said his CIA sources told him Oswald had been in contact with the FBI. When Corso would not be specific, DeLoach threatened to call him before the Warren Commission. Corso now said that the source was a man named John Stanford, secretary of the Communist Party of Texas, located in San Antonio. DeLoach did further inquiry. It turned out that rightwing writer Frank Capell had learned from his sources *on the Commission* that Stanford's lawyer had told Sen. Yarborough that Oswald was a CIA agent! Yarborough then turned over this information to the Commission.[135]

From this secret Bureau inquiry, it appears that the original report actually did originate in Texas. That on its way out, it got altered. Starting as an "Oswald as CIA agent" story, it got changed to "Oswald as FBI informant" story. Since Yarborough relayed the original information to the Commission, I tend to suspect someone like Allen Dulles or John McCloy may have hidden its true import. In Texas, it appears that when it got to Hudkins, it was either scrambled, or he changed it to an FBI informant story. Why? Because something Bugliosi either doesn't reveal or does not know is this: Hudkins was very close to the CIA.[136] And this is probably why Hudkins would not give up his original source, or issue a signed statement.[137] It is superfluous to add that you will not find the name of William Stanford in *Reclaiming History*. Neither will you find the information about Yarborough transmitting his story to the Warren Commission.

The FBI and Odio

As most observers would agree today, two of the most interesting and important steps in the plot were 1) The Odio incident, and 2) Mexico City. What the FBI did in relation to these two episodes further undermines Bugliosi's denial of any cover-up on J. Edgar Hoover's part.

As previously noted, Bugliosi agrees that the incident at Sylvia Odio's apartment happened. He actually calls it deeply troubling.[138] He then does a fairly good job of describing the incident and who Sylvia told it to before the assassination. He then writes the following: "On August 28, 1964, the Warren Commission's chief counsel, J. Lee Rankin, wrote to FBI Director J. Edgar Hoover, stating that 'it is a matter of some importance to the Commission that Mrs. Odio's allegations either be proved or disproved.'"[139] Wisely, Bugliosi makes no comment on how late in the game Rankin wrote this letter. But considering how important she was as a witness, and what the ramifications of her story were, it is a bit shocking. For the Warren Report was going to the printers in less than a month. How could the Bureau be expected to do a thorough, honest inquiry into such a crucial incident under that kind of time pressure?

The answer is something else that Bugliosi underplays: the FBI knew about the visit to Odio *in November 1963!*[140] A woman named Lucille Connell, who was active in the Cuban exile milieu was a friend of Sylvia's. Odio's sister Sarita, who was not there that night, told her about the incident. And here begins a very interesting discrepancy in the FBI probe which, again, Bugliosi underplays.

Connell had two pieces of information concerning the JFK case. As noted above, Sarita Odio had told her about her sister's visit by a man named Oswald. But she also had information about Jack Ruby. After she learned about Odio, she was on the phone to a friend of hers, Mrs. Sanford Pick, on Sunday, the twenty-fourth. Pick worked in a Dallas law firm. After Ruby shot Oswald, she told Connell: "Oh my goodness, Ruby was in our office last week and had power of attorney drawn for his sister."[141] Later that day, in speaking to a friend of hers involved in Cuban exile matters, Connell mentioned the information about Ruby. This woman was a teacher and the son of a local FBI agent was in her class. And this was how the FBI came to contact Connell and learn about the Odio incident.[142]

As the HSCA observed, "It was not possible to resolve the inconsistency of the substance of this and certain related FBI reports."[143] For instance, the FBI says that Connell told them that Sylvia *knew* Oswald and that he had spoken to groups of refugees in Dallas. Nothing is noted about a visit of three men." (Emphasis added.) Connell told the HSCA that she did not recall ever telling the FBI such a thing. Further, Odio herself never told the FBI about any prior knowledge of Oswald or any speaking engagements to Cuban exile groups. And in fact, there is no credible report of Oswald doing this in Dallas through anyone else. Beyond that, there is no reference in the FBI report of Connell of her knowledge about Ruby's visit to the law office. Yet Connell was positive she did tell the FBI about this. Incredibly, the HSCA discovered that neither Mrs. Pick nor the attorney who handled Ruby's case at the firm were questioned by the Bureau! Bugliosi leaves this out. He also fails to mention that because of this FBI failing, this point can never be definitively resolved since the "firm's records on the case were later routinely destroyed."[144]

What is obvious from the sketch above, but what Bugliosi does not want to admit, is that the FBI had no desire to investigate the Odio incident. Which is shocking, since it is such a fascinating and pregnant lead. The HSCA was plain about this. The committee said one of the problems they had in probing the Odio episode was the paucity of material available in the extant files. They then noted: "Both the Warren Commission and the FBI failed to pursue adequately the investigation when several leads still held a potential for development."[145] The committee could find no systematic approach to either identifying by photo the two Cubans who accompanied Leon Oswald to Odio's door, or a "search for the specifically described car the men were seen driving. . . ."[146] But beyond that, once the FBI obfuscated the event with the dubious December reports mentioned above (based upon the first November interview), they apparently stopped any further inquiry. From here until September, the only detectable inquest was a slight one by the Secret Service.[147] Bugliosi makes no note of this gap.

What do I mean by "fascinating and pregnant lead"? For starters, the Cubans told Sylvia that they had come from New Orleans and were about to depart on a trip.[148] When one of the Cubans, Leopoldo, called her back a day or two later, he talked to her about the American with them called Leon Oswald. Leopoldo said Oswald was "kind of nuts," had been in the Marines, and was a fine marksman. He then added that Leon said the Cubans had no guts. Because President Kennedy should have been shot after the Bay of Pigs, and the Cubans should have done it since he was the one holding the freedom of Cuba hostage.[149]

Now right here, any investigator's ears should have perked up. First of all, Oswald was a former Marine, he had just resided in New Orleans, and was now about to depart on his famous trip to Mexico City. But second, the portrait of Oswald as a nut, and as a good marksman are the exact legend that both the FBI and the Commission will use to pin the Kennedy assassination on him. These two Cubans were doing it two months in advance. But further, as I previously noted in the second edition of *Destiny Betrayed*, the name "Leon Oswald," who was the man with the two Cubans at Odio's door, was used by a lookalike for Oswald in New Orleans.[150] So the possibility exists that the man at Odio's door was the real Oswald. And that the man on his way to Houston to board a bus for Mexico was a double. Or visa–versa.

It gets more fascinating. When the Cubans arrived at the Odio residence, they asked not for Sylvia, or her sister Annie, who were both there. They asked for Sarita Odio, another sister, who did not live there. (op cit, HSCA, p. 25) Annie told them Sarita did not live there. But then one of the Cubans mentioned something about the one who was married. Since neither Sarita nor Annie was married at the time, they must have been looking for Sylvia, who was divorced. The Odios were part of the Cuban exile group called JURE, which was headed by Manuel Ray. Ray was a favorite of the Kennedys and was detested by the operational part of the CIA who ran the Bay of Pigs invasion, especially Howard Hunt. Why? Because he was so liberal that Hunt regarded him as a diluted version of Castro. Their pretense for being at Sylvia's was to solicit funds for JURE. They wanted Sylvia to compose a letter in English for them so they could present it to local businessmen. (ibid p. 26) They also said they knew Sylvia's father who was a businessman who had been imprisoned by Castro on the Isle of Pines.

Rankin's aforementioned letter tells Hoover that Odio's story must be "proved or disproved." With Hoover's performance so far, and what Rankin knew about it, the note contained an invisible wink about how to proceed. Hoover sent his agents to interview someone who he knew was involved with anti-Castro activities, Loran Hall. The FBI reported back to the Commission that it was he, Bill Seymour, and Lawrence Howard who had visited Odio. On the basis of this information, the Commission concluded Oswald had not been at Odio's door.

Bugliosi later adds that Hall recanted his story.[151] Again, to be kind, this is not completely accurate. For on October 5, 1977, Hall was interviewed by the HSCA on this specific point. Namely, what he told the FBI when they interviewed him back in September 1964. They asked him if he knew a Mrs. Odio. He said he told the agent he did not recall a woman by that name.[152] Hall asked the agent for a photo of her.[153] Incredibly, the agent said he did not have one with him. Hall did say that he had been in Dallas, but not with Howard and Seymour. He was there with Howard and a man named Alba. He was asked if he was ever directly or indirectly involved with Odio in acquiring military equipment for anti-Castro raids. He said he had not been so involved. So according to Hall, he didn't "recant." The FBI lied. And if they did not bring a photo of Odio, the interview was likely a setup. Since that lack indicates they knew Hall would not identify her.

What all but certifies that Hoover and the Commission cooperated on a cover-up here is that the FBI interviewed Seymour two days after the Hall interview. He told them he had not been in Dallas in September 1963 and had not been in any contact with Sylvia Odio. Yet this report was not compiled until *two weeks later*, on October 2, which is after the Warren Report was published.[154] Bugliosi makes nothing of this peculiar timing.

The FBI and Mexico City

What about the FBI and the momentous event originating about the same time as the Odio incident? That is, Oswald's alleged trip to Mexico City. On the day after the assassination, Hoover was in receipt of at least one of the audio tapes from Mexico City that was supposed to be of Oswald's voice. FBI agents in Dallas had listened to it. They came to the conclusion that the voice was not Oswald's. Hoover mentioned this to President Johnson in a memo of November 23. That tape had been facilitated at the Texas border by FBI agent Eldon Rudd.[155] Rudd was also involved in carrying photos of the famous "mystery man" to Dallas. This is the stocky, six foot gentleman whom the CIA tried to pass off as Oswald in Mexico City. But they knew he was not Oswald. After the assassination, Rudd had to have known the photos were not Oswald because one of them was taken on October 4, after Oswald had departed Mexico City.[156] No surprise, when Rudd later became a congressman he opposed the creation of the HSCA and then refused to testify before that body.[157]

As John Newman noted, Hoover decided to go along with this CIA charade. As we have seen, the FBI knew that the tapes survived past the assassination. Yet they never contradicted the CIA cover story that they had not.[158] Hoover acknowledged just seven weeks after the assassination that the CIA had duped him about Mexico City. On the margin of a memo about keeping abreast of CIA operations inside the USA, he scrawled: "OK but I hope you are not being taken in. I can't forget the CIA withholding the French espionage activities in the USA, nor the false story re Oswald's trip to Mexico, only to mention two instances of their double-dealing."[159]

Hoover Rigs Ruby's Polygraph

Let us conclude this chapter with a discussion of one of the most important areas of the JFK case where it is clear that the FBI concealed evidence. Namely, the polygraph examination of Jack Ruby.

As Arlen Specter told a packed house at Duquesne University in November of 2003, it was never the Commission's idea to give Ruby a polygraph examination. Ruby pushed it on them. Even then Earl Warren was still reluctant to give him one. According to Specter, he persuaded Warren that he should follow through on it.

Predictably, the Warren Commission went to the FBI for its polygraph operator.[160] This was a man named Bell Herndon. It is important to note Herndon's experience and qualifications in light of the peculiar techniques he would utilize in the Ruby test. Herndon was a special agent in the FBI for fourteen years. In 1964 he was the polygraph supervisor and an examiner at the FBI lab in Washington.[161] He had been trained for six months on the machine by a PhD in psychology who specialized in polygraph examination out of the New York FBI office.[162] He then trained under polygraph specialists in Washington. He told the Commission that he had "given, supervised, or reviewed several thousand polygraph examinations."[163] Clearly, Herndon knew his craft and had a good background in how to conduct a proper test. Therefore, he also knew how *not* to conduct a test. He explained to Arlen Specter the three charts then in use on polygraph exams: one for respiratory patterns, one for heart rate and blood pressure, and one called galvanic skin response. GSR measures the response of skin and muscle tissue to internal stimuli. GSR tracings can be highly sensitive to emotions in some subjects.

Now, Specter clearly tried to get Herndon to say that there were no deceptive criteria when Ruby was asked the question, "Did you assist Oswald in the assassination?"[164] Herndon was reluctant to reply at first but he eventually said, "Other than a slight impact in the GSR, there was no noticeable change in his physiological response to that particular question."[165] The reader should keep this reply in mind as we proceed.

Generally speaking, most of the reports in the HSCA volumes are mediocre or worse. But occasionally in those volumes one will come across some valuable information or even an above-average report (for example, the report on Sylvia Odio). The HSCA report on Ruby's polygraph strikes me as being above the norm for Robert Blakey's inquiry.

The three polygraph experts reviewed the surviving relevant data on the Ruby lie detector test and came up with a rather compelling analysis of Herndon's work. Although the criticism is couched in rather mild terms, the content of the report is blistering. The analysis concludes that the Ruby test violated at least ten different rules of good polygraph practice. The violations ranged from the preparation of questions to the actual equipment used to register the reaction charts.[166] One of the extraordinary aspects of this test is that Bugliosi's trusted colleague, assistant DA Bill Alexander, was in the room for all the pretest questions.[167] And the HSCA agreed with Herndon that this was a problem with the examination, namely that too many people were present. Accepted polygraph practice allows for just the examiner and the subject to be in the room. Yet in this particular test, there were eight people present during the actual examination, and ten during the pretest.[168] Herndon himself made this criticism before the Commission. The problem with too many people present is it may create distractions that register on the test chart as a false reading. But further, the HSCA panel noted times when Herndon just lost control over the proceedings due to the ad hoc participation of the observers.[169] Alexander even had off the record conversations with Ruby over the phrasing of a question.[170]

Another criticism was the number of both overall questions asked—which was over a hundred—and also the number of what is termed "relevant" questions. The latter refers to actual questions involving whether the subject is truthful about the matters involved with the case. (They are usually intermingled with what is called irrelevant and control questions.) The HSCA panel believed the sheer number of these questions "showed total disregard of basic polygraph principles."[171] Just how bad was this violation? The standard text in the field recommended three relevant questions in an exam. The Ruby test had fifty-five. One of the panel members said that the most he had ever heard of in nearly thirty years of practice was seventeen. Here is the problem with this violation: ". . . the more a person is tested, the less he tends to react when lying. That is . . . liars become so test-tired, they no longer produce significant physiological reactions when lying."[172] Therefore, the subject could lie and get away with lying. In fact, by the fourth series, Herndon himself admitted that Ruby showed real signs of fatigue to the point of "going to pieces."[173] The panel thought that Ruby's condition was not necessarily due to fatigue but caused in part by "the chaotic nature of the entire situation." Which the operator should have never allowed.

Herndon himself called Ruby's reactions by this point "very erratic." And this is where two more violations by the examiner surface. The panel commented that it is just because of these types of readings that good practice requires the relevant questions be asked a second time, and further, that a second test be used as a cross check.[174] Especially since the test was too long, lasting a total of over five hours.[175]

The panel also criticized the "control" questions used by Herndon. It is one that the operator knows the correct answer to and to which the person will probably lie. This helps the examiner determine what a deception on the chart will look like. But Herndon defined a control question as one to which Ruby would have any kind of emotional response. For example: Herndon used "Have you ever been arrested?" as a control question. Ruby replied in the affirmative. Therefore that was not a lie. So how could this be used as a "control" question? It was just an emotional reply to an uncomfortable question. The panel noted four other "control" questions like this one.[176] One being "Are you married?" The panel thought this was an irrelevant question, one used to just acclimate the subject to the test or to get a stable response. Herndon used it as a "control" question.

In other words, there was method to the madness. First, by wearing Ruby down the charted physiological responses would be less detectable. Second, by confusing the three types of questions, there would be no accurate landmarks with which to make an accurate chart. But the panel went even further.

It seems that Herndon had a fallback plan in case the above tactics failed. He set the GSR device at only a quarter of its maximum reading at the start of the test. He then actually lessened it from there.[177] The panel noted that this was the opposite of accepted practice. The sensitivity should have never been that low to begin with, but it actually should have been increased as the test went on because of its overlong nature. Because of this, the panel considered the GSR reading to be completely useless. It was so bad that they suspected the machine itself was defective. They wrote that Herndon should have had a second machine available. And he should have used it.[178]

The strongest indication that Herndon's violations were deliberate was in his use of a faulty control question to map out a patterned response. When Ruby was asked "Have you ever been arrested?" Herndon testified that the response resulted in a "noticeable rise in blood pressure." The panel disagreed with this because the rise was seven seconds after the answer. Which is at least three times longer than a normal reaction. They believed the reaction was due to a physical movement at the seven second point, which Herndon had actually recorded. The panel then applied the clincher. They wrote that Ruby's reaction to the preceding question—"Did you assist Oswald in the assassination?" to which he replied in the negative—recorded the largest valid GSR reaction in the first test series. Plus, there was a constant suppression of breathing and a rise in blood pressure at the time. So although Herndon opined Ruby was being truthful in this reply, to the panel the possibility was open that he was lying.[179] What makes this even more apparent is that it was the largest GSR reaction when Ruby was relatively fresh at the start, and even though the GSR was at one fourth of its sensitivity. The reader can now see why Herndon was hesitant to reply to this question with Specter.

In light of such a systematic and rigorous bypassing of standard practice, the question arises: Could someone as experienced and knowledgeable as Herndon have set out to violate so many rules without the OK from above?

How does the author deal with all these troubling, even distressing, facts? In the main text of *Reclaiming History*, Bugliosi mentions Ruby's polygraph on two pages. He writes that Herndon concluded that, if one considers Ruby mentally competent, there was no area of deception present in regard to relevant questions. And he states no disagreement with Herndon's conclusion there.[180] In the End Notes, he finally mentions the HSCA panel. He deals with their twenty-one-page report in *four sentences*. He now admits that Herndon made "errors." He specifically notes two: 1) An excess of people in the room, and 2) the surfeit of relevant questions.[181] And that is that for the prosecutor. Bugliosi read the HSCA report. Somehow, Herndon's mixing up the three types of questions, the overlong duration, and the faulty GSR registration, these were not worth mentioning? Recall what the prosecutor said at the beginning about making the critics' arguments the way they would want them made?

This could go on, of course, for many more pages. But the point is made. The FBI was involved in the cover-up almost immediately, and in just about every aspect. From either substituting or getting rid of bullet evidence, to falsifying polygraph tests. It is not a debatable point. It is a provable fact. As noted above, even members of the Commission—like Lee Rankin, Hale Boggs, and Burt Griffin—acknowledged that the FBI served them in a highly questionable manner. For Bugliosi not to acknowledge what the Commission members themselves did seriously compromises the credibility of his book.

CHAPTER TEN

Bugliosi Hearts
the Warren Commission

"The best evidence that Oswald could fire as fast as he did and hit the target is the fact that he did so."

—Commission Counsel Wesley Liebeler

In sequential order, these last three chapters show how the Kennedy case was investigated. First by the Dallas Police, second by Hoover's FBI, and finally the Warren Commission. By taking this approach we pose an important, perhaps crucial, question: What was the state of the evidence when it arrived at the Warren Commission? It appears that the Dallas Police Department (DPD) had dabbled with CE 543, the dented shell which may or may not have been sent to FBI headquarters the evening of the assassination. But, whatever the case, experimentation shows it could not have been fired that day. Because it was exculpatory of Oswald, Hoover concealed the actual results of his continued gunshot residue testing. The Dallas police appear to have intimidated Wesley Frazier and then retrieved a "package" from the Texas School Book Depository that does not correspond to the one in evidence today. The Commission was presented with an autopsy report that was first burned and then rewritten after Oswald was killed. They were confronted with a print on the rifle that was not initially reported in Dallas and not found by the FBI in Washington, but then appeared when the rifle was returned to Dallas several days later.

The above is, of course, only a partial list. I have not enumerated the cover up around Oswald's activities in New Orleans and Mexico City, or the spectacular security breakdown by the Dallas Police in the basement of City Hall. The point is that the Commission was confronted with an evidentiary trail that contained telltale signs of manipulation and concealment. But yet, both the DPD and FBI had declared to all that Oswald was guilty. But now Oswald was dead. In light of this dubious collection of evidence, any fair or judicious legal body would be concerned with granting the murdered Oswald his posthumous day in court. After all, before he even had a lawyer, he had been killed in the arms of people who were supposed to be protecting him. Because of that, at the very least, one expected the Commission to uphold the tradition of the American legal system: Oswald would be presumed innocent and be given a vigorous defense. That defense team would view and study all the evidence concerning their client. They would then be able to use this knowledge to both call and cross-examine witnesses. And they would also be able to present their own experts in certain refined fields. For instance, illustrious New York City medical examiner Milton Halpern would be allowed to study the autopsy evidence and records. Based on that, he would participate in the examination of the pathologists about why they did what they did during Kennedy's autopsy.

And, of course, all these official proceedings would be conducted in the open so that Americans would know their government had nothing to hide about President Kennedy's murder.

Earl Warren: Oswald Gets No Defense

As we know, in a complete reversal of standard jurisprudence, nothing even like the above happened. In each category, the opposite occurred. Oswald was provided with no defense team. He was presumed guilty by the Commission in January, before the first witness was called. Many important documents and pieces of evidence were never presented to the Commission. Important witnesses were not called. Crucial areas of evidence, like the autopsy and ballistics, were never questioned—even though they could have easily been challenged. One of the most surprising twists in *Reclaiming History* is this: lawyer Bugliosi finds nothing wrong with any of this.

What makes this so shocking is that Bugliosi must know that Earl Warren's legacy is based upon the revolution in the criminal justice system that he helped usher into practice. Among the cornerstones of his legacy was that a criminal defendant has a right to counsel. Just eight months earlier, in the famous case of *Gideon v Wainwright*, the Warren Court had established that no state could deprive a criminal defendant of his right to counsel. And in that case, after Clarence Gideon had been convicted without a lawyer, he was acquitted in one hour after he was retried with an attorney. That acquittal also took place before the assassination. Warren would also be responsible for the later and related decisions in the Massiah, Miranda, and Escobedo cases. These all greatly aided in the protection of an accused criminal's rights before the police and in court. In light of all this, it seems bizarre for Bugliosi to not even note the rather savage irony of the Warren Commission not granting the accused a defense. It underlines his antihistorical approach.

What made the rush to judgment all the worse was the incessant pounding home by the press that Oswald was clearly the only gunman involved. How Warren was so unaware of this issue is also puzzling. Dr. Sam Sheppard had been convicted in 1954 of killing his wife. Many noted the incessant negative publicity against the accused during the trial. Sheppard had made a few appeals prior to 1963 that were unsuccessful, but while the Warren Commission was in session, in July 1964, he did finally succeed in getting a new trial. He was later acquitted.

Compared to Oswald, Sheppard's media was not so one-sided. Before Oswald was shot by Ruby, Dallas DA Henry Wade appeared on national television and told tens of millions that Oswald was the killer. And further, it was so obvious that he would try for the death penalty in the case. Then, after Oswald was killed, during the months of November and December, the media carried deliberately leaked stories. They drummed into the public mind the "overwhelming guilt" of the dead Oswald. The day after Oswald was killed, J. Edgar Hoover was the source for an *Associated Press* story declaring Oswald's posthumous guilt. On December 1, the *Washington Post* did a long article that told its readers "all the police agencies with a hand in the investigation . . . insist that the case against Oswald is an unshakable one." *Time* magazine assured its readers that the FBI report "will indicate that Oswald, acting in his own lunatic loneliness, was indeed the President's assassin."[1] *Newsweek* echoed this verdict by stating "the report holds to the central conclusion that Federal and local probers had long reached: that Oswald was the assassin."[2] The *New York Times* also served as a bullhorn for FBI Director Hoover. On December 10, it ran a front-page story that was titled "Oswald Assassin Beyond a Doubt, FBI Concludes."

In other words, Warren was not only going to deprive Oswald of a right to counsel, he was doing it amid a tumult of unfair and prejudicial publicity. As we shall see, there might be an excuse for Warren in this regard. But what is the excuse for Bugliosi? Why does he never bring up these other cases which set such valuable precedents for the rights of the accused? Again, he said he would set forth the critics' arguments as they themselves want them expressed.

The Commission's "Investigatory Mood"

This publicity barrage is even worse because it seems orchestrated by officers in the government who were responsible for finding out who actually killed President Kennedy. That is, both Hoover and Acting Attorney General Nicholas Katzenbach. Since the shabby FBI report was classified and the Commission worked in secret, there was no one to show that the Emperor was wearing no clothes. That is, the "unshakable" case against Oswald was anything but airtight. These irresponsible officials were bamboozling an all too gullible media. The Commission itself criticized the FBI report at an Executive Session of December 16. Representative Hale Boggs said, "There's nothing in there about Governor Connally." To which Senator John S. Cooper replied, "And whether or not they found any bullets in him." Commissioner John McCloy added, "This bullet business leaves me confused." Chief Counsel J. Lee Rankin then summed it all up with, "It's totally inconclusive." What is important to remember about this conversation is that the Commission at this time had done almost nothing. Materials and reports had begun to accumulate but very little of it had been digested. That is because the Commission itself was a part time body. The vast majority of its work was done by its legal staff—which had not been appointed at this time and would not be until early January.

The way Bugliosi deals with the above questions by the Warren Commission is, again, so rich in unintended humor it needs to be quoted. He describes their questioning of the FBI report as constituting a "very investigative mood" for the Commission.[3] He leaves out two things. They are in an investigatory mood because the FBI report had turned out to be a debacle. Second, he doesn't say that the "very investigative mood" didn't last very long—or go very far.

For by January 11, the December 16 "investigative mood" had been muzzled. The Commission was in firm agreement with the FBI and Dallas Police: Oswald did it by himself. We know this by their own records. In a document dated January 11, 1964, and titled "Progress Report," Rankin prepared a work outline to assist in the organization and evaluation of the materials received by the Commission. (He had been assigned to do this by Warren at the December 16 Executive Session meeting.) The second subhead was titled "Lee Harvey Oswald as the Assassin of President Kennedy." The third subhead was "Lee Harvey Oswald: Background and Possible Motives." In other words, the verdict had been decided upon *in spite of* the Commission's previously expressed doubts. And three weeks before the first witness had been called. Bugliosi does not tell the reader that at this same December 16 meeting, Warren stated that he wanted a birth to death biography of Oswald and a similar one on Ruby. Which clearly influenced Rankin's outline.

What happened between December 16 and January 11? Formally, nothing was done. The December 16 meeting was the last executive session before Rankin prepared his fateful outline—from which there would be no turning back. Placing the question in a broader context, the Commission was announced on November 29. The first witness was called on February 2. To paraphrase Walt Brown: What did they do for the first sixty-six days?[4]

Was Warren in a Coma?

They had four executive session hearings, and they hired their support staff. This staff started to sift through the assembled reports of the FBI, Secret Service, and CIA. But in the roughly nine months left of their existence, they would not budge from Rankin's outline. Why? Because at the very first meeting on December 5, during Chairman Earl Warren's first speech, he said that the function of the Commission should be to evaluate evidence, not to gather evidence. And that the Commission could rely upon the reports of "the FBI and Secret Service and others that I may not know about at the present time." He sealed the deal by saying something that would discredit both him and the Commission: "I believe that the development of the evidence in this way should not call for a staff of investigators." In other words, the Commission would accept the work of the Dallas Police, the FBI, and the Secret Service and not investigate or search for new evidence or witnesses with detectives of their own. With what we know today about the work of the bodies the Commission relied upon, this was an error of judgment similar to General Custer at the Little Big Horn.

Just how emasculated was Chief Justice Earl Warren on the Kennedy case? From here, he went on to say that the hearings should not be held in public. He thought that their report would carry more influence done secretly than if it were done in the open. Incredibly, he even wanted the Commission to hear no witnesses or even have the power to subpoena them! He added that this would "retard rather than help our investigation." At this first meeting, Warren was clearly carrying water for President Johnson. For he added that one function of the Commission was to head off legislative committees from holding hearings. Which was LBJ's goal. Further, Warren invited Acting Attorney General Nicholas Katzenbach to the first meeting. Mr. Katzenbach told the Commission a real whopper. He said that the upcoming FBI report on the case "will have no conclusions in it." As noted in the previous installment, this was completely false. The fact that the report was absolutely conclusive shocked some of the Commissioners. The FBI report was so poor that the Commission decided at its second meeting that they could not rely on it. What they needed was the raw data it was based upon, as well as the interview reports of the other agencies involved. Sen. John S. Cooper added, "I think we ought to have a list of people we want to interrogate." Therefore subpoena power was necessary.

One of the most amazing things about *Reclaiming History* is this: Bugliosi has no serious problems with any of the above. Oswald not having representation is not a real problem for him. The Commission not hiring its own investigators and relying on Hoover is not really objectionable to the prosecutor. The Commission not having all the evidence from agencies like the CIA is also OK. To have the bizarre autopsy practices not reviewed by a professional is not objectionable. The proceedings being closed to the press and public, that's not a big deal. Bugliosi doesn't bat an eyelash at Earl Warren not subpoenaing important witnesses like David Ferrie and Sylvia Duran. In fact, the former practicing attorney who found the Supreme Court procedures and actions so outrageous in both the Paula Jones case, and the *Bush v Gore* decision, doesn't wince at any of the oddities and irregularities noted here.

As a result, he can't bring himself to admit a rather troublesome truth about this whole sorry state of affairs. As Chris Sharrett noted: the Nazis at Nuremberg were furnished more of a defense than Oswald was. Of course, if he did admit that, the author would have a lot to explain. (One thing would be: How could you as an attorney condone such a thing Mr. Bugliosi?) This would have created a rather large problem for the author since today we have more data about the inner workings of the Commission than we had before. We also have more information on the commissioners themselves. And this helps explain why people like Hess, Streicher, and Goering got more justice than Oswald.

Bugliosi Defends Katzenbach

But to understand just how far into the prosecutorial zone Bugliosi is, one has to realize that he even defends the Katzenbach and Eisenberg memos. On November 24, after Oswald was killed it appears that Hoover had a phone conversation with Acting Attorney General Nicholas Katzenbach. He called the White House and talked to assistant Walter Jenkins. Both Jenkins and Hoover summarized this in memos written on that day. They both contain similar key passages. Hoover expressed it thusly: "The thing I am most concerned about, and so is Mr. Katzenbach, is having something issued so that we can convince the public that Oswald is the real assassin."[5] The next day Katzenbach issued his famous memorandum. This memorandum is rightly perceived as wishing to cut off any kind of verdict of conspiracy in the case. Bugliosi scores Mark Lane for selective quoting from the memo, even though Lane quotes accurately from it. How does he counter Lane? By selectively quoting the first sentence. Bugliosi quotes thusly, "It is important that all of the facts surrounding President Kennedy's assassination be made public" and he puts a period after this with a closed quote.[6]

This is not the correct academic style because that is not the whole sentence. The rest of the sentence reads as follows: ". . . in a way which will satisfy people in the United States and abroad that all the facts have been told and that a statement to this effect be made now." The second half of the sentence has a direct modifying effect on the first half. Specifically, the spirit of full disclosure is limited by the next phrase: "in a way which will satisfy people," which limits the disclosure. The rest of the memo goes even further than this in limiting what should be said in the way of fact finding: the public must be satisfied that Oswald was the assassin, that he had no confederates, and he would have been convicted at trial. If Bugliosi wanted full disclosure with his readers then the solution would have been obvious. He had over 2,600 pages. Why did he not just print the memo? He couldn't sacrifice one page of slamming those goofy critics to print an important document?

Bugliosi Defends the Eisenberg Memo

The same question could be asked of the prosecutor about another famous memorandum. This one is by Commission staff lawyer Melvin Eisenberg. It is from the first staff meeting. Again, instead of printing it on those thousands of pages he has, the prosecutor selectively quotes from it. Many people consider this memo to be very revealing about the way the Commission decided to proceed. Warren tells the staff that he did not want the job, and his associate justice on the Supreme Court did not want him to take it. LBJ called him in and explained to him how rumors were sweeping the country about a political plot to get him into the White House. Other rumors could lead the nation into a war that could cost forty million lives. Therefore, he could not refuse such a position. The author then says that there was nothing in his address about "suppressing the truth to avoid a war."[7]

If Bugliosi had quoted the next sentence there would have been. It reads, "The President convinced him that this was an occasion on which actual conditions had to override general principles."[8] How could the message have been made much clearer to a bunch of Yale, Stanford, and Harvard law school graduates? The threat of 40 million dead was going to take precedence over the general legal principles he had espoused.

Instead, the author jumps forward to the next paragraph in which, after reading this threat of atomic holocaust and saying it would override normal procedure, Warren now said that "the Commission had to determine the truth, whatever that might be." Question for the Prosecutor: If Warren spent 167 words scaring the staff about not walking into nuclear winter, domestic LBJ led conspiracies, and squelching conspiracy rumors, and then turned and spent all of fourteen words saying they must find the truth, don't you think the bright Ivy League lawyers would understand that an over 10–1 ratio tells them what the boss wants? Or else, why bring the subject up at all? Clearly, that one sentence was CYA, and that is what people like David Belin used it for. The fact that the lawyers got the message is brought home by the Church Committee interview of Sylvia Odio. She told Gaeton Fonzi that when Wesley Liebeler interviewed her in Dallas, he told her that Warren had given them orders that they were supposed to ignore any evidence they found that indicated a conspiracy.[9] Therefore, Warren succeeded in his goal to ward off nuclear war. By not connecting this to exactly why Johnson had scared Warren and how, the reader does not understand just why "normal conditions had to override general principles." But if the reader thinks back to the chapter on Mexico City, that was the basis for the whole Armageddon scenario. The CIA had sent up phony tapes of Oswald in Mexico City meeting with a KGB assassination expert. Therefore, Oswald had killed Kennedy for the Soviets. Of course, Warren never understood how that was all a CIA stage managed illusion. But, it worked.

Power Play

The author mentions the fact that Commission Chairman Earl Warren wished to appoint his friend and colleague Warren Olney as Chief Counsel. But he glosses over what happened to Warren when he tried to do this. In fact, he actually tries to blame Olney's rejection on Sen. Richard Russell.[10] Which, in light of what actually happened, is nonsense. Gerald McKnight was much more forthcoming in *Breach of Trust*. After describing how close Warren was with Olney, McKnight then described the origin of the opposition to him: Hoover hated Olney's guts.[11] How did Hoover find out about Warren's preference so quickly? Through Nicholas Katzenbach, and perhaps Gerald Ford.[12] As we now know, Ford was an informant for FBI official Cartha DeLoach on the Commission. This began closely after his appointment in late November of 1963. But like most informants, Ford insisted that his role should remain secret. He then lied about it after it was exposed. His snitching included panel disputes over the hiring of staff.[13] In turn, DeLoach served as a conduit to Ford for what Hoover thought about those panel disputes. And Ford acted in accordance with his longtime friend Hoover's wishes.

But it wasn't just Hoover who wanted the independent Olney out. Katzenbach did also. He had also jumped on the "Oswald as lone gunman" bandwagon, and he did not want to risk the Commission upsetting that contraption. So Katzenbach installed his man at the Justice Department, Howard Willens, on the Commission to guard against the train jumping off track. [14] How important was Willens in this regard? As Bugliosi notes without comment, one of Willens's functions was to recruit the staff.[15] With what Katzenbach had written in his famous November 25 memo—"The public must be satisfied that Oswald was the assassin"—we can imagine what Willens was looking for as qualifications. When the FBI was informed about Warren's preference for Olney, a lobbying campaign was arranged by Hoover, Katzenbach, and DeLoach to thwart said appointment. According to McKnight, there was a lot to fear. For as the author states in his book, "Had Olney served as Chief Counsel it is very likely that the Warren Commission Report would have been an entirely different historical document."[16]

When Warren tried to appoint Olney, it was Ford and McCloy who joined forces to block him. McCloy just happened to have a list of substitutes on hand. One of whom was J. Lee Rankin. A rump committee was formed which included McCloy, Ford, Allen Dulles and Warren. As McKnight tells it, in just a matter of hours, Rankin now became the consensus choice. Warren was outmaneuvered since Ford and Dulles threatened to resign if Olney was appointed. Rankin was a longtime friend of McCloy, but he was also a working colleague of Hoover whom the Director felt he could get along with. Regrettably, Hoover was right in that regard.

In *Breach of Trust*, McKnight spends about four pages on this key episode. Bugliosi deals with it in three paragraphs.[17] In his discussion of it, he leaves out the role of Ford as the FBI informant. He leaves out the work of Hoover and DeLoach in lobbying the Commission. And, most importantly, he ignores the maneuvering of McCloy, Dulles, and Ford to veto Olney and enlist Rankin, the more palatable FBI candidate.

The Troika Asserts Power

There may be a reason Bugliosi blurs and discounts the above. Because it betrays what the real balance of power was on the Commission. Unlike Bugliosi's insinuation, Richard Russell and John Cooper made no real objection to Warren's appointment of his own counsel. From the Senate, they understood the chair's privilege in that regard.[18] It was McCloy, Ford, and Dulles who cooperated with the off stage actors—Hoover, Katzenbach, and DeLoach—to make sure Olney was not appointed. When broken down and analyzed, this episode provides a window into what the Commission was really about and how it would proceed. What does the window reveal?

1) For all practical purposes, Chief Justice Earl Warren had been made into a figurehead. Bugliosi mentions how LBJ scared Warren into taking the job by suggesting images of mushroom clouds and tens of millions of burnt corpses. But, incredibly, the author makes no comment on how this fear-mongering could have impacted Warren in his fiduciary function. Yet from the way Warren reacted to it—tearfully—and the way he then spoke at the first meeting of the Commission, one would think he clearly got the message: the Kennedy case was not to be dug into or exposed to the public. As others have written, the giveaway as to how compromised LBJ made Warren was the Chief Justice's famous reply to a question about just when the public would see all the documents the Commission had seen. Warren was rather indeterminate. He responded with, "Yes, there will come a time. But it might not be in your lifetime."[19] The reader should note the use of the word "might." One wonders just how many lifetimes Warren was talking about.

2) The real nexus of power within the Commission was made up of John McCloy, Allen Dulles, and Gerald Ford. To anyone who studies American history, this would have been a predictable grouping. Why it is predictable is a key point that is drastically underplayed by the author. But before we get to that, let us use some facts to demonstrate that this power center actually existed and acted. In his microstudy of the Commission hearings entitled *The Warren Omission*, Walt Brown broke down the proceedings by attendance and questions posed. The Commission member who was in attendance at the most number of full hearings was Allen Dulles. The member who posed the most questions was also Dulles.[20] He outdistanced the second place finisher in both categories by no insignificant margin. In fact, Brown's charting of these statistics demonstrates that Dulles, Ford, and McCloy asked nearly 70 percent of the questions. A startling figure, especially since this troika formed a minority of the Commission. Another way to demonstrate their dominance is by tallying up the number of full hearings each member attended. The grand total for all members was 260. The Dulles–McCloy–Ford

troika tallied 145 of those. More than half, even though they formed a minority. The Troika clearly dominated the proceedings.

3)   Since statistics are usually a zero sum game, the reader can guess the next point. The three members left out in the cold were Representative Hale Boggs, and Senators John S. Cooper and Richard Russell. These three attended only sixty-three full hearings. Which is less than 25 percent of the total. They also asked less than 25 percent of the questions posed by the Commission members. One could conclude that the southern wing of the Commission was being both left out and left behind by the Washington–Wall Street Troika.

In light of these facts, one should note that Brown's book was published over a decade before *Reclaiming History* appeared. Bugliosi lists it in his bibliography. There may be a reason why the author does not then inform us of these illuminating figures. See, once the early critics of the Warren Report began to expose the Commission's subterfuges, it was Russell, Boggs, and Cooper who first voiced doubts about the work they had done. In light of the above numbers, this makes perfect sense. Because the figures indicate that those three—the figurative Southern Wing—were not really a part of the Commission's work in any integral way.

Richard Russell Says: No

The case of Richard Russell epitomizes what actually happened. Back in 1967, estimable critic Sylvia Meagher first pointed out the poor attendance record of Sen. Russell.[21] Many writers, both pro- and anti-Warren Commission, have used this to score him as "shirking his responsibilities." Predictably, Bugliosi goes after him on this account.[22] With what we know about both the Commission and Russell today, the senator could have easily pleaded what Corazon Aquino did when she challenged Ferdinand Marcos for the highest office in the Philippines. Her critics charged that she was inexperienced. She replied that the charge was accurate. For she had no experience in graft, kickbacks, blackmail, criminal cover-ups, and bribery. Today, one can make the same case for Russell. After he saw how the neutered Warren was going to conduct the Commission, and after he read the wholly inadequate FBI report of December 9, he decided the proceeding was going to be a stage managed dog and pony show. Which it was. In fact, even assistant counsel Burt Griffin testified that Russell wanted to do an investigation as opposed to an evaluation. One that would be a countercheck on the Commission, to be sure no stone was unturned.[23]

Russell saw the handwriting on the wall early. At the December 5 executive session he took some cryptic notes which indicate that he was upset that Warren and Katzenbach had already bought into the FBI report and were considering no one bought Oswald. This was before it had been completed and submitted. At the December 16 meeting, Russell had warned the Commission that the FBI report needed to be scoured for weaknesses and contradictions. If not, five or six years later it would come back to haunt them. He then saw that the Commission's disagreements with the FBI report were not one of content, but of form. Hoover had not camouflaged his negligent and biased tracks well enough, either in length or in obfuscation. The Commission's cover-up would be longer, and more elaborate: 888 pages of it. Realizing what was ahead, Russell did something that no other Commissioner did. Using people on his own staff, like Alfredda Scobey, and others, like retired Army Intelligence officer Philip Corso, he conducted his own inquiry. Corso found out that the Mannlicher Carcano rifle allegedly used in the assassination could not perform as the official story leads us to believe. Corso also came to believe that there was a Second Oswald, and that Oswald had gone to Russia as part of a fake defector program run by Naval Intelligence. He also came to the conclusion that the assassination was a project of rogue CIA agents working with anti-Castro Cubans. Russell tended to agree with Corso, but he said he could never get the other members of the panel to believe it.[24]

Few people know that the day after the Southern Wing did a rather hostile interview with Marina Oswald, without the Troika in attendance, Russell visited Dealey Plaza with Boggs and Cooper. He took an unloaded rifle up to the sixth floor and simulated firing at JFK. In light of what Corso had told him, he commented rather wryly afterwards that "Oswald must have been an expert shot." Which, of course, he knew he wasn't.[25] What even fewer people know is that Russell actually composed a letter of resignation from the Commission. Dated February 24, 1964, it was never sent to President Johnson. In it, he complains that the Commission "has been scheduling, holding, and canceling meetings without notifying him."[26] If one adds in the Southern Wing's performance with Marina, to their hesitance in signing onto the Single Bullet Theory at the September 18, 1964, Executive Session hearing, it is easy to understand why the Troika didn't want Russell around. Russell disagreed with the Single Bullet Theory based on two strong pieces of evidence, 1) The testimony of John Connally as to hearing the first shot and turning before he was hit, and 2) The Zapruder film. Rankin tricked Russell into thinking that his objections would be noted at this meeting. They were not. There is no stenographic record of this meeting. Harold Weisberg later informed Russell of Rankin's deception.[27]

The emerging record of Russell as the first dissenter—perhaps the first critic—of the Commission is one of the most important developments in the scholarship on the Warren Commission to appear of late. Russell did not criticize the Commission in public until November 20, 1966, in *The Atlanta Constitution.* There he said he harbored a lingering dissatisfaction with the Commission's work and that he disagreed with the Single Bullet Theory. In 1968, he went further and told Weisberg that the Commission had been deceived by the CIA and FBI in two key areas: 1) Oswald's background, and 2) the ballistics evidence.[28]

Russell left the records of his work from the Commission at the University of Georgia Library. Many people, besides Dick Russell, have used them. And there have been several unpublished scholarly papers based upon those records by students like Gary Diamond and Dani E. Biancolli. In twenty-one years, Bugliosi apparently never consulted that archive or read those research papers. This tells us much about what he was up to in *Reclaiming History.*

As critical as Russell was about the Warren Commission, he never got as vituperative or as specific as Hale Boggs did. Boggs famously said that "Hoover lied his eyes out to the Commission—on Oswald, on Ruby, on their friends, the bullets, the gun, you name it."[29] The congressman's regrets about his service on the Commission were well known to his family. In the seventies, his widow Lindy Boggs took over his seat in Congress. In keeping with his wishes, she became one of the early backers of the bill to authorize a new inquiry into the JFK case, which became the House Select Committee on Assassinations. Senator Cooper once expressed concerns over contradictions between the testimonies given by witnesses before the Commission versus the interviews of those very same witnesses to the media.[30]

Senator Cooper also did not buy into the Single Bullet Theory. In an interview he did in 1978 for a British documentary he stated that,

> "Yes there were disagreements. I think the most serious one . . . was whether the first shot went through President Kennedy and Governor Connally, who was sitting in the jump seat in front of him. I heard Connally testify he was not struck by the same bullet. I could not convince myself the same bullet struck both of them."

At this point, realizing the import of what Cooper had said, the interviewer jumped in and asked, "You mean you yourself were not convinced by the Single Bullet Theory?" To which Cooper replied simply, "No, I was not." By which he was saying there was a second gunman and, by necessity, a conspiracy.[31] Cooper's 1978 testimony means that Russell did not stand alone in his dissent from the Troika.

One way to look at why the Troika and Warren did what they did is this: It was the easy way out. By January 11, it had become clear that Hoover, the White House, the Dallas Police, and the press all wanted a verdict of no conspiracy, with Oswald and Ruby as disturbed killers. Further, all the above power centers were alive and kicking. Oswald was dead and gone. The path of least resistance was quite obvious.

But something else was at work here. Clearly, the incredible power of the Establishment and the mainstream media was pulling everything in one direction. But in a very real sense, the Troika *was* the Establishment and the mainstream. This is a significant point that Bugliosi simply does not confront. Beneath the surface of *Reclaiming History* lurks a rather disturbing fact: on one of the most controversial issues of the era, the author is siding with four of the most repellent characters in postwar American history. Those four are J. Edgar Hoover, John McCloy, Allen Dulles, and Gerald Ford. In the last chapter we took some time and informed the reader about much of the rather unappetizing character and practices of Mr. Hoover. You will find much more there about what a despicable ogre Hoover was than you will find in *Reclaiming History*. But as curtailed as his writing on Hoover is, I exaggerate only slightly when I say that in comparison with his discussion of the Troika, it looks comprehensive. Yet, it is hard to understand what the Commission did if one leaves out who McCloy, Dulles, and Ford really were and what they represented. It is also necessary in understanding how the Southern Wing was marginalized and, at the last meeting, duped into thinking their objections would be recorded. The Troika was in control. And, from vast experience, they knew how to manipulate both people and events. In that regard, Cooper, Boggs, and Russell were provincial, almost amateurish. Dulles, McCloy, and to a lesser extent Ford, were masters at pushing levers behind the scenes: both of power and the press. Whether they knew it or not, the Southern Wing was being taken to school in how the Eastern Establishment controlled the national agenda. But to understand that, you need to know something about the unsavory background and acts of these three men. Bugliosi doesn't give it to you. We will soon see why.

"He Is More or Less Inclined to Be a Fascist"

In over 1,600 pages of text, Bugliosi could not find the room to write the above description of John McCloy by Roosevelt New Dealer Harold Ickes. Even though that quote appears in the McCloy biography by Kai Bird, a book that the prosecutor lists in his bibliography. But to understand what the man did while on the Commission you have to understand why Ickes said that about him. So let us do something here which Bugliosi should have surely done in his book. Let us give some background information about the main characters who controlled how the Commission worked.

John McCloy's widowed mother made a middle-class living by being a hairdresser for the upper-class wives of Philadelphia. As a youth, he first met the Rockefeller clan at a vacation resort in Maine.[32] His mother saved the money to send him to Amherst and then Harvard Law School. At Harvard he concentrated on corporate and commercial law. Upon graduation he was advised by a Philadelphia lawyer to go to New York to make his fortune. He did. He eventually worked for three famous Wall Street firms, ending up at Milbank, Tweed, Hadley and McCloy. That firm did a great deal of work for the Rockefeller family, especially in their banking and oil holdings. One of McCloy's early specialties was driving individual corporations into bankruptcy at the expense of holders of common stock—a skill that he exercised in takeovers of railroads during the twenties. This, of course, would benefit families like the Harrimans—who he also represented—since they owned the preferred stock, which could now be purchased by an allied family like the Warburgs, who McCloy also represented. In other words, it was a socialist scam for the ultra-rich. But it allowed McCloy to become wealthy enough to marry into the class he served. He wed an heiress to the Phelps–Dodge copper fortune.[33]

McCloy really made his name in the higher circles by winning the famous Black Tom Terminal case in international court against Germany. Employed by Bethlehem Steel, he reversed a judgment on appeal and showed that an explosion in New York Harbor in 1916 was a product of German espionage. In light of our subject, something else about his life at this time cannot be left out. In 1930, when working on this case for Cravath, Henderson and de Gersdorff, McCloy became friends with Allen Dulles. Dulles headed up the Paris office of another powerful Wall Street firm, Sullivan and Cromwell. So when the two joined forces on the Commission, they had known each other for over three decades.[34] War Secretary Henry Stimson noticed the Black Tom case, and McCloy became Stimson's assistant in 1940. It was that case plus this appointment that seems to have enamored McCloy of his two later preoccupations: national security and espionage. (McCloy was one of the very few who had access to the famous MAGIC intercepts prior to 1942.)

McCloy, the Holocaust, and the Japanese Internment

While at work for Stimson, McCloy was involved in two very questionable decisions. The first was the infamous Japanese internment on the West Coast. He played a key role in implementing this disgraceful episode. There was a dispute between the Justice Department and the military over whether Japanese American citizens should be rounded up, many of their belongings forfeited, their lives disrupted, and then detained in isolated camps. McCloy came down on the side of the military. How unsupportable was McCloy's decision? Even *Hoover* recommended against it.[35] Some argued it was unconstitutional. Since most were American citizens they deserved due process. McCloy shot back with one of the most ill-advised quotes in memory: "If it is a question of the safety of the country or the Constitution of the United States, why the Constitution is just a scrap of paper to me."[36] It was this kind of attitude toward the law which made other Roosevelt advisers like Harold Ickes say about McCloy that ". . . he is more or less inclined to be a Fascist."[37] But that wasn't all. Once the over 100,000 American citizens were in detention, McCloy manipulated evidence during legal proceedings to be sure they stayed there. A legal claim in their appeal was that they had been singled out because of their identifiable race. The Army had more or less admitted this was a reason for their incarceration. McCloy had this point deleted from the Army report admitted into evidence at two legal hearings seeking their release.[38]

But there is little doubt that race was part of McCloy's reasoning. He later wrote a friend that:

> "We would be missing a very big opportunity if we failed to study the Japanese in these Camps . . . before they were dispersed. . . . These people . . . afford a means of sampling opinion and studying their customs and habits in a way we have never before had possible. . . . I am aware that such a suggestion may provoke a charge that we have no right to treat these people as 'guinea pigs', but I would rather treat them as guinea pigs and learn something useful than merely to treat them . . . as they have been in the past with such unsuccessful results."[39]

These sentiments remind some of the attitude of the eugenics "doctors" toward the Jews incarcerated in Eastern Europe at the time. In light of that, one would not be surprised to know that McCloy also argued against ameliorating the Holocaust. Reports had filtered into America as early as 1941 that Hitler was slaughtering the Jews he had captured in the East. Many Jewish groups appealed to the White House to help those in the camps to escape. In 1944 FDR set up an agency to consider such action. McCloy actively opposed efforts to bomb Auschwitz, or the rail lines leading to the camp itself.[40] He even lied about the possibility of doing so. He said it would detract from the war effort. Yet American bombers, in attacking trivial targets near Auschwitz, had accidentally bombed an outlying division of the complex.[41] In August 1944, McCloy responded to a similar plea by the World Jewish Congress with another one of his infamous dictums: the bombing raids, "even if practicable, might provoke even more vindictive action by the Germans."[42] The real reason for McCloy's obstinacy was that the Joint Chiefs thought any such rescue operations "might create a precedent which would lead to other demands and an influx of additional refugees."[43] Which they did not want to deal with before Germany was defeated. McCloy was pimping for the military again. But, as in the Japanese internment case, there is much anecdotal evidence to show McCloy was also anti-Semitic.[44]

McCloy Goes Soft on the Nazis

After the war, McCloy was appointed High Commissioner for Germany. Some, like George Kennan and Walter Lippmann, favored German reunification. McCloy's overall aim was to join the fledgling republic of West Germany into the western alliance. German chancellor Konrad Adenauer wished to leave the de-Nazification era behind and make Hitler a more distant memory. Therefore McCloy agreed to a review of the cases against surviving Nazis convicted at Nuremburg. Even though many had already been reviewed by McCloy's predecessor Lucius Clay just before he left office.[45] The problem for McCloy and Adenauer was that Clay had not been comprehensive or lenient enough. McCloy's new clemency board worked with remarkable speed. In just six weeks, they reviewed over ninety cases, three thousand pages of judgments, and considered written and oral briefs from fifty defense lawyers. But there were two unusual factors that revealed McCloy's actual objective. His board did not review the actual evidence used at the trials, nor did they hear from the prosecution.[46] The board predictably recommended reductions in seventy-seven of the ninety-three cases, including the commutation of seven of the fifteen remaining death sentences. McCloy approved over half of those decisions. This included twenty out of twenty-five former SS officers who had served in Einsatzgruppen, the early mechanized Jewish firing squads.[47]

Afterwards, Eleanor Roosevelt asked McCloy why he was in such a hurry to free so many convicted Nazis. Telford Taylor, a member of the prosecution team at Nuremburg, showed that McCloy misrepresented salient facts in his reply to her.[48] As some later commented, McCloy's lack of sympathy for the Jews trapped at Auschwitz contrasted interestingly with his solicitude for some of their killers.

But that wasn't all. McCloy helped conceal the escape of the notorious Butcher of Lyon, former Gestapo chief Klaus Barbie. Barbie liked to torture his victims before killing them. One of his favorite methods was stringing them upside down from hooks.[49] Another job of Barbie's was to ensure the deportation of French Jews eastward to the death camps. Some believe he overdid it when he emptied an orphanage containing forty-one Jewish children aged three to thirteen and shipped them to their deaths.[50] After the war, the French demanded Barbie be extradited from Germany to stand trial. McCloy helped cover up his true location until he was transported secretly to Bolivia in 1951.[51] There he became a drug lord and arms dealer. Why would McCloy do such a thing for such a person? Military intelligence felt Barbie was a valuable asset in the Cold War against the French communists. Nazi hunter Beate Klarsfeld finally discovered Barbie. His subsequent trial was popularized by documentary filmmaker Marcel Ophüls. Therefore McCloy was interviewed by several people about his past actions concerning the Butcher. He repeatedly said he had no memory of either Barbie or the French attempt to extradite him.

McCloy, Rockefeller and the Shah

In 1952, after resigning his post in Germany, he went to work for his old benefactor David Rockefeller as president of Chase Manhattan Bank. He also became counsel for the Seven Sisters, the name given to the largest American oil companies at the time. Which means he ran oil diplomacy into the sixties and seventies. He later also helped run the Council on Foreign Relations and the Ford Foundation. At the latter, due to the urging of his friend Allen Dulles, he allowed the CIA to use the foundation as a channel to run Agency projects throughout the world.[52] One of the things Dulles arranged through McCloy was secret funding for the Congress of Cultural Freedom. This was a liberal front group that financed various publications in Europe in order to strengthen the anti-Communist left.[53] Dulles and McCloy arranged for this clandestine Ford funding to be known to only four people at the foundation.

McCloy's swan song for the Eastern Establishment was as part of a three-man lobbying effort codenamed Project Alpha. His two partners in Alpha were David Rockefeller and Henry Kissinger. McCloy's firm was paid handsomely for his ultimately disastrous efforts. The objective was to get the Shah of Iran into the USA for medical treatment after the Iranian Revolution of 1979. Nixon and Kissinger had tried to make Iran into a regional power, a surrogate for American interests in the Middle East. So Kissinger considered the Shah both a personal and national friend. President Carter resisted the overtures. But McCloy was indefatigable. He wrote letters, made phone calls, held lunches, and he even arranged for the publication of a book to answer the Shah's critics.[54] The campaign went on for nine months. Carter resisted mightily but, one by one, McCloy and his cohorts converted his closest advisers: Walter Mondale, Cyrus Vance, and Zbig Brzezinski. Finally, cornered and alone, Carter relented. But not before asking prophetically: "What are you guys going to advise me to do if they overrun our embassy and take our people hostage?"[55] Which, as we know, is what happened. McCloy didn't care. He had achieved what Rockefeller paid him to achieve. In so doing he helped Ronald Reagan gain the White House. Thus, McCloy ushered in the Neoconservative Revolution, which culminated in the catastrophe of George W. Bush.

McCloy died unrepentant over any of his reprehensible acts. For example, decades later, when called to testify about his role in the Japanese internment, he appeared guiltless about what he had done. He said that any financial award to those deprived of due process would be "utterly unconscionable."[56] This from a man who made millions pimping for banks, oil companies, and David Rockefeller. After reviewing his career, Jacob Heilbrunn wrote that, in sum, McCloy was a thoroughly despicable character.[57]

Yet the reader of *Reclaiming History* would not know how bad the real McCloy was. Why? Because there isn't one detailed paragraph describing his deplorable acts in Bugliosi's giant book. Somehow, while writing 2,600 pages, he never thought that McCloy's access to MAGIC and his siding with the military over due process in the internment controversy was important to understanding him or his role on the Warren Commission. Yet, he fails to mention that while also serving on the Commission, McCloy had a role in Brother Sam, the 1964 CIA coup operation against President Goulart of Brazil.[58] In the world of *Reclaiming History*, backing the Single Bullet Theory forgives a multitude of sins. Even those the magnitude of John McCloy's.

The Dulles Power Family

As mentioned previously, Walt Brown did a valuable service in breaking down the proceedings of the Warren Commission to see who were the most active and influential members. On pages 83–87 of *The Warren Omission*, he presented the information he had ferreted out in different ways via different charts and matrixes. He came to the conclusion that many of the questions asked by Warren were mere formalities, like "Will you rise and be sworn?" Or he would ask if each commissioner was present. Allowing for that, Brown came to the conclusion that "of Commission members, Allen Dulles was the Grand inquisitor." Brown constructed a formula in which he gave credit for full witness session attendance, partial session attendance, and if the Commissioner asked questions of the witness. He then combined this with the total number of questions asked. After tallying up the totals, he came to the conclusion that the Commission was actually misnamed. If one looks at the sheer level of activity during the proceedings, it should be called the Dulles Commission. Let's quote

Brown in this regard: ". . . the key Commissioner, above and beyond all others, in the process of sifting through the evidence in the murder of President John F. Kennedy, was the former head of the Central Intelligence Agency—and a man who seethed at his removal from that post—by *the late* John F. Kennedy." Bugliosi does not inform you about this fact. As with McCloy, he tells you very little about Dulles the man. Because he was so influential on the Commission, let us fill in what the author leaves out.

Allen Dulles was directly related to three Secretaries of State. His grandfather on his mother's side was John Watson Foster, Secretary of State under President Harrison. His uncle, Robert Lansing, served in that office under President Wilson. His brother, John Foster, eventually served under President Eisenhower. His Uncle Robert and his brother John formed a powerful influence on his life.

Lansing was an Anglophile who favored England in the World War I disputes over freedom of the seas. He so much admired the British that he took elocution lessons to mimic a British accent.[59] Lansing was so in cahoots with the British, he actually worked with English undercover agents in covering their tracks in the breaking of neutrality laws.[60] He brought one of them home, and he regaled young Allen with espionage stories for hours. So Allen developed three proclivities that determined his future: an admiration of England, the ambition to be, like Lansing, an international lawyer, and his love of the spy world.

After Dulles graduated from Princeton, Lansing got him a job in the State Department. He ended up in Berne, Switzerland. It was in Berne, during World War I, that he first entered the world of intelligence.[61] He met dissident leaders of East Europe like Jan Masaryk and Edouard Benes, and "he began running networks of Czechs and Yugoslavs out of the U. S. Embassy."[62] He also met the family of Herbert Field, including his controversial son Noel who, many suspect, the Dulles brothers used as a double agent later in the Cold War.[63] In fact, it was as early as 1918, with the collapse of the Hapsburg Empire that Dulles first formulated the idea of an intelligence network to thwart the expansion of Bolshevism.[64]

Dulles at Versailles, Covering Up the Armenian Genocide

After the war, John Foster Dulles—through his employment at the powerful New York law firm of Sullivan and Cromwell—met Wall Street financier Bernard Baruch. Baruch helped the brothers gain entry to the Treaty of Versailles. With their Uncle Robert, they worked at redrawing the maps of Europe and the Middle East, and figuring the reparations owed by Germany. During the conference, Thomas Lamont of the Morgan Empire made sure that the brothers would be in on the beginning of the American version of the British Round Table Groups. This ended up being called the Council on Foreign Relations.[65] At the age of twenty-seven, Allen Dulles was now where he wanted to be. He was working with the political leaders of the world and, through his brother, with the world's plutocracy of wealth. Until President Kennedy fired him, this is where he would stay.

From 1919–22, Allen worked for the State Department and was stationed in Berlin, Vienna, and then Turkey.[66] While at the last post, he helped cover up the Turkish genocide of the Armenians. He wrote to his superior that "Our task would be simple if the reports of the atrocities could be declared untrue or even exaggerated but the evidence alas, is irrefutable . . . I've been busy trying to ward off congressional resolutions of sympathy for these groups."[67] From 1922–26 he was head of the Near East division of the U.S. Department of State. This is where, after the collapse of the Ottoman Empire, Dulles developed his interest in the nascent new Arab world. And one should add, also with the controversial nation of Palestine. There is evidence that Dulles, like his friend T. E. Lawrence, was really an early Arabist.[68]

There was a problem for Allen in working at the State Department: he didn't make enough money. But he now had a law degree. And his brother was senior partner at Sullivan and Cromwell, making over $300,000 a year in the Great Depression—or over ten million today.[69] So John brought Allen into the firm, and in four years he made partner. Allen's value was in his services derived from overseas connections to top clients like United Fruit, and DuPont.[70] For example, in 1932 he saved a rich oil and mineral field for the Mellon family when he rigged the Colombian presidential elections by bribing one of the candidates.[71] It is these types of clients that Allen would stay loyal to when he became CIA Director by arranging things like the Guatemala coup in 1954 for United Fruit.

Dulles and the Nazis

It was with Sullivan and Cromwell that Allen Dulles now began his clouded, controversial, and hotly disputed association with the upper classes in Germany: those who would eventually bring Hitler to power. Sullivan and Cromwell represented "several provincial governments, some large industrial combines, and a number of big American companies" which would eventually do extensive business with the Third Reich.[72] Allen was a friend of the infamous industrialist Fritz Thyssen who introduced him to Hitler and Goebbels. The latter's sincerity and frankness impressed Allen.[73] Thyssen was one of Der Fuehrer's earliest and most important financial backers—to the tune of 100 million marks. Another of Sullivan and Cromwell's clients who did business with the Third Reich was Standard Oil.[74] Which is one way the Dulles brothers became well acquainted with the Rockefeller clan.

As both economics minister and Reichsbank president, Hjalmar Schacht was the fiscal wizard who helped finance the Third Reich. The Dulles brothers had been personal friends and/or business partners of Schacht since at least 1930.[75] Through Schacht, "Sullivan and Cromwell thrived on its cartels and collusion with the new Nazi regime." One of the cartels was the infamous I. G. Farben chemical company.[76] This Dulles client was another huge early contributor to the Nazis. When Sullivan and Cromwell helped construct Farben's American alliances and its subsidiaries, Farben insisted on secret German control.[77] Through its industrial might and scope, Farben became a crucial contributor to the war effort. For instance, in 1943, Farben was responsible for the entire Wehrmacht supply of synthetic rubber, methanol, and lubricating oil. Plus 95 percent of its poison gas, 84 percent of German explosives, and 70 percent of German gunpowder.[78] As Sen. Homer Boone said during a Senate hearing on military affairs on June 4, 1943, "Farben was Hitler and Hitler was Farben." Allen Dulles was important to Sullivan and Cromwell in this regard. Since he helped draft parts of the Versailles Treaty, he could advise Farben on how to bypass them and illegally rearm Germany.[79] Allen also served as general counsel for J. Henry Schroder, New York, whose Hamburg banking branch was a chief backer of Heinrich Himmler, commander of the SS.[80] Allen tried to fuzz up all this hobnobbing with the Nazis as he socialized with the English upper classes by saying that the USA had no interest in "fights over oppressed races and lost causes."[81]

Dulles and the Nazis: Part 2

In 1940, William Donovan hired Allen to serve in the Office of Coordinator of Information (COI), which would later turn into the Office of Strategic Services (OSS). Stationed in Berne again, Dulles ran agents all across Europe. He had a habit of playing both sides. For instance, in France he ran money to "De Gaulle's Free French guerillas but also to the anti-Gaullist factions of his arch-rival, General Giraud."[82] In Germany he worked with both Nazis and anti-Nazis. It is here again where some of Dulles's most controversial acts occurred. The first was the attempted working out of a sort of "separate peace" with the SS in northern Italy through General Karl Wolff. This was initiated without any knowledge by his superiors and continued like that for weeks. When Dulles finally reported it, Stalin was enraged. He accused Dulles of trying to arrange a private accommodation with Germany based in part on anti-Bolshevism. For this reason, the Joint Chiefs told Dulles to terminate the contacts.[83]

There may be some truth to Stalin's accusation. When the war ended, Dulles became OSS chief in Germany. There he got to know two men who would figure prominently in his efforts to construct the future Central Intelligence Agency: Richard Helms and Frank Wisner.[84] Wisner told Dulles, "Forget the Nazis and get in there and find what the Commies are up to instead." In this regard, Dulles proposed a scheme by which a group of anti-Nazi students would stage a coup in Berlin, take over the city, and then have a force of Anglo-American paratroopers occupy the capital and make it pro-Western—all before the Russian troops arrived. It was wisely rejected by Gen. Eisenhower, or it may have started World War III. For when the Russians got wind of it, they planned on drenching any American occupying force "by accident" with an artillery bombardment.[85]

With this dropped, Dulles found a new way to find out what the Soviets were up to. And to also fulfill his ambition of starting a new war for his clients: the Cold War. He heard that General Reinhard Gehlen was hiding in Bavaria. Gehlen was the commander of the Nazi intelligence apparatus for Eastern Europe. He specialized in military information about the Russian army. He was ready to help the Allies against the Communists. So when he surrendered, he expected to be greeted with open arms. Instead he was arrested as just another ex-Nazi.

Dulles had put out word to be on the lookout for him, so information about Gehlen's arrest soon reached him.[86] Gehlen and his former staffers were now freed and given an office in Wiesbaden. Gehlen was given an army platoon to go to the secret hiding place where he had hidden his files. When one steel case was unearthed, he patted it and said, "Here are the secrets of the Kremlin. If you use them properly, Stalin is doomed."[87] As Gehlen knew, this is what Dulles wanted to hear. Eisenhower was against signing up Gehlen since he thought it would endanger his alliance with Marshall Zhukov, the Soviet Commander in Germany. He was right. Zhukov was actually hunting Gehlen down. Gehlen surrendered to the Allies knowing Zhukov would probably have him summarily executed. He played his cards right. In September of 1945, Donovan and Dulles had Wisner fly Gehlen out of Germany to Washington. From there the Gehlen organization was incorporated into the American military intelligence network, pretty much on Gehlen's terms. It remained intact and under his control, justified under the rubric of mutual defense against the communist menace. In 1949, Gehlen signed a contract for five million dollars a year to work for the CIA.[88] In 1950, John McCloy appointed Gehlen as an adviser to Adenauer on intelligence matters. Via Dulles and McCloy, a man who should have been in the dock at Nuremburg was now allowed to start and then exacerbate the Cold War. For, as many commentators have written, not only did Gehlen exaggerate the Soviet threat, his network was riddled with double agents. Further, the network was a safe haven for former SS officers, including members of the notorious Einsatzgruppen.[89]

Their association with Gehlen tells us much about Dulles and McCloy. Yet in all of *Reclaiming History,* you will find just one reference to the Nazi: a footnote at the bottom of page 1194. Contrary to the appraisal of many other commentators, Bugliosi actually calls Gehlen's network "helpful" to the USA. This is explainable because the author bases his unusual opinion in part on Richard Helms. In accordance with this soft-pedaling, I could find no reference to Gehlen's war crimes in the entire book.[90] Also absent is Gehlen's help in providing a hiding place for former SS officers. And, of course, I could find no reference to the associations of Dulles and McCloy with the former Nazi who was so useful to them in launching and preserving the Cold War.

Dulles Refines the Cold War

After the war Allen Dulles returned to Sullivan and Cromwell. He and Donovan were instrumental in getting the National Security act of 1947 passed. This allowed for the creation of the Central Intelligence Agency. But in 1948, the CIA had no real covert action arm or experience. So from the offices of Sullivan and Cromwell, Dulles oversaw a CIA team headed by Frank Wisner, James Angleton, and Bill Colby. They used millions on a "crash program of propaganda, sabotage, and secret funding" to stop the Italian Communists from gaining significant power.[91] Dulles also participated in his brother's efforts to elect Thomas Dewey as president. If Dewey had won in 1948, Allen would have been CIA Director.[92] In 1948, Dulles helped write the Jackson–Dulles–Correa report to expand the CIA's efforts into covert action areas.[93] Dulles was also part of the group that founded the propaganda channel Radio Free Europe before it was sold to the government.[94] He was also instrumental in negotiations among competing intelligence agencies to make the Director of CIA the head of all US intelligence.[95]

Lisagor and Lipsius make clear an important point about the Dulles brothers' service at Sullivan and Cromwell. The authors note that the anti-communism of Joe McCarthy gave them a means to undercut the bipartisanship from which the GOP had benefited when out of power.[96] The brothers also used a young Richard Nixon, who Allen had met in 1947—perhaps even earlier in 1945—for similar reasons.[97] Besides Joe McCarthy, perhaps no one attacked Harry Truman for harboring communists more than Nixon. The Dulles brothers used the exaggerated rhetoric of these men to rebuild West Germany while protecting their German clients from Justice Department investigations. As with their friend McCloy, anti-communism superseded de-Nazification. From their long experience on Wall Street, the Dulles brothers firmly believed that the national interest was equated with the interests of private enterprise. Their "virulent anti-communism reflected a fear of losing markets for American exports, a shrinking of the realm in which American business could operate."[98] In other words, they manipulated Cold War demagogues in order to advance the pecuniary interests of Sullivan and Cromwell.

Dulles Revolutionizes the CIA

All these ideas came to fruition when Dulles came to power in the CIA. That ascension was a two-stage process. First, the CIA's second Director, Walter B. Smith, read the Jackson–Dulles–Correa report in 1950. Impressed, he invited Dulles to become his Deputy Director in order to reorganize the Agency along that report's lines.[99] In 1952, the Dulles brothers' effort to paint the Democratic Party as soft on communism helped the GOP win the presidential election. The following year, Allen Dulles fulfilled his ambition to become Director of the CIA.

To put it simply: Dulles revolutionized the Agency. The two previous Directors, Roscoe Hillenkoetter and Smith, were military men. They generally believed that intelligence should be used to supplement military action. But Dulles's long experience in the State Department, the OSS, and at Sullivan and Cromwell gave him a much wider and more sophisticated view of what the CIA could be and do. Plus one other thing: in service to the upper classes at Sullivan and Cromwell, Dulles worshipped at the altar of ruthless corporate Realpolitik. With Dulles, the acronym CIA came to stand for Corporate Interests of America. No method was discarded in his pursuit of their ends.

It was Dulles who began the Agency's specialty of engineering the overthrows of governments who wanted to keep their natural resources for themselves (i.e., Iraq in 1953, Guatemala in 1954). It was under Dulles that the CIA began its program of executive action against nationalist heads of state in the resource rich Third World, for example, plotting the murder of Patrice Lumumba in the Congo. It was under Dulles that the concept of preparing death lists of those after a coup became established doctrine.[100] And it was under Dulles that men willing to do this kind of dirty work now rose in the Agency, for example, David Phillips and Howard Hunt. Dulles originated the CIA's use of religious groups as cover organizations. Dulles began the systematic process of using the media to disguise these lethal actions and keep them from the public. That particular project was called Operation Mockingbird. As Director, Dulles's worst traits had free rein because his brother was Secretary of State and Foster had strong influence over President Eisenhower.

What is extraordinary about what Dulles did with the CIA is that it was too much for even certain elements of the Eastern Establishment (i.e., the very people who Dulles worked with and for). In 1956, David Bruce and Robert Lovett composed the Bruce–Lovett Report on the CIA for President Eisenhower. That report is almost nowhere to be found today. But writer Seamus Coogan pointed out to me that Arthur Schlesinger saw it among Robert Kennedy's papers and used it for his biography, *Robert Kennedy and His Times*.[101] RFK had access to it during his service on the board of inquiry into the Bay of Pigs debacle. Bruce and Lovett had served on the forerunner of what came to be known as the Foreign Intelligence Advisory Board: a group of private citizens meant to monitor American intelligence activities abroad. Eisenhower appointed this board in 1956. When they got a look at what Dulles had done with the CIA, they were shocked. These two were scions of the Eastern Establishment. Bruce was a friend of Dulles who married into the Mellon family in 1926, served in the OSS, and was ambassador to France prior to writing this report. Lovett was a member of the Skull and Bones secret society at Yale, became a lifelong partner at Brown Brothers Harriman, served with McCloy under Henry Stimson in the War Department, was Under Secretary of State under George Marshall, and became Defense Secretary in 1950. They were not leftist critics of American foreign policy. And what they wrote demolishes writers like Max Holland who maintain that the CIA was under executive control.

In general, the two men were disturbed by the fact that Dulles had turned what was supposed to be an intelligence agency into a covert action machine that specialized in undermining and overthrowing foreign governments.[102] And no matter how wild the scheme, or how badly it failed, as long as it was anti-Russian and pro-Western it was approved, and if it failed, forgotten. There were no consequences for shoddy work performance. But beyond that, since everything was done in secret, there was no oversight as to what was actually going on. Which meant that the CIA was exerting an almost unchecked, unilateral influence on American foreign policy.[103] Sometimes, not even the American ambassador in that foreign country was aware of what CIA was doing. Lovett and Bruce decided that this could not have been what President Truman had foreseen back in 1947 and '48. And this was why so many foreign countries, especially in the Third World, looked upon the USA with such suspicion and cynicism. And, notably, within one month after JFK's murder, Truman began to write a famous editorial stating that the CIA had evolved into something he did not in any way imagine once he signed the legislation creating the Agency. That editorial would be published in the *Washington Post* on December 22, 1963.

Once Lovett and Bruce—and Joseph Kennedy, who was also on the advisory board—discovered all this, they pressed their case against Dulles until they left. In their last report they wrote that "the CIA's concentration on political, psychological, and related covert action activities have tended to detract substantially from the execution of [a] primary intelligence-gathering mission. We suggest, accordingly, that there should be a total reassessment of our covert action policies."[104]

After his Bay of Pigs testimony, President Kennedy called Lovett in for a private meeting. There can be little doubt that Lovett's testimony and his relationship with Kennedy's father helped convince President Kennedy to fire Allen Dulles. How important was it? Lovett's influence was so profound that after JFK fired Dulles, Robert Kennedy was determined to find out if any other *relative* of Dulles was still at the State Department. When he found out that Allen's sister Eleanor worked there, he ordered Dean Rusk to fire her. Because "he didn't want any more of the Dulles family around."[105]

This is the man LBJ appointed to the Warren Commission. As shown above, he became the most active member of that cover-up. It later turned out that Dulles had nothing but scorn for both the evidence and critical arguments against the Oswald-did-it hypothesis. In 1965, at UCLA, David Lifton questioned Dulles about the Zapruder film and Harold Feldman's essay entitled *51 Witnesses* about many witnesses hearing a shot from the grassy knoll. Dulles not only denied that evidence, he ridiculed Lifton for even bringing it up. He said bizarre things like "There is not a single iota of evidence indicating a conspiracy." When Lifton pointed out testimony, and even pictures, of smoke arising on the grassy knoll, Dulles derisively replied with, "Now what are you saying, someone was smoking up there?" When Lifton brought up Feldman's essay, Dulles—even though he knew full well about it—asked him where it was published. When Lifton answered, Dulles replied, with ridicule: "The *Nation*! Ha, ha, ha, ha, ha." When Lifton showed him frames from the Zapruder film arranged in sequential order to show Kennedy's head going back toward the seat—the opposite direction of a shot from the Texas School Book Depository—Dulles said: "You have *nothing!* Absolutely nothing! . . . I can't see a blasted thing here. You can't say the head goes back. I can't see it going back. It does not go back. You can't say that." Dulles then tried to neutralize this Z film argument by tendentiously saying he had never heard it before,[106] when, of course, the Commission had seen the film dozens of times. They just did not feel that powerful evidence, like Kennedy's violent reaction backwards, merited mention in the Warren Report.

Dulles admitted to being in Dallas about three weeks before the assassination.[107] His very kind, Council on Foreign Relations biographer, Peter Grose, places Dulles as arriving on Long Island on the day of the assassination. But researcher Lisa Pease has discovered some rather odd notations Dulles made about that date. According to notes written on his calendar, Dulles wrote down "the Farm." You have to know something about CIA shorthand to understand what that means. As Jim Hougan discovered, it could actually refer to two places: the CIA training facility in Camp Peary, Virginia, or Mitch Werbell's sixty-acre weapons development laboratory in Georgia.[108] As Hougan notes, the confusion in the names is deliberate. For Werbell was a wizard in creating lethal weapons to be used in counter-insurgency warfare and assassinations, neither of which the CIA wanted to be openly involved with. In discussing a silencer created by Werbell, Hougan noted the following: that the sound pattern created in Dealey Plaza—with shots heard in two directions—could well have been created by two teams using Werbell's partial directional silencers.[109] It would be interesting to hear Dulles explain what he meant by that notation in his calendar at that particular time.

Any objective person would admit that much of this material on Dulles is relevant in evaluating the make-up of the Warren Commission. Especially since he became its most active member. A fact which Bugliosi has to be aware of since Brown's study of the Commission, *The Warren Omission*, is in his bibliography. Yet although you will find Schlesinger's biography of Robert Kennedy in his bibliography, you will not find Robert Lovett's name in Bugliosi's book. Comedian Lenny Bruce's name is in the index, but not David Bruce's. So the influence of their report in the firing of Dulles is absent. Bugliosi's reader doesn't know that Dulles was in Dallas three weeks before the assassination. Or that he was at the Farm the day of the assassination. (Werbell's name is not in Bugliosi's index.) Bugliosi *does* quote from Truman's article, but what he does with it is notable. After a long quote, he just drops it and goes to a new subject. Almost like he didn't want to be accused of not mentioning it.[110] Researcher Ray Marcus received supplementary material about Truman's essay from the Truman Library early in 2006, a year before *Reclaiming History* was published. Which meant that Bugliosi could have also. So the reader never learns that Truman began the essay one week after Kennedy's assassination or that he had a written correspondence with Admiral Sidney Souers about it in which former Naval Intelligence officer Souers wrote to Truman that Dulles had surely allowed the CIA to stray from the conception the two men had of it at the outset. And finally, without this material, the prosecutor cannot tell his readers that Dulles visited with Truman in April of 1964, while he was on the Commission, and tried to get him to retract the editorial! But that's not all. During their conversation, Dulles clearly implied that he thought the reason

Truman wrote the article was due to Kennedy's assassination. Specifically in regards to his Vietnam policy.

With all this missing, the reader cannot ask the obvious question: If you were Oswald's defense lawyer, would Dulles be on the jury? Because not only was he on the jury, he was its most active member.

"The Warren Report: a Gibraltar of Factual Literature"

The exact quote for the above subhead was this: "The monumental record of the President's Commission will stand like a Gibraltar of factual literature through the ages to come." With what we know today, that quote is simply incomprehensible. The informed reader would think it could have only come from an informant of a professional cover-up artist of political assassinations. As we shall see, Jerry Ford was both.

Representative Gerald Ford was the junior partner in the Troika. In more ways than one. He was only fifty-one at the time. Dulles was seventy-one. McCloy was sixty-nine. And while they had been players in the Wall Street–Washington power alleys since the 1920s, Ford had been a congressman from Grand Rapids, Michigan, only since 1949. Yet according to the indices in Walt Brown's book, Ford was a solid second to Dulles in overall participation in the Commission proceedings.[111] What makes this attendance record remarkable is that, although Dulles did not have a full-time job, Ford was supposed to be representing the people of his congressional district. Yet looking at Brown's statistics, in some ways Ford even surpasses Dulles in his participation at the hearings. We must look a bit closer at Ford to understand why.

As Gerald McKnight notes in *Breach of Trust*, the association between J. Edgar Hoover and Ford went back to the forties.[112] McKnight writes that Hoover so much wanted Ford in Washington that he secretly aided him in his first congressional campaign. Appreciative of the help, "Ford reciprocated in his maiden speech by asking Congress to increase Hoover's salary."[113] From there, Ford developed a close relationship with the Bureau. FBI official Cartha DeLoach once noted that "relations were excellent" between the Bureau and Congressman Ford and that Ford had been "in touch with my office on numerous occasions." Hoover and Ford were so close that the Director even sent Ford an autographed copy of his ghostwritten *A Study of Communism*, realizing the conservative views expressed therein would echo with Ford.[114]

This early cultivation paid off in spades when Ford was appointed to the Commission. A week after the first Commission meeting Ford was in DeLoach's office complaining about Warren's "general ineptitude and attempt to force Olney on the Commission as chief counsel."[115] DeLoach noted in a memo that

"Ford indicated he would keep me thoroughly advised as to the activities of the Commission. . . . He also asked if he could call me from time to time and straighten out questions in his mind concerning our investigation. I told him by all means he should do this."[116] Five days later, the two met again and Ford told DeLoach that so far there had been no criticism of the FBI. Over Christmas of 1963, the FBI loaned Ford a briefcase with security lock so he could read the FBI report while on a skiing vacation.[117] While the Commission was still in session, DeLoach arranged a dinner at his home for the Fords and the Director. Hoover followed up on this by writing Ford that his door was always open "any time our help is needed or when we can be of service." In response to this, McKnight notes that it was probably Ford who passed DeLoach an early draft of the Warren Report in July of 1964. The FBI added a note to this copy: "There will be a fourth and final draft made available through a source by July 23, 1964, which will contain the final conclusions and recommendations of the Commission."[118] As noted before, the FBI's atrocious performance in the Kennedy case centered almost instantly on convicting Oswald at any price. Ford quickly joined in that monomaniacal effort.

The year after the Warren Report was issued, Ford published his own book called *Portrait of the Assassin*. Ford arranged for John Stiles, his first campaign manager and Richard Nixon's campaign field director, to be his assistant while on the Commission. Their book was essentially a rehash of the Commission's view of Oswald. It made for dull reading. Consequently, the publisher told them to spice it up. So they added a section about the (probably deliberately) misconstrued Hudkins report from Texas about Oswald being an FBI informant. The problem was that at the time the book was published the records of the Warren Commission executive sessions were classified. Evidently, Ford had little problem with violating the law in order to smear Oswald and make a little money in the process. But in 1973, Nixon chose Ford to replace Spiro Agnew as his Vice President. Ford was now questioned about his use of classified material. He lied under oath about what he had done. He said he only used material in the Warren Commission volumes for that book—which he clearly had not. When later exposed, Ford apologized for his misdeed.[119] Six months after he became president, Ford declassified the material in question. In light of the lying, and the use of Stiles, Jim Marrs is probably correct when he writes that it was Nixon who recommended Ford as a Commissioner to LBJ.[120]

While a congressman, Ford developed a reputation for being one of the CIA's best friends. In 1974, when Nixon resigned under the pressure of the Watergate scandal, President Ford immediately began to prove his reputation.

Many people on the Watergate Committee, like Sen. Howard Baker, suspected that the CIA had played a role in that affair and that Richard Helms had manipulated the FBI inquiry.[121] Consequently, there was a movement to investigate the crimes of the CIA and FBI. Ford gave a speech at the time in which he defended the Agency against the rumors that they had overthrown Salvador Allende in Chile the year before. Which turned out to be true. When asked if this action was not in violation of international law, the new president replied with:

> "I am not going to pass judgment on whether it is permitted or authorized under international law. It is a recognized fact that historically, as well as presently, that such actions are taken in the best interest of the countries involved."[122]

In other words: Uncle Sam Knows Best. *Time* commented, "Ford's words seemed to represent an anachronistic, cold–war view of national security reminiscent of the 1950s." Complained Democratic Senator Frank Church of Idaho: "It's tantamount to saying that we respect no law save the law of the jungle."[123]

In late 1974, even more friction came between President Ford and Sen. Church. James Angleton had badly divided the CIA over the Yuri Nosenko affair. In order to force him to resign as counter-intelligence chief, Director Bill Colby had given a story to the CIA friendly reporter Sy Hersh. This story uncovered some of the illegal surveillance operations Angleton had run out of his shop. When exposed at Christmas time in the pages of the *New York Times*, the story created a sensation. Angleton resigned. Ford called Colby for a briefing. Realizing this would give Frank Church the opening he needed for a full-scale inquiry into the intelligence community, Ford tried to divert that by appointing his vice president, Nelson Rockefeller, to run his own inquest.[124] Called the Rockefeller Commission, this was seen as something of a whitewash. The report contained an annex on the JFK assassination, but since Ford brought back Warren Commission assistant counsel David Belin as Executive Director, this was viewed as something of a joke: two original cover-up men redoing the cover-up. In fact, the report deliberately distorted the testimony of Dr. Cyril Wecht.[125] It was also the first official JFK inquiry to use the discredited "neuromuscular reaction" as a way to explain Kennedy's violent rearward action at the time of the head shot.[126]

The appointment of Belin indicated Ford's stance during the entire eighteen months of what one author has called "the season of inquiry." This refers to the two investigative committees set up in Congress: the Pike Committee in the House and the Church Committee in the Senate. They ended up replacing the Rockefeller Commission. This historical period is as close as the USA has ever come to explaining to the public just what the CIA and FBI have done in the name of national security. Who knows what they would have achieved if Ford had not fought them. Why did he resist an open-ended inquiry? It might be that he understood that his work on the Commission could have been exposed for the sham it was. Why say such a thing? Because Ford did.

On January 16, 1975, Ford held a White House luncheon for the editors of the *New York Times*. Someone asked why Ford had picked such a conservative and defense-minded panel to make up the Rockefeller Commission (for example, Ronald Reagan was a member). The president said he needed people who would not stray from the straight and narrow. If they did, they could stumble upon matters that might hurt the national interest. As Daniel Schorr relates in his book, *Clearing the Air*, the following unforgettable colloquy now followed: The editor asked "Like what?" Ford replied with, "Like assassinations!"[127] Ford then added that this was off the record, but reporter Daniel Schorr deduced that since the Rockefeller Commission was investigating domestic matters, Ford must have meant American assassinations.[128] But later, CIA Director William Colby effectively spun Ford's comment. He told Schorr that the CIA had run assassination plots abroad, but not in America. This deftly neutralized Ford's slip. The committees would now look at CIA assassination plots against foreign leaders. In regards to the JFK case, the Church Committee would only investigate the performance of the intelligence agencies in *investigating* Kennedy's murder.

But even Bill Colby was too open for cover-up man Ford, who had learned his lessons well from McCloy, Hoover, and Dulles. Colby was deemed to open with Congress. After all, when mobster Sam Giancana was murdered before testifying, Colby went out of his way to say the CIA had nothing to do with it.[129] Colby was later fired for being too forthcoming. Ford picked George Bush to replace him at the CIA. And as a further signal of his new "get tough" policy, Ford made a young Dick Cheney his Chief of Staff, and moved Donald Rumsfeld into the Pentagon. It is a little noted fact that, in actuality, the neoconservative movement really began with these moves designed to rein in Henry Kissinger. Because Kissinger was deemed too accommodating to the Soviets.

With all these elements in place, Ford decided to use the 1975 murder of a CIA officer as a way to squelch and smear any further investigation. Richard Welch was the CIA station chief in Athens. He was killed on December 23, 1975, by a group of Marxist revolutionaries called the Revolutionary Organization 17 November. The CIA and Ford blamed his death on the fact that his name had been exposed by an American journal called *Counterspy*. In fact, the leftist rebel group who killed him had issued a communiqué that revealed they knew his name well before that.[130] Author Philip Agee noted that the house Welch lived in was well known as being the home of the CIA station chief in Greece for years before the murder. And Welch had been warned about this by the Agency. Welch's name had been revealed by Julius Mader in the East German publication *Who's Who in the CIA* in 1967. One month before he was killed, a local newspaper, the *Athens News,* revealed his name in print.[131]

All that was brushed aside. In a classic case of political propaganda, Ford and the CIA pulled out all the stops in using Welch's funeral as psychological warfare against any further investigation by the committees. Welch's body was flown into Andrews Air Force Base. But the plane circled the base for fifteen minutes to time the landing for the morning news shows.[132] Ford attended the chapel service, but the press was barred in order to suggest that they were to blame for Welch's murder. Colby issued a statement saying that Welch's death was the result of a "paranoiac attack on . . . Americans serving their country." David Phillips was interviewed by CBS and said that American agents are in less danger today from the KGB than from the "moral primitives" who "condemn my label."[133] Welch's body was buried at Arlington with full military honors. His coffin was carried on the same horse-drawn caisson that carried President Kennedy's. Colby gave the flag draped over it to Welch's widow. As Schorr wrote, "This is the CIA's first secret agent to become a public national hero."[134]

It worked. Henry Kissinger jumped on the committees: "I think they have used classified information in a reckless way . . ."[135] Both the Church and Pike committees closed up shop shortly after the media extravaganza. Ford and the CIA held veto power over what could be published in either report. When Otis Pike defied that agreement, Congress bottled up his report. A copy was smuggled to Daniel Schorr. As he was arranging to have it released, his boss, Bill Paley, lunched with CIA Director Bush.[136] The Pike Report was published in a special issue of *The Village Voice*. Forgetting all about his own use of classified material for his Oswald book, Ford now proposed an FBI investigation to find out who gave the report to Schorr.[137] After Paley's meeting with Director Bush, Schorr was taken off the air by CBS. After a two-hour impromptu interrogation—during which he was not represented by counsel—Schorr was fired by the network. He was later investigated by the House but refused to reveal his source for the report.

Ford's performance with the Pike and Church Committees reveals his character in extremis. When it came to the intelligence community and their role in covert operations—including coups and assassinations—Ford joined whole-heartedly in the cover-up. This sheds retrospective light on his performance for the Warren Commission and his apprentice work with the Troika. But you would never know that from reading *Reclaiming History*. Because you will find not one reference there to either Daniel Schorr or Richard Welch. Therefore you are not informed of how Ford engaged in outright warfare with the Pike and Church Committees. How he exploited the death of a CIA officer to cut off any further inquiry into the crimes of both the CIA and FBI. The Pike Committee is mentioned four times in the book, but only as a source. Bugliosi never chronicles what happened to it at the hands of Ford and the CIA. The influence of Colby's leak about Angleton to Hersh and Ford's creation of the Rockefeller Commission is dealt with in a footnote.[138] In the references to Ford in the book, I could find no mention of the lunch with the *Times* editors and his blurting out the word "assassination" as the reason why he picked who he did for the Rockefeller Commission. Which any objective person would think relevant to his service on the Commission.

Yet, the author often uses Ford as a witness to just what a fine investigation the Warren Commission really was. Well, if you eliminate just about every-thing detailed above, you can do that.

Bugliosi had more than enough space in his book to give us long and full biographies of the Troika. But what he holds back on them, plus what he chose not to reveal about Hoover is, in my view, critical to understanding his work. Since once you understand them, one could fairly conclude they were four of the worst people to hold high office in America for any length of time in the twentieth century. They were all involved—in some ways they helped create—the cult of the national security state. Which often means that Americans should not be privy to the ugly things America does in their name. Well, if one was involved in some of the things these men were, you wouldn't want anyone to know either. Would you want people to know you helped Klaus Barbie escape from Europe? Or that your coup in Guatemala led to a series of rightwing fascist leaders—like General Rios Montt—who eventually killed, raped, or maimed, about 100,000 citizens? Or in Ford's case, that you approved Suharto's 1975 invasion of East Timor, which resulted in the deaths of at least 60, 000 people? (Try and find that in Bugliosi's discussion of Ford in *Reclaiming History.*) Or that, as FBI Director, you ordered the systematic liquidation of the Black Panthers? In large part, this is what "national security" meant to these four.

Now that we are outside the realm of *Reclaiming History* and know the full story of Ford, McCloy, Dulles, and Hoover, the question arises: If President Kennedy was killed by a high- or even mid-level conspiracy, how could these men be trusted to reveal that to the public? The answer is they couldn't have. Not in a thousand years.

CHAPTER ELEVEN

The DA Acquits Everyone

"The issue of conspiracy . . . can be disposed of in one sentence: since we know Oswald killed Kennedy, we also know that no group of conspirators killed Kennedy and framed Oswald for the murder they committed."

—Vincent Bugliosi, *Reclaiming History*

A large part of Book Two in *Reclaiming History* is devoted to Vincent Bugliosi discussing various suspects in the history of the JFK case. Bugliosi here devotes chapters to the Mafia, the CIA, FBI, Secret Service, KGB, the Radical Right, Lyndon Johnson, Fidel Castro, and the Cuban exiles. If one includes Bugliosi's discussion of Ruby's life and career—during which the author discusses the idea of Ruby killing Oswald for the Mob—then this section of the book covers about 265 pages.

Book Two is subtitled, with the author's usual subtlety and charm, "Delusions of Conspiracy: What Did Not Happen." So the reader understands what faces him. Bugliosi is going to argue that none of these agencies or groups or individuals was involved in plotting to kill President Kennedy. He has to do this or his entire twenty-one-year effort goes up in smoke. Before getting to the specific outlines of the author's verdict in these cases, let me make two observations about the preconditions of his argument that inform us of the entering assumptions.

First, as shown in the chapter on Oliver Stone and Jim Garrison, the author's view of Lee Harvey Oswald is very much reliant on the Warren Commission and also Priscilla Johnson's 1978 book *Marina and Lee*. (As noted, the late Fred Haines penned much of that section.) In fact, when Bugliosi was on his book tour in 2007, he spoke at a bookstore in Boston. Priscilla Johnson was there. According to researcher Ed Tatro, after his talk, Bugliosi told the woman that he could not have written his book without her. Which is an accurate statement. Why Bugliosi would want to admit that in public is puzzling. For today, Johnson's ties to the Agency are there to see. For his own polemical reasons, Bugliosi ignores them and uses her anyway.

Why does that figure importantly in this part of the book? Because Priscilla Johnson's portrait of Oswald is an extension and aggrandizement of the material in the Warren Report. Oswald's life is dealt with in two separate sections of the Warren Report (i.e., in Chapter 7 and Appendix 13). These amount to about 125 pages. Now, as everyone knows, the first witness called by the Commission was Marina Oswald. Both the Secret Service and the FBI had basically held Marina under house arrest after the murder of Oswald. And as authors from Sylvia Meagher to Harold Weisberg to John Armstrong have shown and documented, her testimony before the Commission differed from the first things she told those two investigative agencies, for example, about there being a scope on the rifle she saw, and whether she knew or not that Oswald had gone to Mexico. As shown earlier, there was a strong and, at times, vocal, debate inside the Commission on whether or not to use certain witnesses to make the case against Oswald. Because Bugliosi wrote the kind of book he did, he ignores that important debate. The last thing he wants to reveal is that certain junior counsel inside the Commission had severe reservations about witnesses like Helen Markham, Howard Brennan, and Marina Oswald. But the junior counsel were overruled by their higher ups (i.e., Norman Redlich serving as the messenger service for Allen Dulles, John McCloy, and Jerry Ford).

Oswald Not in Mexico City? Sure He Was

Priscilla Johnson found certain articles of evidence that indicated that Oswald actually had been to Mexico; that was too much for Wesley Liebeler.[1] In his discussion of his work on the Commission with the HSCA, Liebeler said that he found this incident rather troublesome.[2] Why? Because it occurred in August 1964, which was nine months after Oswald's possessions had been rounded up and sent to the FBI. And further, it was around the time that Senator Richard Russell was having severe doubts about signing the report. One of the problems he had was the issue of whether Oswald had actually gone to Mexico or not.

What made Johnson's belated discovery even more problematic was that it built upon the previous work of Ruth Paine. Understand the background. Marina had left New Orleans with Ruth Paine before Oswald had gone to Mexico. As we have seen in the chapter on Mexico City, the FBI had a devil of a time trying to prove that Oswald had left for and returned from Mexico. Time after time, they ran into suspect evidence provided by either the CIA or its proxies. The dispute about this evidence—along with the controversy over Soviet defector Yuri Nosenko—was one of the issues that eventually caused a split between the FBI and CIA.

But, as John Armstrong notes, before Priscilla Johnson mysteriously showed up at Marina's door, Ruth Paine had already been producing suspect evidence about Oswald in Mexico. As she did numerous times, *after* the police had inspected the Paine home, Ruth somehow came up with interesting articles that those bumbling cops had missed.

1. A folded card called "Rules for Betting" from a racetrack in Mexico City. This was the only evidence found to show Oswald attended the track while there.[3]

2. A Spanish-American dictionary with a handwritten note saying "watch Jai-Lai game." But the Commission found that you had to be formally attired to attend these matches and the ticket taker said that Oswald was never there.[4]

3. A paperback edition of a Spanish-English, English-Spanish dictionary with more notes about a Jai-Lai game that Oswald did not attend.[5]

4. Six picture postcards with neither writing nor stamps added.[6]

This was turned over on November 30, a week after the police had searched the Paine household for two days. It joins a long procession of evidence—like the Imperial Reflex Camera—that somehow the police missed, but amateur sleuth Ruth later found.

But, the above was not enough to do the job. So way after Ruth Paine left the scene, Priscilla Johnson now became Marina's new escort. And she managed to find evidence that even Ruth Paine had missed. Priscilla arrived in August 1964, near the end of the Commission proceedings. Her ostensible reason for introducing herself to Marina was that she wanted to work on a book project with her. That book, so much admired by Bugliosi, would not be published for another twelve years.

But right after she appeared, like she had telepathic powers, she performed the magic act that so surprised Liebeler. She quickly found three more exhibits that, in nine months, neither the police, Ruth Paine, nor Marina could locate. They were 1) An entertainment guide distributed in Mexico inside of which were 2) two spanking new tickets for bus rides from Mexico City to Monterey and Monterey to Laredo, Texas, and 3) a guide map of Mexico City.[7]

The FBI was given the runaround by the CIA on most of the information provided to the Bureau about Oswald in Mexico. As John Newman notes, Hoover came to believe that the CIA had lied to him about Oswald being there. Seven weeks after the assassination he wrote in the marginalia of a document that the CIA had "double-dealed" him on "the false story re. Oswald's trip to Mexico."[8]

So if the Warren Commission relied on what Hoover realized was dubious info about Oswald in Mexico, and if Priscilla Johnson was a participant in that charade, how trustworthy can either source—Johnson or the Commission— be about Oswald? Yet it is these two sources that Bugliosi and Fred Haines so heavily relied upon in their biography of Oswald. The man who worked on the Commission's Oswald biography from his cabin in Vermont was Wesley Liebeler. When Oliver Stone's film came out, he admitted in a conversation with Alexander Cockburn in *The Nation* that he never believed his work explained why Oswald allegedly did what he did.

Who Is Priscilla Johnson?

What makes this even more one-sided is that the declassified documents of the ARRB make it quite clear now who Johnson was. Johnson worked for a rather small newspaper outfit in 1959 while she was stationed in Moscow. It was called North American Newspaper Alliance, or NANA for short. She was one of the reporters who interviewed Oswald once he defected. On the weekend of Kennedy's assassination, articles about Oswald penned by her went out over the wire and into several large newspapers including the *Boston Globe* and The *Dallas Morning News*. Right after Oswald's death she did an interview with The *Christian Science Monitor*. In April of 1964, she wrote an article for *Harper's* entitled "Oswald in Moscow." In June of 1964 she signed a contract with Harper and Row to produce a book about Oswald and his widow Marina, a book that would not be published for over ten years. At about that time, and before she appeared on Marina's doorstep, she was questioned by David Slawson and Richard Mosk of the Commission. Perhaps no other writer, outside of the Commission staff, had more influence in molding the image of Oswald for the American public than did Priscilla Johnson.

Up until 1967, no one really questioned who the enterprising woman was, but then, something spectacular happened. The daughter of Josef Stalin defected to the USA with help from the State Department and the CIA. When Svetlana Stalin came to America she stayed in the home of Priscilla's stepfather. And Priscilla now became her translator for a book she was going to write.[9] For anyone understanding how a high level defection worked at the time, and how people exposed to Svetlana had to be cleared in advance, the bells and alarms now began to go off around Priscilla. And also her association with Oswald. For instance, NANA was purchased by former OSS operative Ernest Cuneo.[10] It was a home to prominent rightwing and CIA associated reporters like Victor Lasky, Lucianne Goldberg, and Virginia Prewett. Prewett's husband was a CIA agent and was handled by David Phillips. Also, making her interview with Oswald even more suspect, a former security officer for the State Department, Jack Lynch, once wrote that Johnson's encounter with Oswald in Moscow was "Official Business."

As John Newman notes in *Oswald and the CIA*, the man who approached Johnson on her "Official Business" with Oswald in Moscow was John McVickar, who worked at the US Embassy. Newman makes a good case that not only did McVickar tip off Johnson to interview Oswald, but what he did was essentially a briefing and debriefing before and after the interview. McVickar and Johnson talked about things that no one knew about at the time, for example, that Oswald would be transferred to a radio electronics plant by the Russians. He also told Johnson that Oswald had threatened to give up radar secrets to the Russians.[11]

In 1963, Priscilla altered her original 1959 story. For instance, she added a line at the end which referred to Oswald like this: "However I soon came to feel that this boy was the stuff of which fanatics are made." As researcher Peter Whitmey has noted, the image of Oswald in her earlier story is that of a soft-spoken idealist who spoke in terms of "emigrating" instead of defecting. The insertion of the word "fanatic" is much more in line with what the Commission is going to do with Oswald's new image of a disturbed young Marxist zealot. Whitmey notes two other revisions. In 1963, as we have seen, Johnson and McVickar somehow knew Oswald would be going to an electronics plant. She ignores this in 1963 and says he disappeared against her wishes without notifying her. The final statement in her 1963 story was, "I'd wondered what had happened to him since. Now I know." But she did know what happened to him and she and McVickar talked about it. What Johnson was doing with that last sentence was in tune with her suggestion that Oswald's fanatical tendencies had turned him into an assassin. Right after the article in *Harper's* appeared, in which she wrote, "Oswald yearned to go down in history as the man who shot the President," she signed a contract with Harper and Row to do her twin biography of Oswald and Marina.[12] In her testimony before the Warren Commission, on September 6, 1964, in Dallas, Marina told the Commission that the book would be probably be published in December.

It was not. Priscilla first contributed to a book called *Khrushchev and the Arts* which was published in early 1965. She then worked on the Svetlana Stalin book. The advance rights to that volume had already been sold by Harper and Row (the same company handling her Oswald book) for over a million dollars. Svetlana said some interesting things when she temporarily went back to Russia about her sojourn in America. She said "she had been naïve about life in the USA and had become a favorite pet of the CIA." She also said she had not been "free for a single day in the so-called free world."[13]

Finally, in 1977 *Marina and Lee* was published. The timing was interesting. From about 1974 onward, there was a building alarm about what was really going on with the CIA in both the Watergate scandal and the Kennedy assassination. Finally, in 1976, the House Select Committee on Assassinations had been formed to reopen the case. So her book, which recycled the Warren Commission view of both Oswald and the case, appeared right in the middle of that investigation. The publicity surrounding the book was immense. Longtime CIA flack Thomas Powers did an appreciative review in the *New York Times*. (Interestingly, Powers was working on his authorized and very kind biography of CIA Director Richard Helms at the time. On a show hosted by Phil Donahue in 1991 about JFK, Helms appeared with Priscilla and asked her what had attracted Lee to Marxism.)

When Marina testified before the HSCA, they asked her the last time she saw Priscilla. Marian said it was the night before she appeared. When asked what she contributed to the book, Marina said, "I just contribute very little to the book. It was up to Priscilla to fish out all the facts and everything and put them together some way."[14] By this time, suspicions about her were becoming common. Jerry Policoff wrote an article in *New Times* which accused her of working for the State Department. Priscilla threatened to sue Policoff but never did. In 1988, for CBS's Dan Rather, she did an interview in which she concluded that one of the last words Oswald spoke to her in Moscow were, "I want to give the people of the United States something to think about." Rather never asked her why that quote was not either in her original 1959 article or her revised 1963 version. Probably because the insinuation, that somehow Oswald was thinking of killing Kennedy four years in advance, was a bit ridiculous. Even for her and Rather.

On April 20, 1978, Priscilla Johnson was interviewed in executive session by the HSCA. She showed up with her attorney by her side. Her attorney was from a big New York City firm, Wilmer, Cutler and Pickering. Even though she was allowed to see her CIA file two months before the interview, it was clear from the file that Priscilla was cooperating with the Agency on reviews for Russian writers for American publications. But she said she did not recall initiating contact with the Agency in advance of her third trip to Russia in 1962. Which is something the questioner, Michael Goldsmith, clearly did not believe.

Nevertheless, after she contacted CIA about her 1962 trip, Donald Jameson of the Soviet Russia Division wrote a memo about her. He concludes with the following, "I think that Miss Johnson can be encouraged to write pretty much the articles we want." In 1964, the CIA called her for a meeting which lasted for seven hours. She had another meeting with them in 1965. In 1956 she was granted by the Office of Security an Ad Hoc clearance through the status of "Confidential" provided that caution was exercised. Another document dated later in 1975 classifies her as a "witting collaborator" for the Agency. It appears that Priscilla had applied for work with the CIA prior to her 1959 interview with Oswald. And she was in clear contact with them by the time of the assassination, and was cooperating with them on various matters, including cultural assignments and the matter of Svetlana Stalin's defection.

How does Bugliosi deal with all this information about the woman? He quotes the HSCA Report which was written by Robert Blakey and Dick Billings after the entire staff was dismissed in 1979. He then uses her self-serving answers to certain questions by the HSCA.[15] He then uses her as his major source on Oswald.

Bugliosi's Road to Acquittal

Why is this important to this discussion? Because if you abide by the above two portraits of Oswald—Johnson's and the Commission's—you have a cleaned off sociological specimen. That is, Liebeler and Johnson never admitted to any of Oswald's ties to the FBI, the CIA, intelligence operatives in Dallas and New Orleans, or organized crime figures. If you start with this as your touchstone, then it's pretty simple to declare there was no conspiracy because you just reiterate the false Commission line of Oswald as sociopathic loner. Instead of what, say, Philip Melanson described much more accurately as in his fine book *Spy Saga: Oswald an undercover intelligence operative*. By sticking with the outdated and unsupportable Liebeler/Johnson picture, Bugliosi rigs the deck. And by not telling the whole story about Johnson or Ruth Paine, he lessens suspicion about one organization, namely the CIA.

We should add one other point before we begin. From the list of suspects noted above, one can see that Bugliosi includes groups that almost nobody calls out today. For example: the FBI, KGB, Radical Right, and Castro. But also note that, for some reason, Bugliosi left suspects off his list that some prominent researchers do support (i.e., the late Hal Verb and Harold Weisberg). That is, military intelligence. Why he would leave them off and include the KGB and Castro is inexplicable.

Bugliosi: Ruby No More a Mobster than I Am

Let us begin with Bugliosi's discussion of Ruby and the Mafia. Since there have been many authors who have written in this field—Robert Blakey, David Scheim, John Davis, Seth Kantor, Dan Moldea, and Peter Scott among them—one would think that Ruby's association with the Mob would be hard to deny. Which it is. But the ever-inventive author tries to wiggle around it in a number of ways. First, he goes to his old reliable warhorse, former assistant DA Bill Alexander. The guy who forgot about all the frame-ups his DA's office worked on and now doesn't want to address them. What does Alexander tell the author? It's predictable, which is why Bugliosi likes the guy. Alexander says, "We had no organized crime in Dallas. Our local criminals were too tough for them."[16] Hmm. What about two locals mentioned many times by authors like Tony Summers: Joe Campisi and Joseph Civello? According to Alexander, "they never did anything here." How would Alexander know? Because he screened the cases that came through the DA's office. Which is faulty logic. Why? Because local authorities were notoriously inept in dealing with organized crime. And it was not until the Kennedy administration that the FBI and Justice Department began a systematic campaign against the Mob. Further, as Summers points out, Civello was at the famous landmark Apalachin meeting in New York where most of the heads of the Mafia met and were accidentally discovered and busted.[17] Now at this 1957 conference, over fifty Dons were in attendance, including Vito Genovese and Sam Giancana. If Civello was there, he had to have been part of the managing directorate of American organized crime. Did Alexander think he was called to New York to serve up some Campisi-made meatballs?

As Summers also points out, Ruby was personally acquainted with Civello. As one FBI informant stated, Ruby "was a frequent visitor and associate of Civello. . . ." This witness had previously worked for both men, so the information seemed reliable. Summers then adds to the intrigue by noting that Civello was a personal friend of Sergeant Patrick Dean, who so many suspect of having a role in getting Oswald into the Dallas police basement to kill Oswald.

Incredibly, Bugliosi can write that Jack Ruby "was no more of a mobster than you or I. . . ."[18] In a purely technical sense, this may be true. But in a practical sense it is extremely misleading. The evidence for Ruby's involvement with criminal activity, and his associations with both mobsters (like Civello) and mob associates, like Lewis McWillie, is abundant. For instance, everyone knows about Ruby's prolific gunrunning activities. These extend as far back as the late fifties out of the small town of Kemah, Texas.[19] These arms were driven to Mexico and then picked up by followers of Castro. This gun smuggling continued with a man named Eddie Browder out of Florida, as he and Ruby supplied arms to Castro's crusade. And then when Castro rose to power, to his enemies.[20] Later on, Ruby was associated with CIA gunrunning to Castro's enemies through agent Thomas Eli Davis.[21] Eventually, Ruby met a noted gunrunner who actually knew Castro, Robert McKeown. Ruby once offered him $25,000 for a letter of introduction to the Cuban dictator. Where Ruby would get that kind of money and why he needed to contact Castro so badly is a question Bugliosi leaves unstated. Let alone answered.

Although Bugliosi brings up Ruby's trip to Cuba to see McWillie in the main text, he does not mention the fact that Blakey and others believe Ruby lied about his other trips to the island. For instance, Ruby called a man named Clarence Rector in April of 1963. Rector told the FBI that he had known Ruby since 1950. And in 1960 Ruby had mentioned to him that he had previously been to Cuba for the purpose of obtaining gambling concessions for his associates.[22] Because of information like this, Robert Blakey wrote that it was ". . . established beyond doubt that Ruby lied repeatedly and willfully to the FBI and the Warren Commission about the number of trips he made to Cuba and their duration. . . . Their purpose was to courier something, probably money, into or out of Cuba."[23] Now, considering Ruby's gunrunning activities, which Bugliosi severely discounts, this very likely was, at least partly, the source of the funds.

Astonishingly, Bugliosi ignores the fact that *even the Warren Commission* was aware of Ruby's ties to CIA–Mafia activities in regards to Cuba. Burt Griffin and Leon Hubert, who ran the Ruby inquiry, wrote a memo in March of 1964. It said, "The most promising links between Jack Ruby and the assassination of President Kennedy are established through underworld figures and anti-Castro Cubans and extreme right-wing Americans."[24] Remember, Bugliosi wrote in his introduction that he would present the case for the critics as they themselves wished it to be presented. Somehow he missed this important memo written by the Commission on the very subject of Ruby's connections to criminal activity, organized crime, and Cuba. Did he then also miss the next memo written two months later: "We believe the possibility exists, based on evidence already available, that Ruby was involved in illegal dealings with Cuban elements who might have had contact with Oswald." In other words, the Commission itself had discovered that Ruby was in the middle of these illegal arms deals in a nexus that included the Mafia and Cuban exiles. Now recall what the author said, Ruby was no more a mobster than you or I. Question: Do you or anyone you know participate in such dealings? If not, then Bugliosi is flat wrong and Ruby had more dealings with mobsters than you did.

This includes McWillie. Who, of course, Bugliosi tries to diminish in importance to Ruby, and also as a Mafia figure. McWillie is important not just because of his friendship with Ruby, but also because of his residency in Cuba before the revolution. There is an important point to be made about the two that Bugliosi leaves out. They were not just friends. Ruby idolized McWillie. Elaine Mynier, a girlfriend of McWillie, said that McWillie was ". . . a big time gambler, who has always been in the big money and operated top gambling establishments in the United States and Cuba. He always had a torpedo [a bodyguard] living with him for protection." She then added that Ruby was "a small time character who would do anything for McWillie . . ."[25] This is an important passage that, again, I could not find in Bugliosi's massive tome. One did not operate top-flight casinos in Cuba at the time without Mafia clearance. And, in fact, McWillie managed the Tropicana in Havana, which was owned by Santo Trafficante and Meyer Lansky.[26] Even though McWillie managed this jewel in the Mafia crown in Cuba, Bugliosi actually quotes McWillie as saying that he only knew Trafficante enough to say hello to him![27] This is ridiculous. Yet Bugliosi takes it seriously. Clearly, McWillie was trying to conceal just how close to Trafficante he was. Why?

It may be for a reason that Bugliosi again discounts. As many people know, once Castro overthrew the Batista regime, he closed down the Mafia run casinos and actually detained Trafficante. It was around this time that Ruby first got in contact with McKeown. He told McKeown that he represented Las Vegas interests who were seeking the release of some prisoners in Cuba.[28]

This directly relates to some interesting testimony that Bugliosi does what he can to erase. In 1963, after Ruby killed Oswald, an English journalist contacted the American embassy in London. John Wilson told the embassy that he recalled Ruby visiting an American gangster named Santos in Havana in 1959.[29] The HSCA took this testimony seriously and wrote about the incident, "There was considerable evidence that it did take place."[30] If it did, it could easily be related to Ruby's visit to McKeown. What makes that possibility even more fascinating is that McWillie was also a former employee of a main power inside the Delois Green gang—Benny Binion—who had moved to Las Vegas. Binion had also worked at the Tropicana in 1959. Were these the "Las Vegas interests" Ruby was referring to in his talk with McKeown?

Ruby's Busy Day

All the above is crucial to keep in mind when contemplating Ruby's possible role in a conspiracy. It is also important to realize the ample evidence that exists to establish Ruby as at least cognizant of the plot, and perhaps playing a role in it. There is the testimony of Rose Cherami who predicted the assassination in advance and said that Ruby knew Oswald.[31] There is the testimony of Julia Mercer who said she saw a pick-up truck stopping on Elm Street on the day of the Kennedy assassination at about 11:00 AM. The truck was stopped a bit beyond the triple underpass. While stalled behind the truck, Mercer saw a young man go into the back and remove a package she thought was a rifle wrapped in paper. He then walked up the embankment toward the grassy knoll area with the package. As she eventually tried to pass the pick-up, she looked at the driver and he looked at her. She later identified the driver as Ruby to the FBI. This was before the murder of Oswald. As most everyone who relates this story asks: How did the FBI know that Ruby may have been the man in the truck *before* he shot Oswald?[32]

Now let us follow the reported movements of Jack Ruby the rest of that fateful Friday, after the Mercer sighting:

1. Ruby is seen at the offices of the *Dallas Morning News* at about the time of the assassination. An employee said he disappeared for a 20–25 minute span, and then returned after.[33] This was only four blocks from Dealey Plaza, and there is more than one photo taken at the Plaza which resembles Ruby. Was Ruby trying to arrange an alibi for himself while monitoring what happened at the crime scene?

2. After the assassination, around 1:30 PM, two reliable witnesses saw Ruby at Parkland Hospital. The Warren Commission discarded this testimony. The HSCA did not.

3. Later that afternoon, after Oswald was detained and then paraded out to attend his first lineup, there are reports of Ruby being at the police department.[34]

4. That evening, Ruby took some sandwiches to the police even though he was told it was not necessary. He ended up on the third floor interacting with journalists. He followed them to Henry Wade's press conference and there he did something extraordinary. He tried to

pass himself off as a reporter, and he corrected Wade as to the group Oswald was leafleting for in New Orleans. Wade called it the Free Cuba Committee. Ruby quickly corrected that false association with a rightwing group by saying it was actually the Fair Play for Cuba Committee, a leftist organization.

When arranged in the above manner, that is with Ruby's longtime Cuban gunrunning activities with both CIA (Davis) and Mafia (Browder) related figures; when it is established that there is evidence that Ruby knew men like Civello, McWillie, and Trafficante; when it is revealed that even the Warren Commission knew the importance of Ruby's ties into this illegal, black market activity with underworld figures and how this may have crossed trails with Oswald's Cuban activities; and when the evidence of Ruby's activities on November 22, 1963 is arranged in chronological order, it is difficult to deny that all the elements were in place to insert Ruby as an accessory in the Kennedy plot and as a man who could be used to help clean up the mess afterwards because of that knowledge and accessory status. And for Bugliosi to deny that this framework existed, to use the self-serving words of the likes of Alexander and McWillie to minimize it, and then to write that Ruby "was no more of mobster than you or I . . ." this just flies in the face of common sense, logic, and the record.

Let me conclude this section by briefly commenting on Bugliosi's discussion about two parts of Ruby's possible role in a plot, that is, his famous calls with underworld figures which notched up markedly in October and November; and how Ruby would be approached to enter the police basement to kill Oswald.[35]

For the former, I was unsurprised but disappointed to see the author fall back upon the tired excuse that the calls were all over a labor dispute about unfair trade practices with his competitors, some of whom were using amateurs while Ruby used more expensive union members. Years ago David Scheim exposed this stance as a probable cover-up in his book *Contract on America*. Even the non-conspiracy-minded members of the HSCA found it hard to believe that Ruby would have to call people like McWillie and Barney Baker and Lenny Patrick, who were hundreds of miles away, to settle a local and minor labor dispute. As the HSCA noted about these calls, "The explanations provided by several of the organized crime-connected figures Ruby was in touch with have not been corroborated and seem to have lacked credibility."[36]

Per the latter, why Ruby would enter the police basement to kill Oswald, Bugliosi closes his chapter on Ruby with a satirical phone call between Ruby and a Mafia figure he calls "Vito." Bugliosi gives the imagined call some questionable underpinnings: 1) That the man calls Ruby out of the blue, 2) that Ruby did not even know of Oswald prior to the assassination, 3) that Oswald had killed Kennedy for the Mafia, 4) that there was no reason for Ruby to kill Oswald except for this call, and that 5) Ruby would have to be "sprung" from prison in a jailbreak to prevent him from getting a life sentence.

As mentioned above, and the author's discussion of the Discovery Channel's lamentable program, *JFK: The Ruby Connection*, there is ample evidence to argue that these assumptions are all wrong. If Ruby was involved in the lead up to the assassination, and if he knew Oswald, then his acts directly after the Kennedy murder—as listed above—are indicative of a man who is monitoring the situation, both at Parkland Hospital and at the police station. Why would Ruby do that if he did not at least suspect what had really happened? If that is so, the risk existed of Oswald mentioning his name while under questioning. And if Ruby *was* an accessory—as the Mercer testimony suggests—then it would make sense for him to rub out Oswald before he talked. As Bugliosi points out later, an aggravated manslaughter charge—called murder without malice in Texas—carried a maximum sentence of five years.[37] Considering all the extenuating circumstances involved, Ruby could have been out in even less time than that. In comparing that with the penalty for an accessory to a murder plot, the idea of polishing of Oswald had its inherent advantages.

Bugliosi: No Mob Conspiracy

Now, with Bugliosi's attempts to cut off Ruby and Oswald respectively from the Mob and the CIA, and therefore minimize their conspiracy involvement, let us get to the author's specific discussions of why no major group or body was in on the murder of President Kennedy.

Bugliosi first discusses the possibility of a Mafia conspiracy which, at one time, was fairly popular in the research community. As Gaeton Fonzi wrote, one of Robert Blakey's chief aims was to establish the Mob in the public's imagination as the prime suspect in Kennedy's murder. Blakey's lead was followed up by writers like John Davis and David Scheim, among others. Consequently, Bugliosi devotes a chapter to criticizing this theory. He starts out with a history of how the Mob transferred itself from Sicily to the United States and then how it flourished while the FBI ignored it.[38] This takes us up to the installation of RFK as attorney general and the milestone public testimony of Joe Valachi. The author then discusses the idea that the Mob contributed money to the Kennedy presidential campaign and felt they were lied to. (The thesis of Chuck Giancana's goofy book *Double Cross*.) Bugliosi finds this wanting.

What Bugliosi does next has to be seriously underscored to appreciate. As he knows, most people who have written about a Mafia plot don't rely on the aforementioned concept of a financial "double-cross" as a motive for murder. What they rely upon is the concept of self-preservation. That is, the Mob wanted to slow down or maybe stop the Kennedys' unprecedented campaign to eliminate organized crime in America as a powerful force for evil and corruption. This has always been a sensible argument on its face. How does the author deal with it? By saying it is "anemic." Why? Because the Mob would have "no assurance that Robert Kennedy would not continue to be attorney general under LBJ. . . . And if RFK concluded that the mob had killed his brother, it could expect a vendetta by him against them of unprecedented proportions."[39]

And that is about it. Yet again, Bugliosi avoids the historical political backdrop, a recurrent problem he has. Everyone knew that LBJ and RFK—to put it mildly—did not get along. And most Washington insiders understood just how close LBJ and Hoover were (although the author seriously underplays this fact). Most commentators also understand about the relationship between Bobby and Hoover. Now, the Mob had all kinds of lobbyists working on Capitol Hill, like Irving Davidson. So if they were going to contemplate something like this, they would be informed about the pending ramifications. And, of course, we all know what happened. After President Kennedy's murder, Hoover pulled RFK's private phone from his office, and Johnson then marginalized him at the White House. Bobby resigned within a year since, as Jimmy Hoffa noted, he was just another lawyer now. This, of course, does not mean that the Mob killed JFK. But it does mean that Bugliosi's political analysis is shallow and skimpy. Which is a real problem with the entire book.

Bugliosi then argues that the killing of Oswald by Ruby does not have the earmarks of a classic Mob hit. And he is probably correct about that. But, of course, with Oswald in jail and about to be transferred in a day or so, circumstances were not conducive to the usual Mafia orchestration and ritual: the conference meeting, the delegation of a committee to do the job, the letter sent to an uncle, the trip to the location, the following around of the victim, etc.

The author then writes that the National Committee of organized crime would never sanction the murder of such a top official since the risk of retaliation would be too high if they were detected. Which seems reasonable. Except for the fact that this case may have been one in which certain mobsters went outside the committee and worked on their own accord. Which is what Blakey believes happened.

The rest of this chapter deals with the accusations of the likes of Frank Ragano, Lamar Waldron, and Ed Becker about the stories concerning the involvement of Santo Trafficante and Carlos Marcello in the Kennedy murder. Bugliosi spends four pages trying to diminish Becker's story about hearing Marcello utter a not-so-veiled threat against Kennedy. In Marcello's company, Becker commented on RFK's campaign against both him and organized crime. According to Becker, Marcello then said words to the effect: The dog will keep biting you only if you cut off its tail, but if the dog's head were cut off it would die. This meant that if JFK was killed, Bobby would be cut adrift and be much less effective. Marcello then said, in Italian, "Livarsi na pietra di la scarpa." This means: "Take the stone out of my shoe."[40] When Becker replied to Marcello that he would instantly become a suspect if he did such a thing, the Mafia chieftain said words to the effect: Get a nut to do it.

Bugliosi does what he can to discount or minimize this exchange. He ends up conceding that it most likely did happen.[41] He then tries to show that there is no actual evidence that connects the Mafia to the crime. He first mentions the BRILAB tapes, secret audiotapes, done by the Justice Department on Marcello in the seventies. The ARRB got hold of these and there is nothing on them that incriminates Marcello in the Kennedy case.[42] In his End Notes, he goes after the so-called CAMTEX documents made by an FBI informant who knew Marcello in prison. These were used by Lamar Waldron and Thom Hartmann in their book *Legacy of Secrecy*. He characterizes the so-called confession by Marcello there as the ramblings of advancing senility.[43] Which is actually something I agree with him about. Although to refine it down a bit, it is probably that Marcello actually had Alzheimer's disease.

Blakey: Oswald as a Mob Hit Man

The author then scores Blakey for relying on unreliable evidence to connect Oswald to the Mob. By using declassified files of the HSCA, the author shows the rather strained relationship Blakey postulated between Oswald, Oswald's uncle Dutz Murret, and Sam Saia who, according to Aaron Kohn, was a gambler and close associate of Marcello. Yet in interviews done with Murret's wife and son, it became clear that Murret had gotten out of the bookmaking business prior to 1959. Therefore the association with Saia would have been terminated well before the time of the assassination.[44]

But as we will see, the point is not whether or not Oswald was connected to the Mob or Marcello. Most commentators agree that the evidence for this is seriously deficient. But it's the entering premise that is conclusively wrong. Both Bugliosi and Blakey argue only that Oswald was actually a hit man for the Mafia in the Kennedy case. Which is a nutty argument to be on either side of. It should never come up for a variety of reasons. But Blakey makes the even more ridiculous argument that somehow Marcello got wind of Oswald's shot at Edwin Walker and this is how he got the idea to use him in the Kennedy murder![45]

This is the scale of damage Blakey did in his pseudo-inquiry into the Kennedy assassination. Talk about a literally unfounded concept. First of all, the idea that Oswald shot at Walker never surfaced until *after* the Kennedy assassination. There is no evidence that Marina ever told anyone in New Orleans about this. So how could Marcello have heard of it? And that relates to my second point. As already shown, the bullet fired at Walker could not have come from the alleged rifle that Oswald had. But grant Blakey his argument. Why would Marcello want to use a guy who missed a sitting target from a distance of about twenty-five feet for a job that required one to hit a moving target from almost five times the distance?

It is nonsense. But this is the kind of stuff that Blakey was reduced to by the time of the end of the HSCA. Like the Commission, he had locked himself into Oswald as the lone assassin. And come hell or high water, he was not going to move from that position. And this, of course, makes it easy to go after his "Oswald as Marcello Hit Man" goofiness.

Bugliosi: No CIA Conspiracy

I will now proceed to what I think is one of the worst chapters in *Reclaiming History*. This is the next chapter in the book, which reviews the case for CIA involvement in the Kennedy assassination. Here it becomes necessary to reiterate what I said about the author relying on Priscilla Johnson as his authority on Oswald. With Ruby, Bugliosi ignores or discounts the record to say that he had no more relationship to gangsters and illegal activity than you and I. With Oswald he does something similar. Let me quote two parts of this section in order to show just how determined the author is to cut out the very idea of first, conspiracy, and then a CIA conspiracy for the reader.

In his very long footnote on Jeff Morley's attempt to pry loose documents from the CIA about George Joannides and the Agency sponsored Cuban exile group the DRE, Bugliosi writes the following startling statement, ". . . there is no evidence that Oswald had any relationship with the CIA . . . Oswald was clearly not CIA agent or operative material."[46] This is nonsense. Just follow the arc of Oswald's shortened life from the time he first joined the Civil Air Patrol and met David Ferrie to the attempted phone call he made to military intelligence officer John Hurt the night before he was killed and you will see what nonsense it is. As Jim Garrison so memorably described in his book, he was shocked to see that a radar operator like Oswald was getting tested in the Russian language while in the Marine Corps.[47] As Garrison wrote, even though he had been in military service for well over twenty years when he read about this test, he "could not recall a single soldier ever having been required to demonstrate how much Russian he had learned." He then added that as a radar operator, Oswald would have about as much use for the Russian language "as a cat would have for pajamas." The implication being that Oswald was being trained in the language for a future mission. Which, according to Bugliosi, by a wild coincidence, actually happened: the Marine gets a phony hardship discharge and then defects to Russia.

As many authors have outlined, including this one, Oswald's life and career fit perfectly into the profile of an intelligence operative who was first sent to Russia as a fake defector, and then returned to the USA to act as an agent provocateur.[48] After the work of Philip Melanson, John Newman, and John Armstrong, it is the height of folly to deny this today. But by doing so—as with Ruby and the Mob—the author can curtail any possibility that the CIA had a role in Kennedy's assassination. For if Oswald was a CIA operative, then it is easy to see him being maneuvered across a chess board—from New Orleans to Mexico to Dallas—as an unwitting pawn. Bugliosi cannot have that so he just denies or makes excuses for all the evidence that indicates it happened. He even quotes the HSCA Report as saying that once the CIA heard he was in Mexico City the Agency initiated background checks and noticed other agencies of his possible contact with the Soviets.[49] This is highly misleading. As the declassified *Lopez Report* reveals:

1   The CIA sent out the *wrong description* of Oswald to those other agencies.[50]

2   James Angleton had bifurcated Oswald's file so that no one but he would have all the information about Oswald at this time.[51]

3   Because of this there was no on the ground investigation by the CIA as to Oswald's alleged visits to the Cuban and Russian consulates *prior* to the assassination. And the CIA lied about this fact.[52]

If you ignore, obfuscate, or discount all this crucial information then you can say that 1) The *Lopez Report* is a giant dud, and 2) Oswald had no relationship with the CIA. Bugliosi says both in order to stay on his preconceived agenda.

Bugliosi: Kennedy and CIA were Buddies!

Now, let us examine some of the things that the author says in his chapter dealing with the prospect of CIA culpability in the murder of President Kennedy. Right off the bat, one can see that Bugliosi is going to be unbalanced in his treatment of the subject. The author writes that although Kennedy threatened to split the CIA into a thousand pieces he never came close to doing so. This is supposed to minimize any antagonism between the Agency and President Kennedy.[53]

Now consider the record. After the Bay of Pigs debacle, Kennedy created a board of inquiry to investigate what the CIA had actually done to create such a disaster. After it was over, Kennedy decided that the Agency had deliberately deceived him. They realized the operation could not succeed on its own and they wanted him to intervene with American naval power to save the day. As pointed out previously, the Kennedy brothers were strongly influenced by the testimony of Robert Lovett, who had been critical of Allen Dulles during the Eisenhower administration. It was Lovett's testimony and private audience with JFK that convinced him to fire not just Allen Dulles, but Director of Plans Dick Bissell, and Deputy Director Charles Cabell.

But it didn't end there. As David Corn revealed in his biography of Ted Shackley, Robert Kennedy now became an almost de facto Inspector General over many CIA operations. And the CIA really did not like this. Because RFK would demand to see the final blueprints for operational plans and he would then ask many questions and even request revisions. There was also the issuance of NSAM's 55, 56, and 57, which limited the role of the CIA in paramilitary affairs. Kennedy also created the Defense Intelligence Agency to supplement the CIA and to help the Pentagon in his transference of paramilitary operations to the military. In the wake of the Bay of Pigs investigation, Kennedy also issued orders that the CIA would not be able to override the charges of the ambassador in any foreign country. So what Bugliosi says here about Kennedy never trying to take control or reforming the CIA is just not supportable by the record.

Now, the other thing Bugliosi almost completely ignores is how Kennedy's foreign policy shifted significantly from Eisenhower's. Kennedy was not a classic Cold Warrior by any means. In fact, while in the Senate, Kennedy made powerful and famous speeches against the Cold War policies carried out by Eisenhower and Secretary of State Dulles.[54] This is well illustrated in the valuable book by Richard Mahoney, *JFK: Ordeal in Africa*. (As noted, a book conspicuous by its absence in Bugliosi's lengthy bibliography.) But the point is, if you eliminate the splits between the CIA and Kennedy in foreign policy views and aims—for example in the Congo—then you minimize the conflict that arose from them.

In his mini-history of the Agency Bugliosi does two things that are simply inexplicable.[55] First, by using an official CIA source, he tries to say that the Agency had an even *better relationship with President Kennedy than Eisenhower!*[56] To anyone who has studied the Agency to any degree, this statement is so wide off the mark as to be humorous. Secondly, and directly related to it, Bugliosi completely ignores the revolutionary effect that Allen Dulles's appointment as Director had on the Agency. Again, what the prosecutor does is to not fully inform the reader of key historical facts that animate the political calculus of the era. In this case, he leaves out the strong influence of Secretary of State John Foster Dulles on Eisenhower; and how this enabled his brother to alter the Agency in a way that was decisively different from its previous form. How is this left out? The name of John Foster Dulles does not appear in his chapter on the CIA. In fact, if you look in the index, you will see that his name is mentioned twice in the entire volume—and in the first instance, Bugliosi made an error and spelled Allen Dulles as "John Dulles." So, in fact, Foster Dulles is mentioned exactly once in the nearly 2,700 pages of the book. The name of Allen Dulles is mentioned all of four times in this chapter on the CIA.

To me, this is simply indefensible. By leaving out the fact that Allen Dulles took the CIA to a level of covert and paramilitary activity that no one ever dreamed of at the time the National Security Act was signed, the author can ignore the fact that people strongly suspected of being involved in the JFK murder cut their teeth in these Dulles sanctioned operations, for example, David Phillips and Howard Hunt in the Guatemala coup of 1954. By eliminating the influence of his brother on Eisenhower, the author can leave out instances where John Foster Dulles literally cleared the way for an Allen Dulles coup attempt by replacing an ambassador opposed to it, for example, Indonesia in 1958.[57] By not going into any depth about Kennedy's foreign policy beliefs as expressed in Mahoney's extraordinary book, he does not have to delineate the difference between Allen Dulles's relationship with Eisenhower versus his relationship with Kennedy. Some historians, for example, in covering the failed Dulles brothers' coup in Indonesia, do exactly that:

> "Probably at no time since World War II has violence—especially on a militarized level—in the execution of covert American foreign policy been so widespread as during the Eisenhower administration. Especially was this so with respect to U.S. relations with Third World countries. . . ."[58]

They then go further in this regard in relation to a particular area of conflict: "In no part of the Third World were the Eisenhower administration's militarized interventions . . . so extensive (or have been so little chronicled) as in the newly emerged ex-colonial states of Southeast Asia." They then specifically name Laos, Vietnam, and Indonesia. Kennedy eventually reversed the previous administration's intentions in all three. Now Mahoney demonstrates how Kennedy also subverted Allen Dulles's intent in the Congo. And in fact, Dulles likely speeded up the murder of Patrice Lumumba because he knew that Kennedy would never approve it.[59]

This of course leads us to Dulles vs. Kennedy during and after the Bay of Pigs invasion. As mentioned above, it was the White House inquiry after this debacle, plus the influence of another Dulles/Eisenhower antagonist—Robert Lovett—that caused JFK to fire Allen Dulles. Thereby ending an intelligence career that spanned—on and off—forty years. There can be no doubt that Dulles came to epitomize what a certain aspect of the Eastern Establishment thought the CIA should be. Further, that certain operators in the covert operations side owed their careers to the man. If anyone was seriously investigating the antagonism between the CIA and President Kennedy, one would have to spend at least a few pages on this whole falling out between the two and what it represented.

Well, between the text and End Notes, this chapter runs to about fifty-five pages. The author mentions the Bay of Pigs all of three times. And once it is in relation to Oswald. If you can believe it—and by now you can—Bugliosi never once mentions the fact that *Kennedy fired Allen Dulles* as a result of the Bay of Pigs. In this chapter, he never once mentions the board of inquiry that President Kennedy set up afterward to investigate the causes of the failure. Or the fact that Allen's brother would have protected him from any such White House inquiry under Eisenhower. Or that the Dulles–Eisenhower view of the Third World actually caused the preparations for the Bay of Pigs.[60] That it was Allen Dulles who first approved plans to "eliminate" Castro in December of 1959.[61] That it was Dulles, in early 1960, who first proposed paramilitary sabotage operations against Cuban industry.[62] It was Dulles who first brought plans to the White House to build a paramilitary force of Cuban exiles to use in an overthrow attempt. All of these anti-Castro operations occurred under Eisenhower. What is important to remember is that Castro took power in 1959. Yet, by the spring of the next year, Eisenhower and Allen Dulles were intent on overthrowing his government.

The point is this: the CIA attempt to overthrow Castro's government was Dulles's baby. He pushed it on a reluctant Kennedy.[63] Kennedy never forgave himself for approving the hare-brained operation: "How could I have been so stupid as to let them proceed!" he exclaimed. He later called it "the worst experience of my life." Considering what happened with PT-109, that is saying something. As a result, Kennedy ordered a full investigation. He came to the conclusion that he had been hoodwinked. That the CIA never expected the operation to succeed on its own. That they were banking on him sending in the Navy when it looked like it would fail. In fact, Allen Dulles later all but admitted this was the case. In an extraordinarily important article that Douglass quotes—Lucien S. Vandenbrouke's "The Confessions of Allen Dulles"—the legendary spymaster wrote in coffee-stained notes that he understood that what he and Bissell had planned violated Kennedy's ban on direct American involvement. But he was banking that "the realities of the situation" would mandate that Kennedy sanction the amount of force needed to carry the day.[64]

Needless to say, Bugliosi leaves all the above out. Why? Probably because he then doesn't have to explain a very real problem he has: Allen Dulles coldly planned on manipulating Kennedy into a military invasion of a Third World country. Kennedy would not do it. And he never did it in his three years as president. This undermines his point about Kennedy having "even better" relations with CIA as Eisenhower.

Once one establishes this actual acrimony, we see that people who are suspected of being in on the JFK murder were protégés and great friends of Dulles, for example, David Phillips, Howard Hunt, and James Angleton. (Angleton actually carried the urn with Dulles's ashes at the Director's funeral.)[65] Finally, that if those men were involved in any kind of plot against Kennedy, Dulles would be in perfect position to protect them by obstructing any real investigation—which he did.

Vince: Where Is Angleton?

The other way that Bugliosi curtails any kind of conspiracy involving the CIA is through his two ringing denials about Oswald. He first says that "Since it has been established beyond all doubt that Oswald killed Kennedy. . . ."[66] As I have noted throughout this review, in light of the evidentiary record in this case, this statement is preposterous. The second way he achieves curtailment is through this statement: "Oswald was a Marxist, and Marxist being in league with U. S. intelligence just doesn't ring true."[67] (He then goes on to score certain critics, like Jim Garrison and myself, who question this portrait of Oswald). He says that the idea that Oswald was really just posing as a Marxist, but in reality was a CIA agent provocateur is a contention that "cannot seriously and rationally be made." A statement that is pure poppycock. It most certainly can be made, and to any objective person it can be proven. Like almost all other rabid Warren Commission supporters, Bugliosi simply cannot tolerate this view of Oswald since it makes the concept of a CIA conspiracy even more palpable. Oswald was following his marching orders, not knowing that he was being manipulated.

One of the most startling names left out of this part of the book is this: James Angleton. At the time *Reclaiming History* was written, two major works concerning Angleton and the JFK case had already been published. They were John Newman's *Oswald and the CIA,* and Lisa Pease's two-part essay entitled simply "James Angleton" in *The Assassinations.* Bugliosi seems to have read Newman's book since he discusses it. He was a subscriber to *Probe,* which is where the Pease articles first appeared. So it is hard to comprehend how he missed the import of both. But he only mentions Angleton's name four times in the text. Two of them are in footnotes and one appears to be a mistake by the indexer, since I could not find the name on that page. The only substantive part of the book about Angleton is in the discussion of Soviet defector Yuri Nosenko. The problem with this today is that many people think that Angleton was the ultimate control agent of Lee Harvey Oswald. John Newman makes this argument very well in the reissue of his book *Oswald and the CIA.* He states that Angleton was the only person in the Agency who has access to all of Oswald's files. He therefore knew what to do with them on the event of the Mexico City charade and then on the day of the assassination. He even argues that it was likely that Angleton actually designed the plot.[68] If that were so, then does it not make it rather odd that Angleton was then the CIA liaison with the Warren Commission? I could find only four lines on this issue in all of *Reclaiming History.* And those are in the Notes.[69]

One last point on the whole issue of a CIA conspiracy, Bugliosi does note the trial of Clay Shaw. He says that with two minor exceptions the CIA did not at all interfere with the legal proceedings. Which, again, is so off base as to be shocking. As I proved, the CIA was involved in the middle of Garrison's office from 1966 with Bernardo De Torres misleading Garrison. It then escalated throughout the entire over two year delay to get to trial. Finally, as Robert Tanenbaum noted, he saw documents out of Richard Helms's office revealing that he was monitoring and harassing Garrison's witnesses right up to and during the trial.[70] Again, this is all well documented today. For the prosecutor to say it did not happen, well, what can one say?

Bugliosi and the Bureau

Let us briefly note how Bugliosi deals with some other "suspects" in the JFK case. After his pitiful chapter on the CIA, he then goes to the FBI. He begins that chapter with this sentence: "The other federal intelligence agency that many conspiracy theorists have sought to implicate in the assassination is the FBI, the main villain being J. Edgar Hoover, its longtime director."[71] This is a strange comment for a man who has spent twenty-one years researching the JFK case. Its strangeness is accentuated by the fact that Bugliosi then does not name any examples in this regard. I can't either. The closest is the long pamphlet entitled *Nomenclature of an Assassination Cabal,* commonly referred to as *The Torbitt Document.* Today, proper analysis of this pamphlet concludes that it was a disinformation piece.[72] Outside of that long essay, I am hard pressed to find any notable book which presents a case for the FBI being the prime agency through which an assassination plot against President Kennedy was run.

Bugliosi has the same problem. Because the book he does mention here is Mark North's *Act of Treason.* Yet, this is a "Mafia did it" book. Its only tenet supporting an FBI role was Hoover's alleged failure to forward a threat by the Mob against Kennedy. So in fact, North's book is not actually an "FBI did it" book. The other things Bugliosi brings up in this chapter are also tangential. And contrary to what the author says, it is proved without a shadow of a doubt that Hoover was an active agent in the cover-up, as distinct from the conspiracy. This is a distinction, that in their uncontrollable zeal to pile up as many participants in the plot as possible, many Commission advocates fail to make.

Bugliosi on the Secret Service

Bugliosi's next chapter deals with the Secret Service. Again, I can hardly recall any notable book saying that the Secret Service was the main plotter in the JFK case. The only one I can think of is the 1974 self-published effort entitled *Murder from Within.* It is a book that few people even know about, let alone use. Bugliosi seems to understand this, as he did not with the FBI. So he writes that "One other U.S. intelligence agency has had the suggestion of *complicity* in the assassination leveled against it by the conspiracy theorists, the Secret Service, but nowhere near as much as the CIA and FBI."[73] (Emphasis added.) But in his continual efforts to have it both ways, he later changes this to the Secret Service being behind the assassination.[74] Why does he do this, when in fact, there is virtually no one who says this? Probably so he can land another of his straw man broadsides: ". . . the notion that the Secret Service was behind the assassination is, like virtually all the conspiracy theories, ridiculous on its face."[75] Yep, especially when virtually no one is saying it.

Now what does Bugliosi do with his two classifications of the Secret Service as being both "complicit" and/or "being behind" the assassination? As is his usual bent, he severely limits the discussion of both. How does he do that? Consider the following: "With respect to the Secret Service, for all intents and purposes, the inquiry about complicity in the assassination begins and ends with the motorcade route."[76] This is a shocking statement. Even for someone as agenda-driven as the prosecutor. Let us drop just one name to show how Bugliosi's self-imposed limits are nothing but solipsistic: Abraham Bolden. Secret Service agent Bolden has described an assassination plot on Kennedy in Chicago in early November that is very similar in design to what happened in Dallas. That had nothing to do with the Dallas motorcade route. But as demonstrated earlier, since Bugliosi does all he can to curtail any discussion of the plot to kill Kennedy in Chicago, he can ignore that vitally important episode.

Let me drop another name to show how solipsistic Bugliosi's take on the subject of the Secret Service is: Elmer Moore. As mentioned in the chapter on the autopsy, Moore has become one of the most important discoveries of the ARRB. As Pat Speer, Doug Horne, Gary Aguilar and I have noted, it is not unjustified to say that Moore was one of the most important players in the cover-up. The Secret Service agent eventually became a personal valet to Earl Warren. Again, Bugliosi does not have to deal with the very important figure of Moore. Why? For the simple reason that he does not mention him in the nearly 2,700 pages of his book.

Surprisingly, the author glosses over the name of Pat Kirkwood in this chapter. Kirkwood ran an after-hours club called The Cellar located in Fort Worth. Within days of the assassination, it became fairly well-known that Secret Service agents had been at the Fort Worth club well into the early hours of the morning. Drew Pearson mentioned it this way, "Obviously, men who have been drinking until nearly 3 AM are in no condition to be trigger-alert or in the best physical shape to protect anyone."[77] As Jim Marrs notes, this was a clear violation of the Secret Service rules and regulations as expressed in their manual. But James Rowley decided not to discipline any of the agents involved, even though four of them rode on the car behind the presidential limousine. Why? Because if he did it "might have given rise to an inference that the violation of the regulation had contributed to the tragic events of November 22."[78] Which some people have said was the case. Both Ken O'Donnell and Ralph Yarborough noted the slow reaction time by the Secret Service to the fusillade.

Pat Kirkwood later elucidated what had happened. At about midnight the evening before the murder, some reporters called him and said they were out with about *seventeen Secret Service agents*. They asked him if they could bring the agents over. According to Kirkwood, they were still there at 3:30 AM, joking about how local firemen had to replace them in guarding the president at the Fort Worth hotel. After the episode got in the papers, the White House called and told Kirkwood not to talk to anyone because the Secret Service had taken a beating in the press already. So Kirkwood and his manager didn't say anything for years. But later manager Jim Hill said that the agents were clearly drunk since they were drinking nothing but alcohol.[79] It's incredible that Bugliosi deals with all this in one paragraph. In fact, I have related more about what actually happened there than he does. Further, the man who has all kinds of boilerplate condemnation of the critical community, does not condemn this unprofessional and irresponsible behavior. Which actually borders on negligence.

The man who has done the best work on the Secret Service failure in Dealey Plaza is Vince Palamara. Bugliosi mentions his book called *Survivor's Guilt* and briefly discusses it.[80] What the author leaves out from Palamara is rather interesting. Thankfully, Doug Horne put it in Vol. 5 of his series *Inside the ARRB*.

As Horne notes, in the original security design, there was included motorcycle escorts traveling to the side of the limo. At a meeting on November 21, Secret Service agent Winston Lawson did two things: he cut the number of guarding escort motorcycles in half—from four to two—and he then placed them *to the rear* of the car, not to the side.[81] Further, Horne notes that Lawson then tried to camouflage this by saying that it was Kennedy who wanted the motorcycles to the rear.[82] Palamara has also shown that it was standard practice to have motorcycles ride to the side of the limousine. As Horne writes, "If motorcycle patrolmen had been riding abreast of the limousine on Elm Street, their positioning may have obscured the president from shooters firing in front of the limousine."[83]

This weird formation of the motorcycles is backed up by B. J. Martin, one of the cyclists. He said he was given instructions at Love Field to ride to the rear of the limousine. He said he had never heard of such a formation.[84] Dallas motorcycle officer Marrion Baker told the Warren Commission the same thing, "When we got to the airport, our sergeant instructed me that there wouldn't be anybody riding beside the president's car." The HSCA investigated these charges and found them soundly based. They called the formation around the president "uniquely insecure."[85] In addition, Palamara found out that Floyd Boring had told Clint Hill that JFK did not want agents riding on the rear steps of the presidential limousine in Dallas.[86] As Horne writes, this assignment of agents may have obscured the aim of an assassin firing from the rear of the car. Again, the failure to do this was falsely attributed to President

Kennedy.[87] Even though Bugliosi has read Palamara, there is not a word about any of this in *Reclaiming History*.

Just like there is not a mention of the name of Donald Lawton. Lawton is a Secret Service agent who has become famous due to a YouTube film clip. This film was shot by local television in black and white. It depicts both the presidential limo and the follow-up car leaving Love Field. Agent Lawton is running along the rear fender of the presidential limo as the car pulls out of the airport. As he is doing this, agent Emory Roberts calls him back away from the car. Lawton is surprised by the Roberts order. He turns, shrugs his shoulders, and stretches out his arms—three times. Lawton apparently thought he was going to be on the rear steps of the limo. That is, obstructing any shots from the rear of the car. He can't believe he is being called off. In both of these cases, the moving of the cycles to the rear and the calling off of the agents from the rear bumper, the Secret Service said Kennedy requested this. Palamara hotly disputes this. Noting that this is natural since if the cycles and men on the rear bumper had been in place, it would have been much harder for the assassination to take place as it did.

Horne brought up another interesting aspect of the Secret Service performance in regards to the Warren Commission. Arlen Specter had requested of the Secret Service that they obtain videotapes and transcripts of the Malcolm Perry press conference in Dallas on the twenty-second. James Rowley, the Secret Service chief, wrote to Chief Counsel J. Lee Rankin that, "The video tape and transcript . . . mentioned in your letter has not been located. After a review . . . no video tape or transcript could be found of a television interview with Dr. Malcom Perry."

In light of that letter in reply, it is rather odd that the ARRB found a transcript of the Perry conference that was time stamped, "Received US Secret Service 1963 Nov. 26 AM 11 40, Office of the Chief." In other words, Chief Rowley was lying about this transcript. It did exist and he had it even before the Commission was created. But Perry said in that press conference that the wound in the front of the neck was an entrance wound, therefore it came from the front.[88]

Finally, before moving off this issue, there is another way to look at this. According to Abe Bolden, who was with the Secret Service in Washington for a month in 1961, the men on that detail were, for the most part, amateurish in their approach to their jobs. Bolden was once given an AR-15 to stand duty with. He told the agent who gave it to him that he had never used the weapon before. He was told he should just "fake it" for now.[89] Bolden got the feeling that most of these men didn't really think that much of Kennedy and may have even resented him for his stand on civil rights.

Palamara calls what happened in Dallas—the altering of the motorcycle formation and cutting it in half, and the removal of agents from standing on the rear of the car—"security stripping." This clearly resulted in the assassins having a much better opportunity to hit their target than if the proper procedures had been followed. No surprise, Bugliosi apparently did not think any of this was important in discussing the possibility of Secret Service negligence or complicity in the assassination. Further, he makes no note that there was no inquiry into whether it was negligence or complicity. Probably because, as we have seen, Rowley was too involved in the cover-up. And the prosecutor makes no comment on the difference in performance of Secret Service agent Rufus Youngblood who knocked down Lyndon Johnson almost the instant he heard the first shot, and the performance of the agents in the presidential limousine and follow-up car who never knocked down anyone until the fusillade was complete.

Straw Men

After this poor performance on the Secret Service, Bugliosi next reverts back to his straw man approach. That is, he actually spends chapters on consideration of whether or not the KGB, Fidel Castro, or the Radical Right killed Kennedy. Again, the amount of published literature pushing these angles is rather slim considering the vast library of literature on the case. It would have been much more responsible of the author to spend more time correcting the record in his Secret Service or CIA chapters. As per the idea that the KGB did it, well one only has to look at who Bugliosi lists as advocating this idea to see how silly it is to bring it up. In his End Notes, the author surfaces the name of Revilo Oliver, a member of the John Birch Society who wrote about this possibility in their publication *American Opinion*.[90] To somehow put Oliver in the critical community is a wee bit absurd.

Bugliosi spends a large part of this chapter on the famous case of Yuri Nosenko. Nosenko was a KGB defector who came to the USA after the assassination and declared the Russians had no interest in Oswald while he was there. Today, and even back in the sixties and seventies, most informed people agreed with what Nosenko said. For instance, the FBI accepted this as fact. So did much of the CIA. Except for one James Angleton. Angleton imprisoned the man for about three years and applied an array of physical and psychological torture techniques to break him into confessing he was a false defector. Why? Because Angleton's theory—actually another disinformation tract—was precisely the opposite. Namely that the assassination was a KGB hit with Oswald as the assassin. (See two outlets for Angleton, Edward Epstein's

Legend, and Joseph Trento's *Secret History of the CIA.)* In other words, in his manic attempt to smear the critics, Bugliosi is actually using James Angleton as part of the critical community. When, in fact, the truth is the contrary. As noted above, many parts of the critical community feel that Angleton was actually running Oswald as an "off the books" CIA agent. And he used the Nosenko affair, and then Epstein and Trento, to disguise that fact. As we shall see, as with his treatment of Castro, Bugliosi never points this out.

The author's chapter on the Right Wing is similar in its relevancy. In fact, this subject is pretty threadbare in the literature. So Bugliosi takes up about four pages printing Kennedy's famous televised speech made on June 11, 1963, about civil rights.[91] He then starts writing about the resultant murder of Medgar Evers by Byron De La Beckwith. He fills out the rest of this distracting chapter by writing about Joseph Milteer and H. L Hunt. The Milteer story, about how he predicted the way Kennedy would be shot in advance—from a tall building with a high-powered rifle—has been around for decades. It's an interesting story, in part because the FBI seems not to have taken the taped warning seriously. But I know of no credible author who has built any kind of assassination plot or cabal behind it. Or put it in book length form. As per H. L. Hunt, most people who write about him in regards to the assassination tend to place him in the confines of a "Texas" oriented plot, which Bugliosi discusses in his chapter on the LBJ theories.

Castro's Great Speech

As per the advocates of Castro being the culprit, today many feel that works suggesting that Castro did it were and are probably deliberate pieces of disinformation. And such works—like Carlos Bringuier's book *Red Friday,* or Gus Russo's works like *Live by the Sword* and *Brothers in Arms*—were called out as such by the critical community. This calling out of books that look suspiciously "sponsored" is a point which Bugliosi conveniently and completely ignores.

But it should be noted that on the day after the assassination, Fidel Castro made a memorable speech. An English translation of the speech was made public by the Cuban UN delegation in 1963. Castro stated in this speech that Kennedy's murder was the result of a power struggle within the USA; and the reactionary forces had won out. Castro said these forces were disappointed in Kennedy's decision not to invade Cuba during the Missile Crisis. He then notes that the suspect Oswald, who had not been killed yet, had defected to Russia and was working for the Fair Play for Cuba Committee. So the alleged assassin has convenient ties to both communist opponents of America. He then notes that Oswald threatened to give up American radar secrets, yet he was allowed back into the country with financial help from the American government. Further, Castro says that his agents have looked into the matter of a Fair Play for Cuba Committee in New Orleans, and there is none there. But he notes that the FBI and CIA have made a habit of infiltrating these committees with undercover agents. In looking at his profile, Castro notes: How did an American born citizen, educated in American public schools, and who joined the Marines suddenly turn into a Castro sympathizer? He wonders why no one in the American media asks that question. Just like he wonders how someone as ordinary as Oswald got on television and radio to talk about Cuba just months before the assassination. And if he is a fanatic, why does he deny killing Kennedy? He warns that Oswald may be innocent and if he is, he was used as "a cat's paw, in a plan very well prepared by people who knew how to prepare these plans. . . ."

Castro then notes that Kennedy had called off attacks on Cuba from the United States and that the Cuban exiles trained by the CIA never forgave him for this. He then quotes a news story from November 19, three days before, where one of their representatives in the media stated at a press conference that "I believe a coming serious event will oblige Washington to change this policy of peaceful coexistence." Castro asks a question no one in America asked at the time about this Associated Press story: What did this gentleman mean in light of yesterday? Was there a reactionary plot based upon opposition to Kennedy's growing policy of détente with Russia and Cuba? And if that was so, was Oswald being used to get an invasion of Cuba as retaliation for Kennedy's death?

And then Castro goes further. He notes that someone in the State Department has announced they are absolving Cuba of any part in the plot. He notes that Cuba needs no one to do that since they had nothing to do with the crime. But what this reveals is that some people in the American government understand where this anti-Cuba, anti-Russia hysteria is headed. And they are trying to stop it before it is unleashed in full fury. He asks: "Who can benefit from this . . . from this murder if not the worst elements of U. S. society? Who could be the only ones interested in this murder?" He warns Americans that they themselves should demand that "what is behind the Kennedy assassination be clarified."

Bugliosi would have done well to tell us about Castro's wonderfully perceptive speech delivered *within twenty-four hours* of Kennedy's death. No one else in a position to publically say so was this close to the truth at that early date. Many commentators, through French reporter Jean Daniel, have noted Castro's comments when he got the news of Kennedy's death. Very few have noted the import of this brilliant speech. For not only was Castro theorizing that Oswald was likely a phony communist and had nothing to do with Cuba, he was actually showing what had actually happened. And further, he was urging Americans to find out the real facts of the case. In other words, Castro was being a better American citizen that anyone of the Warren Commission was.[92]

Bugliosi Acquits Johnson

Which brings us to Vice President Johnson. Now there *are* people who have written books about the idea that Johnson was a leading part of a cabal to kill President Kennedy. For example, Craig Zirbel, Barr McClellan, and later Philip Nelson. Ed Tatro, a noted researcher from Boston, has been at work for decades on such a book. Furthermore, the idea that LBJ was a leader in this plot has advocates who have not necessarily written at length about it, for example, Walt Brown and George Bailey (Bailey runs the interesting website *Oswald's Mother*).

Surprisingly, in light of all the above, Bugliosi spends only eight pages in the text on this subject.[93] In the End Notes he spends another half page. In other words, he spends more than twice as much space on the Right Wing than he does on LBJ. The same ratio applies with the KGB. He actually spends four times as long on Castro as a suspect. (To be fair to the author, he does touch on this LBJ subject in his chapter called "Other Assassins." There he discusses McClellan, the book *The Men on the Sixth Floor*, Mac Wallace, and the late fingerprint analyst Nathan Darby.[94] It is hard not to conclude that the sillier and less backed the theory is, the more time the author spends reviewing it since it makes it easier to ridicule the critics that way.

In his chapter entitled "LBJ," Bugliosi mentions the Bobby Baker scandal. But he gives it short shrift: three paragraphs, less than a half page.[95] He tries to counter the belief that Johnson was going to be removed from the presidential ticket in 1964 by saying that President Kennedy had said in public that this was not so, and that Arthur Schlesinger also said it was false. This is not altogether convincing. First, the idea that JFK would announce in public that he was going to dump Johnson is a bit wild. Second, according to James Wagenvoord, an editor at *Life*, the impetus behind pushing out LBJ was not President Kennedy but Bobby Kennedy. Wagenvoord has told British historian John Simkin that the magazine was preparing a long story on the subject of the LBJ/Baker scandal at the time of the assassination. The information was coming from RFK's Justice Department. The story was dropped when LBJ became president.[96]

But another potential scandal that Bugliosi completely ignores is the Don Reynolds affair. Reynolds told a senate committee that Johnson had asked him for kickbacks in order to sign a life insurance policy with his company. This testimony was taken the day of the assassination and has since allegedly disappeared.[97]

Now, if RFK had succeeded in forcing LBJ off the ticket, then the possibility does exist that Johnson may have gotten into serious legal trouble because of the two scandals. To me, compared to these two scandals, the other things that the author brings up to render the LBJ argument useless are silly or irrelevant, that is, the myth that Johnson ducked down early because he knew the shots were coming; that Johnson ordered the limo cleaned and rebuilt to conceal or discard evidence; and, of course, the fanciful and ever-evolving Clint Murchison "assassination party" the night before the murder.[98]

In the previously mentioned section of the book, Bugliosi deals with McClellan, Billy Sol Estes, the book *The Men on the Sixth Floor* and the late Nathan Darby's work on the alleged Mac Wallace fingerprint found on one of the boxes on the sixth floor of the depository. To put it briefly, I have no great dispute with Bugliosi's criticism of the first three subjects.

I do have a serious problem with the last. In his horrendous book *Blood, Money and Power*, McClellan used Darby's work to try and prove that Wallace had killed JFK for Lyndon Johnson. Bugliosi writes that he called Darby about his work matching a fingerprint from the boxes to a print taken of Mac Wallace while he was alive.[99] Bugliosi depicts the conversation as going something like this: He calls Darby and says that he told the elderly print analyst that he had trouble buying into his work. Darby asked why that was so. Bugliosi replied to Darby that the unidentified print on the sixth floor was a palm print, not a fingerprint. Therefore no such match was possible.

The clear implication by the prosecutor is that Darby was a charlatan who would do anything that Barr McClellan asked of him for his book. Like matching a fingerprint to a palm print. Or that McClellan had somehow rigged the game by substituting two Wallace prints taken from a previous case and not told Darby that the unidentified print at the Depository was a palm print. When I talked to Bugliosi about this point, he was so confident about it that he actually had me believing he was right and Darby was up a tree. Although, at that time, before his book was out, Bugliosi would not reveal what was actually the problem with Darby's work. When *Reclaiming History* was published, it was Bugliosi's ideas on this issue that I later wrote about in a review of Dean Hartwell's *Dead Men Talking*. Pat Speer read that review and alerted me to the fact that this was another Bugliosi "smoke screen." He pointed me to some research on this, and I wrote an update to the original Hartwell review.

To be kind to Bugliosi, it appears that Speer was right. Bugliosi trusted the Warren Report in his judgment that there was only one unidentified palm print left on the sixth floor in August of 1964.[100] The FBI appears to have fudged this information in their report to the Commission. There were other prints left that the Bureau termed as "not identifiable" or they had "indistinct characteristics." The Bureau also used another trick in disguising the actual information about the prints by using reporting numbers that differed from those official itemized lists.[101] Some of these prints are in the Warren Commission volumes.[102] According to researcher Richard Bartholomew, one of the FBI's tricks on this was to place two prints under one exhibit number.[103] In rereading the long appendix and exhibit section in McClellan's 2003 book, this all now seems apparent. So apparent that it seems again, quite odd, that Bugliosi could not have seen the issue correctly. But if so, it again shows his unwarranted trust for the FBI and his failure to dig deeper into the issue.

Bugliosi as Sherlock Holmes

As the reader can see by now, as with many things in his inflated and oversized book, Bugliosi's approach to this subject—who really murdered President Kennedy and who covered it up—is rabidly one-sided and conclusion driven. His first error is not differentiating between two strophes, that is, the plot to kill Kennedy, and the effort to conceal it afterwards. Secondly, by keeping each power group separate, he can discuss them in isolation from each other. By spending so much time on suspects that merit little—if any—discussion, he can make the critics look silly by erecting multiple straw man arguments. (Although linking the community to the likes of James Angleton and Revilo Oliver is a bit much.) By splitting off Jack Ruby and Lee Oswald from the Mob and the intelligence community he can curtail any conspiracy from either getting started on the ground or uniting with another group. As shown earlier, even Burt Griffin of the Warren Commission contemplated such a thing happening.

In the real world, it doesn't work like this. Power groups do not operate in complete isolation from each other. They intersect each other at many points. Of course, from their perspective, normal middle class people do not see it. They can't. And the mainstream media does not tell them about it, since part of their function is to keep us all in the dark about how the Power Elite actually operates. But every once in a while something extraordinary happens and the media can't completely hide the way the world really works.

One such incident occurred on October 5, 1986, in Nicaragua. On that day, pilot Eugene Hasenfus—a former Marine—was flying a C-123 cargo plane while delivering supplies to the Nicaraguan rebel group called the Contras. That group was termed by President Ronald Reagan the equivalent of "our Founding Fathers." They were fighting the leftist, democratically elected Sandinista government, and the White House said the USA had nothing to do with their efforts. A young Sandinista soldier shot the Hasenfus plane down with a shoulder launched rocket. Hasenfus disobeyed orders by wearing a parachute. The Sandinistas captured him alive. He had a black book on him with a list of phone numbers that connected him to Ilopango Air Base in El Salvador. That base was run by infamous CIA officer Felix Rodriguez.

Thus began the unraveling of a huge conspiracy that included the importation and sale of cocaine, illegal money to a secret army, illegal arms shipments to our alleged enemy Iran, and hostage selling. The giant conspiracy included the CIA, President Reagan, Vice President Bush, the National Security Council, a wealthy class of multimillionaire donors, the Secretary of Defense, the military, including Colin Powell, the Secretary of State, and the Mossad. It was a massive criminal enterprise supposedly run by a lowly Lt. Colonel named Oliver North. But it was later learned that this was just a preplanned cover story and that the upper level conspirators had designed it that way. An honest prosecutor named Laurence Walsh indicted fourteen of the plotters. But as one of his last acts as president, George H. W. Bush pardoned some of his fellow conspirators. So the truth is, we will never know the real extent of this spiraling, multileveled plot.

But the point is, this is the way that the Power Elite works. Centers of power are not separated from each other. They live next door to each other and work together. In the Iran/Contra affair the guy at the bottom was Hasenfus. The giveaway was the black book. In the JFK case, the guy at the bottom was Oswald. The giveaway was the Corliss Lamont flyer he stupidly stamped 544 Camp Street. That flyer has eventually unraveled a wide conspiracy. But unlike with Iran/Contra, there has been no Walsh allowed to uncover and prosecute at least some of it.

By keeping these groups artificially isolated, Bugliosi clouds our view of where the evidence leads and what really happened. What most observers believe today is that the conspiracy before the fact was run by the Agency with aid from the Cuban exiles. The exiles were eager to help since they despised Kennedy for the Bay of Pigs and his refusal to invade Cuba during the Missile Crisis. After Oswald was apprehended, the CIA called in the Mafia, its former partner from the Castro plots: Enter Ruby, exit Oswald. Lyndon Johnson and his friend J. Edgar Hoover had no difficulty participating in the cover up. LBJ was now safe from being kicked off the ticket and possibly indicted; Hoover was now rid of his boss, the hated Bobby Kennedy. Hoover would now cover up Oswald's FBI informant status. LBJ then picked a blue ribbon whitewash committee consisting of the likes of Allen Dulles, Jerry Ford, and John McCloy. Men he knew personally and who he knew would keep the true circumstances of what happened concealed until he was elected. With Hoover as their chief investigator, how could it be otherwise? The last touch on the whitewash was the phony information from Mexico about Oswald and what he did at the Russian and Cuban consulates, and his alleged meeting with the KGB chief of assassinations in the Western Hemisphere. This was used to intimidate Johnson. He then used it in turn to scare the hell out of Earl Warren, whose choice put the temporary seal of respectability on his whitewash panel.

Unlike the grade school picture that *Reclaiming History* implies, this is the real way the Power Elite operates. It's a world the MSM hides from us. But with what has happened to this country of late, adults can now understand America for what it really is. It's not *Ozzie and Harriet*, and it's not heroes in white hats and villains in black. We live in a gangster state where laws are broken with impunity, since the perpetrators know that there is little chance they will ever be caught, and less that they will be punished. They have understood that since 1963.

Summing Up *Reclaiming History*

Contrary to what Tom Hanks and Gary Goetzman and Bill Paxton may think, Vincent Bugliosi's opinion of the Warren Commission is different than other professionals who have studied the JFK case. Bugliosi must know this but he fails to note it in the book. Since 1964, every attorney who has looked at the Kennedy case in an official manner thinks the Warren Commission was wrong. And they have nothing but scorn for how the Commission proceeded. That list would include New Orleans DA Jim Garrison; Gary Hart and Dave Marston of the Church Committee; the first Chief Counsel and Deputy Counsel of the HSCA, Richard Sprague and Robert Tanenbaum; their replacements Robert Blakey and Gary Cornwell; and the Director/Chief Counsel of the ARRB, Jeremy Gunn. Bugliosi likes to belittle Cyril Wecht by saying he was the "odd man out" on the HSCA medical panel. The prosecutor leaves out the fact that, against this backdrop, he is also a bit odd. By an 8–1 tally.

When the HSCA was starting up, Jim Garrison wrote a letter to attorney Jonathan Blackmer. In it, he warned him that traditional methods of crime detection would not work in this case. Therefore he could not really rely on things like fingerprints and handwriting analysis. Garrison had learned the hard way just how thick the cover-up was. It extended to the FBI technical analysts. Bugliosi never learned that lesson. Which is why his book is rather easy to pick apart. I have taken no pleasure in doing so. It was a laborious and tedious exercise. And as stated elsewhere, Bugliosi has done some good work in the past. Here he seems to have been blinded by his chimerical success in a farce of a mock trial. One which every aspect favored him, and his opponent was ill-prepared. Nevertheless he took it seriously. He now doubled down and was bent on declaring war against every Commission critic who ever wrote a book or essay. The result, as noted above, is not pretty. It is also unsound. There are some bits and pieces of value in the volume but not nearly enough to justify its inflated length. It has a good bibliography if one needs to check out the date and publisher of a hard to find book. But none of that justifies the over the top Bela Lugosi-type hamminess and bombast of his vituperative and vicious personal attacks on the critics. Especially when, as we have seen, Bugliosi has settled just about nothing. Certainly not the central question: Who killed President Kennedy and why?

This is the book that Hanks, Goetzman, and Paxton bought into. Did they read the entire work? All 2,646 pages of it? Did they send it out to be peer reviewed? All that seems impossible because they bought the rights within weeks of publication. To do a peer review of *Reclaiming History*, it would take six months to perform the analysis and about three months to collate and write the report. Those are not the kind of things that these three men and Playtone are about. As we have seen, toward the end of his life, that is not what their favorite historian—Stephen Ambrose—was about either. He had become too successful to do that kind of scholarly work. He was too busy promoting himself as a Wise Man. Largely based upon his fraudulent association and interviews with Eisenhower.

Based upon Paxton's boyhood trip to Fort Worth to see JFK, Playtone bought *Reclaiming History*. What came out of that ill-advised purchase does not even resemble its progenitor.

Part 3:
From *Reclaiming History* to *Parkland*, and Beyond

CHAPTER TWELVE

Hanks as Historian: A Case Study

"You can't blame the Marines for teaching Lee Harvey Oswald how to shoot!"

—Congressman Charlie Wilson

The man who made the above comment obviously knew very little about the JFK case. For as anyone who studies it understands, Lee Oswald was not trained by the Marines to shoot. Or at least to shoot very well. And he could have never done what the Warren Commission said he did. As an intelligence agent, he was studying the Russian language and was let out early from his enlistment to go to that country.

But secondly, the man who made that statement is in a state of denial about the aftereffects of a policy in which he was a major player. Which is quite understandable. After all, in the long run, the policy Wilson was pushing ended up being a catastrophe for the United States. It provoked three disastrous wars—two of which are still ongoing—caused the deaths of thousands of Americans, and hundreds of thousands of civilians, and is probably the major cause of the fiscal bankruptcy of the American treasury. Yet Charlie Wilson is a man who Tom Hanks, producer and self-styled historian, chose to make a hero out of in his film *Charlie Wilson's War*. In reading the book the film is based upon, and knowing what we have learned about him, if Hanks was ever going to make a film about the CIA, this was going to be it.

George Crile

George Crile's *Charlie Wilson's War* was originally published in 2003. Crile, who died in 2006, was a journalist and also a producer for the CBS show *Sixty Minutes*. In August 1975, Crile along with *Time* reporter Taylor Branch wrote a long essay for *Harper's* entitled *The Kennedy Vendetta*. It purported to be a study of President Kennedy's Cuban policy from after the Bay of Pigs to right after the Cuban Missile Crisis. It was overwhelmingly based upon interviews done by the authors with CIA officers like Ray Cline and Edward Lansdale, and Cuban exiles like Watergate burglar Rolando Martinez. With the declassified record we have today, the article today seems pretty much superfluous. But what it did do was show that Crile, previewing his forthcoming television tasks, had a propensity to place a strong narrative spin on his materials. Even when they were not well researched, and/or left out many important facts. For instance, the article tried to say that the Bay of Pigs invasion was an operation that Kennedy was somehow enthusiastic about. The authors also tried to say that somehow Kennedy was not really all that upset with the CIA after that debacle. Today, of course, with the declassified records of the ARRB, we know these tenets to be wrong. The authors also allow CIA officer Ray Cline to say there was no CIA controlled attempt to assassinate Castro. But today we have the declassified CIA Inspector General Report on the CIA–Mafia plots to kill Fidel Castro, which reveals the opposite. At the end there is no mention of how these programs were systematically shut down by the president, or of the back channel that Kennedy had set up with Fidel Castro to attempt to establish some kind of détente. Either someone at CBS saw the article and liked it, or Crile pitched it to the network as a news special. Because a documentary special was then broadcast on the subject by CBS in June of 1977. It was entitled the *CIA's Secret Army*. Crile now became a TV documentary producer and was eventually employed by *Sixty Minutes*.

In 1988, Crile produced a *Sixty Minutes* segment which began with Texas Representative Charlie Wilson in Afghanistan firing a Gatling gun. We then saw him on horseback riding with the mujahideen. These were the Afghan rebels who were fighting against the Soviet invasion of their country. When they were producing the segment on location, the cameraman, Peter Henning, told Crile, "You've got a big problem here. . . . You could turn Charlie Wilson into the biggest hero you've ever heard of . . . or a complete clown." During the actual segment there is little doubt about how he is supposed to be perceived. Only when Harry Reasoner does his sign off, only then is there any note of warning as to the dangerous alchemy that Wilson was stirring. At that point,

Reasoner notes that some of the rebels the CIA was training hated Americans as much as they hated the Soviets.

In March of 2001, with Afghanistan now controlled by the radical Moslem group called the Taliban, Crile got Wilson back on camera, this time with Mike Wallace. Wilson now tried to explain that America did not do enough for Afghanistan after the Russians left in 1988–89. Wilson said that America should have stayed longer and helped rebuild the country with a sort of Marshall Plan, and that would have prevented the rise of the Taliban. The important thing about this segment is that it was originally broadcast approximately six months before the attacks of September 11, 2001. But even then, Wilson was trying to disassociate himself from Osama Bin Laden and Al Qaeda. He was saying that they really were not there being trained for combat missions. Bin Laden was really just writing checks.

In 2003, Crile wrote his bestselling book, *Charlie Wilson's War.* Even though it was now almost two years after the 9/11 attacks, America had invaded Afghanistan and Iraq, and the War on Terror had now replaced the Cold War as the CIA's preoccupation, Crile still tried to make Wilson out to be some sort of a hero. In the actual text of the book, there is only the slightest note about the opium trade out of Afghanistan. There is a similar passing note about the danger of supplying weapons to radical fundamentalists. It is only at the end of the book that Crile tacks on a relatively brief Epilogue, which he entitled "Unintended Consequences." After 500 pages of "Charlie is Great," fifteen pages of "Maybe he's not so Great" simply does not balance the scales. Especially since Wilson is a guy who admired Central American dictator Anastasio Somoza. Wilson's closest partner in the Afghan operation, CIA officer Gust Avrakotos, backed the coup of the Greek colonels in 1967. He even advised them to kill Andreas Papandreou, the liberal candidate who was predicted to become the next president before the coup.

None of the above mattered to Hanks, Goetzman, and Playtone. They bought Crile's book fairly quickly. In an interview Hanks did at the film's premiere, the self-styled historian said that once he read the book he felt there had to be a way to make it happen as a film. Because, as he termed it, it was a story he had never seen before, it was undiscovered country. At the premiere, Charlie Wilson said he really did not control anything about his depiction in the film. He only insisted that the Afghan people be portrayed as the heroes they were.

It is amazing that, at the premiere, Hanks could say that he never heard the story contained in Crile's book. Because the film was not released until December of 2007. By that time, the whole story behind what had really happened—the entire breathtaking catastrophe—had become clear to most informed observers. To use just one example: Steve Coll's Pulitzer Prize winning book, *Ghost Wars,* had been published in 2004. Unlike the Crile book, that volume took the story all the way to its ultimate conclusion: the attacks of 9/11. And not only was it much more inclusive in its time span, it revealed the entire architecture of the American intervention. With Crile, one would think that Wilson and Avrakotos ran the entire giant American intervention in Afghanistan. Coll's book shows that those two men were only a part of a much larger, conservative, Republican effort.

Carter Begins It All

Crile's book begins with the Soviet invasion of Afghanistan in December of 1979. It appears like a bolt out of the blue. There is no scaffolding by the author to explain why it happened. Let us supply that explanation here.

Mohammed Daoud Khan had seized power in Afghanistan in 1973 via a coup. Under Daoud, the communist party in Afghanistan (the PDPA) had grown in strength due to his attempts at repression and his suspected role in the murder of one of its leaders. On April 27, 1978, the Afghan army, which was sympathetic to the PDPA, overthrew and executed Daoud. The two leaders of the PDPA took power. But in 1979, one of them, Hafizullah Amin, was involved in a palace coup against the other. This strengthened a rebellion in the countryside that had already begun. A treaty of support had been signed in December of 1978 between Russia and the PDPA. There had been requests for military support early in 1979 and the Russians had sent in small units. In December, Amin requested more help. But by this time, the Russians felt that Amin was involved in the palace coup, was too friendly with rival China, and was talking with the American delegation. Therefore, when the Russians sent in a 100,000 man army in December of 1979, the KGB had Amin assassinated. They then installed another communist, Babrak Karmal, as the new president. In addition to leaving all this out, Crile does not note where and why the rebellion against the PDPA began. Coll explains that it started at the city of Herat, a Moslem stronghold. Because the communist government wanted to educate young girls as well as boys. Therefore, right at the beginning, before the Soviets even invaded, the threat of Islamic fundamentalism was evident to anyone who was watching closely.

In addition to that, Crile does something else that is odd. He leaves the impression that President Jimmy Carter did not sign an authorization for the CIA to take countermeasures until after the invasion. As CIA Director Robert Gates later revealed in his book *From the Shadows,* this is not accurate. Carter signed the authorization, technically called a "finding," six months *before* the invasion.[1] This was confirmed by his National Security Adviser Zbigniew Brzezinski in a famous interview he gave in 1998 to the French journal *Le Nouvel Observateur*. In a memo he wrote to Carter at the time, Brzezinski said that "this aid was going to induce a Soviet intervention."[2] And when the Russians crossed the border, he told Carter, "We now have the opportunity of giving the USSR its Vietnam War." This is almost three years before Wilson made his first visit to the Afghan refugee camps in Pakistan.

Why did Carter sign the finding months in advance? Because in that same year he had suffered a tremendous setback. Because of his ties to David Rockefeller and the Trilateral Commission, Brzezinski had advised Carter to become friendly with the Shah of Iran. For the Shah was a bulwark of stability in the area. But in February of 1979, in the face of spreading riots, Reza Pahlavi had been forced to flee his country. The Iranian revolution had begun and was spinning out of control. The month before the Soviet invasion, Iranian students had stormed the American Embassy and taken fifty-two personnel as hostages. Carter now began to take a beating in the press. Therefore, he now tried to use the Russian invasion to his advantage. He cancelled American participation in the Moscow Olympics of 1980, he cancelled grain sales, and he actually said that the Russian invasion was "the most serious threat to peace since the Second World War."[3] In other words, this eclipsed the Korean War, the Cuban Missile Crisis, and the Vietnam War. It is important to note, the Russians never had more than 120,000 troops in Afghanistan. Under President Johnson, the United States had over half a million men in Vietnam. All of the above is left out by Crile.

Casey Enters the Picture

Largely because of the hostage crisis, Ronald Reagan and the Republicans won the White House in 1980. William Casey now became CIA Director. He was intent on backing the Mujahideen, the holy warriors, against the Soviet Union. And as Coll notes, it did not matter to him how America did it, or who they employed as their allies.[4] Which meant that it would be acceptable to him if they had to employ religious radicals to do it. On the ground, that translated into the fact that Casey would be fine with letting a Moslem nation like Pakistan handle all the supplies and weapons the CIA would be shipping. And, for the first part of the war at least, they would allow the Pakistani intelligence service, the ISI, to handle the training also. The problem with this was that the leader of Pakistan at the time, General Zia-ul-Haq, was an Islamic fundamentalist who encouraged the enacting of Sharia law into his country.

Zia insisted on having complete control of all weapons and supplies the CIA brought into Pakistan. He insisted on controlling the training, and therefore picking who to train and who to favor with the weapons and supplies. And since he himself was a Moslem fundamentalist, the ISI could now choose like-minded personages to train and arm. This meant that the CIA was going to eventually be in cahoots with some very extreme characters like Jalaluddin Haqqani, Gulbuddin Hekmatyar, and finally, Osama Bin Laden. Men, who later on, the United States would be trying to kill. But not only did this not matter to Casey, it did not matter to Wilson either. At one point, he actually called Haqqani, "goodness personified"[5] A truly radical Moslem like Haqqani ended up being a magnet for like-minded religious zealots from Saudi Arabia. And this is where Bin Laden began in earnest to organize his Al Qaeda terrorist group.[6]

Wilson was in a very good position to raise the funding that Casey was able to get for his ambitions. He was on both the Appropriations Committee and, more importantly, its Subcommittee on Defense. But further, he had very good relations with Speaker Tip O'Neill and also John Murtha who controlled that committee.

The Minutewoman

In addition to Wilson and Avrakotos, the third major character in Crile's embroidered and selective book is a woman named Joanne Herring. Herring was an extremely conservative Houston upper-class socialite. When she was growing up, she actually joined a group called the Minutewomen.[7] Herring was a TV personality in Houston and was famous for holding huge parties for other rich Texas Republicans like James Baker, who would become Ronald Reagan's Chief of Staff in 1981. When she married oil man Bob Herring she began to have foreign dignitaries from the Middle East to her home also. In fact, the State Department actually had her on their list as a good hostess to send foreign visitors for a stay.[8] She eventually met the chief of French intelligence, Count Alexandre de Marenches. He introduced her and her husband to the foreign minister of Pakistan. Yaqub Khan proposed that Bob Herring become an honorary consul. Herring declined but suggested Joanne, who accepted.[9] She then met the dictator General Zia and became a roving ambassador for him. As Avrakotos noted to Crile, Herring was important because it was she who got Wilson interested in the plight of Afghan refugees in Pakistan.[10] Herring knew Wilson from her lavish parties, at which she tried to connect with as many political luminaries as possible. But she specifically knew Wilson because "he had passed an important piece of oil and gas legislation that her husband had thought impossible."[11]

Herring got Wilson to meet her friend, the leader of the country, General Zia. Wilson now used his muscle on the Appropriations Committee to begin to raise the CIA's allotment for Afghanistan. To read Crile, one would think this was all done by Wilson, on his own initiative, and with no one watching his back at the White House. In reality, in these areas, it is the president who is supposed to propose these types of CIA budgets, simply because the Agency is an executive office. Congress then approves the request. But there may be an explanation for this. Many years later, author Robert Parry discovered an interesting handwritten memo at the Reagan Library in Simi Valley, California. It was located in the files of CIA officer Walter Raymond. It appears to be written by Reagan's National Security Advisor Robert McFarlane. McFarlane was another Texan who worked with Texas Senator John Tower who, quite naturally, knew Wilson. Reagan had appointed McFarlane National Security Adviser in 1983. McFarlane instructed Raymond to go and visit Wilson and to "seek to bring him into circle" quietly, since he could be very helpful in getting the White House money.[12] Today, this helps us understand Wilson's proper role in the whole affair. He was essentially the White House's secret moneyman in this giant operation. It was after this, in 1984, that the CIA budgets for Afghanistan now began to really soar into, first, the scores of millions, then the hundreds of millions.

But yet, this was really only half the allotment. Because Saudi Arabia had agreed to match whatever the CIA budget was. Therefore, if the CIA got 200 million for one year, it was actually 400 million. In the late eighties the total budget was over a billion dollars. With all this money coming in, the number of volunteers for the Mujahideen went into orbit. The ISI eventually trained and supplied hundreds of thousands of volunteers. And since the Pakistanis got to pick whom to back, it was radicals like Haqqani and Hekmatyar that got the large majority of the supplies. Whereas the moderate and capable commander Ahmad Shah Massoud received a small fraction of what Hekmatyar got.[13] Incredibly, after Massoud was assassinated by suspected Al Qaeda undercover operatives on orders of Bin Laden, Wilson actually called him "a Russian collaborator."[14] Massoud is the man who many commentators, including Coll, believe that the CIA should have backed from the start. He was the only commander capable of keeping the country together and avoiding a civil war after the Russians left. In 2001, the man Wilson called a Russian collaborator was named the National Hero of Afghanistan.

With this tremendous input of cash and weaponry, plus the addition of the Stinger shoulder launched missile to down the Hind attack helicopter, the tide began to turn. In 1985, when Mikhail Gorbachev took power in the USSR, he switched commanders and brought in more elite troops.[15] But by this time, the CIA weapons expert, Mike Vickers, had brought in such excellent communications equipment and such a wide variety of weaponry, that it was only a temporary reprieve. Gorbachev did not want to escalate the war. In order to win, he had to 1) invade Pakistan, and 2) bring in at least twice as many troops. He did not do either.

Before the Soviets left, there was one other thing that General Zia demanded. Wilson was going to run interference for him so he could build a nuclear bomb, even if his agents stole parts from the United States. Which they tried to do but were caught. With help from Reagan and Casey, Wilson actually got Congress not to take any retaliatory action against Pakistan, even though such retaliatory action was embedded in the law.[16] As a result, today Pakistan has approximately eighty nuclear warheads. With its many religious fanatics, perhaps no other nation poses such a threat to detonate a nuclear warhead as Pakistan. And Pakistan is not a signatory to the Nuclear Non-Proliferation Treaty.

Gorbachev's Offer

Gorbachev decided to start negotiating with Secretary of State George Schultz in 1987. A treaty was signed in Geneva in 1988. The Russian army completed its withdrawal in early 1989. The Soviets left behind Mohammad Najibullah as president. Gorbachev advocated a power sharing agreement between Najibullah and the moderate tribes. This was meant to keep the country unified and also to marginalize the influence of the religious radicals that Pakistan had backed.

The United Nations favored Gorbachev's proposal. But the agreement failed, in part because the United States favored a military solution all the way until the end of 1991.[17] Without Gorbachev's agreement in place, after the Russians left, Afghanistan descended into a long and nightmarish civil war. In retrospect, this is startling. Because, by 1988, any interested observer could see that the Pakistanis were backing violent fanatics like Haqqani and Hekmatyar all the way. And they were doing this with much of the money Moslem Saudi Arabia was giving to the effort. In fact, the Saudi intelligence officer, Ahmed Badeeb, was a former teacher of Bin Laden. According to Coll's *Ghost Wars*, Badeeb once said, "I loved Osama and considered him a good citizen of Saudi Arabia." Coll also notes that General Zia had taken much of the Saudi money and set up hundreds of madrassas along the Pakistan/Afghanistan border. These were schools and colleges of Islamic study. And they ended up training thousands of young Taliban students.

In the face of all this, Gorbachev found it surprising that the USA would not vigorously pursue this offer.[18] Did they really want to see Afghanistan become a religious radical haven and a proxy of Pakistan? Also, by this time, the United States was being explicitly warned by people who knew, like Benazir Bhutto. She told President Bush, "You are creating a Frankenstein."[19] And people in the United States Senate knew by then also, for example, Pat Moynihan, Gary Hart, and Gordon Humphrey.[20]

Charlie Wilson didn't see it that way. Even after meeting with a Soviet diplomat who tried to explain to him just how bad Hekmatyar was. After the Russians departed, and Wilson got an earful from the Saudis and the CIA, he began pushing for hundreds of millions to fight Najibullah.[21] Therefore, when we watch Wilson in his 2001 interview with Mike Wallace talking about a Marshall Plan for Afghanistan, or when we view the Playtone film and see Hanks arguing in committee for money for schools, one has to wonder: Who is kidding whom? In 1988 and '89, Wilson had a great opportunity to finally be a visionary statesman. He threw it away in order to be a typical rightwing southern Democrat. One who is always fighting the last war. It's not like he did not have good information in front of him to avoid the upcoming disaster. Even Crile admits he did.[22] So the reason the destruction continued to unfold was not the excuse Wilson proffered with Mike Wallace in 2001, namely that America lost interest after the Russians left. America did not lose interest at that point.[23] But the Bush administration, the CIA, and Wilson were all still fighting the Cold War. They could not buy Gorbachev as a true break with the Kremlin past. Which he was. So therefore, instead of taking his offer and forming a coalition government with the capable and fair Najibullah, they decided to keep the money flowing to the likes of barbarians like Hekmatyar.

Most of us know what happened after that. Unlike what the CIA predicted, Najibullah did not collapse quickly. He held out for three years, until 1992.[24] He then stepped down and took refuge in the United Nations sanctuary. The situation now got even worse. Afghanistan descended into a horrific and terrifying civil war. Hekmatyar and Haqqani now killed more Afghans than they ever did Soviets. But still, the charismatic Massoud held off the two of them from taking Kabul.[25] Even though they shelled half of the city to the ground. With the situation stalemated, Wilson's allies, the Pakistanis, sent in their own troops, the Taliban.[26] They took over the country, dragged Najibullah out of the sanctuary, castrated him, attached him to the back of a truck, and dragged him through the streets of Kabul. They then laid waste to the country and turned it into an anti-American haven: the home of Al Qaeda. After 9/11, the USA had to invade the country, while fighting armies they themselves had equipped and trained.

A Playtone Production

In this film of Crile's book, Hanks cannot use the excuse that he was an actor who had contracted himself out to a studio and was therefore working for someone else. He could use that pretext when he was starring in that fraudulent fantasy about the Catholic Church, Dan Brown's *The Da Vinci Code*. (Although, if Hanks really respected history, he would never even contemplate doing such a thing.) But for *Charlie Wilson's War* he has no such protection. He and his partner Gary Goetzman produced the film. Which means they had final approval of everything. It was their picture. But if one thought that Crile's book was not up to snuff, what can one say about this Playtone picture? Crile at least devotes his brief epilogue to the epic disaster that Wilson and his friends caused. In this film, there is exactly one sentence given over to that subject. At the end, after the Russians have left, Gust Avrakotos shows Wilson a report about some "crazies" moving into Afghanistan. The whole exchange takes place in about twenty seconds. And that is it. The implication being that this just happened in 1989. Which, as we have seen, is simply not true. The Pakistanis were backing radicals almost from the start.

Further, that exchange takes place at a party at Wilson's house. The problem is that Gust Avrakotos never was at any such party. Because he had retired from the CIA before the Russians left.[27] And, as depicted in the film, the party did not take place at Wilson's townhouse either. It was at CIA HQ.[28] And if Gust was not at that party, then he could not have said his celebratory line, "Here's to you motherfucker!" According to Crile, Wilson said that to himself in the privacy of his home as he watched the Russian troops leaving the war zone.[29]

So therefore, how does the film actually end? With Charlie Wilson at CIA headquarters getting a medal for what he did in Afghanistan. This really did happen. But the time was June of 1993. On the wall is a huge sign that says, "Charlie did it." Which was a quote from General Zia. A good question would have been: "Charlie did what?" For Afghanistan was descending into the final bloody throes of its civil war that year. The timing is reminiscent of Karl Rove arranging George W. Bush's landing on an aircraft carrier with the banner "Mission Accomplished," when, in fact, the worst part of the Iraq War was lying ahead.

And the film actually says that the CIA was backing Massoud. As more than one commentator has said, this is just an outright deception.[30] No one who has even read just Crile's book can say that. The last scene in the film dealing with the actual conflict in Afghanistan is Wilson/Hanks attempting to get money for a school. But we know that, after the Russians left, Wilson was still trying to get money for fighting the remnants of their regime.

Concerning that issue, in the film, there is no mention of Gorbachev's coalition government offer. Not even in passing. Which, really, is not that surprising, since it is not in Crile's book either. But at least Crile mentions the dictator Zia pursuing the bomb and Wilson riding shotgun for him. That entire interlude is absent from the film.

To go through the entire film to point out all the differences between what Crile depicts, and what the film depicts would take another essay. To use just one example, Crile does not have Gust making a play for Herring. Nor does he have Gust smashing a window at CIA HQ in front of his boss. But the point is this: Crile's book is a sickening whitewash about Wilson and Herring. Hanks's film is so sugar coated and such a half-truth, it almost makes Crile's book look realistic.

Hidden Agendas?

But that's still not the worst part. Sometimes it takes a while for the truth to surface about why people do the things they do. There is no doubt that Wilson and Herring were conservatives in foreign policy. But in the film, Hanks mouths a line about Wilson making $700 per week. Therefore, not only was Wilson a true patriot, he was a financially strapped and self-sacrificing patriot also. Which enhances his stature for the audience. As mentioned above, at the time of the Soviet invasion, Joanne Herring was married to an oilman. Crile tells you that much. He doesn't tell you the name of the energy firm Bob Herring ran. A fact that must have been known to him.

Herring headed a company called Houston Natural Gas.[31] Four years after his death in 1981, this company became Enron. General Zia was being friendly with the Herrings because he wanted Bob to drill for oil and natural gas in Pakistan.[32] It is uncertain if Herring did that in his lifetime. But there is no doubt that another company named Union Texas Petroleum did so. They got the general's permission in 1978. They were granted a 30 percent concession rate by Pakistan. When Joanne first needed help in fighting the Soviets, she told documentary filmmaker Melissa Roddy she turned to Wilson, "Because he was an old friend of the oil business."[33] Herring also told Roddy that after Reagan was inaugurated, she got an audience with fellow Texan and new Vice

President George Bush. It was only supposed to last fifteen minutes, but it went on for two hours. He was very polite but did not reply formally to her concerns. But a few days later, new Chief of Staff Jim Baker saw her at a party. He took her aside by the arm and confided to her, "We're going to give them a lot of good stuff."[34] This was in early 1981, before Herring had passed away.

In looking at Wilson's Financial Disclosures form for 1981, it is difficult to reconcile his $700 a week salary with his six figure stock holdings in an oil company called Supron. He held between $100,000 and $250,000 worth of stock in that company until May of 1982.[35] How is that possible on that salary? However it was done, in April of 1982, the aforementioned Union Texas Petroleum, with pipelines in Pakistan, purchased a controlling interest in Supron. A few months later, Wilson made his first official visit to Pakistan. Owning that much stock in a company that relied for its business on General Zia must have made Wilson a little more sympathetic to the dictator's demands.

The other oil company that had large interests in Pakistan at the time was Occidental. The day Reagan took office, James Baker sold his daughter's shares in that publicly traded company.[36] But Union Texas was privately held. And its primary law firm was Baker Botts, founded by Baker's great-grandfather. Charlie Wilson's financial interests corresponded with those in the White House. But it didn't stop there. After Wilson stepped down from Congress, he became a lobbyist. The lobbying work he did for Pakistan paid him $360,000 a year. Between the stock and his lobbying work, Wilson became a millionaire.[37]

But there is one last issue that needs to be elucidated. Why did General Zia do what he did? Why was he intent on undermining the cause of Afghan unity and freedom? We have mentioned Zia getting Wilson to protect him in his acquisition of nuclear weapons. And as Coll notes, there is little doubt that the ISI was skimming some of the weapons and supplies that Baker promised and the CIA was sending in by the shipload. But there is one other thing the ISI and Pakistan wanted from the USA.

In 1893, the British drew a geographic line running north and south for 1500 miles roughly parallel, but to the west of Pakistan. It was called the Durand Line. It was supposed to be part of a new border with India. But once Pakistan came into being in 1947 that line came to contain about 40 percent of her territory and much of the region now called Pashtunistan. That line was supposed to expire in 1993, and therefore Pakistan would have ceded much of her territory back to Afghanistan. After the Wilson alliance with General Zia, is it any wonder that the USA was now allying itself with Pakistan on this issue? The State Department was now saying that the Durand Line had not expired in 1993. Therefore, Pakistan did not need to cede any territory back to Afghanistan.[38] And at the time of Zia's death in 1988, Afghanistan was in no condition to demand any restoration.

As we can now see, like he did with Oswald, the late Charlie Wilson never got Afghanistan right. And years after his disastrous misjudgments had been exposed, Hanks repeated—in some ways he worsened—that distortion. As the reader can see, Playtone's heroes (i.e., Charlie Wilson, Joanne Herring, and General Zia are not what Hanks and Playtone depict them to be). And if Hanks told the full truth about them and portrayed the whole story, they would not be heroes at all. As someone from Playtone said, "We just can't deal with this 9-11 thing. Does it have to be so political?"[39] Sometimes the truth about American involvement overseas is like that. That is something the Powers That Be don't want to deal with since they are too invested in maintaining the status quo. Therefore, it's no surprise that the *New York Times* liked the film of *Charlie Wilson's War*. As we can see, Hanks's view of the world and recent history coincides with theirs. The *Times* called the film "a hoot."[40] Yes, it was a joke, but not for the reasons the Gray Lady says it was. But for Tom Hanks to feel he had to tell that story, in that way, reveals all we need to know about his view of America, and also what he sees as the function of history.

CHAPTER THIRTEEN

Where Washington Meets Hollywood

"Top Gun was the single best recruiting tool the Navy ever had
. . . . The CIA was looking for a project that could help them
do something similar."

—David Houle, Television Production Partners

In 2013, not one, but two films that were quite appreciative, even adulatory, of the Central Intelligence Agency were nominated for the Best Picture Oscar. Ben Affleck's *Argo* depicted what was perhaps the one success that the CIA and President Jimmy Carter had in Carter's entire ordeal with the fall of the Shah of Iran and the subsequent hostage crisis which did so much to collapse his presidency. Kathryn Bigelow's *Zero Dark Thirty* portrayed the CIA's operation to hunt down and kill Osama Bin Laden.

But that was topped by an unprecedented event in the history of the Oscars telecast. As veteran Hollywood journalist Ed Rampell noted, on February 24, 2013, the "most bizarre ballyhooing in Motion Picture Academy of Arts and Sciences history took place, turning the show's venue into the Dolby Theater of the Absurd."[1] As Jack Nicholson proceeded to announce the nominees for the Best Picture Oscar, a live telecast on the digital screen took us to the State Room in the White House. Via satellite transmission, Michelle Obama now materialized above Nicholson; her image dwarfing him in size and positioning. She appeared surrounded by young men and women in military regalia. After giving a little spiel about Hollywood Heart in these nominated films, it was Michelle Obama who was handed the envelope with the name of the winning film in it. Therefore, the Best Picture Oscar would be declared in Washington, not Los Angeles. She then announced that *Argo* had won. As Rampell noted, a member of the first family had never announced a winner at the Academy Awards, let alone given out the top honor. In other words, the CIA had been awarded not with just an Oscar, but one given to it by the First Lady, live from the White House.

There were some voices of dissent who questioned the appropriateness of this maneuver. Especially since *Zero Dark Thirty* depicted what many perceived to be a triumph for Michelle Obama's husband. If that film had won, the art of political self-congratulation would have soared to new heights. But for even those taken aback by this unseemly symbolic gesture of the blatantly political intervening in an artistic competition, very few noted that there had been a recent forerunner. At the Golden Globes, held just a few weeks earlier, there was another surprise political visitor. Except this time the personage appeared in the flesh. Former president Bill Clinton introduced Steven Spielberg's film *Lincoln* into consideration. Though not as spectacular, or as brazen—Clinton had been out of office for thirteen years—this should have given some people pause. But looking deeper at the circumstances, it also gave an indication of how and what had happened that paved the way for these two unprecedented crossover events.

The Michelle Obama sanctification of *Argo* was the result, and the triumph, of the longtime efforts of four men. Two of whom almost everyone knows; two of whom almost no one knows. The two that nearly everyone knows are Steven Spielberg and Tom Hanks. The two men who almost no one knows are Phil Strub and Chase Brandon. Since Strub and Brandon worked in the background, let us deal with them first.

Strub vs. Eisenhower

Most of us recall Dwight Eisenhower's famous 1961 Farewell Address. Director Oliver Stone used an abridged version of this televised speech at the start of his film *JFK*. Eisenhower warned of something new that had entered into the American equation of government, business, civil liberties, and democracy. He stated that, prior to World War II, there had been no permanent arms industry. But after the war the United States now had well over three million men and women in the military service. This immense commitment had now created an arms industry that was a huge and full-time corporate entity unto itself. Eisenhower said that the annual budget at that time for this military expenditure surpassed the net income of all American corporations. As a result, this colossal combination of a giant military machine, with an equally giant corporate conglomerate to feed it, had an immense "total influence—economic, political, even spiritual," and this new influence was felt in every city, every Statehouse, every office of the Federal government. He warned that this new military-industrial complex must be watched and guarded against, for to let this new pillar of power gain unwarranted influence would be disastrous. He then said, "We must never let the weight of this combination endanger our liberties or democratic process."

As Eisenhower dourly predicted, the unwarranted influence of what he called the Military-Industrial-Complex, is very much felt in the city of Hollywood. In fact, it is felt there almost every day. And it has not just endangered both liberty and the democratic process, it has already curtailed them. But as Eisenhower further stated, "Only an alert and knowledgeable citizenry can compel the proper meshing . . . so that security and liberty may prosper together." The problem is that almost no one knows who Phil Strub is, what he does, and how he wields an artistic power that literally no other person in Movieland can match. For as the Pentagon's liaison to Hollywood, Strub can force film producers to not just alter their screenplays, but to eliminate entire scenes. And beyond that, he can actually *eliminate* a film from a studio's production schedule altogether. And he has done so. In other words, in many instances, what the public sees in the theater is not what the producers of the film intended them to see. What they watch is Strub's altered and sanitized version. And beyond that, at its most extreme, Strub can deprive the public of their right to even see a film that was once headed into production. Yet, even today, after Strub has been around for decades, 99.9 percent of the viewing public does not even know who Phil Strub is, even though he has an immense impact on what the average person pays to see at the movie theater. And that is the way that Strub and the military wish it to be.

The bottom line is this: Phil Strub pretty much is in control of a monopoly. One that is as complete as that which Bill Gates and Microsoft or John Rockefeller and Standard Oil represented at their pinnacles. Except Strub is not in business for profits or market share. What he wants to do is control the perceptions and the images that Americans think about and see on screen once they are cozily ensconced in the darkness of the movie theater. More specifically, he wants to control how films depict the massive armed forces that Eisenhower was so worried about. How does he do this? By controlling how much of the military's equipment and weaponry the producer gets to use in his film. What determines the usage factor a producer gets from Strub? The contents and themes of his script. And if Strub does not like what is in that script, the producer does not get to rent the essential military hardware he needs in order to make the film. But as law professor Jonathan Turley pointed out, there is a problem here. The property Strub rents out does not belong to him. It was bought and paid for by the American public. And as Turley notes, Congress has never given Strub the authority to curtail free speech or limit artistic expression or shape public opinion.[2] But yet producers continue to bow down to Strub's demands. Even if it means giving up not only their rights and liberties, but the rights and liberties of those who pay to see their products.

How This Monopoly Works

Every year, many films having military type settings and themes are written and scheduled for production. They could be set in the Army, Air Force, Navy, Marines, even the Coast Guard. This means that the film production office then has to get in contact with either the Pentagon or the individual service that it needs to rent props, equipment, planes, ships, or weaponry from. Simply because that is the only place in America that a producer can go to secure these things for film rental. Certainly, one can rent uniforms from say Western Costume Company in North Hollywood. But how does one rent things like tanks, F-14 fighter jets, Black Hawk helicopters, or even an aircraft carrier? The answer is you have to go to the Pentagon. That usually means talking to Phil Strub.

The process goes like this: the company makes its request for assistance, detailing what items will be needed and when the film is set to begin shooting. Once that is submitted, five copies of the script are sent to the Pentagon liaison, Mr. Strub. He keeps one and forwards the others depending on what materials are in the request.[3] If Strub and his colleagues like the script, it is approved, and the request for assistance is forwarded. If they don't like it, they don't approve the request. Then the negotiations begin in order to attain approval.

Once the requested alterations are made, the process is still not completed. Because, quite often, the Pentagon assigns a caretaker to the film's production process. This person is on the set almost every day to see that the director and cast stay true to the revisions agreed to in order to get approval. A person very often used by the Army was Major David Georgi. If on the set alterations are outside the scope of the agreement, there is no problem. But if they are not, someone like Georgi will remind the director and producer of the agreement. As Georgi says, "If they don't do what I say, I take my toys and go away."[4]

And that is still not the end of it. After the film is done shooting and being edited for release, it must be screened in advance by the Pentagon brass. In other words, the film's first public preview is by the generals and admirals in Washington. This is their way of catching anything that still made it through the vetting process.[5] At this point, if there are still any elements that are objectionable, the Pentagon can now object to them. If they are not edited out, the military can do one or all of the following: 1) Take their seal of cooperation off the film, 2) Make it very difficult to get approval for that production company the next time around, and 3) refuse to exhibit the film on military bases in America and abroad.[6]

How far have producers gone in altering scripts to get Pentagon approval and help? It is not just a matter of editing out profanity, or drug usage, or scenes of excessive drinking. Literally whole scenes have been cut out of films. For example, in the Robert Duvall film *The Great Santini,* three scenes were cut out of the script, or so heavily altered that they did not resemble the original screenplay. [7] In the film *Battle Cry,* an entire supporting character, played by actor Victor Millan, was cut down to one line in the completed film. And Millan ended up being uncredited. The reason was that the Pentagon thought since that character's climactic speech was about racism in America, the communists could use it in propaganda wars.[8]

The Truth Makes No Difference

On the film *Thirteen Days* about the Cuban Missile Crisis, the Pentagon did not want to cooperate because they did not like the characterization of Air Force General Curtis LeMay. They objected to certain lines of dialogue by LeMay. In these he compared President Kennedy's decision to construct a blockade around Cuba, instead of bombing the island, to what Neville Chamberlain did at the Munich Conference. When the producers of the film proved with tapes that LeMay had actually said this, Strub's office made another objection. This time they objected to the scene where a U-2 pilot was shot down over Cuba. Again, the producers proved that this actually happened. They produced Kennedy's letter of condolence to the pilot's widow.[9]

After this, there was silence. So producer Peter Almond got in contact with Sen. Fred Thompson through his friend, the director of the film, Roger Donaldson. In turn, Thompson got in contact with Defense Secretary William Cohen. Not even Cohen could move Strub's office to cooperate with a film they did not like. Strub had insisted that the script "painted LeMay and the joint Chiefs in a false and negative light."[10] Strub was smart enough to not come out and say he wanted the facts changed. But according to Almond, the underlying conflict was that ". . . they didn't want to support a major film that showed their leadership taking positions that would very likely have led the world on the descent toward real nuclear confrontation."[11] Even if that was clearly the case, Strub wanted no part of it.

So Almond had to find airplanes elsewhere. In this case, the Philippines. They rented out planes and painted them and pulled them around on the ground to simulate they were taxiing on a runway. They used digital effects to imitate a U-2 in flight. This was all expensive and time consuming. But they were able to make an honest film instead of a dishonest one.

But Strub and the Pentagon got in the last dig. In February of 2001, the film's star, Kevin Costner, offered to hold a special screening of the film at Ramstein Air Base in Germany. The commanders at the base initially accepted the offer. After all, this kind of thing does not happen every day. But as the invite went up the chain it was ultimately rejected. The official reply was rich in irony. Colonel John Whitaker said that the Department of Defense had tried to make sure the film was accurate but these objections were ignored. Whitaker specifically mentioned the inappropriate portrayal of military leaders, specifically Curtis LeMay. Therefore, in their eyes, the film was a work of "historical revisionism."[12]

LBJ's Truth Does Make a Difference

Strub's predecessor in the film office was a man named Don Baruch. Strub's obstinance in extending aid to Almond can be contrasted with Baruch's prodigal generosity with John Wayne in the making of his Vietnam War film *The Green Berets*. Wayne was a dyed in the wool rightwing reactionary. Like many of these types he was what we now term a chickenhawk. That is, while glorifying wars and America's participation in them, he himself found ways to get out of his own commitments. Wayne did not serve in World War II. Wayne also liked to make films that expressed his political beliefs in opposition to others. For example, he so detested the classic Western *High Noon* that he made a film to oppose the themes in it, *Rio Bravo*. (This is one of Quentin Tarantino's favorite films, which tells you a lot about him.)

In 1965, Wayne was getting upset with the opposition to America's participation in Vietnam. President Johnson had won the 1964 election promising that he would not send American boys to fight a war that Asian boys should be fighting for themselves. As more than one commentator has written, "If any American president had ever promised anything to the American people, then Lyndon Johnson had promised to keep the United States out of the war in Vietnam."[13] The problem was that Johnson was being a slick and disingenuous politician about the issue. From almost the moment he took over for Kennedy, he had been planning to expand the war in Vietnam. All he needed to know was if the present American advisory force there could hold on long enough until after he was inaugurated. In fact, Johnson's secret planning group had targeted opening the war in January of 1965.[14] They did not miss this deadline by much. The first week of February marked the air attack codenamed Flaming Dart, the precursor to the gigantic Rolling Thunder air operation.[15] One month later, the first American troops landed at DaNang. Thus began the incredible escalation which would eventually top out with 540,000 combat troops in Vietnam. When Kennedy was killed there were none.

John Wayne visited South Vietnam in 1965. He then purchased the rights to Robin Moore's fiction book entitled *The Green Berets*. Wayne wrote the White House in December of 1966 explaining to President Johnson why he needed this film to explain the war to the American people.[16] He implored LBJ, "Someday soon a motion picture will be made about Vietnam. Let's make sure it is the kind of motion picture that will help our case throughout the world."[17]

But there was a problem with the first draft of the script. Moore's book was rather realistic and did not whitewash some of the activities the Berets were involved in, like torturing prisoners. That is one thing that scored no points with either Strub or Maruch. Therefore, a meeting was held in Washington in April of 1966 between John Wayne, who would direct and star in the film; his son Michael Wayne who would produce the picture; and screenwriter James Lee Barrett.[18] At this meeting, they were advised that any torture by either the Berets or South Vietnamese would have to be written out of the script. Secondly, any reference to cross border excursions into Laos would also have to be eliminated. The reader should note, as with the *Thirteen Days* script, the military was objecting to events that were true! The difference is that Almond and Costner chose not to cut those aspects of the script. Wayne and Barrett did.[19]

For that, they were amply rewarded. In 1967, they were allowed to film at Fort Benning, Georgia, for a period of 107 days. They were allowed to use Army troops as extras free of charge. They were allowed to use hundreds of weapons free of charge. Wayne was not charged for the use of equipment and aircraft, or for the troops operating them either. The bill submitted to Wayne's production company was a fraction of what any other production company would have paid.[20]

Unfortunately for the perpetrators, the Johnson/Wayne conspiracy to glorify the war did not pay off. The film was released about five months after the Tet offensive. Therefore, the public could not connect what they saw on television with what this propaganda film was saying. For example, the last scene of the film has Wayne walk off into the sunset with a young South Vietnamese lad who had previously been the adopted friend of another Beret. The message being that America can befriend and lead the Vietnamese. That wasn't the message Tet was bringing home to America. In fact, the film was so one-sided that Baruch wanted to take the Defense Department credit off the picture because he thought it would hurt the "propaganda value of the film."[21] In other words, he did not want to advertise the fact that the Defense Department was behind such an obvious exercise. The Waynes went along with the request. After all, Baruch had just saved their production company a ton of money.

In summing up this sordid affair, we should quote a memo from Johnson's famous "yes man" Jack Valenti, who was in the White House back then. When Wayne first got into contact with the president, Valenti noted to Johnson, "Wayne's politics are wrong, but if he makes this film it will be helping us." Shortly after, Jack Valenti became president of the Motion Pictures Producers Association. As author David Robb notes in his study of Pentagon influence on films, when Phil Strub's position was being phased out of existence due to budget cuts, Valenti responded rather oddly. He led a successful industry effort that pleaded with Secretary of Defense William Cohen to restore Strub's job. In fact, as Robb also notes, Valenti even offered to prescreen films they had cooperated on to the military at the MPAA offices in Washington. This is how compromised, how slavish, producers were and are with the Pentagon. And for this kind of leadership, Valenti was making well over a million dollars a year before he retired.

The CIA Opens Their Office

As Tricia Jenkins notes in *The CIA in Hollywood*, the Agency came late to actually opening up a direct liaison office with the studios. The Pentagon and the FBI had long been in operation in this manner before Chase Brandon formally opened the CIA shop in 1996. This is not to say the Agency had no presence or interest in Movieland prior to this. For example, veteran black operator Edward Lansdale had gotten writer/director Joseph Mankiewicz to alter the story of Graham Greene's classic 1956 warning about America's growing involvement in Vietnam, *The Quiet American*. In the novel, the character of Alden Pyle is a CIA agent under the cover of an American aid worker. He secretly arranges a bombing with the help of a high level South Vietnamese officer in order to increase the chaos in Saigon. Reportedly, Greene modeled Pyle on Lansdale. For the film, Lansdale got Mankiewicz to change Pyle from a CIA agent into a toy manufacturer. And the bombing is now done by the communists. Finally, at the end, the communists trick the English journalist Thomas Fowler into taking part in a plot to kill Pyle. After his work with Mankiewicz, "Lansdale wrote to his friend President Ngo Dinh Diem of South Vietnam that the film was an excellent change from "the original and should aid in Diem's making more friends in Vietnam."[22]

Another Agency triumph was the recruitment of Paramount executive Luigi Luraschi in the fifties. Luraschi worked to limit the number of awards a film like 1952's *High Noon* would win. He reported on suspected leftist leanings of people in the business. He also worked to install minority actors in certain films so the Soviets could not criticize the movie industry for being segregated.[23] In addition to infiltrating and recruiting certain people into the film colony, the CIA did more traditional propaganda services. For instance, they broadcast dozens of episodes of *Dynasty* into East Germany to sell them capitalism as a way of life.[24]

Robert Gates's Task Force

In 1989, with the fall of the Berlin Wall, there began to be a chorus of people in Congress, like Senator Pat Moynihan, who questioned whether or not there really was a need for the CIA. Two years later, in 1991, CIA Director Robert Gates created a Task Force trying to promote openness about the Agency. One of the reasons he did so was to try and counteract the negative image of the Agency in the media, including TV and film. As Jenkins reveals, the memorandums show "that the CIA faced a serious image problem and wanted to find more media-savvy ways of enhancing its public support under the guise of 'greater openness.'"[25] One of the proposals put forth was the appointment of an official spokesperson to appear on television "to refute media allegations and set the record straight."[26]

Another memorandum argued that "working with Hollywood could help the Agency with its public image."[27] The memo said that the Agency's Public Affairs Office had already helped aid some productions by letting them film some scenes at Agency headquarters in Langley, Virginia. This had helped portray the CIA's "activities accurately and without negative distortion."[28] The memos argued that the Agency should do more of this, that is, trade access for input into screenplays. And the authors specifically stated that, even though they had known for a while that Oliver Stone was making a film about the JFK assassination, the Agency "did not contact him to volunteer an Agency viewpoint."[29] It appears that the combination of the results of this inquiry plus the debacle of the Aldrich Ames scandal provoked the CIA to make a proposal for its own TV series. It was to be called *The Classified Files of the CIA*.[30]

The model for this program was the TV series *The FBI* which had run on ABC from 1965–74. It was largely controlled by the Bureau and was seen essentially as a propaganda outlet. The company chosen by the Agency to produce this show was Television Production Partners (TPP) headed by Jack Myers and David Houle.[31] They were chosen because of their reputation of being supportive of the American lifestyle, plus the fact that they secured their own advertisers in advance, without relying on the network. As the program began to head into production, there began to be problems with just how much control TPP and its appointed producers, Steve Tisch and Aaron Spelling, would have over the content of the show. TPP had given the CIA an extraordinary amount of control. Tisch and Spelling wanted to bring that factor back into traditional boundaries. But still, a contract was signed and the program had been sold to Twentieth Century Fox; but for some reason it was not produced.[32] So the CIA now tried something else.

Chase Brandon Moves the Mountain

Perhaps no person in the history of the Agency has been more responsible for rehabilitating its image in television and the movies than Chase Brandon. Brandon had been a twenty-five-year veteran of the Clandestine Services branch before he became the CIA's first chief of their Entertainment Liaison Office in 1996.[33] He would stay in that position for over a decade. And there is no doubt what his mission was or how he perceived it. Therefore, Brandon was not going into his assignment cold. Further, one of the CIA's former allies in Congress, Senator Bob Kerrey, also urged the Agency to get involved in this kind of image enhancement.[34]

To get an idea of what Brandon perceived as the problem, let us have him describe the trouble as he himself saw it. In talking about the villains in political thrillers, he said, "They are always fomenting revolution or serving as hit men. There is always some ugly representation of us as a conspiratorial government overthrow apparatus."[35] Brandon also said:

> "Year after year, as moviegoers and TV watchers, we've seen our image and our reputation constantly sullied with egregious, ugly misrepresentations of who we are and what we stand for. We've been imbued with these extraordinary Machiavellian conspiratorial capabilities."[36]

He went on to say that "The real work that people do at the CIA is eminently more intriguing than some nonsense that some screen writer whips up out of the muse of his imagination."[37] When Brandon took his job he said the CIA finally realized that if the Agency did not work directly within the system ". . . we were leaving ourselves open for misrepresentations. We have been systematically typecast as the bad guys in one movie after another." He concluded with this: "So we decided to help the industry portray the Agency more accurately and fairly portray the CIA in scripts."[38] Clearly, Chase Brandon did not want to see any more major productions like *JFK, Air America,* and *Three Days of the Condor.* He immediately set about his task of moving the mountain. Whatever side of the argument one tallies in on for this issue, it is hard to deny that he was quite successful in achieving his goal.

Brandon decided to get the entire Agency management team involved in his efforts to reverse what he thought was the demeaning image of his employer in TV and films. This went all the way up to and included CIA Director George Tenet. Brandon's first real success was a Paramount Studios production for Showtime cable television film, *In the Company of Spies.* Brandon was involved with this film for over a year. He actually saw several drafts of the script and bounced it back to the writers with his ideas. Both the filmmakers and the actors met with high officials in the Agency at Langley. The result was so much appreciated by the CIA that the picture premiered at Langley with 500 Showtime, Paramount, and CIA guests on hand. The Agency even invited Washington luminaries like Alan Greenspan, and John Podesta and journalists like Cokie Roberts and Andrea Mitchell to attend.[39]

From there, things got even better for Brandon. He actively worked on a TV series called *The Agency.* Producer and writer Michael Beckner again submitted drafts of each script to the CIA representative. Brandon was so pleased with these scripts that he forwarded them up the chain to clear access to the production team to actually enter into CIA HQ and film there. This included the highest administrative levels at Langley. As with the Pentagon approval process, Beckner revealed that he understood how to get access. He said that his scripts were not like a lot of the previous ones: ". . . it also wasn't like a lot of films that featured CIA agents who eventually go rogue only to come back and try to assassinate the president."[40] This show was so CIA-friendly that an original CIA assigned technical advisor became an associate producer of the series.

Brandon and Tenet liked Beckner's series so much that it also was supposed to premiere at Langley. The problem is that the attacks of 9/11 cancelled the showing. Considering what we know from reviewing both the book and the film of *Charlie Wilson's War,* this should have been a disaster for the CIA. For, in many ways, the attacks were a classic case of what the CIA calls "blowback." The attacks originated in the rather unwise CIA support given to religious extremists who should never have been given that kind of unlimited weaponry, supplies, and money. But because of the characters of those manning the White House, President George W. Bush and Vice President Dick Cheney, these horrendous and irresponsible failures were shoved under the rug. Unlike what President Kennedy did after the Bay of Pigs, there was no presidential review process which resulted in the termination of those responsible for the debacle.[41]

With this kind of support, Brandon now used Beckner's show to actually deflect criticism of the CIA for its failure to predict and combat the new War on Terror. For example, the tag line of the series was, "Now, more than ever, we need the CIA." Further, the series actually depicted the Agency as *refusing* to torture suspects, and even refusing to turn them over to countries like Israel and Saudi Arabia that would.[42] This, of course, is not at all accurate because, as many reporters have shown, it was actually the CIA leading the way in the art and science of torture. To the point of even choosing to do it on the territory of client states, so they could not personally be prosecuted later. It was actually the FBI, the State Department, and parts of the Pentagon which argued against it.[43]

But not only was it Chase Brandon aiding the effort to conceal the disastrous decisions made in the Afghan war. So were certain conservative elements in Hollywood. They now joined forces directly with the administration to support this blowback called the War on Terror.

Bruce Ramer is one of the most powerful entertainment lawyers in the film colony. He was been at the firm of Gang, Tyre, Ramer, and Brown for over four decades. He is, for all intents and purposes, that firm's managing partner. His company is one of the top three entertainment law firms in Hollywood. At one time or another, Ramer's client list has included the likes of Bob Zemeckis, Demi Moore, Rob Minkoff, George Clooney, Clint Eastwood, and, key to our narrative, Steven Spielberg. In fact, the shark in Spielberg's movie *Jaws* was named Bruce.[44] In the movie business, an agent or lawyer is measured by his client list. But Ramer is also a former president of the American Jewish Committee and also a member of the Council on Foreign Relations. He has been associated with the Corporation for Public Broadcasting through both the Bush and Obama administrations. Ramer hosted a meeting "featuring Bush administration officials in his Beverly Hills office in the days following 9/11 to discuss ways the film and TV businesses could help fight terrorism."[45] It is not certain if Karl Rove was present at Ramer's meeting, but it has also been reported that Rove journeyed to Los Angeles for this purpose also.[46] As one person at these meetings stated, what Rove wanted was the film industry, TV industry, and music industry to produce propaganda. Rove was putting a lot of pressure on these leaders of the entertainment industry for "the kind of support

Hollywood gave the United States during World War II."[47] This exceptional Washington/Beverly Hills effort, plus Brandon's growing record of success, constituted a real turning point for the CIA's liaison.

Brandon Goes Wide

Chase Brandon now worked directly on the TV series *Alias*. That show was created by Spielberg's friend J. J. Abrams. The show's star, Jennifer Garner, actually did a recruiting commercial for the CIA.[48] It is hard to believe, but to demonstrate how far Brandon had come in reversing the CIA's image in the movies, he actually *appeared* in a DVD segment of the film *The Recruit*. He explained how to apply for the Agency, and how difficult it is to be accepted. And the film's producer, Jeff Apple, also appeared on screen and endorsed the recruitment message. Which, of course, amounted to having a joint Hollywood/Langley commercial in the film's feature menu.

The triumph of Chase Brandon's career was probably his work on the film *The Sum of All Fears*. This film was based on a Tom Clancy novel depicting what could happen if a nuclear weapon fell into the hands of a terrorist group. Ben Affleck played a CIA analyst working to identify the group, a neo-Nazi ultra-wealthy Austrian who leads a like-minded band of compatriots. They are intent on starting World War III by using the bomb against America and then blaming the Russians, thereby having both superpowers destroy each other. Which will pave the way for them to try and control a European revival.

Brandon was literally on the set advising things on a day-to-day basis.[49] Affleck plays a CIA Russian specialist who is the hero in the story and it is his analytical abilities that literally save the world. Affleck worked directly with the CIA's Russian analysts. Director Phil Alden Robinson actually met Director George Tenet. This might explain how the portrayal of the Director in the book got changed. In the book, the man is an inept political appointee who has little input into solving the crisis. In the film, he is a highly competent and demanding leader who advises Affleck never to go beyond what he can actually prove. The film was begun before 9/11, but not released until after the attacks. As more than one critic pointed out, it was an excellent tonic for the aftermath. It depicted the CIA as being much wiser than the politicians it served and, unlike the true facts, being well aware of the danger being posed by splintered terrorist groups outside of the Cold War axis. Again, Brandon was part of the publicity package for the film.[50]

How successful was Chase Brandon? By 2007, CIA attorney John Rizzo stated that the Agency now had a "very active" network of people in Hollywood helping "in whatever way they can to give back."[51] This undoubtedly was made possible by Brandon's direct work with writers and producers, and his insistence on being on the set so he could interface with actors and directors. For example, in 2006, Tom Cruise and Abrams met with CIA officers to discuss ways to present the Agency "in as positive a light as possible for *Mission Impossible III*." Brandon worked closely with Bob Towne on the script.[52] When he retired in 2007, his successor Paul Barry said he took all documents from his office with him.[53] Barry stayed on the job only until 2008. Apparently, Brandon had achieved what the CIA always wants to achieve: a self-sustaining program. This is one which they do not have to pay for, or deny the existence of. If that is an accurate assessment, they owe much to Spielberg and his close friend Tom Hanks.

The Secret of Steven's Success

Steven Spielberg achieved his spectacular success by becoming, in more than one critic's phrase, a "poet of suburbia." In films like *Close Encounters of the Third Kind* and *E.T.* he took average middle class people from the suburbs, placed them in incredible circumstances, and had them act in rather admirable, perhaps heroic, ways. It is a formula that paid him phenomenal dividends in that it allowed millions of people to easily recognize and identify with the characters in his films.

But yet, as Joseph McBride makes clear in his biography of Spielberg, this is rather paradoxical. Simply because it is not what the famous director felt like as he was growing up: first in Phoenix and then in Saratoga, California, to the west of San Jose. Those two areas were made up predominantly of WASPs when Spielberg lived there. But Spielberg's family was Jewish. Further, he was small and frail in junior and senior high school. He has neatly described his dilemma in all this: "I was Jewish and wimpy when I grew up. . . . In Arizona too, where few are Jewish and not many wimpy."[54] He complained about the insularity and peculiarity of his upbringing to his mother, "Everyone else's mother is normal. They go bowling. They go to PTA meetings and they play bridge."[55] It is this outsider quality that Spielberg always felt and which he was very sensitive and self-conscious about that molded his approach to his films. As his mother later said, "The conventional always appealed to Steven, maybe because we weren't." Clearly, this is one of the reasons that Spielberg later became a poet, and a romantic one, about middle class life. Because it's the life he always wanted, but felt he never had.

As most of us would be, the director was even more frank about this once he achieved his success. In a quote we should remember because of the discussion at hand, he said, "I never felt comfortable with myself, because I was never part of the majority. . . . I felt like an alien. . . . I wanted to be like everybody else."[56] Amplifying this idea, he was even more explicit about it: "I've always worked to be accepted by the majority. I care about how I'm perceived."[57] As a child, he wanted his parents to hang Christmas lights outside. They tried to explain to him that they could not do that since Christmas was not a Jewish holiday. So they were going to put decorations out for Hanukkah. He told them not to, since people would think they were Jewish. Which they were.[58]

Spielberg was born in 1946, therefore he grew up in the sensational six-ties. In that tumultuous decade he went from being an adolescent to a young man, which is when most young men develop a political identity. Spielberg says about this period in his life, "I grew up in the sixties, but I was never with flower power, or Vietnam protests, like all my friends. I was always at the movies."[59] (Why would the two areas, political protest and film, be mutually exclusive?) Although he says he admired President Kennedy, the only film tribute he could think of for the deceased head of state was a three-minute documentary about his famous rocking chair.[60]

When Spielberg's family moved to Saratoga, California, his parents divor-ced after he graduated from high school. The young man moved to Los Ang-eles and went to film school at Long Beach State. He made a short film which brought him to the attention of Sidney Sheinberg, head of television at Univer-sal Studios. Sheinberg offered him a seven-year contract. So Spielberg dropped out of college after a bit more than two years. Today, he regrets that decision because he says college could have helped him. If he had stayed in college, "I might have delayed my career by a couple of years, but I think I would have had a much more well-rounded education."[61]

That short film Sheinberg saw was 1968's *Amblin'*. This was a film about two young people hitchhiking across the country: a young man and a girl who meet on the road accidentally. Although it was made at the height of the sixties cataclysm—the year both Martin Luther King and Bobby Kennedy were assassinated, and Richard Nixon was elected president—it was really a boy-girl film. If it is about anything, it's about a young man pretending to be a free spirit, but the girl finding out at the end that he isn't. As time went on, Spielberg came to despise the film. He said he couldn't look at it anymore because, "It really proved how apathetic I was during the sixties." When he watched it, it demonstrated to him why, "I didn't go to Kent State . . . or I wasn't protesting when my friends were carrying signs and getting clubbed. . . ."[62] He then added that the film was devoid of any meaning or overtones because he was immersed in movies up to his nose and the film is a slick by-product of that mentality.

The Success Spreads

To many people, this carried over to his first feature film, 1974's *The Sugarland Express*. With its (partially) true story about two outlaws traveling across Texas with a captured policeman in tow, some commentators saw this as a kind of triple diluted version of *Bonnie and Clyde*. Stephan Farber gave the film a blistering review in The *New York Times*. He called the film "perfectly synthetic—pure Hollywood—from first frame to last." He wrote that the film was "slick, cynical, mechanical, empty. . . . Everything is underlined; Spielberg sacrifices narrative logic and character consistency for quick thrills and easy laughs."[63] He said it reminded him of "a shifty campaign speech designed to please every segment of the public." Farber honed in on what Spielberg later came to conclude about himself, that, like many other young filmmakers of the era, the young twenty-eight-year-old director knew a lot about making movies, but "Unfortunately, they are ignorant of everything else. They haven't had time to read a book; they are technical wizards with pea-sized brains."

The Sugarland Express was not a big commercial hit. But, as everyone knows, Spielberg's next film was. *Jaws* became the first of the modern "summer hit blockbusters." It altered the way summer escapist fare was released and advertised. It marked the beginning of a move toward massive ad campaigns and what is called "saturation booking" (i.e., booking a film its first week in thousands of theaters). The film's success was also a milestone for the director. Spielberg fully expected to be nominated for an Oscar for his work on the movie. He was so confident that he brought a film crew into his office to shoot his reaction to now being part of the club of which he always wanted to be a member.[64] Although he did not get the nod, this indicates something about his persona. Some directors, once they become successful, use their success to get away from the Hollywood scene and factory system, for example, Stanley Kubrick. Spielberg never did anything like that. As he said about himself, he wanted to be part of the majority.

As McBride notes in his biography, what people consider Spielberg's serious films, *Amistad, Schindler's List, Munich, Lincoln,* and *The Color Purple,* are all projects that other people brought to him. For instance, *Schindler's List* was purchased by Sheinberg for Spielberg in 1982. Spielberg had never even heard of the book by Thomas Keneally. It then took him ten years, and constant badgering by Schindler survivor Leonard Page, to finally make the movie. He even tried to pass the project on to other directors, like Roman Polanski, to make.[65] Ironically, it was the film that he didn't want to make that finally brought him the Oscar he so much wanted and the respectability he always craved. In fact, he said later that if he had not won that award he probably would have been shattered.[66]

Steven, Clinton, Obama and the War on Terror

It was the prestige that this film gave him that now allowed Spielberg entry into the political circles of world leaders. He met with the two most powerful leaders in the world at that time, President Bill Clinton and Russian president Boris Yeltsin. He was also feted by several other world leaders who wanted to talk to him about the film. Very soon after the film's premiere, Spielberg began talks with film executive Jeff Katzenberg and former talent agent and music impresario David Geffen to form their own studio called DreamWorks. This time period, with his growing friendship with Clinton, and his alliance with Katzenberg and Geffen, really became the beginning of Spielberg's becoming a political force. Because his two partners, Katzenberg and Geffen, were two of the biggest contributors to the Democratic Party in Hollywood. Spielberg quickly joined their efforts. From 1997 to 2009, Spielberg and his wife, actress Kate Capshaw, gave almost $700,000 to political candidates. Like Katzenberg, almost all of it went to Democrats.

That kind of money gets the donor a lot of access. So does agreeing to direct a pet project of the president's. When Spielberg presented the Washington premiere of *Amistad,* President Clinton asked him to direct a documentary short called *The Unfinished Journey,* which Spielberg did. Over time, the two became fast friends. Clinton stayed at Spielberg's Pacific Palisades home on his visits to California. And, likewise, Spielberg now became a frequent guest at the Clinton White House.[67] All of this eventually paved the way for Clinton's surprise appearance at the Golden Globes to introduce his close friend's film about Abraham Lincoln. And it was around this time, the late nineties, that Spielberg became attached to the *Saving Private Ryan* project, which cemented his friendship with Hanks, and led to their contributions to Ambrose's World War II museum in New Orleans. Spielberg had now achieved what he always wanted to from his boyhood days back in Phoenix. He was not just a Hollywood insider, but a Washington insider. He was now finally part of the majority. In fact, he was a full-fledged member of the club that he always felt detached from.

His backing of Ambrose shows that his understanding and interest in history is at about the level of his friend, Tom Hanks. This is furthered by McBride's revelation that Spielberg purchased the rights to Scott Berg's biography of Charles Lindbergh, sight unseen, in 1998. Quite naturally, the film has not been made. Spielberg apparently only knew about the man's trans-Atlantic flight. None of the assistants in the office informed him that Lindbergh later became a leading isolationist during World War II, a Nazi sympathizer, and was an anti-Semite. Further, that he fathered a secret family with three children by a German woman at the same time he was married to Anne Morrow in the United States.

Spielberg's association with the White House continued through the Barack Obama years. And as with Clinton's appearance at the Golden Globes, this helped pave the way for Michelle Obama's Washington/Los Angeles digital appearance at the Oscars. Spielberg hosted two dinners for Obama in 2008. He also directed a short for the Democratic convention that year. Again, this kind of track record, and money, gets someone access. Therefore Spielberg was sent VIP tickets for Obama's inauguaration.[68] Later, for a White House Correspondents' Association Dinner, Spielberg appeared in a humorous short kidding Daniel Day Lewis's method acting approach with Barack Obama as Barack Obama.

It is both relevant and interesting to note Spielberg's gushiness about Obama at the time of his first inauguration:

> "He's young, he has tremendous optimism and courage about this country, and the most important thing is, he's got great ideas. He's a president of ideas. . . . This is more than just a presidential election, this is really a new beginning.[69]"

To most commentators, Obama's disappointment has been precisely because he has not been a new beginning. He hasn't been much of a new anything. In fact, many of his national security ideas are holdovers from George W. Bush. A man who many historians, like the illustrious Sean Wilentz, rank as perhaps the worst president ever. And does not Obama's comment on the passing of the reactionary British Prime Minister Margaret Thatcher remind one of what Bush would have said:

> With the passing of Baroness Margaret Thatcher, the world has lost one of the great champions of freedom and liberty. . . . Here in America, many of us will never forget her standing shoulder to shoulder with President Reagan, reminding the world that we are not simply carried along by the currents of history—we can shape them with moral conviction, unyielding courage and iron will. Michelle and I send our thoughts to the Thatcher family and all the British people as we carry on the work to which she dedicated her life—free peoples standing together, determined to write our own destiny.

Finally, let us note how Spielberg reacted to the reception to his film *Minority Report*. That film proposed a future world where all sorts of crime prevention techniques, both technical and human, are allowed. Even where sages predict crimes and people are arrested before they commit them. Although the film's script was finalized and production completed before the 9/11 attacks, it was released in the summer of 2002. Therefore, with the passage of the Patriot Act, the ideas in the film became quite topical. Spielberg responded with a statement as dismaying as his rather naïve predictions about Barack Obama. He actually seemed to back the Patriot Act: "Right now, people are willing to give away a lot of their freedoms in order to feel safe." He then proceeded to back President Bush in this rollback of personal rights, "As George W. Bush says, root out these individuals who are a danger to our way of living. I am on the president's side in this instance." He did attach a qualifier—how much freedom should we give up?—but it was of degree, not kind.[70]

As McBride notes, Spielberg did not even come out against Bush's 2003 invasion of Iraq. During the run up to the Iraq war, he said, "I'm not an advocate of pulling back the CIA's and the FBI's far-reaching powers right now. I think this is a time of war." Even though it was clear before it happened that the excuses for the Iraq War were invented and manufactured. Spielberg even said those transparently false pretenses were "solid and rooted in reality."[71] It actually took two years for the man who had no political identity in the sixties to come to his senses. In 2005, he told the German magazine *Der Spiegel* that he was now against the war and the restrictions placed on citizen's freedoms. This was one year after two government reports, one by David Kay and one by Charles Duelfer, demonstrated that, unlike what Bush and Secretary of State Colin Powell had proclaimed, Iraq had no stockpiles of weapons of mass destruction.

Like Director, Like Star

As we have seen, Tom Hanks also grew up in Northern California. He also felt like an outsider. Not because of his religion or physical stature, but because his fractured family gave him little stability. As his biographer has said of him, although he liked to masquerade as a free spirit, like the young man in Spielberg's film *Amblin'*, he spent much of his time searching for the idealized family life he missed as a child. He tried joining a Christian Fundamentalist church. This worked for a while. But there was something else that nourished him through his troubled youth. As has been mentioned, he was an avid television watcher, particularly of programs such as the documentary miniseries *The World at War* and the anthology series *Biography*. This is where he got his sense of history. For, as with Spielberg, Hanks dropped out of college.[72] Therefore, his sense and appreciation of history didn't develop beyond these middlebrow types of visual presentations. But it's clear that once he garnered enough weight in the industry, these kinds of Hallmark Hall of Fame productions became the model for his ideas about what history was and how it should be presented to the public. In the Ambrose success tradition, it was to be a homogenized, pasteurized form of nourishing milk for the public. Even when—as we have seen with *Charlie Wilsons' War*—what he bought into was a complete distortion of what the real history was.

As we have seen, Spielberg and Hanks bought into Ambrose as a historian and were quite generous in their donations to his National World War II museum. Douglas Brinkley was Ambrose's protégé at the University of New Orleans. When Ambrose resigned, Brinkley became the Director of the Eisenhower Center there. Apparently, he was appreciative of the actor's support of his mentor. For he actually wrote an article for *Time*, trying to extol and explain what Hanks's qualities were as a history buff.[73] In this article Brinkley has to stoop to stating that Jacques Cousteau "first lured a TV-obsessed teenage Hank to take biology seriously." His favorite book was Truman Capote's *In Cold Blood*. This engineering of the nonfiction novel is supposed to be the basis for the actor/producer's miniseries productions like *The Pacific*. There is no full disclosure in the article about the Ambrose/Brinkley association, or how that would explain why a professor like Brinkley would somehow aggrandize someone like Hanks. Somehow *Time* did not think that was important.

Like Spielberg, Hanks was quite enthusiastic about Bill Clinton and his presidency. He was also a visitor at the White House on more than one occasion. He was so star struck, he had a hard time believing Clinton was actually talking to him.[74] But Hanks went even beyond Spielberg in this regard. He actually intimated that someday he might run for office himself. Therefore, in 2004 when he presented at the Oscars, the orchestra played "Hail to the Chief" when he came onstage.[75] He backtracked slightly on this by saying he would need to learn more about law and economics. (This author would add history to that all too short list.)

Hanks also did not say anything about President Bush's clearly fabricated reasons for invading Iraq. Which meant he was putting the troops Hanks says he cares so much about in harm's way needlessly. In other words, he was playing with their lives for no credible security reason. Even worse, his staff had created those reasons out of whole cloth. But apparently that was no big deal. Because Hanks appeared with Bush at a dedication for the World War II Memorial he had helped sustain.[76]

Like Spielberg, Barbara Streisand, and George Clooney, Hanks continued in the transfer of his allegiance from Clinton to Barack Obama. In 2008, he went on YouTube and gave Obama an endorsement that almost made

Spielberg's look mild. For some reason, he tried to compare Obama becoming president with George Washington handing the keys to the White House to John Adams in 1797. In 2012, he said he was endorsing him again and he actually went beyond that. He narrated a seventeen-minute campaign ad that featured tributes from Joe Biden and Rahm Emmanuel.

With these kinds of associations in the foreground, and with Chase Brandon and Phil Strub in the background, it's no wonder that Hollywood has been brought to heel by the likes of Clinton and Obama. As Robert Reich noted in *Locked in the Cabinet*, his fascinating memoir about working in the Clinton White House, what they were doing in public was essentially a diversion for the media. When Reich actually tried to get positive programs through for things like job retraining, they would not pass Congress. This was explained to him by chairman of the Budget Committee, Marty Sabo, a Democrat. He told the befuddled Secretary of Labor, "We're owned by them. Business. That's where the campaign money comes from now. In the 1980s we gave up on the little guys." When Reich persisted in trying to get big money for programs to help the poor better themselves and give breaks to the middle class, the president smiled and said words to the effect: Bob you don't understand. We're Eisenhower Republicans here.

And that, unfortunately, is the sorry truth about what has happened to the American political system today. With the choices the public has in front of them, it's not a matter of reviving America, or reforming the system, or trying to do what is needed to improve schools, hospitals, or housing. It is simply a matter of which political party will delay America going to hell in a hand basket. What celebrities like Hanks and Spielberg do with their puerile understanding of history and politics is legitimize the brutal hegemony of the two party system. At the same time that hegemony marginalizes people who really want to change things, for example, Howard Dean, Ross Perot. It also discourages the founding of any new political party that really understands what needs to be done. It's people like Hanks and Spielberg who keep this dead puppet show alive with images of Michelle Obama reigning over Tinsel Town as CIA associated movies garner nominations and awards. One of them glorifying her husband's killing of Osama bin Laden, a victory that allowed him to begin a drone program that initially disguised its inability to discriminate between actual targets and innocent civilians.[77] When Chase Brandon was working with Michael Beckner, he actually got him to test out ideas for him. One of those ideas was that the CIA had a Hellfire missile fired from a Predator drone. Another was that the CIA had a biometric detection system that was so sensitive it could detect a terrorist entering the country. Beckner could not understand why Brandon was pushing this idea on him. The CIA liaison admitted they didn't have that kind of technology yet. But he added, he wanted that show inserted anyway. Because, "Terrorists watch TV too."[78] In other words, Beckner was to run a program for pure propaganda, counter-intelligence purposes.

If you can do something like that, then the system has been rigged. You can retire. Which is what Chase Brandon, with the help of Hanks and Spielberg, was able to do.

CHAPTER FOURTEEN

Playtone and *Parkland*

"We're going to do the American public a service. A lot of conspiracy types are going to be upset."

—Tom Hanks to Douglas Brinkley

In discussing what actually became of the Hanks/Goetzman attempt to make an HBO miniseries out of Vincent Bugliosi's *Reclaiming History*, we must not lose sight of what we learned in the last chapter. That is the huge influence that Chase Brandon, and to a lesser extent, his successor Paul Barry, had on film and television depictions of the CIA. Brandon went into his position with a clearly defined goal: to revive and purify the image of the CIA on television and in films. In large part, he succeeded in achieving his goal. To the point that the Agency had people in the industry now who saw it as their duty to "give back" to them. In addition to the programs and films we have already discussed, there are television shows on the air like *24, Covert Affairs, Homeland*, and *The Americans*. Although *24* was discontinued, at the time of this writing it is scheduled to return in 2014. Also scheduled for 2014 is a miniseries called *The Assets*. This program will be scripted by two veteran CIA officers, Sandra Grimes and Jeanne Vertefeuille. It will look at the end of the Cold War through the eyes of the CIA and its agents. *The Americans* is a series just started up in 2013. It was also created and produced by a former CIA agent named Joe Weisberg. That is an important point to note. For Weisberg's executive producer is a man named Graham Yost. Yost is a close working associate of Tom Hanks. He has worked with Hanks as far back as 1998's *From the Earth to the Moon*. But he also worked on Playtone's two World War II miniseries, *Band of Brothers*, and *The Pacific*. In fact, he served in the same function on the latter series as he does on *The Americans*, executive producer. Which means he is the liaison between the TV network and the production entity.

On *Charlie Wilson's War*, Playtone hired former CIA officer Milt Bearden as their technical advisor. Bearden was the CIA station chief in Islamabad who ran their side of the Mujahedeen war against the Soviets. In 1999, he wrote an infamous editorial for the *New York Times* in which he said that the danger posed by Osama Bin Laden had been blown out of proportion. Further, in referring to Bin Laden's following (Al Qaeda) he wrote that the romantic mythology about it "has become more dangerous than the man himself."[1] He then went on to say that America should renounce any unilateral military plans it has against Bin Laden and instead practice more restraint with the Taliban. Bearden is the CIA officer who revealed in a panel talk with *Washington Post* writer Steve Coll that he had cut off aid to the most moderate, reliable and effective Afghan freedom fighter, Ahmad Shah Massoud, in the last two years of the war, since Massoud had decided the Soviets were leaving anyway.[2] Therefore, Massoud wanted to preserve his forces for what he knew would be a new battle for control of Afghanistan. If Massoud had won out, there likely would have been no civil war and no Taliban.

In spite of these rather unwise comments, Bearden has built quite a retirement career for himself. He does consulting work for multinational companies, he has written three books, he does many media appearances, and he is employed by film companies as a technical advisor. For *Charlie Wilson's War*, Bearden said months in advance of the picture's release that the film would "put aside the notion that because we did that [supplied arms], we had 9/11."[3] The film did put that issue aside, but unfortunately for history and America, 9/11 *is* what happened as a result. And that is an issue about their film that Historian Hanks and CIA officer Bearden, for differing reasons, would like to forget.

Reclaiming History Disappears

In 2011, Hanks made an appearance in Dallas to promote his (silly) film *Larry Crowne*. He was asked about the status of the Bugliosi adaptation. He said that he wanted to do the project, "But there's really only one way to do it, and that's to have a substantial amount of time so you go in much, much deeper than ever before. . . . That gets to be very expensive. . . ." He then added that he could not say Playtone was definitely doing the project. His implication was the HBO brass was resisting it for budgetary reasons.[4] These sentiments were later echoed on a TV interview show the actor did.

If Hanks is to be taken at his word, he seems to be saying that HBO did not want to fork over big bucks for the miniseries. Which begs the question: Why did they do that with all of Playtone's other projects, but not this one? Tom Hanks essentially pioneered the very long form, very expensive TV miniseries for cable. His productions have cost anywhere from sixty million to well over a hundred million dollars. And these are projects that are inherently expensive to produce, since they deal with epic subjects, large casts, and many extras. With very few exceptions, that would not be the case with *Reclaiming History*. So, how could a series about the JFK case be more expensive than those productions?

A couple of industry insiders have explained to me that they did not think *Reclaiming History* was ever a "go project" either at Playtone or at HBO. They explained that since they were in the business, they had never seen a screenwriter assigned to the book either at HBO or at Playtone.[5] And this was as far back as 2010. What makes this rather notable is that *The Pacific* actually set a record for cost of a cable miniseries. In fact, it may be a record for miniseries cost ever. It reportedly came in at 217 million dollars,[6] which meant that each one-hour installment was budgeted at over $20 million. What makes that figure even more astonishing is that the series had no big name actors or actresses involved. But there may be an attached problem that Hanks did not mention. *The Pacific* was a serious ratings disappointment for HBO. Budgeted at almost twice as much as *Band of Brothers,* the opening night ratings pulled less than half the viewers.[7] Hanks's comments about the reluctance of HBO to back *Reclaiming History* came over a year after *The Pacific* debuted. Perhaps HBO felt that they did not want to back another miniseries that cost anywhere near that much. Especially one that was essentially a recycling of the Warren Commission. And therefore did not promise any big attraction in the first place.

Parkland Appears

Once the decision was made to deep-six *Reclaiming History* as a miniseries, the focus shifted to the medical aspects of the Kennedy assassination. But not at anything that occurred at Bethesda, Maryland, where the actual horrendous autopsy took place. But at Parkland Hospital, the Dallas hospital at which President Kennedy was taken after he was shot. Kennedy died there after futile attempts to save him. Kennedy was only there perhaps for ninety minutes. Therefore, how could one make a dramatic film out of such an event?

The answer to that question is this: They didn't. I secured one of the early drafts of the film *Parkland,* and unless there were later attempts to radically revise the script and/or concept, what Playtone had done is turned the Kennedy murder into an exercise in, to use a proper medical term, anesthesia. But before turning to the script, let us discuss the writer/director. He is a man named Peter Landesman.

Landesman started his literary career as a novelist. He then became a *New York Times* investigative journalist for a number of years. By far his most controversial story was a front pager for *New York Times Magazine* published on January 25, 2004. Entitled "Sex Slaves on Main Street" it attempted to depict the international human trafficking in young girls from places like Mexico and Eastern Europe into the United States. The long article was criticized from a number of angles and sources, but most famously from Jack Shafer in *Slate.* Shafer and others pointed out some rather obvious inconsistencies and anachronisms in the piece, which surprisingly, Landesman's editors did not.[8] The debate featured veiled accusations that Landesman's article was shot so full of question marks about both his characters and events, and the magnitude of the problem, that it was at least exaggerated, at worst, partly fiction. The debate over the article went on for sixteen months. It was so heated that Landesman's editor, Gerald Marzorati, chimed in to defend the *Times.*

Incredibly, after all this, Landesman managed to market his seriously flawed story as the basis for a screenplay. The film, entitled *Trade,* starred Kevin Kline. It was produced by Roland Emmerich (*Independence Day, The Day After Tomorrow*). The film was first released at the Sundance Film Festival in 2007, and went into limited release afterwards. It did quite poorly at the box office. Although Landesman did not write the actual screenplay, his article did get a "based upon" screen credit.

What happened next with Landesman was even odder. Even though the first film he was associated with bombed, he zoomed up the ladder. In 2011, it was announced, on more than one film industry site, that Landesman was being hired by producers Scott Z. Burns and Lorenzo di Bonaventura to write the screenplay for a film tentatively entitled *The Mission.*[9] This was a South American hostage drama about the rescue of former presidential candidate Ingrid Betancourt, and several others, from a revolutionary Colombian group of guerillas. Betancourt was kept captive for over six years.

What was so notable about the announcement is that the film was to be produced in part by McLarty Media. This was the entertainment arm of the giant Washington D.C. consulting firm called McLarty Associates. Mack McLarty was Bill Clinton's chief of staff until he was replaced by Leon Panetta in 1994. He then became a member of the National Economic Council. As most people know, Clinton was more successful than Republican presidents in getting through Western Hemisphere free trade agreements. Therefore, McLarty was a key figure at the Council in the creation of both the North American Free Trade Agreement (NAFTA), and the Free Trade Area of the Americas (FTAA). He served as a liaison between Clinton and David Rockefeller on the last.[10] These agreements had been an all-consuming goal of David Rockefeller for decades.

The Rockefeller connection is firmed up by the fact that when McLarty started in the Washington consulting business, he was working very closely with Henry Kissinger, and his already established firm, Kissinger and Associates. In fact, the temporary name of the firm McLarty ran was Kissinger-McLarty Associates. Because of Kissinger's long-term and close ties to Rockefeller, Kissinger-McLarty was a corporate member of the Council of the Americas. That organization was a business group set up by David Rockefeller in the sixties. Its goal was to achieve exactly what the ostensible Democrats Clinton and McLarty helped it to achieve: a giant free trade zone throughout North and Central America. Once he was schooled by Kissinger in the business, McLarty splintered off and formed his own company. McLarty Associates' film and entertainment arm is a major player in helping to get films produced, for example, *The Kite Runner, Body of Lies*, and *Mission Impossible: Ghost Protocol*.[11] The Landesman scripted film about the abduction of Betancourt was likely being made at the behest of the Colombian government as a way of propagandizing against the abducting rebel group called FARC.[12] Rather early in his career, Landesman was involved with some very big players in both Washington and Hollywood. And as of this writing, it appears that he has the national security angle tied up for now in Hollywood.

Playtone's Approach to JFK's Murder

As mentioned above, I was fortunate (or unfortunate) enough to be sent an early draft of Landesman's script for *Parkland*. This marks another remarkable step up for Landesman. Since he did not just write the script, he also directed the movie. To put a major production in the hands of a man who not only had never directed before, but who had never written a produced screenplay before, is a rarity in Hollywood. But having read the early script, I can say, Landesman delivered for Playtone. The script is as much a distortion of the facts as *Charlie Wilson's War* was. And as with that film, Hanks and Playtone have given us another turning and twisting of an important historical event. And this one has Hanks's imprint all over it. His son, Colin Hanks, plays Malcolm Perry.

James B. Dale, the star of *The Pacific,* plays Robert Oswald. Paul Giamatti, star of *John Adams,* plays Abraham Zapruder.

The script is supposed to be based upon *Reclaiming History.* But as with Spielberg's *Lincoln* and the credit given to Doris Kearns Goodwin's *Team of Rivals,* that credit is very loosely grounded. As with *Lincoln,* Bugliosi's book was only a departure point. One could more aptly compare it to *Four Days in November,* the very much abridged paperback reissue of *Reclaiming History.*

Landesman's script does not really have a protagonist; not even a central character. The approach he took was something like a Robert Altman film, for example, *Nashville.* He took a major event in a large city and concentrated on a relatively brief period of time. Here it was Kennedy's visit to Dallas. The focus is almost exclusively on the forty-eight-hour period from Kennedy's arrival at Love Field to the murder of Oswald. There are essentially four locations to the story: 1) Parkland Hospital, 2) the Dallas FBI station, 3) Dallas Police Headquarters, and 4) Abraham Zapruder's home, office, and the film labs where he developed and copied his film. Although there is no central character, there are lead characters. At the hospital it is Dr. Charles Carrico. At the FBI station it is station chief Gordon Shanklin and FBI agent James Hosty. At the police station it is Robert Oswald, Marguerite Oswald and Captain Will Fritz. In the Zapruder locations it is Zapruder, his friend and business partner Erwin Schwartz, and Secret Service agent Forrest Sorrels.

Before we begin to critique Landesman's script, I understand that, at the time of this writing, the film is in postproduction. Therefore it is not completed. Further, I cannot be sure that the version of the script received was the final shooting version. But even weighing all of that, there is still value in discussing this draft because it is clear from the choices Landesman made that from the beginning, he was headed for a certain result. And it did not matter what the facts were that happened to be in the way of achieving that result.

At the Hospital

Some of the most important medical evidence in the JFK case was originally developed at Parkland Hospital. For instance, on November 22, 1963, both Drs. Malcolm Perry and Kemp Clark held a joint press conference. During that press conference Perry said that President Kennedy's neck wound was an entrance wound. He said this three times.[13] Well, that scene is not in this script. But further, although Landesman spends a lot of time describing the efforts to revive Kennedy in Trauma Room One, and he describes Perry cutting a tracheotomy over a wound in Kennedy's neck, still it's not described by Perry as an entrance wound there either. This is an important deletion. Because if it were described as such it would mean there was more than one gunman since Oswald was behind Kennedy at the time of the shooting.

Although he cuts out the Perry-Clark press conference, Landesman does have a scene in this script depicting assistant press secretary Malcolm Kilduff's press conference announcing Kennedy's death. Except in his version it is very much shortened. And in the screen directions, Landesman does something revealing. Landesman quotes Kilduff as saying that Kennedy died of a gunshot wound in the brain. Then comes the following script direction: "Kilduff points to his head. Just the head in general." As anyone who has seen either a snapshot, or the film of this press conference, that is not what Kilduff does. He points quite clearly to the right front of his head. Whether or not that has any forensic value is a different question. But he is not just pointing to his head "in general."

This relates to one of the most bizarre distortions in Landesman's script. At three different places in the screenplay Landesman refers to a large hole in Kennedy's skull: once while Kennedy is in the limousine being driven to Parkland, and twice in Trauma Room One. For instance, he has Dr. Robert McClelland staring into Kennedy's face while he is being operated upon. He actually writes that the doctor was eighteen inches away from JFK and staring right at him. He then adds that McClelland was mesmerized by Kennedy's exposed brain. A few pages before this, Landesman has Dr. Carrico "wince at the sight of . . ." Kennedy's head since "the right frontal quarter" was simply gone. Which would indicate a shot from the rear that exited through the front.

The problem here is that this is not what either doctor testified to under oath before the Warren Commission. McClelland said that the right *posterior* portion of the skull had been extremely blasted. It had been shattered by the force of a bullet so that the parietal bone protruded up through the scalp. He also said the occipital bone was fractured along its lateral half.[14] Carrico said much the same. He swore under oath that there was a rather large defect in "the posterior skull, the occipital region. There was an absence of the calvarium or skull in this area. . . ."[15] The words "posterior" and "occipital" both refer to the back of the skull and both doctors have gone on record with photos illustrating this location. Which indicates a shot from the front that exited out the rear of the skull. Therefore, what Landesman does here with, first, Carrico and McClelland, and then Kilduff is to consciously reverse the medical evidence for a headshot from the front of Kennedy. A shot that, like with the evidence at Perry's press conference, could not have originated with Oswald.

Zapruder and His Film

The script essentially follows Zapruder from the time he goes to Dealey Plaza on Friday morning to when Time-Life representative Richard Stolley bought the film from him on Saturday. This includes multiple screenings of the film on Friday and Saturday. Each time the film is screened Landesman's screen directions point the viewer away from the actual images on the film and toward the eyes of the viewers in the scene. After the second or third time this happens, it becomes rather obvious what Landesman and Hanks are up to. They actually don't want the viewer to see the famous "back and to the left" movement of Kennedy's entire body, as it jerks with incredible speed and force toward the back seat. When an odd pattern like this is repeated, it leaves out the happenstance possibility. Whether this will be maintained for the theatrical release is something I cannot answer. But that is the way the script reads.

When Dick Stolley tracked down Zapruder late Friday night, the Dallas dressmaker put him off until the next morning. Zapruder understood the monetary value of the film he had taken. It was from, by far, the best angle, and it had the clearest view of what had happened inside the car. The only instants missing were those when the car disappeared behind the Stemmons Freeway sign. Therefore Zapruder pushed for a five-figure deal for the film's photo rights. This was later altered to include all film rights also. And then the price went to $150,000.[16] While the actual reason the price went up is ignored in the script, Landesman inserts something into the Stolley-Zapruder negotiations that I have never seen anywhere else, even after consulting with various sources and experts on the matter.

It has always been a matter of contention as to why Time-Life never actually allowed the public to see what is obviously the most important part of the Zapruder film. That is, the sequence described above: the violent and unforgettable rearward motion of Kennedy's body after being hit at Zapruder film frame 313. Well, in this script, while Zapruder is negotiating with Stolley, he tells him that he does not want to have the actual frames 313 and onward published. And he makes this unconditional. In other words, take it or leave it. As this author has noted, no author or commentator has ever said this about the negotiations, including Dick Stolley. Even people who have seen the contract, like Assassination Records Review Board analyst Doug Horne, do not note it as a clause in the agreement. What actually happened is that Time-Life representative C. D. Jackson ordered Stolley to buy all the rights to the film after he watched a copy on Monday the twenty-fifth.[17]

After agreeing to pay Zapruder this sum, Time-Life never exhibited the film in public. And it never showed the actual film frame 313 onward in any of its magazines in a photo essay. In 1975, when a copy of Robert Groden's version of the film was shown on ABC television by host Geraldo Rivera, it created a national sensation. In an obvious attempt to get themselves off the hook for concealing vital evidence from the public, Time-Life now returned the film and all rights back to the Zapruder family for the price of one dollar.[18] Therefore, what Landesman and Hanks appear to be doing here is to be shifting the blame. That is, in their universe, it wasn't the management of Time-Life that was involved in censorship. It was that dressmaker Abraham Zapruder, who died in 1970. If only it were true.

Robert, Marguerite, and Oswald's Guilt

As seen above, the script distorts the evidence to maintain the Warren Commission's conclusions. But it really does not examine the case assembled by the Dallas Police against Oswald by the time of his death. Therefore, the way it imputes guilt to the man who never had a lawyer, let alone a trial, is through two members of his family: his brother Robert and his mother Marguerite. Landesman and Hanks use Robert to portray Oswald as being absolutely guilty: almost as soon as he hears the announcement of his brother's name on the radio. The script has Robert Oswald see the rifle in evidence at police headquarters and mentally recognize it as Oswald's.

There is a serious problem with this. It could not have happened. Prior to the assassination, the last time Robert saw Lee was at a 1962 Thanksgiving family reunion of the three brothers: Lee, Robert, and John Pic. The alleged assassination rifle supposedly arrived in Dallas in March of 1963. In that month, Robert moved to Malvern, Arkansas.[19] In April of 1963, Lee and Marina moved to New Orleans. Oswald did not return to Dallas until the first week of October. By that time, Robert had made a job related move to Denton, Texas.[20] Robert Oswald explicitly admitted that he never again saw his brother after the Thanksgiving reunion in 1962—until the day after the assassination.[21] In spite of this, in another script direction by Landesman, he says that when the alleged murder weapon is seen by Robert at the police station, Robert thinks, "He's seen that rifle before." The obvious question to anyone who knows the case is: How could he have seen the rifle before if he never saw Lee between the time it was allegedly ordered and the day after the assassination?

There are other problems with this characterization of Robert Oswald in the immediate aftermath of the assassination. When Commissioner Hale Boggs asked Robert if he could think of any reason why Lee would have killed Kennedy, Robert said, "No sir; I could not."[22] When Boggs asked him then if it came as a great shock to him, Robert replied, "Yes sir; it certainly did, and I might add that the Lee Harvey Oswald that I knew would not have killed any-body."[23] Robert was exposed to nothing but FBI agents and Dallas Policemen on the day of the assassination. After getting a haircut at the Statler Hilton, the barber said he thought Oswald deserved a fair trial; Robert was so glad to hear that he gave the man a tip.[24] Robert actually told Commissioner Albert Jenner that he was not sure whether or not Lee "could have possibly done this."[25] In fact, upon meeting Ruth and Michael Paine, he concluded that they were somehow involved in it.[26] Further, he later concluded that Jack Ruby was paid to kill Lee and that he also knew him beforehand.[27] By February 20, 1964, at his appearance before the Warren Commission, he did say that he was now persuaded by the circumstantial evidence that Lee had killed Kennedy.[28] But this was nearly three months after the time frame of Landesman's script when all the big guns of the media had already pronounced Oswald guilty.

The probable reason that Hanks and Landesman overplay his characterization is that they want to use their version of Robert to ridicule Oswald's mother, Marguerite. For what they do to Marguerite, the word ridicule is probably too mild. They actually want to demean the woman just as much as the Warren Commission, Arlen Specter, and reporter Hugh Aynesworth did. Why? Because she actually wanted Lee to have a lawyer. Since she thought he might be innocent. Maybe Hanks forgot: in America the defendant is innocent until proven guilty.

From the very first moment Landesman introduces her, it is quite clear he has been instructed by his employers to turn her into a stand-in for the Commission critics: she is both bizarre and an attention seeker. For instance, Landesman draws a scene where she and Robert meet alone at Dallas Police headquarters. Almost immediately she tells Robert that she knew Lee was a secret agent of some sort. She then tells him to watch himself since the room they are in is bugged. Robert then ridicules this and says, "You're insane." From reading Robert's Warren Commission testimony, this scene, to say the least, is very much exaggerated. According to his testimony, he and his mother never met alone. They were always with either the Paines, Marina Oswald, FBI agents, or reporters.[29] Robert also said that Marguerite never confided in him about Oswald's status as an intelligence agent at the station. He said that he did not recall this happening until either days, or even weeks, later.[30] And he did not say he thought she was crazy for thinking that. He said he told her she should tell the Secret Service.[31] And he did not tell the Commission that Marguerite thought the room they were in was bugged. Lee told Robert that the phone *they* were talking on was tapped. This is when he also told Robert not to form any opinion about him based on this "so-called evidence."[32]

The attribution of guilt is capped off through Robert in two ways. First, a Dallas detective tells him that his "mother's a piece of work" and his brother was a "good shot." Further, that it was gutsy to kill an unarmed man in the back. For Oswald it was like shooting fish in a barrel. This is pure flapdoodle. Oswald was not anywhere close to being a good shot. And the record shows he could not have done what the Commission said he did. Second, later, Landesman has Robert Oswald utter some utter banalities about why his brother killed JFK; which are completely unjustified in any way by his sworn testimony before the Commission. And these clichés—which refer to him as always identifying with the underdog and wanting to be a star—would be much more appropriate for the Paines to utter. Who Robert thought were involved in the crime in some way. Now, before leaving the subject of Robert Oswald, there is no doubt that as time went on, Robert became more convinced of Oswald's guilt. But this draft of the script does not deal with those later matters. So it is fair to criticize it on those grounds.

Oswald and the FBI

For the most part, Jim Hosty and Gordon Shanklin represent the FBI in the film. When Oswald is announced as being the main suspect in the killing of Officer Tippit, Hosty says that he has been tracking Oswald for several months prior. This is true. But when someone asks him why, he replies: "I couldn't tell. Just a sorry sonofabitch." This is more of Landesman doing his masters' bidding. Someone should tell Hanks and Landesman: the FBI does not track citizens because they are bums or not suitably employed.

As John Newman notes, the FBI, quite sensibly, first took notice of Oswald at the time of his defection to Russia in 1959.[33] This was proper and rather standard. As former intelligence analyst Newman notes, there was a notation to examine what kind of security threat he posed if he returned to America.[34] In other words, did the KGB turn Oswald into a Russian agent while he was there? And also, did the former Marine give them any military secrets while he was in Russia?

Also, Marguerite had sent her son money while he was in Russia. But she found out he was not getting these funds. She complained about this to the State Department.[35] She also talked about it with the FBI. The Bureau then began investigating the matter in 1960. This included sending FBI agent John Fain to interview Marguerite.[36] Marguerite thought Oswald was lost in Russia someplace. So the FBI began investigating where he could be. This led to the famous memo by J. Edgar Hoover saying that someone might be impersonating Oswald in Russia.[37] So, in other words, by 1960, a year after Oswald's defection, the Director of the FBI was writing memos about Oswald. Then, in 1961, Marguerite told Fain that her son wanted to come home.[38] This resulted in FBI HQ in Washington reviewing intelligence files on Oswald. Then Washington sent a memo to the Dallas FBI office warning of Oswald's likely return.[39]

When Oswald did return, the FBI and CIA were both involved in programs to counter the Fair Play for Cuba Committee (FPCC) based in New York.[40] The FBI then interviewed Oswald upon his return to the USA in June of 1962.[41] That interview was conducted by Fain. Oswald was reportedly uncooperative. Fain asked him to take a polygraph test, which Oswald refused to do.[42] Fain then wrote a memorandum about the results of the interview, and then interviewed Oswald again two months later. John Fain retired in October of 1962. When the Oswald case was taken up again, it was Jim Hosty who became the agent in charge of it. And he therefore knew about all of the above. In light of all this, for Landesman to write that Hosty did not know why the FBI had a file on Oswald, and that it was opened because he was some kind of a "poor sonofabitch" is just utter and complete poppycock.

The time period Hosty took over the Oswald case until the assassination of President Kennedy is an even more interesting time frame for the FBI's Oswald case. Because, as noted above, the FBI was running its own attempt to discredit the FPCC. Which is what Oswald appeared to be a part of in New Orleans in the summer of 1963. Then, before he returned to Dallas in October of 1963, Oswald allegedly visited Mexico City. The combination of these two activities should have brought him to Hosty's attention upon his return to Dallas. Especially since Oswald was arrested in New Orleans for getting into an altercation with an anti-Castro Cuban on the street. While in jail, Oswald *asked* to be interviewed by an FBI agent. While in Mexico City, he allegedly visited both the Cuban and Russian consulates. At the latter he supposedly spoke with Valery Kostikov who, according to the CIA, was the man in charge of KGB assassinations in the Western Hemisphere. Therefore, Oswald should have been flagged by the Bureau and reported to the Secret Service in advance of Kennedy's visit. He was not. And, as Newman explains, there are many irregularities with how Hosty handled the Oswald file, which contributed to the Secret Service not knowing about Oswald in preparation for Kennedy's visit.[43] One of the most bizarre things the FBI did was to remove the Bureau's FLASH warning on Oswald's file on October 9, 1963. This was just a few days after he allegedly returned from Mexico. Therefore, after four years, this warning was removed almost at the *same time* the first cables from the CIA arrived at the FBI about Oswald being in Mexico City.[44]

All of these oddities about Hosty's handling of the Oswald case have led many to think that perhaps it happened that way because Hosty knew Oswald was actually an FBI informant. In fact, after Hosty was disciplined by Hoover for his ineffective performance with Oswald, which allowed him to be on Kennedy's motorcade route, he was transferred to Kansas City. There, according to FBI agent Carver Gayton, Hosty told him that such was the case: Oswald was a paid FBI informant.[45]

If that is true, then this makes the famous incident of the destruction of Oswald's note, which he left at the FBI office in Dallas, quite compelling. What Landesman does with this is pretty much consistent with the rest of what we have examined. Sometime in early November, Oswald visited the FBI office and asked for Hosty. Receptionist Nannie Lee Fenner told him he was not there. Oswald then left her with a note inside an envelope for Hosty.[46] To this day, no one knows for sure what the note said because it did not survive the weekend. Hosty was ordered to destroy the note by Shanklin. But in 1975, the cover-up around the note and its destruction broke into the local Dallas papers. There was an FBI investigation in which over fifty people were interviewed.[47] It was found out that Shanklin and other higher-ups knew about the note before the assassination.[48] It was decided in Washington that to prevent further controversy, Hosty should destroy the note. What makes this even more fascinating is that Hosty's name, address, phone number at the FBI, and the license plate of his car were all in Oswald's notebook. Yet when the FBI forwarded their report, including this information, to the Commission, the Hosty citation in the notebook was omitted.[49] This further contributed to the suggestion that Oswald was an FBI informant, and Hoover was trying to conceal that fact.

Landesman reduces this all to mush. The signs that Oswald was an informant are cut out. Shanklin then calls Hosty into his office with the note already on his desk. There is no indication how he knew about it, and if so, why there was no action taken on it before. Oswald being in the FBI office in November and leaving a note for Hosty, this is all dismissed as a screw-up that will look bad in the press. Shanklin then orders Hosty to not just destroy the note, but the whole Oswald file. In other words, the script does Hoover one better. Oswald was so inconsequential, and cover-ups are so much a part of American life, the FBI can just bury his whole file with all sixty-nine items in it.

These are problems of the script's errors of commission. There are things though that are in the script's time frame that Landesman just ignored. Marina Oswald, who was at the police station while Oswald was in jail, is pretty much written out of the script. Probably because, in those forty-eight hours, she was protesting her husband's innocence and telling the Secret Service he had never been to Mexico and had no rifle with a scope attached.[50] There is no scene of Jack Ruby being at Parkland Hospital. Even though two credible witnesses placed him there.[51] There is no mention of the Secret Service not just abandoning the presidential limousine outside the hospital, but apparently of a Secret Service agent sponging the interior down.[52] Incredibly, there is no discussion at all about the failures to protect either Kennedy or Oswald that weekend. There is no noting, for example, of the Secret Service drinking hard alcohol until 3 AM on Thursday night.[53] Or of the threats against Oswald the Dallas Police knew about prior to his murder. One by Ruby himself.[54] There is no depiction of the press conference on Friday evening with Jack Ruby in the background correcting DA Henry Wade about which Cuban group Oswald belonged to.[55] The list could go on and on.

No screenwriter can do something like this on his own. Something like this happens only when the orders come down from above. As Hanks noted at the premiere of his miniseries *The Pacific,* he is not a "hands off" producer. He and Goetzman are on top of their productions. Therefore, as with the debacle of *Charlie Wilson's War,* we can thank Playtone for this abomination of the record. As noted above, this script may not remain intact when the film is released. In fact, it will not be the same. The details may not even be similar. But what this review shows is this: from the start, this project had an almost violently rigid agenda to it. Like Bugliosi's book, it was going to, first, uphold the Commission; second, it would demean the critics as being a bunch of fruit-cakes who didn't deserve the time of day. In doing so, as with the Afghanistan example previously reviewed, we have demonstrated one thing beyond question. Tom Hanks is no historian. He is a mythologist.

CHAPTER FIFTEEN

My Dinner with Giorgio

"Well, that's not his fault. It's the footnote editor's."

—Giorgio DiCaprio

What happens when two comic book creators get involved with a film project about the assassination of President Kennedy? You guessed it. You get a picture that is the film version of a comic book. But in this case, as we shall see, it is what was called Underground Comics. And that is the second calamity about to befall the American public from Hollywood in relation to the murder of JFK.

I know something about this upcoming fantasy because both Paul Schrade and I tried to prevent the disaster in advance. Let me relate the background to it.

Paul Schrade is a true American hero. He was at the Ambassador Hotel the night Robert Kennedy was assassinated. In fact, he was actually one of the people shot that night. Fortunately, he recovered. Later on, when the actual circumstances of the shooting were explained to him, he quickly understood that it was not possible for the alleged assassin, Sirhan Bishara Sirhan, to have done all the shooting that night. At least not by himself.[1] He then worked to get a reopening of that case. Miraculously, he almost did it.[2] To this day, forty-five years later, he is still hard at work both commemorating Robert Kennedy's life and trying to get a true reexamination of the circumstances of his death.

Earl Katz is a documentary film producer who, over the last decade, has made some notable films, for example, *Unprecedented: The 2000 Presidential Election*. Since he and Schrade navigate in the same political circles in Los Angeles, they are familiar with each other.

DiCaprio Buys Waldron's Comic Book

In the fall of 2010, *Entertainment Weekly* announced that Leonardo DiCaprio and his production company Appian Way had purchased the rights to the book *Legacy of Secrecy* by Lamar Waldron and Thom Hartmann.[3] Shortly after this, Katz was moved into Appian Way to plan a documentary to accompany the feature film.

The announcement was not exactly correct. Because Leonardo DiCaprio was not the man who was the motivating force behind the purchase of the Waldron/Hartmann book. (Some would call it a novel.) The man pushing for Leonardo to buy the book was the actor's father, Giorgio DiCaprio. If Giorgio was not part of Appian Way, his son would not be making this film. Before Leonardo became a famous actor, and his father became part of his office, Giorgio was very active as a comic book writer, editor, and West Coast distributor. Except he was involved with what was termed "underground comix," that is, small press comic books which are often satirical and have a socially relevant point. Some other practitioners in the field were Robert Crumb, Dori Seda, and Gilbert Shelton. As he became more involved in managing Leonardo's career, Giorgio phased out of his former occupation.

In a similar way, before Waldron began writing about the JFK case, and later Watergate, he was in the comics and graphic novel business.

For instance, he founded the Atlanta Fantasy Fair. He was the convention chairman until 1987. For some reason, he invited Newt Gingrich to speak there in 1985. He was the author of a graphic novel called *Light Runner*, wrote the comic book *Speed Racer*, and created and wrote the comic book *Micra*. The last stands for Mind Controlled Remote Automation. It was about a college student who volunteered to be the remote pilot of an android body.[4]

In 2005, Waldron and Hartmann published *Ultimate Sacrifice*. A book which is considered today, at best, an eccentricity, at worst, a diversion. But Waldron had Hartmann as his partner. Therefore, he had someone in the media world to give him access on both radio and television. With Hartmann promoting him, he was able to keep a profile. Therefore this bizarre book was kept in the media and even was featured on *Discovery Channel*. Hartmann himself was featured on a segment of Nigel Turner's *The Men Who Killed Kennedy*, with the likes of Daniel Marvin and the late Tom Wilson. In 2008, the two now produced a sequel. This was called *Legacy of Secrecy*. It essentially had the same far-out theory behind it: President Kennedy and his brother Robert were planning a coup in Cuba for December of 1963. The Mob found out about it. They then killed Kennedy and used the cover-up around the cancelled coup to conceal the circumstances surrounding their murder of the president. But yet, in the second book, the authors now branched out into the Martin Luther King case, the Robert Kennedy case, and even Watergate.

I have done extensive writing about the first two books and also Waldron's third book about Watergate, which he wrote alone.[5] The two books about Kennedy's assassination are so weakly founded in fact as to be properly labeled as fantasies. There simply is no credible evidence that Kennedy was going to launch an invasion of Cuba in December of 1963. And no one who looks at the documents Waldron supplies as evidence agrees with his interpretation of them. They all amount to contingency planning. Secondly, as most people understand, at the time of his death, Kennedy was working hard toward a détente with Castro. He was pursuing back channel communications which he hoped would soon lead to an exchange of emissaries. In fact, at the time of the assassination, Castro was meeting with one of Kennedy's back channel representatives, French reporter Jean Daniel.[6] Third, in *Legacy of Secrecy*, Waldron and Hartmann offer up what they term as three "confessions," which they say prove the Mob killed Kennedy. As I exposed in my review of that book, the so-called confessions have little or no credibility. The one by Santo Trafficante was likely fabricated by his lawyer Frank Ragano.[7] The one they attribute to John Roselli is devoid of any content or specificity, and is also third party hearsay. And the one they rely upon the most, by Carlos Marcello, amounts to the fruity and senile ravings of an old man who is suffering through strokes, and is likely in throes of Alzheimer's disease.

I was privy to these documents about Marcello's "confession" and his mental health problems in prison way before Waldron saw them. This was done through the work of National Archives researcher Peter Vea. Vea included in his package of documents various reports by the prison guards who said Marcello was talking to himself and actually knocking his head up against the wall. Clearly, the man was in a state of mental deterioration which continued downward until his eventual release. When Marcello died in 1993, his relatives noted that he was pretty much senile by the time he was released from prison in 1989. Which meant that the onset of the senility took place while he was in jail and talking to the FBI informant to whom he confessed the Kennedy assassination.

In my review of *Legacy of Secrecy*, it was noted just how bizarre these conversations were that Marcello had with the FBI informant. As presented in their book, Waldron and Hartmann have Marcello saying that he met with Oswald in person and in public at his brother's restaurant.[8] They then top that. They say that Marcello set up Ruby's bar business and Ruby would come to Marcello's estate to report to him. So after being seen in public with both men, the savvy Don has the first kill Kennedy and the second kill Oswald. But yet, the authors did not note in this section that elsewhere in their book they contradict this confession they try and propagate. Because they write that Oswald did not kill Kennedy.[9] And, in fact, in an updated version of the book, they actually named Watergate burglar Bernard Barker as the actual assassin. Does this claim not discredit the "Marcello confession"? And by their own hand? But further, why would a powerful mobster like Marcello hire a man who was as poor a shot as Oswald for a job like killing Kennedy, who was a moving target at a distance? This certifies the mental affliction Marcello was suffering from at the time.

But Waldron was nothing if not energetic. He began to call media outlets about his "newly discovered confession." Some TV outlets actually had him on. At the Lancer Conference in Dallas in 2007, he pursued Canadian journalist David Giammarco with his discovery. Giammarco was a friend of Kevin Costner and Waldron thought the actor would be interested in doing a film based upon the Marcello "confession."[10] All this industry finally paid off for Waldron. Giorgio DiCaprio saw him in one of his television appearances. And the two fell in love. Giorgio would now get his son Leonardo to play the FBI informant. Katz would be brought in to do an accompanying documentary. This was fortunate for Waldron. Because by this time, so many people in the JFK research community had become doubters about him and his ideas that he could not even get an invitation to any conferences. Waldron had to approach the promoters and request time from them.[11]

Meeting Earl and Giorgio

As noted above, Paul Schrade knows Katz. When Paul read about the purchase of *Legacy of Secrecy* he did his homework on the book. Like many, he thought its central premise, about the invasion of Cuba, was absurd. Since he had never heard of any such operation while he was working with RFK. Paul heard about my reviews of the two volumes. To try and spare the filmmakers a lot of embarrassment, and the public a lot of tedious silliness, he arranged a meeting with himself, me, and Katz at Appian Way. There followed a second meeting, which included Giorgio. These took place in late April and early June of 2011 at DiCaprio's office in West Hollywood.

Before we attended we asked that 1) The discussions be taped, and 2) that Waldron not be in attendance. No one likes to see their work attacked in the company of their prospective backers. Therefore, we knew how Waldron would react. He would get defensive, argumentative, and probably start shouting. But Katz and DiCaprio wanted him there. They made up a couple of silly excuses for him to be there. One was that there was a new edition of *Ultimate Sacrifice* out with some new information in it. And second, there was new information about what the informant learned from Marcello. These ended up being nothing but pretexts. There was no new information in the edition of *Ultimate Sacrifice* presented to Schrade and me. Second, the new information about Marcello was that he had talked about some other things he had done with the informant. Which has nothing to do with JFK and were described only in the most general terms.

We later deduced that the reason Waldron was there was because Katz and DiCaprio knew very little about the JFK case. And further, they had little knowledge of all the myriad problems inherent in the book. In other words, they had bought the book sight unseen. Therefore, they needed Waldron there to defend their making of the film. And, as we predicted, Waldron got defensive, argumentative, and started shouting. It got so bad that we threatened to leave twice. It was fortunate for Appian Way that we were not allowed to tape the meetings, because Lamar would not have come off very well to the listener. To indicate just how disruptive Waldron was, our presentation to Appian Way took about sixty-five minutes in a run through. Once we got there, we passed out a notebook containing the presentation.[12] Waldron, who said he would only comment about every ten pages, ended up breaking in on about every other page. With all of his interference, a presentation that should have taken a bit over sixty minutes, took over three hours—and that was just for *one third* of the presentation. Waldron clearly resembled a lawyer objecting to every other question in court simply to break up the opposing lawyer's line of argument. Except in this case, the jury—Katz and DiCaprio—had already made up their minds. Except we didn't know that. But we should have. Because when I said something about this, since Waldron was speaking even more than I was, Katz said, "Let him talk." Right there, we should have known that neither Earl nor Giorgio gave a damn about the serious faults in the book. Or that it would seriously misrepresent who the Kennedys were and what happened to them. This was all in fact just a dog and pony show so that they could say they did have us there. And that message could be relayed to Bobby Kennedy Jr.

As noted above, one of the most shocking things about meeting these two men was to find out not just how little they knew about the JFK case, but how unfamiliar they were with the property they had purchased. One of the main problems with the Waldron/Hartmann novelistic scenario is this: in their book, they say that CIA Director of Plans Richard Helms had to have known about the upcoming invasion of Cuba. Yet, this is vitiated by his own book, *A Look Over my Shoulder.* There he talks about presenting an arms cache allegedly taken by the CIA from Venezuela. This is supposed to reveal that Castro is violating a pledge to Kennedy about not exporting revolution to South America.[13] Helms took weapons from the cache to both RFK and President Kennedy for them to see Castro's perfidy. This was supposed to represent over three tons of armaments Cuba was sending into the country. Clearly, Helms wanted the Kennedys to do something about Castro exporting revolution into South America. But yet, neither Kennedy shows any real reaction to the discovery Helms finds so bracing. Further, CIA analyst Joseph B. Smith discussed this alleged weapons find. He said that after reviewing it, he came to the conclusion it had been planted by the Agency.[14] I told Katz that this episode by itself undermines the Waldron/Hartmann thesis because the date of this visitation is November ninth. This is just two weeks before the authors of *Legacy of Secrecy* say that Kennedy had scheduled the invasion of Cuba—which Helms knew all about. The obvious question then is: If such an invasion was planned, and if all the parties knew about it (i.e., Helms and the Kennedys), why would Helms go to all the trouble of planting the exported weapons if he knew the invasion was a bit over two weeks away?

The reaction by Katz was very revealing. He said words to the effect, well, it was like Bush not reacting when he was told about the 9/11 attacks. In retrospect, Paul and I should have left right then and there. I had to clarify the relevance of what I just said: The point was, why did *Helms* do what he did if he knew the invasion was imminent? The obvious answer of course was Helms didn't know an invasion was imminent because it was not. Waldron then chimed in with a tactic he would use throughout the several hours we were there. He began to attack Richard Helms! This, of course, was a way for him to distract from the real point. Which was why would such a dastardly man, who just invented evidence to provoke an invasion of Cuba, do such a thing if he knew he already had one going? Neither the befuddled Katz, nor the misleading Waldron ever answered that question.

Another piece of evidence in the notebook was a letter that was declassi-fied by the ARRB from Desmond Fitzgerald to McGeorge Bundy.[15] This was a review of American Cuban operations in the second half of 1963. It was written by Fitzgerald, but reviewed by Helms as part of bringing President Johnson up to speed on that subject. Fitzgerald had taken over the Cuban Desk at CIA at the beginning of 1963, so he and Helms would know what was going on in that theater. Not only does the letter not mention any invasion, the letter says there were only five CIA/Cuban exile raids into Cuba in the entire second half of 1963. And the Agency only had a cadre of fifty exiles in their employ at the time. We asked, "Why would there be no mention of any invasion by Helms or Fitzgerald in this letter? And what kind of invasion could one mount with fifty men?" Waldron now tried a different tack. He tried to say that it was only through his efforts that this document was declassified, since he wrote the ARRB about getting all these 1963 Kennedy/Cuba documents out. So even if these documents vitiated his argument, somehow Waldron wanted credit for that.

We then presented another declassified ARRB document. This one was another letter from Fitzgerald to Helms about 1963 Cuban operations. It was again meant to bring Johnson up to speed on this subject. In this one the two discussed Manuel Artime and his Central American AM/World operation.[16] This was part of the effort to get the Cuban exile operations out of the USA mainland and offshore. It was done to honor the promise Kennedy had made after the Missile Crisis to not launch any invasion of Cuba from America. Artime's operation was probably the most expensive one of these the CIA had going. But in this letter, Fitzgerald and Helms ridicule Artime as a braggart and a waste of money. They say that, if he is lucky, he gets off one operation every three months. Because of this, they recommended all these efforts just be dropped as a waste of time and money. This, of course, put another nail into the whole Waldron/Hartmann scenario. For Artime is actually someone they think was actually in on Kennedy's assassination. If the CIA is recommending to LBJ that he be completely cut off, then why would Artime slit his own throat? Waldron now said that the problem is that we needed more documents on this whole Artime issue. The implication being that somehow the ARRB was covering this all up.

More than once throughout the two meetings, Paul Schrade asked a question he was quite interested in finding the answer to. Throughout the two books—*Ultimate Sacrifice* and *Legacy of Secrecy*—Waldron and Hartmann make reference to certain men in RFK's entourage who knew about the upcoming invasion. Yet, they are never named. As noted, Schrade was quite close to RFK. Yet Robert Kennedy never said one word about this subject to Paul. Even to say that he was wrong to contemplate any such thing. Further, Paul knew almost every one of RFK's former advisers when he was Attorney General. Not one of them ever said anything about it. So, Schrade asked Waldron for their names. Waldron said they were in his book. Which is not really accurate. Because the people named in the book who the authors say knew about the invasion were Secretary of State Dean Rusk and Cuban exile Harry Williams and Helms. As we have seen, Waldron and Hartmann seem to be wrong about Helms. Rusk only knew about this invasion after the fact. And Williams was dead. Schrade went away empty-handed.

Which brings up Harry Williams. Williams was a Cuban exile who was active in the CIA's programs against Castro. Since he was relatively liberal, the Kennedys liked him. After RFK's assassination, authors William Turner and Warren Hinckle began their book *The Fish is Red* on the CIA's war against Cuba. Turner found Williams. He interviewed him for about eight hours. In preparation for this meeting, I spoke to Turner about these interviews. Turner said that not once in any talks he had with Williams did the man say one word about any such invasion of Cuba in 1963. Waldron responded by saying it was hard to explain the operation without giving away the name of Juan Almeida, who was supposed to be the leader of the invasion on the island. This was bizarre. Because *Ultimate Sacrifice* is over 800 pages long. And a large part of the book discusses this mythical invasion. In the first edition of the book, Almeida was never mentioned.

We also brought up the issue of how Waldron and Hartmann treated Edwin Black's milestone article, "The Plot to Kill JFK in Chicago." This was published in the *Chicago Independent* in 1975. Although Waldron and Hartmann rely on this article in *Ultimate Sacrifice* for about eleven references, there is an odd thing about the footnotes. Every footnote is wrong. They are all to a book by George Black called *The Good Neighbor*. Therefore, the question was, how could the authors repeatedly screw up both the name and source of such an important reference for their book? To the point that the reader could never find the original essay to see the material himself? The reply was stunning. Waldron blamed this on the footnote editor. He said that the book *The Good Neighbor* is actually used as a footnote, and this was repeated throughout all references to Edwin Black. The editor did not catch the error.

First of all, I have never heard of a footnote editor. Most authors have book editors. They check the entire book: text, bibliography, and footnotes. But let us grant the position. No editor actually writes an author's original manuscript. It was either Waldron or Hartman who did that. Are we to believe neither one of them noticed they were misappropriating an important source? George Black's book has nothing to do with the plot to kill JFK in Chicago. Could both men have missed this on each and every pass through the manuscript? But further, in granting the footnote editor excuse, would not such a person be expert at what he does? If that is what he concentrates on each day? In the mislabeled George Black footnotes, there is an obvious giveaway about them. In each one, there is no page number listed. Are we to really think that a footnote editor 1) missed that obvious lack, and 2) never once got back to the authors about it? Incredibly, Giorgio actually came to Waldron's aid on this with the quote that heads this chapter. He blamed the footnote editor also. Waldron then tried to redeem his misattribution by saying that the article was online now. So Black got his credit. He apparently did not know the following important fact: When my review of *Ultimate Sacrifice* came out, it corrected all this by properly sourcing Edwin Black's article. Several people then asked for the source. Which was supplied through Jim Douglass, who had given it to me. In other words, Black's article is now on the web through Douglass and me. If that review had never appeared, it might never have been online because no one could find it with *Ultimate Sacrifice* alone.

Let us conclude the description of this episode with one last vignette. Douglass and Hartmann do all they can to discount the importance of Mexico City in the plot to kill Kennedy. Which is very hard to do today. When we brought up the importance of John Newman's book, *Oswald and the CIA*, in regard to this crucial point, the advance planning to kill JFK, Waldron reacted almost violently. He screamed about former military intelligence officer, John Newman, "What does he know about the Mafia!" Neither Katz nor DiCaprio asked their man the obvious question: "Lamar, what does the Mafia have to do with Mexico City?" The fact they did not says all one needs to know about how much review either man did of the book they were adapting.

The problem with DiCaprio and Katz going ahead with this misguided exercise is not just that it is wrong. It is not just that no one in the research community buys it. What is wrong with it is this: What the material states is actually contrary to the truth. Because what most researchers believe today is that a large part of the reason for Kennedy's death is his desire to get a rapprochement with Castro. If that is correct, then what this film will be doing is misrepresenting the actual facts about both Kennedy and the reasons for his death. Isn't fifty years of that enough?

Apparently, Giorgio and Earl don't think so.

Afterword

"I'm Tom Hanks. The U.S. government has lost its credibility, so it's borrowing some of mine."

—Tom Hanks in *The Simpsons Movie*

As the reader now understands, it is natural for the government to call on Hanks since, in many ways, he is part of that government. Which is really something that no artist should ever be. But alas, Hanks has taken that role upon himself with no qualms. Therefore, the apparent joke stated above has no humor to it. Since, after examining some of his works based upon history, Hanks has about as much credibility as the State Department.

Many years ago, the great Orson Welles was asked what he thought about the ". . . current tendency in Hollywood for actors to form their own companies." Welles answered in his usual candid manner:

"It's turned out to be very bad I think. Great surprise. If anybody said to me twelve years ago, what will happen to films if all the actors get into business for themselves, I would have said, liberation from the studio system. And it's been just the opposite I think. Very bad. Because that's when they really get commercial . . . like Louie B. Mayer in his prime."

Mayer was the man who perfected the "star system" while running Metro-Goldwyn-Mayer. He was famous for demoting the young Irving Thalberg because Thalberg favored intelligent literary adaptations, whereas Mayer liked star-studded entertainments. Therefore MGM produced pictures like *Father of the Bride, Mrs. Miniver,* and *The Yearling.* As film scholar Neal Gabler wrote in his award-winning book, *An Empire of Their Own,* Mayer was one of several European Jews who immigrated to America from Europe and became studio moguls. Ironically, once they were ensconced in power, they began to construct their version of the American Dream on film. And they began to market these films as commodities instead of works of art. One of the subthemes of this book is that Hanks and his friend Spielberg also saw themselves as outsiders when they were growing up. And once they got into positions of power in the film business, they used that power to become insiders, part of the majority. Not just in Movieland, but in Washington. Therefore, once one evaluates the overall output of Playtone and Spielberg's DreamWorks studio, in my opinion, there would be very little that Louie Mayer would object to in the two canons. If anything, he might find the overall product a bit too juvenile. I won't even comment on what Welles would have thought of it.

Hollywood and the ARRB

From 1994 to 1998, the Assassination Records Review Board declassified over 2 million pages of documents concerning President Kennedy's assassination. The fact that the Warren Commission declared Oswald guilty, yet the government was concealing so much information, should give the public pause about the JFK case. But the fact that since that process was completed there has been no TV series, miniseries, or film based on showing the public what was in these documents, may be even worse.

Part of the problem may be the way that the ARRB was formed. In 1991, Oliver Stone produced and directed his startling film based on the investigation of Kennedy's death by New Orleans DA Jim Garrison. No film in my experience ever created such an uproar—even before it was released. Stone was pilloried in the press six months before the public even saw his film. The big guns of the media, the *New York Times,* the *Washington Post, Newsweek,* etc., pulled out all the stops to make sure that there were doubts about the picture's credibility before the audience saw the film. That huge controversy kept up all the way through to the Academy Awards program. Before that show, Warren Commission counsel David Belin anonymously took out an advertisement in the film trade journal *Variety* advising voters not to vote any Oscars for the picture. Whether or not his ad hurt the picture at that year's awards is irrelevant. The fact that he was so intent on secretly hurting the film was something that was unprecedented. No director in the history of motion pictures took as many punches for a movie as Stone did for *JFK.* It was a gutsy and patriotic act. And it gave us the ARRB.

But there seems to have been a by-product to that colossal controversy. After David Talbot's book *Brothers* became a bestseller, many observers, including me, thought that the book was a natural to be made into either a feature film or a documentary. So did Talbot. He hooked up with a hot production entity, Lionsgate, and a distinguished producer, Sid Ganis—then the president of the Academy of Motion Picture Arts and Sciences. The studio began to pitch the project to the TV networks.[1] There were meetings with HBO, Showtime, ABC, and Starz. Although there was much excitement about the proposed film, nothing happened. Chris Albrecht, the programming chief at Starz, wanted to make the book the centerpiece of his new season. But it didn't happen. Yet, the producer of *24,* Joel Surnow, did get his version of the Kennedy story on Reelz Channel even though many commentators thought *The Kennedys* was not in the class of Talbot's book. There was some hubbub in the press about Surnow having a hard time selling his series. There has been very little said about the abandonment of the Talbot project or what that says about the New Hollywood.

Oliver Stone predicted what would happen to *Brothers*. He told Talbot, "*Brothers* will never get made in this town."[2] So far, he is right. Maybe, after the ordeal he endured, he understood what the problems would be. As film historian Joseph McBride told me, Stone was blindsided by the scope and savagery of what happened to him in 1991.[3]

He shouldn't have been. Anyone who understands what happened to Jim Garrison from 1967–69 and beyond could have predicted it. In 1966, Jim Garrison was the darling of New Orleans.[4] He was a very successful District Attorney with a promising political career in front of him. He very likely could have become the governor of the state, or a senator in Washington. After four years of attacks, smears, politically motivated show trials, and electronic surveillance, he lost the DA's office to a man, Harry Connick, who brought that office into disrepute. When I interviewed the late John Volz at this office in New Orleans, he said as much. Connick was not half the DA Garrison was.[5] But that didn't matter. The Power Elite in New Orleans, with some help from Washington, wanted Garrison out. And they moved heaven and earth to do so.[6] They wanted him removed for two reasons. First, they wanted no more legal proceedings to ever come out of New Orleans concerning the JFK case. Connick, who had worked with the Justice Department against Garrison, guaranteed that would not happen.[7] But secondly, and just as important: They wanted to make an example of Jim Garrison. They wanted to say to any other local DA with any desire to look into the JFK case: "Don't even think about it. Look what we did to the toast of New Orleans."

And this was one of the reasons behind the fury and the length of the attack on Oliver Stone. It was to show any other Hollywood producer and/or director, "Hey, you live in La La Land. The real power in this country is in New York and Washington. So don't try that again." Not only did Talbot feel that preemptive impact. So did Emilio Estevez. When his film *Bobby* was screened at the Producers Guild back in 2006, Kennedy researcher Pat Speer attended. Estevez answered questions afterward. Speer asked him why he showed Sirhan killing Kennedy from the front when coroner Thomas Noguchi's autopsy showed that RFK was killed by a fatal shot delivered from behind. There was a murmur that went through the crowd when he asked this question. Estevez explained that he was aware of a lot of evidence that suggested there was more than one assassin firing at the Ambassador that night. But he didn't want to make that kind of film, because "I didn't want to go through what Oliver Stone had to go through."[8]

Giorgio DiCaprio and Tom Hanks don't have to fear this kind of reaction. For the works of respectively, Lamar Waldron and Thom Hartmann, and Vincent Bugliosi on the JFK case, really don't raise the hackles of the Powers That

Be. Concerning DiCaprio's production, two of the favorite fall guys in the JFK case after Oswald have been Fidel Castro and the Mob. Those are assassins the MSM can live with. So can the Establishment. Why? Because it doesn't extend to them, either in the conspiracy or the cover-up. After all, according to the authors, the JFK cover-up extends out from the proposed invasion of Cuba, which the authors call C-Day. Therefore, the Mob killed Kennedy, and the Kennedy brothers constructed their own cover-up. Both the MSM and Power Elite can live with that. It is neat, clean and antiseptic.

In fact, when the DiCaprio film debuts, there is little doubt that someone like Robert Blakey will be there to talk about it in a sanguine and tolerant way. Most knowledgeable people know that this is how the whole "Mob did it" idea really got started.[9] It was a way for Blakey to get away from all the evidence that indicated JFK's murder was an inside job.[10] Therefore, Blakey is accepted by the Establishment. His ideas don't rock the boat. "Tsk, tsk. Oh those terrible mobsters. Good night. See you tomorrow."

Bugliosi Doubles Down—Twice

Both Vincent Bugliosi and Gerry Spence made terrible mistakes in choosing to participate in what can only be called a grotesque fantasy of a trial for Lee Harvey Oswald. As we have seen, in no way did it even approach what a trial would or should have been. Bugliosi can talk around this issue as much as he wants. He is simply blowing smoke when he tries to say it was in any way genuine.

But then he did something worse. He actually took the guilty verdict seriously. Which may be even more startling. Bugliosi must know that the sideshow he was a part of did not even approach the forensic standard of a real trial. He also must have known that Spence was ill prepared for the task. But for some reason, perhaps his acquaintance with David Phillips who was egging him on to write a book on the case, that is what he did.[11] But two things intervened. First there was Stone's film; then there was the ARRB. Bugliosi decided to double down on both issues. He was going to skewer *JFK,* and then say that there was nothing in those 2 million pages of documents the ARRB declassified that altered the outcome of his phony trial. When, in fact, it altered everything about it. With a skilled and knowledgeable attorney, today, witnesses like Cecil Kirk, Charles Petty, and most of all, Ruth Paine, would have been reduced to mush. But since there is a media blackout on these materials, Bugliosi can say otherwise. Who will dispute him? Chris Matthews? Bill O'Reilly?

Tom Hanks was the perfect foil for *Reclaiming History,* just as he was the perfect foil for *Charlie Wilson's War.* As we have seen, the latter was a "feel good" mythology that tried to erase the disastrous outcome of a huge foreign policy miscalculation. Bugliosi's book is a "feel good" mythology about perhaps the most egregious cover-up in the history of political assassinations. But yet, this fits in with Hanks as Historian. Urged on by the late Stephen Ambrose, and his son Hugh Ambrose, Hanks and Goetzman glorified the American effort in World War II for their film of *Band of Brothers.* When any historian sees that series back to back with *Saving Private Ryan,* he has to be troubled. For the simple reason that not only is the latter a confection in its details, but the former is a confection in its gestalt.

Why? Because America did not win the war in Europe and Dwight Eisenhower was not the great liberator of the continent. The battle for Europe was won on the steppes of Russia. The Nazi invasion of the Soviet Union in 1941 entailed over 80 percent of the German Wehrmacht: Three million men. To this day it is the largest land invasion in history. The man who did the most to stop that invasion was Russian commander Georgy Zhukov. Through a combination of Hitler's mistakes and Zhukov's brilliance, the great German military machine was, for the first time in the war, stopped cold. It was then pushed back. Amazingly, Zhukov commandeered the defenses of Leningrad, Moscow, Stalingrad, and the climactic tank battle at Kursk. It was those four battles that broke the back of the German army. If Hitler's invasion of Russia had succeeded as planned, and a million or more men could have been transferred back to Western Europe, the Allied invasions of both Italy and France may very well have been stopped.

But the point is: This is real history. How many Americans know who Zhukov was? Yet, in reality, his name should be ranked above Eisenhower both in his battlefield achievements and his importance to history. In fact, Zhukov should rank with the greatest generals ever: Napoleon, Alexander, Hannibal, Lee. But he's not American. Therefore, someone like Stephen Ambrose knew he could never sell a lot of books writing about him. Therefore, he's relatively unknown. Hanks and Goetzman did the same distortion with *The Pacific.* How can anyone take ten hours to tell the story of war against Japan and not show the discussions that led to the dropping of the atomic bombs on Hiroshima and Nagasaki? Well, Tom Hanks can. And did. If you can do something like that, then how difficult is it to say Oswald killed Kennedy? When, in fact, not only did he not, but it was impossible for him to do so. The only way one can make it happen is to alter the factual record. Which both Bugliosi and *Parkland* do. In fact, all that Bill Paxton, or Hanks, or Goetzman had to do was ask the attorneys who looked at the case professionally after the Warren Commission. Lawyers like Jeremy Gunn of the ARRB, Bob Tanenbaum and Richard Sprague of the HSCA and Dave Martson and Gary Hart of the Church Committee, these men all disagree with Bugliosi on the Kennedy case.

The Decline of America and Its Cinema

Many political commentators, and many historians, believe that America has entered a period of decline, both economically and politically. The economic collapse of 2007–08 was triggered by the fact that Washington was bought off to allow Wall Street to slowly but surely erode and replace the Wall Street reforms made by Franklin Roosevelt in the first years of the New Deal. It was the gutting of the Glass-Steagall Act, and the allowing the sale of a new economic invention called the derivative that were largely responsible for the real estate collapse of 2007 and the stock market crash of 2008. The effect of those twin debacles, combined with the slow erosion of the standard of living of the middle class, has brought America to a point where the country of Barack Obama does not resemble the country of John F. Kennedy. At a time when police forces are shrinking, libraries are open only four days per week, cities are going bankrupt, schools are cutting back on teachers, and also days in the school year, Playtone is spending 200 million dollars on World War II combat films. This may make Hanks, Goetzman, and Spielberg feel good about themselves, but what does it do for everyone else caught in the spiral of national decline?

America used to have a relevant cinema. From 1964 to 1975, American cinema took a back seat to no other country. The record of achievement of that era is truly amazing. Consider just some of the films of that period: *Dr. Strangelove, Hearts and Minds, The Parallax View, The Conversation, Chinatown, Five Easy Pieces, Bonnie and Clyde, The Spy Who Came in from the Cold, Badlands, MASH, Who's Afraid of Virginia Woolf, Midnight Cowboy, The Wild Bunch, Cool Hand Luke, Petulia, Dog Day Afternoon, Little Big Man, The Collector, Patton, The French Connection, The Graduate, The Last Detail, Easy Rider,* etc. That doesn't even begin to exhaust the list of fine films released in that period. These films were not just aesthetically daring. But they had something to say about American life and history. *Little Big Man* was a gripping and honest look at the genocide of the American Indians. *The Conversation* was a powerful and prophetic preview of the dangers of the total surveillance society. *Easy Rider* was a beautiful film depicting how America was splitting into two countries at the end of the sixties. Do we have anything like this today on anywhere near a regular basis? Yet, shouldn't we have a cinema like that today? Don't we need one?

In 1995, Susan Sontag wrote a famous essay published in Germany called "A Century of Cinema." It was an eloquent and painful elegy for an art form which she saw as in "ignominious, irreversible decline."[12] As David Denby wrote, "The 1995 article was Sontag's last published piece on movies; in retrospect, it was her farewell to film criticism."[13] She said that to her the current cinema was a "disincarnated, lightweight cinema that doesn't demand anyone's full attention." Therefore, she was leaving. That memorable essay was then reprinted in the *New York Times*.[14] She essentially said that the great hopes that lovers of cinema had for a truly relevant, interesting, and enriching art form had dissipated. And she added, rather fatally, that "No amount of mourning will revive the vanished rituals. . . ." What she was referring to was the excitement that cinephiles had when going to a film, like say, Roman Polanski's *Chinatown*. At one time, she said there were new masterpieces released almost each month. She concluded by saying that "the lowering of expectations for quality and the inflation of expectations for profit have made it virtually impossible for artistically ambitious directors" to operate.[15] Therefore, the excitement about expectations was now gone. How is it possible to look forward to a film by Michael Bay? And what does Michael Bay have to say about the American scene today? Dustin Hoffman echoed that feeling. At the press conference for *Kung Fu Panda,* a film writer asked him, "How did you go from *The Graduate* to *Kung Fu Panda*?" The actor replied, "It's called the decline of culture and it's impacted your profession too."[16]

The Value of a True Historian

The work of Vincent Bugliosi on the JFK case is irrelevant today. Just like the film Playtone made of his book is irrelevant before it arrives. Because neither tells us anything about 1) What really happened to President Kennedy or 2) what happened to America as a result of Kennedy's death. And because Hanks really doesn't know what history is, or how to write it, these issues completely elude him to the point that he's oblivious to it. Hanks's understanding of history is about at the level of the History Channel. Except Hanks could make his own cable channel, call it the Military Channel. Or maybe the NASA Channel. After all, Tom is proud of those American flags on the moon. They only cost $60 billion each to put there. But the point is, we don't need nostalgia about the past in America today. What we need is acknowledgement about where we are now and how we got there. Hanks and Goetzman can't help us there because they are fans of the status quo. They are satisfied with the Democratic Party as it is. Hanks and Spielberg and George Clooney and Dave Geffen and Jeff Katzenberg think people like Barack Obama and the Clintons are fine. They actually invite them to their awards ceremonies. In doing so they look askance at things like NAFTA, death by drone, the war with Iraq, and

Obama's association with Robert Rubin, etc. As mentioned in Chapter 14, Bill Clinton helped achieve the free trade dreams of David Rockefeller. As Donald Gibson shows in his fine book, *Battling Wall Street*, Rockefeller and John Kennedy didn't share the same economic vision for America in the sixties. And anyone who knows history would be aware of that.

But people who think that the Clintons and the Obamas are the best we can do today cannot understand who President Kennedy, Senator Kennedy, Martin Luther King, and Malcolm X really were, or what they meant. Nor can they understand, as Pete Hamill wrote, why peasants in Mexico have three pictures on their walls: one of Christ, one of Che Guevara, and one of John F. Kennedy. That is why one real historian, like John Newman, is worth a hundred Vincent Bugliosis; a hundred Tom Hankses; a thousand Gary Goetzmans. In every major city, one will find prosecutors just as skilled as Bugliosi. In every major regional theater, one will find actors as talented as Tom Hanks. As instructor Rawley Farnsworth said, Hanks was not even the most talented actor at his high school.[17]

But one historian like John Newman empowers us all. Because he liberates us from the myths of the past, which help us deal with the present and future. As Michael Morrissey once wrote, the biggest lie ever told in post-war America is that Oswald shot Kennedy. But the second biggest lie is that Lyndon Johnson stayed true to Kennedy's Vietnam policy. Yet, this is something that both historians—like Stephen Ambrose—and the public and the media bought into. And they did it for decades. Which, as James Blight shows in his book *Virtual JFK*, is how Johnson designed it.[18] John Newman's book, *JFK and Vietnam*, shattered that lie forever. By doing so, he liberated us all from a pernicious myth that should have never enslaved us into going to war in Southeast Asia.

Three years later, in 1995, Newman wrote *Oswald and the CIA*. This book defined the relationship of Lee Harvey Oswald to CIA Counterintelligence Chief James Angleton. No one had ever done this nearly to the extent Newman did. By doing that, the historian showed us that Angleton should never have been the liaison between the CIA and the Warren Commission. Because that allowed him to conceal his own relationship with Oswald.

This is the kind of truth we need today. And it's the kind of history we need today. It's the kind of cinema we need today. And it's the kind of television we need today. One good film based on either of Newman's books is, for me, worth the entire output of Playtone.

In 1961, President Kennedy, at the behest of his brother Robert, appointed Newton N. Minow the chair of the Federal Communications Commission. On May 9, 1961, Minow gave what many consider one of the great political speeches of the twentieth century. It is a speech that today is almost forgotten.

But it is a speech we need to remember if we are to survive as a country. At the convention of National Association of Broadcasters, that is the people who create TV programming, Minow said the following:

> When television is good, nothing—not the theater, not the magazines or newspapers—nothing is better. But when television is bad, nothing is worse. I invite each of you to sit down in front of your own television set when your station goes on the air and stay there—without a profit and loss sheet or a rating book to distract you. Keep your eyes glued to that set until the station signs off. I can assure you that what you will observe is a vast wasteland.

That was in 1961. It took John and Robert Kennedy to pick a man who would go into the lion's den and tell them that what they were making was a bunch of junk. And the public deserved better. With all the travails, scandals, murders, lawlessness, robbery, and embezzlement that have taken place since, we need a *lot* better today.

As described in this book, after Chase Brandon and Playtone, the New Hollywood almost guarantees we won't get it.

ACKNOWLEDGMENTS

I would like to thank Ray McGovern and Mel Goodman, two former CIA analysts, for helping me on my chapter on *Charlie Wilson's War*. Afghanistan is a complex subject and they helped me straighten out some points in the narrative.

As much as I firmly disagree with *Reclaiming History,* I valued the conversations I had with Vincent Bugliosi while he was preparing it. I actually enjoyed talking to the man and appreciate many of his personal qualities. He is bright, witty, and at times, self-effacing.

As the reader will see from examining the footnotes to this book, like my previous work, the revised and expanded edition of *Destiny Betrayed,* there are many references to *Probe Magazine.* As time goes on, the achievement of that journal grows even higher in stature and scope. I therefore again thank all the writers who contributed their time and efforts to making that journal the finest ever in the field of JFK, RFK, and MLK studies.

Before I started this book, I had no real conception about the CIA's direct influence in the New Hollywood. For instance, I had never heard of Chase Brandon. Lisa Pease helped point this out to me and showed me in which directions to go in order to pursue the matter. In so doing, I can only say that what I discuss in this book about Brandon's influence probably underestimates what the man achieved. It is surprising, actually it is almost startling, how eager young producers and filmmakers were to embrace him and cooperate with his agenda. I can only hope that what is contained in this book will inspire other writers to forge even farther in this crucial area of study. If we are to understand what has happened to our culture, especially our film and television world, we have to comprehend the impact of Chase Brandon's years in the movie business. When the CIA does not just review script content, but actually suggests story lines and writes whole scenes and sequences, then something has gone wrong with the creative process.

Notes

In the notes that follow, references to the Warren Report appear as WR, with the page number(s). References to the Commission volumes are cited by the volume and page numbers. References to the Final Report of the House Select Committee on Assassinations appear as HSCR. Citations to the 12 volumes of appendices and hearings appear as HSCA and the volume and page number.

Books cited in these endnotes are listed by author(s) only. If a book is used for only one or two footnotes, the full citation is given in the footnotes. The full citations to all other books appear in the Bibliography. If a periodical is used for only one or two references it is cited in the footnotes. If it is used for more than that it is cited in both the footnotes and bibliography.

Introduction

1. *Reclaiming History*, by Vincent Bugliosi, (W. W. Norton: New York) 2007. All references in this book to Bugliosi's work are to this original hardcover edition.
2. See Jerry Policoff's "How All the News About Political Assassinations in the United States Has Not Been Fit to Print in the New York Times" at the website www.ratical.org
3. Email communication with Jerry Policoff of May 6, 2013.
4. James DiEugenio, *Destiny Betrayed*, 2nd Edition, pp. 155-56, and 193-208.
5. *The Atlantic*, June, 2007, "A Knoll of One's Own."
6. *Los Angeles Times*, May 13, 2007.
7. See Chapter 9b, at Patspeer.com
8. See, Roger Feinman's "When Sonia Sotomayor's Honesty, Independence and Integrity were Tested" at ctka.net
9. Martin Cannon, "Letter from America," *Lobster*, No. 28, December 1994.
10. Ibid.
11. Ibid; author's 1994 interview with Peter Scott in San Francisco.
12. This would include this author, Peter Vea, William Davy and Joan Mellen.
13. For a brief example of this, see Garrison's October 1967 interview in *Playboy* which is posted at the Lancer website.

[14] See Gary Aguilar's critique of *Reclaiming History* in the Nov/Dec issue of *Federal Lawyer*.

[15] DiEugenio, op. cit, pp. 302–03.

[16] Turner and Christian, p. 304.

[17] Ibid.

[18] Ibid.

[19] Bugliosi, *Reclaiming History*, End Notes, pgs. 550-52. From here on this will be abbreviated as EN.

[20] Ibid, p. xxxix.

[21] WR, pgs. 807–08.

[22] HSCA Vol. 8, pgs. 197 ff.

[23] Ibid, p. 213.

[24] EN, p. 645.

[25] Thompson, pgs. 175–76.

[26] ARRB interview of 2/13/96

[27] Bugliosi, pgs. 429–47.

[28] Horne, Vol. 3, p. 806

[29] Ibid.

[30] Ibid.

[31] See the thread entitled "Vincent Bugliosi, DVP and CTKA" at Spartacus Educational begun by this author on August 22, 2010.

[32] This last came about because of Aguilar's coruscating review of the book in the Nov/Dec 2007 issue of *Federal Lawyer* and an ensuing round of personal letters between the two men in the summer of 2008 which Aguilar told this author about.

[33] This invitation was extended by both Wecht and Aguilar, and is referenced in a letter to the prosecutor by Aguilar of August 29, 2008.

[34] Reuters News Service, May 7, 2013.

Chapter 1

[1] The details about Bugliosi's early life are taken from his *Playboy* interview of April 1997 conducted by Lawrence Grobel (hereafter referred to as Grobel interview); and from the book *The Assassination of Robert F. Kennedy* by William Turner and Jonn Christian, p. 243.

[2] Ibid, Contemporary Authors.

[3] Turner and Christian, p. 244. Although Bugliosi's admirers like to bandy this winning record about, as a matter of perspective, it should be noted that most big city DA have a high winning percentage. Mainly because, due to finite resources, they usually take cases they think they can win, and most defendants cannot afford an expensive criminal defense attorney. In his 1976 race against John Van de Kamp, these numbers were questioned as being undocumented and non-specific.

[4] Bishop, p. 8.

[5] Bugliosi and Gentry, p. 452.

[6] Ibid, p. 143.

[7] Ibid, p. 207.

[8] Ibid, p. 229.

[9] Bishop, p. 11. The entire county, over ten thousand square miles, has less than twenty thousand people in it today.

[10] Ibid, p. 398.

[11] Ibid

[12] Bugliosi, pgs. 1295–1335.

[13] Bugliosi and Gentry, pgs. 104, 108.

[14] Garrison, pgs. 199–200.

[15] Bugliosi and Gentry, pgs. 140–41.

[16] DiEugenio and Pease, p. 228.

[17] Bishop, p. 79.

[18] Ibid, p. 90.

[19] Bishop, p. 345.

[20] Sanders, p. 64.

[21] Bugliosi and Gentry, pgs. 320–30.

[22] Bugliosi and Gentry, p. 294. See also Tate-LaBianca Murders Blog entry for 1/13/2006.

[23] Bishop, p. 326.

[24] Ibid.

[25] Ibid, p. 351.

[26] Ibid.

[27] Ibid, p. 397.

[28] Ibid.

[29] Bugliosi and Gentry, p. 294.

[30] Ibid, p. 251.

[31] Bishop, p. 306; Sanders, p. 229.

[32] Sanders, p. 283. For the comparisons to Hitler, see Bugliosi and Gentry, pgs. 407, 651. The opinion registered here about *Helter Skelter* today is not unusual among those who have followed that case assiduously over the decades. The reader can discern this by visiting websites and forums on that case.

Chapter 2

[1] Tavis Smiley Show transcript, March 16, 2009.

[2] Ibid.

[3] Ibid.

[4] See Patspeer.com Chapter 9b.

[5] HBO press release of September 18, 2007.

[6] Ibid.

[7] Ibid.

[8] Ibid, p. 29, p. 53.

[9] Ibid, p. 47. When Hanks won the Oscar for his role as a homosexual in *Philadelphia*, he saluted Farnsworth and his classmate John Gilkerson, and exposed their sexuality. This inspired the romantic comedy film *In & Out*.

[10] Ibid, p. 49.

[11] Ibid, p. 52.

[12] See Alec Baldwin's elegy for Bloom at *Huffington Post*, February 26, 2008.

[13] The only other actors who have done this are Spencer Tracy, Katharine Hepburn, and Jason Robards.

[14] Gardner, p. 199.

[15] Ibid, pp. 199–200. One of the worst things about writing this book was having to sit through this soporific, prosaically written, and aesthetically dull miniseries. That *From the Earth to the Moon* won best miniseries signifies one thing: television's Emmy Awards are as

meaningless as the Oscars. Hanks introduced each episode with a superfluous little speech. Watch closely and you will see that he did not even bother to change suits for most of them.

[16] Ibid, p. 227.
[17] See *Buffalo Reporter*, online edition, September 3, 1998.
[18] *The New Yorker*, April 26, 2010.
[19] Ibid.
[20] Ibid.
[21] *Los Angeles Times,* May 9, 2010.
[22] Blog of James Bacque, entry dated April 10, 2010.
[23] Ibid.
[24] Ibid.
[25] Ibid

Chapter 3:

[1] Bugliosi, p. 368.
[2] *Los Angeles Times*, April 2, 1993.
[3] Bugliosi, p. xxiv.
[4] *New York Times*, January 22, 1993.
[5] *Baltimore Sun*, April 2, 1993.
[6] O'Toole, pp. 27-28.
[7] This talk is available at the C-SPAN Video Library.
[8] Bugliosi, p. xvi.
[9] Ibid.
[10] Ibid, p. xvii.
[11] Ibid, xxiv.
[12] My descriptions of the trial come from the most current DVD release of the program, *On Trial,* in 2008. With extras, plus Edwin Newman's introduction, it runs about five and one half hours. The reader can watch the segments as posted on You Tube by David Von Pein.
[13] Benson, p. 54.
[14] Summers, p. 23
[15] Ibid.
[16] This information is taken from Patricia Lambert's important article, "Secret Service Report 491" in *The Continuing Inquiry*, Vol. 2, Nos. 3 and 4, October and November of 1977.
[17] Ibid.
[18] WR, pgs. 645–46.
[19] Bugliosi, p. xvi.
[20] *Dallas Morning News*, June 21, 2013.
[21] WC, Vol. 7, p. 11.
[22] Armstrong, p. 857.
[23] Ibid, p. 858.
[24] Lane, *Rush to Judgment*, p. 278.
[25] WC, Vol. 11, pgs. 435–36.
[26] Armstrong, p. 858.
[27] WR, pgs. 175-76.
[28] Ibid, p. 175.
[29] Scottsdale Police Department press release made at the time of Kirk's death in 2011.
[30] See Kirk's entry at the Find A Grave online site.

31 *Probe*, Vol. 7 No. 6, p. 17, "Max Holland Rescues the Warren Commission and the Nation" by Gary Aguilar. The Harris essay is called "Proof at Last" and is at the Acorn website.

32 Remington, p. 165; WC Vol. 7, p. 498.

33 Ibid.

34 Email from Speer to the author dated June 23, 2013. See also Chapter 7b of his valuable online book at patspeer.com.

35 See HSCA Report, p. 80.

36 WR, p. 98.

37 *Boston Globe*, January 12, 2007.

38 Ibid.

39 Crenshaw, p. 176.

40 Kurtz, p. 100.

41 DiEugenio and Pease, p. 274.

42 Kurtz, p. 31.

43 Hurt, p. 83.

44 Ibid.

45 Ibid.

46 WR, p. 740.

47 Ibid, Chapters 7 & 8, for a review of this aspect of Oswald's life.

48 Ruth had been saying these same things in public for decades. See Len Osanic's 50 Reasons for 50 years, Episode 19 on YouTube.

49 Bugliosi, p. xxiv.

50 WC, Vol. 2, p. 508.

51 *Medicolegal Investigation of the President John F. Kennedy Murder* (Springfield: Charles C. Thomas) 1978.

52 HSCA, Vol. 11, p. 512.

53 Bugliosi, EN, p. 13.

Chapter 4:

1 Bugliosi, p. xiv.

2 Ibid, p. xv.

3 Ibid, p. xvi.

4 Ibid, p. xli.

5 Bugliosi, pgs. 1057, 1063, 434.

6 Ibid, p. 443.

7 Ibid, p. 435.

8 Ibid, p. 873.

9 Ibid, p. xxviii.

10 Meagher, pgs. 107–09.

11 Bugliosi, p. xxviii.

12 Ibid, p. xxxviii.

13 Ibid, p. xxxix.

14 Ibid, p. 1515.

15 Ibid, p. 1258.

16 Ibid, p. 1275.

17 Ibid, p. 1277.

18 See the essay by David Mantik in *Probe*, Vol. 2, No. 3, p. 3; essay by Milicent Cranor in *The*

Fourth Decade Vol. 2, No. 4, p. 22; patspeer.com chapter 12c; the visual essay by Harris is at ctka.net, under the section "Dale Myers: An Introduction."

[19] EN, pgs. 346–47.

[20] Bugliosi, p. 965.

[21] Ibid, p. 237.

[22] Meagher, pgs. 95–100.

[23] WC, Vol. 3, p. 295.

[24] Decker Exhibit 5323, WC Vol. 19, p. 507.

[25] WR, p. 645.

[26] Bugliosi, p. 190.

[27] HSCA Vol. 1, pgs. 463–64.

[28] WR, p. 119.

[29] *Probe*, Vol. 5, No. 6, p. 10, "When Did Oswald Order the Rifle?" by Raymond Gallagher.

[30] WC, Vol. 7, p. 366.

[31] Op. cit. Armstrong.

[32] Op. cit. Gallagher.

[33] WC, Vol. 17, pgs. 677–78.

[34] Op. cit. Armstrong, p. 449.

[35] WR, p. 119.

[36] Op. cit. Armstrong, p. 439.

[37] Meagher, p. 105.

[38] WC, Vol. 25, CE 2562

[39] When it was pointed out to the longtime Warren Commission advocate Lattimer that he had just contradicted the Commission's case, he changed his story.

[40] WC, Vol. 19, p. 205.

[41] Op. cit. Gallagher.

[42] Armstrong, p. 472.

[43] See website giljesus.com, section entitled "The Rifle."

[44] Ibid.

[45] WC, Vol. 7, p. 368.

[46] Crescent Firearms shipping form number 3178, dated February 9, 1963.

[47] Armstrong, p. 472.

[48] WC, Vol. 7, p. 289ff; p. 525ff.

[49] Ibid, p. 526.

[50] Ibid, p. 527.

[51] Ibid.

[52] Commission Exhibit No. 2585

[53] Armstrong, p. 453.

[54] Report of Agent Charles Kunkel dated December 3, 1963, "Activities of the Oswald family from 11/24-11/30/63."

[55] HSCA interview of Mitchell Westra, 2/20/78.

[56] WC, Vol. 11, p. 226.

[57] FBI interview of Ryder, 11/25/63

[58] WC, Vol. 11, pgs. 262–75.

[59] Ibid, pgs. 253–61.

[60] Meagher, pgs. 369–70.

[61] George Michael Evica, *And We are All Mortal*, (University of Hartford: West Hartford, Connecticut) 1978, p. 8

[62] Op. cit. Jesus website.

Chapter 5:

1. Thompson, pgs. 163–64.
2. See pgs. 129–34.
3. Kurtz, p. 46.
4. EN, p. 431.
5. Op. cit. Kurtz.
6. Thompson, p. 175.
7. See Commission Exhibit 2011, and FBI Airtel of 6/20/64.
8. Op. cit. Thompson.
9. DiEugenio and Pease, p. 284.
10. Ibid.
11. EN, p. 545.
12. EN, p. 442.
13. Shaw's press conference is in various versions on YouTube.
14. The Harris essay, entitled "The Connally Bullet," is housed at ctka.net.
15. Ibid
16. Bugliosi, p. 814; EN, pgs. 439, 442–43.
17. Summers, p. 72; Hurt, p. 105.
18. Ibid, Summers.
19. Bonar Menninger, *Mortal Error*, (St. Martin's Press: New York) 1992, p. 114.
20. Thompson, p. 145.
21. WR, p. 647.
22. WC, Vol. 4, p. 253.
23. Op. cit., Thompson, p. 144.
24. Gerald Posner, *Case Closed*, (Random House: New York) 1993, p. 270.
25. Bugliosi, p. 928.
26. Letter dated September 11, 1996, emphasis in original.
27. See Michael Griffith's website, article entitled "The Dented Bullet Shell" dated 4/26/01.
28. Kurtz, p. 51.
29. Ibid.
30. Ibid.
31. Memo from Hoover to Rankin, June 2, 1964.
32. Ibid.
33. See Eaglesham's website, "The Sniper's Nest: Incarnations and Implications."
34. See Nov/Dec 2007 issue of *Federal Lawyer.*
35. Bugliosi, pgs. 811–14.
36. "The Enduring JFK Mystery" by Lisa Pease at consortiumnews.com, November 22, 2005.
37. See National Association of Criminal Defense Lawyers journal, *The Champion*, July 2004, article entitled "Comparative Bullet Lead Analysis: A Case Study in Flawed Forensics."
38. Ibid, p. 14.
39. Ibid.
40. Ibid.
41. Ibid, p. 17.
42. Ibid, p. 19.
43. See the article "Death of the NAA Verdict" by James DiEugenio at ctka.net
44. Ibid.
45. EN, pgs. 433–38.
46. Remington, p. 230.
47. Ibid, p. 232.

48 DiEugenio and Pease, p. 77.
49 Bugliosi, p. 326.
50 EN, p. 435.
51 Ibid.
52 *USA Today*, May 24, 2007.
53 EN, p. 436.
54 Ibid.
55 McKnight, p. 49.
56 General offense report of 4/10/63.
57 Armstrong, p. 507.
58 Ibid.
59 FBI Memorandum of 3/27/1964 from Jevons to Courad.
60 Op. cit. Brown.
61 Commission Exhibit 1.
62 McKnight, p. 56.
63 Armstrong, p. 511.
64 Ibid, p. 512.
65 Ibid, p. 510.
66 Commission Exhibit 1785.
67 Thompson, pgs. 163–64.
68 Ibid.
69 WR, p. 187.
70 WR, p. 405.
71 Commission Exhibit 1403, p. 1
72 FBI Report of June 4, 1964.
73 Dallas Police report of 4/11/63
74 Op. cit., Brown.
75 McKnight, p. 58.
76 Bugliosi, pgs. 690–91.
77 Ibid, p. 694.
78 Ibid, pgs. 690–94.
79 Ibid, p. 694.
80 Armstrong, p. 520.
81 Bugliosi, p. 694.
82 Armstrong, p. 515.
83 Ibid, p. 509.
84 Bugliosi, pgs. 694–95.
85 *Probe*, Vol. 5 No. 1, "The Paines Know" by Carol Hewett, p. 12.
86 Bugliosi, p. 695.
87 Op. cit. Hewett, p. 14.
88 Ibid.
89 WC, Vol. 1, p. 18.
90 DiEugenio, pgs. 194–95.
91 Op. cit. Hewett, p. 17.
92 Ibid, Hewett.
93 WC, Vol. 9, p. 314, 249; WR pgs. 282–83; George deferred to his wife for this date and she said it was April 13th.
94 FBI report of April 10, 1963.

[95] WC, Vol. 9, p. 248.
[96] Russell, p. 201.
[97] Op. cit. Hewett.
[98] Marrs, p. 287.
[99] Op. cit., Russell.
[100] Op. cit. Hewett, p. 16.
[101] Ibid, p. 11.
[102] Commission Exhibit 1403, p. 777.
[103] EN, p. 379.
[104] Ibid.
[105] Meagher, p. 130.
[106] DiEugenio, p. 203; Armstrong, p. 502.
[107] Armstrong, p. 501.
[108] Ibid, p. 502.
[109] Bugliosi, p. 228.
[110] Armstrong, p.503.
[111] WC, Vol. 1, p. 16.
[112] WC, Vol. 1, pgs. 146-48. Australian researcher Greg Parker postulates that this is a photo of Oswald holding a shotgun above his head in Minsk.
[113] Bugliosi, p. 1485.
[114] WC, Vol. 1, p. 14.
[115] Armstrong, p. 515.
[116] Epstein, p. 144.
[117] WR, pgs. 187–89.
[118] Op. cit. Epstein.
[119] Epstein, p. 145.
[120] Ibid.
[121] WC, Vol. 5, p. 588.
[122] Armstrong, p. 520.
[123] Bugliosi, p. 351; Meagher, pgs. 238–41.
[124] Bugliosi, p. 164.
[125] Letter from Turner to Gary Aguilar, July 17, 2007.
[126] Dallas Police Report of 11/23 from Doughty and Brown to Anderson.
[127] Dallas JFK Archives, Box 8, Folder 10, Item 5.
[128] FBI Memorandum of November 27, 1963.
[129] Letter from Hoover to J. Lee Rankin, March 10, 1964.
[130] Letter from Redlich to Dulles, July 2, 1964.
[131] Larry Hancock, *Someone Would Have Talked* (JFK Lancer Productions and Publications: Southlake Texas) 2006, p. 73.
[132] Bugliosi, p. 964.
[133] FBI Report of Charles Givens, 11/22/63.
[134] FBI Memo of Jevons to Conrad 2/27/64, McKnight, p. 211.
[135] Bugliosi, p. xxviii.
[136] WC, Vol. 8, p. 235.
[137] Hurt, p. 99.
[138] Michael Griffith website, "Was Oswald a Poor Shot?" posted 8/27/96
[139] Hurt, pgs. 99–100.
[140] Bugliosi, p. 1384.

[141] Lane, *Rush to Judgment*, p. 124.

[142] Ibid.

[143] HSCA, Vol. 11, pp. 231–32.

[144] McKnight, p. 113

[145] Commission Exhibit 1381. Bugliosi alludes to a location for this interview in the Commission volumes, but his source for it appears to be wrong.

[146] McKnight, p. 399.

[147] EN, p. 469.

[148] Meagher, pgs. 72–74.

[149] Ibid, p. 73.

[150] Commission Exhibit 2003, pgs. 59, 60.

[151] WR, p. 154.

[152] WC, Vol. 6, p. 340.

[153] WC, Vol. 6, p. 393.

[154] Ernest, p. 176, E-book version.

[155] WR, p. 154.

[156] Op. cit, Ernest, p. 218

[157] Ibid, pgs. 36, 219.

[158] Ibid.

[159] Ibid, p. 215.

[160] Ibid, p. 212.

[161] The author did a timing experiment on this point.

[162] Op. cit., Ernest, p. 79.

[163] Email communication with Ernest, July 3, 2013.

[164] Op. cit., Ernest, p. 75–76.

[165] Op. Cit., Ernest, p. 207.

[166] Ibid.

[167] EN, pgs. 468–69.

[168] McKnight, p. 114.

[169] Ibid.

[170] Ibid, p. 115.

[171] Bugliosi, p. 831.

[172] Ibid.

[173] WC, Vol. 4, p. 103.

[174] Bugliosi, p. 31.

[175] Ibid, p. 23.

[176] WC, Vol. 6, p. 330.

[177] WR, p. 622; Summers, p. 76

[178] WC, Vol. 3, p. 164, Bonnie Ray Williams; WC, Vol. 6, p. 337, Billy Lovelady; WC, Vol. 3, p. 200, James Jarman.

[179] Meagher, p. 226.

[180] Commission Exhibit 2003, p. 27; Commission Document 5, p. 329.

[181] WC, Vol. 19, p. 499.

[182] Commission Document 87, p. 780.

[183] WR, p. 143.

[184] WC, Vol. 6, p. 354.

[185] Sylvia Meagher, "The Curious Testimony of Mr. Givens," *Texas Observer,* August 13, 1971.

[186] WC, Vol. 5, pgs. 35–36.

[187] See Chapter 4, at patspeer.com, "The Strange Reliance on Charles Givens."

[188] Bugliosi, p. 823; see also the author's Source Notes, p. 101.

[189] Ibid.

[190] WC, Vol. 6, p. 355.

[191] McKnight, p. 115.

[192] Ibid.

[193] Ibid.

[194] Jerry Rose, "Important to Hold that Man," *The Third Decade*, Vol. 2 No. 4, p. 17.

[195] Mark Bridger, "The Myth of the Depository Roll Call," *Dealey Plaza Echo*, Vol. 11 No. 2, p. 38.

[196] Ibid, p. 40.

[197] EN, p. 93.

[198] Armstrong, p. 921.

[199] Ibid, p. 925.

[200] EN, pgs. 451–52.

[201] WC, Vol. 3, p. 465.

[202] Garrison, p. 200.

[203] Ibid, p. 201.

[204] EN, p. 453.

[205] Ibid.

[206] Ibid, p. 456.

[207] Dallas Municipal Archives, Box 9, Folder 1, Item 17; Armstrong, p. 871.

[208] WR p. 15.

[209] Bugliosi, p. 103.

[210] Ibid.

[211] Ibid.

[212] HSCA interview of former DPD officer Paul Bentley, 6/15/78

[213] Dale Myers, *With Malice,* (Oak Cliff Press, 1998) pgs. 274–78

[214] Bugliosi, p. xviii.

[215] Meagher, p. 255.

[216] Ibid, p. 254.

[217] These were Lee Farley and Robert Morrow. Both men are much taller than Oswald, therefore it would seem they would be able to traverse the distance faster.

[218] Meagher, p. 254. Markham is a controversial witness, but most would agree she did not become hysterical and unreliable until after the shooting.

[219] Author interview with Harris in Dallas at the ASK Conference in 1992.

[220] EN, p. 51.

[221] Meagher, p. 261.

[222] John Armstrong, "Harvey, Lee and Tippit: A New Look at the Tippit Shooting," *Probe*, Vol. 5 No. 2.

[223] Bugliosi, pgs. 669–685.

[224] Armstrong, op. cit. p. 483.

[225] WR, p. 173.

[226] Ibid.

[227] Remington, pgs. 340–454.

Chapter 6:

[1] Bugliosi, p. 451.
[2] Ibid, p. 462.
[3] Ibid.
[4] Ibid, p. 451.
[5] Ibid.
[6] Ibid, p. 452.
[7] Ibid, p. 455.
[8] Fetzer ed., *Assassination Science*, p. 252.
[9] McKnight, p. 295.
[10] Ibid, p. 296.
[11] EN, p. 296.
[12] McKnight, p. 294.
[13] EN, p. 297.
[14] Bugliosi, p. 458.
[15] Ibid.
[16] EN, p. 347.
[17] WR, p. 98.
[18] WR, p. 112.
[19] Thompson, pgs. 74–75.
[20] Ibid, p. 77.
[21] Bugliosi pgs. 458–64.
[22] Ibid, p. 467.
[23] Ibid, p. 468.
[24] patspeer.com, Chapter 9b, Part 3, "The Case Against Vincent Bugliosi." Speer shows here that Bugliosi's choice of witnesses is so selective that when one examines and analyzes exactly what they say, the author has next to zero support for this thesis.
[25] Bugliosi, p. 470.
[26] Ibid, p. 471.
[27] Hurt, p. 136.
[28] Bugliosi, p. 481.
[29] Thompson, p. 79.
[30] Bugliosi, p. 484.
[31] Ibid, p. 486.
[32] Horne, *Inside the ARRB*, Vol. 2, p. 600.
[33] Bugliosi, p. 487.
[34] Ibid, p. 382.
[35] Crenshaw, p. 176.
[36] Bugliosi, p. 382.
[37] Ibid, pgs. 384–85.
[38] DiEugenio, p. 301.
[39] Crenshaw, p. 179.
[40] Law, p. 150.
[41] Crenshaw, p. 180.
[42] Ibid, p. 179.
[43] Ibid, p. 181.
[44] Ibid.
[45] EN, p. 220

46 Crenshaw, p. 181
47 DiEugenio, pgs. 300–04. See also, Appendix A of the first edition of that book. It is also available online.
48 Ibid, p. 302.
49 Crenshaw, p. 228.
50 Law, p. 41; Livingstone, p. 215; Fetzer ed. *Murder in Dealey Plaza*, hereafter referred to as *MIDP*.
51 Law, p. 79.
52 *MIDP*, p. 208.
53 Law, p. 215; Livingstone, p. 214.
54 patspeer.com, Chapter 11.
55 Hurt, p. 60.
56 Law, p. 102.
57 Bugliosi, p. 423.
58 Law, p. 195.
59 Ibid, p. 194.
60 See the DVD, *Into Evidence*
61 McKnight, p. 158.
62 Law, p. 295.
63 Ibid, p. 293.
64 Ibid, p. 294.
65 Ibid, p. 295.
66 Commission Exhibits 385, 388,
67 patspeer.com Chapter 13 part 2.
68 EN, p. 357.
69 Law, p. 187
70 Ibid, pgs. 191, 226.
71 Ibid, p. 226.
72 McKnight, pgs. 92, 179–80.
73 Crenshaw, p. 185.
74 Ibid, p. 187.
75 McKnight, p. 162.
76 Ibid.
77 Ibid; Livingstone, p. 190.
78 McKnight, p. 165.
79 Ibid.
80 Bugliosi, pgs. 276–80.
81 Crenshaw, p. 183.
82 patspeer.com. Chapter 10, p. 9.
83 *New York Times*, 11/25/66.
84 Op. cit., Speer, p. 14.
85 Ibid, pgs. 23–24.
86 Bugliosi, p. 392.
87 Op. cit. Speer, Chapter 13, p. 3.
88 Thompson, p. 111. For a visual juxtaposition of the difference, see patspeer.com, Chapter 13, "Solving the Great Head Wound Mystery."
89 Jim Hougan, *Secret Agenda*, pgs. 315–20; see also, *Probe Magazine*, Vol. 3 No. 1, "The Formation of the Clark Panel" by Lisa Pease, p. 14.

90 Email communication to the author from Pat Speer, June 14, 2013.

91 *MIDP*, p. 451.

92 Ibid, p. 449.

93 ARRB interview of February 26, 1996.

94 Law, p. 257.

95 Ibid, p. 267.

96 Ibid, p. 166.

97 *MIDP*, p. 439.

98 Op. cit. Law, p. 120.

99 EN, p. 221.

100 Ibid, p. 222.

101 Livingstone, p. 38.

102 *MIDP,* p. 207.

103 Livingstone, pgs. 244–45.

104 Ibid, p. 245.

105 Ibid, p. 36.

106 Ibid.

107 *MIDP*, p. 443.

108 Livingstone, p. 239.

109 Ibid, p. 245.

110 *MIDP*, p. 238.

111 patspeer.com, Chapter 13, p. 10.

112 *MIDP,* p. 443.

113 Livingstone, p. 240.

114 *MIDP*, p. 446.

115 Fetzer, ed. *Assassination Science*, p. 120.

116 Ibid, p. 115.

117 Ibid, p. 112.

118 Ibid.

119 *MIDP*, p. 266.

120 Op. cit. Fetzer, p. 112.

121 Quoted in *MIDP*, p. 11.

122 Law, p. 120.

123 Ibid.

124 Ibid.

125 *MIDP,* p. 268.

126 Livingstone, pgs. 352–53.

127 Horne, Vol. 3, p. 797.

128 Ibid, p. 814.

129 *MIDP*, p. 284.

130 Ibid.

131 Ibid, p. 212.

132 Law, p. 257.

133 Harrison Livingstone, *High Treason II* (New York: Carroll and Graf, 1992) p. 226.

134 Groden and Livingstone, p. 42.

135 Ibid, p. 43.

136 Ibid, p. 47.

137 Ibid, p. 50.

[138] Harrison Livingstone, *Killing the Truth* (New York: Carroll and Graf, 1993), p. 195.

[139] Op. cit., Groden and Livingstone, p. 231.

[140] Horne, pgs. 1097, 1099. Agent Floyd Boring first said he found this in the follow-up car. Which would be just about proof positive the shot came from the front. He then called Horne the next day to say he was wrong, it was in the president's car.

[141] DiEugenio and Pease, p. 252

[142] Horne, pgs. 1097, 1099.

[143] Horne, Vol. 1, p. 41.

[144] DiEugenio and Pease, p. 253.

[145] Ibid.

[146] Ibid, p. 255.

[147] Ibid.

[148] Commission Exhibit 387.

[149] Commission Exhibit 391.

[150] HSCA, Vol. 7, p. 115.

[151] Op. cit., Commission Exhibit 391.

[152] EN, pgs. 283–84.

[153] See Pat Speer's DVD, *The Mysterious Death of Number 35* for Baden placing an autopsy photo upside down on an easel; Gary Aguilar corrected Baden on there being no FBI photographers at the autopsy.

[154] Horne, p. 806.

[155] Ibid.

[156] Ibid, pgs. 807–08.

[157] Horne, p. 809.

[158] Ibid, p. 785.

[159] Ibid, p. 810.

[160] *Probe*, Vol. 4 No. 3, "How Three Investigations of the Medical/Autopsy Evidence Got it Wrong" by Gary Aguilar and Kathleen Cunningham, p. 20.

[161] Ibid.

[162] Ibid.

[163] Ibid, p. 21.

[164] *MIDP*, p. 272.

[165] Op. cit, Aguilar and Cunningham, p. 21.

[166] Ibid.

[167] Livingstone, p. 192.

[168] Law, pgs. 228–29.

[169] *MIDP*, p. 116.

[170] Treasury Department memo of January 7, 1964

[171] McKnight, p. 402.

[172] Bugliosi, p. 425.

Chapter 7:

[1] *Probe*, Vol. 6 No. 3, "What Harry is Hiding," by James DiEugenio, p. 16.

[2] HSCA memorandum of April 19, 1978, from Betsy Palmer to Robert Blakey.

[3] Op. cit. DiEugenio, pgs. 17–20.

[4] Bugliosi, p. 1377.

[5] DiEugenio, p. 169.

6 *New Orleans Times Picayune*, April 1, 2012.
7 Ibid.
8 Ibid.
9 Ibid.
10 *New Orleans Times Picayune*, January 10, 2012. See also the website "Resurrection after Exoneration" for another look at Connick.
11 Bugliosi, pgs. 1358–59.
12 *New York Times Magazine*, August 6, 1995.
13 *Probe*, Vol. 2 No. 6, "Connick Continues to Defy ARRB," p. 15.
14 DiEugenio, p. 322.
15 Ibid, pgs. 229–37.
16 Ibid, pgs. 243–49.
17 Ibid, p. 289.
18 Ibid, p. 244.
19 Bugliosi, p. 1348.
20 James Kirkwood, *American Grotesque*, (New York: Simon and Schuster, 1970) p. 17.
21 For a chronicle of Shaw's covert career with the CIA, and his career as a free trade advocate for the power elite, see DiEugenio, pgs. 382-86.
22 Bugliosi, p. 1397.
23 Ibid.
24 Ibid.
25 Summers, p. 302.
26 NODA Memorandum of April 18, 1967.
27 Bugliosi, p. 1397.
28 Davy, p. 6.
29 Armstrong, pgs. 122–25.
30 *Probe*, Vol. 5 No. 5, "He's Back! The Return of Gerald Posner," by James DiEugenio, p. 15.
31 Armstrong, p. 125.
32 DiEugenio, p. 310.
33 Ibid, p. 81.
34 Ibid, pgs. 81-82.
35 Davy, p. 6
36 DiEugenio, p. 84.
37 Bugliosi, p. 1404.
38 Ibid.
39 DiEugenio, pgs. 113–14.
40 Ibid, pgs. 114, 341.
41 Garrison, p. 24.
42 DiEugenio, p. 113.
43 Ibid, p. 111.
44 Ibid, p. 158.
45 Garrison, pgs. 85–86.
46 DiEugenio, p. 387.
47 EN, p. 887.
48 FBI Memo of 3/22/67.
49 FBI Memo of 2/24/67.
50 For a compilation see DiEugenio, pgs. 387–88.
51 Davy, p. 302.

52 DiEugenio, p. 388.
53 *Probe*, Vol. 3 Nos. 3 and 4, "David Atlee Phillips, Clay Shaw and Freeport Sulphur" and "JFK, Indonesia, CIA and Freeport Sulphur" by Lisa Pease.
54 NODA Memorandum of 10/9/68.
55 Davy, pgs. 85–87.
56 Davy, p. 87.
57 NODA Memorandums of Marcy 27, and 29, 1967; Davy pgs. 185-86.
58 Davy, pgs. 28, 31.
59 DiEugenio, pgs. 105, 115.
60 Ibid, p. 363.
61 Ibid, p. 364.
62 Davy, p. 103.
63 DiEugenio, pgs. 88–93.
64 DiEugenio, p. 186.
65 EN, pgs. 858–70.
66 Bugliosi, p. 858.
67 Ibid, p. 859.
68 Mellen, pgs. 225, 227, 229, 231.
69 Bugliosi, p. 859.
70 Ibid, pgs. 859–60.
71 Mellen, pgs. 223, 225.
72 EN, p. 861.
73 Mellen, p. 231.
74 Ibid, p. 238.
75 Mellen, pgs. 232–34.
76 Ibid, p. 234.
77 Davy, p. 111.
78 Mellen, p. 224.
79 Ibid, p. 237.
80 Ibid, p. 238.
81 Ibid, p. 225.
82 Ibid, p. 227.
83 Davy, p. 110.
84 Bugliosi, p. 1421.
85 Ibid, p. 1417.
86 Newman, *JFK and Vietnam*, p. 72.
87 Ibid, p. 226.
88 Ibid, p. 446.
89 DiEugenio, p. 370.
90 Ibid, 369-71.
91 Bugliosi, p.1408.

Chapter 8:

1 EN, p. 115
2 Ibid, p. 114
3 WC, Vol. 4, p. 203.
4 Bugliosi, pgs. 114–15.

5 *USA Today* online, 7/29/08

6 Ibid.

7 Ibid.

8 Ibid.

9 Ibid.

10 *Dallas Morning News* online 9/19/08.

11 *CNN.com* online 8/15/05

12 law.com 3/8/04

13 Op. Cit. *USA Today.*

14 *Khou.com* online, 3/1/08

15 WR, p. 14.

16 WR, p. 15.

17 Ibid.

18 WR, p. 604.

19 Meagher, p. 225.

20 WC, Vol. 6, p. 377.

21 Meagher, p. 58.

22 Weisberg, p. 58.

23 Meagher, p. 225.

24 WR, p. 133.

25 WC, Vol. 9, p. 424.

26 WC, Vol. 22, p. 751.

27 Weisberg, pgs. 51, 52, 59.

28 Ibid, p. 58.

29 WC, Vol. 6, p. 360.

30 Ibid, p. 361.

31 Griggs, p. 203.

32 Henry S. Bloomgarden, *The Gun*, (New York: Bantam, 1976), p. 113.

33 Griggs, p. 200.

34 WC, Vol. 4, p. 97.

35 Ibid, p. 77

36 See giljesus.com, "The Gunsack."

37 Meagher, pgs. 48-49.

38 WR, p. 135.

39 WC, Vol. 4, p. 7. See also Commission Exhibit 631.

40 Ibid, p. 8. See also Commission Exhibit 634.

41 See Speer's article, "Proof the FBI changed Documents and Vincent Bugliosi was Wrong" at the Mary Ferrell Foundation website.

42 See patspeer.com, Chapter 4, "Sack of Lies."

43 WR, p. 136.

44 FBI Airtel of 12/6/63.

45 Commission Document 5, p. 165.

46 WC, Vol. 4, p. 93.

47 Commission Document, 897, p. 163.

48 See subhead at giljesus.com called "The Tape" under "The Paper Gunsack."

49 WC, Vol. 4, pgs. 99-100.

50 Ibid, p. 92.

51 WC, Vol. 4, p. 268.

52 Griggs, pgs. 176–77.
53 Ibid, p. 178.
54 Ibid.
55 Ibid, p. 179.
56 WC, Vol. 3, p. 231.
57 Meagher, p. 59.
58 Griggs, pgs. 181–82.
59 Meagher, p. 61.
60 Griggs, p. 185.
61 patspeer.com, Chapter 4b, "Sack of Lies" and 4c.
62 Commission Exhibit 2003.
63 Ibid.
64 O'Toole, p. 187.
65 Ibid, p. 186.
66 Ibid, pgs. 178–79.
67 Ibid, p. 180.
68 Ibid.
69 Commission Exhibit 2003.
70 Ibid.
71 Commission Exhibits 446, 447.
72 WC, Vol. 2, pgs. 226, 251.
73 Ibid, p. 248.
74 Ibid, p. 225.
75 Commission Document 205, p. 147.
76 WC, Vol. 2, p. 225.
77 Lee Farley, Spartacus Educational, post of December 4, 2012.
78 WC, Vol. 2, p. 228.
79 WC, Vol. 7, pgs. 393–95.
80 Armstrong, p.797.
81 Griggs, pgs. 205-07.
82 EN, pgs. 407–10.
83 WC, Vol. 4, p. 93.
84 Ibid.
85 Benson, p. 96.
86 EN, pgs. 307-09.
87 O'Toole, p. 205.
88 EN, p. 308.
89 EN, p. 311.
90 Michael Griffith's website, article entitled "Extra Bullets and Missed Shots in Dealey Plaza."
91 *MIDP,* p. 82.
92 O'Toole, p. 100.
93 Meagher, p. 99.
94 EN, p. 419.
95 Confidential source at the ARRB.
96 Bugliosi, pgs. 802–03.
97 Meagher, p. 121.
98 Ibid, p. 123.
99 Ibid, p. 122.

[100] Bugliosi, p. 800.

[101] WC, Vol. 4, p. 273

[102] Meagher, p. 122.

[103] Ibid, p. 123.

[104] Bugliosi, p. 801.

[105] Meagher, p. 124.

[106] Hurt, p. 109.

[107] Bugliosi, p. 801.

[108] EN, p. 414.

[109] Hurt, p. 107.

[110] Bugliosi, p. 802.

[111] Hurt, p. 109. Researcher Pat Speer has gone through the literature on this, and at a conference in Dallas in 2007, he confirmed it could be done and was done in other cases. Since this was the year his book came out, Bugliosi could have done the same.

[112] Meagher, p. 74.

[113] WC, Vol. 2, p. 251.

[114] Gary Savage, *JFK: First Day Evidence* (Monroe Louisiana: Shoppe Pess. 1993) p. 365.

[115] WR, pgs. 613, 636.

[116] WC, Vol. 3, pgs. 257–58.

[117] Ibid, p. 257.

[118] Ibid, p. 262.

[119] Ibid, p. 259.

[120] Meagher, p.72.

[121] Summers, p. 74; WR, p. 622.

[122] WR, p. 626.

[123] WR, p. 613.

[124] Ibid, p. 619.

[125] WC, Vol. 4, p. 468.

[126] WR, p. 636.

[127] WC, Vol. 7, p. 306.

[128] WR, p. 636.

[129] Summers, p. 76; WC, Vol. 3, p. 189.

[130] WC, Vol. 6, p. 380.

[131] WC, Vol. 3, p. 202.

[132] WC, Vol. 3, p. 171.

[133] Don Thomas, "Bugliosi Parses the Testimony" at Mary Ferrell Foundation.

[134] Savage, p. 140.

[135] *The Fourth Decade*, Vol. 5, No. 1, p. 4

[136] Ibid.

[137] Ibid, p. 5.

[138] Ibid.

[139] Bugliosi, pgs. 284, 1125.

[140] Hurt, p. 188.

[141] Bugliosi, p. 1078.

[142] Ibid, p. 1119.

[143] Ibid, p. 1133.

[144] Ibid, p. 1122.

[145] Ibid, pgs. 1072-73.

[146] Commission Exhibit, 2002, p. 51.

[147] Bugliosi, p. 1072.

[148] Meagher, pgs. 404-05.

[149] Ibid.

[150] WR, p. 221.

[151] WC Vol. 13, pgs. 135–37; Vol. 12, pgs. 323–29, 332–34; Vol. 12, pgs. 192–93.

[152] Bugliosi, p. 1073.

[153] See the DVD *Evidence of Revision,* Part 1, Section 7 at YouTube.

[154] Summers, p. 460.

[155] WR, p. 352.

[156] Summers, op. cit.

[157] Marrs, p. 418.

[158] Summers, Op. cit.

[159] Marrs, p. 419.

[160] Benson, p. 413.

[161] Summers, op. cit.

[162] Bugliosi, p. 1073; WR p. 209.

[163] WR, p. 354.

[164] Commission Exhibit 2287.

[165] Commission Exhibit 2313.

[166] WC, Vol. 15, p. 663.

[167] WC, Vol. 13, p. 204.

[168] WC, Vol. 15, p. 655.

[169] WC, Vol. 13, p. 205.

[170] WC, Vol. 5, p. 199.

[171] Ibid, p. 186.

[172] Ibid.

[173] Ibid, p. 199.

[174] HSCA, Vol. 9, pgs. 138-39; Summers, p. 463.

[175] Ibid, p. 134.

[176] Ibid.

[177] Ibid.

[178] Ibid, p. 139.

[179] Ibid, p. 136.

[180] See Part 7 of *Evidence of Revision*, on YouTube at 9 minute mark.

[181] Bugliosi, pgs. 272–73.

[182] O'Toole, p. 176.

[183] Kantor, p. 144.

[184] Ibid, p. 146.

[185] Ibid, p. 127.

[186] Summers, p. 465

[187] HSCA, Vol. 9, p. 139.

[188] Ibid.

[189] Ibid, p. 140.

[190] Summers, p. 463.

[191] HSCA, Vol. 9, p. 143.

[192] Kantor, p. 20.

[193] EN, p. 126.

[194] Marrs, p. 431.

[195] This clip is available on YouTube.

[196] Jim Marrs at the 2012 Lancer Conference in Dallas, based on a police interview.

[197] Benson, p. 485.

[198] Marrs, pgs. 423–34.

[199] Bugliosi, p. 1466.

[200] Griggs, p. 94.

[201] Benson, p. 96.

Chapter 9:

[1] Bugliosi, p. 1234

[2] Ibid, pgs. 1235–36.

[3] Ibid, p. 1238.

[4] EN, p. 695.

[5] EN, p. 704.

[6] Summers, *Official and Confidential*, pgs. 279-80.

[7] Ibid, p. 278.

[8] Gentry, p. 571.

[9] Summers, op. cit., p. 279.

[10] Gentry, p. 536; Summers, p. 316.

[11] Summers, p. 330.

[12] Ibid, p. 279.

[13] Gentry, pgs. 501–03.

[14] Ibid, p. 605.

[15] Ibid, p. 570.

[16] Talbot, p. 1.

[17] Ibid.

[18] Summers, p. 315.

[19] Ibid, p. 332.

[20] Gentry, p. 94.

[21] Gentry, p. 136.

[22] Summers, p. 38.

[23] Gentry, p. 99.

[24] Ibid, p. 101.

[25] Ibid, p. 88

[26] Ibid, p. 163.

[27] Ibid, pgs. 202–04.

[28] *The Nation,* June 26, 1976, "What the FBI Knew and Hid" by John Lowenthal.

[29] Summers, p. 167.

[30] *New York Times,* "Harvey Matusow, an anti-Communist Informer, Dies" February 4, 2002.

[31] Gentry, p. 354.

[32] Ibid, p. 441.

[33] Summers, p. 384.

[34] Ibid, pgs. 208–13.

[35] Summers, p. 315.

[36] Ibid, p. 317.

[37] It is available online at the Mary Ferrell Foundation.

38 Hurt, p. 144.
39 Ibid, p. 156.
40 McKnight, p. 56.
41 Summers, p. 321.
42 Antony and Robyn Summers, "The Ghosts of November" *Vanity Fair*, 12/94, p. 90.
43 Summers, p. 317.
44 O'Toole, p. 213.
45 Gentry, p. 547.
46 *Vanity Fair,* op. cit. p. 117.
47 Ibid.
48 Ibid.
49 Ibid, p. 88.
50 Ibid.
51 Ibid, p. 90.
52 Ibid.
53 Ibid.
54 Gentry, p. 548.
55 Summers p. 330.
56 Ibid. p. 139.
57 EN, p. 115.
58 WR, p. xii.
59 Email from Kritzberg to Robert Morrow dated May 11, 2011.
60 WR, p. 81.
61 These are "Phantom Identification of the Magic Bullet: E. L. Todd and CE 399" and "The
    Mystery of the 7:30 Bullet." They are both housed at JFK Lancer website. The author will be
    referring to both of them in this section.
62 Thompson, p. 156.
63 WC, Vol. 24, p. 412.
64 Ibid.
65 Thompson, p. 155.
66 Ibid, p. 176.
67 Ibid, p. 155.
68 Commission Exhibit 2011.
69 EN, p. 431.
70 Ibid.
71 Bugliosi, p. 471.
72 Ibid, p. 457.
73 Harold Weisberg, *Never Again*, (New York: Carrol and Graf, 1995), p. 342.
74 Hurt, p. 131.
75 McKnight, p. 228.
76 Ibid.
77 Hurt, p. 132.
78 McKnight, p. 231.
79 Hurt, p.132.
80 Ibid, p. 133.
81 McKnight, p. 228.
82 Hurt, p. 134.
83 Ibid.

[84] McKnight, p. 229.
[85] Ibid, p. 230.
[86] Hurt, p. 135.
[87] Ibid, p. 138.
[88] EN, pgs. 315–17.
[89] McKnight, p. 232.
[90] WR, p. 117.
[91] Bugliosi, p. xxxix
[92] Harold Weisberg, *Whitewash II* (Hyattstown Md: Self-Published, 1966), p. 215.
[93] Ibid, p. 4.
[94] Marrs, p. 456.
[95] Ibid, p. 457.
[96] WC, Vol. 5, p. 105.
[97] Hurt, p. 129.
[98] McKnight, p. 151.
[99] Ibid, p. 152.
[100] Op. cit. *Whitewash II*, p. 207.
[101] DiEugenio and Pease, p. 240.
[102] Armstrong, p. 125.
[103] *Probe*, Vol. 5, No. 5, p. 17.
[104] Ibid.
[105] Mellen, pgs. 232–34.
[106] JFK Lancer Conference of 2003, Olivier Presentation.
[107] DiEugenio, p. 181
[108] FBI Memorandum of March 2, 1967.
[109] Davy, p. 194.
[110] Ibid, p. 100.
[111] Newman, p. 310.
[112] Summers, *Official and Confidential*, p. 325.
[113] WC, Vol. 26, p. 783
[114] Probe, Vol. 4 No. 3, John Armstrong, *The FBI and the Framing of Oswald*, p. 23.
[115] Armstrong, p. 910.
[116] NODA Memorandum, of December 19, 1966.
[117] Armstrong, p. 304.
[118] Garrison, p. 182.
[119] Ibid.
[120] Newman, p. 317.
[121] Op. cit., *Vanity Fair*, p. 132.
[122] WC, Vol 10, p. 61.
[123] Mellen, p. 59.
[124] DiEugenio, p. 160; Mellen, pgs. 59–60.
[125] Op. cit., *Vanity Fair*.
[126] Robert Groden, *The Search for Lee Harvey Oswald*, (New York: Penguin, 1995) p. 230.
[127] Op. cit., *Vanity Fair*, p. 132.
[128] Bugliosi, p. 720.
[129] Ibid, p. 1222.
[130] Ibid, p. 1216.
[131] Ibid, pgs. 1218–19.
[132] Ibid, p. 1220.
[133] Op. cit., *Vanity Fair*, p. 132.

134 *Probe,* Vol. 3 No. 6, "Dodd Part 2: New Orleans and the Cover-up" by Lisa Pease, p. 15.
135 FBI Airtel of 2/10/64.
136 Mellen, p. 152.
137 Bugliosi, p. 1217.
138 Ibid, p. 1295.
139 Ibid, p. 1303.
140 HSCA, Vol. 10, p. 34.
141 Ibid, p. 28.
142 Ibid.
143 Ibid, p. 34.
144 Ibid.
145 Ibid, p. 30.
146 Ibid.
147 Ibid, p. 35, at footnote 139.
148 Ibid, p. 19.
149 Ibid.
150 DiEugenio, pgs. 248–49.
151 Bugliosi, p. 1306.
152 HSCA, op. cit., p. 22
153 Ibid, p. 23.
154 Meagher, p. 387.
155 Newman, pgs. 653–54.
156 Armstrong, p. 657.
157 Ibid, p. 671.
158 DiEugenio and Pease, p. 224.
159 Ibid.
160 WR, p. 808
161 WC, Vol. 14, p. 580.
162 Ibid.
163 Ibid.
164 Ibid, p. 587.
165 Ibid, p. 588.
166 HSCA, Vol. 8, p. 197.
167 Ibid, p. 201.
168 Ibid, pgs. 208-09.
169 Ibid, p. 210.
170 Ibid, p. 212.
171 Ibid, p. 209.
172 Ibid, p. 209.
173 Ibid, p. 212.
174 Ibid, p. 213.
175 Ibid, p. 217.
176 Ibid, p. 214.
177 Ibid, p. 213.
178 Ibid.
179 Ibid, p. 218.
180 Bugliosi, p. 1129.
181 EN, p. 645.

Chapter 10:

1 *Time*, December 13, 1963.
2 *Newsweek*, December 16, 1963.
3 Bugliosi, p. 331.
4 Walt Brown, *The Warren Omission*, (Delmax: New Castle, Delaware, 1996) p. 59.
5 HSCA, Vol. 3, pgs. 471–73.
6 Bugliosi, p. 364.
7 Ibid, p. 367.
8 Memorandum of Melvin Eisenberg of January 20, 1964, First Staff Meeting.
9 DiEugenio, p. 352.
10 Bugliosi, p. 327.
11 McKnight, p. 41.
12 Ibid, pgs. 42–43.
13 Associated Press story of August 8, 2008.
14 McKnight, p. 42.
15 Bugliosi, p. 331.
16 McKnight, p. 44.
17 Bugliosi, pgs. 327–28.
18 McKnight, p. 45.
19 Summers, p. 101.
20 Brown, pgs. 83–85.
21 Meagher, p. xxx
22 Bugliosi, p. 455.
23 HSCA, Vol. 11, p. 274.
24 Dick Russell, *On the Trail of the JFK Assassins* (New York: Skyhorse Publishing 2008), pgs. 126–27.
25 *Flagpole Magazine*, "Sen. Richard Russell and the Great American Murder Mystery," November 19, 2003.
26 Ibid.
27 McKnight, p. 296.
28 Op. cit., Russell.
29 *Texas Observer*, November, 1998.
30 Marrs, *Crossfire*, p. 477.
31 DVD entitled *The Assassination of President Kennedy.*
32 James Chace, "The Proconsul," *New York Review of Books*, October 8, 1992.
33 Jacob Heilbrunn, "The Real McCloy" *The New Republic*, May 11, 1992.
34 Bird, pgs. 76–77.
35 Ibid, p. 149.
36 Heilbrunn, p. 42.
37 Bird, p. 161.
38 Op. cit. Heilbrunn.
39 Bird, pgs. 165–66.
40 Heilbrunn, p. 43.
41 Bird, pgs. 213–14.
42 Heilbrunn, p. 43.
43 Bird, p. 204.
44 Ibid, p. 207.
45 McCloy, p. 331

46 Ibid, p. 336.
47 Heilbrunn, p. 44.
48 Op. cit. Chace.
49 Bird, p. 346.
50 Ibid.
51 Ibid, p. 352.
52 Ibid, p. 427.
53 Ibid, p. 428.
54 Ibid, p. 644.
55 Ibid, p. 652.
56 Heilbrunn, p. 43.
57 Ibid, p. 41.
58 Bird, pgs. 550–53.
59 Mosley, pgs. 35, 38.
60 Ibid, p. 37.
61 Ibid, p. 39.
62 Jacob Heilbrunn, "The Old Boy at War," *The New Republic*, March 27, 1995, p. 33.
63 Mosley, p. 49.
64 Op. cit., Heilbrunn.
65 Laurence Shoup and William Minter, *Imperial Brain Trust*, (New York: Monthly Review Press, 1977), pgs. 5, 26.
66 Mosley, p. 71.
67 Christopher Simpson, *The Splendid Blond Beast*, (Monroe, Maine, Common Courage Press, 2002) p. 34
68 Mosley, p. 71.
69 Lisagor and Lipsius, p. viii.
70 Mosley, p. 77.
71 Lisagor and Lipsius, p. 129.
72 Mosley, p. 88.
73 Op. cit., Heilbrunn.
74 Mosley, op. cit.
75 Lisagor and Lipsius, p. 122.
76 Ibid, pgs. 125–27.
77 Ibid, p. 136.
78 *New York Times,* October 21, 1945.
79 Op. cit. Heilbrunn, p. 34.
80 Ibid.
81 Ibid.
82 Mosley, p. 144.
83 Ibid, p. 184.
84 Ibid, p. 226.
85 Ibid, p. 230.
86 Ibid, p. 233.
87 Ibid, p. 234.
88 Bird, p. 353.
89 Ibid, p. 354.
90 Christopher Simpson, *Blowback*, (New York: Collier Books, 1989), p. 44.
91 Ibid, p. 90.

92 Mosley, p. 245.

93 Ibid, p. 246.

94 Lisagor and Lipsius, pgs. 163–64.

95 Ibid.

96 Ibid, p. 165.

97 Mosley, p. 243.

98 Lisagor and Lipsius, P. 165.

99 Mosley, p. 268.

100 See the article "CIA Death Lists and Guatemala Killing Fields" by Robert Parry at the online magazine, The Consortium.

101 Arthur Schlesinger, *Robert Kennedy and His Times*, (Boston: Houghton Mifflin Company, 1978) pgs. 474–78.

102 Ibid, p. 475.

103 Ibid.

104 Ibid, p. 477.

105 Mosley, p. 473.

106 David Lifton, *Best Evidence*, (New York: Carroll and Graf, 1988), pgs. 34–36.

107 DiEugenio, pgs. 197-98.

108 Jim Hougan, *Spooks*, (New York: William Morrow and Company, 1978) p. 29.

109 Ibid, p. 36.

110 Bugliosi, p. 1195.

111 Brown, pgs. 83–87.

112 McKnight, p. 42.

113 Ibid.

114 Ibid.

115 Ibid, p. 43.

116 Marrs, p. 466.

117 McKnight, p. 43.

118 Ibid, p. 44.

119 Marrs, p. 467.

120 Ibid, p. 466.

121 Schorr, p. 139.

122 *Time,* September 30, 1974.

123 Ibid.

124 Schorr, p. 143.

125 Gary Shaw and Larry Harris, Cover-Up, (Cleburne, Texas: Self-Published, 1976), p. 29.

126 Ibid.

127 Schorr, p. 144.

128 Ibid.

129 Ibid, p. 155.

130 Ibid, p. 191.

131 John Ranelagh, *The Agency*, (New York: Simon and Schuster, 1986) p. 473.

132 Schorr, p. 191.

133 Ibid.

134 Ibid.

135 Ibid, p. 194.

136 Ibid, p. 201.

137 Ibid, p. 208.

138 Bugliosi, p. 1236.

Chapter 11:

1 Armstrong, p. 696.
2 HSCA, Vol. 11, p. 221.
3 Armstrong, p. 695.
4 Ibid.
5 Ibid.
6 Ibid.
7 Ibid, p. 696.
8 DiEugenio and Pease, p. 224.
9 Priscilla Johnson McMillan" by James DiEugenio, at ctka.net
10 Ibid.
11 Newman, pgs. 84-86.
12 Op. cit. DiEugenio.
13 Ibid.
14 Ibid.
15 EN, p. 368.
16 Bugliosi, p. 1102.
17 Summers, p. 468.
18 Bugliosi, p. 1102
19 Armstrong, p. 177.
20 Ibid, p. 178.
21 Hurt, pgs. 401–05.
22 HSCA, Vol. 9, p. 200.
23 Marrs, p. 394.
24 Armstrong, p. 948.
25 Marrs, p. 393.
26 FBI Memorandum of March 26, 1964.
27 Bugliosi, p. 1111.
28 Marrs, p. 396.
29 Summers, p. 440.
30 Ibid, p. 441.
31 DiEugenio and Pease, pgs. 225-28.
32 Garrison, pgs. 217–18; Hurt, pgs. 114-15.
33 Hurt, p. 184.
34 Hurt, p. 185.
35 Bugliosi, pgs. 1103–1107; 1142–44.
36 HSCA, Vol. 9, p. 201.
37 Bugliosi, p. 1466.
38 Ibid, pgs. 1145–57.
39 Ibid, p. 1160.
40 Ibid, p. 1169.
41 Ibid, p. 1171.
42 Ibid, pgs. 1173–75.
43 EN, pgs. 658–59.
44 Bugliosi, p. 1178.
45 Ibid, p. 1180.
46 Ibid, p. 1199.
47 Garrison, p. 22.
48 DiEugenio, Chapter 7, "On Instructions from His Government" and Chapter 8, "Oswald Returns: Strange Bedfellows."

49 Bugliosi, p. 1199

50 Newman, *Oswald and the CIA*, p. 398.

51 Ibid, p. 393.

52 *Lopez Report*, pgs. 156–57.

53 Bugliosi, p. 1189.

54 DiEugenio, see especially Chapter 1 and 2.

55 Bugliosi, pgs. 1189-95.

56 Ibid, p. 1190.

57 Audrey and George McT. Kahin, *Subversion as Foreign Policy* (New York: The New Press, 1995) p. 98

58 Ibid, p. 8.

59 DiEugenio, p. 29.

60 Trumbull Higgins, *The Perfect Failure*, (W. W. Norton: New York, 1989) pgs. 49-50.

61 Ibid, p. 46.

62 Morris H. Morley, *Imperial State and Revolution*, (Cambridge University Press: Cambridge, 1987) p. 95

63 Peter Kornbluh, Bay of Pigs Declassified (New press: New York, 1998). See the entire Introduction, pgs. 1 and 3, for the next two quotes.

64 See DiEugenio, Chapter 3, where these matters are all explored in depth.

65 DiEugenio, p. 76.

66 Bugliosi, p. 1195.

67 Ibid.

68 Newman, pgs. 635–37.

69 EN, p. 675.

70 DiEugenio, p. 294.

71 Bugliosi, p. 1215.

72 DiEugenio, pgs. 323–24.

73 Bugliosi, p. 1239.

74 Ibid, p. 1241.

75 Ibid.

76 Ibid.

77 Marrs, p. 246.

78 Ibid, p. 247.

79 Ibid, p. 248.

80 Bugliosi, p. 1243.

81 *Inside the ARRB*, Vol. 5, p. 1402.

82 Ibid, p. 1403.

83 Ibid, p. 1404.

84 Ibid.

85 Ibid, p. 1405.

86 Ibid, p. 1406.

87 Ibid, p. 1409.

88 Horne, Volume 2, p. 647.

89 Bolden, p. 42.

90 EN, p. 713.

91 EN, pgs. 720–23.

92 This speech is today available online at ratical.org as part of a book by Martin Schotz, *History Will Not Absolve Us.*

[93] EN, pgs. 1273–80.

[94] See pages 919–25

[95] Bugliosi, p. 1273.

[96] This information is at Simkin's website Spartacus School.net and and Doug Horne's blog.

[97] Simkin, ibid; the Reynolds episode is also in Robert Caro's book, *The Passage of Power.*

[98] Bugliosi, pgs. 1275-80.

[99] Ibid, p. 922.

[100] WR, p. 566.

[101] See Richard Bartholomew's monograph, "Conflicts in Official Accounts of the Cardboard Carton Prints."

[102] WC, Volume 17, Commission Exhibit 656.

[103] Print 22, Box B.

Chapter 12:

[1] Stanley Heller, "Brzezinski and Charlie Wilson's War," *Counterpunch*, December 26, 2007.

[2] Ibid.

[3] Ibid.

[4] Interview with Coll, on radio program *Democracy Now*, June 10, 2004.

[5] Crile, p. 521.

[6] Chalmers Johnson, "An Imperialist Comedy," at Tom Dispatch.com, January 6, 2008.

[7] Crile, p. 65.

[8] Ibid, p. 66.

[9] Ibid, p. 67.

[10] Ibid, p. 64.

[11] Ibid, p. 69.

[12] Robert Parry, "Hollywood's Dangerous Afghan Illusion," *Consortiumnews.com,* April 7, 2013.

[13] Melissa Roddy, "Tom Hanks Tells Hollywood Whopper in Charlie Wilson's War" at Alter.net, December 20, 2007.

[14] Ibid.

[15] Crile, pgs. 343–45.

[16] Ibid, pgs. 477–79.

[17] Steve Coll, "Gorbachev was Right," *The New Yorker*, September 29, 2009.

[18] Ibid.

[19] Evan Thomas, "The Road to September 11th," *Newsweek*, October 1, 2001.

[20] Op. cit., Roddy.

[21] Crile, p. 514.

[22] Ibid.

[23] Bruce Cameron, "Why Afghanistan Really Fell Apart," *Consortiumnews.com,* February 10, 2010.

[24] Ibid.

[25] Ibid.

[26] Ibid.

[27] Crile, p. 454.

[28] Ibid, p. 504.

[29] Ibid, p. 506.

[30] Op. cit. Roddy.

[31] *New York Times*, October 13, 1981.
[32] Melissa Roddy, *Huffington Post*, July 13, 2013.
[33] Ibid.
[34] Ibid.
[35] Ibid.
[36] Ibid.
[37] Ibid.
[38] "The Durand Line," *The Nation*, November 3, 2012.
[39] Roddy, Alternet, op. cit.
[40] *New York Times*, December, 21, 2007.

Chapter 13:

[1] Ed Rampell, "Hollywood's Year of Living Clandestinely," *Counterpunch*, Volume 20, Number 5, p. 9.
[2] Turley in the foreword to Robb, p. 18.
[3] *Mother Jones*, September 20, 2004, Interview with author David Robb.
[4] Ibid.
[5] Ibid.
[6] Ibid.
[7] Robb, pgs. 249–57.
[8] Ibid, pgs. 292–94.
[9] Ibid, pgs. 54–55.
[10] Ibid, p. 54.
[11] Ibid, p. 53.
[12] Ibid, p. 56.
[13] Logevall, p. 253.
[14] Ibid, p. 257.
[15] Ibid, p. 337.
[16] Robb, p. 281.
[17] Ibid.
[18] Ibid.
[19] Ibid, p. 284.
[20] Ibid, p. 280.
[21] Ibid, p. 277.
[22] Jenkins, pgs. 8–9.
[23] Ibid, p. 7.
[24] Ibid, p. 9.
[25] Ibid, p. 35.
[26] Ibid.
[27] Ibid.
[28] Ibid.
[29] Ibid, p. 36.
[30] Ibid, p. 37.
[31] Ibid, p. 38.
[32] Ibid, p. 47.
[33] "An Offer They Couldn't Refuse" by Matt Alford, in *The Guardian*, November 14, 2008.
[34] Ibid.
[35] Robb, p. 149.

36 *New York Times*, September 2, 2001.

37 Ibid.

38 Jenkins, p. 32.

39 Ibid, p. 56.

40 Interview by Jenkins with Beckner, December 2, 2009.

41 DiEugenio, pgs. 41–50.

42 Jenkins, p. 65.

43 Jane Mayer, "Zero Conscience in Zero Dark Thirty," *The New Yorker*, 12/14/2012.

44 There is little doubt about what Spielberg meant by this assignation. As Bob Tanenbaum noted to the author, Ramer was not a founding member of the firm. He got his name situated on the title because he threatened to leave. Tanenbaum knew this since his wife's father, who did help found the firm, was involved in hiring Ramer. (Personal interview with Tanenbaum, August of 2004.)

45 *Variety*, March 28, 2007.

46 *New York Times*, November 30, 2008.

47 Ibid.

48 Jenkins, pgs. 74–75.

49 Ibid, p. 85.

50 Ibid, p. 89.

51 Ibid, p. 94.

52 Ibid, p. 112.

53 Ibid, p. 3.

54 McBride, p. 73.

55 Ibid, p. 75.

56 Ibid, p. 18.

57 Ibid, p. 20.

58 Ibid, p. 55.

59 Ibid, p. 127.

60 Ibid, p. 130.

61 Ibid, p. 141.

62 Ibid, p. 164.

63 *New York Times*, April 28, 1974.

64 McBride, p. 256.

65 Ibid, p. 426.

66 Ibid, p. 436.

67 Ibid, p. 469.

68 Ibid, p. 470.

69 Ibid, p. 471.

70 Ibid, pgs. 490-91.

71 Ibid, p. 491.

72 Gardner, 1999 edition, pgs. 29, 51, 185. It should also be noted, Hanks was also a Star Trek fan, to the degree that some of his friends said he was actually a Trekkie. See, p. 53.

73 *Time*, March 3, 2010.

74 Gardner, 2007 edition, pgs. 254–55. The rest of these references in this section will be from the 2007 edition also.

75 Ibid, p. 251.

76 Ibid, p. 252.

77 David Sirota, "A Tale of Two Presidents," *Salon*, June 21, 2013.

78 Jenkins, p. 69.

Chapter 14:

1 *New York Times*, August 13, 1999.
2 See discussion of *Ghost Wars* at Woodrow Wilson Center on YouTube. In this author's opinion, Coll's book is a much more accurate look at the subject of Afghanistan and the Soviet invasion than Crile's.
3 Matt Alford and Robbie Graham, "An Offer They Couldn't Refuse," *Guardian UK*, November 14, 2008.
4 *Dallas Morning News*, June 25, 2011.
5 Two confidential sources to the author in 2010, and 2011.
6 Jo Piazza, *AOL News*, August 27, 2010.
7 Robert Seldman, *TV by the Numbers*, March 16, 2010.
8 See especially "Assessing Landesman" at *Slate*, June 9, 2005. This article contains links to most of the entire controversy.
9 Mike Fleming at *Deadline*, June 29, 2011.
10 David Rockefeller, *Memoirs*, (Random House: New York, 2002), p. 437.
11 See McClarty Associates website under Film and Entertainment tab.
12 2012 Confidential source.
13 See ARRB Medical Document No. 41 at the *History Matters* website.
14 WC Vol. 6, p. 33.
15 WC Vol. 3, p. 360.
16 See Civil Lawsuit filing, AARC vs. LMH Company, November 23, 1998.
17 Ibid, see also The Official Zapruder Film Time Line at jfk.org, The Sixth Floor Museum.
18 Douglas Horne, *Inside the ARRB*, Volume 4, p. 1203.
19 WC, Vol. 1, p. 310.
20 Ibid.
21 Ibid, p. 312.
22 Ibid, p. 314.
23 Ibid.
24 Ibid, p. 460.
25 Ibid, p. 457.
26 Ibid, p. 346.
27 Ibid, p. 449.
28 Ibid, p. 314.
29 Ibid, p. 456; Commission Exhibit 323, p. 5.
30 Ibid, p. 316.
31 Ibid.
32 Ibid, pgs. 462, 468.
33 Newman, *Oswald and the CIA*, p. 151.
34 Ibid, p. 152.
35 Ibid, p. 151.
36 Ibid, p. 153.
37 Ibid, p. 143.
38 Ibid, p. 217.
39 Ibid, p. 218.
40 Ibid, pgs. 243–44.
41 Ibid, pgs. 264–65.
42 Ibid.
43 Ibid, see especially pages 270–73, pgs. 300, 311, 317
44 DiEugenio and Pease, p. 222.

45 Ibid, p. 123.
46 McKnight, p. 255.
47 Ibid.
48 Ibid, pgs. 258-59.
49 Ibid, p. 276.
50 Charles Kunkel Secret Service Report on Oswald family, 11/24-11/30.
51 Meagher, pgs. 394-97.
52 *Murder in Dealey Plaza*, edited by James Fetzer, (Catfeet Press: Chicago, 2000) pgs. 62, 420.
53 Marrs, pgs. 246–47.
54 Ibid, p. 417.
55 Ibid, pgs. 415–16.H

Chapter 15:

1 See DiEugenio and Pease, pgs. 530–631.
2 Ibid, pgs. 563–66.
3 Jeff Labrecque, "Leonardo DiCaprio to tackle JFK Assassination in Legacy of Secrecy," *Entertainment Weekly*, November 19, 2010.
4 Although Waldron has tried to erase this previous career from his official past, some of these comics and graphic novels are still available on amazon.com.
5 The reviews of *Ultimate Sacrifice* and *Legacy of Secrecy* are at ctka.net; the review of *Watergate: The Hidden History* is at Robert Parry's Consortiumnews.com.
6 DiEugenio, pgs. 71–76.
7 See Anthony and Robbyn Summers, "The Ghosts of November" *Vanity Fair*, 12/94.
8 Lamar Waldron and Thom Hartmann, *Legacy of Secrecy*, (Counterpoint: Berkeley, 2008) p. 50.
9 Ibid, p. 121.
10 Author's interview with Giammarco in September of 2012.
11 Conversation with Larry Hancock at 2010 Lancer Conference in Dallas.
12 These notebooks were the only thing anyone at the meeting brought in preparation for the discussion, Waldron.
13 Richard Helms, with William Hood, *A Look Over My Shoulder*, pgs. 226–27.
14 Joseph Burkholder Smith, *Portrait of a Cold Warrior*, p. 383.
15 DiEugenio, p. 70.
16 Ibid.

Afterword:

1 David Talbot, "The Kennedys in Hollywood," *Salon*, April 1, 2011.
2 Ibid.
3 Author interview with McBride, July 20, 2013.
4 DiEugenio, Chapter 9.
5 Author's 1994 interview with Volz in New Orleans.
6 DiEugenio, Chapter 14.
7 Ibid, pgs. 299–306.
8 Email communication from Speer, dated July 22, 2013. Afterwards, Estevez told Speer he was specifically aware of the fine work Lisa Pease had done on the RFK case.
9 When I brought this point up about Blakey at Appian Way, Waldron jumped in and said

that "No, it was Peter Noyes's *Legacy of Doubt.* That was a *New York Times* bestseller, it says so on the jacket." It is true that Noyes's book did proffer in a vague way some sort of Mob did it concept. But it had so little impact, it is often ignored. But, as it often is with Waldron, one has to track down many of his grandiose claims. The Noyes book does not show up on any *New York Times* bestseller list from that era. And in the paperback issue (there was no hardcover) it does not say it was such.

10 DiEugenio, p. 340.
11 Ibid, p. 364.
12 David Denby, "Susan Sontag's Life in Film," *The New Yorker*, September 12, 2005.
13 Ibid.
14 Susan Sontag, "The Decay of Cinema, *The New York Times*, February 25, 1996.
15 Ibid.
16 This press conference is on YouTube.
17 Gardner, 1999 edition, p. 48.
18 James Blight, Janet Lang, David Welch, *Virtual JFK* (Rowman and Littlefield Publishers: London, 2009) pgs. 305–10.

Bibliography

Government Reports

Oswald, the CIA and Mexico City, more commonly referred to as "The Lopez Report." The HSCA report on Oswald in Mexico City was written in 1978 by Dan Hardway an Ed Lopez. It was almost fully declassified in 2003. Yet the appendix title "Was Oswald an Agent of the CIA?" is not available.

Report of the President's Commission on the Assassination of President John F. Kennedy (the *Warren Report*) (Washington D.C.: U.S. Government Printing Office, 1964), with accompanying 26 volumes of exhibits and testimony.

U. S. House, Select Committee on Assassinations, Report, with twelve accompanying volumes of hearings and appendices (material on Kennedy case as opposed to Martin Luther King Jr. case) (Washington D.C.: U.S. Government Printing Office, 1979), 95th Congress, 2nd Session, 1979, H. Rpt. 1828.

Periodicals

Aguilar, Gary, "Max Holland Rescues the Warren Commission and the Nation," *Probe*, Vol. 7 No. 6.

Aguilar, Gary and Kathleen Cunningham, "How Three Investigations of the Medical/Autopsy Evidence Got it Wrong," *Probe*, Vol. 4 No. 3.

Armstrong, John, "Harvey, Lee and Tippit: A New Look at the Tippit Shooting," *Probe*, Vol. 5 No. 2.

Black, Edwin, "The Plot to Kill JFK in Chicago," *Chicago Independent*, November, 1975.

Bridger, Mark, "The Myth of the Depository Roll Call," *Dealey Plaza Echo*, Vol. 11, No. 2.

Bugliosi, Vincent, interview in *Playboy*, April 1997.

Chace, James, "The Proconsul," *New York Review of Books*, October 8, 1992.

Coll, Steve, "Gorbachev was Right," *The New Yorker*, September 29, 2009.

Denby, David, "Susan Sontag's Life in Film," *The New Yorker*, September 12, 2005.

DiEugenio, James, "He's Back! The Return of Gerald Posner," *Probe*, Vol. 5 No. 5.

DiEugenio, James, "What Harry is Hiding," *Probe*, Vol. 6 No. 3.

Gallagher, Raymond, "When Did Oswald order the Rifle?" *Probe*, Vol. 5 No. 6.

Hewett, Carol, "The Paines Know" *Probe*, Vol. 5 No. 1

Heilbrunn, Jacob, "The Old Boy at War," *The New Republic*, March 27, 1995.

Heilbrunn, Jacob, "The Real McCloy," *The New Republic*, May 11, 1992.

Heller, Stanley, "Brzezinski and Charlie Wilson's War," *Counterpunch*, December 26, 2007.

Lambert, Patricia, "Secret Service Report 491," *The Continuing Inquiry*, October-November, 1977.

Meagher, Sylvia, "The Curious Testimony of Mr. Givens," *Texas Observer*, August 13, 1971.

Pease, Lisa, "The Backyard Photo Experts," *Probe*, Vol. 3 No. 2.

Pease, Lisa, "Dodd Part 2: New Orleans and the Cover-Up," *Probe*, Vol. 3 No. 6.

Pease, Lisa, "No Lt. Columbo in Mexico City," *Probe*, Vol. 4 No. 1.

Rampell, "Hollywood's Year of Living Clandestinely," *Counterpunch*, May 2013.

Robb, David, Interview in *Mother Jones*, September 20, 2004.

Rose, Jerry, "Important to Hold that Man," The Third Decade, Vol. 2 No. 4.

Sprague, Richard, Interview in *Probe*, Vol. 7 No. 2.

Summers, Anthony and Robyn, "The Ghosts of November," *Vanity Fair*, December 1994.

Books

Armstrong, John. *Harvey and Lee* (Arlington, Texas: Quasar Ltd., 2003).

Benson, Michael. *Who's Who in the JFK Assassination* (Citadel Press: New York, 1993).

Bolden, Abraham. *The Echo from Dealey Plaza* (Broadway Books: New York, 2009).

Bird, Kai. *The Chairman* (Simon and Schuster: New York, 1992).

Bishop, George. *Witness to Evil* (Dell: New York, 1971).

Brown, Walt. *The Warren Omission* (Delmax: Wilmington, 1996).

Bugliosi, Vincent. *Reclaiming History* (W. W. Norton and Company: New York, 2007).

Bugliosi, Vincent and Curt Gentry. *Helter Skelter* (W. W. Norton and Company, 1994).

Coll, Steve. *Ghost Wars* (Penguin Books, New York, 2004).

Crenshaw, Charles. *Trauma Room One* (Paraview Press: New York, 2001).

Crile, George. *Charlie Wilson's War* (Grove Press: New York, 2003).

Davy, William. *Let Justice be Done* (Jordan Publishing: Reston, Virginia, 1999) .

DiEugenio, James. *Destiny Betrayed*, Second Edition (Skyhorse Publishing: New York, 2012).

DiEugenio, James and Lisa Pease. Editors, *The Assassinations* (Feral House: Los Angeles, 2003).

Douglass, James. *JFK and the Unspeakable* (Orbis Books: New York, 2008).

Epstein, Edward. *The Assassination Chronicles* (Carroll and Graf: New York, 1992).

Fetzer, James. Editor, *Assassination Science* (Catfeet Press: Chicago, 1998).

Fetzer, James. Editor, *Murder in Dealey Plaza* (Catfeet Press: Chicago, 2000).

Fonzi, Gaeton. *The Last Investigation* (Thunder's Mouth Press: New York, 1993).

Gardner, David. *Tom Hanks: The Unauthorized Biography* (Blake Publishing: London, 1999) Reissued in 2007 as *The Tom Hanks Enigma*.

Garrison, Jim. *On the Trail of the Assassins* (Sheridan Square Press: New York, 1988).

Gentry, Curt. *J. Edgar Hoover: The Man and the Secrets* (W. W. Norton: New York, 1991).

Griggs, Ian. *No Case to Answer* (JFK Lancer Productions and Publications: Southlake, Texas, 2005).

Groden, Robert and Harrison Livingstone. *High Treason* (Berkley Books: New York, 1990).

Hurt, Henry. *Reasonable Doubt* (Holt, Rinehart and Winston: New York, 1985.)

Horne, Douglas. *Inside the ARRB* (Self-Published: Charleston, S.C. 2009).

Jenkins, Tricia. *The CIA in Hollywood* (University of Texas Press: Austin, 2012).

Kantor, Seth. *The Ruby Cover-Up* (Zebra Books: New York, 1978).

Kurtz, Michael. *Crime of the Century* (University of Tennessee Press:Knoxville, 1993).

Lane, Mark. *Rush to Judgment* (Holt, Rinehart and Winston: New York, 1966).

Law, William Matson. *In the Eye of History* (JFK Lancer Productions and Publications: Southlake, Texas, 2005).

Lisagor, Nancy and Frank Lipsius. *A Law Unto Itself* (Paragon House: New York, 1989).

Livingstone, Harrison. *Killing Kennedy* (Carroll and Graf: New York, 1995).

Logevall, Fredrik. *Choosing War* (University of California Press: London, 1999).

Marrs, Jim. *Crossfire: The Plot that Killed Kennedy* (Carroll and Graf, 1989).

McBride, Joseph. *Steven Spielberg: A Biography* (University Press of Mississippi: Jackson, 2011).

McKnight, Gerald. *Breach of Trust* (University Press of Kansas: Lawrence, Kansas, 2005).

Meagher, Sylvia. *Accessories After the Fact* (Bobbs-Merrill: New York, 1967).

Melanson, Philip. *Spy Saga* (Praeger: New York, 1990).

Mellen, Joan. *A Farewell to Justice* (Potomac Books: Dulles, Virginia, 2005).

Mosley, Leonard. *Dulles* (The Dial Press: New York, 1978).

Newman, John. *JFK and Vietnam* ((Warner Books: New York, 1992).

Newman, John. *Oswald and the CIA* (Skyhorse Publishing, 2008).

O'Toole, George. *The Assassination Tapes* (Penthouse Press: New York, 1975).

Remington, Rodger. *Biting the Elephant* (Trafford Publishing: Victoria, British Columbia, Canada, 2009).

Robb, David. *Operation Hollywood* (Prometheus Books: Amherst, NY, 2004).

Russell, Dick. *The Man Who Knew Too Much* (Carroll and Graf: New York, 2003).

Sanders, Ed. *The Family* (Da Capo Press: Cambridge, Massachusetts, 2002.

Schlesinger, Arthur. *Robert Kennedy and His Times* (Houghton Mifflin: Boston, 1978).

Schorr, Daniel. *Clearing the Air* (Houghton Mifflin: New York, 1977).

Schreck, Nikolas, *The Manson File* (World Operations: Berlin, 2011).

Summers, Anthony. *Conspiracy* (McGraw-Hill: New York, 1980).

Summers, Anthony. *Official and Confidential* (Putnam: New York, 1993).

Talbot, David, *Brothers: The Hidden History of the Kennedy Years* (Free Press: New York, 2007).

Thompson, Josiah. *Six Seconds in Dallas* (Bernard Geis Associates: New York, 1967).

Turner William and Jonn Christian. *The Assassination of Robert F. Kennedy* (Random House: New York, 1978).

Weisberg Harold. *Whitewash* (Dell: New York, 1966).

Online books
Atkins, Susan, *The Myth of Helter Skelter*.

Patspeer.com, *A New Perspective on the Kennedy Assassination*.

<u>E-Books</u>
Ernest, Barry, *The Girl on the Stairs*
Denny, George, *The Vince Bugliosi Story*

Films

Evidence of Revision by Terrence Raymond, Etymon Productions, 2011.
Into Evidence, Forensic Sciences and Law Education Group, Duquesne University, A CORTON Production, 2004.
The Jim Garrison Tapes, by John Barbour, Blue Ridge/Film Trust, 1992.
The Mysterious Death of Number 35, Directed by Braddon Mendelson, Noisivision Productions, 2008.

Index